Casebook of Interpersonal

Psychotherapy

Casebook of Interpersonal Psychotherapy

EDITED BY JOHN C. MARKOWITZ

AND

MYRNA M. WEISSMAN

Oxford University Press, Inc., publishes works that further
Oxford University's objective of excellence
in research, scholarship, and education.

Oxford New York
Auckland Cape Town Dar es Salaam Hong Kong Karachi
Kuala Lumpur Madrid Melbourne Mexico City Nairobi
New Delhi Shanghai Taipei Toronto

With offices in
Argentina Austria Brazil Chile Czech Republic France Greece
Guatemala Hungary Italy Japan Poland Portugal Singapore
South Korea Switzerland Thailand Turkey Ukraine Vietnam

Published by Oxford University Press, Inc.
198 Madison Avenue, New York, New York 10016
www.oup.com

Oxford is a registered trademark of Oxford University Press

Library of Congress Cataloging-in-Publication Data
Casebook of interpersonal psychotherapy / edited by John C. Markowitz, Myrna M. Weissman.
    p.; cm.
  Interpersonal psychotherapy
  ISBN 978-0-19-974690-3 (alk. paper)
    1. Interpersonal psychotherapy—Case studies. 2. Depression, Mental—Treatment--Case studies.
I. Markowitz, John C., 1954- II. Weissman, Myrna M. III. Title: Interpersonal psychotherapy.
[DNLM: 1. Psychotherapy—methods—Case Reports. 2. Depressive Disorder—therapy—Case Reports.
3. Interpersonal Relations—Case Reports. 4. Mental Disorders—therapy—Case Reports.
5. Psychiatric Status Rating Scales—Case Reports. WM 40]
  RC489.I55C37 2012
616.89´14—dc23   2011026859

Printed in the United States of America
on acid-free paper

This is the fourth official volume of interpersonal psychotherapy (IPT) written by at least one of the original developers. The first author of the first volume, the original IPT manual published in 1984, was the major developer of IPT, my late husband Gerald Klerman. Gerry charted the origins, theory, and strategies of IPT fresh from the first clinical trials (Klerman et al., 1984). IPT was his idea.

The second volume (Weissman et al., 2000), published in 2000, which still carried Gerry's name because it contained mainly his thoughts, came after his death in 1992. It was co-authored with John Markowitz, who was Gerry's last psychiatric resident IPT trainee at Cornell. This manual updated the methods based on the numerous clinical trials that had occurred in IPT since 1984, and extended IPT beyond major depression to other disorders.

In 2007 John and I published the third volume (Weissman et al., 2007), still based on the same strategies but geared to the practicing clinician, incorporating many of the scripts we had developed over the years. This book fleshed out the clinical methods and highlighted the clinical approach while summarizing the background, theory, and efficacy data.

In 2011 John and I completed editing this fourth volume of IPT. We felt this book was needed to incorporate the experience and insights of the many scientists and clinicians in the United States and abroad who were using IPT, and to meet the growing demand for examples of IPT in different clinical situations. We wanted detailed case descriptions to help clinicians understand the procedures discussed in the manuals. Our authors responded enthusiastically: not one declined the invitation, and they responded flexibly and constructively to our requests. Represented among the authors are the best and the brightest of IPT clinicians and researchers.

The planning of this volume began in 2009. With the death of my husband, Marshall Nirenberg, in 2010, John graciously agreed to take the lead in completing this volume. He did all of the work in seeing that the organization, length, and flow had coherence, and that the volume was completed on time. Each chapter is organized around a case to illustrate a particular procedure or adaptation. The novice IPT reader is encouraged to read any one of the first three manuals to understand the theory and strategies of IPT.

We thank the expert contributors who generously gave their ideas and clinical experiences, and the Department of Psychiatry at Columbia University for providing a rich intellectual setting for carrying out this work. We thank the organizers of the International Society of Interpersonal Psychotherapy for the venue for meeting with the many talented IPT investigators and clinicians from all over the world. John thanks Barbara for her support and patience throughout the editing process.

Finally, we thank the patients and their families who shared their lives, suffering, and interpersonal challenges with us. Their identities in the case descriptions have been altered to protect their privacy.

Myrna M. Weissman and
John C. Markowitz

REFERENCES

Klerman GL, Weissman MM, Rounsaville BJ, Chevron ES: Interpersonal Psychotherapy of Depression. New York: Basic Books, 1984

Weissman MM, Markowitz JC, Klerman GL: Comprehensive Guide to Interpersonal Psychotherapy. New York: Basic Books, 2000

Weissman MM, Markowitz JC, Klerman GL: Clinician's Quick Guide to Interpersonal Psychotherapy. New York: Oxford University Press, 2007

CONTENTS

SECTION 3 Treating Major Depression in Diverse Populations

SECTION 4 Using Interpersonal Psychotherapy in Differing Formats

ABOUT THE EDITORS

John C. Markowitz, M.D., is a Research Psychiatrist at the New York State Psychiatric Institute, Professor of Clinical Psychiatry at the Columbia University College of Physicians & Surgeons, and Adjunct Clinical Professor of Psychiatry at Weill Medical College of Cornell University in New York City. He received his medical degree from Columbia in 1982 and completed psychiatric residency training at the New York Hospital-Payne Whitney Clinic in 1986. He was trained in cognitive-behavioral therapy (CBT) at the Center for Cognitive Therapy in Philadelphia and in interpersonal psychotherapy (IPT) by the late Gerald L. Klerman, M.D., at Cornell.

Dr. Markowitz has conducted clinical research involving psychotherapy and pharmacotherapy of mood, anxiety, and personality disorders. He has collaborated with James Kocsis, M.D., on chronic depression research and with the late Drs. Klerman and Samuel Perry on HIV-related research at Cornell. Since moving to Columbia University/New York State Psychiatric Institute in 2001, he has also focused on personality disorders and posttraumatic stress disorder (PTSD). He is currently funded by the National Institute of Mental Health to study the efficacy of psychotherapies for chronic PTSD. He has lectured widely and conducted many workshops on IPT and other topics. Dr. Markowitz is the author, co-author, or editor of eighteen books and more than two hundred seventy peer-reviewed articles and chapters.

Myrna M. Weissman, Ph.D., is a Professor of Epidemiology in Psychiatry, College of Physicians and Surgeons and the Mailman School of Public Health at Columbia University and Chief of the Division of Epidemiology at New York State Psychiatric Institute (NYSPI). She is a member of the Sackler Institute for Developmental Psychobiology at Columbia. Until 1987, she was a Professor of Psychiatry and Epidemiology at Yale University School of Medicine. She has been a Visiting Senior Scholar at the Institute of Medicine, National Academy of Sciences, Washington, D.C. She received a Ph.D. in epidemiology from the Yale University School of Medicine in 1974.

Dr. Weissman developed interpersonal therapy (IPT) with her late husband, Gerald L. Klerman, at the beginning of her career. She has maintained an interest in disseminating and training IPT since his death in 1992. IPT manuals have been translated into numerous languages and an international society of IPT meets every two years to share new developments. Dr. Weissman is also a member of the Institute of Medicine, National Academy of Science. She has been the author or a co-author of over five hundred fifty scientific articles and chapters and eleven books, and the recipient of numerous grants from National Institute of Mental Health, private foundations, and numerous awards. In April 2009, she was selected by the American College of Epidemiology as one of ten epidemiologists in the United States who has had a major impact on public policy and public health. The summary of her work on depression appears in a special issue of the *Annals of Epidemiology*, "Triumphs in Epidemiology."

CONTRIBUTORS

Charles D.R. Baily, M.A.
Teachers College
Columbia University

Kathryn L. Bleiberg, Ph.D.
Weill Medical College of Cornell University
New York, NY

Carlos Blanco, M.D., Ph.D.
Department of Psychiatry
Columbia University College of Physicians and Surgeons
New York State Psychiatric Institute

Eve Caligor, M.D.
Center for Psychoanalytic Training and Research
Columbia University

Ori Elis, M.A.
Department of Psychology
University of California, Berkeley

Iljie K. Fitzgerald, M.D., M.S.
Department of Psychiatry and Biobehavioral Sciences
University of California, Los Angeles

Ellen Frank, Ph.D.
Distinguished Professor of Psychiatry and Professor of Psychology
University of Pittsburgh School of Medicine
Western Psychiatric Institute and Clinic

Elizabeth P. Graf, Ph.D.
Mount Sinai School of Medicine
New York State Psychiatric Institute

Nancy K. Grote, Ph.D.
School of Social Work
University of Washington

Meredith Gunlicks-Stoessel, Ph.D.
Department of Psychiatry
University of Minnesota

Marcela Hoffer, L.C.S.W., M.A., M.S.
New York State Psychiatric Institute at Columbia University

Juliette M. Iacovino, M.A.
Department of Psychology
Washington University in St. Louis

Jessica A. Keith, Ph.D.
Bay Pines Veteran Affairs Healthcare System
Bay Pines, Florida

Roslyn Law D. Clin. Psychol.
SWL & St George's Mental Health NHS Trust

Jessica C. Levenson, M.S.
Western Psychiatric Institute and Clinic
University of Pittsburgh Medical Center

Laurie Reider Lewis, Psy.D.
Private Practice, Stevensville, Maryland

Roberto Lewis-Fernández, M.D.
Department of Psychiatry
Columbia University College of Physicians & Surgeons
New York State Psychiatric Institute

Jonathan Lichtmacher, M.D.
Department of Psychiatry
University of California, San Francisco

Joshua D. Lipsitz, Ph.D.
Ben Gurion University of the Negev, Israel
College of Physicians and Surgeons,
Columbia University

Sue Luty, Ph.D.
University of Otago
Christchurch, New Zealand

John C. Markowitz, M.D.
Columbia University College of Physicians & Surgeons
Weill Medical College of Cornell University
New York State Psychiatric Institute

Robert Maunder, M.D.
Department of Psychiatry
Mount Sinai Hospital
University of Toronto

Mark D. Miller, M.D.
Department of Psychiatry
Western Psychiatric Institute and Clinic
University of Pittsburgh Medical Center

Monica S. Mills, M.A.
Department of Psychiatry
Washington University School of Medicine

Laura Mufson, Ph.D.
Columbia University College of Physicians and Surgeons
New York State Psychiatric Institute

Christine Nanyondo, M.A.
World Vision

Robin Nusslock, Ph.D.
Department of Psychology
Northwestern University

Sapana R. Patel, Ph.D.
Department of Psychiatry
Columbia University Medical Center
New York State Psychiatric Institute

Paula Ravitz, M.D.
Department of Psychiatry
Mount Sinai Hospital
University of Toronto

Charles F. Reynolds III, M.D.
Institute on Aging
University of Pittsburgh Medical Center

Elisabeth Schramm, Ph.D.
Department of Psychiatry and Psychotherapy
University Medical Center
Freiburg, Germany

Holly A. Swartz, M.D.
Department of Psychiatry
Western Psychiatric Institute and Clinic
University of Pittsburgh Medical Center

Dorothy J. Van Buren, Ph.D.
Department of Psychiatry
Washington University in St. Louis

Helena Verdeli, Ph.D.
Teachers College
College of Physicians and Surgeons
Columbia University

Myrna M. Weissman, Ph.D.
Department of Psychiatry
College of Physicians and Surgeons
Columbia University
New York State Psychiatric Institute

R. Robinson Welch, Ph.D.
Department of Psychiatry
Washington University School of Medicine

Denise E. Wilfley, Ph.D.
Department of Psychiatry
Washington University School of Medicine

Jami F. Young, Ph.D.
Graduate School of Applied and Professional Psychology
Rutgers University

Allan Zuckoff, Ph.D.
Departments of Psychology and Psychiatry
University of Pittsburgh

Casebook of Interpersonal Psychotherapy

1

Introduction

JOHN C. MARKOWITZ AND MYRNA M. WEISSMAN

Interpersonal psychotherapy (IPT) is a time-limited, diagnosis-targeted, empirically validated treatment that has been tested in numerous randomized controlled outcome studies (Weissman, Markowitz, & Klerman, 2000, 2007). National and international treatment guidelines recommend it as a first-line treatment for major depressive disorder and for bulimia nervosa, and it shows promise as a treatment for other psychiatric diagnoses as well. Developed in the 1970s (Weissman, 2006, 2007), IPT remained for perhaps too long an almost purely research intervention. Although results of IPT trials were repeatedly published in psychiatric and psychology journals, only a handful of clinicians actually practiced it. This was due in part to the paucity of programs in psychiatry, psychology, and social work in the United States offering training in evidence-based psychotherapy, and particularly in IPT (Weissman, Verdeli, Gameroff, et al., 2006).

In the past decade or so, the success of IPT in the research arena has led to its increasing dissemination among practitioners. The International Society for Interpersonal Psychotherapy (ISIPT; http://www.interpersonalpsychotherapy.org) has held three highly successful and well-attended meetings for researchers and clinicians. IPT workshops are conducted at professional meetings and as freestanding events in the United States and around the world. Various IPT manuals have been translated into Danish, French, German, Italian, Japanese, Portuguese, and Spanish. With greater clinical interest comes the need for greater information about IPT. Clinicians learn techniques from IPT manuals (Weissman et al., 2000, 2007) but often want more. There is a dearth of videotapes illustrating IPT practice. This casebook is intended as a response to this need for more clinical information.

A casebook can serve several functions. As a companion to the IPT treatment manual (Weissman et al., 2007), this book expands available clinical illustrations of treatment techniques, providing a wealth of additional clinical material. This casebook offers detailed narratives from master clinicians, specialists in particular areas and adaptations of IPT, in action with actual (appropriately disguised) patients. The goal has been to put you in the office with them, to observe and to understand the process of IPT cases over expert shoulders — in other words, to let these experts teach through demonstration. We believe the casebook fills a clinical need for further, fuller exploration of the conduct of IPT.

IPT has a simple paradigm: it defines the patient's problems as a treatable medical diagnosis, and links the patient's affective distress to interpersonal situations in order to help the patient better understand and handle them. This model has worked extremely well and flexibly in a variety of situations, as the current volume should demonstrate. Nonetheless, psychotherapy must always be tailored to the specifics of the encounter, and it makes sense to adjust the model to different diagnoses, cultural situations, chronicity of symptoms, treatment formats, etc. The cases in this book describe the various adaptations of IPT and also depict problem areas that inevitably arise in working with patients. These are not clean, idealized treatments, but real-life, warts-and-all portraits of IPT. The authors have illustrated not only broad themes and particular techniques of IPT, but also turning points in treatment: some hint of why treatment has worked in a particular clinical context. We hope that these case presentations will provide useful clinical and conceptual examples to clinicians who are interested in IPT in particular, and in psychotherapy more generally.

The book contains four sections: Mood Disorders, Other Psychiatric Disorders, Treating Major Depression in Diverse Populations, and Using IPT in Differing Formats. We begin with mood disorders because major depressive disorder was the original target of IPT (Klerman, DiMascio, Weissman, et al., 1974; Weissman, 2006) and remains the diagnosis both best supported by outcome research and for which IPT is probably most widely used. Authors present cases to illustrate each of the four IPT problem areas—grief, role dispute, role transition, and interpersonal deficits. Other chapters present adaptations of IPT for dysthymic and bipolar disorders.

The second section comprises chapters in which cases illustrate the application of IPT to non-mood disorders: bulimia, posttraumatic stress disorder, social phobia, and borderline personality disorder. The third section explores adaptations of IPT for particular patient subgroups, including adolescent and geriatric depression, depressed patients with medical illness, and patients in different cultural settings. The final section deals with variations in IPT formats: maintenance IPT, inpatient, group, and telephone delivery.

Each chapter follows the same general format. It opens with a brief discussion of the empirical evidence supporting IPT for the patient population of interest. The authors do not undertake lengthy reviews of the empirical literature, but this introductory section should inform the reader of how confident he or she can be in treating this kind of patient with IPT. Where appropriate, there follows a discussion of the rationale for and adaptations of IPT for this patient population.

This brings the reader to the heart of the matter: a detailed case illustration of IPT applied to a particular clinical diagnosis or setting. Cases derive from actual practice and are generally complex. The authors have attempted to illustrate the problems they faced as therapists treating often severely ill patients, and the maneuvers they employed to resolve them. Elements of the case history include:

1. History of present illness
2. An interpersonal inventory, cataloguing the patient's key relationships, supports, interpersonal difficulties, and patterns of relating
3. Psychiatric, family, and medical history
4. Differential diagnosis and indication for IPT
5. The therapist's thinking in developing a formulation, and a description of the formulation actually presented to the patient
6. Detailed exposition of the middle phase of treatment, describing specific interventions employed and problems that arose: What did the patient say? What did the therapist say? Then what happened?
7. Termination, including discussion of the issue of maintenance treatment and any follow-up therapists had on the patient's subsequent course
8. Use of rating scales demonstrating change in symptoms, functioning, and other domains
9. The authors then discuss their cases, making observations specific to the treatment population and on the benefits and limitations of the course of treatment

The range of material shows how widely IPT has spread in its relatively short existence. Different diagnoses require differing expertise and clinical wisdom. Mixed through the cases the reader will find a series of clinical dilemmas that may compound the conduct of IPT, or any therapy: working with patients' negative affects (Markowitz & Milrod, 2011), emerging clinical risks, comorbidities, cultural factors, therapist and patient disagreements, and the like. Therapists describe their own emotional reactions to difficult clinical situations. We have enjoyed and learned from reviewing our expert colleagues' excellent, if not always easy, treatment reports. We trust that you will as well.

Mood Disorders

2

Complicated Grief

ROSLYN LAW

It is relatively rare that an interpersonal focal area receives specific attention in the IPT literature. Most published outcome studies do not report the breakdown of interpersonal problem areas in a manner elucidating process and outcome with different interpersonal themes. The grief focus is more richly served, however, both in conceptualizing this focal interpersonal problem area and in evaluating the relative benefits of using IPT compared with alternative approaches that target complicated bereavement.

The IPT therapist selects grief as an interpersonal focus when the onset of the patient's symptoms is associated with the death of a significant other and manifests in a bereavement-related depression (Weissman et al., 2000). The reaction differs from the predictable sorrow associated with bereavement—the experience of deprivation and desolation. The DSM-IV echoes this distinction by excluding immediate bereavement reactions in making the diagnosis of major depression. Clinicians may diagnose major depression only if symptoms persist for more than 2 months after the death or are characterized by marked functional impairment, morbid preoccupation with worthlessness, suicidal ideation, psychotic symptoms, or psychomotor retardation (DSM-IV-TR, 2000).

Distinguishing grief following bereavement from bereavement-related depression can be difficult. Some symptoms of grief, including neurovegetative symptoms and sadness, are considered normal following the death of a loved one. The characteristic reactions of a bereavement can closely resemble those we see in depressed patients: persistent sadness, a sense of emptiness, loss of interest in normally enjoyable activities, disturbed sleep, and impaired memory and concentration are all common. Estimates of the proportion of individuals who meet diagnostic criteria for major depression following bereavement have ranged from 30% to 60% in the month after a death. Estimates a month later are roughly half as high, and half again at the end of the first year after bereavement. However, for this smaller number of 7% to 16%, major depression persists into the second year of bereavement (Zisook et al., 1991a, 1991b, 1993a), suggesting that some individuals have great difficulty moving on and endure the added burden of a depressive episode.

Bereavement-related depression is more likely to occur when patients suffer multiple bereavements, have delayed onset of symptoms, or neglect to use social support at or after the time of the death. For some the grief is so consuming they need look no further for an interpersonal focus in IPT: the deaths of a spouse or child are typically rated as the most stressful life events one can face. For others, delay in symptom onset and complicated ramifications in other relationships can obscure the picture. If the sequence of events appears interrupted, with depressive symptoms emerging only after a delay, patients may struggle to connect their loss to their symptoms and to see the logic of working on one to alleviate the other. Many depressed patients find themselves gripped by a terrible dilemma: Does being happy now mean I didn't love him or her then? Does being depressed prove I did?

One patient opened her first IPT session by saying, "It all started when my husband died . . .," but still expressed surprise when the therapist suggested the grief focus two sessions later. When asked why, she said that she had seen others recover from similar losses more quickly and so had ruled out bereavement as an explanation for her current distress. In other cases, the manner of the death and the availability of support can interact to obstruct recovery. One young man was present when the person who subsequently killed his friend arrived in their home. Aware of this individual's potential for unpredictable behavior and afraid for his own safety, he fled before the individual entered the house. Returning hours later, he discovered the murder scene and was distraught to have, in his view, abandoned his friend to this fate. He believed his friends subsequently blamed him for not having done more and withdrew from all contact with them. He essentially lost his best friend and wider network in one event and, suddenly and simultaneously bereaved and isolated, had few social resources to help him recover from his depression.

There is debate in the literature on the overlap between depression and complicated grief. Complicated grief is not currently a DSM-IV diagnostic category. ICD-10 classifies it as an adjustment disorder. Some authors have argued that complicated or traumatic grief should be considered a distinct disorder rather than a variant of depression (Boelen et al., 2003; Horowitz et al., 1997; Prigerson et al., 1997, 1999).

Estimated comorbidity of depression and complicated grief ranges between 24% and 54% (Prigerson et al., 1995). Diagnosis of complicated grief refers to a cluster of symptoms similar but not identical to those of major depression, which have been estimated to characterize 10% to 20% of bereaved individuals (Middleton et al., 1996). The symptoms of complicated grief include extreme focus on the loss and reminders of the loved one; intense longing or pining for the deceased; problems accepting the death; numbness or detachment; preoccupation with the sorrow; and bitterness about the loss. This chapter focuses on IPT as an intervention for bereavement-related depression. Readers interested in the treatment of complicated grief specifically and the evolution of treatments integrating IPT and cognitive-behavioral therapy (CBT) strategies should read Shear et al. (2005) and Simmons et al. (2008).

Levenson et al. (2010) analyzed comparative outcomes across the focal interpersonal problem areas in IPT for depressed patients (N = 182) and found no difference in time to remission as a function of focal area. Use of IPT, and where necessary medication, yielded equivalent clinical success across the four interpersonal themes. Markowitz et al. (2006) reported retrospective evaluations of progress in interpersonal problem areas by patients with dysthymia and posttraumatic stress disorder (PTSD), using the Interpersonal Psychotherapy Outcome Scale (IPOS). This retrospective analysis revealed less improvement for those who worked on grief than those facing interpersonal transitions and disputes. The authors noted, however, that the rate of endorsement of focal problem areas by the patient sample was high, suggesting a broader definition of the focal areas than therapists would have employed, and consequently may reflect a more general evaluation of working with grief and loss than the specific work outlined in the IPT model. This broader definition of grief is a common issue for therapists new to IPT and should be addressed through careful attention to specific, clear formulation and negotiation of treatment goals.

Reynolds et al. (1999) examined IPT for bereavement-related depression in older adults, usually following the loss of a spouse. They found that IPT plus nortriptyline, nortriptyline alone, and placebo yielded superior remission rates than IPT plus placebo. There was little evidence of an additive effect of IPT with medication over medication alone, although the study authors noted that the small sample size of 17 for combined treatment was underpowered to demonstrate such a difference. Combined treatment of IPT and medication did demonstrate greater treatment retention than the other interventions.

CASE EXAMPLE

Ellen was thirty-two years old, unmarried, and lived alone. She had been raised Catholic and continued to attend church occasionally, describing her faith as private but important to her. She had not been involved with the church community since leaving school. She had had a boyfriend, Pete, for two years and no children. She worked as a classroom assistant with children with special educational needs. Ellen presented with a fluctuating two-year history of agitated depressive and anxiety symptoms that began following her father's death in a traffic accident.

History of Present Illness

Ellen had first experienced anxiety and depressive symptoms two years earlier in the immediate aftermath of her father's death. She had attributed this to the normal process of grieving. Ellen's father had been drinking on the night of the accident, had driven off the road late at night, and died at the scene. A pedestrian was badly injured but survived. Ellen was tormented by her suspicion that her father's death had not been an accident, that he had committed suicide. He had been under stress for some time following the collapse of his business and had been distressed, agitated, and drinking when speaking to her on the night of his death. This uncertainty complicated the task of mourning for Ellen and her family, and made her reluctant to discuss her loss with anyone. Ellen felt that her uncertainty about the circumstances of her father's death prolonged her distress. She described trying not to think about it by keeping busy, and managed this for brief periods but inevitably returned to feeling low and anxious.

Twenty months after her father's death, Ellen suffered a broken ankle in a cycling accident. Unable to work immediately after the accident, she experienced a marked increase in depressive symptoms that prevented her planned return a few weeks later. She lost all interest in social activities and became very withdrawn, very tearful and depressed, feeling preoccupied and guilty. Ellen told her mother that she wished she had died in the cycling accident and could be with her father again. She was encouraged to speak to her general practitioner (GP), who prescribed antidepressant medication and referred Ellen to a National Health Service primary care service for psychotherapy.

Initial Assessment

On presenting for treatment, Ellen was offered an initial assessment appointment in which to describe her recent experiences and current symptoms. To measure the range and severity of symptoms, Ellen completed standardized measures of depressive and anxiety symptoms and a review of interpersonal relationships. She completed the Patient Health Questionnaire-9 (PHQ-9; Spitzer et al., 1999), a brief self-report measure of depressive symptoms that reflects the diagnostic criteria for Major Depression in DSM-IV. Items are rated 0 to 3, with a maximum score of 27. Ellen scored the maximum, 27. The GAD-7 (Spitzer et al., 2006), a measure of anxiety symptoms, is another self-report with items rated 0 to 3, with 3 indicating greater severity. Ellen scored 19 of a possible 21.

To collect information about Ellen's interpersonal world, she completed a questionnaire asking about her current significant relationships. The Significant Others Scale (Power et al., 1988) measures the types of support available—emotional, practical, and social—and satisfaction with the support provided. Ellen's responses revealed that she generally felt able to confide in and spend time with a number of friends but was not doing so at present. She commented that she had talked to them about her feelings in the past but not about her current concerns. She described feeling close to her sister but not having a confiding relationship, which was "not what we do in our family." Ellen reported ambivalent feelings about her mother and boyfriend. She rated her ability to talk to and spend time with her mother as low but expressed some desire to be more at ease with her. She said their relationship had been difficult and unsettling since her father's death.

Ellen said she could talk to Pete about anything and spend time with him, but that this was what he wanted rather than her own wish for the relationship. Hence she rated her ideal as being less close to him, which she said made her feel guilty. This assessment provided an initial insight into Ellen's interpersonal experience and served as foundation for the more detailed interpersonal inventory carried out during IPT. This combination of assessments in routine practice made the dual goals of IPT—reduced symptom distress and improved social functioning—evident from the start of the work, helped the patient to understand the model, and helped to monitor treatment progress.

Having established that Ellen was severely depressed and that her symptoms were related to a significant interpersonal loss, I explained the nature, framework, and objectives of IPT and gave Ellen a patient information sheet to provide her an overview of the therapy. By providing this advance information I hoped to encourage a collaborative, mutually informed approach to the treatment. Ellen found the approach acceptable and we made arrangements to complete an IPT assessment.

During the first IPT session we reviewed Ellen's current difficulties and the fluctuating course of her depressive symptoms over the prior two years. To thoroughly and collaboratively review her symptoms, we completed the 17-item Hamilton Depression Scale (Ham-D; Hamilton, 1960) to complement the self-report measures from the initial assessment session, and drew out a timeline together. The Ham-D score was 29, again indicating severe depression. This process provided an overview of Ellen's depression and allowed us to consider the relative impact of significant events over the past two years.

Ellen reported a broad range of depressive symptoms, including feeling low and tearful every day and lacking pleasure in any activities. She had no motivation for social or daily routines: she no longer dressed or left her bedroom until midday and rarely left home or saw friends. She described feeling very anxious and agitated much of the time. She couldn't keep her mind on anything, which prevented her planning to do more with her time because she became so easily confused and found this very embarrassing when in company. She described feeling irritable with friends and resentful that others could carry on with their lives.

Ellen reported marked feelings of guilt that she had let her father down by not responding to his distress and was now letting her family down by being a burden and drawing attention to their private grief. She said she wanted to conceal her distress from her family. She and her father had always been the "emotional ones" in the family, while her mother and younger sister, Louise, had always been contained and seemed to cope better. Ellen said that she felt ashamed to have told her mother about her wish to die and felt that her mother had only sent her to her GP "to get fixed" and prevent anyone else finding out. She assumed her mother and sister were coping with her father's death better than she was, but had not discussed it with them. Although she was sure they didn't need her, she felt ashamed that she didn't know how they felt and criticized herself for being so "indulgent" and "self-absorbed" with her own distress. Preoccupied with her loss and by her uncertainty about the circumstances of her father's death, Ellen felt unable to move on or accept that he was really gone.

Ellen wanted to die but found this thought very distressing and feared what would happen if she tried to kill herself. She believed in an afterlife, and as we spoke she clarified that she wanted to die to see her father again. However, she also believed suicide would be sinful: she would "not go to heaven" and would be separated from him forever. This belief prevented direct self-harm, but not a marked reduction in self-protection. She reported placing herself in dangerous situations in the hope that she would die and no longer have to face the struggle she now felt life to be. For example, when unable to sleep she walked through the streets at night in dangerous areas of the city with little regard for her own safety. Cycling was her main means of transport, and on the infrequent occasions she still cycled she disregarded road signs, inviting a collision. This had led to her cycling accident. Ellen said her mind would often wander when cycling, often to thoughts of her father and her frustration with her mother. She then found it hard to concentrate but didn't care if something happened to her.

We discussed how her urge to die fit with her belief about an afterlife but also followed from the diagnosis of major depression on which we had agreed. Ellen admitted that she had not connected depression to her wish to see with her father again. We discussed her distress at not knowing if her father had killed himself, and whether her own death might have the same effect on those she would leave behind. Ellen initially thought her friends and family would not realize that she had acted deliberately, saying, "They would never imagine I'd do something like that." I emphasized this response, noting how differently she was thinking and behaving as a result of the depression. On continuing to discuss her thoughts of death, Ellen found it hard to imagine her mother could be unaware if she acted to harm herself, as they had already discussed her suicidal feelings before she saw her GP. Ellen said she would hate to cause them the pain she now felt.

Following this discussion she agreed not to take late-night walks or to cycle alone while in treatment, and to discuss in sessions occasions when she felt tempted to harm herself. We clarified that she had no other methods of self-harm in mind and had not acquired other means of hurting herself. We identified a telephone help line she could use if she felt at risk and identified the signs and triggers that marked her vulnerability. Ellen could not imagine talking to anyone she knew about her wish to die, having been upset by her mother's alarm at her first admission. We agreed to talk more about whom she could turn to when she felt upset, although she insisted no one would understand.

We reviewed Ellen's current symptoms and worked back over the current episode to place them in an interpersonal context. We discussed details of past depressive episodes to better understand Ellen's vulnerability to depression and to assess her familiarity with the diagnosis and potential to respond to treatment. Ellen felt perplexed and confused by her unfolding reaction over the preceding two years. She could not understand why she had initially seemed to cope "normally" with her father's sudden death but had so worsened after the cycling accident. To explore the impact of different events and their connection to her depressive symptoms we drew out a timeline (Fig. 2.1), marking dates and descriptions of significant events and change in symptoms during the episode. We deliberately extended the start of the timeline to the year before her symptoms arose to allow consideration of potential precipitating factors, and added details of previous depressions to better understand her recent experience in the context of her depressive history. As Ellen's story involved several themes around which IPT might frame an intervention—bereavement, role transitions, and implicit and explicit role disputes—the timeline allowed us to explore the relative contribution and resonance of the different themes.

Before completing the timeline, Ellen believed she had mostly been coping until her cycling accident. She had described "dips" but had quickly brushed these aside in her initial narrative. In drawing out the timeline, however, she noted that she had had recurring difficulties in close family and work relationships and had consulted her GP twice following her father's death. Both consultations had occurred months after the death in the context of disagreements and work stress. She recalled feeling tired and irritable and described the medication as "vitamins for her brain" to get her back on her feet. Ellen had been prescribed antidepressants once in the past with good effect, following the breakup of a relationship, and felt comfortable with the

Timeline

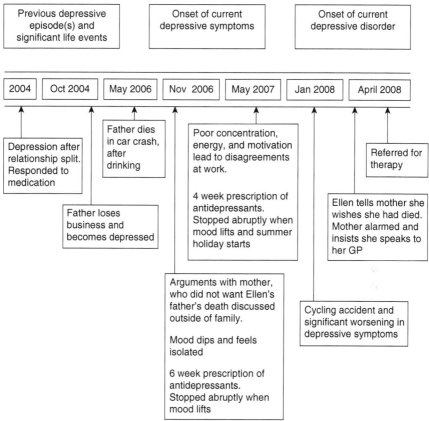

Figure 2.1 Timeline

idea that she sometimes needed a boost. This had been Ellen's only previous episode of significant physical or mental ill health: she was not "someone who got sick." I commented that taking medication also appeared to allow Ellen to dismiss her distress as minor and to avoid looking at the reasons for her continuing distress. She said she thought that she must have been coping as she had stopped taking antidepressant medication quickly when she had begun to feel better, but she could see that this had offered only a very temporary solution. We discussed the increased risk of recurrence associated with such partial treatment of depression. Ellen said she had been unaware that her attempts to resume independent function could inadvertently undermine her objective. She had felt annoyed with other people for not understanding her loss and had imagined that the family and work conflicts were the reason her mood and energy had been low. Ellen became tearful, explaining that she had told no one how much she missed her father, expecting her family would not listen and her friends would not understand.

Ellen described feeling confused by her current distress, saying she had struggled, physically and psychologically, to get back on her feet after her cycling accident. She described life as very difficult since her father's death: she missed him and wished she could see him again. She did not regard this as depression, and couldn't imagine she could have felt any differently. Ellen found the circumstances of his death unbearable and found it impossible to set aside questions of whether it had been accidental. Ellen's father had been found marginally over the legal limit for alcohol when he died, but his distress in the days leading to his death made Ellen question alcohol as the sole explanation. She described feeling both numb and intensely angry in the months after his death, but reported few opportunities to talk about this. When she tried to raise her suspicions with her mother, she was told she must never suggest such things again and must not speak to anyone outside of the family about the death. Her mother told Ellen that it was "already shameful enough" without her making it worse for everyone. Ellen initially felt guilty for upsetting her mother and tried to push the questions out of her mind. She tried hard to distract herself by keeping busy at work and through physical activity. When, following the cycling accident, neither strategy remained available to her, she found it impossible to cope and described a heavy weight descending on her. She felt as though everything had broken when her ankle did.

I encouraged Ellen to describe her symptoms as fully as possible. When she had done so, we matched her descriptions with the symptoms of depression and discussed the similarities to and differences from bereavement. I aimed to show Ellen that I understood her depression, how we could address it in IPT, and how she could develop IPT expertise. We noted the symptomatic overlap between Ellen's experience and bereavement-related depression but did not select the focus before having discussed other possible interpersonal foci. Ellen described marked social withdrawal over the preceding months, increased conflict with work colleagues, and irritation and frustration with her family, and latterly the first period of her adult life when she had not worked. It was important to explore the interpersonal disputes and transitions that had taken place.

I presented the diagnosis of depression to Ellen and described the nature and course of the disorder, particularly emphasizing the potential to treat depression. Ellen described relief at having her distress recognized. She said she had tried to conceal her feelings from those around her but could only do so by avoiding company, which had left her isolated. She felt reluctant to consider her reaction to her father's death anything other than the inevitable consequence of losing someone she loved, but acknowledged that she appeared to be struggling more than others in coming to terms with her father's death. Ellen admitted she didn't really know how her family was coping with the death, as she had mostly avoided discussing it with them. She said that it was not her mother's or sister's style to talk about emotional matters. She and her father had done so, and she said such emotional discussion was part of what she missed. She agreed with some surprise when I pointed out that while her father had been alive she had also discussed her feelings with friends, but had stopped doing this since his death even though they remained available to her.

Sick Role

Having agreed on the diagnosis, we explicitly talked about depression as a treatable illness that provided a framework for understanding her current difficulties. I encouraged Ellen to acknowledge the impact depression was having and to think about initial changes she could make in her life to begin to promote recovery, emphasizing the potential for improvement with treatment and targeted change. I emphasized that Ellen was currently unwell, through no fault of her own, and acknowledged how much more difficult life felt at the moment. I encouraged her to consider what tasks or routine she could temporarily give up to reduce the burden she felt while also exploring opportunities for more pleasurable or relaxing activity. Ellen identified feeling chronically sluggish and tired as a particular difficulty. She found it hard to get started in the morning often because her sleep was broken, disrupted by dreams about her father's accident that left her drained, agitated, and tearful. Reviewing her evening routine in detail revealed that she often sat alone until late into the evening, often doing nothing, sometimes looking at photographs and videos of her father. This had initially been comforting, but she often broke down in tears and found it difficult to relax and sleep afterwards.

We agreed that Ellen needed to remember her father but that this routine appeared to trigger rather than relieve her symptoms. I stressed the importance of rest in order to start to recover, and we discussed how to change her evening routine to make it easier to relax. As Ellen acknowledged that this routine no longer offered any comfort, I asked her to consider putting the photographs and videos away temporarily while considering who could support her in remembering her father and establishing a more relaxing routine before bed.

Ellen suggested that she resume her yoga practice, which had previously kept her relaxed and fit, and which she previously had found absorbing and enjoyable. She initially planned to do this at home but agreed to consider rejoining classes she had previously attended. I picked up on this suggestion to stress the social approach to recovery. I explained that Ellen had previously relied on others' company and support to sustain her daily routine, but that since becoming depressed she had withdrawn from company and assistance when she most needed it. Ellen readily acknowledged feeling overwhelmed. She agreed to ask her boyfriend Pete to support her to get out of bed and dressed in the morning, as she had found such encouraging prompts helpful in the past. We agreed to monitor the effects of these changes in discussing her symptoms in each following session.

Interpersonal Inventory

To fully understand the interpersonal context of Ellen's depression, we completed an interpersonal inventory. I asked about her significant current relationships, including supportive and problematic relationships, explaining that by understanding the interpersonal context of her depression we would clarify the most useful focus for our sessions. Ellen reported finding social contact frustrating and irritating. She occasionally pushed herself to attend family events, especially when Louise invited her, but found them difficult and quickly sought to leave. Ellen's father was never mentioned at these events and she would feel her awareness of his absence build until she could no longer tolerate it and would retreat to her home. She felt irritated when friends or family talked about things that she considered trivial and appeared to ignore what she felt to be so important. She didn't believe her family was interested in or her friends could understand her current distress and confusion about her father's death, so she did not openly voice her feelings. She said that this withdrawal had not been characteristic of her before her father died, but that she felt silenced by her confusion, reinforced by her mother's insistence that she not discuss her father's life and death outside of the family. Ellen believed her mother was ashamed of the circumstances of her father's death and coped by blocking any reference to it.

Ellen identified her mother, sister, and boyfriend as her most significant relationships and noted that this represented a change in the context of her depression: she would normally have included more friends, but had seen much less of them in recent months. I explained that the interpersonal inventory would provide an opportunity to understand her important current relationships and their relationship to her current depression. This discussion expanded the information collected in the interpersonal relationship questionnaire: it included not only relationships Ellen felt happy about but those she found challenging or that triggered depressive symptoms. We drew a diagram to summarize these relationships (Fig. 2.2). Interpersonal inventory diagrams, like the IPT-A closeness circle (Mufson et al., 2004; see Chapter 12), are widely used by IPT practitioners in the United Kingdom as a visual reminder of the range of interpersonal relationships available to the patient.

Ellen described her mother first. She said that she got less emotional support from her mother than she would like and felt constantly concerned lest she upset her. She described her mother as very contained and organized, someone who always had a plan about what to do. Ellen had found this helpful in the past but daunting since feeling depressed, and had become reluctant to share her concerns with her. Ellen described her mother as a "no-nonsense" person and said that her father used to tease her about this, which often brought out a softer side to her. Since his death,

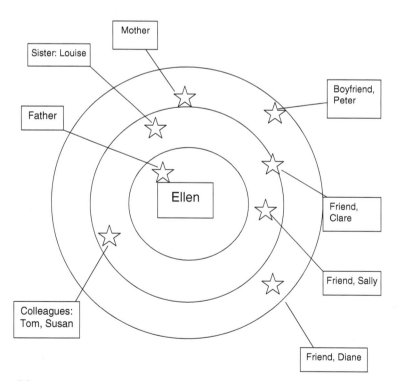

Figure 2.2

however, Ellen had not seen that side of her mother and felt as though she had retreated behind an angry wall. Ellen's mother had been diagnosed with depression when she and Louise were children but Ellen had little memory of it and her mother did not discuss it. Although she said she trusted her mother, she felt reluctant to speak openly to her. Ellen imagined she would be quickly rebuffed and that appearance would be more important than how she felt. Ellen recalled the sharp exchanges when she had tried to discuss her distress or concerns about her father's death and said she would not risk provoking them again. Ellen sought to limit her time with her mother, seeing or speaking to her once every few weeks, as she easily irritated her. On saying this she became tearful and said she also missed her.

I asked her what had prompted the tears. She replied that she felt she had lost both her mother and father: as they had not been able to mention her father's death without one or the other becoming upset or angry, they had retreated from each other. This was a change in their relationship: in the past her mother had been an encouraging, supportive figure to whom she turned for practical advice. Her mother had provided practical rather than emotional support, but this had usually sufficed, as her father and friends had given her emotional support. Ellen said she had enjoyed this odd role reversal in her parents, and they had been able to joke about it in the past.

Ellen next identified her partner, Pete. She immediately described feeling ambivalent towards him, uncertain about their future together, but unable to make any change at present. The relationship had been better when they first met, and he had been very supportive when her father died, soon after the relationship had started. Ellen had found it comforting to have someone around then, especially as her family had not spoken openly about their loss. On her mother's instructions the funeral had been for family members only, limiting the opportunity to talk to people who knew her father. Ellen wondered about Pete's support, and whether she had confused friendship with greater intimacy because she had felt so alone at the time. It felt good to talk to someone about her father, but she had never voiced her suspicions about his death, as she felt this would be disloyal to both her father and mother. She knew that Pete found it difficult to understand why she could not get over her father's death, and this made her feel guilty and at times even more alone. She felt guilty that he appeared more committed to their relationship than she did: she saw him as a companion, whereas he saw her as his partner. She now tolerated rather than enjoyed their time together, while he seemed eager for her company.

They saw each other two or three times a week and made daily contact, usually initiated by Pete. Ellen was aware that she made little effort to sustain the relationship, and felt she took his attention for granted. She felt ambivalent and guilty about having a sexual relationship when her feelings were uncertain, but had felt this necessary to maintain Pete's emotional support. Their sexual relationship had almost entirely ceased as she had become more depressed, and on one level she felt relieved to have depression as an excuse. This had not been true in her last significant relationship, and she had been "broken-hearted" when that ended, leading to her first antidepressant prescription. Although she no longer wished to be with her ex-partner, she remembered what it felt like to be in love and knew she had never felt that for Pete. She described feeling trapped but afraid to break the routine and ungrateful for considering it. We discussed whether this guilt might be part of her depression. Ellen acknowledged routinely feeling responsible for others' feelings and to blame for burdening them.

Ellen spoke affectionately about her sister Louise and her friends Sally, Diane, and Clare. She felt guilty that she was not speaking to them or seeing them as often as in the past. She described Louise as maintaining regular contact, "checking up" on her weekly, offering practical help with shopping and suggestions for getting out, which Ellen rarely took up. It was not the family style to mention feelings, but Ellen found this a little easier to do with Louise than her mother. In the past, Ellen and Louise had laughed at their mother's insistence that family business remain private, but they still had trouble talking to one another and tended to fall back on light-hearted companionship and providing each other with practical help: decorating, babysitting for Ellen's niece. Personal discussion grew difficult once Ellen became depressed, as she feared that expressing feelings would be painful and upsetting. She felt guilty that she was not supporting Louise as much as she ought and did not really know how their father's death had affected her.

Ellen had spent much less time socializing with friends since meeting Pete and her father's death. She had attributed this to starting a new relationship but now realized that the change had been much greater since her father's death. I asked Ellen to describe how the change happened. She reported periods when she would try to see her friends regularly, particularly when she had taken antidepressants, but typically found this effort difficult to sustain and now avoided socializing. She did not know what to say about her father's death and preferred to avoid the possibility of discussion. When I asked Ellen if she thought her friends would still expect her to talk about her father after two years, she seemed surprised and said it hadn't occurred to her that they would focus on this less. She said it was more likely that they would talk about their own lives and acknowledged sometimes missing having other topics of discussion. Her friends still kept in touch, but now sent text messages or emails rather than calling at her house or phoning. She had kept them at a distance, torn between loyalty to her mother and wishing to see them. Ellen felt she sometimes used her mother's insistence on family privacy as an excuse because she felt so much less interested in socializing. In speaking about her friends, Ellen became sad in the session and said she missed her time with them. She especially missed Sally, who had often cycled with Ellen and her father. Ellen worried she would ruin their image of her father if she told her friends the circumstances of his death.

Ellen also spoke about her father. She had always felt that they were one team in the family and her mother and sister another. Ellen described herself as resembling her father in being adventurous and sociable and enjoying a good chat. They both enjoyed physical exercise and activity and she helped him around the home and garden. He had been physically fit, and they had often bicycled together. She had greatly enjoyed their time together and often used it to discuss their lives and feelings. Her father had been a great support when her last relationship broke down, and she had encouraged him through a series of business ventures. Her father had never been able to settle in a job for long because he got bored or saw a better opportunity elsewhere, and had moved through a range of careers, each time believing it would be the one for him. Ellen described knowing that each plan was ill fated but having enjoyed being carried along by his enthusiasm and confidence. Her father had managed a restaurant, imported wine, and become a property developer, each job less financially successful than the last. Ellen acknowledged that her father occasionally drank too much, which at times made him unreliable, contributing to his business difficulties and causing arguments with her mother. He was a man who "really went for it" when he did something, drinking included. Ellen found his energy exciting but feared that it had finally contributed to his death. She felt guilty that she had missed signs that he was struggling at the end of his life and harshly criticized herself for not having done more. Ellen expressed a wide range of emotions during this discussion, becoming animated and excited when describing her father's energy and low and tearful when describing his disappointments and conflict. I asked if she had followed his emotions so closely when he was alive. She became tearful, saying that she had looked up to and admired him and couldn't believe his life had ended in such a "shabby and tragic way."

Ellen was dissatisfied with her family's communication, particularly their failure to discuss her father. He was mentioned only on anniversaries, which made her angry and sad: as if he appeared "only to have existed on the day he entered the world and the day he left it." She wanted to talk much more about him but feared this would upset others or that they would reject her wish to converse. Ellen was also confused by her own wish—if she raised her preoccupations and concerns about his death, she felt guilty and disloyal; yet if she spoke about her good memories, she felt sure none of her family would listen.

Ellen described good relationships with two work colleagues, Tom and Susan. Susan was the classroom teacher and she and Tom were both classroom assistants for children with special educational needs. She enjoyed her job and felt guilty that her absence had left them short-staffed. Her work performance had deteriorated over the past year because of memory problems and low energy. This had increased tension at work, as her colleagues had to cover for her without adequately understanding why she was struggling. Feeling she had not left work on good terms, she was embarrassed and reluctant to resume contact, fearing her colleagues would be angry and frustrated with her.

Formulation

In formulating with Ellen I said, "You have described feeling increasingly low and anxious for two years and have described all of the symptoms of depression over recent months following your cycling accident. When you initially felt low, you thought this was a natural reaction to your father's sudden death. You had had a close relationship, but had felt much more distant from him in the months leading to his death, when his drinking became more frequent and the routine between you changed. You tried to speak to him about this change and felt very hurt and angry when you were rebuffed.

"The change in your relationship with your father before his death, and your deep concern that you missed signs that he felt more desperate than you had understood, have made it very difficult for you to grieve his death. Your anxiety and depression have led you to doubt the choices you made and have left you feeling guilty and responsible. The uncertainty and shame you feel have made it difficult for you to talk to anyone about your feelings and fears. When you tried to talk to your mother, she quickly closed down the discussion and insisted that you not speak to anyone else. You've been caught in a terrible dilemma. At a time you have most needed to talk and get support, something you would often have turned to your father for, you have felt least able to. For a while you tried to manage by keeping active and busy, but you haven't been able to do that since your cycling accident, which I think is why you have felt so much worse in these last weeks. You have felt the full weight of your grief and depression, and as you have become even more withdrawn, you have had little to protect you against that. I think this gives us a way of understanding how depressed you have become since your father died and how we might work together to resolve your current difficulties. By focusing on the depression surrounding your bereavement we can support you in moving on in your mourning, rather than feeling so hopeless and stuck, and to reconnect with the people who are still available to you."

Ellen was tearful listening to the interpersonal formulation but said she felt relieved to have an opportunity to talk about her father and the tremendous loss she felt. We agreed to focus on her mourning for her father, and on planning changes in her remaining network to ensure that her needs were better met in future and to protect against the isolation that had characterized her preceding year.

Grief Focus

In the middle sessions of IPT, the grief focus has two main objectives: to mourn and come to terms with the loss of a relationship, and to connect with remaining or new relationships for support and to find a new direction. Ellen was evidently stuck in the process of mourning and had disengaged from most of her relationships. She had been unable to clarify the narrative of her father's death and was tormented by questions. The shame she felt for herself and for her father prevented her from using the supports previously available in her life, and trapped her in an unproductive cycle of angry rumination. It was important to help her be zetetic and inclusive rather than ruminating on her relationship with her father, and to enable her to engage those who cared for her as a means of reviving her formerly diverse and engaged life.

To reconstruct her paternal relationship, I asked Ellen to tell me what memories she had been having. To maintain relevance to her current symptoms, I encouraged her to speak about parts of the relationship that had most influenced her symptoms, both positively and negatively, in the past week, and then encouraged her to elaborate. I aimed to support Ellen in recalling readily available memories and those more difficult to tolerate in order to create a whole rather than edited version of her relationship. As she remained preoccupied with her father's final days and the events surrounding his death, we followed this lead. Ellen initially described distress and confusion about the end of her father's life, repeating, "I just didn't listen. I let him down when he needed me most." She called this a daily preoccupation and reported spending hours picking over the final days of his life, thinking of ways she could have understood and supported him. Such unproductive, cyclical reflection is common in depression. The IPT therapist promotes an interactive reconstruction, facilitating understanding and reflection through the very act of having to communicate. She tearfully repeated, "He wouldn't be dead if I had listened." This feeling compromised her sleep and made her guilty. Tormented that she had missed an opportunity to save him by calming his distress, she accused herself of killing her father through her inattention.

As Ellen described particular torment over her final phone call with her father, I asked her to tell me all she could remember about it. Ellen said her father had been drinking and crying before she answered the call. His crying made him difficult to understand. He repeatedly apologized for having made such a mess of things and said he would fix it all. I encouraged her to describe how she felt at the time and now. Initially Ellen only reported feeling guilty and reiterated that she had not listened. We again reviewed the call, and I asked her to think about what was said, how she felt, sounded, and moved. When she started to visualize herself during the call Ellen was surprised to recall having felt helpless and frustrated at the time. She recalled rolling her eyes and remaining standing because she did not want the call to continue. Ellen immediately criticized herself: it was "terrible to have been so uncaring when he was obviously so upset." I encouraged her to try to remember if that was how she had felt at the time, as she had described many other examples of the warmth between them. Ellen became quiet for several seconds and then said, "I had had the same call with him over and over in those last few weeks and I was worn down by it." She explained that her father's property deal had fallen through suddenly, and he had lost his investment. Ellen initially felt sympathetic but with each subsequent call became more frustrated and "wanted to shake him into action and make him pick himself up with a new plan like he had always done in the past."

Ellen recalled feeling at the time like they were on familiar territory and she just had to wait for him to get through the dip as he had done before. She now felt guilty and callous to have responded this way. We talked through her past experience of her father's business failures to try to understand her reaction. Ellen acknowledged having had many such conversations about previous failed deals. She said she felt guilty because she now believed she had underestimated his distress on this occasion. After several similar conversations with him, she had seen his mood recover the next day. She had therefore told him to sleep it off and that she would speak to him another time. Ellen expressed intense guilt at having "dismissed" her father, and was convinced that this had somehow caused him to drive while over the legal limit and die. She insisted she should have anticipated trouble and had failed to prevent it.

We contextualized the call in her wider relationship with her father and noted that she had often joked him along when he had been drinking because he was difficult to reason with at such times. Ellen cried, admitting she found her father's drinking disappointing and often sought to distance herself when he drank. Because he rarely remembered their discussions afterwards, she had come to think it pointless to talk to him when he was drunk. Ellen insisted there must have been something during the last call to signal her that things were different. I asked whether she perhaps wished rather than believed there had been something, as it was so difficult to imagine that her life could change so dramatically without warning. Ellen nodded and said she had described it to Pete immediately afterwards as "another of Dad's wobbly calls."

Her father's drinking had grown more frequent in his final year. The once infrequent "wobbly calls" had become regular and intrusive. Ellen eventually admitted that she hadn't known what to do and had wished "it would end." At first Ellen guiltily equated this to wishing her father's life was over. I encouraged her to continue to think about what she wanted to end. She gradually acknowledged wanting to have her "old Dad" back to talk to and do things with, and feeling frustrated and unhappy about how his drinking had changed their relationship. As we reviewed the pattern of communication, Ellen noted how often she had closed discussions when her father was drunk. As we reconstructed the last calls, she acknowledged that her father had been unable to converse constructively and simply circled around the same apologies and self-blame. Ellen had tried to speak to Sally once or twice about how difficult she found her father at that time, but felt disloyal and had stopped. I noted that keeping things private appeared important in her family and appeared to prolong her depression. Ellen responded with surprise, saying that perhaps she was more like her mother than she realized.

Ellen initially felt concerned her father could have read her disapproval. I asked her how much this mattered if he recalled so little of what had been said. Surprised, Ellen acknowledged it unlikely that he would have remembered anything, especially as she tried so hard to conceal her feelings. When I asked if she had ever expressed disapproval, Ellen became silent. She said that she had always imagined that they spoke openly, but that she mostly had supported rather than challenged him. Before he lost his previous business, she had spoken bluntly to him about his increasing drinking and chaotic plans. She found this very difficult to do as she had always supported his adventures and expected his next fresh plan to turn things around. She hoped he would understand that she was motivated by concern and was devastated when her father dismissed her as "being just like my mother" and worrying over nothing. Ellen remembered feeling hurt that he ignored her point of view and angry that the camaraderie and mutual respect she had so valued in their relationship seemed to evaporate when they disagreed. I noted that Ellen had previously made this comparison herself; she said she had noticed this too. She had thought her father had intended it as an insult, "but maybe we all felt a need to rein him in and I just took longer to get there." Very tearfully, she said she had "wished the drunk, helpless Dad would disappear and let the old one come back." We reviewed depressive guilt, which could make her feel punished for something she had thought and create a certainty out of a period of great confusion and frustration. Noting how difficult it was for Ellen to avow disapproval or anger, I suggested that feeling this way was unsurprising given how deeply she had felt the loss of a treasured bond. Ellen agreed that when her father drank she felt angry to be deprived of enjoyable company and forced to tolerate a poor replacement.

Ellen explained she had been too ashamed to tell her mother and Louise about the final telephone call, fearing that they too would blame her for her father's death. She withdrew from her mother and sister, feeling responsible for their distress. Her mother's demands for family privacy had prevented her from talking with outsiders, compounding her isolation. Prompted by Ellen's feelings about her mother and sister, we discussed the family's behavior after her father's death. Her mother had sounded "unnaturally calm" when she telephoned Ellen that her father had been in an accident. She did not initially say that her father was dead but asked her to come to the hospital. Ellen arrived with Pete and was embarrassed when her mother asked him to leave, describing it as "a family matter." Ellen felt angry that the person who could support her had been sent away. This happened before she knew her father had died in the accident, and that everything else was "wiped out" when her mother announced he was dead. Her mother remained very contained in the hospital, but Ellen and Louise cried. Ellen said she panicked when she realized he had been drinking and driving. She slowly realized that her mother knew or assumed that her father had been drinking, and this was why she had sent Pete away. She "initially felt relieved" that her father had not been "even more exposed" but then began to worry that she had missed a sign and that his death might not have been accidental.

The funeral was a small and private service, which she thought made the family seem ashamed of her father. She felt she hardly recognized him from the eulogies. Her mother warned her not to mention her father's drinking to the family who attended, and Ellen said it felt as though it was all for someone else. She felt bitter that family members who had had little to do with her father in life were free to discuss and remember him, while his immediate family closed down and acted as if he hadn't existed.

When her family seemed to forget or ignore her father, Ellen felt it her duty to hold him in mind. This common feature of bereavement-related depression creates a terrible dilemma for the person trying to sustain the past in an evolving and changing present. She felt angry and guilty that in respecting her mother's wishes she was allowing her father to be forgotten. She repeated: "I let him down when he was alive, so I must now make it up to him." We discussed how this appeared to sustain her depression in two ways—making it impossible for her to acknowledge the end of her father's life and to relate to her mother, who seemed to Ellen overly willing to do that very thing. Ellen said she couldn't imagine being happy again, because it would mean she hadn't loved him and would vindicate her mother's criticism of his life and death. We discussed how her behavior demonstrated her bond with her father. I asked if the way she lived now was a fitting testimony to the energetic and active relationship they had had for much of his life. Ellen immediately responded that he would be horrified to see her now, and would push and cajole her to get out and get on with her life, as he had done so many times when alive. Ellen appeared struck by the difference between the way her current, depressed life reflected their relationship and what she imagined her father would want. We discussed how her response was shaped by depression rather than a legacy of the relationship. We reviewed her role when her father was alive—defending him when others, particularly her mother, thought him foolish or reckless; and in his life as in his death, how difficult it had been for her to concede his difficulties as well as his strengths. Ellen remarked that she had enjoyed his energy and enthusiasm and had considered him a "flawed hero," but in the months before his death had been aware only of his flaws. Ellen felt uncomfortable remembering her father in this way because it recalled the criticism her mother leveled at him. Ellen said getting angry at her mother had been easier than acknowledging her father's flaws, but as she remembered her own frustration she began to understand her mother's disappointment and anger, and noted that her own anger dissipated.

I encouraged Ellen to consider options between sessions for engaging others in the process of remembering her father. She was initially reluctant to talk to anyone but conceded feeling guilty that she did not know Louise's feelings about their father's death. She described having become so self-absorbed that she sometimes felt others didn't exist. At times she had wished to withdraw completely, finding it too difficult to have to consider other people when she felt so overwhelmed. There was "no room left to think about anyone else." Despite their cautious communication, she had felt close to Louise and had missed her company while depressed. Ellen had not told Louise about her therapy and asked if doing so might reveal how much she had been struggling with their loss. Struck by how different it felt to think about "their" rather than "her" father, Ellen felt guilty but also motivated to ask about how her sister was coping.

As Ellen felt nervous about starting the conversation, we explored what she would be comfortable saying and what she feared to discuss. Ellen rehearsed what she wanted Louise to know about depression and agreed to consider inviting her sister to join one of her sessions. Ellen was surprised that once she decided to talk to Louise, it became much easier to imagine the conversation. She had been touched by her sister's concern and had not pushed her to talk, but thought it would help them both to tell Louise more. Ellen noted that she had become more practiced in talking about her depression in our weekly sessions. Her main objective was to ask how Louise had coped.

When they spoke, Ellen was surprised to discover that Louise already suspected Ellen was depressed but had felt unable to ask her about it. Ellen had not expected Louise would feel relieved to ask her, but understood when Louise said she would feel less helpless if she knew how to help. Ellen told Louise her guilt about their father's death, recounting the phone call, but did not mention her suspicions that their father had killed himself. To her astonishment, Louise already knew about the call, as their father had spoken to Louise after calling Ellen. Louise reported that their father had declared Ellen quite right to ignore him, and that he was going to bed as she suggested. She didn't know why he had gone driving later. This discussion left Ellen very unsettled. She said she believed Louise, felt relieved that her father had appeared calmer following their conversation, but still felt her questions about his death remained unanswered.

While continuing to expand the range of Ellen's positive and negative memories of her father in therapy sessions, we also explored the relationships available to Ellen outside treatment. She found it novel to talk as she did in therapy and increasingly difficult to "close it back down again" between sessions, as had been her habit. I suggested that this habit had not helped her and had sustained her depression. Ellen said she had initially worried that therapy was making her worse, as she felt so sad when talking about her father, but she noted that she recovered more quickly after each session, and at Session 9 commented when she did not cry in the session. We noted that her sleep had started to improve, she stopped having nightmares, and in consequence she had more energy during the day. We distinguished feeling depressed from feeling sad in our weekly symptom review, a distinction Ellen actively picked up. After speaking to Louise, Ellen responded to calls from her friend Sally, who lived nearby, and rejoined her yoga class. She said she enjoyed feeling curious about other people again. She still missed her father very much but no longer wanted to die to be with him. She was surprised how quickly this had changed, remembering how strong and frightening the feeling had been only a few weeks before.

Sally had recently had a baby and Ellen was able to spend time with her without feeling that she had to be the center of attention. Ellen found that she enjoyed the company and was reassured that Sally's routine rarely allowed for more than brief visits or walks around the park. She began to spend a little more time with her mother, tending her garden for her as she had previously done with her father. Recognizing her own frustration with her father and her struggle to make headway in talking to him altered her perspective on her mother's response. Ellen was still reluctant to open discussion but could manage contact that had a practical focus, acknowledging that she and her mother had never talked easily despite enjoying each other's company. I asked if Ellen would like to change her relationship with her mother. She said talking would feel too unfamiliar; she found discussion much easier with others in her life. I commented that she was rediscovering her social skills in company and in her relationships, and that she could always revisit this option if she chose to.

After a couple of weeks of more regular contact with Sally and Louise, Ellen felt an increasing need to discuss her father with someone else who had known him. She had become more comfortable doing this in sessions, recalling both happy and difficult memories. Ellen decided to speak to Louise again about her continuing uncertainty about her father's death. She still felt unsettled, but better able tolerate the feelings this evoked. When they spoke again, Louise also wanted to know more about the accident and remembered a police liaison officer having invited them to contact her if they had questions. Supporting one another, they met with the officer, who described the accident investigation and why the position of the car suggested that their father had lost control while driving. She also told them that the accident scene was a notoriously dangerous stretch of road where three other serious accidents had occurred, one also fatal. The officer reported that the pedestrian knocked down in the accident had recovered fully. Ellen found this meeting distressing, as if she were hearing the news of the accident for this first time, but, as at the time of his death, she and Louise comforted each other. Ellen told Louise her fears that her father had killed himself and described feeling she was letting go of a weight in saying it aloud. Louise said she had no idea Ellen had been thinking this way or feeling to blame. Ellen described her "gentle concern" as unexpected and calming.

After 12 of her 16 therapy sessions, Ellen had regained considerable energy and began to consider returning to work. First she contacted her colleague Tom, who told her she was missed at school. Ellen, encouraged by her experience with Louise, explained how much she had struggled after father's death. Tom admitted he had not understood what she had been going through and was pleased she was returning. Ellen started a gradual return to work and found that although it was demanding, her energy and enthusiasm increased each week. She returned full time within a month.

While Ellen was returning to work, she unexpectedly announced that she had ended her relationship with Pete. She reported no longer needing the practical support he had offered and felt it unfair to mislead him about her feelings any longer. She described the split as upsetting and worried that she would dip back into depression. Her symptoms had fallen below the clinical threshold for caseness for two weeks and Ellen felt keen not to rush to assume she was better—as in the past—and potentially put her recovery at risk. She had spoken to friends before ending the relationship and met them immediately after speaking to Pete. They were supportive, insisting upon making plans to see her so that she would not feel lonely. Ellen deliberately agreed to their plans, wanting to avoid isolation after having felt it for so long. In the final weeks of therapy, Ellen described enjoyment and excitement about her new routine and confidence that she had chosen correctly. In response to Ellen's concerns we looked in detail at how her decision had affected her symptoms and actively distinguished depression from distress. She saw that while she had been upset and tearful, she had not withdrawn or lost interest and had in fact sought out company. Her guilt was appropriate to the situation and assuaged by her sense of having "done the right thing." She was clear that she did not feel suicidal and reassured that she had made great progress and was responding to this ending very differently from the loss of her father.

Ending

This relationship change gave us a natural opportunity to talk about the end of the therapy and our work together. In the ending phase of IPT, the therapist notes the approaching end of the therapy sessions, helps the patient to face the separation, consolidates the patient's sense of new skills and confidence by reviewing and evaluating the progress made in therapy, and helps the patient to plan for the future. Ellen described significant improvement in her mood and across the range of depressive symptoms but remained apprehensive about the depression returning. She scored 3 on the PHQ-9, below the cutoff for depression. Her score on the GAD was 6, down from 19, indicating slightly elevated anxiety that she attributed to taking on so many new things and the prospect of therapy ending. She described feeling anxious before events but rarely having difficulties once she arrived or got involved. Her Ham-D score was 5, indicating remission.

Ellen said she wanted to consider the depression just a reaction to a bad event and not part of her makeup. We continued to talk about how Ellen would distinguish distress from depression, and revisited the psychoeducation about depression I had presented early in therapy. We reviewed that depression can recur and the importance of continuing to use the skills she had developed to protect against future episodes. Ellen found this frightening to think about, although her recent experiences had boosted her confidence that she could manage, and she felt she understood depression much better than she had before treatment. This highlighted a risk for Ellen, her tendency to withdraw from difficult interpersonal situations. Her isolation had helped to maintain the depressive episode; after therapy it would increase her relapse risk if she did not work to stay well. After past episodes she had abruptly stopped medication, with a resulting rapid return of symptoms. The discussion about ending therefore began by reviewing both the progress Ellen had made and the concerns and vulnerability she faced in the future.

We reviewed how Ellen had felt in the past after stopping her medication. On both occasions she had tried "to be happy all the time" and "put on a face" to cover what she was still feeling because she so wanted to feel better. She said she had felt better but had lacked the confidence in her recovery she had now. We carefully examined how she was feeling now through a detailed discussion of her symptoms, to clarify the extent of the change she had achieved and to open discussion on staying well. We used psychoeducation to reinforce Ellen's understanding and expertise as she faced the fourth phase of IPT, independent practice. We also discussed in detail Ellen's ongoing responsibility to help herself remain well in the context of a recurring illness. I highlighted her vulnerability when Ellen withdrew from support, how this extra burden of coping on her own had prolonged and worsened her symptoms. We acknowledged that very likely she would face changes and losses again in the future, and looked at how she could use her newly developed strategies and skills to manage events while minimizing the chances of another depressive episode. I explicitly linked our discussion of patterns of recurrent depressive illness to good practice guidelines on the role of medication and the time course for such treatment. We discussed the vulnerability of partially treated depression and clarified the recommendation to continue medication for at least two years following a second episode. Ellen was initially uncomfortable about continuing treatment when she felt well, but responded well to visual illustrations of different stages of remission and recovery. Acknowledging that she had already spent two years unwell with partially treated depression, she agreed she would rather continue to invest in her own well-being than risk revisiting distress and disruption. Ellen agreed that she responded to medication as she did to difficult emotions and communication: avoid as much as possible. She said she had learned to face the feelings she feared and therefore felt confident that she could similarly change her behavior towards medication.

At the end of therapy, Ellen noticed her greater consciousness of informing her friends and sister that therapy was terminating, and having them support her through it. She still did not like to be the focus of attention but felt better able to tell them how she felt. She was not used to focusing the conversation on herself and acknowledged the need to work on that. She said she had learned it was acceptable to talk about herself without criticizing herself for selfishness or self-absorption. We acknowledged her progress in choosing whom she could talk to and whom she could trust with her confidences.

Ellen reported an example of an upsetting event to illustrate the progress she had made. A friend with whom she had re-established regular contact had a miscarriage. Ellen described feeling very sad for her friend but said the incident made her realize how much better she was. When very depressed she would have fallen apart at this news, but now could comfort her friend and feel sad, as opposed to depressed. Her friend's raw distress made her aware that it had been weeks since she could remember feeling that way herself. We scrutinized the distinction between predictable, normative emotional reactions and depressive symptoms, and Ellen mapped out how she would determine a depressive recurrence. She retraced the initial days of the recent depressive episode and pinpointed markers she would look for in the future. To further protect herself, she included Louise in checking her warning signals. They agreed upon a plan of action, emphasizing ways in which Ellen could maintain contact with supports around her and address difficulties as they arose rather than struggling at length on her own.

Ellen had been maintaining her mother's garden since the middle of therapy. This felt relaxing, and made her feel closer to her father. She started to notice that this was too solitary an activity and that she found more pleasure in company. Accordingly, she invited her mother and sister to join her in gardening, which they did readily. The garden ended up getting less attention but Ellen got a lot more, and this improved her mood greatly. Ellen had not spoken more openly to her mother about her depression as treatment ended. She felt she had regained their former relationship and happily enjoyed her company again, but did not expect to pursue a more confiding relationship. Ellen was pleased to confide more to Louise, commenting that "perhaps our family just works one relationship at a time." We acknowledged that while IPT had not transformed her relationship with her mother, she had regained the practical intimacy and support they had previously shared and had deepened her bond and communication with her sister.

At the start of therapy, Ellen's daily routine had been severely disrupted. In the final sessions, she reported going to bed at a reasonable hour, sleeping every night, rising and dressing for breakfast every day, and having a daily plan. She no longer spent evenings watching videos of her father, and now felt guilty she did not think of him more. A couple of days could now pass without a thought of him because she had so much more to address in her day. Her energy was much better and she no longer needed to nap despite rising earlier. Ellen felt excited that she could function without depression and now wanted to do things all the time. She said she no longer thought of death and became tearful in recalling that she had wanted to die to be with her father. She spoke quietly of wanting to live her life before seeing him again. As IPT ended, Ellen remained in remission. She reported greater satisfaction in her relationships with her sister and friends. Ellen still felt reluctant to talk about her father in front of her mother but now could more willingly accept that their coping styles differed. She felt satisfied that she could talk with Louise and Sally, but noted she felt less need to do so and felt more able to look forward to her own plans, less tied to the grief that had preoccupied her.

DISCUSSION

This case illustrates how IPT can provide a supportive framework in treating bereavement-related depression. The introduction of the diagnosis appeared a key intervention in this case, as in many grief cases. This did not dismiss or override the understandable and predictable sadness of bereavement, but rather clarified that Ellen was struggling with the added burden of depression. This manoeuvre helped her understand the enormity of her distress and to start to confront the necessary and unnecessary losses she faced. This distinction was a crucial point that she had not been able to consider before, having felt all was lost in her unrecognized depressed state. Considering the differences as well as the similarities between bereavement and depression helped her to allow herself relief from some of the burden.

IPT has an explicit interpersonal focus that evidently contrasted with Ellen's initial response. This can be a challenge in grief work, when anger and resentment can be directed towards others simply because they are still alive. The fact of existence can become a point of contention, over and above individual relationship issues and expectations. The slow, careful inventory of relationships aimed to engage Ellen in remembering the other people in her life rather than just gathering information. The discussion deliberately focused on both the experience of relationships in the context of the depressive episode and her memories of earlier periods. We thus made a connection with Ellen outside of her depression, in areas of competence and relationships she had temporarily forgotten. This piqued her curiosity and motivation to re-engage with others and resume her own life again.

One distinctive feature of the grief focal area in IPT is the intensity of the affect in and between sessions. Affect is a routine focus in IPT but often appears to be felt more deeply by both patients and therapists in grief focal work. It is crucial that therapists allow time and space for patients to express this, and that the therapist and perhaps even other people in the patient's life demonstrate their capacity to stay with the patient despite sadness, anger, and fear (Markowitz & Milrod, 2011). This demands a slow, confident pace to the work at times, but without it attempts to re-engage with the routines and activities of everyday life may be unavailing.

Affect is often related to unspoken fears or unresolved issues in the relationship with the deceased, as in Ellen's suspicions of suicide, guilt at not having supported her father, and anger at her mother's apparent rejection of her father in her own grief. These issues are often difficult to express openly and require gentle but persistent therapist attention. The IPT model provides an tolerant, constructive, and effective framework for working with bereavement-related depression, helping patients to understand and manage the impact of one of the most difficult interpersonal events any of us can face, and to explicitly and deliberately engage with the network who remain while remembering, in full richness and diversity, the person and relationship that has been lost.

3

Interpersonal Psychotherapy for Major Depression

Role Dispute

JONATHAN LICHTMACHER AND ILJIE FITZGERALD

INTRODUCTION

When IPT focuses on a role dispute, the therapist links acute major depression with non-reciprocal ideas about what the patient and a significant other owe to each other in a relationship. Role dispute-focused IPT may be considered unilateral couples therapy (Weissman et al., 2000, p. 76). The role dispute may be with a marital or domestic partner, a boss, parent, friend, or child, among other relationships. The therapist helps the patient associate the patient's feelings of depression with interpersonal interactions between himself or herself and the significant other and encourages the patient to try out new, assertive behaviors and communications. The patient and therapist use role-play to test out new communications in session to prepare the patient for a successful outcome. Optimism that the patient will get better, permission to try new behaviors in interpersonal relationships, a renewed sense of agency, clarification and validation of feelings, and successful new experiences are key to the antidepressant effect of role dispute-focused IPT (Miller & Markowitz, 1999).

In this chapter we present a case example of role dispute-focused IPT and demonstrate supervision in an outpatient teaching clinic where IPT is offered to all patients with depression as part of an evidence-based treatment program. The therapist is a third-year psychiatry resident learning IPT as a required part of the residency training curriculum.

Residents see patients with non-bipolar, acute major depression for sixteen weekly, individual sessions with a goal of achieving remission from depression. Supervision groups, consisting of three residents and one or two faculty members, meet weekly

in a group supervision format. Supervision entails reviewing cases and
clips from video recordings of recent sessions. Video recording brings imm.
the supervision, offers an opportunity to stop the action and discuss in
moments in the therapy, and allows specific instruction about technique. Cli.
obtain consent from the patients for the video recording and its intent: clinical , .i-
vision and teaching (Lichtmacher, Eisendrath, & Haller, 2006).

CASE EXAMPLE

History of Present Illness

Joy, a thirty-seven-year-old, bisexual-identified financial analyst, presented to our
psychiatric evaluation clinic with the chief complaint of "being stuck." Joy, who had
chronic, severe hypertension and a long history of poor medication adherence, had
suffered a small myocardial infarction eight months earlier. Afraid for her long-term
health, Joy had decided to leave her high-stress job and look for a new one. A generally social and gregarious person, she now stayed superficially connected with a core
group of five or six friends who were mothers at her daughter's preschool. Joy
reported a depressed mood, anhedonia, feelings of guilt and low self-worth, decreased
energy, poor appetite, and impaired concentration for the past three months.
Reporting that she did not want to get out of bed in the mornings, she described
herself as "basically lazy and unmotivated." She summarized, "I guess I'm just in a
rut." Notably, Joy reported that her job loss had led to increased conflicts over the
sharing of child care with her ex-partner, whom she had left two years earlier. She
spent most evenings and weekends at the apartment of her supportive boyfriend,
Ben, but was increasingly feeling that she did not deserve his kind attention.

Joy came to the evaluation clinic seeking therapy that would target her depression
and help her move out of the "rut" in which she found herself. She felt she no longer
had control over her life. Though she wanted to go back to work, she lacked the motivation to search for a new career.

Psychiatric, Family, and Medical History

Joy denied a history of psychiatric diagnoses, hospitalizations, substance abuse,
or individual treatments prior to this presentation. She had briefly gone to couples
therapy "years ago" and found it "somewhat helpful," specifically because she felt
that she had "learned some tools for how to express myself." She denied a family
history of psychiatric disorders, substance abuse, psychiatric treatments, or suicide
attempts.

Joy's medical history was significant for hypertension diagnosed when she was
seventeen years old. Poor adherence to her blood pressure medication regimen over
several years had contributed to her recent heart attack. She had brought herself to
the emergency room with jaw and arm pain, and after the heart attack was diagnosed
she spent several days in the hospital for treatment and observation. Fortunately, she
had no functional sequelae from the heart attack, but she did have to take a medication to prevent arrhythmias. Notably, both of her parents had hypertension, and two

, her grandparents had died from strokes that had resulted from chronic hypertension.

Differential Diagnosis and Indication for IPT

Joy met DSM-IV criteria for major depression in the setting of multiple social stressors, including job loss, a new relationship, conflict with an ex-partner, and a chronic medical illness (American Psychiatric Association, 2000). She was reluctant to say that she was depressed, but was frequently tearful in her first session. Her diagnosis was supported by a Beck Depression Inventory-II (BDI-II) score of 25, indicating moderate depression (Beck, Steer, & Brown, 1996). (Scores on the BDI-II range from 0 to 63, with less than 10 consistent with remission and greater than 30 consistent with a severe depression.)

As a third-year psychiatry resident learning IPT for the first time, I presented my initial session with Joy to my supervision group using video recording. Joy had readily signed the consent for recording. After I reviewed the tape with my supervisor and fellow residents, we agreed that IPT offered an opportunity for the patient to focus on the interpersonal aspects of her depression in her roles as a partner, mother, and unemployed professional.

After the first interview, I believed that IPT for depression was indicated for several reasons. First, Joy had a DSM-IV diagnosis of non-psychotic, unipolar major depression. Second, she was significantly distressed related to a dramatic change in her social roles due to a chronic medical condition, suggesting a role transition focus for the treatment. Third, she was able to contract with me to get better using a time-limited model; and fourth, she connected with my initial formulation that her depression might be linked to interpersonal stressors.

Interpersonal Inventory (Sessions 2 and 3)

At the second visit, after checking in with Joy about how things had been going since we last met and reviewing her current symptoms of depression, I described IPT in more detail to her, clarifying that we would focus on the ways in which her interpersonal interactions might make her more susceptible to getting depressed. Responding to Joy's expression of shame about being depressed, I likened having depression to having the flu. Using a medical model helps patients see depression not as a personal failure, but as something serious that requires attention and is treatable. Joy had high expectations of how she should be functioning, which both were a consequence of and contributed to her depression. Giving the patient the **sick role** excuses the patient from her normal social roles when depression prevents her from performing them, shifting the patient's stance from self-accusation to blaming the illness (Klerman, Weissman, Rounsaville, & Chevron, 1984).

THERAPIST: It seems like you expect to be able to function in all the ways you used to before your depression began, and then you blame yourself when you can't.
JOY: Yeah, pretty much.

THERAPIST: Well, depression is an illness, like the flu. If you had the flu, don't you think you would take some time to get better?

JOY: That's true.

THERAPIST: What I'd like to suggest is that together we tackle your depression and get you feeling a lot better. The model is a 16-session, weekly psychotherapy specific to depression. How does that sound?

JOY: That sounds really good, but do you think it will work?

THERAPIST: I do. I have a lot of confidence in the model, and there is good research supporting it for depression, so I'm recommending it.

JOY: OK.

THERAPIST: Next week bring your calendar and any specific dates when you anticipate you will be away. I will do the same. Together we will count out 16 sessions and set an end date for the therapy.

JOY: OK. That sounds fine.

After we made a contract to do IPT, I asked Joy to begin her interpersonal inventory. The interpersonal inventory catalogs the patient's relationships with the significant people in her life. The information it provides helps the therapist understand interpersonal contributions to the current depressive episode and develop an interpersonal formulation for the therapy (Klerman et al., 1984; Stuart & Robertson, 2003). I asked Joy to "tell me about all the important people in your life currently—what you like about the relationships and what you would like to be different." The specific wording of this instruction conveys to the patient that she can want her relationships to be different and that she can have agency in making changes.

Joy's interpersonal inventory included several significant current relationships. First, she had been romantically involved for the past year with her boyfriend, Ben. Joy and Ben started dating immediately before her heart attack. Joy described their relationship as "drama-free" and in particular appreciated Ben's "non-pushy" encouragement to take care of her own physical health, from reminders to take her blood pressure medications to encouraging her yoga sessions for stress reduction. Joy was hesitantly optimistic about their relationship. She appreciated Ben's warmth, caring, and "low-maintenance" attitude. At the same time, Joy felt unsure about whether Ben genuinely wanted to be with her, in part due to the reversal in roles from her previous relationship, in which Joy had felt that she was the caretaker at her own expense.

Joy's romantic relationship with her ex-partner, Laura, had ended two years before. Joy and Laura now shared care of Maxine, their five-year-old daughter. Joy and Laura had met through mutual friends soon after Laura had gone through a bitter divorce. Joy initially appreciated Laura for her sharp intelligence, liveliness, and self-assurance. However, she often felt manipulated by Laura, who dominated their relationship. Joy had complied with Laura's exacting demands for doing all the household chores; drove Laura everywhere she needed to go, because Laura claimed driving gave her a headache; and moved with her to a neighborhood that Laura preferred, despite Joy's wish to stay put. Laura had had a baby just prior to the start of their relationship. After a brief and exciting courtship, Joy and Laura became enmeshed in a complicated relationship that involved co-parenting Laura's young daughter, Maxine.

Joy complained of feeling "diminished" and "voiceless" through her partnership with Laura. She had nevertheless felt unable to express her frustration or assert her needs. Joy and Laura raised Maxine together until their breakup. Laura had begun expressing her desire to have an open relationship in which she could date other people. Joy had refused this proposed arrangement and moved out. Joy stated that she would have cut off all ties to Laura were it not for Maxine. As Joy had never formally adopted Maxine, she had no legal rights to custody.

Maxine lived primarily with Laura, but Joy brought her home to her own apartment, back in her old neighborhood, two nights each week as part of an informal arrangement. Laura's many rules for how to raise Maxine affected Joy's parenting and constituted an ongoing stressor. In the past few months, since Joy had stopped working, Laura's increasingly frequent requests that Joy be available for last-minute child care led to growing "frustration" and "anger" for Joy. At the same time, Joy feared that if she challenged Laura, Laura would cut her off from their daughter. Joy denied any history of physical violence in the relationship.

I asked Joy about her extended social network. Joy described her support network as "some friends from my life before I met Laura, but I haven't seen them in ages," daily superficial chats with a core group of mothers at Maxine's school, and some new couples she had met through Ben. I wanted to know more about the cultural context of Joy's different social communities and inquired about whether Joy's bisexuality affected her different relationships. Joy's school community included lesbian, gay, and heterosexual parents who were well integrated socially in the context of school and related activities. Her lesbian friends, with whom she had forged bonds during her relationship with Laura, were generally accepting of her bisexuality as well. Ben's friends were mostly heterosexual. Joy acknowledged that her bisexuality was not something she discussed openly with them, nor did it come up as a general topic of discussion. In addition, she denied that her bisexuality played a central role in her acute depression. Further discussion about Joy's bisexuality felt to me to be more intrusive than clarifying.

Rather, Joy complained of feeling disconnected from her friends, despite their best intentions. She linked her increasing sense of social isolation to her depression, stating that depression exacerbated her baseline stoicism. Even before the onset of this depressive episode, she had always felt that to express her feelings and needs would bother others, and she did not want to worry her friends unnecessarily. She had a longstanding pattern of "minimizing my own needs" to others. Though Joy smiled as she made that statement, my own spreading feeling of sadness intruded in the moment and helped me better understand Joy's depression. I was reminded that in her first visit Joy had said she came to our clinic seeking "someone objective who can listen to me." Social support and the perception that help is readily available protect against depression (Henderson, 1980; Henderson, Duncan-Jones, McAuley, & Ritchie, 1978; Paykel, Myers, Dienelt, et al., 1969). Joy had many friends, but may have had internal barriers to reaching out for help.

From the second IPT visit, I began sessions by asking, "How have things been going since we last met?" This question helps keep the patient focused on the present (Weissman, Markowitz, & Klerman, 2007). In the third session, Joy reported that she was doing "better." She noticed that her appetite had improved and she had more energy in the morning. In this session Joy's interpersonal inventory extended to her parents, retired physicians who lived across the country. Her father had been a surgeon, her mother a neurologist. Joy described her father as "warm and caring, but not home much." She described her mother jokingly as "more clinical than maternal."

Joy related that her mother showed concern for her after her heart attack by sending medical literature about exercise and calling her weekly to remind her to take her medications, but not inquiring about any other aspect of her life except to ask about Maxine. In addition, Joy complained that her mother had mailed prescriptions for anti-anxiety medications for her to try, though she had not asked for them. When she learned that Joy was going to see a therapist, her mother tried to convince her that psychotherapy was a waste of time. During her intake appointment, Joy made clear that she was "not interested in being prescribed medications for my depression," and wanted to try a "talk therapy" by itself before considering any pharmacological recommendations.

I asked about Joy's early relationships—what she liked about them and what she would have liked to have been different—as a way to understand the quality of those relationships and how she handled negative and stressful interactions. As a pre-teen, Joy saw herself as the family peacemaker amid frequent arguments between her parents. At age 12, she discovered the secret of her mother's infidelity, which nearly ended her parents' marriage. Joy never told anyone about this. In high school, Joy was an average student who was very socially involved, though she had no close confidantes. As a junior, she met her first girlfriend. She kept her bisexuality secret from her family out of fear of rejection. She never discussed it with family until her relationship with Laura. Even then, her sexuality was just not discussed. In contrast, Joy's sister's boyfriends were a frequent topic of discussion for the whole family.

Joy further contrasted her own and her younger sister Faith's relationship with her parents. Although Joy had moved out of state for college, Faith continued to live in the same town, on the same street where they grew up. Joy had always felt that Faith had been the favored child. Yet, when she visited her family once or twice a year, Joy was the one who did the household maintenance tasks her father could no longer do himself, such as cleaning out the rain gutters or setting up his online bill payments. One of Joy's complaints was that her primary family continued to rely on her to referee and solve family problems, even from afar.

When asked what she would like to be different in the relationship with her mother, she wished that her mother would not call her to referee disagreements with her sister. She wished her mother "could just be real with me."

THERAPIST: What do you mean?
JOY: I mean, I wish she would act like a mother. You know, to want to hear about my personal experience of things, to listen. I feel like she is constantly demanding my allegiance, but holding me at arm's length.
THERAPIST: Have you ever shared that feeling with her?
JOY: Sure.
THERAPIST: What happens?
JOY: What happens is that we fight or I get angry and she turns off.

Session 4: Formulation

At the end of the interpersonal inventory, my supervisor and I considered two possible foci: role transition and role dispute (Klerman et al., 1984). A role transition refers to a major life change that results in a change of social roles. Joy clearly had several life changes: the heart attack, leaving her job, and medical disability. However, as the interpersonal inventory progressed, it became clear that although Joy's heart attack and medical leave were significant stresses related to her depression, she was now medically asymptomatic and anticipated going back to a less stressful job if she could regain the energy and motivation to look for one, and wanted to take her medications more reliably; she was still occasionally missing doses. Nevertheless, my supervision group appreciated that a role transition seemed a reasonable focus for the treatment, though not the only one.

Joy's mood symptoms and angry and sad affect in sessions seemed linked to her recent stressful interactions with her demanding ex-partner and phone conversations with her mother. During the interpersonal inventory, Joy had recounted her difficulty in expressing anger or resentment towards her ex-partner, often denying or minimizing these emotions, though her affect (tears) and body language (crossing her arms and sitting back in her chair) indicated otherwise. This consistently happened when she described something Laura expected of her that she did not want to do, but ended up doing anyway, such as waking before dawn to walk Laura's dogs. The non-reciprocal nature of their relationship arose in almost all their communications. Joy's pattern was to refrain from asserting herself and then to end up feeling more frustrated, discontented, and, ultimately, depressed. In sessions, Joy laughingly pointed out "how ridiculous" and "outrageous" Laura had been in a recent communication. She also put herself down for not speaking up. By taking the time in the sessions to review Joy's feelings moment to moment in these communications with Laura, Joy and I were able to see that these painful exchanges with Laura directly influenced her mood. This association between her interpersonal stressors and her depression seemed more consistent with a role dispute. My supervision group agreed.

THERAPIST: As we have talked, I've noticed a pattern in your relationships with your ex-partner and your family which makes you susceptible to feeling unheard and subsequently depressed.

JOY: Yes, I totally agree.

THERAPIST: With your mother and Laura, you have what we call an interpersonal role dispute. A role dispute is when two people have non-reciprocal ideas about their mutual roles in the relationship, and in your situation, it's Laura and your mother whose expectations are prevailing.

Joy listened quietly, and I realized that I had her full attention.

THERAPIST: What do you think? Does this ring true for you?

JOY: Yes, you make a lot of sense. I think I've always had this problem. Why do I keep getting involved and intervening when it's not my problem to solve? Some of my friends have even complained that I get too involved taking care of things that I'm not responsible for.

THERAPIST: Like what? Can you share an example from the past week?

JOY: Well, earlier this week, my Mom called me to complain that Faith wasn't helping her get her broken kitchen faucet repaired. I ended up spending an hour calling her and then my sister, and back and forth multiple times, trying to help them resolve it. This happens all the time, at least a couple of times a month. I feel resentful that they keep coming to me to solve their problems from three thousand miles away, and also ineffective because they never resolve anything anyway.

THERAPIST: So why do you do it?

JOY: [bitterly chuckling] I guess I feel like I have to solve the problem. I feel compelled to intervene.

THERAPIST: Or what?

JOY: I don't know. A train wreck.

THERAPIST: So, it's hard to say "no." It's almost as though you feel that you have to take care of the needs of all the people in your life before you can take care of your own, or else everything will fall apart.

JOY: That's exactly how I feel. I guess that's why I'm here! I don't want to keep doing this, living like this.

THERAPIST: OK, Joy, so it looks like we are on the same page about the focus of our therapy sessions. You are in a role dispute with your mother. You have very different ideas about what you owe to each other in the relationship.

JOY: Yes. Definitely.

THERAPIST: There is a parallel with your relationship with Laura as well, like your walking the dogs at dawn, when you really don't want to.

JOY: Yes.

THERAPIST: And in both situations, you are losing out.

JOY: Yes. That's right.

THERAPIST: OK, your task for the rest of the therapy is to bring into sessions things that happen in the intervening week that you have strong feelings about. Does that sound reasonable?

JOY: Yes. I think that makes a lot of sense.

Joy and I agreed on the formulation and formed a contract for the remainder of the therapy. I set the frame for future sessions by asking her to bring in specific "here-and-now material." This was not a new idea in the therapy: from the very beginning, I had started sessions by asking, "How have things been going since we last met?"

IPT: Middle Phase

During the middle phase of IPT, I used specific interventions to address interpersonal communication and behaviors. **Communication analysis** of an interpersonal encounter helps connect the patient's affect to the incident. The therapist has the patient describe the interaction in great detail, at each step asking the patient to reflect on her feelings moment to moment, helping the patient link incidents to affects. The clinician then creates opportunities for the patient to explore options, to try out new communications and behaviors between sessions. The IPT therapist might ask: "What would you have liked to have happened?" or "What else might you have said?" **Clarification** and **attention to affect** are prominent therapeutic tools. **Role-play** gives the patient the opportunity to try out new interpersonal strategies with the therapist. In the middle phase, Joy had a chance to reevaluate her attitudes toward her mother's limitations and to "rewrite" the relationship contract between herself and her ex-partner (Weissman et al., 2007).

Session 5

During the week between sessions, Joy had visited her parents for her mother's birth-day. Joy related the following interaction that occurred on the car ride back to the airport.

JOY: It was not a good visit, and we had the usual terrible goodbye.

THERAPIST: Tell me about it.

JOY: On my last day there, on the way to the airport, my Mom started in on me again.

THERAPIST: What do you mean, "started in on" you?

JOY: She said, you know, real quiet, like I was a patient, that even if I didn't care about my blood pressure, she did. And she didn't want me to have another heart attack. And I told her to stop worrying about it. I had it under control. And I do. I don't want to die.

THERAPIST: What did you say?

JOY: [sharply and loudly] "God, stop reminding me about it, Mom! It's under con-trol!" [sarcastically] "If I have another heart attack, I have another heart attack!"

THERAPIST: What were you feeling at that point?

JOY: Well, I was definitely pretty annoyed.

THERAPIST: Just annoyed? Was she raising your blood pressure?

JOY: [after a pause] I guess I was actually kind of angry. As in, "Obviously I don't want to die, Mom, but your constant nagging isn't helpful."

THERAPIST: So you were understandably angry with your mom. Any other feelings come up?

JOY: Well, I think I was also probably angry with myself. Like, why do I keep having the same kinds of arguments with her? They always end up the same way, with my feeling depressed and guilty, and neither of us satisfied.

THERAPIST: So you felt angry; and also depressed and guilty? [I purposefully clari-fied the link between the interpersonal communication and the patient's feelings, using the patient's words.] What happened after you said that?

JOY: She got all huffy and quiet, and refused to speak, right up until she dropped me off at the airport. Then, when I was getting out of the car, she reminded me again to take my medications. I said a curt "bye" and she drove away.

THERAPIST: What were you hoping for from your mother?

JOY: I don't know. I guess . . . for us to have a better goodbye.

THERAPIST: What would "a better goodbye" look like?

JOY: Her not focusing on my medical stuff, but asking about other parts of my life instead. The thing is, she's always been clinical first. She made that clear the whole time I was growing up. And I guess I stupidly keep hoping that she'll get away from the medical lingo and medication details, and instead show that she cares about me as a mother, not as a doctor. And then I get so angry, like I did in this case, even though I know it won't do any good. She will never change. I keep acting like a teenager with her, even though I know better. Then I feel guilty.

THERAPIST: (Silence)

JOY: (Silence)

THERAPIST: I can see how that would make you angry, when your mother treats you more like a patient than a daughter.

JOY: (Silence)

THERAPIST: Why do you think your mother is making medical interventions?

JOY: (after a pause) I think, she thinks, she is showing caring.

THERAPIST: Well, looking back, what else might you have said to her in that moment?

JOY: I wish I had said, "I am a person, Mother. I wish you would take an interest in me personally, in my personal life, and not just treat me like a clinical problem to be solved with medication. I'd like to have a better week with you and not have our visits end in silence."

THERAPIST: What would it feel like to say that to her?

JOY: Well, I imagine it would feel risky.

I presented a video recording of this communication analysis to my supervision group. The patient's appreciation that her mother wouldn't change, followed by silence, seemed significant to me, because it didn't seem to be a depressing idea to the patient, as I would have expected. It was more like an epiphany. Other members of the supervision group agreed. One resident noted that the communication analysis "felt significant" because the patient was authentically connected to her feelings. I shared with the group my own insight that Joy's ability to articulate what she would have liked to say to her mother helped her clarify her feelings to herself. The supervisor suggested that the communication analysis had enabled the patient to draw her own conclusion that her mother's behavior would not change, and that her own expectations of her mother might need to change. At the same time, he suggested that there was still the possibility that Joy could alter the relationship with her mother, by addressing her more directly. Later in the therapy, after another similar interaction with her mother, this time by phone, Joy thought that the conversation went better because she was more patient with her mother.

JOY: I tried something different. I thanked her for the medications she had sent. That felt weird, I think to her too. Then I told her I'd like to change the subject to something else. And she was sort of silent. I realized it was unexpected.

THERAPIST: What did that feel like?

JOY: It actually felt better; I mean, she is not a spontaneous person. But I was not angry. I felt in charge of myself. It was a good experience, though I am not sure what to do at this point.

THERAPIST: You seem to be actively trying to figure out what you owe to your mother and what you owe to yourself. I am confident that you can be successful.

For Joy, the idea that she was in a process of figuring something out was appealing. Being in touch with her anger and sadness through the communication analysis, and having me validate her feelings, seemed to mitigate them in the moment and allow for change.

Session 7

In IPT, Joy's success experience with her mother informed her role dispute with Laura as well. Joy's anecdotes about her mother, coincident with her going home to celebrate her mother's birthday, gave way to a renewed desire to vent about the day-to-day contentious interpersonal incidents with Laura over their daughter's care. Joy came to the seventh session appearing withdrawn. She initially explained that she was worried about Maxine, who was sick with the flu. When I asked her when she had most recently seen her daughter, she paled as she said she had actually been with her for the past four days:

THERAPIST: What happened?

JOY: On Friday, I got a call from Laura. She said she really needed me to take care of Maxine, because Maxine was sick and she couldn't stay with her. Laura had appointments and errands that she had planned during the day.

THERAPIST: And what did you do?

JOY: Well, I'm home, so I think that Laura expected me to step up. But I also felt obligated to go over and take care of Maxine. She was sick! But then . . . well, I ended up staying over there for three nights, even though I really wanted to bring her home with me.

THERAPIST: What happened?

JOY: Laura insisted that Maxine stay at her house. Even though I was supposed to have Maxine over the weekend and wanted her with me in my home, Laura said that she wanted to make sure that Maxine was as comfortable as possible, and that she would help take care of Maxine as well. Of course, it turned out that Laura wasn't around at all, and Maxine and I were alone at her house almost the whole time. It kind of felt like I could justify being anywhere, if Maxine was there. At the same time, I guess . . . I was afraid Laura would freak out on me if I pushed the issue and said I wanted to bring her home with me.

THERAPIST: What were you afraid of?

JOY: Well, she's always rigid about her rules, and I didn't want to provoke her and cause a scene, especially while Maxine was present. And then, of course, last night it all came to a head anyway. One of Laura's rules dictates that Maxine can only watch one hour of children's TV each week. But after I put Maxine to bed, she snuck out of bed to join me on the couch. When Laura returned home, she found us watching TV together and she became very upset. She went from zero to 95 in less than 5 seconds. She *freaked* out, and immediately looked like she was going to cry.

THERAPIST: What did that feel like?

JOY: I felt angry and protective of Maxine.

THERAPIST: What did you do?

JOY: Well, I *wanted* to tell her that Maxine was sick, and that she'd watched an additional half-hour of TV with me, and that her rule needed to be more flexible. I wanted to point out that I had been flexible and gave in when she asked me to stay at her house, because Maxine was sick. I *wanted* to tell her that I was sick of the emotional blackmail and that I didn't want to be controlled or manipulated any more. But, of course, I didn't say any of that.

THERAPIST: [looking questioningly and sympathetically at Joy] Why "of course?"

JOY: I don't know. What I did instead was apologize. Ugh!!! [looking frustrated, clenching hands]

THERAPIST: It sounds like you were pretty angry with Laura, and maybe upset with yourself as well.

JOY: Yeah. I guess I was pretty upset. I wish I didn't always feel like I have to give in to her.

THERAPIST: What do you think makes it hard to respond to her the way you would like to respond?

JOY: I don't know. I am never quite ready to stand my ground with her. I feel so angry, so misunderstood and invalidated that I shut down, just to keep control of things.

THERAPIST: And then you feel depressed.

JOY: Yes.

THERAPIST: And you blame yourself, even though anybody might get angry under those circumstances.

JOY: Yes. I totally blame myself.

THERAPIST: That is depression talking.

JOY: (Silence)

THERAPIST: What are you feeling right now?

JOY: Like a loser for doing this for so long.

THERAPIST: I wonder if we could try role-playing this incident right now, here in this session. The difference is that this time, say what you wished you had said last night, what you want to express.

JOY: [somewhat hesitantly] Um, OK. I'll try it . . . but I don't know if it will be helpful. And I guess you'll be Laura in this?

I nodded and at this point, positioned my chair so it directly faced Joy.

THERAPIST-AS-LAURA: Were you *actually* letting Maxine watch TV?

JOY: Well, Laura, you can see that I was.

THERAPIST-AS-LAURA: [voice rising slightly] Don't you remember the rule about TV? Why would you let her do this?

JOY: She's been feeling so sick and down, and I think she just wanted to stay close to me.

THERAPIST-AS-LAURA: But Maxine shouldn't be watching TV! Don't you care about our daughter's well-being?

JOY: [with a more assertive tone] The whole reason I let Maxine stay with me on the couch was because I care about her well-being. She's sick and feeling pretty awful, and even though I knew you would freak out about it, I felt like it was important for her to feel comfortable right now.

THERAPIST-AS-LAURA: I can't believe that you're acting like this was for Maxine. You just wanted to upset me, and you didn't care that you were harming our daughter.

JOY: Here we go again. Get over yourself. This is about Maxine, this isn't about you. The only reason I even stayed here for the past 3 days is because I love Maxine and care about her. I'm sick of feeling like I'm never good enough. You don't have the right to make me feel this way. [deep inhale and exhale]

Joy repositioned her chair, sat back, and regarded me for a moment.

JOY: Wow. That . . . that felt really good.

THERAPIST: What felt good about that?

JOY: I guess I've always had difficulty expressing how I'm feeling, especially when I feel bad. And I just tuck it inside when I'm upset or feel like I'm not good enough.

And Laura is really good at pushing that button. But, even though we were just pretending, to be able to verbalize to her that this is *not* OK . . . that felt cathartic. Like I can breathe a little freer now.

Role-play continued to be an effective tool for Joy. She found that by allowing herself to identify and access her emotions during frustrating interpersonal interactions, and then "rewriting" the interactions during sessions, she felt more empowered and less depressed. Nevertheless, as the sessions progressed, Joy continually expressed ambivalence about asserting herself in real-life interactions with Laura. I appreciated Joy's bind. Joy had psychological barriers to asserting herself, and as we had discussed earlier in the treatment, a practical concern in that she did not want to jeopardize her relationship with Maxine.

I brought this dilemma and my own frustrations back to the group. As a new therapist, I was beginning to feel overwhelmed by the challenge of "fixing" this complicated family in short order. I wondered whether Joy was too enmeshed with Laura for a brief treatment to help her. The other residents in the supervision group shared my frustration. I wondered if family therapy was indicated and wanted to suggest it to Joy. The supervisor was not against family therapy down the line, but he reminded us that IPT with a role dispute focus is akin to family therapy for one. In IPT, the therapist is a catalyst for change in the office, but the patient is the catalyst for change outside the office.

In the next session, I asked Joy if she had considered family therapy for the three of them. Joy responded, "I know we need it. We are just not there yet. Laura and I are too far apart to even have a discussion about that." I felt good that I had raised the idea of adjunctive family therapy to Joy. It was a recommendation I could return to later, perhaps at the end of treatment. We discussed this the following week, when I showed my tape in supervision. The supervisor encouraged me to continue to look for opportunities for Joy to challenge this difficult dilemma of asserting herself with Laura without losing access to Maxine and to role-play in preparation for a success experience that might help Joy feel more in control of the relationship and of her mood.

Session 11

Joy opened the hour by happily telling me that she had "done it": she had definitively asserted her own needs in a tense situation with Laura. The dispute centered on a longstanding child care agreement that Laura wanted to break at the last minute. Joy and Laura had agreed months prior that Laura would care for Maxine on Memorial Day weekend because Joy planned to go away for the long weekend with Ben and some friends. Laura's new girlfriend had invited Laura to accompany her to New York City on a business trip. Two weeks before, Laura told Joy that she couldn't take care of Maxine that weekend after all, and that Joy would have to take care of her. Joy protested, reminded Laura of the agreement, and said she had already booked a hotel room. According to Joy, Laura seemed surprised that Joy didn't give in right away, and she agreed to take care of Maxine that weekend. However, as the weekend approached, Laura called and emailed Joy with friendly but persistent requests that Joy cancel her trip. She eventually implied that Joy was interfering with her new relationship. Joy initially stalled Laura, but worried that she would give in. She felt herself becoming depressed at this prospect.

Then she reported having surprised herself by emailing a reply to Laura in a "calm, non-provocative, detailed, and clearly written response" delineating their agreement. She also wrote that she felt that her own time was valuable, just as Laura's was. She pointed out the imbalance in their relationship; she included a couple of written examples of how she felt devalued by Laura, one of which she'd discussed at the most recent IPT session; the other she had recognized and processed on her own. She also expressed her hope that they would have continued joint success in raising Maxine to be the amazing little girl that she was, reiterated her devotion to her, but emphasized that she also needed to take care of her own needs and time, especially in light of her recent health problems. She brought a copy of the email to the session and confidently read it aloud to me.

After reading the email, and calling to confirm that Joy was really not going to change her mind, Laura begrudgingly stopped asking Joy outright to cancel her trip, although she did drop several more hints. Although Joy's first reaction was to feel guilty and consider canceling her trip, she did not, and reported that she "felt good about holding my ground and taking care of my needs instead of hers." She went away for the long weekend and had a wonderful time with Ben.

In our clinic we give patients the BDI-II at the twelfth week. In Joy's case, the BDI-II came at the eleventh session. She scored a 13, consistent with a partial remission from major depression. Joy looked like a different person. Her mood was improved and she was significantly brighter and calmer than when she first arrived.

Termination Phase (12–16)

The termination phase is an opportunity to review the successes in the treatment (Weissman et al., 2007). Nevertheless, in the last few sessions of any brief psychotherapy a patient may present with her original symptoms and complaint. The therapist must determine whether this represents a true recurrence of a major depression or a temporary reaction to ending the treatment relationship. It would be unhelpful to overreact to minor symptoms, or to confuse sadness at separation with depression, and to unnecessarily extend sessions beyond the agreed-upon end date. Instead, the therapist can help the patient distinguish between appropriate sadness and depression. A true recurrence may suggest a need to reevaluate the diagnosis and the utility of the model for that patient.

Session 12

Joy was angry about a recent handoff of Maxine, for which Laura was four hours late. Joy felt that to assert her needs here would potentially endanger the agreements they had made about the times she would be out of town in the near future: "I didn't want to push my luck." In addition, Joy reported a return of her fatigue and renewed hopelessness about her ability to manage "the three people in my life—Maxine, Ben, and Laura." I made a point of acknowledging how angry Joy must have felt.

I brought the session to supervision. I had refrained from talking with Joy about the termination phase of the treatment, because she seemed so depressed. Joy's presentation reminded the other residents in the group of how she looked at the beginning of her IPT course. Using the video-recorded session for reference, my supervision group noted that Joy's affect became especially tender whenever she talked about Maxine. A resident confided that those moments on the tape made him feel real sadness for Joy and for Maxine, who was caught in the split between her parents. Other residents agreed. The supervisor asked the residents to reflect on where this feeling of sadness was rooted. He suggested asking Joy how she felt about her role as a parent. I brought this back to Joy in Session 13. Joy shared her hopelessness regarding the potential sequelae of her interpersonal interactions with Laura, not just for herself but for Maxine. Joy worried that her daughter would take on some of her own negative relationship patterns and end up feeling manipulated and having low self-esteem. Explicitly naming these feelings in the therapy appeared to increase Joy's resolve about her self-agency and her role as a mother. She herself acknowledged the active role she had already taken as a mother to provide a secure environment for Maxine.

In the same session, I reviewed the IPT formulation of role dispute and how it related to Joy's specific symptoms of depression. This was a prelude to acknowledging Joy's accomplishments in the therapy. Joy responded animatedly that she felt good about the work. I asked her about ending:

THERAPIST: What do you think it will be like when we aren't meeting any longer?

JOY: I think I've learned a lot. I think I'll be fine.

THERAPIST: Are there any interpersonal scenarios you're imagining may come up?

JOY: Well, sure. I mean, I'm sure things will come up. But I'll be fine. Thank you so much for helping me.

THERAPIST: I really believe that you *will* be fine. Your progress here, as we've continually reviewed, has been really positive and consistent. I have every confidence that you're going to build upon the progress you've made during the past thirteen weeks. Part of that is going to be thinking about what future challenges to prepare for and what future successes are going to look like. What do you think?

JOY: I hope that I'll keep doing well. I think these sessions have been very helpful.

It appeared that Joy's representation of sadness and frustration in the 12th session was fleeting and not a recurrence of depression.

Session 14

Joy's bright affect and energetic greeting in the waiting room were notable. In session, Joy described an experience she had earlier in the week when she had consistently refused Laura's last-minute request to transport Maxine back and forth to a play date. The therapist used this as a launching point to again review Joy's successes in asserting her own needs that had led to this, and again expressed her confidence in her continued stability after their termination, now two weeks away. This led to a much deeper discussion about the end of therapy:

THERAPIST: I really have to reiterate that I have such great confidence in how you're going to take care of yourself and your own needs after we end our therapy in two weeks. It's been very inspiring for me to hear about the hard work you've been putting in, week after week, to take better care of your own needs in some difficult relationships, and to hear about all the successes you've had. Equally confidence-inspiring has been your willingness to keep trying and not feel dispirited if a certain plan of action didn't work the way you had hoped. For some folks, especially when they are depressed, the idea of putting in the kinds of efforts you've put in might seem almost impossible.

JOY: You know, it's true. When I was depressed and first started coming to see you, I never would have imagined that I would be able to handle myself and my relationship with Laura this way. I feel so much . . . healthier!

THERAPIST: As you know, we take a six-week break at the end of this treatment and then follow up for a check-in. What will it be like for you not to meet every week?

JOY: I think it will be fine.

THERAPIST: I also think you will be fine. If you feel a little off, or sad around the time of our visits, that would be completely normal.

JOY: OK.

THERAPIST: We should also talk about what to do if you start feeling depressed again. What are some Joy-specific warning symptoms of depression that you want to be aware of?

JOY: At this point, I've been feeling so consistently good that I really hope that depression won't strike me again, but if it does, I know that the first thing to go is my self-confidence, particularly around demanding people like Laura. I also recognize, what now seems so obvious to me, that when I get depressed, the last thing I want to do is ask for help from good people like Ben or friends, because I think I can handle it. And the way I handle it is to feel terrible and assume the blame in situations when I know I'm not at fault, and then lose even more self-confidence, and then feel even worse. So I need to keep doing what I've been doing lately, getting support from Ben and other people and *not* always trying to fix things which leads to me feeling guilty when they don't work.

THERAPIST: Like what?

JOY: Well, like this incident with Laura earlier this week. Before I started seeing you, I would have gone out of my way to take Maxine to her play date and pick her up, even if it meant rescheduling my own life, and would have resented Laura for asking me to do it but never would have said anything, and then just felt more down and depressed.

THERAPIST: And now, instead . . .?

JOY: Now, I set a boundary, and it was clear, and Laura didn't like it, but no matter how much she tried to make me feel like I was to blame for the situation, I didn't cave in, because I really wasn't to blame for it. She's the one who wanted to schedule a last-minute appointment that coincided with the play date. And because I didn't cave in, I don't feel like crap about it. I actually . . . I actually really feel good! Like I handled it in a good way, and it's a little easier to set the boundary every time now.

THERAPIST: And what do you think it will be like after we stop meeting?

JOY: I'll certainly miss having this hour with you every week, because it's been very helpful for me, and I really like seeing you and checking in every week. What I've been realizing, though, is I can do it more and more on my own now. The last few sessions, I've been able to come in and tell you about problems that I solved from start to finish, and so we didn't have to try to do the problem solving during the appointment, like we did before.

THERAPIST: And now?

JOY: [smiling more and more broadly] Well, it's kind of strange, but the word that comes to mind is "healthier." I was depressed and not taking care of myself, and now because of all the work I've done in here, I've gotten better. So even though I'll miss seeing you, I think I'm at a point where it's not necessary the way it was before. [pause] Wow, that's actually kind of nice!

THERAPIST: It's very nice!

Joy completed the full sixteen-week course of IPT with a BDI score of 5. In this clinic, patients are scheduled to come back for a six-week check-in. Joy canceled her six-week check-in appointment because she had obtained a full-time job and did not want to jeopardize her new job by asking for an hour away. She assured me on the phone that she was doing quite well, had sustained her progress, and still felt "healthy." She also promised to call me should she ever experience a relapse in depressive symptoms. I imagined that once Joy settled into her new job, she would have the kind of relationship with her work where she also took care of herself. An alternate course might have been to come in for monthly maintenance sessions of IPT with me (Frank, Kupfer, Buysse, et al., 2007; Frank, Kupfer, Wagner, et al., 1991).

DISCUSSION

For new therapists learning IPT, a significant challenge is lack of experience with some of the nonspecific factors of psychotherapy, such as managing, but not interpreting, transference and counter-transference, tolerating negative affects, using language to alleviate anxiety, and avoiding advice giving (Markowitz, 1995; Markowitz & Milrod, 2011). Additional challenges include worry about making a non-IPT intervention, concern that video recording will harm the patient and embarrass the resident, and belief that a brief treatment for a profoundly depressed patient may be insufficient. However, IPT is a flexible treatment that can accommodate the style of the therapist. Video recording is an essential component of residency psychotherapy training that leads to better therapist skills and better care (Abbass, 2004). Although IPT is not a panacea, it can be a very effective treatment for complex cases of depression, as this case reflects.

Even for otherwise experienced therapists who are new to IPT, keeping the frame of the treatment with an end date, an interpersonal inventory, and IPT formulation using one of the four foci can be challenging at first. Clinical flexibility and a clear view to the goal of treatment, remission of depression, are learned through supervision and experience with the model.

A common challenge, and a particular one for me early in the therapy, was Joy's desire to focus significant time on the history of her parents' marriage during her childhood. Whenever Joy expressed dissatisfaction with her current relationship with her mother, she would return to details of her parents' arguments from more than two decades before and then excuse her mother's perceived cold behavior as a consequence of the bad marriage. I came to IPT with the preconceived idea that I should be making the patient's early emotional traumas the focus of the treatment. The supervisor noted that IPT would be "a different kind of therapy altogether," and suggested that focusing on early traumas interfered with Joy's here-and-now experiences and feelings, which are part of the IPT framework. The supervisor encouraged me to stay with the IPT frame. When the patient spent too much of a session relating a childhood experience, I was encouraged to say, "Next time, let's talk about how that experience affects your life today."

The other challenge for me was my concern that a brief treatment would not suffice to deal with the complex relationships that included a child and patient who had so many social stressors. I appreciated how the interpersonal inventory enabled me to take what felt like an overwhelming case and develop a formulation based on current interpersonal patterns of behavior. I also appreciated that antidepressant strategies in IPT, combined with nonspecific factors of all therapies and a predetermined end date, catalyze positive change in depressed patients.

SUGGESTED READING

Lichtmacher JE, Eisendrath SJ, Haller E: Implementing interpersonal psychotherapy in a psychiatry residency training program. Academic Psychiatry 2006;30(5): 385–391

Markowitz JC: Teaching interpersonal psychotherapy to psychiatric residents. Academic Psychiatry 1995;19:167–173

4

Major Depressive Disorder

Role Transition

PAULA RAVITZ AND ROBERT MAUNDER

Relationships are essential for survival, growth, development, and health. IPT, a therapy that centers on interpersonal experience, is therefore appealing and clinically relevant and can be powerfully helpful to patients whose symptoms occur in the context of stressful life events (Frank & Levenson, 2010; Weissman, Markowitz, & Klerman, 2007). The goals of IPT for treating depression are to relieve symptoms through improving interpersonal functioning and resolving interpersonal problems (Markowitz, Bleiberg, Christos, & Levitan, 2006; Ravitz et al., 2008).

This chapter describes a case of IPT treatment of major depressive disorder with a focus on *role transitions*. Social roles are central to our sense of identity, and we all hold numerous roles. A single individual may be a partner, child, parent, sibling, neighbor, and community member, besides having vocational roles as a colleague, employee, employer, or professional. Social roles determine the "rules of engagement" (e.g., around communication, sharing of responsibilities) and expectations we have of one another. A change in one's social role, for example the change that accompanies losing a job, moving to another city, becoming partnered, ending a spousal or long-term romantic relationship, adjusting to a disabling or disfiguring medical condition, or becoming a new parent, can generate a shift in or loss of one's sense of self. These role transitions also evoke changes in one's needs for or access to social supports. A role change can be stressful enough to provoke an episode of major depression, especially in individuals with limited social support, insecure or disorganized attachment, or a history of or genetic vulnerability to depression (Bifulco et al., 2006; Bifulco, Moran, Ball, & Bernazzani, 2002; Bifulco, Moran, Ball, & Lillie, 2002; Constantino et al., 2008; Markowitz, Milrod, Bleiberg, & Marshall, 2009; Ravitz et al., 2008).

CASE EXAMPLE

Barbara is a thirty-seven-year-old married mother of two daughters. She has been struggling with chronic major depression in partial remission, which began shortly after the birth of her second child seven years ago. Prior to her daughter's birth she was a manager at a social service agency but has not worked since she became depressed. Her depression was initially treated six years ago with ten sessions of cognitive-behavioral therapy (CBT; Beck, Rush, Shaw, & Emery, 1979), a sound evidence-based choice, but she had terminated early. Her Beck Depression Inventory (BDI; Beck, Steer, & Brown, 1996) scores diminished from the severe to the moderate range (from 32 to 24) during her course of CBT, but not to a degree that would be considered a treatment response. Afterwards, during a year-long period of medication optimization, her BDI score further decreased to 19. Pharmacotherapy had involved five trials of antidepressants (at optimized doses for sufficient duration [i.e., four to six weeks]). Some were discontinued due to intolerable side effects, others due to a lack of therapeutic benefit. Her symptoms improved on a combination of sertraline 200 mg and bupropion 150 mg, but she had significant continuing depressive symptoms and still did not meet criteria for response, much less remission. Thus, she was referred for IPT. With IPT, we would aim to identify and resolve interpersonal problems associated with the onset and perpetuation of this lengthy current depressive episode in order to reduce symptoms and improve her interpersonal functioning.

The tasks of the first phase (Sessions 1–3) of IPT include establishing a therapeutic alliance, conducting a comprehensive psychiatric assessment, providing psychoeducation about depression and IPT, and conducting an interpersonal inventory (Weissman, Markowitz, & Klerman, 2007). The IPT guidelines also call for evaluating the need for medication in the beginning treatment phase; however, in this case, pharmacotherapy optimization had been recently undertaken by a mood disorders expert. Although she arguably could have continued with further pharmacotherapy trials, the patient, her pharmacologist, and I felt it was worth trying to add IPT at this juncture. Given the chronicity of her symptoms, a combination of psychotherapy and pharmacotherapy was indicated, continuing the sertraline and bupropion (see Chapter 6).

Gathering the history of the present illness, social history, and interpersonal inventory facilitates the formulation of an interpersonal case conceptualization that uses the biopsychosocial model to integrate an understanding of the patient and organize the therapeutic work of the middle phase (Markowitz & Swartz, 2007; Stuart & Robertson, 2003).

Session 1

THERAPIST: The purpose of this first session is to begin to get to know you. I will be asking you many questions to learn about your struggles, symptoms, concerns, life circumstances, what kinds of psychiatric care and psychotherapy you've tried, and details of your past relationships. I'm gathering this information to provide you and your referring physician with an opinion regarding whether IPT can be helpful.

Barbara quietly nods, flushed with emotion, eyes welling with tears. Although the tasks of the beginning phase require the therapist to be quite active in order to gather and communicate a lot of information, it was essential to respond to the affect in the present moment.

THERAPIST: Barbara, I can see you're upset. I wonder if you can tell me what's behind the tears.
BARBARA: I'm kind of scared you'll not be able to help, or you'll see me as a complainer.
THERAPIST: Ah, okay. It sounds like you're worried this won't be helpful. Maybe you're concerned that I won't understand you. I want to do all I can to begin to get to know you so that, together, we can sort out what will most help you to recover and feel better. Your telling me about your concerns today helps me to understand that you really wish to be helped but worry that others will dismiss your concerns.

Barbara conveyed a sense of interpersonal sensitivity. Attentive to the importance of establishing a good therapeutic alliance, I chose in my response to reframe her fear of being seen as a complainer as an apprehension that I might be someone who would invalidate or dismiss her concerns. I aimed in this first session to reassure her of my intention to help, in the service of the important task of establishing a therapeutic alliance.

BARBARA: (appearing more settled) Yes, that's true. I've had experiences with people, a past therapist and colleagues, where this has been the case.

Her earlier cognitive psychotherapy trial had terminated prematurely, and that therapist's diagnostic impression of Barbara had been that she had chronic depression with features of borderline personality. Barbara, however, had no history of self-harm or difficulties with anger or impulsivity, and had been able to work and maintain long-term relationships.

THERAPIST: Good for me to know. I'll want to hear more about you, about these difficulties, and about your relationships. Would it be okay for me to ask you some questions to learn more about your struggles and experiences?
BARBARA: Yes, that'd be okay.
THERAPIST: Let's start with you telling me what brings you here and what you're hoping to get from therapy.

Barbara described her longstanding struggles with depression and her wish to feel better and to return to work. It was important not to overlook this prelude to beginning the tasks of the first session, in which she provided important information that allowed me to start to conceptualize her difficulties and interpersonal sensitivity. It provided an opportunity to establish a therapeutic alliance by acknowledging her affect and validating her concerns, which helped her to feel psychologically safe enough to continue to speak about her relational experiences, her problems, and her worries. As we proceeded with the interpersonal inventory, I listened carefully for the antecedent relational experiences that predisposed her to the heightened sensitivity and negative expectations that she held of others, as she described her current relationships.

The history of Barbara's present depressive episode dated back seven years, in the postpartum period following the premature birth of her youngest daughter, Karen, who had multiple developmental challenges (see Chapter 13). Barbara's daughter required several hospital admissions during her first year of life. Barbara took maternity leave from her job that year. When it came time to return to work, she could not, due to ongoing depression. She reported continued struggles with daily periods of tearfulness and sleep difficulty with terminal insomnia. She initially lost her appetite, which had returned over the past year. She experienced significant weight loss to a level well below her baseline prior to the pregnancy, some of which she had gained back. She also endorsed symptoms of low energy, poor concentration, and a loss of self-esteem. She had strong feelings of guilt that she attributed to being an inadequate parent. Not only did she feel responsible for her daughter's difficulties, which she feared were caused by complications during birth, she also believed that she should have been better able to manage the challenges of parenting Karen, given her capacities and strengths as a social services manager. Barbara spoke of missing the sense of competence she had felt in the workplace and expressed a wish to return to work as one goal of her treatment. She denied current or past suicidal thoughts, nor had she thought of self-harm or harming others. She had never experienced panic symptoms, substance abuse, psychosis, or manic symptoms. After her course of CBT and prior to starting pharmacotherapy a year before, she received intermittent counseling from her family physician. She was initially reluctant to take medications, but she eventually agreed because of her ongoing symptoms of depression. Since starting pharmacotherapy she felt somewhat improved; however on the BDI self-report measure of depression, she continued to score a 19, in the moderate range of symptoms on the BDI-II (Beck et al., 1996).

Barbara's psychiatric history included two episodes of untreated major depression prior to Karen's birth. The first was in high school, when Barbara's mother expected her to help care for a younger brother who, like Karen, had autistic disorder. Tensions and disagreement arose when Barbara wanted more autonomy and less responsibility at home as a teenager. She had had many heated arguments with her mother, and although she had expressed her anger and protested against her mother's demands, the situation remained unchanged. She spoke of learning that speaking up "just wasn't worth it." In her early twenties, Barbara had another depressive episode following the death of her grandmother, to whom she had been very close. In both cases the depressive episodes lasted approximately four months and according to her report resolved spontaneously. When I asked if she had considered seeking professional help during these periods, she replied that the stigma of mental illness and both her own and her parents' lack of awareness were barriers to recognizing the symptoms as a clinical problem that warranted treatment.

Barbara described her CBT as unhelpful (although her depressive symptoms lessened by 25% during its course). She did not feel she could trust her therapist, and didn't feel he understood her. They ended up agreeing to terminate treatment after several months and she was not interested at the time in an alternative referral.

Barbara was physically healthy and had no contributory medical illness. Her thyroid functioning and other baseline blood work were within normal range. She denied any history of past or current substance use or abuse.

The therapist can elicit an interwoven family psychiatric history, social history, and interpersonal inventory during the beginning phase of IPT. For the interpersonal inventory, the therapist can spend several sessions, if necessary, gathering information about important current relationships along with significant losses. There are many ways of going about this inquiry (Frank, 2005; Frank et al., 2010 Mufson, Dorta, Moreau, & Weissman, 2004; Stuart & Robertson, 2003; Weissman et al., 2007). The therapist asks the patient to describe each significant individual and their relationship. Important relationships are revisited in greater depth during the middle phase of therapy. This "first pass" gives a sense of the patient's social network and begins information gathering about those in the inner circle, along with significant relationships that are distant or absent. When conducting the interpersonal inventory, helpful areas to explore include interpersonal expectations, understanding (or misunderstanding) of others' intentions, the patient's capacity to take alternative perspectives, the patient's awareness of his or her impacts in interactions, and how the patient characteristically handles situations of disagreement or conflict in which he or she may assert or confront others. Examples of interactions with significant others are often characteristic of patterned interpersonal problems or attachment style, and they shed light on potential future therapeutic opportunities.

Conducting an interpersonal inventory provides information about social, emotional, and instrumental supports, the quality of important relationships, and how they have changed in the context of life stressors and in response to the patient's depression. Through watching for nonverbal, affective cues and lapses in narrative coherence as the patient describes her important relationships, we can better understand which relationships currently trouble the patient while detecting patterns of relating and how relationships have shaped her as a person. In all phases of IPT, we use therapeutic opportunities to work on problematic relationships and interpersonal patterns—through the interpersonal inventory of the beginning phase, through communication analyses throughout the middle phase, and by hearing the stories patients tell about their experiences, interactions, and expectations in relationships.

Although no one in Barbara's family had been formally diagnosed or treated for a psychiatric disorder, she described her mother as intermittently depressed and recalled episodes when she would stay in bed for weeks on end, neglecting to look after Barbara and her younger brother. Her mother did not work outside the home, but Barbara flushed with emotion when she commented on her mother's many hobbies, including playing cards and jogging with friends. She described her mother as "caring, but selfish." When asked for an example, Barbara said that when she and her children visited, her mother wouldn't bother to curtail her hobbies to spend time with her grandchildren. She described her father as a "quiet man" and good financial provider who worked as a traveling salesman. When home, he was not involved with the family and often read, falling asleep in his chair most nights. Because of his developmental disability, Barbara's younger brother was severely limited in his verbal communication. Barbara often babysat for him. She stated they were close, that she loved him and tried to look after him even though she was only one year older. Her memory of her childhood was one of neglect, and she tearfully recalled that little attention was paid to her. Barbara felt her parents' approval was contingent on her looking after her brother and undertaking many of the household chores. As an indication of the magnitude of her contribution, she noted that when she married and moved out of her parents' home, her brother was moved into supervised housing.

Learning these details helped me to begin to formulate an understanding of Barbara's interpersonal expectation that others might overlook or dismiss her needs. Alerted to this, I listened carefully to her descriptions of other important relationships and interactions in which this pattern might recur. Barbara's expectation of disappointment was forged in her experience with her parents; however, what was true "then and there" is not necessarily so in the "here and now." It would be important to identify opportunities for her to have experiences that disconfirm her low expectations of others. I was aware of the importance of our therapeutic alliance (McBride et al., 2010), which needed to be a strong bond forged through agreeing on the goals and tasks of therapy (Bordin, 1994), and providing support and responsiveness without being overly directive (Constantino et al., 2008; Daly & Mallinckrodt, 2009; Horvath & Symonds, 1999). The beginning tasks of IPT provide a means to an important end: agreement on which interpersonal problem area will become the focus of therapy.

Continuing the interpersonal inventory, I learned that Barbara's husband of ten years worked as a bookkeeper, and that she had been the primary financial provider before her sick leave seven years ago. The family now struggled financially, living in a two-bedroom apartment. Although Barbara described her marriage as loving and unconflicted, she and her husband had not slept in the same bed since Karen was born. Barbara slept with Karen, who was unable to sleep on her own. Although their family had faced many challenges, Barbara thought that these challenges brought them closer together; she and her husband agreed on most things and shared many of the child care and household responsibilities. She described Kenneth as quiet, kind, and supportive. They rarely argued, and when they disagreed he tended to accede to her requests. She described both of her children in glowing terms, with much pride, smiling as she spoke. Her elder daughter, Danielle, was ten years old, an outgoing, creative, athletic, good student who got along well with her peers. As for Karen, Barbara and Kenneth first noticed when she was about a year old that she didn't do the things that Danielle had at that age, like playing peek-a-boo, mimicking expressions and gestures, making eye contact, or responding when her name was called. Their pediatrician referred them to a child development specialist, who diagnosed autistic disorder. Although Karen had pervasive and severe difficulties with communication and reciprocal social interactions, Barbara thought she was affectionate and that they were especially close.

When I asked Barbara who knew of her depression, she answered that Kenneth was the only one. She "hadn't bothered" to tell her parents or any friends or colleagues, as she feared they would judge her negatively and did not expect that they could help or understand. She had lost contact with former friends and colleagues over the past seven years. When she was feeling well, Barbara tended to be highly self-sufficient; and, the current depression had led to social withdrawal.

Always an excellent student, Barbara had received a master's degree in occupational therapy. At the social service agency, she had been promoted to a management position in recognition of her capacity, conscientiousness, and responsibility. The esteem and sense of mastery she derived from her professional achievements contrasted starkly with her experience of parenting, in which she described feeling inadequate, guilty, and disappointed that she could not do more to help her younger child. With the pediatrician's help, the family had secured part-time paraprofessional help in school: Karen was in a special needs classroom at the same school as her sister Danielle. Neither of Barbara's parents nor anyone in the extended family provided any further help or respite care.

Towards the end of the first session, we discussed depression and IPT. Barbara met DSM-IV criteria for major depressive disorder, recurrent and chronic, of moderate severity. I tried to validate and de-stigmatize her experience of how the depression was affecting her physically, emotionally, interpersonally, cognitively, and occupationally. With the intention of instilling hope, we discussed that although she had tried numerous antidepressant treatments, including pharmacotherapy and a partial course of CBT, other talking therapies with empirical support remained that might well be helpful, including IPT. Although the medications had reduced her symptoms on the BDI-II from 25 to 19, adding IPT could provide further benefit, with the goal of attaining full remission of symptoms (APA Workgroup on Major Depressive Disorder, 2010). I confidently prescribed IPT, telling Barbara that it was in the consensus treatment guidelines for depression in Canada, the United States, the United Kingdom, and other countries (APA Workgroup on Major Depressive Disorder, 2010; American Psychiatric Association, 2000; National Institute for Clinical Excellence, 2004; Parikh et al., 2009), with numerous research studies supporting its antidepressant efficacy (see Chapter 1). I explained that we would monitor her therapeutic progress, interpersonal problems, and symptoms weekly. I asked her to pay close attention to her mood fluctuations in the context of her day-to-day interpersonal interactions and stressors, which we would focus on in therapy. I explicitly communicated the goals of IPT: to remit her depressive symptoms and improve her interpersonal functioning so that she could better recruit or use supports. I also told her that we would choose a specific interpersonal problem area to focus on, linked to the onset or perpetuation of her depressive symptoms.

Based on the chronological link between Barbara's younger daughter's birth and the onset of her depression, I formulated the focus on her role transition. Her depression was associated with significant life changes: from a working mother of one child, to losing her vocational role in the workplace as a source of esteem and collegial support, to being a stay-at-home parent of two children, one of whom had significant challenges with severe communication impairments and pervasive developmental problems.

Case Formulation

Barbara had biological, psychological, and social factors contributing to the current depressive episode: a prior history of depression, a family history of depression, as well as a history of early neglect and invalidating experiences in which her needs and emotions were overlooked, predisposing her to insecure attachment. Social stressors included the loss of her vocational identity, which had formerly given her a sense of control and esteem, coupled with the challenge of parenting two children, one with special needs, in the face of limited extended familial supports.

Psychologically, Barbara's self-sufficiency had been adaptive in her early life, avoiding dependence on parents who were often either unavailable or unresponsive to her needs. This reinforced a pattern of attachment in which she did not seek support or emotional closeness with others whom she expected to be similarly unhelpful (Bowlby, 1969). In keeping with this pattern, as an adult Barbara usually chose not to communicate her needs or emotions to others. Her reluctance to seek validation, solace, and support in close relationships may in turn have perpetuated disappointments, isolation, and despair. During the therapy we would work to find strategic, selective opportunities for her to clearly express her emotions, needs, and expectations (within realistic and reasonable limits) so that she could experience help, caring, and understanding from others. If she did not find these new experiences rewarding, we would challenge this difficulty with the intention of making her aware of how she tended to respond to the present as though it were just like her past experience. Following standard procedure for role transitions, we would explore changes, losses, challenges, and opportunities, with particular focus on interpersonal aspects of her experience—mourning losses associated with her past role and recognizing opportunities in the new one.

Session 3

Reaching agreement on the focus and goals of treatment, towards the end of session 3:

THERAPIST: Barbara, over the past weeks you've told me about yourself, your life, and your relationships. Moving forward in our work, we need to focus on the interpersonal experiences that are most closely linked to your current depression and distress. What are your thoughts on this?

BARBARA: Well, I'm relieved. As I said, my goal is to return to work. Ever since I left, I've been unhappy.

THERAPIST: Can you help me to understand what's interfered with your return?

BARBARA: Actually I wanted to, but between the depression and feeling like Karen really needs me, I don't know what to do.

I understood her wish to return to work as part of the role transition. She was missing positive aspects of how her life had been in her old role, prior to this life change. In the middle phase we would brainstorm about returning to work, exploring both the challenges and the opportunities that existed in the new role.

I also wanted to discuss the biopsychosocial understanding of her current depression.

THERAPIST: Your daughter's birth and her subsequent developmental problems have presented some overwhelming challenges, and this, combined with the loss of the job that had been so important to you, is contributing to your depression. In IPT, we understand stressful life changes as a role transition. These changes are understandably upsetting. Your past depressions and your description of your mother's struggles with her mood suggest that you also have a biological vulnerability to depression. You have numerous strengths and have been able to cope with many challenges in your life; but for the past seven years, despite many attempts to recover from the depression, you've been struggling. You're missing work and are under pressure with the challenges of your current circumstances, so these will be important to focus on in therapy.

We contracted to meet once a week for thirteen more weeks (for a total course of sixteen sessions) and to focus on her role transition, including her wish to return to work. Her depressive symptoms would be tracked weekly with the BDI-II to ensure that we were also progressing towards the goal of remission. Towards the end of this session, I asked Barbara to attend to her interactions in between our sessions so that we could learn about the links to her mood states and learn more about her relationships and, importantly, about her communication.

In the context of Barbara's primary role transition, from working parent to stay-at-home parent of two children, one handicapped, a secondary interpersonal problem had reactivated and flared: a worsening of longstanding disagreements with her mother. The role transition took precedence because it was overall more important to the patient and was temporally linked to the symptom onset. In IPT, the focus should answer the "why now" question and constitute the interpersonal problem area most closely linked to onset of the current depression, most affectively charged, with the best potential for therapeutic resolution. I imagined we would be able to integrate some work on Barbara's relationship with her mother into our role transition focus. As is always true, we began with a preliminary hypothesis and agreement on the focal problem area, knowing that our formulation would evolve over time.

Addressing the interpersonal problem area of role transitions requires exploring life changes—positive and negative aspects of what was and is. We use the onset of the current episode as the moment from which we look backward and forward to see these changes. Patients often recall the past fondly and see the present and future in a negative light. The therapeutic process usually begins with grieving for positive aspects of what has been lost. We also discuss the challenges of the new, present circumstances and changes in social roles. Patients often come to recognize that all is not lost, as they appreciate positive aspects of their former roles that have carried on. Simultaneously, we find ways to redefine and better cope with the challenges of the new role, trying to help patients build or recruit supports and find other ways to mitigate the negative aspects of their circumstances. Experiences of control or mastery in the new role and the discovery of new relational opportunities bring a sense of achievement, triumph, and overcoming adversity that often leads to finding a "silver lining" in the new role. Patients find that experiences of mastery, adaptation, and improved relatedness all have antidepressant effects. In Barbara's case, her wish to return to work provided a prospective new role; however, it is important not to jump to premature conclusions or to assume this option is the only or best resolution of the role transition that triggered her depression. During the middle phase, we engage in iterative exploration of challenges and opportunities of the role transition in order to allow consideration of her options and choices. IPT conceptualizes this as a process of decisional analysis in which to discover the best options for sustained improved mood and relationship satisfaction.

In Barbara's case, early middle session tasks included exploring how Barbara's roles had changed since the birth of her second child; her sense of what has been lost; and the challenges and opportunities of the new role. Throughout this process, I tried to help her to recruit or better use social supports and to improve the quality of her relationships by examining communication, reciprocity, understanding, and expectations in her interactions.

Session 4

THERAPIST: How've you been since we last met?

BARBARA: Okay, I guess. I've been arguing with the school principal. She thinks we should send Karen to a different school, but I don't want to. I like that both our girls are at the same school. I don't think it's fair.

THERAPIST: This sounds like a challenge. You want to preserve stability for your daughters by not changing schools, and the principal is suggesting that things should change.

BARBARA: Yes, I've had enough changes in my life. I told you I want to get back to work. Things seemed so much simpler when I was a working mom.

Here was an example of a choice point in a session: we could either stay with the details of the interaction and pursue a communication analysis of the encounter with the principal, or segue into exploration of the losses and challenges associated with this life change. Communication analysis involves unpacking the details of a conversation to discover what was actually said, along with associated moment-to-moment mood states, expectations, and awareness in an interaction. In early middle sessions of a role transitions case, it is important to seek therapeutic opportunities to explore changes, whereas in the late middle sessions it can be more productive to explore communication, with a view to changing interpersonal behaviors, understanding and interacting in different ways to better manage current relationships and challenges. I chose to explore the changes associated with her role transition in keeping with the focus of the treatment at this point in the course of therapy

THERAPIST: Can you tell me about how things have changed since you stopped working?

BARBARA: Sure, it's been 24/7 for the past seven years. I'm always worried, and I feel like I'm always fighting. . . . fighting for our youngest daughter to get care, and have fair access to normal stuff—opportunities and support.

THERAPIST: That sounds exhausting.

BARBARA: Damn straight it is. But I'm pretty good at it.

THERAPIST: Tell me more.

BARBARA: Well, when she was little it was scary. We didn't know what was wrong, and we ended up in the hospital over and over again. These days, we've got things sorted out, but day to day it's challenging. It's been a ton of work, but we now have some help and she's been able to attend school.

THERAPIST: So, you've really stepped up to a lot of challenges and had some success.

BARBARA: Yes, I think that all that management experience really came in handy.

THERAPIST: So, some aspects of what you did when you worked as a manager are still quite actively present. All has not been lost.

BARBARA: Yes, but I miss it.

THERAPIST: Can you tell me more about what you miss?

We went on to explore what had changed, what she missed, the challenges and frustrations. How is she coping with these challenges, and importantly, in what ways do others support, help, or understand her? In whom does she confide? How and whom does she ask for help?

Over the second month of treatment, Barbara spoke of the moment-to-moment challenges of each day. A tireless advocate for her daughter, she had negotiated with social service agencies and the school system for her child and family to secure extra services. She was clearly an effective negotiator and was using managerial skills to recruit resources for Karen. Barbara was effectively dealing with numerous challenges of her current circumstances. She went on, however, to identify some things that negatively affected her mood. She felt guilty about not spending enough time with her elder child, Danielle. Although she obtained help from the school and social service agencies for Karen, she felt unsupported by her parents and felt disconnected from Kenneth. It became clear that she rarely asked for help and did not really confide in others. There remained aspects of the role transition that required work. We noted that over the course of treatment, experiences of mastery and of interpersonal effectiveness as an advocate for her youngest daughter coincided with decreases in her depression scores.

Barbara and I explored what she missed about her role as a working mother and social service agency manager. Although she felt accomplishment and satisfaction in having been promoted in recognition of her hard work, organizational skills, and attention to details, she also recalled feeling frustrated that her job had limited her time with her family. She recalled tensions in the workplace that she was happy to no longer face. She cherished having more time with her children and her husband. Barbara appreciated what a devoted father Kenneth was, in stark contrast to her own father, who had been so often physically or emotionally absent. She compared the choices she made as a parent to those of her mother. Barbara was sensitive to Danielle's needs and identified with her, having been sibling to a brother with special needs. She spoke with satisfaction of her family values and wishes to better balance her time, energy, and attention between both children. We noted that when her moods were lowest, she often felt alone, overwhelmed, or overlooked.

Although Barbara had initially expressed a wish to return to work, over the course of treatment this shifted. During the middle phase, as she attended to links between her mood and interpersonal aspects of her experience, she revised her idea of the new role she desired. It became clear to Barbara that she valued her role as a stay-at-home mother, as she articulated some positive aspects of her current experiences and adopted a less idealized view of her former job. It also became evident that the role transition from working mother to stay-at-home mother had triggered interpersonal difficulties that were related to unfulfilled expectations and unfulfilled needs for support that contributed to negative mood states, and these offered a productive area of therapeutic attention.

Session 6

Barbara began Session 6 by tearfully telling me about an upsetting conversation with her mother. They had planned a visit for the following summer weekend, and her mother told Barbara she planned to play cards most of that Saturday. Hearing this,

I recognized a therapeutic opportunity for a communication analysis of the non-shared role expectations Barbara had with her mother. I would apply the IPT conceptual guidelines related to disputes, while keeping our primary focus of role transition in mind. In exploring the interactions, we would try to clarify the issues in dispute and the sense of shared understanding of one another, with the aim of identifying communication problems to work on.

THERAPIST: I can see how upsetting this is for you. I'd like to better understand the details of this conversation. Can you tell me how it began?

BARBARA: Sure. Well, I called her to talk about our plans. The children were so excited, and it's rare for our family to get away together. My parents live in the country and don't get to see their grandchildren all that often. I imagined they'd want to spend time with the kids, but no—so typical of my mom, her leisure always trumps.

THERAPIST: Tell me more. What were you feeling as you were talking on the phone with her?

BARBARA: Well, at first when I called her I was feeling good, excited about the visit. But when my mom started telling me about her plans, it was a bit of a heart sink and it pissed me off. I should have known better than to expect her to be at all considerate. The kids will be so disappointed, and she's so oblivious.

THERAPIST: How did you respond?

BARBARA: I just said, "fine," and quickly got off the phone.

THERAPIST: Ah, okay. Did you express to her any of what you just said in here?

BARBARA: I think she knew how I felt.

THERAPIST: And how was your mood after you ended the telephone conversation?

BARBARA: Actually, I felt angry and sad, and I was more irritable with the children. And that night I couldn't fall asleep. I kept thinking about how awful it is that our kids are so excited to be visiting their grandparents, and how I'm going to have to explain to them why their grandmother isn't bothering to go out of her way to make it special for them, to make them feel welcome, or cared about. This is so typical of her!

THERAPIST: So you were left feeling pretty terrible and you didn't convey to your mother how this bothered you. This is important and clearly linked to your mood and difficulty sleeping.

When patients bring in examples of interactions and communications that negatively influence their mood, it is important to use this material and tie it to the focal area. In this case, the dispute with her mom had flared in the context of the role transition, presenting an opportunity for therapeutic work in the service of helping Barbara better recruit the support she needed from her mother. In talking to me, Barbara was able to articulate her anger and reasonable expectations for spending time together during their visits. While validating Barbara's experience of her mother as disappointingly oblivious to their family's needs or emotions, I framed this conflict as an opportunity to modify her new role to include more direct expression of her feelings and wishes.

Communication analysis can help to clarify patterned interpersonal problems and to identify potential areas for change. This often leads to evaluating and revising interpersonal expectations regarding what is reasonable and realistic. Role-plays then practice and re-script what might occur in a follow-up interaction. This sets the stage for interpersonal behavioral change—helping patients to author what they wish by clearly expressing emotions and needs and clarifying misunderstandings. In some cases this can produce dramatic change, in others an existential acceptance of the limitations of others, and of what might not change.

THERAPIST: What would you like your mother to understand?

BARBARA: She should know how inconsiderate she is. I want her to know I'm pissed and she's being terrible.

THERAPIST: She doesn't get how this feels for you, and for the kids.

BARBARA: I just want her to know that the kids actually are so excited to see her, and they want to spend time with her. If she spent time with them during our visit, it'd mean so much to them . . . and to me. Plus I imagine she'd also enjoy it.

THERAPIST: How do you think she'd respond if you told her what you just said here—about how upsetting and disappointing it feels, and your wish for her to be with her grandchildren on this visit?

BARBARA: I don't think she realizes at all how this affects us. Well, if I put it a way that emphasized the good stuff she's missing, I imagine she might actually change her mind.

THERAPIST: And if you expressed your anger and disappointment?

BARBARA: I worry it'll devolve into an argument—like what happened when I was a teenager.

THERAPIST: Well, let's take a moment to brainstorm on how it might go differently at this point in time, as an adult, married mother of two, one of whom has special needs . . . something your mom should be able to relate to?

BARBARA: Yeah . . . she SHOULD. I can imagine telling her how hurtful it feels and that I really want her to be more considerate of me, us, the grandkids!

We went on to do a role-play in which she practiced expressing her feelings and expectations to her mother. This included communicating her disappointment, anger, and wishes for more time together in their upcoming planned visit. I periodically checked in and validated her feelings, explored the anticipated response, during which she refined and clarified her expectations, helping her to prepare for a future interaction with her mother. This process provided her with an experience of clearly voicing her expectations and emotions within the safety of the therapeutic alliance. Towards the latter part of the session, I invited her to consider taking action on what we had worked on through the communication analysis and role-play.

THERAPIST: Could you have that conversation?

BARBARA: Yes, but then again she might just maintain status quo and not change her plans.

THERAPIST: How would that be for you?

BARBARA: Well, I think it'd be better to tell her about how I feel and to try to ask and have her not change, than to not ask at all.

THERAPIST: What's your sense of your mother not holding you and the kids in mind about this weekend?

BARBARA: Well, actually now that I'm a mom, I can relate to wanting, needing to sometimes check out and just not think about the kids. I think she goes to an extreme, though. I think it's just too overwhelming for her. But she really misses out on having much of a connection with us. But as a mother you have to push through and persist and be there for your kids.

THERAPIST: So you partly understand her behavior, yet it's disappointing and you understandably feel angry that she's not putting family first. Now that you're a mother, and she's a grandmother, there might be some opportunity for things to change.

BARBARA: Maybe. I'm not holding my breath, but I'm willing to give this a try. In a way, there's not much to lose, and maybe something to gain.

Barbara communicated more directly with her mother, expressing her anger, hurt, and disappointment and her wish for more time during their visit. Her mother responded by changing her plans. Barbara came to the following session excitedly talking about how much they had all enjoyed the weekend. This therapeutic opportunity, derived from a communication analysis, role-play, and interpersonal behavioral experiment, allowed Barbara to engineer an experience of effectively communicating her wishes and needs to significant others. Emboldened by this success, she began to express her feelings and ask others more directly for help. She began to confide in and communicate more with Kenneth, who told her he missed the emotional and physical intimacy of their relationship. Here was another example of how the role transition involved challenges and opportunities for relational change. As Barbara improved her communications with her spouse, his reciprocal response led to greater closeness, more collaboration in their shared roles as parents, a return of sexual intimacy, sharing the same bed, and a sense of growth in their relationship. It was a valuable example of breaking the vicious cycle of distancing non-communication. As we had done with Barbara's conflict with her mother, we were able to address an interpersonal dispute that had arisen as a result of Barbara's role transition. We did not change the focus of therapy (from role transition to disputes) but used IPT techniques related to disputes in the service of finding new ways for Barbara to interact with others in her new role. Important aspects of this new role were her abilities to be assertive, to express her emotions and needs clearly, and to better recognize her own legitimate needs for support. Over the course of treatment, her weekly self-reported depressive symptoms consistently decreased and she no longer met diagnostic criteria for clinical depression.

Termination

The concluding phase of IPT, over the last several sessions, involves reviewing and consolidating gains, reflecting on how the central focus has been resolved, contingency planning, and emotionally processing the end of the therapeutic relationship. I tried to prepare her for the upcoming termination phase towards the end of Session 13:

THERAPIST: We have three more sessions. Over the next few weeks, I'd like us together to reflect on this experience of therapy, on your sense of what's changed and what you are taking away from this process. As well, if there are areas that remain a concern, we can discuss them along with feelings, frustrations, or disappointments in therapy or in other relationships. Sometimes feelings can emerge, such as sadness about this coming to an end, or worries about how you will be after this ends. It will be important and helpful for us to be able to discuss these feelings and to do some contingency planning in the event that the depression returns.

BARBARA: Well, I feel a whole lot better, closer to my husband, and kind of pleased with how well our daughter is doing as a result of our hard work; and I'm not feeling depressed any more. Say, did I mention that I've joined a book club with some of my old friends? And I've started working part-time as a production assistant for my friend. It has way more flexibility than my old job.

THERAPIST: That's terrific news! I'm pleased to hear how much better you are feeling and doing.

Barbara was aware that her weekly scores on the BDI-II had gone from 19 at the start of our treatment to 6, indicating remission: she no longer met DSM-IV criteria for major depressive disorder. I was looking forward to entering the termination phase, to reflect on how she had resolved her role transition. However, Barbara telephoned several days before our second-to-last session and left a message expressing appreciation and satisfaction for the care she had received. She stated that she didn't feel the need to attend the final two sessions and had called to cancel. I had thought we had a good therapeutic alliance, and given that her symptoms of depression had remitted, I felt confident that the therapeutic focus had been relevant and helpful. I was also aware that endings can be evocative and can open up therapeutic opportunities. I was surprised that her tendency to avoidance had arisen again at this point. I telephoned her back and requested that she attend at least one final session so that we could wrap up, consolidate her gains, exchange feedback, and say goodbye to one another. I was also prepared to explore her wish not to meet for our final sessions. She agreed and returned for her next scheduled session.

I began, as always, by requesting she fill in the BDI-II, to which she stated that she'd rather not. In the session, I tried to make sense of her wish for early termination and her protest against doing the symptom self-report. Although my request to track symptoms could certainly be viewed as benign and therapeutic, I told her it was not necessary to complete the questionnaire and gently inquired about it. I wanted to explore her affective experience of ending therapy, including negative affects. She flushed with emotion at my asking.

THERAPIST: Barbara, you seem flushed with emotion. Can you tell me what you're in touch with right now?

BARBARA: (tearfully) I'm not sure. I thought you were going to be mad at me and insist that I fill it out.

THERAPIST: (passing the Kleenex). Ah, okay. Can you tell me more? I'd like to better understand what's going on, as this is clearly touching a nerve for you.

BARBARA: Well, I know this might sound foolish, but I kind of feel like a kid or something—like when my mom would only agree to let me hang out with my friends if I agreed to babysit my brother.

THERAPIST: So, something about feeling anger and a reaction to care being contingent on you doing something in return?

BARBARA: Yeah. I never really thought about it, but I guess I felt obligated to fill out this form in order to get therapy, and I hate feeling like I have to. I never spoke up, but it feels good letting you know. (Appearing calmer) I really appreciate your not insisting on it for today's session. It's a huge relief actually. I know it sounds like a small thing, but it kind of feels big. And I guess I feel worried about ending, worried that I'll feel worse once this stops.

THERAPIST: I'm glad you could tell me how you feel. I wonder if this is another example of your being able to communicate your emotions and expectations—in this case your wish that care not be contingent on your filling out a form. Like we've talked about, what has been true in the past (that care was contingent, with minimal reciprocity of giving and getting in relationships), is not necessarily so in the present and future.

Barbara and I went on to complete the last two sessions. In the ending sessions, we used a wide-angle lens to examine the course of acute treatment. Rather than examining the week-to-week interactions and life events in a close-up, detailed manner, we focused our attention more broadly. In exploring her feelings about concluding IPT, Barbara expressed some sadness about our treatment ending, saying she would miss our meetings. She worried that this indicated a return of depression. We carefully examined how this sadness differed from her depressed mood: it was neither pervasive, nor functionally impairing, nor accompanied by neurovegetative symptoms. Rather, I reflected that this was an expected emotional reaction of mild sadness to the end of our therapeutic process and separation in a relationship we had both come to value. We went on to review the numerous positive changes she had made, which included resolving her daughter Karen's school situation, rekindling emotional and physical closeness with her husband, being more active socially, and being more assertive with her mother, as she had come to feel more competent.

In contingency planning, Barbara understood that if clinical depression returned, my door would be open for reassessment, booster sessions, maintenance treatment, or another course of IPT if indicated. She expressed some worry about whether she would worsen once therapy ended. Throughout treatment I had made efforts to point out that her improvements resulted from the changes she had made and the work she was doing in therapy. She had achieved the goals of treatment.

DISCUSSION

Barbara's depression had remitted with no further changes in pharmacotherapy. In focusing on her role transition, with its losses, challenges, and opportunities, she developed a sense of pride and joy in her role as a mother. She no longer idealized her old role, and she recognized that she was currently using positive aspects of her managerial capacity as a highly effective advocate for her daughter. At the same time, she had shifted her interpersonal patterns of relating to a more assertive and affiliative style, expressing her emotions, needs, and expectations. This involved interpersonal learning through a process of trials and discoveries with more direct communication—expressing her expectations of more from some, and revising her understanding with an existential acceptance that although others, like her mother, had limits, they were worth testing.

With respect to resolving the central focus on role transition, she was able to talk about her distress over losing positive aspects of her old role as a working mother of one, coupled with her wish to regain the sense of agency she possessed in the workplace. Some of the middle sessions included discussions of return to work, during which she clarified that it wasn't really the return to her former specific job and workplace that she sought as much as the feeling of mastery. During the latter middle phase of our work, she spontaneously brought in ideas about potential opportunities in her newly configured role, and she began to explore alternative part-time work. We had been able to discuss both positive and negative aspects of the old and new roles, helping her to regain a sense of mastery in her new role as a powerful advocate for her disabled child and loving, devoted mother of two children. Unlike her experience growing up as the older, neglected sibling in a similarly configured family, she was able to derive satisfaction from the very different choices she had made in contrast to her parents—attending to the emotional and instrumental needs of both her children in partnership with her husband. At the same time, she was able to find ways to communicate more directly with both her husband and be more assertive with her mother, improving these relationships.

Barbara had tried one other empirically supported antidepressant psychotherapy and numerous medications that had not fully relieved her symptoms. Addressing the interpersonal aspects of her experience of her altered social role appeared central to her recovery. Over a relatively brief interval, without medication changes, the depression lifted as we focused on her relationships with her children, her husband, her mother, and herself. She found ways to derive self-esteem and improved relatedness in her new role. The simple focus and structured approach of IPT facilitated growth, change, and recovery.

In the final two sessions, Barbara's discomfort with negative affect revealed itself when, feeling anger, sadness, and worry emerging because she felt that her care was contingent, she opted for the avoidant strategy of canceling the last two sessions. Her flexibility in reconsidering that strategy and re-examining those old expectations allowed us to reach a new understanding of the interpersonal forces that had contributed to her depression. I was reminded of lines from T.S. Eliot's *Little Gidding*: "We shall not cease from exploration/And the end of all our exploring/Will be to arrive where we started/And know the place for the first time" (Eliot, 1943).

ACKNOWLEDGMENTS

I wish to gratefully acknowledge Dr. Clare Pain and Dr. Alan Ravitz for their help with reviewing this case report.

5

Major Depressive Disorder

Interpersonal Deficits

SUE LUTY

Interpersonal deficits or sensitivity is the most difficult problem area to work directly with in IPT. It has been considered the IPT focal area of last resort. As IPT focuses on life events, therapists employ this non–life-event problem area only when none of the other focuses is present: the term "interpersonal deficits" really means that the patient has *no* life events and a paucity of attachments. These patients tend to have few social supports and difficulty in tolerating relationships, which puts them at risk for depression and complicates the therapeutic alliance. They see the depression as coming out of the blue. It is prudent to try to ensure that none of the other IPT problem areas exist, as it is easier to work on actual life events in the other problem areas. Moreover, depression triggered by life events usually leads to social withdrawal, so the patient may present with social isolation that should not be labeled "deficits" but considered an expectable part of the depressive picture of grief, a role dispute, or role transition.

Because depressive symptoms can exaggerate personality traits, a good history of prior functioning is crucial. The therapist should avoid prejudging personality in the presence of an Axis I disorder, as it is often very difficult to accurately discern it. Nonetheless, the therapist may try to distinguish between depression and personality during the first phase of IPT, as the interpersonal inventory allows extensive and detailed exploration of prior functioning. A decrease in number and quality of relationships when depressed suggests that the depressive symptoms have played a role in the change in functioning, whereas a lifelong history of few relationships, social awkwardness or solitary activities, avoidance, shyness or aloofness, could suggest personality or even chronic depression. It is important to understand the context. Keep in mind that some people's seeming "personality" can change dramatically when depressive symptoms lift. In summary, the definition of interpersonal deficits relates loneliness and social isolation to an individual's episode of major depression and should be used as a problem area only in the *absence* of life events (i.e., grief, role dispute, or role transition).

When interpersonal deficits is the primary problem area, and the patient is socially awkward, the therapist needs to consider how threatening or challenging it will be to directly address the problem. More often than not it is best done "through" another problem area if another can be plausibly invoked, for example working on adapting to a transition while shoring up interpersonal skills and supports. Remember that social awkwardness in the context of an individual's depression may lead him or her to feel scrutinized by the therapist. Patients may avoid material that exposes them to perceived scrutiny from others and provokes anxiety. The therapist needs to adapt the pace and explicitly lower the goals of therapy: you are not trying to turn an intro- vert into a social butterfly! (And such a goal would terrify such a patient.) Other socially awkward individuals may not actually wish for or need interpersonal rela- tionships. These instances will make forming a therapeutic relationship harder, and finding interpersonally meaningful material may prove elusive. The therapist's stance thus requires attention to the therapeutic relationship and avoiding having the patient experience him or her as pushy or critical. Therapists vary in finding patients with interpersonal deficits easier or more difficult to work with. Experience matters, as does good supervision.

Judicious choice of language for describing interpersonal deficits as a problem area is important for patients, as "deficits" sounds derogatory. It helps to use terms such as "sensitivity," "loneliness," or "isolation." Phrases for promoting change can also be challenging: I suggest "working on addressing isolation" or "working on loneliness" or "adding depth to your world." To an aloof patient, the therapist can describe "your unique individual world" as one that "therapy can enhance positively so that you are less depressed"—perhaps even avoiding the use of the word "interpersonal." Certainly one option is to seek alternative paradigms for considering patients' relatedness to others; the most common one I have found involves computer- and Internet-based technologies, although we do not want to promote complete isolation.

In short, be careful when deciding on deficits as a primary problem area, but when it is carefully chosen and addressed directly or indirectly, results can be rewarding.

The following case illustrates many of the difficulties of working with an individ- ual whose key problem area is interpersonal deficits. This case illustrates the com- plexities of defining and exploring interpersonal deficits with a patient whose depressive symptoms had accented a unique personality style. I will describe the his- tory, formulation, process of therapy, and the difficulties and successes in working with such a patient. An example of using the therapeutic relationship to advance the treatment and issues taken to supervision will also be outlined.

CASE EXAMPLE

History of Present Illness

Tom, a 28-year-old male third-year university art student, was referred to me by his general practitioner for treatment of depression. Tom had visited the doctor saying that he was low in energy, tired all the time, and not functioning. He described increasing bouts of anxiety described as shaking, tightness in his chest, sweating, and an overwhelming feeling of being "crippled," as he had felt more and more despondent about his inability to produce artwork. Over the past two months he had increasingly worsening mood, loss of enjoyment, and poor concentration, and had found it more and more difficult to summon the energy to attend his university lectures and practical sessions. As a result he had spent more time in bed and had eventually stopped attending college altogether.

He described feeling lonely and isolated, feelings that worsened when his flatmates were socializing and bringing home friends and girlfriends. He said he felt different from everyone in his flat and unable to connect with other, younger students in his department. After he stopped attending lectures, he felt so low and tired that he went to his GP, thinking he might have a physical illness, "perhaps iron deficiency." The GP elicited the full range of depressive symptoms and referred him because Tom did not want antidepressant medication and the GP knew we were recruiting for a psychotherapy study. The referral letter indicated increasing isolation in an already isolative individual, withdrawal from his studies, no obvious life events, and a frustration with his symptoms.

Beginning Session: BDI = 28

In our first meeting I sought to clarify his depressive symptoms, confirm the diagnosis, address safety issues, and then discuss treatment options. In the waiting room I noted a tall, dark-haired male who appeared nervous. He had difficulty making eye contact as I greeted him. He was dressed casually in frayed jeans with holes in them, skate shoes, a long brown torn jersey with sleeves pushed up, and a T-shirt underneath. On his left arm was an intricate tribal-type tattoo commonly seen in New Zealand. He also had pierced ears, sported a goatee, and wore a necklace, some rings, and small dark-rimmed glasses. He entered the consultation room slowly in front of me, sat down on the chair I indicated, and leaned forward, elbows on knees. He gave a small sigh and looked awkward, apparently still finding it hard to make eye contact. This was my first observational clue about a possible problem area. Why did he find it hard to make eye contact: Was this part of his mood disorder? Was he shy? Ashamed? Overwhelmed? Intimidated?

When we settled into my room, I explained I would be taking a history to confirm his diagnosis and to help us work out how to proceed. We first talked of his current symptoms and how they had impaired his functioning dramatically. He had a full range of depressive symptoms that I could clearly confirm, and I noted on his symptom report form that his BDI score was 28, indicating moderately severe depression. Besides acknowledging his depressive symptoms, Tom outlined his recent past and his functioning. I learned that he had started his art course two and a half years previously, after a period of transient jobs. He quickly became aware he was the oldest in his course by about four years. Tom had supplemented his formal study earning money by selling his paintings every weekend in a local trade market where he had a regular stall. On these weekends he painted, watched the world go by, and conversed with customers. He stated that although he had always had "a bit of a confidence thing," this had worsened over the past year as he talked less and less with customers, found it increasingly difficult to relate to the younger college students, and became more isolated. I wondered to myself whether this shift was part of his current symptomatic picture and therefore depression-related isolation, or whether his difficulty relating constituted his role as an older student not fitting in.

Tom described generally feeling that his "time was running out" and that he isolated himself because he could not endure the scrutiny of others, felt different, and did not fit in. He said he had never been good at small talk but that this had become more of an issue. He had tried meditation, which had helped his sleep a bit, but he felt despairing and disconnected and that he was closing in on thirty with little to show for his life. Again, while he appeared to be describing himself as lonely and isolated, I also wondered about the relevance of lack of role transition to adulthood for him. As a twenty-eight-year-old, he had made no move away from the student role, and since he would have graduated from high school around eighteen or nineteen there was no clearly defined shift out of tertiary education—but within this role he had become increasingly socially awkward, something that had been an issue for him growing up even before the onset of his depressive symptoms.

Throughout our first meeting Tom appeared nondescript and very shy. He hesitated and struggled in answering some of my questions, often looking puzzled or frowning when I asked him to elaborate or explain. He seemed to find it difficult to provide clear explanations. He at times made complex, somewhat philosophical comments to elaborate on themes. I began to worry that he would be hard to work with and also acknowledged my dismal lack of philosophical background knowledge. Towards the end of the session he asked whether I had read Nietzsche. Help! I thought. What is this about? I haven't read him. Is he testing me? Is he serious? Is he trying to find a common ground for our therapeutic relationship or trying to make me look stupid? I really wasn't sure how to answer. I said I was curious why that would interest him. "Because I want to be able to relate to you." Help! I thought again: What other personal things is he going to ask me, my marital status, my religion? I noted that this would be essential to take to supervision.

From an interpersonal perspective, I wondered if he came across this way outside the clinic room and decided I would try to explore this with him at a later stage: this might be a relevant factor in his isolation from others, but he might experience my raising it now as confrontational and critical since we had not yet developed a therapeutic relationship for me to confidently bring this up yet.

PAST PSYCHIATRIC HISTORY

Tom described having had two similar but less severe prior depressive episodes. The first came during his early teenage years, when he felt lonely and isolated after starting at a new high school. He had moved from a small primary school where he had "one or two friends" and he remembered finding it increasingly hard to relate to his peers, saying he knew he came across as being different from them. He described depressive symptoms including low mood, negative thinking patterns, insomnia, difficulty concentrating on his schoolwork, and tearfulness. He also remembered beginning to question his existence. Around this point he began to take an interest in things artistic and philosophical. He began to develop friendships with two or three like-minded peers, and his symptoms resolved after a few months without treatment. From this I began to form the impression that he was probably isolative and was aware of this but capable of forming interpersonal relationships of some sort.

The second episode occurred after his first year at university. Tom had graduated with university entrance requirements from high school and wanted to study art, but pressure from his father had quickly quashed this (it was "contrary to his father's wishes"), so he decided to study political science, partly to appease his father. When Tom found he did not like political science and dropped out after his first year, he felt relieved but then scorned by his father, who had asked him, "What sort of person gives up after their first year?" He felt himself a failure. Tom developed depressive symptoms similar to his first episode and visited his GP this time, who gave him medication. He immediately experienced side effects of nausea and insomnia, however, and so stopped taking it after three or four doses. Fortunately, once again his symptoms resolved spontaneously. This experience had put him off medication, which he vowed he would take no more. I was interested that both of these episodes had occurred during a transition, once from primary school to high school and once after dropping out of university and failing to adapt to his first "chosen" course of study.

I was aware that he seemed to have the ability to form relationships, but that his father clearly strongly influenced his decisions and his feelings. I wondered how he functioned and performed in front of others and whether he had experienced any episodes of overt anxiety, or frank panic, and certainly wanted to check for episodes suggesting mania or hypomanic symptoms. He denied problems presenting in class or in social situations, and had never had an episode of elevated mood. Beginning to form a sense of his personality style, I questioned him about his likes, dislikes, strengths, weaknesses, and difficulties in relationships, and whether he did or said things that caused problems with others or that others had commented on perhaps in a negative way. He told me others would think him loyal and honest and interesting, but perhaps a bit serious or even odd. He commented that his circle of friends was always small and "alternative"; that he would often have what he called "healthy debates" with his friends, usually around the arts, music, literature, and philosophy, but never arguments; and that he was morally opposed to violence and cruelty. He added that he connected to the beauty and spirituality of nature and enjoyed walks in the mountains, mountain biking, and back-country skiing, which gave him time to reflect on life with a small group of friends, and where he didn't need to talk if he didn't want to. This gave me a real sense of his creativity and ability to relate to others. I concluded he had a rather serious personality style with no clear Axis II diagnosis, perhaps a bit narcissistic, schizoid, and obsessional. I sensed that this had perhaps predisposed him to social withdrawal and to seeming socially awkward and odd when depressed.

ALCOHOL AND DRUG HISTORY

Tom told me he did not drink to get drunk as he did not like feeling out of control. He consumed three or four bottles of beer if he went out—up to three times a week at the most. He had tried but did not like marijuana and had not used any other drugs.

BACKGROUND HISTORY

Tom grew up in a small rural town. He described his father as a strong, determined man who had always "ruled the roost" working in real estate. He was well known locally, a confident and outgoing person who expected his son to excel at team sports, especially rugby. Tom said he wasn't interested in rugby, which is unusual in the Kiwi (New Zealand) culture: Was his nonconformity to expected cultural norms a reason for his withdrawal? His father criticized him for liking the "namby-pamby" arts and compared him unfavorably to his only sibling, a high-achieving, athletic younger sister, a strong hockey player and rower. In contrast, Tom described his mother as "ineffectual" and meek around his father. He remembered her baking and staying at home but displaying little warmth and affection.

He fondly recalled his early childhood years before he went to high school, when there was "less pressure" to succeed. He described family holidays with his parents and his sister camping and playing cricket with friends on the beach. His parents would stay by the tent and read books and "let us get on with our holiday." He vividly recalled once, after having sat for hours, watching the waves and listening to the birdlife, that his father made "a smart comment about daydreaming," which seemed an important fact for me to note: another example of the nature of the relationship with his father. As a child he read books, and said he was generally happy with one or two friends at primary school.

After starting at a large local boy's high school and feeling initially isolated, he made three or four friends towards whom he gravitated because they were "different." He excelled at his studies, and his small but close group of school friends became interested in philosophy and debating, in addition to arts and music. His friends were considered "alternative" but not way out, though "I was the most 'out there.'" "Meaning?" I asked. "The way I dressed. Back then op shop [secondhand clothes shop] gear was unusual" was his reply. After his "fiasco" studying political science, he left university at the age of almost twenty. When his depressive episode then resolved, he decided to take time off from study and tour the country on his own, walking, taking photos, and painting. His father's intense negative reaction to this decision remained imprinted in his mind for years to come: "He told me I would never get anywhere and he was ashamed of me." I reflected here with him that his father had played a pivotal role in the development of his sense of self, and this would have been highlighted by having a cold and distant mother. I resolved to focus on this and other negative experiences with his father during the interpersonal inventory as a likely problem area to explore and work with (i.e., disputes with father).

In his travels, he drifted in and out of jobs: first fruit picking, then training in the coffee industry as a barista (coffee maker), which he enjoyed "because there was a sense of creativity." For relaxation, in addition to art he had taken up back-country mountain biking because it got him to remote spots quickly and he could continue walking if he wanted to. Tom had maintained contact with his three close school-mate friends, but they had moved away to pursue careers and travel overseas. Nonetheless, he maintained regular contact with them via e-mail and Facebook. Regarding more intimate relationships, he said girls had always given him attention because he appeared interesting, and he had "slept with one or two" but had found it difficult to relate to them and often kept his distance as they "would talk of inconsequential things"—he said this with an air of near-arrogance, and I pondered again his personality style of superiority in relation to others. I wondered whether there were similarities between him and his father.

Tom did describe a close sexual and interpersonal relationship with Marie, a girl he met when he first started his university political science course at age twenty.

He described her as being more like him than anyone he had met till then. They shared a passion for music, the outdoors, and philosophy, and quickly became intimate. He said he felt intensely spiritually connected to her, but after eight months she had moved away to pursue a music career. He appeared mildly tearful reporting this, but quickly covered his emotions; I was left guessing as to his inner state. I decided to ask him: "You looked sad when you just spoke of Marie." He told me "these things happen" but lowered his gaze. He denied any relationship between Marie's departure and the onset of his depression after he left university over five months later. I was finding it hard to link any clear life event to his depression despite a general sense of him not adjusting to changes in his life, as he did not acknowledge these changes as particularly important.

Tom reported one or two sexual encounters over the ensuing few years, but few lasted more than "a few months." In the past year he had begun to fantasize about a female friend of one of his flatmates, but when he approached her to get to know her, she indicated that she was not interested in him "that way." In his depressed state, this was the final straw in emphasizing his difference from others, and he had felt devastated and rejected. Again there was no clear relationship between the onset of his symptoms and this rejection, although I could see that this had added to his symptoms.

My Feedback After Initial Assessment

I explained to Tom that I could see he was deeply troubled by his symptoms, and that they and their impact on his functioning were valid reasons to consider therapy. I added that IPT could help him address his current functioning and give him strategies for change; it would not address the past, but would perhaps explain some of his current issues. "Good," he said. "I have no sentimentality." I thought to myself: How will he deal with interpersonal issues, and how will I pull for affect if he is so distant? I returned to interpersonal deficits as a problem area but pondered how I could address his isolation. It still seemed to me that he had difficulty in fulfilling his role as a healthy adult male and that maybe I could work on this as a transition, getting to his social discomfort "deficits" via the role transition focus.

His background history had helped me to consolidate my thoughts about his personality and how he presented himself when depressed. He had had difficulty adapting to his role as an adult and had disputes with key figures in his life. I found it hard to pinpoint a life event clearly related to his current circumstances, so a suspicion of deficits emerged as he gradually found his adult role harder and harder and became depressed. Interestingly, he did not formally identify the lack of transition to adulthood to me; rather, he focused on his inability to relate to others and his sense of difference from them.

In summary, I wondered about Tom having facets of several problem areas, although not grief, as no one had died. Certainly he appeared to have disputes and lack of reciprocity in current relationships with his peers, and in the past and currently with his father. His issues with intimate relationships were also relevant. Concerning role transitions, he seemed awkwardly unsatisfied with his life trajectory, which I conceptualized as his having failed to transition to life as a healthy adult and being an older art student. And there was a lifelong tendency to isolation with very few friendships, which appeared to relate to his early attachments with both parents (Bowlby, 1973).

WHAT I TOOK TO SUPERVISION

I approached my first supervision after seeing Tom feeling despondent. "He's odd," I said. "He seems distant yet sad, a bit aloof and a bit scary. He has had a troubled childhood with distant parents: no wonder he finds emotional connection difficult. And now it's been worsened by depressive symptoms; I can't imagine how I can work with him. He doesn't seem to have any close friends, only some solitary activities— I can't get him to talk to his mountain bike or art brushes!" This was an interesting bit of countertransference and a theme that recurred but also changed as he worked in therapy. I also worried that because I am a female therapist, albeit over ten years older than he, he might start to regard me as either his mother or a potential romantic partner. How would I handle this sensitively and appropriately, without rupturing the therapeutic relationship?

My peer supervision group gave me unanimous encouragement as feedback. First, I had over ten years of experience of working with patients in IPT and had already worked with challenging and difficult personalities. They encouraged me to always bring issues to supervision, to use my IPT knowledge and experience, and to take heart. They told me: "He turned up; he asked for therapy, it's the first time he's asked. There has to be a beginning time for everyone." I thought I would go to our first formal IPT session prepared.

What I Covered During the First Four Sessions

ORIENTING HIM TO IPT

I explained to Tom what IPT was, that we would meet for thirteen weekly sessions. I was careful to very briefly describe the four problem areas to him without highlighting and pre-empting our choice of problem area. I still had a lot of material to explore with him and by briefly explaining what each problem area is, I would keep the process of my exploration transparent. After I outlined the four problem areas he gave a wry smile: "Yeah, that's me what you just said—all of it. I have difficulty with close relationships, I haven't got many friends, I don't really look for them; I don't get on with my father, but I am lonely, very lonely. I want to learn to get on with others and make friends and do something with my life. In the past I've had connections with people, but it's much harder now, especially as an older student." I noted that he was articulate and intelligent and seemed to think about his problems in terms of work and love. I agreed with him but said we would spend the first few sessions working out which problem area best related to his depressive symptoms so that we could clearly choose the focus most helpful in ameliorating his depression.

I told myself that during the first few sessions leading to the formulation I would have to be careful to avoid focusing too strongly on his past and his relationship with his parents. I needed a salient formulation that utilized the here and now for him while emphasizing his isolative nature in a constructive way. Understanding his inventory and obtaining information about all his relationships, current and past, would be crucial in orienting the direction of therapy.

INTERPERSONAL INVENTORY

I asked Tom to tell me about the current and past important people in his life from a social and interpersonal perspective.

"Well," he paused and thought. "Ha-ha, my three flatmates obviously." Pause. "My lecturers." My senses became alert: he ranked his university lecturers second on his list of important people! He might consider academics important, but it appeared that his social contacts were few and limited.

He then looked at me blankly, so I had to prompt him: "Anyone else?"

"People who look at my art, but they don't feature right now." I told him I would note that down and we could talk about when they did feature and what had changed. He then paused, looking a bit resigned and reluctant.

"I suppose I have to put down Mum and Dad." I noted this reluctance and his bland expression, which seemed a dismissal of their importance in his life. "My sister." He brightened when he mentioned her, I noted.

He stopped again, so I asked him about any other relatives "My aunt—she was good to me when I traveled."

I tried to prompt him by asking about other students at his school, classmates, and friends he biked with—it felt like pulling teeth, but I knew I would have to be careful pushing him or even giving nonverbal cues that I was flummoxed by his lack of depth in defining and describing his interpersonal world.

"Yeah, there's a group I've biked with over the past year, but I stopped a few months ago, but yeah, you can put them down. I don't know them really well. And I suppose Hugh and John, my two mates from school, I still have contact with them on the Internet and by texting—does that count?"

I said yes, it would be helpful to talk about his past relationships, as they could tell us both about the patterns in his relationships and also how his relationships had changed. Internet and texting are modern forms of communication, and hence still an interpersonal relationship. I told him we could use this material to think about working in therapy. I then wondered with him about his past intimate relationships, such as his girlfriend in his first year at university. "Yeah, true, she was pretty important there for a while." He paused, then told me he could not come up with anyone else. I again noted to myself the sparseness of his relationships. I told him we could always add to the list if he thought of someone else, then invited him to choose someone from the list to start with. I explained we would try to get an idea of the quality of the relationship, both good and bad, how it developed, and if the relationship had changed with his symptoms. I was curious who he would choose and suspected it would not be his parents.

He started by describing his three flatmates, James, Simon, and Michael, whom he had known for two years. He justified this decision by telling me he saw them most days, so they were probably most important as far as frequency went. They had advertised in the local paper for a fourth flatmate and he replied. It was a typical student flat, untidy, but his room was his "space." He said he spent a lot of time in his room, emerging at mealtimes and conversing with his flatmates about music, art, or politics when cooking or if they all watched TV. He didn't go out regularly with them, but they would occasionally ask him to student parties and go to the occasional gig together. He liked them all, even though they were a bit younger. He could not give me much more detail apart from describing superficial conversations and saying they really did not have much in common because they were into partying and drinking, which was not his style. He denied any conflict in the flat but also had a somewhat superior air when speaking of his flatmates.

He talked then of how he felt definitely the odd one out in the flat, as the others all had girlfriends. Most recently, one had brought home a female friend, Hannah,

whose look he had liked—the first time since Marie he had felt a connection. I asked
what he liked about Hannah. "She was strong and forthright, and she spoke to me,
and was interested in my painting. I sensed she would not reject me. She had a mys-
terious quality that I also liked. We could sit and talk about music in a deconstructive
way that appealed to me." Again he showed some emotion, albeit tinged with serious
intellectualization. I made a note to really explore in another session the facets of
music, art, and biking that got him emotionally charged. I also considered
that a detailed description of how he interacted might prove helpful and that
dialog with his flatmates at home and with others at a party would be good material
to work with.

We talked about other students in his year he occasionally communicated with.
He said in a matter-of-fact tone that he felt other people quickly rejected him, adding,
"But I can't be bothered with people who use small talk." For the first time I sensed
what it would be like to meet him as a peer. I asked what he meant. He explained,
"Well, all this rubbish about the weather or the latest rugby score or who knows
who—it's a waste of time." I asked how he started up a conversation. "Well, I don't
really; I wait to see what they have to say and then respond if . . . well, if they seem
interesting . . ." I asked how he would know they were interesting; he said he just
would. When I asked him to elaborate on what he looked or listened for, he looked
at me blankly.

I decided that I was on the right track and that it would be interesting to walk
through his having a conversation with someone and seeing what led to it continuing
or not, what he brought to the interaction, and how he felt. I filed this away for later
use and carried on with the inventory.

He wanted to talk about his lecturers next—I had half-thought he had included
them in his list tongue in cheek, but he really seemed to consider them important.
He described enjoying talking with them and showing them his art, but did not
socialize with them. He came alive when describing them as people whom he could
have a healthy debate with and relate to. I asked him about conflict but he said, "Not
really, it's debate with valid alternate views." What about these relationships was positive for him? I wondered aloud. "I respect them, and they respect me." So respect
and acceptance are important to you? "Yes," he said, "You've got it. It doesn't happen
a lot." He looked at me directly and I sensed an opportune moment between us: "It's
going to be important here, isn't it, that I relate to you in a way that you feel respected,
and if there are times I say something that isn't right for you, that you let me know so
we can talk about it." He smiled at me and said thanks.

In supervision group afterwards, I reflected on how my comment seemed the right
thing to say, but that I wasn't sure how he would respond. Verbalizing my intentions
and my stance at the moment he looked directly at me was almost a challenge from
him, but he replied with a genuine smile. I have often reflected back as this being
when I first saw the real person beneath his aloof, distant exterior.

Okay, who would he talk about next? I reread to him the list he had given me. He
told me about the sea of acquaintances who came to his art stall and who were easy
to converse with, but whom he hadn't seen since stopping showing his paintings. He
told me that, yes, these relationships were now absent from his life and he missed the
connections he made as people stopped and admired his work. He liked talking with
them about art and depth and definition, and sometimes the same person would
return, and a few regulars would bring him a takeaway coffee. These seemed to be

superficial but important relationships, and we remarked on the mutual respect that came from these past relationships. I asked if he wanted this to change, and he agreed that it would be good to show his artwork again if he could get motivated.

Next on the list were his parents and his sister. He started with his father and initially described him in sarcastic, rather dismissive terms. Upon telling me how he felt he had not lived up to his expectations, however, he appeared near tears. I reflected that he seemed to find it hard to talk about his father. He agreed. I asked how the relationship had changed over the years and he mulled over this. His affect softened when describing their early relationship, which he portrayed as distant but not critical, as opposed to being critical now. He said he had no interest in improving his relationship with his father, not feeling it was worth it. I decided not to push as I would have to go with his wishes, but noted to myself that even if we did not work on this relationship there might be changes that would generalize to this.

He spoke more warmly of his mother, but described her as always a bit anxious and "fluffy"; she had been a "homebody," had her own issues, would be considered a rather nervous person, and probably had been depressed on several occasions because he knew she took "happy pills." He acknowledged that his father had bullied her and that he could never be with a woman like his mother. He wished she were more assertive but again did not wish to change his relationship with her, feeling she could not change and anyway he had never been particularly close to her.

He reported having always been close to his sister, Jude. When younger, they played fantasy Star Trek or cowboy games together. As she was only eighteen months younger, they walked to and from the village primary school together and traveled on the school bus when both went to high school. His sister was now a married physiotherapist, living in the city, and in intermittent contact. He occasionally visited her for meals, got on well with her husband, and said that he would see more of her if he had the time yet did not want the relationship to change. He seemed less uptight when talking of her, with a more connected stance when he smiled. It was the first sustained emotional warmth he had shown.

He spoke of his married maternal aunt Cathy, who lived in a northern town 300 km away. She was outgoing, outspoken, and challenging, but also very warm towards him. There were again some smiles when describing her. When he had traveled around the country, he stayed for some time with his aunt and uncle and worked picking fruit. He stated that he was satisfied with his relationship with them: "She was good to me and I relate to her and him."

We discussed his biking group. He had been invited along for a mountain ride during his time studying political science. He had enjoyed the buzz but did not talk much to the other folk. They informally arranged to meet on Tuesday nights thereafter. He had intermittently ridden with them but seemed not to have formed what he regarded as close connections with any individual in the group. He did say that one member of the bike crew had been "into music," and they had long conversations; when he stopped going, he found he missed those conversations. He stated that he preferred biking solo because he could stop and start when he wanted.

With his two close school friends, Hugh and John, he still had ongoing contact via e-mail and Skype, plus they played online chess and scrabble on Facebook. They swapped tips about bands, and about 6 months prior Tom had had visited Hugh to see a live band. Another brief glimmer of excitement in his eyes made me note that his relationship with music might merit consideration.

We were left with his girlfriend when he was twenty and his general relationship with the opposite sex. I had pondered his sexuality, but he mentioned a few one-night stands and brief encounters with women in addition to the relationship with Marie. He met Marie at a concert at a pub in town during his first semester at university. He had gone with some acquaintances to see a well-known band and struck up a conversation with "this hot-looking chick": he remembered her having striking eyes and long dreadlocks and smiling a lot. Speaking with her, he learned she had been playing the opening act as a guitar soloist and was in her final year at broadcasting college. They quickly discovered a mutual passion for music and very similar tastes. She knew philosophy and could debate and challenge him. He liked her respect for his opinion and ability to stand her ground. They quickly became intimately involved and spent a lot of time together. Asked if he remembered what he felt for her, he admitted a closeness that he had never had before or since. When prompted he said, "Yes, I guess it could be love if that's what you want to call it," then smiled at me. When asked if that was a good feeling he said yes, but then quickly closed off his expression. He then wistfully added that he wished he could recreate it. I chose not to push for more affect here as he seemed a bit uncomfortable, merely acknowledging that it was good for us to seek positive memories, as they could shape our goals in therapy. I told him that we would be starting the middle phase of therapy in the next session, that I would reflect on his formulation with him as I saw it next time, that we would need to agree on this, and that it would be our work in progress, not something I forced on him.

By the fourth session we had amassed an inventory of his current and past significant relationships, and I had discussed the formulation in supervision. I began the session by discussing the formulation with him.

FORMULATION

"As a child, Tom, you felt shy and solitary, and felt second-best to your sister. You distanced yourself from your father and felt distanced from your mother. The few friends you had at school were similar to you, but not the popular group, so you felt more distance and isolation from others. You maintained contact with your two schoolmates and after doing well at school, you briefly felt a strong acceptance from another human being and in an adult role in your relationship with Marie. When you changed your course of study and decided to travel against your father's wishes, you experienced conflict and rejection. Plus your mother, who'd been depressed, remained passive. From an interpersonal perspective, you began increasingly to isolate yourself and look inward for gratification: through expressing yourself artistically, listening to music, and other solitary pursuits. Fearing further rejection, you learned to avoid social intimacy by rejecting first. Yet at your core you felt the need to **transition** into a healthy adult role, to connect to others and not just to nature. You struggled with this; then after a further intimate rejection from your flatmate's friend, you came to view yourself as rejected by the world. You continue to have a dispute with your father, blaming him for your shortcomings. You place others as inferior to yourself, which probably helps you feel more in control, but it seems from what you have told me that you have disputes with those who do not tolerate your philosophical stance."

I then explained that we would work on his resolving his interpersonal issues in the remaining sessions and as a consequence his life and mood symptoms would improve.

As I spoke he nodded or verbally agreed, but in parallel process I wondered whether he would agree or disagree, as he tended to reject others who did not share his views. (I took this to supervision as an interesting countertransference of my need to avoid setting him up to reject me.) He agreed that he was lonely and isolated and that this was a huge issue. He also acknowledged having had disputes with a number of individuals in his life, and having not transitioned to healthy adulthood. I reflected that we needed to carefully choose which problem area to work on. His stated biggest issue was his loneliness and social isolation and this was what he wanted to work on, but if we solely focused on this he could find it challenging. His statement that he wanted to learn to get on with others and find a relationship was encouraging from an IPT perspective, but with such limited interpersonal skills my role was to help him set realistic goals. I wondered if it might be pertinent to consider defining his issue as struggling to transition to a healthy adult role and within that role having deficits and disputes. I told him—by now we could share some humor—that I was not a dating agency and wouldn't turn him into a social butterfly, and that we both had to be realistic about what we could achieve, as he had always been somewhat of an outsider and distant from others. Resolving his depression would lead to him getting on with others and vice versa, so we could look at him recreating the persona of his youth who took people at face value, without prejudging them. We agreed that this would require changes in his interactions with others and work on his part to create opportunities for socializing, but that this would occur at his pace, even though we had a limited number of sessions, and I would not force him to do anything that made him feel uncomfortable. We deliberated practicing in some sessions and perhaps trying out some techniques within the confines of the therapeutic relationship. "You mean like acting out situations?" he asked.

"Well, sort of. We can have a talk about scenarios and have a go at getting you feeling more comfortable in different settings."

Middle Sessions: BDI = 25

So we began the middle sessions. My first task was to obtain a more detailed account of how he interacted with others. I spent this session trying to find material to work with: I asked whom he had seen and what he had been doing. He told me he had been out once to the pub with his flatmates for a boring evening, that he watched TV one night, and had been to the library. He had been to a coffee shop on his own a couple of times and played his guitar on a few occasions in his bedroom. It all seemed sparse and mundane, and I wondered how I could find interpersonal encounters for us to examine.

I recognized the need to use the transition to healthy adult as a way of gaining more material. I said it would be helpful to understand where he saw his current role, how he functioned in that role, what kinds of things he did, and whom he encountered. I said I was particularly interested in the times he noticed his mood shifting and what he was doing at the time, and any interpersonal action or dialog that he could remember from the moments of mood change. He grinned and said,

"You mean a bit like a diary and we can deconstruct it." (I think he was teasing me a bit here by using the word "deconstruct," but I went along with it.) I said, "Yes, that's the sort of thing I mean."

The following week I asked him how his week and his mood had been, and whether he had thought about his role and how he fit into his interpersonal world. He said he noticed a flow to his week, that he often slept late, then got into a daily routine. He played his guitar, then went out for a coffee to his favorite coffee shops and critiqued the coffee. He said this quite seriously but with an undertone of humor, explaining that it was a bit of a game for him to rate cups of coffee he drank on a 1-to-10 scale and banter with the barista who had made it. He said he hadn't done much with his flatmates but that they were going to a party in a couple of weeks that he might go to if he was invited. I asked whether he thought he would be invited and how this might be conveyed to him. He said he would like to go as he was feeling more confident socially and it might be a good setting for him to try out talking with others. I was hoping to generate material for us to work with both about his initiation of interactions with his flatmates and how he related to others in a social setting such as a party. He also mentioned the "sea of acquaintances" he would bump into on his wanderings. We discussed concentrating over the next few sessions on exploring the interactions he had with others as they cropped up and also what happened in the coffee shops. This would prove a helpful focus both for his challenges and successes in interaction, and it gave me some interesting working material.

He explained that when he conversed with others he did not want to be superficial and wanted to relate in an adult way. However, he felt self-conscious when he did, often feeling that others did not like him much, so he felt a crippling inability to know what to say. When I asked what he meant, he said he really struggled with others' "irrelevant small talk" and did not see why people talked about the weather, the rugby, or some such trivia, and that he would rather discuss philosophy, poetry, or music. Over these sessions I learned that his approach to getting to know someone was to jump straight into a debate or in-depth discussion (just as he had on meeting me) rather than exchange a "Hello, how are you?" or "How's such and such?"—he completely avoided small talk.

I wondered how confrontational others might find this (as I had). I considered how to tackle this and took it to supervision. Knowing that telling him I thought he was confrontational would not be a good idea, I planned to get him to describe his perceptions and accounts of people's reactions to him and to use role-play as a way in. Sure enough, when asked how his interactions panned out, he said that people usually ended the conversation before he did. His next comment was telling: "I am other people's adversary when I don't want to be . . . people just tend not to like me." This came out hesitantly and while looking at the floor. "That's hard for you, isn't it?" I responded, and asked how he felt about that. He initially avoided the reply, saying that if people couldn't accept him it was their fault; but then paused: "But I do want to talk with them, and it frightens me that I have traits like my father, but I want to be a pacifist and I do want to keep the conversations going." I knew this was an important moment to carefully explore his behaviors that put people off, and to help him distance and work on them. I asked him which of his father's traits he thought he had and if he wanted to work on them. He admitted having pushed his emotions to the back of his mind and that he ended up trying to be clever to get people to like him but that it came across differently.

I saw an opening when he said this, as in supervision we had discussed how I could use the way he related to me as a template for behavior outside the sessions. I said yes, that at times in sessions I could get a bit confused (I was careful to sound as neutral as possible) by his philosophical language, and I wondered if other people had similar reactions outside the sessions. He wanted me to give him an example so I had to think on my feet—not coming across as critical was crucial. I returned to our first meeting, when he had asked me if I had read Nietzsche, and how it threw me a bit, and I wondered if he said that to people he didn't know and how they reacted. He thought for a while and slowly said: "Yes, well, I do see people looking uncomfortable or bored and I always thought it was them not liking me, but maybe it's how I come across." "How might you be coming across?" I asked. "Can you think of a word to describe how your suddenly saying, 'Have you read Nietzsche?' might be for some-one else?" He paused: "Well, it's obvious, it sounds sarcastic or arrogant, and that's the bit that reminds me of my father." This was a very reflective observation. In IPT I would not interpret this transference, but rather reflect it back to his interpersonal functioning outside of the session.

I therefore used this to wonder with him whether he could think more about how others react or respond to him. I said it would be good if he came back with an example that we could look at in detail, as he understandably linked this rejection by others to worsening his mood. I pointed out that these interactions with the "sea of people" would generalize to many others, and that day-to-day conversations with his flatmates might also be useful for us to examine.

The other important aspect to the next two sessions was looking for what Tom enjoyed in life and how this improved his mood. His first four sessions and inventory had made clear that in the past this had involved his connection to nature, outdoor pursuits, and showing his artwork, but I sensed that currently the coffee shop visits filled this niche. I asked him to describe recent times when his mood improved, and sure enough these proved the most beneficial he reported. He recounted joking with the baristas, which were his favorite and less favorite shops, and how with his back-ground coffee training he could compare a well-made, well-presented coffee with a bad one. He brightened when describing his bantering with them and rating their coffee. A clear sense of humor emerged from these discussions, and he seemed more relaxed, with a less condescending air. We explored what else happened when he was having his coffee. He would nod at people he recognized and feel more relaxed being on his own without needing to talk to people.

I told him I sensed this was a comfortable setting for him and that he seemed to enjoy telling me about it. He agreed. I wondered with him what various people in the shops were doing. He reflected that some just appeared deep in thought, others were talking and "yarning," others reading or working on laptops, some were on the phone. He began to pay more attention to observing others and listening to conver-sations around him, seeing what themes arose. He opened one session saying, "Well, I went to the café again and did my homework like you said." (What homework? I never set homework.) He grinned: "Well, I listened to people talking and thought about what we talk about and how they all talk about the most inconsequential things sometimes, and how I just don't do that anymore and I need to relearn it."

Able by now to share humor, we joked that it might be off-putting if he wrote notes about what people talked about or stared too hard at people, but that the examples he observed could provide useful frameworks for practicing beginning to converse with more people in a less confrontational manner. We used some of the material he brought to practice and role-play meeting in a coffee shop, talking about the latest news, the rugby, a hypothesized mutual friend and how he knew her, the latest music or bands. At times I would have to stop him and say that I didn't understand him, or to talk about how it felt when he went philosophical on me. I began to see more humor evolve in our conversations: for example, he said something obscure and philosophical, stopped, grinned, and said, "Ah, adversarial philosophy again there—mustn't do that."

These practice sessions were great, and he began to spend more time conversing with his "sea of acquaintances." He also found it interesting that his flatmates were more open with him as he had begun to ask them more about themselves, their day, etc. During the sessions he wondered how he could plan small tasks such as striking up a conversation with someone he didn't know, and trying to get it to last longer than five minutes, then ten minutes, and so forth, and to think about how he felt during it. While I do not actively set homework in IPT, this was very helpful: he began to notice that when he was interested in someone, he or she would reciprocate and open up. After five sessions of detailed role-plays in sessions, observations and better interactions outside the sessions, he began to appear more open and smiling, and his BDI score had dropped to 14. We agreed that he was acting more as an equal to others rather than superior, and transitioning to more healthy adult behaviors. He talked of a lightening in his sense of self, which was an incredible change for him. He also began to attend more of his lectures, talked more to others in his class, and started mountain biking again.

In one clear breakthrough, he openly wept in a middle session recounting a party from which he walked home alone feeling very sad and in tears. During the walk he had been wishing he could find a girlfriend, as although he had been able to interact with others at the party, he had been acutely aware of how many couples there were. This drove home his single status. We carefully explored his lonely feelings, and I helped him visualize new interactions that might slowly evolve. We anticipated that from better interpersonal relations would emerge healthier ways of interacting and engaging with the opposite sex. I linked this back to his transitioning from being an adult with interpersonal sensitivity and depression to an adult without interpersonal sensitivity and without depression. He left this session hopeful, and I sighed in relief. I felt I was sitting on the edge of my seat. He was trying hard—this proved to me how sad he really was about where his life had come. I was mindful about his risk of harm and made sure each session to explore this with him.

Termination Phase: BDI = 10

In Session 10, Tom commented that he recognized we were nearing the end of therapy, as we had three more sessions planned. He said that he had been thinking of traveling away from the city for a while to reconnect with nature and meet people, and to expose himself to other new interpersonal situations, and what did I think of this? I encouraged him to talk about how he felt about ending therapy as we entered our final three sessions, that he might have strong feelings about this, and that yes, planning ahead might be helpful.

At the end of thirteen weeks of therapy I saw a very different person. Tom smiled spontaneously and brought up material without my having to probe. He was still more solitary than not, but felt content. His comment about therapy ending was: "It was like having this mentor. You were interested and strong but not dismissive of me, and you accepted me for what I was without criticizing me. I was so embarrassed when I cried in front of you, but I saw the tears in your eyes and I knew you cared about me, and I thought that if one person can, then others can."

I was curious about how Tom would fare afterwards. Nine months on I saw him for a brief review after therapy. He had a girlfriend—a like-minded person he had met while traveling. The sparkle in his eye was a measure of his well-being before we went into the therapy room and his BDI of 5 reflected this. I heard after that he had already greeted our new secretary with a smile and a "How are you?" "What a nice young man," she said to me after he left.

DISCUSSION

This case highlighted for me a sense of richness about the different processes in IPT and how to work with someone who has severe interpersonal discomfort through a different interpersonal problem area. It taught me not to assume when I first see patients that they will be too hard to work with. Supervision was very helpful, and I also learned that to give a little bit of myself interpersonally during sessions can help and that my reactions can be healing for patients. My use of his comments about the role of his relationship with his father was a good example of addressing the issues interpersonally without interpreting the transference.

In retrospect, I might have done some things differently with Tom, such as clarify further the avoidance of a direct focus on interpersonal sensitivities, as I am not sure how much I emphasized the use of the role transition as a conduit. I also wonder how important it was to pace the sessions and whether I could have anticipated some interpersonal struggles and prepared Tom for them: for example, prior to the party, which was a jump for him socially. Having an optimistic positive stance with Tom, who had interpersonal "deficits" as part of his interpersonal problems when depressed, gave me the opportunity to practice role-plays carefully in a variety of interpersonally challenging situations. This optimistic stance contributed to giving Tom the power to transition to a healthy adulthood using IPT for depression.

6

Interpersonal Psychotherapy for Chronic Depression

JOHN C. MARKOWITZ

Acute major depressive disorder is an impairing, painful, and potentially lethal condition. It is a debilitating state, characterized by low mood, low energy, constant self-doubt, and a sense of oneself as personally defective and inadequate, in addition to sleep and appetite disturbances, anxiety, and guilt. Chronic depression[1] is even worse (Wells et al., 1992). The misery just continues: chronicity itself compounds the individual's problems. The person becomes resigned to feeling terrible, accepting depression as part of who he or she is: part of life, part of personality. Although the DSM definition requires a duration of at least two years for depression to be considered chronic (APA, 2000), it frequently lasts for decades. Individuals may not recall a time when they did not feel depressed. No wonder, then, that individuals with chronic depression come to see depression as part of who they are.

INTERPERSONAL ASPECTS OF CHRONIC DEPRESSION

Chronic depression has malign interpersonal sequelae. Individuals lead chronically miserable lives. The disorder tends to engrain dysfunctional interpersonal patterns: social discomfort, avoidance of confrontation, risk aversion (Leader & Klein, 1996). There is generally the sense that one's feelings are "bad": patients often consider anger, ("selfish") desire, sadness, and other normal emotions as evidence of their pathological selves. They consider, sometimes from experience, that others do not want to hear

1. As the DSM-V is planning to discard the diagnosis of dysthymic disorder because of its minimal distinctions from chronic major depression, this chapter will follow that lead and consider chronic major depression as a single diagnosis.

about their feelings, which would brand them as dysfunctional and which hence must be hidden to avoid rejection. Chronically depressed individuals often minimize social contacts. In social situations they try hard to pass as "normal," covering their misery with a blandly cheerier façade that makes them feel like "frauds." Feeling unlovable, they attribute any social success to this façade, which only further reinforces the sense that hiding their true feelings is necessary (Markowitz, 1998).

Feeling indecisive and inadequate, and constantly self-doubting, the chronically depressed person is unlikely to project social confidence. Chronically depressed individuals tend to put other people's needs before their own, feeling selfish or bad about putting their own needs first. They tend to expect that anyone who gets too close will detect their unworthiness and other defective qualities. Hence they keep a social distance and often have a paucity of social supports. Any relationships they have feel fragile, based on the charity of others: were the individual to contradict or anger a friend, that would immediately end the friendship. Hence individuals with chronic depression abhor confrontation. It is naturally difficult to confront others if you mistrust your own feelings and see them as pathological.

Chronic depression may develop in childhood, and patients may present for treatment in their forties claiming never to have known euthymia. Growing up with depression retards social skills. The patient may learn dysfunctional interpersonal behaviors from his or her family of origin. Alternatively, chronic depression may begin later in life and erode social functioning: many such patients have striking "amnesia" for their premorbid function. In either case, social dysfunction is a hallmark of chronic depression.

Chronicity of depressive symptoms may be paralyzing, keeping individuals from assertively pursuing a career or forming relationships. Wanting to stay out of the spotlight and unnoticed lest their depressive defects show, they are risk averse, which often reduces the life events with which they present. Chronic depression encourages social isolation, limiting the network of social supports that might protect against depression (Markowitz et al., 2009). They are frequently unmarried and not in relationships. Patients describe themselves as "lagging and lacking," not keeping up with their peers because of some inherent inner defect.

PSYCHOTHERAPY RESEARCH ON CHRONIC DEPRESSION

No psychotherapy has worked brilliantly for chronic depression, which is clearly harder to treat than acute major depressive disorder (Hollon et al., 2002; Markowitz, 1994). We published a manual on the adaptation of IPT for dysthymic disorder in 1998 (Markowitz, 1998) and tested it in randomized controlled trials. Outcome research showed that IPT decreased symptoms of chronic depression, but neither our studies (Markowitz et al., 2005, 2008) nor other IPT trials (Browne et al., 2002; Feijó de Mello et al., 2001) showed dramatic benefits for IPT relative to comparators such as supportive psychotherapy or medication. As an acute treatment, pharmacotherapy showed advantages over IPT (Browne et al., 2002; Markowitz et al., 2005). Other psychotherapies have not shown consistent benefits relative to pharmacotherapy either (Kocsis et al., 2009; Ravindran et al., 1999). There are suggestions that IPT may augment the benefits of pharmacotherapy (Feijó de Mello et al., 2001; Hellerstein et al., 2001), although no large-scale trials have yet been undertaken to demonstrate this.

Thus, the outcome literature suggests that chronically depressed patients deserve trials of pharmacotherapy, which has in several trials appeared more efficacious than empirically validated psychotherapies like IPT and CBT. On the other hand, pharmacotherapy may not suffice. Chronicity of depressive symptoms is one indication for combining medication and psychotherapy (Rush & Thase, 1999). Patients who respond to antidepressant medications may still have residual difficulties with interpersonal functioning for which psychotherapy may provide an essential rehabilitation. IPT is an intuitively appealing choice for chronic depression since interpersonal difficulties are so much a hallmark of the disorder. Although IPT by itself has had limited success in treating chronic depression, IPT with medication is a reasonable choice (Markowitz, 1993).

ADAPTATIONS OF IPT FOR CHRONIC DEPRESSION

We adapted IPT in a treatment manual for chronic depression (Markowitz, 1998). The approach resembles that for acute major depressive disorder but adjusts for some of the problems therapists face in treating patients with more chronic symptoms. These include the following:

1. *Pervasive and infectious pessimism.* Chronically depressed patients are often daunting for therapists. They are more than usually pessimistic about their own prognoses, deeply skeptical that anything will change the feelings and outlook they report having always had ("There was one Tuesday, fifteen years ago, when I felt a little better, but then everything went south again"). They often have comorbidity, including anxiety, substance, and at least apparent personality disorders (Blanco et al., 2010)—although the latter, cluster C conditions such as avoidant and dependent personality disorders, may reflect chronic depression as much as any personality diathesis. In short, these patients are not only discouraged but discouraging. Hence, they are not ideal patients with whom to start IPT training; rather, therapists who have gained confidence in successfully treating acute major depressive disorder can graduate to these more challenging patients.
2. *Paucity of social supports and social skills.* IPT therapists encourage patients to mobilize their social supports, which protect against symptomatology. Yet chronically depressed patients often have few, or none. Further, their repertoire of social skills is limited. Although the usual IPT techniques (Weissman et al., 2007) may help these patients, therapists must apply them more rigorously and repetitively:
   - First, the *naming and validation (normalization) of affects* such as sadness, anger, and disappointment
   - Then *exploration of interpersonal options*, many of which may strike chronically depressed patients as unfeasible new territory (e.g., expression of desires, confrontation)
   - Repeated *role-play*, to help patients develop the words and tone they need to effectively communicate their newly validated feelings

- *Psychoeducation* to reinforce the construct that chronic depression is a treatable condition distinct from who the patient is.

  Therapists need to be empathic and encouraging in conducting what often constitutes a rehabilitation program for social skills.

  A time limit for acute treatment—that is, short-term treatment to quickly relieve dysthymic symptoms—helps to push the patient to action. The therapeutic gambit of improvement in twelve or sixteen weeks seems incredible to the decades-depressed patient, yet can help to achieve it. If acute treatment is helpful, however, most patients will need continuation and maintenance therapy to consolidate and extend their initial gains. It takes time to develop a "new track record" while euthymic (Markowitz, 1998), to develop active momentum and a sense of agency rather than passivity.

3. *Lack of life events.* In choosing a focus, IPT therapists prefer any upsetting event that provides an active interpersonal focus (i.e., role dispute, role transition, or grief) to the eventless "interpersonal deficits." A life event allows the therapist to shift the patient from self-blame to blaming external circumstances and the depressive syndrome itself. Yet chronically depressed patients often present with a paucity of life events, which in part reflects their constricted social circle. They have few friends with whom to have disputes (or to grieve), often lack a romantic relationship, and take a risk-averse stance that minimizes the likelihood of life events that could trigger role transitions. Thus there is often little acute change for the therapist to capitalize upon. Moreover, the IPT linkage between recent life events and recent onset of mood symptoms that works so well for acute depression fits less well for patients who have been depressed as long as they can remember.

Because chronically depressed patients present with chronic stasis rather than acute events, they tend to qualify for the no-interpersonal-event "interpersonal deficits" category of IPT, which generally works least satisfactorily. In developing an adaptation of IPT for chronic depression, we therefore developed a novel strategy. As many such patients see chronic depression as a way of life, their unhappy fate, and who they are, we emphasized the medical model of chronic depression to these patients: "This *isn't* your personality, it's a treatable illness." We then turned the time-limited acute treatment (sixteen weekly sessions) into an "iatrogenic (or therapeutic) role transition" in which patients could test new interpersonal strategies that might lead to more adaptive handling of encounters with others, and consequent success experiences (Markowitz, 1998). These successes in turn were likely to improve their mood.

In our experience, even those chronically depressed patients fortunate enough to respond dramatically to antidepressant medication—the *Listening to Prozac* (Kramer, 1993) phenomenon—often have some difficulty in adjusting to their happier new world (Markowitz, 1993). They lack social skills and may still have an overly pessimistic outlook. They may not want to "rock the boat": feeling "less bad" may seem sufficient, and taking an interpersonal risk might bring back greater pain. Thus medication relieves depressive symptoms, but an intervention like IPT seems tailor-made for helping the less symptomatic chronically depressed patient adjust to a less miserable, less pessimistic—even potentially happy—life.

CASE EXAMPLE

Alex, a thirty-year-old, married, Roman Catholic white businesswoman, presented with the chief complaint: "Basically, I've been on and off antidepressants for a dozen years since I was depressed in college."

History of Present Illness

Alex reported having been depressed for years, born of parents in a troubled, battling marriage. She doubted herself constantly, had trouble making decisions, and was highly self-critical. Her sleep was often broken, although appetite and energy were adequate. She had passive suicidal feelings at times but had never acted on them. She had occasional panic attacks. She denied alcohol and drug use. Although she had earned an M.B.A. and had fared fairly well at the same company for four years, she lacked the aggressiveness she saw in her colleagues in pressing for new accounts, asking for raises, and getting the perks she deserved.

Work, however, was not her main concern. Alex had been involved with Mike, her husband of two years, for six years. Mike was a law student who constantly argued with her. Although she often felt fairly sure she was right, she felt indecisive and self-doubting enough that he generally won their arguments, leaving her feeling frustrated and confused. Mike had arranged what amounted to a long-distance relationship. He had opted for a law school in New England rather than an equally excellent school in New York City where she worked. He demanded that she spend every weekend in his city, even though she was exhausted by the end of the work week. When she visited him, he dragged her to "frat-boy drinking parties" she disliked. She resented that she worked hard as their breadwinner while he partied; he called her a wet blanket.

Although both said they loved each other, they argued more than they agreed. Mike had an elaborate schedule for how their marriage should proceed, where they should live, when they should have children, and so forth. Alex had an equally organized plan, but the timing differed. Continual attempts to discuss this led to him out-arguing her, always leaving her frustrated and uncertain.

Meanwhile, the couple had barely had sex since early in their dating relationship. Although Alex was an attractive, slim woman who worked out regularly, Mike accused her of being overweight as a reason for avoiding sex. This hurt her feelings and contradicted her own view of herself, but played at her own fears and doubts. When, after a year or so, that argument had gradually lost currency, he then insisted that they could only have sex using multiple forms of birth control because of his extreme fear of pregnancy. Even with double condoms, an IUD, and birth control pills, he avoided sex, finding varying excuses to blame her. She knew there was something wrong with his stance, but so disliked confrontations and felt so unsure of whether she was right or wrong that the problem dragged on, unresolved, for years.

She had been taking sertraline 50 to 100 mg for the past five years, which she had felt was modestly beneficial to her mood and energy but still left her depressed and hopeless. She had stopped the medication six months previously and had gradually noticed a mild worsening in her symptoms, which led her resignedly to seek treatment.

Her 24-item Hamilton Depression Rating Scale (Ham-D; Hamilton, 1960) score upon presentation was 19. She reported minimal alcohol intake and denied other drug use.

Family History

Family history was notable for maternal, paternal, and her maternal grandfather's depressive episodes. The parents, who had immigrated when Alex was *in utero*, had separated several times but remained married in a bitter, contentious relationship wherein the father yelled at the mother, criticizing her weight and intelligence, often in the presence of Alex and her younger brother. Her mother was chronically depressed, and her father drank heavily. There was no other family history of mania, psychosis, substance abuse, or suicide.

Past Psychiatric History

In retrospect, Alex had been depressed since her childhood, meeting criteria for DSM-IV dysthymic disorder of early onset. Early memories were anxious, sad, and lonely. She had been a good student but painfully shy, with few close friends. She had been embarrassed to bring friends home to her warring parents. Although a pretty high school student, she avoided dating. She denied alcohol and drug use. She experienced a single episode of major depressive disorder in her freshman year of college when her first attempt at a romantic relationship quickly went awry. She was seen three times at the student health service, declined antidepressant medication, and eventually pulled together enough to complete the semester at something lower than her usual baseline. She had never planned or attempted suicide, and there was no suggestion of hypomania or mania.

She had briefly flirted with an eating disorder in high school—in response, she said, to her father calling her mother fat. She had occasional panic attacks at times of stress. She took a controlled, organized approach to life compatible with obsessive-compulsive personality disorder.

Besides the recent sertraline, Alex had had adequate trials of two other serotonin reuptake inhibitors in adequate but not high doses, with minimal response. She had also undertaken four unsuccessful psychotherapies of varying length. Both psychodynamic and cognitive approaches had been unavailing, as had a brief couples therapy with her then-fiancé. Alex had evidently worked methodically in these treatments and felt frustrated by her inability to change anything about herself or her situation. Therapists had given her diagnosis of depression in passing but had said little about the disorder or its prognosis. The word "dysthymic" was new to her.

Past Medical History

Generally healthy, with no history of thyroid disease or sexually transmitted infections. Alex was taking birth control pills, but no other non-psychotropic medication.

Mental Status Examination

Alex was an alert, petite, attractive, slim brunette woman, appearing her stated age, with appropriate makeup, dressed in blue blouse and skirt. Her movements were somewhat controlled, and her speech was fluent and unpressured, if somewhat monotonal and deliberate. Her mood was mildly to moderately depressed and anxious, with constricted affect for much of the interview. She gave way to tears briefly near the end of the interview but then resumed control. She showed no affective lability. Thinking was goal-directed, if somewhat obsessive and intellectualized. Alex denied psychotic symptoms and active suicidal ideation, conceding that life did not always feel worthwhile. She reported suggestions of obsessive-compulsive behaviors, such as having a favorite, magic number. In terms of her insight, she recognized being depressed and frustrated with past treatment, but had doubts about her prognosis. Sensorium was clear, with full orientation.

Impression

A thirty-year-old married businesswoman with longstanding, perhaps lifelong dysthymic disorder, with at least traits of and perhaps mild syndromal obsessive-compulsive disorder (Table 6.1). She was apparently functioning fairly well at work.

Alex has evidently never had aggressive trials of antidepressants, and might benefit from pressing the dosage higher. She appears a good candidate for IPT: she has relationships (a blessing for a chronically depressed patient, from the IPT perspective), and they are replete with conflict. IPT might focus on either a role transition or a role dispute.

Plan

As an initial plan, we discussed:

1. Discontinuing birth control pills, which might be worsening her mood and seemed unnecessary in the absence of sexual contact and her spouse's requirement for other forms of contraception. She agreed to discuss this with her gynecologist.

Table 6.1 DSM-IV DIAGNOSES

Axis I	Dysthymic disorder (300.4)
Axis II	Rule out Obsessive-compulsive personality disorder
Axis III	Birth control pills
Axis IV	Marital and family stress
Axis V	52–Global Assessment of Functioning score consistent with moderate symptoms and impairment (1–100 scale where lower scores indicate lower functioning [APA, 1994])

2. Checking her thyroid function, which had possibly never been previously tested

3. Beginning venlafaxine, a medication she has not yet tried that has noradrenergic as well as serotonergic effects. We reviewed potential side effects, benefits, and likely course.

4. Beginning a twelve-week course of IPT as a more focused antidepressant psychotherapy. We made an appointment for the following week. Despite an impressive income, she was concerned about cost, as her insurance covered only half my fee. She ambivalently agreed.

Session 2

Alex appeared promptly. She was somewhat brighter and less hopeless, although she reported persisting depressed and anxious mood, and her affect remained constricted and controlled. She had gotten her thyroid tests, which were normal, but had not yet contacted her gynecologist.

To my question, "How have things been since we last met?" she reported tolerating venlafaxine without side effects and feeling "maybe a few more 'happy' moments, it might be starting to work." We agreed to increase the dosage. She volunteered that she had felt slightly more hopeful after the evaluation session, but quickly felt worse after Mike called and they struggled over weekend plans. I pointed out that her mood seemed connected to how she interacted with other people, which would be an important theme in our treatment.

We spent much of the session collecting an **interpersonal inventory.** Alex had a few friends from college, graduate school, and her job, but they really constituted extended acquaintances rather than people in whom she could confide. Her husband's friends provided most of their social life, but she saw them as mostly distasteful immature types whose company she tolerated. She could confide in her mother, but feared burdening her because her mother was still more depressed than she ("I can handle it better"). Nor did she want to upset her younger brother, although they did have a warm relationship. Her father had never been approachable: he was always demanding, argumentative, and irritable; a provider, but emotionally disengaged from other family members. Because of his workaholic business career, he had rarely been around anyway. Alex agreed with my suggestion that there had been no one to talk to growing up, and that she had kept everything bottled up inside herself.

We resumed discussing her difficult relationship with her husband. Mike was no easy confidant himself. While she worked long hours, he had been coasting through his final two years of law school partying, spending their money, and taking numerous vacations with his school pals but without her. She conceded that the two of them were very different. She described them as "close, we love each other, but he hates New York and I love it, he's for spending money while I would save," etc. They had agreed that she visit him in New England every weekend while his school was in session in return for his eventually returning to New York after graduation.

This agreement amounted to a formal legal contract in their minds. She resented having to commute to his party weekends, but had already invested two years in doing so and at this point felt it would have been for naught if she reneged: he would then not have to honor his part of the deal. Indeed, most of their agreements had to be hammered out in lengthy debates in which she felt unsure, gave ground to his endless, withering arguments, and ended up feeling hemmed in and resentful. It was partly, she conceded, that he was a good debater, and partly her own self-doubt that was the problem. The arguments enraged her: Alex felt that she was probably right to feel taken advantage of, but couldn't win the debates, was tired of fighting, and didn't let herself feel her full anger "because it would be unbearable."

I asked: "What's wrong with being angry?" She related anger to her father's drunken, screaming outbursts at her mother, a bad thing. "What good does it do?" she asked. Anger was disorganizing. She tried to keep things "civilized and rational," taking a stolid, polite stance. We agreed that this didn't seem to be working, and that her disputes with her husband left her frustrated and confused. "There's something wrong with me, I know. I'm just defective," she said. I ventured that the problem might not be that she was defective, but that chronic depression made her feel that way. That defective feeling was a symptom. Meanwhile, anger was a normal emotional response to having someone frustrate and bother you: "If a rational argument works, great; but if the other person doesn't listen, what else can you do? It's helpful to have more than one option for responding." This led to a discussion of anger as a healthy signal of frustrating situations, and an emotion that could be put into words. I remarked that it often felt good to get frustrations off one's chest, and that if she felt angry and didn't express it, she was likely to feel uncomfortable, anxious, and perhaps more depressed. She cautiously if somewhat skeptically agreed.

Alex role-played expressing her frustration to her husband. "I know you have fun on weekends, Mike, and I want you to have fun, but it makes me angry that you expect me to drag myself to see you and join in when I'm exhausted after a week of work." On review, we agreed that the content was what she wanted to communicate, but that her tone of voice was still very measured and "rational." Although it meant stretching her usual affect, with further role-play she was better able to sound angry as well as to explain why she felt that way.

I suggested that this was a great time to take social risks. If they paid off, she was way ahead; and if they didn't, at least she had tried, and we could discuss what had gone wrong and look for alternative approaches. She cautiously agreed.

IMPRESSION

This was an encouraging session. Alex remained depressed but seemed somewhat remoralized by the initial session. She took to role-play and was able to work on her constricted affect. Although she feared confrontations, which had been and remained painful to observe in her parents' relationship, she seemed to understand the need to confront her husband, and seemed likely to do so.

Session 3

Alex was alert, prompt, and well groomed, in a more colorful outfit. She had normal movements, none involuntary, and fluent, unpressured speech. Her mood was less depressed (6–7 on a scale of 10, versus 2–3/10 at baseline) and mildly anxious, with controlled affect. She was half-smiling, giving way to controlled sadness and anger, and eyes welling by session's end. Her affect was nonlabile and there was no thought disorder. She denied suicidal ideation and her sensorium was clear.

"How have things been since we last met?" Alex reported "doing okay" and denied venlafaxine side effects. She noted that her mood had improved somewhat, and mused that she was not sure if depression comes from biochemical vulnerability or life situation "or I guess it's both." She expressed doubts about whether her marriage was worth all the effort she had invested in it. Mike now wanted to go to a Colorado beer fest with his friends that coincided with her brother's wedding. Alex said Mike knew how important this family occasion was for her, and he went drinking all the time—too much, perhaps. There would be other beer fests. Nonetheless, Mike argued that since he wanted her to come to the festival and she wanted him to come to the wedding, they were both equally disappointed and should keep their independent commitments.

This was a typical disagreement in which she felt in the right, yet emerged feeling indecisive, frustrated, and half-convinced by specious arguments. She expressed her sense of being a "weak" person in arguments, not sure whether Mike was not right. She said that her friends blindly supported her and her family already had a low opinion of Mike, so she resisted discussing their marital differences with them further. He's "so childish, selfish! Even when he *has* compromised a little, it requires an exhausting effort." Alex felt stuck, not wanting to be alone, "not wanting to feel I've wasted all this effort on marriage for nothing." I validated her feelings, saying that they were understandable and something to weigh against what it would be like to continue this sort of relationship indefinitely. "And you're also right that the marriage is contributing to your feeling depressed," I said.

At this point it was tempting to dig further into the marriage, but I felt I should give Alex a **formulation** in order to structure the remainder of treatment:

THERAPIST: Can we pause for a moment? You've given me a lot of helpful informa-
    tion so far; I want to make sure I've gotten the picture of what's going on with you.
    From what you've told me, you've been depressed for about as long as you can
    remember, long before when the depression worsened in your freshman year in
    college. We call that kind of lingering depression *dysthymic disorder*, and it's a
    treatable, medical problem that's not your fault. In fact, we're going to try to make
    it better in just the next nine weeks. There are already some hopeful signs that
    you're improving, although I expect you to be skeptical until you're really feeling
    better, and perhaps have felt so for a while. Both medication and psychotherapy
    can be helpful in treating dysthymic disorder.

    This kind of chronic depression has the kind of symptoms we've already
    been talking about: self-doubt and self-criticism, indecisiveness, sleeping
    problems, and a discomfort with feelings like anger and your own wishes that
    makes it hard to be in confrontations. (It doesn't help that your husband is
    such an arguer!) Feeling this way with dysthymic disorder makes it hard for
    you to stand up for yourself in interpersonal encounters: the "weakness" and
    "defectiveness" are dysthymic symptoms. We know that there's a connection
    between how you're feeling and how you handle situations with other people:
    depression makes it hard to handle situations, and when encounters with other
    people go badly, it's depressing, right?

ALEX: Right.

THERAPIST: And yet if you've always felt this way, it's hard to tell what's depression
    and what's you, where the depression is getting in your way. What we're going to

do over the remainder of this twelve-week treatment is to help you through a *role transition, to help you see what's the healthy you and what's the depression.* If you can learn to trust your healthy emotions and use them to handle encounters with Mike and other people better, things should go better, and you should feel better. At the same time, we'll be giving the medication a chance to work. So it's a transition from thinking this is the way you are to feeling better. Does all that make sense to you?

It did. She agreed to the formulation, and we scheduled a next session.

IMPRESSION
Another encouraging session: Alex is a little rigid but a quick learner. Her symptoms seem to be improving—whether from the medication, IPT, or both doesn't really matter at present. I opted for an iatrogenic role transition despite the presence of clear role disputes—with both her husband and father—because Alex's symptoms so long predate her marriage and she seems so clearly to be struggling over which of her feelings and symptoms she should trust.

PLAN
We increased the venlafaxine dosage as she was having no side effects.

Session 4

Alex arrived looking generally brighter but still self-doubting. We began by repeating her Ham-D, which had dropped to 11. She was slightly surprised but pleased to see this progress, on which I congratulated her. She reported "doing okay. Still some problem sleeping, but that may just be from the depression." She said she generally felt okay "when not thinking about my marriage."

Alex raised her concern that she is too compulsive and not flexible enough, a criticism her husband had made. She reported having gone home following our last session and noticing she was upset. She wrote Mike a long email—"in direct conversation things tend to get too emotional"—in which she clearly spelled out feeling hurt about the wedding situation. To his credit, Mike came home early from work so that they could have a long discussion. She emphasized a point we had discussed, that she really needs to have him acknowledge her feelings if the relationship is to work. He then agreed to attend the wedding, saying he "didn't realize it was so important to you"! (Alex and I agreed this was a remarkable explanation, given their long arguments about this.) He then complained that she was not emotionally available, too compulsive and inflexible.

We briefly discussed her mild obsessive-compulsive symptoms. She then conceded that it was hard for her to be emotionally available, having accumulated lots of anger at Mike over the years. I agreed that she had a lot to be angry about:

THERAPIST: And it's never simply resolved: even when Mike concedes a point, he doesn't just apologize, but comes back with conditions, etc. It sounds exhausting.

ALEX: It is. But my choices seem to be to keep working to make baby steps [to improve the relationship] or to give up.

THERAPIST: That may be true.

We reviewed her options for accelerating improvement in the relationship. Both rational proposals and angry arguments had been unsuccessful. I asked if she had ever given him an ultimatum. She had, several years before, after moving to New York, "but I guess not since"—and never about their sexual difficulties. She noted that "it would be very frustrated to have invested so much energy in this relationship and not have it work out."

THERAPIST: Yes, that's true. You're being very patient. The fact that you have to invest so much energy to get so little return . . . When do you think he's going to really get it?

ALEX: I don't know. Maybe it's hopeless.

We discussed the pros and cons of in-person communication over email: she agreed that email might allow her to control affect better but also was less direct and more open to misinterpretation. We role-played both the content and tone in which she might address Mike, during which she raised the stakes by saying, "You know, I can't put up with this forever."

IMPRESSION

Alex is improving steadily, tolerating venlafaxine well, and really trying to address the marital thorn in her side despite her doubts. She sees the wedding concession as a victory, albeit one too hard to win, and is voicing clearer anger at Mike (which I'm normalizing) and less at herself. Good signs are that she is generally insightful and quick to convert our discussions into interpersonal actions. She sounds clear, if deliberate, in her communication. The prognosis appears good for her, if not for the marriage.

Session 5

Alex is alert, prompt, and well groomed. She has normal movements, none involuntary, and fluent, unpressured speech. Her mood is mildly depressed and anxious, with reactive, nonlabile affect. There is no thought disorder. She denied suicidal ideation. Sensorium is clear.

She reported feeling a little worse. "My brother's wedding is next week, and Mike will come, after all, but it was a struggle. He seemed to get it, and is also willing to go to take a future weekend beach vacation because he knows it's something I like. He does seem to be trying." On the other hand, achieving these victories had again seemed Pyrrhic: it required hours of discussion, and he criticized and caviled even as he conceded these decisions, leaving her with a bad taste in her mouth. Alex reiterated that she loved Mike, but she found their relationship exhausting. He continued to avoid sex.

Alex reported tolerating medication without side effects except possible exacerbation of chronic sweating. She was willing to continue the medication and to increase it to 225 mg daily. On the whole, she concluded, she is feeling less depressed, but Mike gets her really upset. She seemed angrier and sadder as she recognized that she is right to be upset about her marriage.

Session 6

THERAPIST: How have you been since we last met?

ALEX: Good. The wedding was nice, although I had to intercede between Mike and my father. Both of them can be so difficult, and I'm always caught in the middle. I have to protect Mike from my Dad.

This led to a discussion of continuing tension with Mike, as well as her father's irritable, critical, and unsociable behavior. Mike had now reneged on the beach plans, saying that he hadn't realized that her family might join them, and that that voided their contract. Alex sighed: "Everything's an argument, everything's a negotiation with him."

We discussed whether she was being overly reasonable and placating with Mike rather than fully expressing how angry his pattern of argument and criticism made her. He continued to see their marriage as a formal legal "contract" and was constant "litigating" with her. She had had it. "I keep thinking: if only I could explain it right, maybe he would get it." I suggested that she seemed clear in her communication on her part, whereas Mike seemed to like to argue but not really to listen or communicate. She related her anger that in their one attempt at couples therapy, the therapist seemed so evenhanded, never contradicting Mike:

ALEX: Why didn't she tell him he was being an asshole? . . . I try to listen to him but he doesn't listen to me. It makes me so angry!

THERAPIST: You're right to be angry. You need to trust your own feelings, although depression can make it hard to do so. It's not nice that Mike plays on your depressed doubts to his own advantage. Do you do that to him?

No, she did not. Alex was sounding angry in a fuller, less controlled (but nonlabile) way than before. Mike never made sacrifices for her, whereas she frequently sacrificed for him.

ALEX: I want him to make things up to me. He's kind of conceding he's been wrong in the past, but wants to start over with an even scorecard, and I'm just too angry to do that right now.

THERAPIST: Have you said that to Mike?

She had not. We then role-played how she might communicate this to him. I commented: "You know, you're really sounding much less controlled, much more appropriately angry." Instead of getting obsessionally stuck in the argument of the moment, she recognized her objection to Mike's more general argumentative strategy: she listened thoughtfully, whereas he played to win. We spent the rest of the session reviewing what she wanted to say to Mike and in what tone. By the end of the session

Alex had reached an ultimatum: "I'm not ready to take this kind of behavior for much longer!" She was going to give him until the end of his term to get his act together.

IMPRESSION

Further progress: Alex is doing well at the halfway mark. I reminded her that we were halfway through treatment as a further spur to her tackling of her marriage.

Session 7

Alex arrived late, having called ahead to say she was stuck in terrible traffic. She was perhaps overly apologetic. That aside, she seemed bright, euthymic, and more emotionally engaged. She denied depression, seemed just slightly hesitant and anxious, but on the whole looked proud of herself.

ALEX: Well, things have been good. [She had learned the IPT method: I didn't even have a chance to ask my opening question.] Things have been good. I practiced what we discussed and really told Mike how I felt. He seemed to get the point. In fact, he's now talking about starting therapy himself, which I take as a good sign. It's a concession that not everything's my fault.

THERAPIST: That's great! Tell me all about how you did this!

She recounted having said to Mike pretty much everything we had discussed in the prior session. "When he saw I wasn't hesitating, he really backed off. The funny thing is that I did still feel a little unsure inside, but I went for it anyway, and it really worked. I do feel like I got a lot off my chest." I validated her emotional response and reinforced her ability to assert herself with her husband. From her description, the interchange was unlike any they had had before.

Session 8

We repeated the Ham-D at the start of the session, which was now at 5. I noted that this constituted remission: she really had the depression under control. Alex denied meaningful side effects on venlafaxine 225 mg daily. She reported feeling euthymic but a little worried about whether it would last. She also described, and showed in her affect, sadness and anger.

ALEX: I'm still angry, wary, not sure how much Mike owes me for all his past mistreatment. We can't just start things over as if nothing had happened in 6 years. And the romance, the erotic vibe is still missing. He *is* trying, at last, and yet I'm too mad to show appreciation at times. Last weekend I went up to see him at law school, and when I came in the door his cell phone rang, and he spent fifteen minutes on the phone talking to his buddies rather than greeting me. I was furious. Then he said he was disappointed that I hadn't appreciated how he cleaned up the house for me, and that he was at home rather than in a bar. He had some points, those were nice things he didn't usually do, but I was too angry to really give him credit.

THERAPIST: Why was that?

ALEX: Because his ignoring me for a stupid frat-boy conversation made that hard to appreciate. Was I wrong?

THERAPIST: What do you think?

ALEX: As usual, Mike has an argument, with some pieces of evidence to back him up. But I think I have a point, too. He's so selfish, he always putting himself first and not stopping to think of my feelings.

THERAPIST: That's where you are right now. You need to trust how you feel. I certainly understand why you felt angry. So did you tell him?

ALEX: Yes, I think you'd be proud of me. I told him that his ignoring me ruined the other things he had done, which is unfortunate: I could see he had tried, but then why did he have to undo the positive by acting as if I hadn't arrived? That he really hurts my feelings when he treats me like I'm not even there. And furthermore, I said I really needed him to get his act together by the time he graduates, which is less than six months away. That means his stopping carping about everything, to really listen to what I'm saying and pay attention to my feelings. That also means our having a sex life. I said this forcefully [as she was saying it now] but not too shrilly, just the way I wanted it to come out. It sounded good, and I felt good. And he heard it.

THERAPIST: That sounds great! No wonder you're feeling good.

Alex raised her doubts about whether Mike was really capable of changing. She then went on to talk about her wish to confront her father, who also intimidated her and ignored her feelings.

At the end of the session I reassured her that while her mood might shift in response to life circumstances, she was likely to remain better—although it might take some time feeling euthymic for her to believe it. I encouraged her that creating a "new track record" while euthymic, taking advantage of her gains to build further momentum, would increase her self-confidence over time.

IMPRESSION

Euthymic and doing well interpersonally. She has a real question of whether her husband, whatever his intentions, is capable of meeting her halfway.

Session 9

Alex was alert, prompt, and well groomed, with more relaxed movements and fluent, unpressured speech. Her mood was euthymic and mildly anxious, with more reactive, nonlabile affect. She had no thought disorder. Sensorium was clear.

Mike had sent her a long email complaining that she was ignoring his attempts to change things. Alex brought this in to discuss: she disagreed with much that he said, found it self-serving, and yet remained confused as to how to move forward. She noted Mike's insistence on developing a contract of rules for starting over in their relationship, of which his letter was an example. Mike complained that therapy was making her a more difficult, angrier, and less pliant wife, and wanted to know: "Do you promise you'll be the same after tomorrow's session?"

She described herself as needing a moral compass but increasingly feeling vindicated in her own feelings. We role-played how she might handle Mike when he asked about her feelings after the session.

IMPRESSION

Alex continues to feel better while also feeling a little overwhelmed by the changes she is making. I kept putting the ball in her court, emphasizing she has to be the one to decide things.

Session 10

Alex reported still feeling euthymic, and seemed a little more confident that this improved state might persist.

As predicted, Mike immediately wanted reassurance after our last session. "I confronted him, said this wasn't going to work, and he gave in. He is seeing a therapist, although I'm not sure what he's doing in those sessions. . . .What's cool is, I'm handling things differently than in the past. We're no longer having exhausting fights, and I'm also not giving up and letting him win rather than fight. I told him I could meet with him and his therapist if he'd like."

We discussed her continuing shift in feelings towards her husband. "I'm not depressed, but I'm unsure where I'm going and our marriage is going, confused at times . . . I'll have to see how I feel, I guess, but I can't just forgive him instantly. He does seem to be making a little progress, but it's not clear that he's really going to be able to have sex or really learn to communicate. On the other hand, it would be sad to give up after having invested so much time, effort, and suffering, blood, sweat, and tears in him."

Why had she put up with this for so long? She spontaneously linked her marriage to her parents' difficult relationship, and not wanting to separate as they had. She blamed both her father and to some degree her mother for the bad parental marriage. "And Mike always projected such certainty that he was right about things . . . but I'm not buying that any longer."

We again discussed and role-played her wish to express her feelings to her parents about how she had felt growing up, and how their marriage had affected her. She had never really confronted her father for not being around and for being so hurtful. She worried it might ruin their already tenuous relationship. "Or strengthen it. You're on a roll!" I commented. We did, however, review contingencies for what might go wrong in such a talk, and how she might broach this to her parents.

We then broached the topic of acute treatment termination and what Alex would like to do. I emphasized that she had already made great progress, achieving the goal of acute treatment of euthymia. I noted that some patients liked ongoing contact, sometimes at reduced frequency, to consolidate their gains, but that she should decide what she wanted to do. (Given her sensitivity to men imposing conditions on her, this stance seemed important.) Alex raised questions about the cost of therapy and said she would think about it. She paused, then thanked me, saying that she had gotten a lot out of treatment already. I mentioned that the idea of separation could evoke sadness, but that sadness differed from depression.

Session 11

Alex reported that her mood remained good. Work was going particularly well and she might qualify for a bonus. Moreover, things were going better with Mike. He was less frustrating in discussions, seemed to make an effort to ask her how she felt at times. Nonetheless, he was still avoiding sex, saying he was worried about pregnancy despite contraception. It wasn't clear that he was really discussing this with his therapist—he refused to discuss it. Much as she didn't want to give up on the relationship, she mused about whether he was really capable of change, whether she was wasting her time.

She had in the meantime confronted her father, with partial success. She had set up a time to speak to him, and he had listened more than usual as she told him that she'd like to have a better relationship, but that she was hurt and angry at the way he had treated the whole family growing up. He denied that much bad had happened, at which point she said that if he took this stance, they couldn't have much of a discussion. He was initially angry, taken aback, but then said he would think about it. The next day he had called and said it was helpful she had confronted him.

We agreed that she was continuing to find alternatives to either going along with the other person's rules or fruitlessly arguing. I noted that she seemed less bound by her dysthymic outlook, more confident and more secure in her own feelings. She had "changed the equation" with Mike, and perhaps could do so with her father as well.

Session 12

Alex was as usual prompt to the session, well groomed and bright. Her Ham-D was now 4. Her mood was euthymic and very mildly anxious; her affect was still slightly constricted at points, but on the whole far fuller than twelve weeks earlier.

Nothing much had changed in her marriage. Mike still seemed to be trying hard to be conciliatory, and he was seeing his therapist more often. She felt less angry at him but more dubious that things would really improve. They had had sex only twice during the interval of therapy, both times at her urging. He continued to shrink from intimacy, telling her he was "just really fucked up." Although this was better than his blaming Alex for all their difficulties, it was still discouraging.

She thanked me for having helped her to this point. I said it had been a pleasure working with her, that I had been impressed by her fortitude, by her bravery in taking interpersonal risks, and by the considerable progress she seemed to have made in understanding and trusting her feelings, communicating them to others, and improving relationships. She asked whether we could continue to meet every two to three weeks for maintenance treatment. I agreed, asking her what goals she had in mind. She talked about resolving her marital situation, improving her family relations, and perhaps building some other social supports, noting that she did not have a lot of friends to turn to.

IMPRESSION

Euthymic at the end of acute treatment. The iatrogenic role transition to euthymia appears accomplished. Alex's marital role dispute is somewhat improved, and she really did as much as could be expected to improve it; much of the problem appears to lie with her husband. Mild obsessive-compulsive traits persist at a diminished level.

PLAN
Begin maintenance IPT, meeting every two to three weeks for the next year, and have her continue venlafaxine 225 mg qd.

Follow-up

Over the next year, Alex continued antidepressant medication and IPT, the latter generally at three-week intervals. Her business career flourished, her relationships with her mother and brother improved, and she began to develop some friendships at work. Despite intermittent attempts to approach her father, they remained fairly distant. Mike graduated from law school and moved back to New York. Although less argumentative, he was unable to tolerate much intimacy despite individual therapy and a couples/sex therapy the couple began. She did report feeling more confident, and more assured that her good mood would persist.

Five months after the graduation deadline, having repeatedly weighed her feelings and her options, Alex stuck to her ultimatum and sadly told Mike that it just wasn't going to work. He was first angry and recriminating, but Alex held her ground, and they both ended up tearfully agreeing that things were not satisfactory. After moving out, she initially worried that she was getting depressed and shifted IPT frequency to every two weeks, but soon stabilized again, and felt stronger having learned she could tolerate such changes. Like many chronically depressed patients, euthymia took some time to feel secure, and led her then to look back sadly on lost years of depression and decreased productivity. She adjusted, however, mourned the past (a completion of a role transition), and focused on moving ahead.

An attractive and intelligent woman who now showed far more emotional range and appropriate self-assertion, she began dating a few months later and started a new, healthier relationship. This relieved her fears that it was "too late" to start over. At the end of the one-year follow-up, her obsessive traits seemed greatly diminished (cf., Cyranowski et al., 2004). She then opted to continue medication and to check in every six months with me. She remained euthymic, had remarried, and (having briefly stopped her antidepressant) had a healthy young child at a further three-year follow-up.

DISCUSSION

Chronically depressed patients can be discouraging, but the combination of antidepressant medication and IPT may provide a potent intervention that literally gives them a new lease on life. The case of Alex proceeded relatively smoothly, and her outcome was excellent. Whether her initial mood improvement resulted from medication, psychotherapy, or the combination, IPT was obviously instrumental in helping her learn to tolerate and understand her affects and to use them to improve her relationships. She tried to resolve and eventually dissolved her role dispute while successfully navigating the role transition to euthymia.

Not all chronically depressed patients respond so easily, but many will respond to combined pharmacotherapy and IPT. Combined treatment has never shown less efficacy than monotherapy for depression (Manning et al., 1992; Rush & Thase, 1999). An advantage of the current case was Alex's marriage: in IPT, we prefer a bad relationship to the absence of relationships. Many chronically depressed patients are single and isolated and would have to be mobilized to find relationships, whereas here the marriage provided a ready laboratory for Alex to explore her interpersonal options. Alex also quickly remoralized in treatment, her hopelessness fading. She showed a readiness to risk change in order to improve her situation. Therapists always hope for such patient qualities, and treatment is obviously more difficult—but still rarely impossible—in their absence. For some chronically depressed patients, an occupational gain, such as asking for a raise, may provide a less threatening initial treatment focus than interpersonal intimacy. Work has a job description patients can understand, whereas dating and other relationships can seem overwhelming, uncharted territory for chronically depressed individuals. An initial success experience (Frank, 1971) at work that helps the patient achieve euthymia may provide greater confidence for subsequent gains in relationships.

Under all circumstances, the therapist must remain encouraging and therapeutically realistic, keeping in mind that the patient is chronically hopeless and waiting to see the therapist give up, as others around him or her have. It is helpful to think ahead both pharmacologically and psychotherapeutically: If this medication is ineffective, what should the next step be? Where does the therapy appear to be heading? Which affects and relationships is the patient avoiding? When the patient sees that you are not giving up, that you really believe the prognosis is good, and that other options remain, it provides an important model for the patient's own outlook.

SUGGESTED READING

Markowitz JC: Psychotherapy of the post-dysthymic patient. Journal of Psychotherapy Practice and Research 1993;2:157–163

Markowitz JC: Interpersonal Psychotherapy for Dysthymic Disorder. Washington, D.C.: American Psychiatric Press, 1998

Markowitz JC, Kocsis JH, Bleiberg KL, Christos PJ, Sacks MH: A comparative trial of psychotherapy and pharmacotherapy for "pure" dysthymic patients. Journal of Affective Disorders 2005;89:167–175

7

Interpersonal Social Rhythm Therapy (IPSRT) for Bipolar Disorder

Review and Case Conceptualization

ROBIN NUSSLOCK AND ELLEN FRANK

Approximately 4.4% of the U.S. population will experience a form of bipolar disorder during their lifetime (Hyman, 2000). Bipolar disorder is a condition of contrasts in both mood and functioning. In some cases, bipolar disorder is associated with high levels of achievement and creativity, as illustrated by the high number of musicians, writers, and actors with a documented bipolar diagnosis (Goodwin & Jamison, 1990). Research finds people with bipolar disorder overrepresented in samples of highly accomplished creative individuals, and people with a history of clinical hypomania report more creative, educational, and occupational attainments across the life course than people with no psychiatric diagnosis (Johnson, 2005). However, bipolar disorder also may severely impair many areas of functioning, such as erratic work performance, high rates of divorce, and substance abuse (Carlson, Kotin, Davenport, & Adland, 1974; Goodwin & Jamison, 1990). Indeed, this illness has been ranked the sixth leading cause of disability among physical and psychiatric disorders worldwide (Murray & Lopez, 1996).

Treatment for bipolar disorder advanced considerably with the introduction of lithium carbonate in the 1960s and anticonvulsants in the 1980s. Whereas patients with bipolar disorder tended to follow deteriorating courses in the pre-pharmacological era (Cutler & Post, 1982), patients treated with lithium or anticonvulsant mood stabilizers often remain out of the hospital for extended periods (Goodwin & Jamison, 2007; Patel, DelBello, Bryan, et al., 2006). Nonetheless, there is increasing recognition that pharmacotherapy alone may forestall but does not always prevent relapses of bipolar episodes (Miklowitz, Simoneau, George, et al., 2000). Despite the use of mood-stabilizing agents, relapse rates may run as high as 40% in one year,

60% in two years, and 73% in five or more years (Gitlin, Swendsen, Heller, & Hammen, 1995). Moreover, poor medication adherence limits the efficacy of medications in 50% to 67% of individuals with bipolar disorder within the first year of treatment (Keck, McElroy, Strakowski, et al., 1998).

Recognizing the limitations of pharmacotherapy alone, a 1996 report by the National Institute of Mental Health (Prien & Rush, 1996) recommended developing adjunctive psychosocial interventions as a central research focus for bipolar disorder. The importance of psychosocial interventions also reflects the fact that environmental variables play an important role in determining whether an individual at risk develops bipolar disorder, and the timing, frequency, and polarity (depressive vs. hypomanic/manic) of bipolar episodes (Ellicott, Hammen, Gitlin, et al., 1990; Nusslock, Abramson, Harmon-Jones, et al., 2007). Over the past fifteen years, researchers have begun to answer this call, and at least three psychosocial interventions for bipolar disorder have shown promise as adjuncts to pharmacotherapy: cognitive-behavioral therapy, family-focused therapy (FFT), and interpersonal and social rhythm therapy. Growing evidence highlights the efficacy of these interventions: a recent meta-analysis (Scott, Colom, & Vieta, 2007) reported a significant reduction in relapse rates (~40%) for individuals with bipolar disorder engaged in psychosocial treatment. Findings from the multisite Systematic Treatment Enhancement Program for Bipolar Disorder (STEP-BD) indicate that each of the three psychosocial interventions enhances life functioning (Miklowitz, Otto, Frank, et al., 2007) and hastens recovery from a bipolar depressive episode relative to a lower-contact control intervention (Miklowitz et al., 2007).

This chapter focuses on interpersonal and social rhythm therapy (IPSRT; Frank, 2005) for bipolar disorder, which our group has spearheaded over the past few decades. We review the theoretical foundation and empirical support for IPSRT, then provide a detailed case illustration to elucidate the mechanisms of IPSRT.

THEORETICAL FOUNDATION FOR INTERPERSONAL AND SOCIAL RHYTHM THERAPY

One of the most prominent clinical features of bipolar disorder is its rhythmicity— that is, mood episodes that cycle on a more or less regular basis, often in conjunction with the changing light/dark cycles of the seasons (Soreca, Frank, & Kupfer, 2009). The relationship between bipolar I disorder and sleep abnormalities is well recognized, depressive episodes being associated with long sleep and anergia and manic episodes associated with (and even precipitated by) sleep loss (Goodwin & Jamison, 1990). The human circadian timing system regulates not only rhythms of physiological variables such as core body temperature, hormone secretion, and sleep–wake cycles, but also rhythms of psychomotor performance, cognitive function, and mood (Linkowski, 2003). Indeed, almost all of the functions that constitute symptoms of depression and mania (changes in mood, energy, interest, appetite, capacity for concentration, etc.) show relatively regular circadian variation.

Thus it appears logical to seek clues to the pathophysiology of bipolar disorder in the function of the circadian timing system (Wirz-Justice, 2006). Over the past few decades, considerable interest in sleep and circadian rhythm disturbances (such as body temperature, melatonin, and cortisol) has fostered theories and models relating these parameters directly to affective illness. Interest in the chronobiology of affective illness has been accelerated by recent identification of clock genes that regulate twenty-four-hour rhythms (Hastings & Herzog, 2004; Pace-Schott & Hobson, 2002; Takahashi, 2004). The ability of both central and peripheral clocks to adapt to environmental challenges may be important for mood regulation (McClung et al., 2005).

This interest in biological rhythms has led to a complementary interest in *social* rhythm disturbances and in directly examining the role of lifestyle regularity in affective disorder. A growing number of clinical investigations now support a relationship among these *social* rhythms, mood changes, and mood episodes in patients with affective illness (e.g., Haynes et al., 2005; Malkoff-Schwartz et al., 1998), as well as in individuals at risk for affective illness (Meyer & Maier, 2006). Taking changes in sleep/wake or social rhythm regularity as proxies for circadian rhythm disturbance, one can tentatively conclude that associations exist between circadian rhythm disturbance and clinical state in bipolar disorder during both depression and mania (Wehr & Goodwin, 1981; Welsh et al., 1986; Wirz-Justice, 2006). We have proposed a social rhythm or zeitgeber theory (Ehlers, Frank, & Kupfer, 1988; Ehlers, Kupfer, Frank, & Monk, 1993) postulating that life events that disrupt daily rhythms or schedules will be especially likely to precipitate bipolar symptoms and episodes. This theory suggests that individuals with bipolar disorder have a predisposition to circadian rhythm and sleep/wake cycle abnormalities that may account, in part, for bipolar symptoms. This model defines a *social zeitgeber* as a personal relationship, social demand, or life task that entrains biological rhythms such as circadian rhythms or the sleep/wake cycle. It is hypothesized that life events (both positive and negative) involving the disruption or loss of a social zeitgeber can trigger bipolar episodes by dysregulating biological rhythms (Ehlers et al., 1988).

According to our model, individuals with, or at risk for, bipolar disorder display abnormalities in sleep/wake regulation even outside manic or depressive episodes. These abnormalities represent a vulnerability for episode onset through a cascade in which life events that disrupt social zeitgebers lead to destabilization of social rhythms and sleep/wake/rest/activity patterns like what most humans experience when forced to lose a night or two of sleep (e.g., when a major project is due or an ill relative requires care throughout the night), or when shifting from a highly scheduled existence (e.g., a school term) to one with few external demands (e.g., summer vacation). This destabilization is experienced as a series of somatic symptoms. In the case of *loss* of social zeitgebers, these may include decreased energy and interest, oversleeping, and worsening mood, typically followed by re-entrainment to a new routine and recovery of energy, interest, and a normal sleep/wake/rest/activity pattern. *Disruption* in social zeitgebers, especially when associated with sleep loss, often triggers a transient increase in interest, energy, and mood, typically followed by a "crash," leading to an effort to recover the sleep debt. According to our model, however, individuals who have bipolar disorder—perhaps because of trait disturbances in behavioral and circadian rhythms—cannot re-equilibrate following these challenges and remain in states of pathologic entrainment we label "major depression" and "mania." Once established, depression and mania, in turn, impede efforts to re-equilibrate.

Empirical support for a social rhythm or zeitgeber perspective comes from several fronts. With respect to life events, Wehr et al. (1987) have demonstrated that sleep reduction can lead to mania in individuals with bipolar disorder, and sleep deprivation has significant antidepressant effects in individuals with both unipolar and bipolar depression (Leibenluft et al., 1993; Leibenluft & Wehr, 1992). Malkoff-Schwartz et al. (1998, 2000) found that manic patients had significantly more preonset stressors characterized by social rhythm disruption (e.g., change in sleep/wake cycle) than did depressed patients with bipolar disorder. Wehr et al. (1987) argued that sleep loss may be a common causal pathway in the genesis of mania. Other research has shown that social rhythm disruption precipitates depressive symptoms and episodes among bipolar individuals (Sylvia et al., 2009).

Given the difficulty of measuring physiological rhythms in large numbers of subjects, and the reality that physical and social environments influence these rhythms, we developed the Social Rhythm Metric (SRM; Monk et al., 1991), a self-report instrument for measuring daily activity and social rhythms. The SRM has been used to examine changes in social routines in mood disorder patients (Frank et al., 1997, 2005) and their relationship to light exposure in depression (Haynes et al., 2005). Meyer and Maier (2006) showed that individuals at risk for bipolar disorder have lower SRM scores (less regular routines) and greater sleep duration variability than controls without specific risk for bipolar disorder. Shen et al. (2008) replicated this finding in a sample of over 400 undergraduates with bipolar spectrum conditions and, in a prospective follow-up study of several years' duration, showed that low social rhythm regularity significantly predicted first prospective onset of major depression, mania, and hypomania. Among participants in STEP-BD, Gruber et al. (2009) found an average variability in sleep time of 2.78 hours (SD = 3.03) over the course of a single week, comparable to the jet lag associated with moving from the east to the west coast of the United States each week. Supporting the social zeitgeber hypothesis, these findings suggest that instability of social and sleep/wake rhythms may be a risk factor for the affective instability that characterizes bipolar disorder. Conversely, reducing variability and consolidating social rhythms appear to protect against recurrence (Frank et al., 2005; Miklowitz et al., 2007).

DEVELOPMENT OF IPSRT

The articulation of the social zeitgeber theory and the development of the SRM led to the development and testing of IPSRT (Frank, 2005), which integrates IPT for unipolar depression with a behavioral intervention that focuses on social rhythm and sleep/wake regulation (Klerman et al., 1984; Weissman, Markowitz, Klerman, 2000). In IPSRT, the clinician helps the patient recognize the relationship between disruptions in social rhythms and the onset of previous episodes and then uses standard behavioral techniques, including psychoeducation, self-monitoring (via the SRM), successive approximation, and reinforcement (via the observed link between regular routines and improved mood), to facilitate and maintain increases in social rhythm and sleep/wake regularity. IPSRT addresses the interplay between the interpersonal and biological spheres by helping patients to see how interpersonal stressors and social role transitions can disrupt daily routines important to maintaining circadian integrity. As in IPT, therapists aid patients in resolving interpersonal disputes and negotiating role transitions. At the same time, they teach patients how to regularize irregular daily routines and how to maintain such regularity even in the face of external challenges.

In particular, IPSRT focuses on (1) the reciprocal relationships between life stress and the onset of mood disorder symptoms, (2) the importance of maintaining regular daily rhythms and sleep–wake cycles, and (3) the identification and management of potential precipitants of rhythm dysregulation, with special attention to interpersonal triggers. Therapists instruct patients to monitor their social routines and rhythms using the SRM (Monk et al., 1991) and, ideally, to begin to see the interplay among instabilities in daily routines, patterns of social stimulation, sleep/wake times, and mood fluctuations. IPSRT then implements behavioral strategies to help patients alter activities that promote rhythm irregularities (minimizing overstimulation, monitoring the frequency and intensity of social interactions). Patients are encouraged to make life changes in order to protect the integrity of their circadian rhythms and sleep/wake cycles.

The interpersonal techniques employed in IPSRT are similar to those in IPT for unipolar depression (Klerman et al., 1984; Weissman, Markowitz, & Klerman, 2000). The therapist determines the important individuals in the patient's life (the interpersonal inventory). In outlining this "cast of characters," the therapist probes the quality of the relationships and aspects of them that the patient would like to change. The therapist identifies an interpersonal problem area during the initial phase of treatment to serve as the interpersonal treatment focus. IPT defines four key areas: unresolved grief, role disputes, role transitions, and interpersonal deficits. In IPSRT, we added a fifth problem area, grief for the loss of the healthy self, in order to increase acceptance of the illness and improve treatment adherence in a patient group that finds these both difficult issues.

We expected the IPT components to contribute a specific antidepressant effect and hypothesized that helping patients stabilize their social rhythms would decrease the risk of new affective (especially manic) episodes (Frank, Swartz, & Kupfer, 2000). Thus, IPSRT is an integrated therapy that allows interpersonal and social rhythm strategies to function synergistically. We expected that the IPT-induced resolution of interpersonal conflict would also contribute to more stable rhythms, and that stable rhythms would promote more stable life circumstances and interpersonal relationships.

EMPIRICAL SUPPORT FOR IPSRT

Growing evidence suggests that IPSRT has a prophylactic effect as an adjunct to long-term maintenance pharmacotherapy. A randomized clinical trial compared IPSRT with an intensive clinical management control condition as both an acute and maintenance treatment for patients with bipolar I disorder (Frank et al., 2005). After accounting for significant covariates of outcome, we found that receiving IPSRT in the acute treatment phase of the trial was associated with significantly longer time to recurrence during the maintenance phase of the trial. At the end of the acute treatment phase, patients assigned to IPSRT demonstrated significantly higher social rhythm regularity than those in the control condition. Consistent with the social zeitgeber hypothesis, the length of the illness-free period during the maintenance phase of the trial was significantly related to how much patients increased the regularity of their social rhythms during acute treatment, indicating that increased regularity of social routines mediated longer survival without a new affective episode. A post-hoc analysis examined the effect of IPSRT and control clinical management on rates of suicide attempts among individuals with bipolar I disorder who were followed for an average of 1.4 years (Rucci, Frank, Kostelnik, et al., 2002). Both IPSRT and clinical management were associated with lowered suicide attempt risk. The low number of suicide attempts precluded comparing the efficacy of IPSRT to clinical management. A small pilot study of patients at particularly high risk of relapse or recurrence integrated the central tenets of FFT and IPSRT (Miklowitz et al., 2003) and found that patients given this combined therapy along with medication showed longer time to relapse than was observed in matched controls given clinical management. Consistent with previous FFT and IPSRT studies, however, the combined treatment improved depressive more than manic symptoms. Finally, in the large, multicenter STEP-BD study, participants receiving IPSRT demonstrated shorter time to and greater likelihood of recovery from bipolar depression than participants assigned to the control psychosocial intervention (Miklowitz et al., 2007).

Each of the empirically validated psychosocial treatments for bipolar disorder attempts to stabilize social and sleep/wake routines. In FFT (Miklowitz & Goldstein, 1997), the clinician emphasizes the importance of regular and sufficient sleep and of establishing regular household routines. Likewise, most versions of cognitive therapy for bipolar disorder (including Basco & Rush [1996], Lam et al. [2003], and Scott et al. [2001]) include psychoeducation about the importance of regular sleep/wake and rest/activity rhythms.

CASE EXAMPLE

We present the case of Adam, a patient with bipolar disorder treated with acute and maintenance IPSRT over several years. Adam's case describes the four phases of IPSRT: initial, intermediate, maintenance, and final treatment phases.

Initial Treatment Phase

Adam was born in Wisconsin and got along well with his parents and brother during his childhood. Adam's mother was a teacher and his father worked in the auto industry. Adam was a talented student but struggled socially, as his interests differed from many of his peers. At eighteen, Adam's future seemed bright. A precociously gifted classical musician, he had been accepted to one of the nation's foremost music colleges. He would have the opportunity to study cello with a world-renowned performer, despite having grown up in a tiny Wisconsin town and having heard only two live symphonies in his life. His interest in classical music had marginalized him as early as junior high, but knowing that he would finally achieve what he had dreamed of for as long as he could remember eclipsed all his past suffering. And there had been a lot of suffering: moments when, out of the blue, he was consumed with a heart-stopping anxiety so terrifying that he was certain he would die, days when he was so irritable that his mother lost her endless patience and he felt abandoned by the world, months when he was so sad he could hardly speak.

At college he made many friends, people who seemed to care just as intensely as he did and were willing to talk about their passions from the minute classes ended until the sun rose the next morning. Then there were the concerts! Just a subway ride away was one of the world's leading symphonies. Whenever he wanted, he could go hear leading musicians play his favorite pieces. He seemed to have boundless energy. Indeed, within a few weeks of arriving at college he found that he really didn't need to sleep. He could spend all afternoon playing his cello and almost all night talking with classmates. When he finally made his way back to his room, he still had energy enough to do his homework and practice some more. His brain was filled with new compositions he wanted to write, day after day, week after week. The sound of rain hitting the sidewalk cement sounded like a Mozart concerto. As he walked back to his dorm room just before dawn, the shadows of the twisted old trees on campus had the weight and intensity of the minor chords. He had never experienced anything like it! When it came time to plan his first-semester final project, he was a bit secretive with his advisor, who, because Adam's work to date had been so exceptional, decided to just wait and see what this brilliant young man devised.

To his advisor's horror, the project Adam presented was a complex and stunning multimedia installation, which he had completed in a single night. Instead of simply composing a musical piece, he incorporated an installation of women's underwear, stolen one piece at a time from the drawers of his dorm mates. The music was incomprehensible and disorganized. Neither his advisor, nor the administration, nor the women whose underwear he had taken were amused. When the dean interviewed Adam the following day, it was apparent that this was not just some drug-induced joke. Adam was having his first manic episode. Besides his sleep disruption and loss of judgment, this episode included a flight of ideas about music-related projects he wanted to do. He described these ideas coming a "million miles per minute" and reported frustration that, as soon as he had one "brilliant" idea, he would lose it and have another. Adam's rapid and pressured speech at times took the form of "rhythmic chants," and he grandiosely claimed he was going to be the next Beethoven.

Escorted by school officials, Adam presented to the psychiatric emergency room. During the screening interview he was euphoric and hyperactive, his thoughts impossible to follow. He was diagnosed with bipolar disorder, admitted to the inpatient psychiatric unit, and initially treated with lithium, with lorazepam and diphenhydramine as needed to reduce agitation and hyperactivity. He had to be placed in seclusion two days after hospital admission because of severe agitation and hyperactivity. Fortunately, his manic symptoms began to improve after two to three days, with a reduction of his flight of ideas and reduced hyperactivity and agitation. After seven days Adam had stabilized enough for discharge to the outpatient IPSRT team, to which he presented a series of challenges.

First and foremost, Adam denied that anything was wrong with him or that he needed treatment. He was distraught over having spent the past week in a psychiatric hospital, stating that people did not understand his brilliance. Second, Adam continued to present symptoms of mania, even though they did not warrant continued inpatient treatment. Before we could begin standard IPSRT, it was clearly important to stabilize his mood. We attempted this in three ways. First, Adam agreed to continue to take lithium. Although he made it clear to the treatment team that he did not need any medications, he agreed to take it to "humor" us.

Second, we spent considerable time teaching Adam about bipolar disorder and the symptoms he was experiencing. When he presented at the psychiatric emergency room, Adam had never heard of bipolar disorder and had no context for understanding what was happening to him. Thus, one aspect of Adam's individualized case formulation was that he lacked information about mood disorders and his treatment plan would need to include extensive psychoeducation, starting at the most basic level. Adam was initially quite defensive about discussing bipolar disorder and refused to see his behavior as either irrational or problematic. He continued to consider his final project a "masterpiece" and ridiculed people for not understanding its meaning, which, he stated, was an exposition on music and the body. Accordingly, we needed to walk a fine line during the initial sessions, trying to help Adam gain perspective on his current state while not appearing to challenge his autonomy or discount his artistic talents as bipolar disorder.

Third, and related to point two, we tried to help Adam recognize the importance of regularizing his sleep and social rhythms. Interestingly, Adam was much less defensive about discussing sleep disruption, saying he recognized it was "weird" that he had not needed much sleep to feel rested over the past few months. He was curious about why this might be, which provided a way to begin educating Adam about bipolar illness: he found focusing on a concrete behavioral symptom rather than the global disorder less threatening. To his credit, Adam took concrete steps during the first three or four treatment sessions to increase his sleep and to regularize his routines.

An important protective factor was that at the time of his first manic episode Adam had minimal exposure to, or interest in, alcohol or illicit substances. Bipolar disorder is associated with higher rates of both alcohol and substance abuse/dependence (Angst, Stassen, Clayton, & Angst, 2002; Goodwin & Jamison, 1990). Many substances (e.g., cocaine, amphetamines, alcohol, nicotine) activate cortico-striatal regions such as the ventral striatum that have been implicated in risk for mania (David et al., 2005; Due et al., 2002). Furthermore, alcohol and substance abuse/dependence are generally associated with a more severe and pernicious bipolar course. A very early treatment goal was to highlight for Adam the likely negative implications that would arise from using illicit substances, especially substances that activate the dopaminergic reward-related brain activity implicated in bipolar disorder (e.g., cocaine, amphetamines). We pointedly praised Adam for avoiding alcohol/substances thus far in his life.

Over the first three or four sessions, Adam's manic symptoms continued to abate, making it possible to begin treatment in earnest. This initial treatment phase had three goals. The first was to orient Adam to treatment and individualized treatment planning. We provided a general explanation of IPSRT and what would happen if he agreed to try this treatment. We tailored this explanation to Adam's minimal understanding of bipolar disorder and minimal illness history. Because Adam had bipolar I disorder, we emphasized that IPSRT is used along with appropriate pharmacotherapy. We described briefly the evidence for links among interpersonal problems, social rhythm disruption, and bipolar disorder episodes. We explained that we would want to learn about his relationships and the day-to-day pattern of his life and work with him to modify these relationships to maximize both mood and circadian stability and social rhythm regularity.

Next, we sought a more comprehensive history of Adam's developmental experience, family relationships, family history of psychiatric illness, past and current symptoms, current stressors, and life goals in order to develop a case conceptualization. A case conceptualization is central to tailoring IPSRT to the needs of the individual patient. Our goal was to be able to articulate the interpersonal problems, rhythm disruption, and bipolar symptoms Adam was experiencing. This included completing an illness history timeline. Although this was Adam's first manic episode, he did report a history of severe depression that began when he was twelve or thirteen years old. He reported week-long periods when he could not get out of bed, had no motivation, cried much of the day, and felt like there was a "black hole" in his chest. He attributed much of his depression to not feeling like he belonged. When all the other boys his age focused on sports, he was interested in classical music, which, he noted, did not make him many friends. Adam reported feeling socially isolated during his childhood. Moreover, his parents (particularly his father) and peers did not respect his talents in music and other creative media. He felt like "the odd duck." He reported getting some advice from the school counselor but never formal treatment. He noted that he grew up in a religious household where he was encouraged to pray when he felt down rather than seek any psychological treatment.

Adam could not provide much information on his family's psychiatric history. Like many Midwesterners, he noted, his family and peers kept a "stiff upper lip" and did not discuss emotions and feelings. There were days, if not weeks, when his mother seemed distant and "cold," but he couldn't say if she was depressed because "no one talked about it." An aunt—his mother's sister—had multiple psychiatric hospitalizations. However, his mother had a falling out with her sister before Adam was born, and Adam had met her only a few times as a child. Early in treatment, Adam stated, "I wish there was more psychiatric history in my family; that way I wouldn't feel like such an odd duck."

Our next goal for the initial treatment phase and developing a case formulation was to complete the interpersonal inventory (Klerman et al., 1984). This inventory focuses on understanding the nature of the patient's relationships, any consistent positive or negative patterns, and particularly whether problems in relationships are linked to the onset or persistence of the current episode of illness, either through their psychological impact or their impact on social rhythms. Adam's interpersonal inventory presented certain challenges. Although eighteen years old when he entered treatment, developmentally Adam was more like a fifteen-year-old. This at times frustrated the therapists, as we often had to repeat or re-explain concepts to Adam. However, once we better understood how Adam processed information, we were better able to tailor our descriptions to Adam's learning style. We even at times connected IPSRT concepts to music concepts, of which Adam had great mastery.

Further complicating the situation, many of Adam's important relationships were back home in Wisconsin, but his current interpersonal context was the college community. The interpersonal inventory began by exploring his relationship with his parents and revealed a strong supportive relationship with his mother, of whom he was extremely fond. His relationship with his stern, disciplinarian father was more difficult. Adam had always disappointed his father, who devalued Adam's musical accomplishments and yearned for sons more interested in "masculine" pursuits. Adam's younger brother was good at sports and was, as Adam put it, "Daddy's boy." This created considerable conflict between Adam and his brother and father. His mother worked constantly to try to improve Adam's relationship with his father.

Although Adam had been at college only months when he entered treatment, he had formed many strong, supportive relationships. His fellow music students were much more understanding of his eccentric behavior than his auto-worker father had been, and several of them expressed a desire to help facilitate his reentry into college life. They accompanied Adam to clinic appointments and represented an important resource for his treatment. Adam's romantic relationships also proved challenging to his mood. The interpersonal inventory revealed that Adam had always been attracted to very flamboyant and not particularly supportive partners. Their frequent rejections and dramatic reconciliations did little to add to Adam's mood stability. The IPSRT team identified this as an area that would require considerable work in the future, once he had completed his role transition to being a stable college student.

Our final initial phase goal was to gauge Adam's daily activity and social rhythm and sleep/wake regularity. We had Adam complete the SRM every day for a full week. We instructed Adam not to alter his sleep/wake schedule or social routine when filling it out in order to provide a snapshot of his current profile, although by the time we introduced the SRM Adam had already begun to make positive changes in his sleep/wake routine from the chaos of his pre-hospitalization lifestyle. Importantly, to understand Adam's typical profile, we delayed the SRM until his manic episode had subsided and he had returned to school. We explained that the SRM was a way of understanding when he did each of a series of five activities (getting out of bed, first contact with another person, starting work or school, having dinner, and getting into bed for the night) that we believe are key to setting the body's clock. We believe that individuals who have bipolar disorder have exquisitely sensitive clocks (rather like a fine wristwatch), clocks that require exquisite care (you wouldn't toss your Piaget into a drawer with a bunch of junk; you would take care of it). We explained that like most chronic illnesses, bipolar disorder requires lifestyle changes to keep it under control. Just as someone with diabetes needs to alter his or her diet and someone with severe asthma needs to alter the living environment, people with bipolar disorder appear to benefit from very regular routines, both short term (for immediate improvement in mood) and long term (to prevent recurrences). We continued that another risk for new episodes of mania or depression can be how much or how little social stimulation one gets, so we would want to monitor that along with his schedule. Indeed, as we were talking, Adam clearly related the onset of his mania to the increasing chaos in his schedule and his enormous increase in socializing once he found himself in an environment surrounded by people who shared his interests.

Adam's first SRM recordings, with a total score of only 2.6, yielded two pieces of information. First, his profile still showed substantial variability in both his social routine and sleep/wake schedule. Adam's bedtime for the seven-day period varied from 9 p.m. to 4 a.m., and his sleep duration varied from four hours to ten hours. There was also significant variability in when Adam awoke, ranging from 8 a.m. to 1 p.m.

It was also apparent that Adam had no set daily schedule. The only anchor for his social routine was his class schedule. Unfortunately, this schedule changed almost daily. Some days his classes started early in the morning, other days not until the afternoon. Thus, Adam's social and sleep/wake schedule was irregular and inconsistent. Adam noted that this profile differed from when he had attended high school in Wisconsin. There he had a strict midnight curfew and a consistent daily school schedule. He had always naturally stayed up late and slept late, but he couldn't do what came naturally in high school because he would have been late for classes. With few close high school friends who matched his artistic energy, he typically had no social pressures to stay up late and party. Thus his social rhythms and sleep/wake profile in high school were far more regular than in his first few months at college.

Based on the data gathered in the initial IPSRT phase, we generated this case conceptualization: Adam is a highly gifted and creative student with a history of several depressive episodes and one episode of severe, psychotic mania. Adam had connected the depressive episodes to feelings of social isolation and alienation from the mainstream interests of his community. Upon entering a college that highly values the arts and music, Adam finally found his community of peers, people who valued his thoughts, ideas, and skills. Adam dove into these opportunities with all his being and found himself intellectually and emotionally stimulated. This stimulation resulted in many deep conversations that went late into the night, a release of his creative potential, and a wave of excitement and enthusiasm for life. While this scenario does not sound atypical for a college freshman, for someone vulnerable to bipolar disorder it can be very risky.

The late-night conversations, abundant new opportunities, and irregularity in social routines and sleep/wake cycle precipitated a storm for Adam. The heightened excitement and energy started to turn into days without sleep, the creative thoughts started to accelerate and become disorganized, the goals and aspirations for art projects lost focus and touch with reality, and soon Adam was spiraling into mania. As Adam wanted to stay in school as his mania remitted, his primary interpersonal problem area was role transition. Adam had gone from his parents' home and very stable (even boring) routine in Wisconsin, to an unstable, irregular, highly stimulating environment.

This was not to say that Adam needed to spend his life in an environment that did not support his creative potential. It did mean, however, that to stay in school he would need to incorporate some qualities of his high school lifestyle into his college lifestyle. In particular, Adam would have to add more routine to his schedule and minimize disruption in his sleep/wake cycle. He would need to begin identifying early warning signs of getting too "high" or "low" in his moods, and to develop strategies to manage mood swings.

The therapeutic goals of Adam's case conceptualization revealed two overarching themes. The first was Adam's need to recognize that he suffered from bipolar disorder, and that to minimize his risk of another episode he would have to change his lifestyle. These are no small tasks for an eighteen-year-old. However, without this understanding and consequent action, Adam would remain at increased risk for a severe and devastating illness course. Second is that Adam would likely struggle with the fifth IPSRT problem area, "grief for the loss of the healthy self." As Adam transitioned out of his manic episode he became acutely aware of the implications of his behavior and that he had an illness he would have to cope with for the rest of his life. He felt shame at having been in a psychiatric hospital, for having embarrassed himself in front of his teachers and peers, and for "letting my family down." He felt understandable rage at being limited by a "ridiculous illness" he certainly hadn't asked for.

We had this exchange with Adam soon after presenting our case conceptualization to him. It is relevant to his struggle with "grief for the loss of the healthy self":

ADAM: I can't believe what happened. I am so ashamed.

THERAPIST: I know, Adam, I know.

ADAM: And now I have bipolar disorder; this is terrible.

THERAPIST: I know this is tough, Adam. But having bipolar disorder is not the end of the world.

ADAM: Sure it is. . . How do you mean?

THERAPIST: Well, our goal is to help you live with bipolar disorder, rather than bipolar disorder "living you."

ADAM: How do I do that?

THERAPIST: In therapy we will be working together to teach you strategies for better managing your moods, relationships, and sleep schedules, with the goal of not letting the disorder get the better of you.

ADAM: Sounds like a lot of work.

THERAPIST: It is, Adam. But we believe it will be worth it in the end. We really do understand how hard it is to not be doing what everyone else in your dorm is doing, but we've seen what a difference these strategies can make for young people with bipolar disorder. Let's consider it an experiment that we'll try for a month or so and see how it goes. Are you willing to give it a month?

ADAM: I guess.

This exchange gives a feel for Adam's ambivalence about bipolar disorder. On the one hand, he is clear that having bipolar disorder is "terrible" and likely "a lot of work." On the other hand, he gives subtle cues that he may be willing to do the work to gain more control over his life and moods. This captures the central struggle in "grief for the loss of the healthy self": the struggle between the desire to go back to the "good old days" when things were easier, and the acceptance that things are now different, and that with some work he or she can create a life worth living.

The initial treatment phase lasted six sessions. Having established a case conceptualization and presented it to Adam (in less technical language than we describe it here), we were ready to begin the intermediate phase, where the bulk of the IPSRT intervention occurs.

Intermediate Phase of Treatment

The intermediate phase involved twenty-one weekly sessions while Adam continued on the same dosage of lithium, lorazepam, and diphenhydramine. His intermediate phase focused on three areas: addressing psychoeducation, Adam's social rhythm disruption, and Adam's primary interpersonal problem area, role transition. Throughout the intermediate treatment phase we also worked with Adam on grief for loss of the healthy self to help manage the sadness and guilt stemming from his first manic episode and to accept his having bipolar disorder.

Psychoeducation is particularly important for patients like Adam who have minimal understanding and experience with the illness. Psychoeducation is essential to establish a treatment commitment from patients. IPSRT asks patients to make lifestyle changes that may conflict with their immediate desires and goals. As a bright and energetic college freshman, Adam understandably wanted to stay up into the wee hours talking with friends and exploring ideas. This is particularly understandable when everyone around him seemed able to live that lifestyle without consequences. An objective of IPSRT psychoeducation was to help Adam better understand bipolar disorder and appreciate that, in his moods, thoughts, *and* circadian system, he is more sensitive than others.

As Adam's manic symptoms abated, he became more aware of the irrationality and implications of his recent behavior and more willing to recognize that something had gone awry. Although still quite defensive about the term "bipolar disorder," he started to actively seek information in session about his episode, some of which he recalled only vaguely. Psychoeducation focused on helping Adam better understand the signs and symptoms of hypo/mania and depression. We helped Adam identify the early warning signs, or prodromes, of manic and depressive episodes. In medicine, prodromes are defined as the early signs and symptoms that herald a full episode (Molnar, Feeney, & Fava, 1988). Individuals with bipolar disorder, as well as their relatives, can report prodromes reliably (Keitner, Solomon, Ryan, et al., 1996; Lam, Wong, & Sham, 2001). Two clinical advantages of targeting bipolar prodromes are: (1) full-blown bipolar episodes may overwhelm the patient's coping strategies, whereas the strategies may be highly effective in managing prodromal symptoms and (2) the prodromal period (Smith & Tarrier, 1992) represents a window in which an intervention might protect the patient from relapse. Good coping skills during prodromes have been associated with higher social functioning (Lam & Wong, 1997), which predicts longer intervals between episodes (Gitlin et al., 1995).

Reflecting on the early stages of his manic episode, Adam identified several prodromes. A central manic prodrome was his lack of need for, and inability to, sleep. He would lie down to sleep but "just stare at the ceiling." This linked to another manic prodrome, which was heightened energy. He felt like the "Energizer Bunny" and could keep "going and going." At first this lack of sleep and heightened energy were fun, but eventually they "became too much to handle." In therapy, we had Adam describe the cognitive, affective, and behavioral states associated with these prodromes in detail so he could recognize them if they returned. We then focused on specific behavioral deactivation strategies to address these prodromes before they spiraled into hypo/mania, including "modifying high activities," "restraining oneself," and "engaging in calming activities" (Lam & Wong, 1997).

Another important psychoeducational component was helping Adam identify situations or events likely to trigger bipolar episodes. Concerning depression, Adam focused on the social isolation of his high school years and described comments by peers and family that he felt minimized or negated things he found important, such as the arts. To help Adam manage his depression we focused on sensitivity to criticism, validated his anger and hurt, and helped him put into words his frustration regarding the peer and family comments. We role-played conversations he might have with his parents about his creative pursuits and helped him find his voice in communicating with friends and family. The goal was to build a greater sense of interpersonal effectiveness and self-respect. For triggers of mania, Adam began to appreciate how the significant life transitions, sleep disruption, and opportunities associated with coming to college put him at risk (a topic we will return to).

The second focus of the intermediate phase of treatment was addressing Adam's social rhythm disruption. The social zeitgeber or social rhythm theory (Ehlers, Frank, & Kupfer, 1988; Ehlers, Kupfer, Frank, & Monk, 1993) postulates that life events that disrupt daily rhythms or schedules will likely precipitate bipolar symptoms and episodes. As Adam's first college semester gravely disrupted both his social and sleep/wake routines, an important component of our work, both in managing his acute symptoms and as prophylaxis against relapse, was helping him to stabilize his social rhythms. Central to this work was the SRM. We had Adam continue to complete the SRM weekly throughout treatment. This provided data on Adam's social rhythm profile. Perhaps more importantly, it provided a mechanism for Adam and the IPSRT team to collaboratively seek patterns in his routines/rhythms, and links between life events and routine/rhythm disruption as well as links between his social rhythms and his mood. Thus, the SRM is not only an assessment instrument but also a tool to help patients see their social rhythm and sleep profile objectively and to monitor their own progress in regularizing their routines. As noted, the first week we asked Adam not to alter his routines in order to objectively assess his SRM profile. In the intermediate phase, however, we developed concrete social rhythm and sleep–wake goals and used the SRM to facilitate them.

Our first objective was to help Adam normalize his sleep/wake routine. With his collaboration, we identified a reasonable time for him to awaken on a daily basis. This took into consideration his natural circadian rhythm—he was a "night owl"—and his daily obligations. We settled on 9 a.m., as he did not typically begin classes until 10:30 a.m. We agreed that Adam would wake up at 9 a.m. regardless of how little he slept the night before. Research indicates that setting a standard wake-up time may more effectively regularize sleep routine then setting a standard bedtime (Buysee et al., 2010). If Adam had been emerging from a depressive episode, we might have instructed him that even if he got only two hours of sleep in a particular night, he was to wake up promptly at 9 a.m. Even though Adam would likely be tired the next day, his need for sleep, or sleep drive, would be high that night, facilitating a full night's sleep and re-entrainment of his circadian rhythm. We would still have highlighted the need to go to sleep at a regular time—something like 1 a.m.—and to strive for a full eight hours of sleep, but we would have particularly attended to his need to wake promptly at 9 a.m. on weekends as well as weekdays. Given how severely manic Adam had been, however, we needed a more complex approach that gave equal weight to a regular wake time and a regular bedtime to ensure sufficient sleep. To Adam's credit, he worked hard at this task and noticed significant improvement in regularity of his sleep/wake schedule over about a two-week period. As can be imagined, this was a challenge because Adam continued to be drawn to late-night conversations with peers and hated being up three hours before anyone else on Saturday and Sunday mornings. To address this, Adam actually recruited some close friends into his therapeutic work on stabilizing his sleep routine. We agreed that he would talk with three of his closest school friends to "teach" them some of what he had learned in treatment. We role-played these conversations before Adam spoke with his friends to help him manage his anxiety about being so open and frank with them about his bipolar illness. Fortunately, Adam's friends were very responsive and willing to actively participate in his treatment. They agreed to help "wrap up" evening activities at a reasonable hour. They also agreed to check with Adam in the morning to ensure he had awakened by 9 a.m., which was easy to coordinate as they all lived on the same dorm floor. Perhaps most importantly, they agreed that at least one of them would get up early on Saturdays and Sundays so he wouldn't be tempted to go back to bed. Within a month Adam's SRM score had risen to just over 4, a level we have found protects against new episodes.

A second strategy for helping Adam regularize his social rhythm was to encourage him to get a part-time job. Adam was fortunate that his parents were paying for his college education; however, this meant that he had lots of free time and little structure to his day. We predicted that a part-time job would help Adam replicate the regular routines and schedule of his high school years. Adam found a job at a local bookstore flexible enough that he could schedule his hours around his classes and have consistent daily structure from 10 a.m. to around 6 p.m.

Two primary components of IPSRT are management of mood symptoms and intervention in the interpersonal problem area linked to the onset of the patient's affective episode (Frank, 2005). For Adam, this primary interpersonal problem area was a role transition. The conceptualization of the interpersonal problem area constitutes one of the unique and important contributions of Klerman et al. (1984) to the treatment of patients with mood disorders. As they indicate, role transitions can include both apparent losses, such as divorce or the departure of children from home, and apparent gains such as a new job, promotion, marriage, or the birth of a child. Both losses and gains require the person in transition to readjust and change. Sensitive to even modest shifts in daily and interpersonal routines, individuals with bipolar disorder can find role transitions particularly stressful. This was true for Adam, who went from a structured lifestyle in Wisconsin to chaotic creative overstimulation. For many, this seems a perfect scenario, but for Adam, it was the perfect stressor. The combination of social rhythm irregularity, significant sleep disruption, new interpersonal relationships, and heightened creativity and goal-striving led to dysregulation and ultimately mania. Our first goal in addressing this role transition was helping Adam understand this chain of events so he could appreciate the types of situations that put him at risk. Adam described how, upon arrival at college, his predominant emotion was excitement. He "wanted to talk with everyone." Whereas in Wisconsin he felt he had one or perhaps two people who understood him, now he felt he had a whole community. He felt accepted, and with acceptance came a willingness to "let go and unleash my creative potential." He went from being the "odd duck" in his Wisconsin high school and his family, to feeling his creative pursuits were accepted and even admired. Women were also taking more interest in him, and even though he did not begin a relationship prior to his manic episode, he was excited by the prospect. Soon after arrival he noticed that he did not need much sleep (three or four hours) to feel rested. Thus began the dance between sleep loss, heightened energy and creativity, staying out late to talk about ideas, further sleep loss, and ultimately dysregulation leading to mania. With no context for understanding what was happening, Adam could not put on the brakes and disengage from the drive to mania. In this section of therapy, we sought to help Adam create a context for understanding so that when he next faced such circumstances and prodromes, he would have a concrete game plan to prevent things from getting out of control. This plan involved multiple therapeutic strategies: (1) psychoeducation to help define and identify prodromal warning signs of manic symptoms; (2) cognitive and behavioral deactivation strategies to regulate his thoughts and mood during prodromal periods; (3) recruiting friends to help identify early warning signs to assist Adam; (4) continued monitoring of social and sleep/wake routines; and (5) medication management to reduce the chance that Adam would stop taking his medication either during euthymic or episodic periods.

Intimately connected to our work on role transition with Adam was work on the grief for loss of the healthy self. A core part of Adam's work in treatment was coming to accept that things had changed. To minimize the risk of another manic episode, Adam needed to make unwanted lifestyle changes. And who could blame him? Adam wanted to return to school with the same intensity and energy with which he had begun. Not only was Adam grieving his manic episode, for which he felt embarrassment and shame, he also was grieving the end of those first few months of school, arguably the best months of his life, before things spiraled out of control. Adam recognized that there were more costs than benefits associated with returning to such a lifestyle. As Adam stabilized, he and his IPSRT team sought to strike the optimal balance between enjoying his friends and creative conversations and endeavors and maintaining his treatment strategies and routinized social and sleep–wake routines in order to minimize relapse risk. Again, a tall order for an eighteen-year-old, but we found ourselves impressed with Adam's commitment to treatment and the authenticity and dignity with which he faced his challenges.

We had the exchange below eighteen weeks into the intermediate phase (twenty-four weeks into treatment overall). Comparing this to the earlier interchange makes clear that Adam had made strides.

ADAM: You know, I think I am going to be OK.
THERAPIST: What do you mean?
ADAM: With this bipolar thing. It's tough, and I don't like it, but it is what it is. And my friends have been really cool about it. They don't give me a hard time about any of it.
THERAPIST: Did you expect that they would?
ADAM: Of course. I did some really objectionable things . . . like stealing Mia's underwear. And I was really irritable and awful with them when I was at my worst. But they seem to understand that that wasn't really me. And they've been so great about helping me get up and haven't pushed me to do stuff they now realize isn't good for me. The only thing I'm really still worried about is this tremor. I just don't have the same fine finger control I had before I started on this medicine. Do you think it will ever go away?
THERAPIST: Honestly, I'm not sure. It may, but it may not. Do you feel like the only way you can express yourself musically is through your instrument?
ADAM: No, actually not. I was getting very excited about composing before I ended up in hospital and I'm still excited about it . . . maybe a little too excited. It kind of scares me now.
THERAPIST: Well, one of the things we can do together is talk about how to keep the excitement in check. Enough to enable you to create, but not so much you can't sleep or calm yourself down when you need to.

This is often how "grief for the loss of the healthy self" resolves. We wouldn't expect Adam to feel lucky to have bipolar disorder, but "it is what it is" indicates that Adam was *integrating* bipolar disorder into his life, his social relationships, and his self-concept. Also, with help from his therapist, he found satisfying creative outlets despite the limits his disorder and its treatment imposed.

Maintenance Phase of Treatment

Adam continued to make progress. After twenty-seven weekly sessions (six during the initial phase and twenty-one during the intermediate phase), Adam and his IPSRT team together decided to enter the maintenance phase. This phase involved a gradual tapering of sessions from weekly to once every three weeks over the course of three months. During this phase we continued to focus on the four topics of the intermediate phase: psychoeducation, social rhythm disruption, Adam's role transition to college, and his grief for the lost healthy self. After six months in treatment, Adam better understood bipolar disorder, IPSRT, and the importance of continued treatment. Thus, by the time of the maintenance phase, Adam was taking a more proactive role in guiding individual sessions. He continued to complete the SRM regularly, finding this useful not only to monitor his social and sleep routines, but also to maintain good sleep and social rhythm regularity. He continued to bring SRMs to session and reviewed which events and situations challenged his routines, sleep/wake schedule, and level of stimulation. His biggest challenge remained his desire to stay out late with friends Thursday through Saturday evenings, which, understandably, he did on various occasions. When he did, however, he was mindful of his mood, energy, and sleep needs. To the best of our knowledge, he continued to abstain from drugs and alcohol, despite peer and societal pressure to indulge. We periodically checked with Adam about this, reminding him of the dangers of mixing alcohol and lithium, as well as the negative effects that alcohol and drug abuse/dependence can have on the course of bipolar disorder.

An important aspect in addressing his "grief for the loss of the healthy self" was his meeting with the school officials and professors who had observed his first-semester manic episode. We spent at least two full sessions helping Adam prepare for these conversations, rehearsing what he was going to say and role-playing different scenarios. Adam agreed that simple honesty would be best about his situation and his struggles with bipolar disorder. To Adam's surprise, the officials were understanding and expressed interest in ensuring that he had the needed support to continue his education.

During the maintenance phase we worked to establish a "rescue" protocol to minimize risk for future relapse. Such protocols can involve various interventions. One that we found helpful with Adam was the availability of low-dose sedating antipsychotic medication to induce sleep when he had difficulty falling sleep for more than one or two nights. Consistent with circadian instability and its role in the onset of new bipolar episodes, we believe that one or two nights of missed sleep can trigger mania.

Another goal during maintenance was medication management and adherence. Unlike patients with recurrent unipolar depression, who frequently may achieve long periods of stable mood maintaining the same dose of medication, many patients with bipolar I disorder require frequent adjustment of doses either upward or downward, as well as occasional to frequent changes in their entire medication regimen. Adam's IPSRT therapist saw him more frequently than his pharmacotherapist (who saw him monthly), and thus played an important role in promoting medication adherence and communicating to his pharmacotherapist information relevant to medication management.

A key to successful treatment of patients with bipolar disorder is the review and management of all common medication side effects (including weight gain and sexual dysfunction). We did our best to check with Adam at each treatment visit about side effects and tried to provide help in managing them. The role of the IPSRT therapist, a psychologist, was to provide psychological support to help Adam manage side effects. We also worked on interpersonal effectiveness strategies to help Adam communicate his side effects to his psychiatrist. We made it clear to Adam that he should report any physical or medical side effects to his psychiatrist or a physician so they could consider adjusting his medication. In our experience, directly addressing side effects improves the chance that a patient will adhere to the treatment regimen. During treatment, Adam experienced polyuria (excess production of urine), a common side effect of lithium. Working with his psychiatrist, we helped Adam develop behavioral strategies to reduce the amount of urine in the bladder and to minimize exposure to the cold, which can exacerbate polyuria.

Final Phase of Treatment

We feel ambivalent about concluding treatment with patients who suffer from what is almost always a lifelong condition. Having been schooled in the short-term psychotherapies, we understand the value of focused, goal-oriented treatment directed to the patient's present problems that does not foster dependency. On the other hand, taking a chronic disease management perspective in treating bipolar disorder, we argue that in most, if not all bipolar cases, true termination should not take place.[1] We took this latter perspective with Adam. Adam was very young when he entered treatment, and we felt that he could benefit from continued support and monitoring. Because Adam had decided to remain in school, he would face the stressors and triggers that had precipitated his first manic episode throughout his college career. We felt that continued therapy would help him better navigate these stressors, and Adam agreed. However, we did gradually taper to monthly to six-week check-up sessions that focused on IPSRT techniques and medication adherence, and he continued to see his pharmacologist monthly as well.

It has been six years since Adam entered IPSRT. His integrity and commitment in engaging in treatment has been inspiring. Adam graduated from college and, this past year, returned to Wisconsin to be closer to family. He has found a gratifying, stable, well-paying position teaching music at a local college, where he greatly enjoys his students and has time and support to continue his composing. It was not bipolar disorder that precluded Adam from pursuing his dream of being a performing musician. Many factors contributed to this decision, including the desire for stability, and recognition of how difficult it is to make a living as a performing artist. Thus, we would not discourage individuals with bipolar disorder from pursuing such dreams

---

1. We are not arguing that an individual with bipolar disorder should necessarily continue IPSRT indefinitely. We are saying that given the chronicity of bipolar disorder, it is important for individuals with bipolar disorder to have ongoing contact with mental health professionals and medication management.

and aspirations. Many famous artists and composers throughout history have had well-documented struggles with bipolar disorder yet had brilliant careers. We suggest, however, that in pursuing their aspirations, individuals with bipolar disorder strive for social, circadian, and emotional stability, and carefully consider how challenging those goals are in the life of a performing artist.

We would like to report that Adam's path has been smooth sailing since first entering IPSRT, but that would be atypical of bipolar illness. Adam had two further hospitalizations for mania and one for depression over the past six years. One manic episode required Adam to leave college for a semester and return to Wisconsin for a few months. These episodes challenged Adam's core identity, his faith in himself, and his ability to manage his illness, but he did not give up. He has also enjoyed protracted periods of euthymia and stability and is currently in a two-year relationship with someone who admires and respects his creative talents and gifts. Adam continues to face his illness with dignity, self-respect, and a delightfully ironic sense of humor. He recognizes that having bipolar disorder requires a lot of work to maintain stability. But as Adam puts it, "I am willing to take on the fight and I'm in it for the long haul."

Other Psychiatric Disorders

8

Interpersonal Psychotherapy for Eating Disorders

DENISE E. WILFLEY, JULIETTE M. IACOVINO, AND DOROTHY J. VAN BUREN

Eating disorders are serious illnesses associated with significant morbidity and mortality, including medical complications related to malnutrition (e.g., osteoporosis, cardiac arrest) and obesity (e.g., type 2 diabetes, high blood pressure), psychiatric comorbidity, reduced quality of life, low self-esteem, and impaired social functioning (Rieger, Wilfley, Stein, et al., 2005). Anorexia nervosa (AN), bulimia nervosa (BN), and binge eating disorder (BED) affect approximately 0.9%, 1.5%, and 3.5% of U.S. women and 0.3%, 0.5%, and 2.0% of U.S. men, respectively (Hudson, Hiripi, Pope Jr., & Kessler, 2007; Wilfley, Stein, & Welch, 2003) (see Table 8.1 for DSM-IV criteria.) AN has the highest mortality rate of any mental disorder (5%), which results from both suicide and complications related to semi-starvation (Steinhausen, 2002).

Despite the harmful effects of eating disorders, these illnesses are often undertreated (Hudson et al., 2007). Nonetheless, prognosis with treatment is good, particularly when initiated during the early stages of illness. The dissemination of effective and acceptable treatments for eating disorders is thus fundamental to improving the quality of life of hundreds of millions of individuals globally.

Empirically supported therapies for eating disorders characterized by recurrent binge eating are cognitive-behavioral therapy (CBT) and IPT. CBT focuses on changing disordered eating cognitions and behaviors, while IPT seeks to alter maladaptive interpersonal patterns that are associated with eating disorder symptoms. While both therapies possess strong empirical bases, evidence suggests that IPT may show some advantages over CBT, as an interpersonal focus may be more acceptable to a broader range of individuals, and may be more effective for individuals with certain

Table 8.1. DIAGNOSTIC CRITERIA FOR EATING DISORDERS

Bulimia Nervosa	Binge Eating Eisorder (DSM-IV-TR research criteria)	Binge Eating Disorder (Proposed DSM-V criteria)	Anorexia Nervosa
A. Recurrent episodes of binge eating. An episode of binge eating is characterized by both of the following: 1. eating, in a discrete period of time (e.g., within any 2-hour period), an amount of food that is definitely larger than most people would eat during a similar period of time and under similar circumstances 2. a sense of lack of control over eating during the episode (e.g., a feeling that one cannot stop eating or control what or how much one is eating) B. Recurrent inappropriate compensatory behavior in order to prevent weight gain, such as self-induced vomiting; misuse of laxatives, diuretics, enemas, or other medications; fasting; or excessive exercise. C. The binge eating and inappropriate compensatory behaviors both occur, on average, at least twice a week for 3 months.	A. Recurrent episodes of binge eating (see **Bulimia nervosa**) B. The binge-eating episodes are associated with three (or more) of the following: 1. eating much more rapidly than normal 2. eating until feeling uncomfortably full 3. eating large amounts of food when not feeling physically hungry 4. eating alone because of being embarrassed by how much one is eating 5. feeling disgusted with oneself, depressed, or very guilty after overeating C. Marked distress regarding binge eating is present. D. The binge eating occurs, on average, at least two days a week for six months. E. The binge eating is not associated with the recurrent use of inappropriate compensatory behavior (i.e., purging) and does not occur exclusively during the course of bulimia nervosa or anorexia nervosa.	A. Recurrent episodes of binge eating (see **Bulimia nervosa**) B. The binge-eating episodes are associated with three (or more) of the following: 1. eating much more rapidly than normal 2. eating until feeling uncomfortably full 3. eating large amounts of food when not feeling physically hungry 4. eating alone because of being embarrassed by how much one is eating 5. feeling disgusted with oneself, depressed, or very guilty after overeating C. Marked distress regarding binge eating is present. D. The binge eating occurs, on average, at least once a week for three months. E. The binge eating is not associated with the recurrent use of inappropriate compensatory behavior (i.e., purging) and does not occur exclusively during the course of bulimia nervosa or anorexia nervosa. **Rationale** Binge Eating Disorder is one of the disorders in the DSM-IV appendix. It is recommended that it be formally included as a disorder in DSM-5. The rationale for recommending inclusion of binge eating disorder (BED) in DSM-5 is based on a comprehensive literature review (**Wonderlich, Gordon, Mitchell, Crosby, & Engel, 2009**). Below we address several key recommendations offered by Kendler et al. as they apply to BED.	A. Refusal to maintain body weight at or above a minimally normal weight for age and height (e.g., weight loss leading to maintenance of body weight less than 85% of that expected; or failure to make expected weight gain during period of growth, leading to body weight less than 85% of that expected). B. Intense fear of gaining weight or becoming fat, even though underweight. C. Disturbance in the way in which one's body weight or shape is experienced, undue influence of body weight or shape on self-evaluation, or denial of the seriousness of the current low body weight. D. In postmenarcheal females, amenorrhea, i.e., the absence of at least three consecutive menstrual cycles. (A woman is considered to have amenorrhea if her periods occur only following hormone, e.g., estrogen, administration.)

D. Self-evaluation is unduly influenced by body shape and weight.
E. The disturbance does not occur exclusively during episodes of Anorexia Nervosa.

Specify type:

Purging Type: during the current episode of Bulimia Nervosa, the person has regularly engaged in self-induced vomiting or the misuse of laxatives, diuretics, or enemas

Nonpurging Type: during the current episode of Bulimia Nervosa, the person has used other inappropriate compensatory behaviors, such as fasting or excessive exercise, but has not regularly engaged in self-induced vomiting or the misuse of laxatives, diuretics, or enemas

Consistent with Kendler et al's recommendation for making decisions about diagnoses in the Appendix, the Eating Disorders Work Group addressed the question, "Should the BED diagnosis should be a) deleted from the appendix, b) promoted to the main manual, or c) retained in the appendix. Synopsis of the Review of Validators.

The following comments are organized according to the structure of the table of validators provided by Kendler et al. (2009) and based on a literature review (Wonderlich et al., 2009). BED has been compared to both other eating disorders (i.e., anorexia nervosa, bulimia nervosa) and obesity in validational studies. Overall, BED distinguishes itself from other eating disorders and obesity across a wide range of validators, including high priority validators.

In terms of **antecedent validators,** there is evidence from family history studies that BED tends to run in families and is not a simple familial variation of obesity.

Furthermore, in comparison to other eating disorders, BED shows a relatively distinct demographic profile with a greater likelihood of male cases, older age, and a later age of onset.

Regarding studies of **concurrent validators,** BED is also differentiated from obesity in terms of greater concerns about shape and weight, more personality disturbance, and a higher likelihood of psychiatric comorbidity in the form of mood disorders and anxiety disorders. Also, BED is associated with lower quality of life than obesity.

Finally, in terms of **predictive validators,** BED may be differentiated from other eating disorders in terms of its lower level of diagnostic stability and greater likelihood of remission. In clinical course, BED also shows a greater likelihood of medical morbidities (e.g., self-reported weight gain and metabolic syndrome indicators) than is typically seen in other eating disorders, or in obesity. Finally, in studies of treatment response, there is evidence that individuals with BED have a more positive response to specialty treatments than to generic behavioral weight loss treatments in terms of reduction of eating disorder psychopathology.

Specify type:

Restricting Type: during the current episode of Anorexia Nervosa, the person has not regularly engaged in binge eating or purging behavior (i.e., self-induced vomiting or the misuse of laxatives, diuretics, or enemas)

Binge-Eating/Purging Type: during the current episode of Anorexia Nervosa, the person has regularly engaged in binge eating or purging behavior (i.e., self-induced vomiting or the misuse of laxatives, diuretics, or enemas)

Table 8.1. (CONTINUED)

Bulimia Nervosa	Binge Eating Eisorder (DSM-IV-TR research criteria)	Binge Eating Disorder (Proposed DSM-V criteria)	Anorexia Nervosa
		These findings suggest some evidence of clinical utility of the BED diagnosis in terms of treatment selection; for example, antidepressant medication is useful in the treatment of BED, but is not generally useful in the treatment of obesity. **Level of change:** Major. **References:** Literature review **(Wonderlich et al., 2009)**. **Criterion D:** In the DSM-IV appendix, it was suggested that the frequency of binge-days, as opposed to binge episodes, be assessed, and a minimum average frequency of twice/week over 6 months be required. A literature review indicated that criteria identical to those for Bulimia Nervosa would not change caseness significantly. Therefore, Criterion D for BED is recommended to be similar to criterion C for Bulimia Nervosa. Level of change: Clarification /Modest/substantial. References: Literature review (Wilson & Sysko, 2009). **Literature Cited:** **Wilson GT, Sysko R: Frequency of binge eating episodes in bulimia nervosa and binge eating disorder: Diagnostic considerations. Int J Eat Disord 42:603-610, 2009.** **Wonderlich SA, Gordon KH, Mitchell JE, et al.: The validity and clinical utility of binge eating disorder. Int J Eat Disord 42:687-705, 2009.** **Severity Criteria** Frequency of binge eating (episodes per week). This disorder is currently listed in Appendix B of DSM-IV: "Criteria Sets and Axes for Further Study." The work group is proposing that this disorder be moved from the Appendix to a free-standing diagnosis in DSM-5.	

comorbidities (e.g., depression, low self-esteem) (Chui, Safer, Bryson, et al., 2007; Tanofsky-Kraff & Wilfley, 2010; Wilson, Wilfley, Agras, & Bryson, 2010). Furthermore, data suggest that interpersonal problems play a large role in the development and maintenance of eating disorders (Jacobs, Welch, & Wilfley, 2004; Pike et al., 2006, 2008; Rieger et al., 2010; Steiger, Gauvin, Jabalpurwala, et al., 1999; Stice, 2002; Stroud, Tanofsky-Kraff, Wilfley, & Salovey, 2000; Tanofsky-Kraff & Wilfley, 2010; Tanofsky-Kraff et al., 2007; Wilfley et al., 2003; Zaitsoff, Fehon, & Grilo, 2009). Thus, IPT shows promise as an efficacious, theory-based, empirically supported treatment for eating disorders that can be widely disseminated.

This chapter provides an overview of the theoretical and empirical bases of IPT for the treatment of eating disorders. Through the presentation of an in-depth case study of the treatment of an individual with BED, the reader is introduced to the use of IPT in the treatment of eating disorders in clinical practice.

EMPIRICAL EVIDENCE FOR THE EFFICACY OF IPT FOR EATING DISORDERS

IPT is the only treatment for BN and BED that has consistently shown comparable long-term outcomes to CBT (Agras, Walsh, Fairburn, et al., 2000; Wilfley et al., 1993, 2002; Wilson et al., 2010). In a multisite randomized controlled trial of IPT for BN, Agras et al. (2000) found that while IPT yielded lower remission rates than CBT immediately after treatment, by eight and twelve months of follow-up they demonstrated equivalent outcomes. Although it has been recommended that clinicians inform their patients of the slower pace of improvements in IPT (Agras et al., 2000; Tanofsky-Kraff & Wilfley, 2010; Wilson & Shafran, 2005), research versions of IPT (Agras et al., 2000; Fairburn, 1993, 1995) tend to de-emphasize the links between interpersonal problems and eating disorder symptoms. For example, Fairburn et al.'s version of IPT did not address eating disorder symptoms following assessment of the eating disorder, and excluded the use of role-playing or problem-solving, major aspects of IPT for depression, in order to distinguish IPT from CBT. Focusing on these connections and using the full range of therapeutic techniques consistent with IPT (e.g., role-playing; Stuart, 2006) throughout the course of treatment, rather than limiting their use, increases the effectiveness of IPT (Arcelus et al., 2009; Tanofsky-Kraff & Wilfley, 2010).

Two studies by Wilfley et al. (1993, 2002) compared group formats of IPT and CBT for the treatment of BED and found them equivalent in reducing binge eating, eating pathology, and general psychopathology in both the short and long term. Reductions in binge eating and eating disorder pathology were largely maintained in these participants over five years (Bishop, Stein, Hilbert, et al., 2007). Furthermore, a recent study (Wilson et al., 2010) found that individual IPT and CBT-guided self-help were associated with significantly better outcomes than behavioral weight loss.

IPT for the prevention of excessive weight gain (IPT-WG) focuses on reducing loss-of-control eating in adolescent girls, a potential risk factor for eating disorders (Tanofsky-Kraff, Wilfley, et al., 2009; Tanofsky-Kraff, Yanovski, et al., 2009). IPT-WG demonstrated greater efficacy than a standard-of-care health education condition in a recent pilot study (Tanofsky-Kraff, Wilfley, et al., 2009). See Chapter 20 for more information on IPT-WG.

For BN and BED, IPT demonstrates a number of advantages relative to CBT, such that patients rate it as more acceptable and report greater expectations of success in IPT (Agras et al., 2000; Chui et al., 2007; Wilson et al., 2010), which is associated with more positive treatment outcomes (Constantino, Arnow, Blasey, & Agras, 2005). Additionally, IPT may be more effective for racial/ethnic minority patients such as African-Americans, as studies have found African-American participants are less likely to drop out of IPT (Wilson et al., 2010) and experience greater reductions in binge eating when randomized to IPT (Chui et al., 2007). Finally, IPT has been found to have greater efficacy for patients with more severe eating pathology and lower self-esteem (Wilson et al., 2010), and thus may be preferable as a first-line treatment for such individuals.

RATIONALE FOR IPT'S EFFECTIVENESS IN THE TREATMENT OF EATING DISORDERS

The application of IPT to the treatment of eating disorders is tied to a strong body of evidence linking the development and maintenance of eating disorders to interpersonal problems. Eating-disordered individuals report social difficulties and interpersonal problems such as loneliness, social isolation, low perceived social support, interpersonal sensitivity, poor social adjustment, and chronically unfulfilling relationships (Hamann, Wonderlich-Tierney, & Vander Wal, 2009; Jacobs et al., 2004; Tanofsky-Kraff & Wilfley, 2010; Wilfley et al., 2003).

Difficulties with peer and family relationships are hypothesized to play a role in eating disorders. Interpersonal problems in peer relationships are associated with disordered eating pathology, even independent of the influence of depression and low self-esteem (Zaitsoff et al., 2009). Family teasing related to weight, shape, and eating, low parental contact, parental pressure, and problems with affective expression and communication have been identified as prospective predictors of eating disorders (Tanofsky-Kraff & Wilfley, 2010). Furthermore, family discord and changes in family structure have been found to differentiate eating-disordered individuals from healthy and psychiatric controls (Pike et al., 2006, 2008).

In addition to social problems, the literature also supports a role for self-disturbances such as low self-esteem, poor emotional regulation, and negative affect in the etiology of eating disorders (Polivy & Herman, 2002; Stice, 2002). The combination of interpersonal difficulties and disturbances in self-concept may create an environment in which disordered eating develops as a method for coping with social stressors, serving to reduce negative affect and negative self-evaluation in response to unfulfilling social interactions (Rieger et al., 2010). Disordered eating may in turn exacerbate interpersonal problems by increasing social isolation and a lack of fulfilling relationships, creating a feedback loop that maintains the eating disorder (Rieger et al., 2010).

Supporting such a feedback mechanism are experience-sampling studies of women who binge eat in which negative social interaction, self-criticism, and negative affect tend to precede a binge and to increase following it (Engelberg, Steiger, Gauvin, & Wonderlich, 2007; Steiger et al., 1999; Wegner et al., 2002). IPT for eating disorders seeks to break this cycle by supporting the development of healthy interpersonal skills that can replace symptoms in the promotion of a positive self-image (Fig. 8.1).

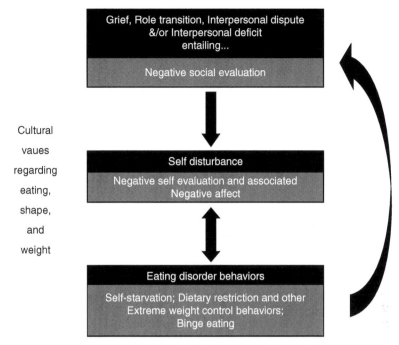

Cultural
vaues
regarding
eating,
shape,
and
weight

Figure 8.1 IPT-ED: a maintenance model of interpersonal factors for eating disorders (Rieger et al., 2010)

ADAPTATION OF IPT FOR EATING DISORDERS

The implementation of IPT for eating disorders differs from traditional IPT for depression in several ways. First, IPT for eating disorders links interpersonal problems to eating disorder symptoms and changes in body weight, rather than depressive symptoms. The trajectory of therapy depends on the specific type of eating disorder being treated, and thus may differ for an individual suffering from BN versus BED. Second, depressed individuals with the IPT focus of interpersonal deficits have traditionally been conceptualized as having few to no social ties. In eating disorders, however, it is more common to identify interpersonal deficits for patients who experience *poor-quality* social ties, or chronically unfulfilling relationships (Tanofsky-Kraff & Wilfley, 2010; Wilfley et al., 2003). Thus, a clinician working with a patient with eating disorders with interpersonal deficits will often focus on helping the patient develop more satisfying relationships, rather than initiating new ones.

IPT for depression was originally formulated to treat a discrete depressive episode and thus focused on life events that contributed to its onset (Markowitz, 2003). IPT for eating disorders (IPT-ED) conceptualizes symptoms as recurring and chronic and thus centers on interpersonal factors that maintain, as well as trigger, eating disorder symptoms. Finally, IPT-ED uses a timeline to chart interpersonal events, eating disorder symptoms, and weight change over time to enhance the interpersonal inventory. This provides the clinician the opportunity to concretely depict the connections between the patient's interpersonal ups and downs and the waxing and waning of eating disorder symptoms.

STRUCTURE OF IPT

Like IPT for other disorders, IPT-ED consists of three phases: initial, intermediate, and termination. Typically, IPT-ED spans fifteen to twenty treatment sessions over four to five months. The IPT-ED clinician addresses maladaptive patterns in *current* interpersonal relationships, which are linked consistently throughout treatment to eating disorder symptoms. As IPT-ED is a time-limited treatment, success depends on the clinician's ability to quickly identify problematic interpersonal patterns, to link them to eating disorder symptoms, and to facilitate the client's awareness of these connections while conducting the interpersonal inventory. Thus, patient and clinician must identify the problem area(s) and treatment goals as early as possible.

Initial Phase

The initial phase of IPT-ED typically lasts one to five sessions and includes diagnosis of the eating disorder, the identification of interpersonal problem areas, and the delineation of treatment goals. The patient's current and past eating disorder symptoms are assessed by a standard diagnostic instrument, a formal eating disorder diagnosis is made, and the patient is assigned the "sick role." The sick role identifies the patient as needing help, and excuses him or her from those responsibilities that cannot be managed because of his or her symptoms, particularly the excessive caretaking that is often characteristic of individuals with eating disorders. By assigning the sick role, the patient is given permission to focus fully on the process of recovery.

Next, the clinician and patient discuss treatment expectations. The clinician assures the patient that he or she has been diagnosed with a known disorder with effective treatment options and a good prognosis. The clinician then explains the rationale of IPT, emphasizing that therapy will focus on identifying and altering current dysfunctional interpersonal patterns related to the eating disorder symptoms.

To determine the precise focus of treatment, the clinician conducts an interpersonal inventory with the patient. The inventory provides a framework for clarifying the interpersonal issues that sustain the eating disorder symptoms and that will define the treatment goals. The interpersonal inventory chronicles the patient's important life events, interpersonal relationships, social support, and eating disorder symptoms. The interpersonal inventory is crucial to the development of an effective treatment plan. It enables the clinician to connect stressful interpersonal events to changes in the patient's self-concept as they relate to eating disorder symptoms, to outline problematic interpersonal relationships, and to identify potential sources of social support.

The clinical importance of conducting a comprehensive interpersonal inventory cannot be overemphasized. Accurate identification of the patient's primary problem area(s) is often complicated and is crucial to successful treatment. In original implementations of IPT, up to three sessions have been devoted to completing the interpersonal inventory; however, conducting a longer (approximately two hour) first session to complete the entire interpersonal inventory may increase the effectiveness of IPT-ED. This extended initial visit enables patients to understand the rationale for IPT, and to see connections between their symptoms and their interpersonal functioning more quickly. Often by the end of this first, extended session, the therapist is able to propose a tentative interpersonal formulation.

In the interpersonal formulation, the clinician links the patient's eating disorder to at least one of the four interpersonal problem areas: interpersonal role transitions, interpersonal disputes, grief, and interpersonal deficits. While the clinician and patient may identify multiple interpersonal problem areas, the time-limited nature of IPT-ED requires that therapy focus on the one or two areas most relevant to the patient's eating disorder symptoms. In addition, the clinician and patient should identify specific goals to work on during treatment. These goals should be developed collaboratively by clinician and patient, and should relate directly to the patient's identified problem areas and disordered eating behaviors. It is useful for the clinician to put these goals in writing, much like a treatment contract. The goals developed at this stage will be referenced at each future session and will guide the day-to-day work of the treatment.

Intermediate Phase

The intermediate or middle phase usually consists of eight to ten sessions and is considered the "work" of treatment. During this phase, the clinician's major role is to focus on how the patient is working on goals between sessions. Phrases such as "moving forward on your goals" and "making important changes" are used to promote the patient's responsibility for his or her own recovery, and to reinforce that fulfilling goals requires persistence. While the patient may at times initiate discussions that stray from treatment objectives (e.g., details of a binge, discussions about weight and shape concerns), the clinician re-engages patients by sensitively but firmly redirecting discussions to focus on agreed-upon goals. This strategy has been supported by research on IPT maintenance treatment for recurrent depression, which has demonstrated that the clinician's ability to maintain focus on interpersonal themes is associated with better outcomes (Frank, Kupfer, Wagner, et al., 1991) (see Chapter 19).

Throughout the therapeutic process, but particularly during the intermediate phase, IPT focuses on affect evocation and exploration (Wilfley, MacKenzie, Welch, et al., 2000). This is particularly relevant for patients with eating disorders because disordered eating often serves to regulate negative affect. The IPT clinician should assist patients in acknowledging and accepting painful emotions, experiencing suppressed affect, and using affective expression to facilitate healthy interpersonal interactions (Wilfley, et al., 2000; Wilfley, 2008). Furthermore, clinicians should assist patients in expressing their emotions in interpersonal relationships more constructively by helping patients identify, understand, and express their emotions appropriately so that their needs are met (Tanofsky-Kraff & Wilfley, 2010).

Termination Phase

The four- or five-session termination phase is a time for reflection on what has been achieved during treatment, and what is to be accomplished in the future. Prior to the start of termination, the clinician should clearly address it and establish open communication with the patient regarding his or her feelings about ending treatment. Some patients may experience a sense of grief or anxiety, while others may seem unaffected by termination. The clinician's role is to attend to the patient's reactions and to encourage healthy emotional expression.

IPT does not assume that the patient's work toward changing his or her interpersonal patterns ends with treatment. Thus, in addition to reflecting on accomplishments, clinicians and patients should collaboratively develop additional goals for patients to work on following termination. In addition, relapse prevention should be addressed during the termination phase. The therapist should help the patient identify signs of relapse (e.g., negative mood, chaotic eating, dietary restriction) and develop an action plan. Again, clinicians should explicitly connect interpersonal stress and eating disorder symptoms when discussing relapse prevention. The collaborative nature of this phase is crucial for instilling a patient's sense of efficacy and security. Patients must feel that they have the tools necessary for maintaining their recovery. However, clinicians should be cautious to identify warning signs that may indicate a need for the patient to again seek professional help.

CASE EXAMPLE

Initial Phase

Muriel was in her early thirties and the married mother of a school-age child with cerebral palsy when she presented for treatment. She stated that she was experiencing problems with her weight and eating, which she felt had increased over the past four years with her son's entry into the special school system. Muriel reported feeling simultaneously bored and overwhelmed by the number of household tasks that she felt she needed to address while her son was in school, and by the number of appointments related to care for her son's medical condition.

Muriel noted that she first began to have concerns about her shape and weight when her father started making critical comments to her about the weight she had gained during her freshman year in college. While in college, she began to restrict her caloric intake and exercise specifically in an attempt to lose weight. Although she had occasional periods when she overate and felt badly afterwards, her first episode of binge eating occurred when she was on bedrest during her pregnancy. She stated that she was worried about weight gain, lonely, bored, and anxious about the health of her fetus. In addition, she resented that her family did not attempt to take care of her during this difficult time in her life despite the fact that she was "always there for them." However, she never expressed these feelings to her family since "they had so much to deal with themselves."

Muriel's responses on the Eating Disorder Examination, a structured interview designed to assess eating disorder pathology based upon DSM-IV criteria (Fairburn et al., 1993), were consistent with a diagnosis of BED. During assessment, Muriel reported binge eating on average once or twice a day most days of the week. These episodes of binge eating were followed by intense feelings of self-loathing. She was most likely to binge eat at night after her son was in bed, during the day when he was napping or at school, or after a stressful visit with her mother.

Muriel also endorsed significant symptoms of depression on the Beck Depression Inventory (BDI = 30). Muriel reported a positive family history for depression and had been diagnosed and successfully treated for postpartum depression with medication and brief counseling following her son's birth. Though hesitant to resume taking medication, she was open to pursuing psychotherapy for treatment of both her eating and mood problems.

In the first session, Muriel was informed of the "good news/bad news" results of the clinical assessment. The "bad" news was that she did indeed meet diagnostic criteria for BED and for recurrent major depression, and had been trying to deal with these extremely difficult problems by herself for a very long time. The good news was that IPT was a treatment available to her that had demonstrated efficacy in improving symptoms of both her eating disorder and depressed mood. Although initially resistant to receiving this diagnosis (and the assignment of the "sick role"), Muriel was responsive to the rationale for treating these problems within an interpersonal framework. Furthermore, she readily engaged in the process of linking her eating and mood symptoms to relationships and significant life events throughout the course of conducting the interpersonal inventory.

Interpersonal Inventory

In addition to her husband, Peter, and her child, Gabe, Muriel's significant relationships included her divorced parents, her younger sister Rachel, and an extended family of aunts, uncles, and cousins. She reported no close friendships outside of her family, although she and her husband regularly attended a Baptist church. Muriel noted that her family moved a great deal while she was growing up due to her father's work, leaving her with no long-term friendships. Also, Muriel felt that the demands of her extended family and of her special-needs child left her with little time to pursue friendships outside of the family.

When asked to describe the quality of each of her significant relationships, Muriel responded that following her parent's divorce, she felt that she became her mother's caregiver, a role her father had fulfilled prior to the divorce. Following the divorce, Muriel's mother became severely depressed and depended upon Muriel for emotional as well as functional support. Muriel resented that her younger sister, Rachel, did not share this responsibility with her, but she also felt guilty for having these feelings given Rachel's history of mental illness.

Rachel was diagnosed with schizophrenia when Muriel was a sophomore in college. Muriel quit college to be close to her family and to provide emotional support to her mother following Rachel's diagnosis. Once Rachel's condition stabilized, Muriel hoped that family members would turn some attention to Muriel's needs, or at least, now that she had her own child to care for, take over some of the caretaking roles in the family that Muriel had assumed since leaving college and since her parents' divorce. Muriel expected family members to spontaneously offer to help her, as she often stepped in to help them without being asked. She believed that they did not provide her with support or help because they either did not care or because they were too overwhelmed with their own problems to help her.

Muriel's relationship with her father was strained. While she was angry with her father for hurting her mother and putting Muriel in a caretaker role, she also felt sorry for him since the woman with whom he had had an affair left him following his diagnosis with cancer. Muriel's father had a child from his relationship with this woman, for whom he often asked Muriel to babysit. Muriel felt that her father expected her to be a "big sister" to this child, but she resented this expectation given the child's parentage and the circumstances of his birth. Muriel felt that she could not speak up to her father for fear of angering him (he had been verbally abusive when she was growing up and she feared his anger), and because of her religious training to "honor" her mother and her father.

In her own marriage, Muriel reported that since her son, Gabe, had started school, she and her husband Peter had begun arguing. Muriel felt that Peter should be doing more to understand Gabe's needs and to be more of a father to him: take him on out- ings, express an interest in his school curriculum, and take him to some of his phys- ical therapy appointments. However, Peter thought that Muriel should be their son's primary caregiver as she did not work outside the home. Muriel also resented Peter's pursuit of interests outside of the home. However, since these activities were work- or church-related, she felt she could not ask him to stop or limit these so that she could pursue her own interests. Anything that Muriel wanted to do outside of taking care of her son or extended family members seemed to her to be indulgent in com- parison to Peter's pursuit of "legitimate" goals such as providing for their family and providing leadership within their church.

Muriel described difficulty expressing anger appropriately within her signifi- cant relationships. She would often withdraw from others and binge eat, letting resentments or hurts build up until she became enraged, shouting and saying hurtful things. These periods of uncontrolled rage frightened her and caused others to be confused by or dismissive of her anger, saying things such as, "You're just crazy, that's what you are." These outbursts and the negative effects they had on her self-esteem and on her relationships caused her to try to hold her anger in even more tightly, resulting in an unfulfilling cycle of pent-up resentment and angry outbursts.

Interpersonal Problem Formulation

To highlight the connection between certain life experiences, the quality of interper- sonal relationships at those times, and eating disorder symptoms, the therapist asked Muriel to recount both her earliest and most recent episodes of binge eating. As noted above, the first episode of binge eating that Muriel could recall occurred when she was on bedrest during her pregnancy and her family did not respond with the type of caretaking that she thought they should given her medical condition; and most recently after she had spent the day taking her mother (who had never learned to drive) to her doctor's appointment, picking up her mother's prescription medica- tions, and doing her mother's laundry while Gabe was in school. Muriel described how she went back home following this time with her mother and binged while wait- ing for the school bus to arrive. When asked to describe the emotions she was having prior to this most recent binge, Muriel noted that she felt overwhelmed by her role as her mother's caretaker and she resented that other family members did not see that she had more than enough to take care of herself and did not offer to pitch in and help out with Muriel's mother.

The therapist then began to fill in other events from Muriel's life, linking each increase in eating disorder symptoms with changes in mood and major disruptions in the roles she assumed or were expected to assume in her interpersonal relationships (see Table 8.2 for a chronological history of significant life events, mood fluctuations, relationships, and problems with eating and weight).

Table 8.2. Life Chart Chronological History

Age	Eating Behavior, Weight Status, Other Psychiatric Problems	Relationships, Events, Circumstances	Mood/Emotions
3		Sister born and family moves every two to three years for father's job	
15	Normal weight and eating	Father transferred from job on East Coast to Midwest	Sad about the move but glad that new job meant end to father's frequent job transfers and family moves
17		Graduated from high school	Looking forward to college
18	Began to overeat and gained weight first semester in college	Father teased and criticized her for weight gain	Frustrated, ashamed of weight gain
19	Began to "over" exercise and lost some weight although still overeating on a weekly basis	Met future husband; made cheerleading squad	"In love" for first time; enjoying cheerleading and starting to make friends
20		Younger sister's psychotic break; hospitalized for suicide attempt; diagnosed with schizophrenia; family resources diverted to sister's treatment; quit school to be with family	Sad, scared, wanted to help family, sad to leave school
21	Stopped exercising; still overeating; weight starts to creep up	Married and moved across town from family	Stressed about sister's continued illness; traveling back and forth from job to parents' home to own home
22	Began binge eating once or twice a week	Difficult pregnancy; bedrest for last month Long days at home alone while husband at work	Sad that family wouldn't come visit or help out—not allowed to be the "needy" one in family
23	Decreased appetite; not sleeping; treated for postpartum depression	Son born with cerebral palsy; parents divorce in wake of father's disclosure of long-term affair with woman from church; mother sinks into depression	Depressed; suicidal; leaned on faith and antidepressants
24	Weight gain; binge eating returns a couple times per week	Father diagnosed with cancer; girlfriend leaves him; mother refuses to reconcile	Feels sorry for father; impatient with mother's bitterness; takes on caretaking for father and son

Table 8.2. (CONTINUED)

Age	Eating Behavior, Weight Status, Other Psychiatric Problems	Relationships, Events, Circumstances	Mood/Emotions
28	Weight gain begins to escalate; binge eating increases to one or two times per day	Husband begins to distance from her and child; leaves all decisions regarding medical therapy and special needs education to her; sister's condition stabilizes on new medication—gets own apartment near their mother	Misses time and support from husband; expects sister to help with father and mother as her condition improves; sees sister as "selfish" when she doesn't "step up" to help their parents
30	Binge eating at night after son was in bed following visit to mother's to take her to drugstore	Husband working long hours and volunteering at church and spends no time alone with son; mother depressed; father receiving cancer treatment; sister trying to rely on mother and father but neither are capable of providing the support she needs	Angry with husband regarding abdication of parental role with son; resents mother's lingering depression following divorce of parents; angry at father for his sudden dependence upon family following his abandonment of them with the divorce; angry that sister cannot put her own needs aside and help take care of mother and father; guilty for being angry at family members who she sees as vulnerable due to their various mental and physical illnesses; bored with role of homemaker; overwhelmed by the medical and social needs of son; lonely because no friends

By the end of Session 1, the therapist and Muriel agreed that there was a strong interpersonal link between her binge eating and mood disturbances. The therapist proposed the following problem formulation (interpersonal disputes) for Muriel to consider: (1) Muriel's mother and husband Peter expected Muriel to be the primary caretaker in their relationships, which made her feel overwhelmed and resentful, particularly when the caretaking was unreciprocated; and (2) she had difficulty appropriately recognizing and expressing emotions, especially anger, in intimate relationships, making it difficult for her to resolve disputes with significant others. Muriel agreed that these problems in interpersonal functioning were contributing to her current disturbed eating patterns and depressed mood and that these would be appropriate areas upon which to focus treatment. The therapist agreed to put this formulation and goals for treatment in writing (Fig. 8.2) for their review and discussion at the next session.

Excerpts from transcripts of this second session illustrate the presentation of the treatment goals to Muriel in a collaborative manner. The therapist works to elicit Muriel's agreement with the salience of the proposed problem area, and her commitment to working on the treatment goals for the remainder of the sessions. Although presenting problem areas and therapy goals in a collaborative manner is a hallmark

Problem Area #1 (Interpersonal Disputes):
During our meetings you have described how you binge eat when you and your husband or other family members disagree regarding how best to deal with a situation and/or when you do not feel quite up to the task being asked of you, or when you feel forced or obligated to deal with a situation that you do not want to deal with. You are likely to binge eat when you feel uncomfortable with the conflict or the anticipation of the conflict that might result if you choose not to deal with a situation in the way you think is expected of you.

Also, during our meetings you have described how you are the emotionally "sensitive" member of your family. This sensitivity has been a great gift in that it causes you to be an empathic and caring family member and friend. However, it often causes you to feel responsible for carrying the emotional "burdens" of family. Since you may be the first to recognize distress or conflict in a relationship you may feel the need to intervene or diffuse the situation, even if it means putting your own needs and feelings on the back burner in a particular situation. This pattern of tuning into others rather than into yourself can cause you to become disconnected from what is going on for you emotionally. You may find yourself feeling drained or inadequate or lashing out in anger without warning. These feelings can cause you to want to withdraw from others just when you could use social support the most. Over time you have learned to rely on binge eating rather than on other people in an attempt to soothe or satisfy your longings and emotional ups and downs.

Goal #1:
When you start to binge-eat, pause to think about your own emotions or hunger level and think about the situation you are trying to adjust to or deal with. Remind yourself that binge eating may provide some respite from problems or feelings of inadequacy or conflict in the short run, but in the long run it diverts energy from acknowledging the difficult situations confronting you and from taking actions or making plans to change the situation. As you return your attention to the situation at hand you will be able to acknowledge your own wants and needs during these challenging interactions. In this way you will be able to make plans or begin to implement changes that are necessary to manage the situation or dispute and not get sidetracked by the negative feelings that arise from binge eating.

Goal #2:
During our work together you will be able to stop this cycle of binge eating by stepping back and noticing when you are feeling lonely, angry, frustrated, bored, or sad for yourself versus having these feelings for others. You will be able to make conscious choices to deal with these feelings and situations in ways other than with food. As you find ways to receive emotional support from others to balance your skill at providing such support you will rely on binge eating less and on your social network more.

Figure 8.2 Problem formulation and treatment goals

of IPT, this stance is particularly important given Muriel's pattern of accepting other people's requests with unspoken resentment:

THERAPIST: As we discussed last time, I've written up a couple of goals—
MURIEL: Okay.
THERAPIST: I think maybe based on what we talked about in our last visit, they seem like they might be in the ballpark. And so I wanted us to look at those together today.
MURIEL: Okay.

THERAPIST: A couple of warnings: sometimes because they're so nicely typed—

MURIEL: Mm-hmm.

THERAPIST: —people feel like they have to go, "Oh, okay," when they see them, but that's not the plan. The reason they're typed is so we can really think through the goals together and make them what you want to work on. So you're going to read them a couple of ways: one is, you're going to read this piece of paper as something we definitely can change . . .

MURIEL: Okay.

THERAPIST: Two is, you're going to read it in terms of, does this really summarize what we've talked about and what we've come to learn about the connection between your binge eating, your emotions, and your relationships, okay?

MURIEL: Okay.

THERAPIST: And three, would you benefit from working on these goals? Okay, so let me give you something to set this on so that if you want to make notes, you can. [Patient and therapist read silently for a minute]

MURIEL: Yep, you hit everything on the—right on the head.

THERAPIST: In what way?

MURIEL: Just like #2—the uh, "lashing out in anger without warning"—

THERAPIST: Mm-hmm.

MURIEL: It's a constant with my husband. I'm so angry with Peter. I'm just constantly— even when I tell myself, "Okay, just—calm and relax and smile" or, you know, try not to take everything he says so personal, it always—to me, it is personal.

THERAPIST: So the more you try to kinda ignore it, the more it bubbles up out into anger?

MURIEL: Yeah, it's like whatever I have to do is inconsequential or not worth a second thought, and, like last week was one of those times when I really could have— I never really ask Peter to watch Gabe . . . this was one of those times when I really could have used his help, because I really wanted to see everybody [at a social event for volunteers at her son's school], to be around people, you know, for the friendship of it, but I didn't want to eat around them so I didn't ask him; but as the night went on, I felt more negative about the situation than I felt positive, and—and I just sat there feeling angry at him, and lonely, and eating anyway [laughs].

THERAPIST: Yeah, so that's a great example of how the second treatment goal emerged, and if we work on this goal, you think that might be helpful? Working on this goal would mean letting Peter know that you were nervous about going but still wanted to go and that you were annoyed that he didn't offer to watch Gabe. Working on this goal would mean reaching out to Peter for help with these kinds of situations. Working on this goal would help you recognize that when you need people most for a social outlet is when you often want to withdraw from them because you are worried about your eating or about something else that might not be quite right. But by working on this goal you would kinda flip that over: instead of withdrawing and binge eating, you might take the risk, ask your husband for help so that you could be with people—because it sounds like you wound up thinking, if you had gone you would have had a nice time. And then that resentment wouldn't build up towards your husband, and then you certainly wouldn't have been lonely and angry and binge eating.

MURIEL: Yeah, he doesn't even know I'm coming to see you, I have to tell him . . .

THERAPIST: I think one of the things in both of these goals is turning more toward checking in with yourself, paying attention to your feelings, and then, when possible, um, turning toward people rather than food for help or for support. So it sounds like when you look at these, the first person who comes to mind is Peter, with whom you would want to practice these goals, right? But it seems like such a negative interaction pattern has gotten going with him that it feels pretty hard to be optimistic about doing that.

MURIEL: Yeah, I'm just thinking, who can I talk to? I could talk to my Mom, but, I don't know; there's just that hesitance there of knowing that it makes her feel bad too, sometimes, that I feel bad. I don't want to be an emotional dump for her. Even though the couple times that I have just broken down and talked to her, she's asked me how come I haven't talked to her before, you know, she always listens. But there's still a part of me that's still mindful that she has a lot of load to carry, and she's barely making it, and I ask myself, "Why are you dumping your crap on her?"

THERAPIST: We definitely need to work on increasing your circle of social support, but it sounds like you certainly could make more use of your Mom and of Peter, so there are two paths to increasing your circle of support: finding ways to more effectively use your husband and mother as social support people, and increasing the circle of people you can turn to for support. Now, working on [interpersonal] disputes in your relationship with Peter is going to be tough, because there are a lot of patterns that have gotten established. But the payoff is real big, because he's your husband and someone you love a whole lot even though you hate how he acts a lot of the time. So, looking at these goals, do you think you want to work on these even if they would be hard?

MURIEL: Yeah, these definitely do hit the nail right on the head.

THERAPIST: Do you think?

MURIEL: Yeah. They really are [imperceptible].

THERAPIST: In what way are you thinking?

MURIEL: Just like I said, the overwhelming parts of my life that I've been feeling all week, both of these just flat-out sum them up.

THERAPIST: So what I'll ask you to do is to, um, read these every day and be working on them, and then when we get together from now on, I'll ask you how your eating has been and how working on these goals has been. And we'll hopefully see things improving for your eating as things improve with these important people. . .

Intermediate Phase

In Session 3, the therapist checked in with Muriel regarding her week and used this opportunity to connect the occurrence of eating disorder symptoms with a troubling interpersonal situation. Once this connection was noted, the therapist worked with Muriel to keep the session focused on examining the interpersonal interaction and her feelings about that, rather than the specifics of the binge episode:

THERAPIST: So, how did your week go in terms of the relationships with Peter or your mother, you know, like we talked about last time?

MURIEL: Yeah, well, not so good. My Mom called, and I was trying to get some things done, you know, while Gabe was at school, like, umm, while I still had some time and, well, she called all crying and stuff. All upset, you know?

THERAPIST: Yeah . . . mm-hmm.

MURIEL: She'd seen my Dad, and, well, umm . . . It's just, I don't know. I wanted to help, you know, but like I wanted to say, "Get over it already," too . . . I just had so much to do and . . .

THERAPIST: Did it create binge eating for you?

MURIEL: I ate like a freakin' pig.

THERAPIST: Oh [laughs].

MURIEL: I even had cookies in my purse when I went to wait for Gabe's bus!

THERAPIST: Wow, wow.

MURIEL: [sighs] So, I think I've gained weight. I have to stop eating these cookies with—I make them with pudding mix. And the pudding mix is what gives you all the extra—my Dad like gained twenty pounds when I showed him how to make it . . .

THERAPIST: Oh. Mm-hmm. So . . . although I wouldn't wish that kind of situation with your mom on you, it sounds like it made a really—well, you really—made the connection between this interaction and all those emotions and the binge eating. And so, that's really—the neat thing about that is that we don't have to wait around and see if interactions with your mother and how you, you know, how you can let her know about what you need or about what you can really provide to her, how these things are going to be really important for us to work on . . .

MURIEL: Yeah, it's really there, that connection.

By the sixth session, Muriel was regularly making connections between her episodes of binge eating and difficulties in her relationships with her family and husband. Although she was reporting fewer binge episodes, she was still experiencing at least one binge each week, and she still found it difficult to shift to a more equitable balance of giving and receiving caretaking in these relationships. While discussing a recent outing with her mother during which her mother had become faint, Muriel began to reveal concerns about her mother's frail health and how these fears often made it difficult to turn to her mother for emotional support. Muriel felt that her mother had enough to worry about without hearing Muriel's concerns. However, Muriel often binge ate after these "one-sided" outings during which all concerns were directed toward her mother. As Muriel explored this pattern with the therapist, she became extremely tearful discussing the months after her son's birth when she was struggling with postpartum depression but did not receive support from her family. As illustrated below, the therapist encouraged the expression of feeling regarding her desire for support and her disappointment at not receiving it:

MURIEL: It horrified me so much that I was at that point of actually contemplating killing my child first, then myself. It was so selfish. [cries] I'm sorry, I've never told anybody.

THERAPIST: I'm glad that you're telling me.

MURIEL: [continues to cry]

THERAPIST: That's a heavy burden to carry all by yourself.

MURIEL: Now people tell me they saw it. And now people tell me they were watching me but, like I told you, my family is all or nothing.

THERAPIST: Yeah, oh my gosh.

MURIEL: And they didn't wanna—they saw me struggling and they saw me trying. I felt so alone. And I felt like I had to smile or try to make things better so that everybody else wouldn't know how hard it was. Peter was already making me feel bad about that. [sighs]

THERAPIST: In what way? How was he making you feel bad?

MURIEL: He made this comment to me one day, he told me that I had six months to get it together. Or things would change and he would leave. And I lost it, I mean I just—going through that depression with the baby and trying to make ends meet in a cramped apartment and baby stuff everywhere and you couldn't really clean because it was shuffling stuff where I was cleaning up, and he had the nerve to stand there and tell me I had six months to get stuff together, when I couldn't do any better. It wasn't even a point of trying, I could barely put one foot in front of each other, and nobody was taking care of me. I couldn't even take care of myself. There's a part of me that's still guilty right now because if I had—I just felt like if I had been a stronger person or if I—if there was some reserve, some place that I could have dug deeper in or I should have been able to see, or I should have been able to notice before that, even though I know that cerebral palsy isn't my fault, there's a part of me that says, "You should have been a better mother, you should have saw it," or I could have prayed harder. [cries]

THERAPIST: Yeah, my gosh, that's a really hard time to think about, you were so depressed and exhausted and trying so hard to make everyone think you had it all together, and instead of help you got watched or threats but no real, you know, help; and you kept thinking if only you could do better it wouldn't be so hard, as if you were the one who was doing something wrong. . .

MURIEL: Yeah [sighs]. That's how I always feel.

THERAPIST: Well, I can see how you would feel that way since, umm, your family seems to take a "wait and see" approach when they see someone struggling, you know, but that doesn't necessarily mean you're wrong if you need help and aren't getting it. Since you're so good at helping out without being asked, I would think that would make you feel kind of bad or make it hard to figure out "why do I need to ask for help and no one else needs to?" You know?

MURIEL: Yeah, like I'm having to beg or something or with my husband, how could he not see me struggling? How could he speak to me that way?

THERAPIST: It sounds like you're still having feelings about that, and, um, well, do you think, if you do have those feelings, how maybe that might make it hard to try to rely on him now, you know, after all that . . . What kind of feelings do you have now as you think back or, um, or what kind of feelings do you remember having then, you know when you "lost it?". . .

In the weeks after the emotionally charged Session 6, Muriel was able to work more directly on both resolving disputes and improving her communication with her husband. With encouragement and coaching, she was able to talk with him about her concerns and to make direct requests for his help with their son's care. As a result, the quality of their marriage improved considerably and her binge-eating episodes decreased.

THERAPIST: So Peter has been trying, at your, uh, request, suggestion, encouragement, um, been trying to spend more time with Gabe?

MURIEL: Trying.

THERAPIST: And you even talked about the church with him, and kind of said, "Look, we've got these people who bring these really ill-behaved kids to church activities, why aren't you bringing our son who has the potential actually to be well-behaved?"

MURIEL: Mm-hmm, yeah. Just we need to pay attention to him! We need to include him! That's my biggest thing [. . .]

THERAPIST: You're talking to Peter now like, "Look, you're the Dad." You're saying "We," like "What kind of family life are we giving Gabe?" You know? Like, "We need to do this as a family." Even though, sometimes, you know, you have to lead by example.

MURIEL: Yeah.

THERAPIST: Because Peter's not nearly as adventurous as you are or feels as competent as you do with Gabe. And it sounds like mistakes just really freak Peter out [. . .]

MURIEL: Yeah.

THERAPIST: So it sounds like you're doing a really nice job of, um, telling Peter what you want, talking to him as if he's already on board or part of the team, and leading by example [. . .] And he's working—I mean, he's a slower, uh, burn, you know—but he's working on it.

MURIEL: Yeah. It's been going pretty, pretty good, 'cause I don't just go into a rage, you know? Now I say, "No, I'm angry with you for doing that . . ." Just, some of the behaviors he does are just flat-out inappropriate or just nerve-wracking [. . .]

THERAPIST: Yeah, exactly, you can still be a team and still get angry [. . .] and that's what it sounds like you're working on: how to communicate being angry and communicate that you want Peter to do something different—

MURIEL: And not turn in on myself and sucking it up and doing the exact opposite and binge eating.

THERAPIST: Yeah, right.

MURIEL: 'Cause I can't do that anymore.

THERAPIST: Right, you can't do everything that you wish other people would do, and you can't browbeat everyone into doing it. So that's really—I think you're doing a nice job of recognizing the dilemma that you find yourself in sometimes based on what your Dad taught you about that. But also realizing that you have all sorts of good people skills to find another way. And I think you're doing that with Peter most times now, saying, "How are we gonna handle this? We've got a problem, our son needs X, Y and Z." Instead of telling Peter what he has to do or just doing it all by yourself and yelling at Peter that you're having to do it all. So that "we-ness" is a big step of breaking out of that martyr or aggressor pattern that people can get into.

MURIEL: Mm-hmm.

Buoyed by her success in improving her relationship with her husband through more direct expression of her needs and concerns, Muriel began to extend this pattern of interacting with other family members. For example, in Session 10, Muriel described a significant change in her pattern of responding to a request from her father to watch his child:

MURIEL: My Dad had called during that, um, nap, and I was half-asleep/half-awake, and he asked me can I watch his son, my little half-brother, who's, um, a couple years younger than Gabe. But, um, I don't know, I always had mixed feelings about that. My Daddy has this attitude like, "Well, we're family," and we're just supposed to pile together and get along like little puppies.

THERAPIST: Oh. Hmm. As if the circumstances don't matter.

MURIEL: Yeah. And to a certain extent, it doesn't because family is family. But don't expect me to act like I grew up with this child. That we grew up in the same household. I'm in my thirties, I have a husband, my own marriage, my own child, our own problems [pause]. It would be different if I was seventeen, still living at home, and this was my mother's child she had later in life.

THERAPIST: Mm-hmm.

MURIEL: But it's not.

THERAPIST: Exactly.

MURIEL: Just even with the babysitting. You know how we've just been talkin' about, about defining those boundaries?

THERAPIST: Mm-hmm.

MURIEL: Not being afraid to say no, or quit sucking it up. And I found myself doin' that [just sucking it up] when he was asking, he said, "Yeah, I need to drop him off around 3 o'clock Sunday."

THERAPIST: Oh. As if you said "yes" already.

MURIEL: Yeah, and um, and I paused—there was a big—I remember a big pause in there after that and you know, I was about to say, just go ahead and say, "Yes." And he said, "and I should be able to leave outta there around ten o'clock." And I remember shooting up saying, "At night?!"

THERAPIST: So three to ten o'clock—

MURIEL: [Simultaneously] Ten o'clock at night!

THERAPIST: With a little guy, when you've got your own bedtime routines and stuff.

MURIEL: Much less! And that pregnant pause there like it was an expectation. And then I had to get off the phone real fast 'cause Gabe needed me and I hadn't said, "Yes," but I hadn't said, "No."

THERAPIST: Mmm.

MURIEL: So I tried to call him back to tell him "no" and he didn't answer so I drove by the new house, and he wasn't there.

THERAPIST: Mmm.

MURIEL: So either he was gone or with one of his little lady friends or whatever, but um, I left a note on the door, a very simple note that you couldn't take or blow out of proportion. It just said, "Daddy, I was half-asleep when you called, and I realize what a long stint of time this is. I can't watch [child] for that long of a period." But um, and I said, "[child] will just have to go back home with his mom," and it said, "I'm sorry."

THERAPIST: Mm-hmm.

MURIEL: Point blank. If he wanted to get mad, you know, it wasn't a negative or nasty tone, but—

THERAPIST: Yeah, you weren't saying, "How dare you!"—

MURIEL: Yeah.

THERAPIST: Yeah, good for you!

MURIEL: So I wrote him the note; he never called. So I called my aunt to tell her what happened and what I told my Dad in the note. When I first told her, she said, "You're feeling guilty, quit worrying." She said, "Quit hanging yourself up."

THERAPIST: Oh, she did? Good!

MURIEL: She said, "Muriel, you gotta put your foot down." And I said, "Yeah, Auntie, I'm getting a little counseling about that [laughs] and some other things."

THERAPIST: Oh, I'm so glad that you talked to her about your worry, you know what I mean, and I'm guessing that helped you not binge over this on—

MURIEL: Saturday. Yeah. I said, "Okay Muriel, you're doing good!"

THERAPIST: Great!

In the latter sessions of the intermediate phase, Muriel also began to explore avenues for developing friendships. She joined a book club and began to more regularly attend the parent volunteer functions at her son's school, and she and her husband joined a Bible study class at their church for couples.

Termination Phase

One useful tool for work on relapse prevention is to conduct a review of goals with patients, as illustrated in Figure 8.3. This review allows the patient to put into his or her own words changes that he or she has made that have led to improvements in interpersonal relationships and eating disorder symptoms; to communicate to the therapist areas of concern that remain and require discussion before treatment ends; and to articulate plans for maintaining and building upon the positive changes made during the course of treatment.

It is often tempting for clients with BED to focus on the need to improve "diet" behaviors at the expense of interpersonal skills, so one important therapist task in these later sessions is return the focus to the interpersonal changes the patient has made that relate to improvements in the binge eating—as illustrated in this excerpt from Session 19:

MURIEL: Plus I realized too that I had slacked up on, uh, making my little salads ahead of time.

THERAPIST: So if you'd had something quick—

MURIEL: Uh-huh, to just go ahead and grab. And, it makes a difference, I'm really, really seeing that.

THERAPIST: So you're saying "no" to old eating habits and you are also saying "no" to unreasonable requests that you don't want to do.

MURIEL: Yeah.

THERAPIST: And how's that been going?

MURIEL: It's been going pretty, pretty good. Um—

THERAPIST: 'Cause it kinda had creeped back up with Gabe being sick, and then you were needing to get back to, you know, setting limits. Did you include some of these ideas for staying on track on your goal reflection sheet?

MURIEL: Yeah.

THERAPIST: And how was that?

Goal #1:

When you start to binge-eat, pause to think about your own emotions or hunger level and think about the situation you are trying to adjust to or deal with. Remind yourself that binge eating may provide some respite from problems or feelings of inadequacy or conflict in the short run but in the long run it diverts energy from acknowledging the difficult situations confronting you and from taking actions or making plans to change the situation. As you return your attention to the situation at hand you will be able to acknowledge your own wants and needs during these challenging interactions. In this way you will be able to make plans or begin to implement changes that are necessary to manage the situation or dispute and not get sidetracked by the negative feelings that arise from binge eating.

---

1) In what ways have you worked on this goal?

Making myself pause and think until it has become a habit. When I can tell and feel the emotions of it, I seem to take some other action. Either telling myself no, telling others no, or by finding something else to do if it feels too out of control.

2) How has work on this goal been connected to decreasing your problems with binge eating?

I can (out loud) say to myself, "You're just frustrated, not hungry," and feel the difference in my body's response. Hunger feels a little painful and a binge trigger makes me feel like I want to run away for something that has scared me.

3) In your social network (e.g. family, friends, work), what changes have you noticed as a result of your work on this problem?

My husband is off my back, my family seems to listen better. I'm getting a lot of compliments on how I look much better. People smile at me more & it is still hard for me to be comfortable with the attention. My attitude is better. Physically feel better, more energy

4) In what ways have you been unable to work on this problem and how can we assist you in making changes in this problem area?

When the binge panic occurs, sometimes I just want to give in and say "to hell with it." I need to get more options and the motivation to use them.

5) What specific plan do you have for continuing work on this problem?

TOPS and the YMCA. Online healthy eating/physical activity support group. Reading more about healthy eating. Use exercise as a stress response.

Figure 8.3 Sample Session 18 review of goals

MURIEL: It was pretty . . . enlightening. I've seen where I've grown.

THERAPIST: Oh, mm-hmm.

MURIEL: There was that panic about everything in the past, um, I don't wanna say it's all a, "hey, easygoin' " type of feeling now, but it just—I don't know, I just feel that it isn't all gloom and doom.

THERAPIST: Mm-hmm.

MURIEL: Uh, I feel—I used to say 100 percent or so better but it really feels 300 percent. I'm really feeling that much better.

THERAPIST: Oh, 300 percent better!

MURIEL: Yes.

THERAPIST: Mm-hmm.

MURIEL: And, um, I'm just really seeing that everything is a moment at a time, a day at a time. Um, I don't have to invent good things to make the day bearable. I think that was kinda like one of my biggest revelations. It felt like I had to constantly try to see some good, and it seemed like all of my energy, even though I was feeling bad, was directed toward not having a "pity party," and trying to find some goodness in things.

THERAPIST: Mm-hmm.

MURIEL: And now, and, um, now things are really going okay.

THERAPIST: Oh wow. Mm-hmm.

MURIEL: Uh, I've got a lead on a job. My cousin, she uh—

THERAPIST: Really?

MURIEL: Yeah. Weird. And you know how part of you is thinking like, "Don't get too excited about it." But at the same time it's like, this might just work out . . .

DISCUSSION

Muriel was seen for twenty sessions over six months. Her self-reported binge days were zero over the last three months of treatment and her BDI score was down to 2 immediately after treatment, indicating no clinically significant symptoms of depression. Although IPT-ED proved an effective intervention for Muriel, alternative or adjunctive treatments were considered. These included: (1) pharmacotherapy, given the severity of her depressive symptoms at presentation and her previous good response to medication; and (2) marital therapy, given the intensity of her marital distress at intake. However, she opposed medication and noted that her husband would be unwilling to engage in couples counseling. Fortunately, Muriel embraced the identified problem area and treatment goals and benefited from this course of therapy, demonstrating what many clinical trials have indicated: that IPT is a viable and effective treatment modality for individuals with eating disorders characterized by recurrent binge eating.

9

Interpersonal Psychotherapy for Posttraumatic Stress Disorder (PTSD)

ELIZABETH P. GRAF AND JOHN C. MARKOWITZ

INTRODUCTION

Originally developed as a treatment for major depression, IPT has been successfully adapted for a variety of psychiatric disorders (Markowitz, 2006; Weissman et al., 2007). Formal empirical research on IPT for anxiety disorders is still in its nascence, but preliminary data and clinical reports support further investigation into the use of IPT for these populations (Bleiberg & Markowitz, 2005; Lipsitz et al., 2006, 2008; Lipsitz, Markowitz, Cherry, et al., 1999). This chapter provides the evidence and theoretical rationale for using IPT to treat PTSD. A detailed case example illustrates technique, and the discussion that follows raises clinical issues central to treating patients with PTSD.

EMPIRICAL RESEARCH SUPPORTING IPT FOR PTSD

PTSD is an anxiety disorder triggered by exposure to a traumatic event. The syndrome is characterized by re-experiencing symptoms, avoidance, emotional numbing, and increased physiologic arousal (APA, 1994; Table 9.1).

Prolonged exposure and cognitive-behavioral therapy are currently the first-line psychotherapies for PTSD (APA, 2004). These treatments emphasize exposure, involving repeated *in vivo* or evoked imaginal reminders of the traumatic event, following the theory that processing the traumatic experience serves as the mechanism of change (Foa & Kozak, 1986; Foa et al., 2000). Based on strong empirical support

Table 9.1. DSM-IV CRITERIA FOR POSTTRAUMATIC STRESS DISORDER

A. The person has been exposed to a traumatic event in which both of the following have been present:

    (1) The person experienced, witnessed, or was confronted with an event or events that involved actual or threatened death, serious injury, or a threat to the physical integrity of self or others.

    (2) The person's response involved intense fear, helplessness or horror. *Note*: In children this may be expressed instead by disorganized or agitated behavior.

B. The traumatic event is persistently reexperienced in one (or more) of the following ways:

    (1) Recurrent and intrusive recollections of the event, including images, thoughts or preoccupations. *Note*: In young children, repetitive play may occur in which themes or aspects of the trauma are expressed.

    (2) Recurrent distressing dreams of the event. *Note*: In children there may be frightening dreams without recognizable content.

    (3) Acting or feeling as if the traumatic event were recurring (includes a sense of reliving the experience, illusions, hallucinations, and dissociative flashback episodes, including those that occur upon awakening or when intoxicated). *Note*: In young children, trauma-specific reenactment may occur.

    (4) Intense psychological distress at exposure to internal or external cues that symbolize or represent an aspect of the traumatic event.

    (5) Physiological reactivity on exposure to internal or external cues that symbolize or resemble an aspect of the traumatic event.

C. Persistent avoidance of stimuli associated with the trauma and numbing of general responsiveness (not present before the trauma), as indicated by three (or more) of the following:

    (1) Efforts to avoid thoughts, feelings, or conversations associated with the trauma

    (2) Efforts to avoid activities, places, or people that arouse recollections of the trauma

    (3) Inability to recall an important aspect of the trauma

    (4) Markedly diminished interest or participation in significant activities

    (5) Feeling of detachment or estrangement from others

    (6) Restricted range of affect (e.g. unable to have loving feelings)

    (7) Sense of foreshortened future (e.g. does not expect to have a career, marriage, children or a normal lifespan)

D. Persistent symptoms of increased arousal (not present before the trauma), as indicated by two or more of the following:

    (1) Difficulty falling or staying asleep

    (2) Irritability or outbursts of anger

    (3) Difficulty concentrating

    (4) Hypervigilance

    (5) Exaggerated startle response

Table 9.1. (CONTINUED)

E. Duration of the disturbance (Symptoms in criteria B, C, and D) is more than one month.

F. The disturbance causes clinically significant distress or impairment in social, occupational, or other important areas of functioning.

Specify if:
Acute: if duration of symptoms is less than three months
Chronic: if duration of symptoms is three months or more
Specify if:
With delayed onset: if onset of symptoms is at least six months after the stressor.

(American Psychiatric Association, 1994)

for prolonged exposure, psychotherapies that employ an exposure paradigm have monopolized the current treatment armamentarium for PTSD. However, not all patients respond to exposure therapy, and not all patients agree to undergo the emotionally distressing confrontation of traumatic reminders required for successful treatment (Bradley et al., 2005; Scott & Stradling, 1997; Simon et al., 2008; Van Minnen et al., 2002).

For these reasons, Bleiberg and Markowitz adapted IPT for PTSD, developing a fourteen-week, manualized, individual psychotherapy (Bleiberg & Markowitz, 2005). Unlike most recognized PTSD interventions, IPT does not require or encourage exposure to traumatic memories. Instead, similar to IPT for depression, the therapist selects a current problem area (grief, role transition, or role dispute) and focuses the treatment on resolving this interpersonal problem. Rather than reliving traumas, the patient focuses on difficulties in current relationships or daily life circumstances. The problem area of "interpersonal deficit" is avoidable in IPT for PTSD because the traumatic event itself guarantees the presence of a role transition.

Preliminary findings for IPT for PTSD have been promising in both individual and group psychotherapy formats. In the first pilot study, Bleiberg and Markowitz treated fourteen patients diagnosed with PTSD with fourteen individual weekly sessions of IPT. At study termination, on the Clinician-Administered PTSD Scale (CAPS; Blake et al., 1995), the primary outcome measure, scores had decreased by at least 50% (the *a priori* criterion for treatment response) for ten (69%) of the study patients. Twelve of the fourteen study patients no longer met DSM-IV criteria for the diagnosis, and all patients completed the treatment protocol. Based on these results, Markowitz et al. are currently conducting the first NIMH-funded, randomized trial of IPT for chronic PTSD, comparing IPT to prolonged exposure and to applied relaxation therapy.

Several studies have adapted IPT for PTSD to group format (IPT-G): Robertson et al. (2007) conducted a small, open trial of group IPT with thirteen subjects, all of whom completed treatment. They showed significant social improvement and a significant decrease in depressive symptomatology. Reductions in PTSD symptoms were moderate, with the greatest improvement seen in the avoidant symptoms of PTSD (Robertson, Rushton, Batrim, et al., 2007). This finding is interesting inasmuch as the protocol does not directly encourage patients to confront the situations they are avoiding. In a larger sample, Krupnick et al. (2008) conducted a randomized trial of IPT-G with twenty-four women in the group IPT condition and sixteen in a wait-list control condition. IPT-G patients received sixteen two-hour sessions, in groups with three to five members. At study termination, 70% of patients who completed active treatment no longer met PTSD criteria, compared to 30% of the waitlist condition (Krupnick et al., 2008). Ray and Webster demonstrated improvements in social and overall functioning using IPT-G for a sample of nine male Vietnam veterans (Ray & Webster, 2010). Campanini et al. (2010) reported significant reductions in PTSD and anxiety and depression symptoms, and improvements in social functioning and quality of life measures, in forty patients with violence-related PTSD treated with IPT-G who had failed to respond to psychopharmacological intervention. These preliminary findings suggest that IPT and IPT-G may represent helpful alternatives for patients who either refuse to participate in or do not respond to other empirically supported treatments. Randomized controlled studies will determine whether IPT has comparable efficacy to prolonged exposure for treating PTSD.

THEORETICAL FOUNDATION

Exposure-based therapies operate under the theory that trauma symptoms will not improve without repeated exposure to the traumatic event. This exposure allows the patient to process, work through, and integrate the memories, thus alleviating symptoms (Amaya-Jackson et al., 1999; Cloitre et al., 1997; Foa & Kozak, 1986). While this treatment is efficacious, some patients' avoidance is so entrenched and the prospect of facing their fears so terrifying that they are unwilling to participate in the treatment. IPT for PTSD does not require the patient to relive traumatic memories. The treatment encourages the patient to focus on the identified interpersonal problem area, actually guiding the patient away from re-experiencing the trauma during sessions.

IPT's here-and-now relationship focus emphasizes the interpersonal repercussions of the trauma, a potentially important alternative avenue to understanding PTSD. Although PTSD impairs social functioning (Amaya-Jackson et al., 1999; Cloitre et al., 1997; Davidson et al., 1991; McFarlane et al., 1994), prolonged exposure targets the avoidance symptoms without directly addressing the relationship disturbances and affect dysregulation that are equally central aspects of the syndrome. Prominent symptoms of PTSD include affective detachment, social withdrawal, and a loss of trust in people and the environment. Social isolation reinforces and maintains the alienation, interpersonal hypervigilance, and perceived lack of safety the disorder creates. Potential advantages of IPT for PTSD include "opportunities to reverse interpersonal avoidance, increase social support, undergo corrective emotional experience with others that potentially modulate trauma-related interpersonal distortions, and improve demoralization and helplessness that inhibit motivation to overcome trauma-related fears" (Markowitz et al., 2009, p. 137). IPT helps patients to identify, tolerate, and use their previously buried or detached affects to handle interpersonal situations adaptively. Indeed, a key aspect of the treatment involves helping patients to re-engage feelings from which PTSD has distanced them. Working directly on relationships allows the patient to resolve conflicts with significant others, work through mistrust through positive experiences of mastery, and build social support.

IPT for PTSD may also address relationship difficulties that preceded the development of PTSD. Poor social support has been demonstrated to be a key risk factor for the development of PTSD (Brewin et al, 2000; Ozer et al., 2003). In addition, individuals who develop PTSD are more likely to have pre-existing problems with attachment and intimacy that react with and attenuate reactions to trauma (Stovall-McClough & Cloitre, 2006). The IPT emphasis on interpersonal relationships allows patients to work on problems that may have contributed to developing PTSD. Thus, this treatment might bolster future resilience through improved interpersonal functioning.

Relationship difficulties are also exacerbated by the core affective symptoms of PTSD. Patients with PTSD suffer from both affective numbing and difficulty in modulating and controlling anger. Exposure treatment does not directly address either symptom. However, treating these aspects of the clinical presentation is particularly important, as high levels of anger and difficulty with its expression predict both greater PTSD severity and poorer response to exposure treatment (Foa et al., 1995; Jaycox et al., 1996; Riggs et al., 1998, Van Minnen et al., 2002). As Van Minnen et al. (2002) state: "It is as assumed that angry feelings inhibit emotional engagement and thus prevent activation of the anxiety network, a process assumed to be necessary for successful anxiety treatment. Furthermore, it is believed that feelings of anger. . ., unlike anxiety, do not habituate and may even increase through exposure therapy, increasing the risk of dropout" (p. 441). Whereas exposure therapy views anger as a problem that interferes with treatment, IPT emphasizes the exploration, validation, and expression of anger as an appropriate—patients who have been traumatized often have good reason to feel angry—and crucial part of the therapeutic process. Anger is a potentially useful interpersonal signal that someone is bothering you, a signal the patient ignores at his or her peril.

In addition to helping chronically dysregulated patients learn to modulate their emotions, IPT may be particularly well suited for patients who are characteristically numb and disengaged, as exposure therapy may be contraindicated for patients who suffer from significant dissociative symptoms. Lanius et al. (2010) argue that patients with this symptom profile suffer from emotional overmodulation and that this particular group of patients does poorly in exposure therapy. Within this subtype of PTSD, prolonged exposure can "lead to an actual increase in PTSD and related symptoms, including dissociation, emotion dysregulation, and an increase in the patient's overall distress and functional impairment" (Lanius et al., 2010, p. 644). The heterogeneous nature of the PTSD population demands careful diagnostic and treatment planning, allowing for alternative treatments for patients who are unlikely to do well in prolonged exposure, even though it is efficacious for PTSD.

Unlike prolonged exposure, IPT focuses on affect and encourages the patient to experience emotion directly in the context of a safe relationship. The patient with PTSD often vacillates between feeling numb and feeling emotionally flooded. As such, the affective and interpersonal work helps the patient to gain more control over his or her emotions, to feel less frightened by them, and to understand and express emotions as effective signals in interpersonal relationships. Anger usually reflects feeling harassed by someone, and sadness typically indicates separation or loss; these are potent but not dangerous cues to reading one's environment. As the patient learns to tolerate a fuller range of emotions, detachment and numbing often recede and experiences of anger become more modulated. With an increased sense of mastery and self-efficacy, some traumatized patients spontaneously begin exposing themselves to feared situations, even without having been directly instructed to do so (Bleiberg & Markowitz, 2005). In this way, unlike exposure therapy, IPT directly addresses the affective and interpersonal components of the syndrome; improvements in avoidance may be a secondary result of improved functioning in other domains. Furthermore, the IPT approach has greater flexibility: frequently, the patient is most distressed by current interpersonal circumstances, not the past trauma. IPT allows the therapist to tailor the treatment to the patient's current needs, rather than rigidly insisting on processing past trauma.

CASE EXAMPLE

History of Presenting Problem

Allan is a twenty-two-year-old, single, unemployed African-American man who lives with his aunt. Allan sought treatment as part of a research study six months after he was "kidnapped" and held at gunpoint for twelve hours before his attackers released him. At intake, Allan stated that his **chief complaint** was "nightmares and feeling nothing." In describing his trauma, he reported that a female acquaintance had called him at work, asking to meet for coffee. Allan went downstairs expecting a routine social encounter, but instead was greeted by a group of men, forced into a van, and taken to a desolate underpass. As this ordeal evolved, Allan came to understand that the lead perpetrator was in a relationship with this woman. The man had discovered that she was unfaithful to him and demanded her lover's name. To protect her real lover's identity, the woman gave Allan's name and directed her jealous boyfriend to his location. Allan was beaten up and certain that he would be killed, and he still does not understand why his life was spared. After the men released him, Allan went to the emergency room for treatment of minor physical injuries he sustained during the attack. Allan opposed pressing charges and refused to help the police for fear for his own safety. Nonetheless, the police initiated an investigation, finding and prosecuting the main perpetrator. The man was arrested and imprisoned pending trial. Allan found himself the key witness in a case he did not want to pursue. Compounding matters, he began receiving threatening phone calls from friends of his attacker pressuring him not to testify.

During his first session, Allan reported that he feared going outside and was spending his days playing video games in his apartment. Allan's cousin, who had shared the apartment, had died in a car accident two months prior to the kidnapping. Allan's aunt refused to clear out his possessions, so time spent at home provided constant reminders of this loss. At his first meeting with the district attorney, Allan tried to explain that he could not testify due to his emotional instability. The DA referred him to a court-appointed social worker, who became so concerned by his symptoms that she called 911 and had him taken to the emergency room. Humiliated by his ER stay, he cataloged the experience as further evidence that people and systems could not be trusted. As a result, Allan stated it would be very difficult to trust a new therapist and made it clear during his first session that he did not expect therapy to be helpful. In addition to skepticism about therapy, Allan felt that as long as the legal case was ongoing, both his mental health and his physical safety were in jeopardy.

When Allan entered treatment, he was suffering from nightly nightmares, avoided the area near where the kidnapping occurred, and feared answering the telephone. He had withdrawn socially and occupationally. Allan quit his job as a production assistant because it reminded him of the attack, and he stated he was too depressed and frightened to look for work again. He cut off contact with most of his social relationships because of an intense feeling that other people could not be trusted. Furthermore, Allan reported that he "didn't care" about anything anymore and was unable to feel pleasure. Allan's therapist was new to IPT for PTSD, and in listening to his history, she found it daunting to figure out how to connect with this young man. His interpersonal and emotional detachment left a flat feeling in the room that made it tempting to join in his hopelessness. It became important to remember that his very act of seeking treatment meant that he engaged the possibility of getting better, allowing the therapist to remain hopeful for both of them.

During his research study evaluation, Allan received Axis I diagnoses of PTSD, major depressive disorder, single episode, and an Axis II diagnosis of borderline personality disorder. Allan's baseline CAPS (Blake et al., 1995) score was 81 (exceeding the study inclusion criteria of 50 and indicating extremely severe PTSD [Weathers et al., 2001]). His Hamilton Depression Scale (Ham-D; Hamilton, 1980) score was 21, supporting his diagnosis of moderately severe major depression. Meeting study inclusion criteria, Allan was randomly assigned to fourteen weekly sessions of IPT treatment.

Psychiatric History

Allan had sought supportive psychotherapy at a mental health clinic immediately after the kidnapping but stopped after only a few sessions because he did not find it helpful. He denied any other history of outpatient treatment and denied ever having taken psychotropic medications. Allan had one psychiatric ER visit after his first appointment with the court social worker, when he was evaluated and released from the ER. He denied any other history of psychiatric hospitalizations, violence, or suicide attempts. Allan denied past episodes of major depression or PTSD. He denied any recreational drug use and acknowledged two or three alcoholic drinks per week.

Family History

Allan reported no known family history of mental illness. He was an only child. His parents separated when Allan was five. Allan's mother obtained full custody, and she remarried shortly after the divorce was finalized. Allan reported frequent and frightening physical abuse by his stepfather from the time he was five until his teens. When Allan went to his mother for comfort and protection, she blamed him for the abuse. In addition, he felt that she held him responsible for the difficulties she had in her relationship with her stepfather. Allan stayed in touch with his biological father, a lawyer, while growing up, but he never lived with him.

Based on his study evaluation, Allan's history had suggested relatively acute, adult-onset PTSD. When the therapist probed his background, however, Allan nonchalantly revealed this pattern of early abuse; thus, his history suggests greater chronicity to his PTSD symptoms than he initially portrayed. Many patients with PTSD have such difficulty trusting their interviewers and verbalizing their traumatic experiences that they reveal their full histories in bits and pieces over the course of the treatment. The therapist should listen for hints of prior trauma and continue to clarify the patient's history throughout the early phase of therapy.

Medical History

At the time of treatment, Allan had no known current or history of significant medical illness.

Initial Sessions

A diminutive young man, appearing his stated age, Allan presented at his first session wearing large, dark aviator sunglasses. He was guarded, his affect was constricted, and he described his mood as "dead." Allan's speech was within normal limits and his thought process was goal-directed. He appeared alert and oriented. His insight appeared fair and his judgment appeared adequate.

In reporting his symptoms, Allan was barely audible, and the therapist had to work hard to elicit his narrative. She introduced the concept of IPT and gave a rationale for his symptoms: Allan had suffered a severe trauma, and his nightmares, distrust, and avoidance were all part of PTSD, a treatable medical illness. He responded to this intervention with a raised eyebrow and a shrug of his shoulders. Allan stated he was not convinced but was willing to give this therapy a try because "I have no other options."

In the initial phase of therapy, the therapist conducted an interpersonal inventory to assess Allan's current social functioning, social supports, and the impact of the trauma on his relationships. Allan stated that he had no close friends. He reported having acquaintances that he saw at parties but could not name specific, meaningful relationships. Allan reported that even these relationships had become more distant following the kidnapping, but denied having had close friendships before the trauma. Allan reported one romantic relationship that had lasted a year; although the relationship had ended several years before, he still had strong feelings for this woman and had not recovered from the breakup.

At the time Allan began treatment, his most frequent social contact was his aunt. Allan reported that she was the one person in his life who had cared about him and proven herself trustworthy. However, she was in the midst of her own crisis, grieving the recent loss of her son. Allan reported that his aunt also had nightmares and often woke him in the middle of the night with her screams. Like Allan, his aunt spent her days locked in their small apartment, where she cried for hours, praying to be taken to join her son in heaven. Allan recognized that his constant exposure to his aunt's distress exacerbated his symptoms. However, he did not believe it would be worthwhile to speak with her about her behavior, nor was it his style to say anything.

He did not want to compound her burden and doubted she would understand what he was going through.

Allan reported a "disappointing" relationship with his mother, and that the kidnapping brought up his angry feelings about her behavior during his childhood. Recently he had tried to confront her about her refusal to protect him from his stepfather's abuse. She responded dismissively: "I'm sorry you felt that way." Although Allan reported he currently "felt nothing" towards her, he described this conversation with barely contained rage. To Allan, his mother's statement meant that she both minimized his suffering and denied responsibility for her mistakes as a mother. "Whatever; I don't care," he said with a sigh. As Allan's emotions had been so frequently discounted or ignored, validating his feelings would become a very important part of his therapist's role.

Describing his relationship with his father, Allan stated proudly: "We are exactly the same person." Although he did not see his father often as a child, he felt much more connected to him as an adult. Allan described feeling tremendous anxiety, however, about his father's reaction to his kidnapping. Despite Allan's insistence that his attorney father stay out of the court case, the father tried to pull strings regarding the investigation. He called Allan weak and foolish for not wanting to testify. Again, Allan denied feeling angry, but his tone of voice became heated and loud in relating this story.

By the third session, the therapist helped Allan select the IPT focus of role transition, presenting a formulation for his current symptoms. While the loss of Allan's cousin led the therapist to consider grief as a potential problem area, the role transition focus seemed most appropriate to helping Allan process and recover from the many life changes that had occurred as a result of his trauma. Not only had Allan suffered a terrible trauma, but as a result, he had left his job and begun avoiding his former life. Furthermore, Allan was multiply traumatized, and this most recent event reactivated unresolved feelings about his early abuse. Besides focusing on the symptoms of PTSD, IPT would necessarily address the interpersonal and occupational consequences of his response to his current and earlier traumas. In just three sessions, Allan had already described feeling powerless in multiple situations—during the kidnapping, with the DA, and in his relationship with his mother. This sense of helpless inefficacy seemed to fuel Allan's PTSD symptoms. In addition, his chronic distrust, likely linked to his previous trauma history, was creating significant barriers to his becoming intimate with others and engaged in his life.

In the formulation, the therapist stated, "You are going through what we call a role transition—in thinking about the kidnapping, there is a before and after. You are transitioning from how things were before to a new role where you have to rebuild your relationships, get through this court case, and find a new job. part of helping you to feel better will mean understanding all of the ways that your life has changed and figuring out how to adjust to your life now. Feeling like you can't trust people is a symptom of PTSD. You had experiences when you were young with your mom and stepfather—anyone who was in that situation would feel less trusting as a result. And then we have what happened to you now, which added on top of that. We can expect that this will also affect your ability to trust me. But this is something that we can work on, and we can also figure out where you want to go from here. We can talk about what you would like to get out of what you've gone through and what you would like to happen next."

Though the IPT formulation is meant to reassure and to provide an organizing framework for the treatment, Allan responded with his characteristic interpretation of the interpersonal world around him. "I'm just another case that you're fitting into a manual for your research," he lamented. "This isn't about whether I get better, it's about whether or not you prove your research." At this point, it was important for the therapist to tolerate her own frustration and avoid becoming defensive; Allan could not openly accept the formulation because it would mean allowing himself to feel hopeful and vulnerable. Attacking the manual was a manifestation of his distrust and disengagement. The therapist explained that the point of the treatment was to understand his individual experience, to help Allan with his unique set of vulnerabilities and possibilities. She again underscored and empathized with his pervasive feelings of distrust. But the sunglasses stayed on throughout these early sessions. While Allan's skepticism and distancing behavior made the initial sessions more challenging, the therapist also saw how vulnerable he felt, and how desperately he was clinging to these protective maneuvers. Many patients with PTSD are characteristically closed off in early sessions and, like Allan, so disconnected from their emotions that they are unsure of and confused by what they feel. Therapists can anticipate this and also predict an efflorescence of emotion as treatment progresses.

Thus the beginnings of the sessions in this early phase of treatment were stilted, with Allan's brief recounting of the week's events (in answer to, "How have things been since we last met?") punctuated by long silences and a vacant expression. The content of the sessions remained sparse, as Allan's internal emptiness was mirrored by his lack of activity and engagement in his day-to-day life. Although staying inside and "doing nothing" was meant to protect Allan from perceived intruders, the therapist worked to help him realize that this strategy was worsening his symptoms. Getting better would involve taking a more active life role. The therapist encouraged Allan to reach out to the friends and acquaintances that he had been ignoring, emphasizing the benefits of social support. Though not overtly rejecting these suggestions, Allan often seemed miffed and irritated by the therapist. The therapist began to feel hapless, perhaps responding to Allan's internal feelings of inefficacy. By pointing out his irritation, however, the therapist made space for Allan to acknowledge what was upsetting him. Allan said he found frustrating the therapist's opening question, "How have things been since we last met?" He grumbled, "You ask me the same question every time, and it makes me want to say nothing." Like the other important figures in Allan's life, by Session 5, the therapist had already disappointed him. The therapist responded to his frustration by encouraging Allan to consider how he would like to begin the sessions. She also explained the rationale for the opening question, attempting to model flexibility while simultaneously retaining the function of the opening question. Although in ways it seemed that Allan was repeating an interpersonal pattern with his therapist, he was also trying something different. Typically, Allan walked away from conflict or threw up his hands in surrender the minute he became frustrated. Here he was testing the therapist, gauging whether she would let him down as everyone else had or might somehow rise to his challenge. His eyes peered over slightly lowered shades.

Allan arrived for Session 6 without his sunglasses, although without this concrete protection, his stony facial expression further hardened. Yet Allan took the therapist's explanation of the opening line to heart (and the therapist took his complaint seriously by staying silent rather than asking the usual opening question).

Rather than shutting down at the beginning of session, Allan spontaneously began describing examples of interpersonal situations that bothered him during the week: As a favor, Allan had taken his young cousin and her visiting friend on a tour of New York City nightlife. He took them to an arcade and sat at the table while the two girls played games that he paid for. "It was boring, I felt like a chaperone," he stated, exasperated. Exploring this situation, the therapist questioned why he agreed to a plan that did not interest him, and why he decided not to participate once he had agreed. Allan answered that he preferred not to get emotionally involved. He had decided it was best not to care about anything. He stated matter-of-factly, "If I don't care, I can't get hurt." While Allan felt protected by this attitude, the therapist encouraged him to consider the negative impact of "not caring." Allan recognized that his cousin and her friend ended up thinking he "was an asshole. They didn't think I liked them." Despite setting out to do something nice for them, he ended up alienating them. "I just give them 'the face,' and I don't know why." Together, Allan and his therapist realized that "the face" was the equivalent of his dark sunglasses. His opaque expression was meant to keep his feelings of vulnerability and anger private and concealed.

The therapist observed that Allan had given her "the face" in sessions when frustrated with her opening question. She pointed out that once Allan articulated his frustration, they were able to work together to resolve this conflict. Until then, it had been clear something was bothering him, but it was impossible for the therapist to read his mind or to rectify the situation. She suggested that this style of communication might partially explain why he so often felt disappointed by others. After recognizing how this pattern occurred in session, Allan was able to more fully acknowledge his role in the encounter with his cousin. Rather than feeling like a victim, Allan began to consider that by changing his behavior, he might be able to influence his environment and his relationships. The session then emphasized helping him to consider options for expressing his feelings to her and role-playing alternative conversations.

Middle Sessions

In the middle phase of treatment, the therapist used this knowledge of Allan's interpersonal style to refine the original IPT formulation. Allan's early trauma had taught him that trust is elusive and people are fundamentally disappointing. His traumas, and the interpersonal betrayal accompanying them, brought these beliefs into stark relief. In an effort to protect himself, he had adopted "the face" and the corresponding emotional attitude of "not caring about anything." While he intended this strategy to prevent pain, it dramatically limited Allan's ability to engage in life and in relationships. The therapist explained to Allan that part of his role transition would mean regaining access to feelings he had kept hidden behind "the face" for so long, and that such feelings, while potentially frightening, were useful in understanding and handling interpersonal encounters.

Predictably, as Allan gained awareness of a greater range of feelings, as his numbness began to recede, a fountain of anger soared. Fully experiencing this emotion for the first time increased Allan's discomfort, leading him to question the therapy, and his therapist, yet again. Although Allan's affect was less constricted and he engaged more fully in sessions (and increasingly in his life), he felt more overwhelmed by his feelings, and hence did not yet report symptomatic improvement. At week seven, Allan's CAPS score of 76 (baseline = 81) and Ham-D of 19 (baseline = 20) remained virtually unchanged. It is not uncommon for patients with PTSD to remain so symptomatic at this point in treatment, perhaps precisely because they are more in touch with uncomfortable, previously warded-off feelings. Qualitatively, however, Allan's symptoms had changed. Previously less aware of his emotional states, he now reported more disturbing affective experiences. As his emotional distress increased, his avoidant symptoms were decreasing, without the therapist having directed him to stop avoiding trauma reminders. Although his overall score remained the same, this difference represented a real shift.

Allan's expression of anger was a crucial aspect of the therapeutic process. He had made every possible attempt to avoid this emotion since he was a child, and thus lacked the skills to tolerate it. As this emotion overwhelmed and flooded him, it became clear that Allan needed help learning how to manage this feeling and how to assert himself appropriately. Based on his negative experiences with the DA, Allan had become even more determined not to testify, but he was afraid to tell her so. He worried that she would push and manipulate him into testifying. The therapist helped Allan to name the emotion ("You're angry"), to understand why he was feeling it, and to consider options and role-play, practicing possible ways of responding if the DA tried to strong-arm him into court. Echoing his earlier words to his therapist, he practiced saying, "You don't care about what happens to me, you only care about your case." Emboldened by the session, Allan called and informed the DA that he had decided not to testify. The role-playing exercise, and his real-life implementation of his newfound skills, was intended to help Allan gain a sense of power and feeling of mastery. When Allan confronted the DA, however, she threatened to arrest him if he refused to testify. This outcome illustrates a difficulty that may arise in IPT, as significant others do not always respond appropriately even when the patient's communication improves. This makes it important to explore contingencies, such as, "What could go wrong, and what could you do then?" as part of considering options and role-playing. Although the case ultimately settled without his having to testify, Allan used this example as further evidence of the unjustness of the world, and the manipulative nature of women in general.

Whereas Allan's early sessions had a numb, disengaged quality, Session 8 was filled with affect. Allan questioned, "How can feeling this anger be a good thing when it gets you nowhere?!" In this moment, it was crucial for the therapist to join in Allan's upset, to share his displeasure and his anger at the DA's tactics. She rejoined: "This is outrageous! No wonder you're angry!" After a pause, however, she also encouraged Allan to think about whether he might have gained anything by expressing himself. At the very least, expressing his anger and disappointment got his feelings off his chest and out in the open. The feelings could be discussed, and Allan no longer had to suffer alone. The DA now knew his position, and he was free to continue to express his frustration. Even though his feelings did not alter the outcome of his case, it might influence how the DA treated victims in the future.

In discussing his frustration with the DA, Allan also began to acknowledge his hurt and disappointment towards his father. Initially he had idolized his father, stating that they "were exactly the same." Now he began to avow anger towards his father for pressuring him to testify rather than comforting and protecting him. Allan said he was too frightened to confront his father, as he did not want to lose their relationship and equally afraid that his father would respond by redoubling his attempts to "nail" Allan's attacker. But for the first time, he expressed a range of emotions towards his father he had heretofore been suppressing: "He doesn't listen to me or care what I am feeling. He just wants me to do what *he* thinks is right. I don't want to talk to him because I am afraid I will snap if he brings up the case."

During Session 10, instead of defining himself as "the guy who doesn't care about anything," Allan complained that he cared too much: "I feel bipolar, like I'm flipping out for no reason." He reported having been insulted at dinner by a female friend. Allan retaliated, insulting her back, then quickly felt remorseful and frightened by his reaction. In the past, Allan would "walk away" in this situation, but his therapist had been encouraging him to handle conflicts more directly. Allan stated, "Now, every time I don't like what people say, I try not to just ignore them and walk away, I just blow up." The therapist had to work to ensure that this experience did not prove so aversive that Allan would resume his former stance and abandon this new strategy. She spoke of the importance of practice in learning to express his anger. She pointed out that Allan had been suppressing his anger for so long that it was bound to feel more intense in the beginning. She also reassured Allan that the more he allowed himself to feel his feelings, the less he bottled them up inside, the less intense they would feel when he did express them. To this point, he had only truly felt angry or sad when he reached a breaking point and exploded; exploding left him feeling frightened and out of control. The therapist worked to help Allan realize that it is okay to feel angry, and occasionally to act on it, particularly when he felt insulted or slighted. Allan was not "flipping out for no reason" but rather having an appropriate (albeit strong) reaction for good reason. Normalizing his affect and repeated role-play helped to calm him and allowed him to begin engaging more with relationships that he had let drift due to his PTSD symptoms.

With the therapist's encouragement, and with increased confidence from role-play, he began seeking social activities and reconnected with his college roommate. This new social activity decreased his isolation and depression but also thrust him headfirst into situations that generated more conflict. Like many patients with PSTD who begin to reconnect with their emotions, Allan's surge of anger meant that he frequently found himself feeling irritable and angry in his interpersonal interactions. While this experience frustrated Allan, it also provided ripe opportunity to practice asserting his anger more appropriately outside sessions.

Termination

As is common in time-limited treatment, Allan began to feel the pressure of the upcoming termination, which led him to participate more fully in therapy. Whereas at the start Allan had had difficulty connecting life events and his feelings, he now arrived full of examples, ready to work and eager for more time. The sunglasses remained tucked in his pocket, and he exhibited a fuller range of facial expressions. As Allan began to express his emotions, his PTSD symptoms improved: although his symptoms would not be formally assessed until week fourteen, he reported fewer nightmares and less anxiety. The therapist pointed out that though Allan found the emotions uncomfortable, his re-experiencing symptoms had diminished significantly.

Furthermore, this process seemed to free Allan to take a more active stance in life. Rather than staying home playing video games under the shadow of his depressed aunt, Allan decided to enroll in a school program that would allow him to develop a vocational specialization. The therapist emphasized all areas of progress in his role transition, a reminder that Allan was improving his relationships and career despite his difficulty in tolerating his increased emotional experience: "Because you developed PTSD, you got really numb, and now as you're getting better, your feelings are coming back very strongly. The more you continue to deal with them, and express yourself, the less overwhelming it will feel, and look how useful the feelings are in telling you how to handle your life." Now that the court case had settled, Allan no longer had an objective reason to fear further attack, and this allowed him to feel a sense of resolution before he finished with his therapist. Termination provided an opportunity for Allan to revisit his accomplishments in IPT and to discuss how he might continue to work on himself in the future. The therapist prepared Allan for his likely reaction to the final session, predicting that he might feel tempted to walk away, to avoid the pain of ending treatment in the way that he had characteristically avoided difficult interactions in the past.

In that final Session 14, Allan reverted to his old stance, appearing somber and shut down. Though "the face" had returned (sans shades), the therapist immediately pointed out, "This is a difficult situation, but you did not walk away from it." As he had so often expressed during treatment, Allan stated, "I just want to get away, start over, not have to care." Acknowledging that Allan was still suffering, the therapist responded, "Before, you were the person who didn't care about anything, and that wasn't working so well. Now, caring about things, taking your life seriously, that's a strength—being able to have feelings and to care is a wonderful quality in a man and it will help you in your relationships." The therapist revisited Allan's role transition, reminding him of how he had developed PTSD (linking the traumas to his difficulty expressing himself in relationships), and how he had worked to relieve it. She also used the final session to allow Allan space to discuss his feelings about ending therapy. They discussed his apprehension about the future and his feelings of disappointment in ending the relationship. "At least coming here, I feel like I'm working towards getting better. I'm not sure how to deal with feeling upset on my own. I'm not sure what I will do at 4:00 on Thursdays." As this was one of the first times Allan had allowed himself to trust anybody, it was essential to help acknowledge the loss he was facing and the anxiety and the sadness it triggered. (It is also important to help patients distinguish between appropriate sadness and depression.) Allan had difficulty incorporating that he had *mixed* feelings: that he could feel upset about leaving treatment while simultaneously recognizing the gains he had made. This tension contributed to his difficulty in tolerating the final session. The therapist helped Allan to acknowledge his mixed feelings and modeled saying goodbye, saying she had enjoyed working with him, had been impressed by his progress, and would miss him.

DISCUSSION

Allan received treatment in a research study in which his symptoms received serial assessment. We recommend this as part of any treatment. Primary outcome measures consisted of the CAPS (Blake et al., 1995) and the Ham-D (Hamilton, 1980). A CAPS of 39 or less is considered subthreshold (Blake et al., 1995), and we defined *a priori* a 30% symptom reduction as a treatment response. At termination, Allan's CAPS and Hamilton scales had declined significantly; his CAPS score was 39, a 52% reduction, and his Ham-D score was 12, a 40% reduction, consistent with only mild depression. Thus he met criteria for treatment response, albeit not remission. Indeed, Allan's PTSD symptoms had greatly diminished: he no longer suffered from nightmares, flashbacks, or affective numbing. Further, Allan no longer met criteria for borderline personality disorder. No longer anhedonic, he was re-engaging in interpersonal relationships and resuming a professional role. By the end of treatment, he was facing conflicts with friends more directly and contemplating confronting his parents and his aunt.

As acute IPT is a short-term treatment, patients will often leave therapy with interpersonal issues to continue working on. It is unrealistic to expect patients to resolve all interpersonal conflicts in fourteen weeks. Rather, the goal of IPT is to help the patient build a foundation for approaching interpersonal problems differently, a template that will continue to empower the patient over time and serve to prevent relapse. Although Allan would need to continue tackling these issues, his functioning at termination differed dramatically from before treatment, and the momentum the therapy generated left him highly motivated to continue such work. Despite major improvement by the end of therapy, he still met SCID DSM-IV criteria for mild PTSD (Spitzer et al., 1994). In particular, Allan continued to avoid the locale where the kidnapping had occurred, was unwilling to answer his phone, and still experienced mild hyperarousal symptoms. As testament to his ability to continue working on his problems after therapy concluded, however, at Allan's three-month follow-up, his CAPS score was 14, an 80% reduction from baseline, and his Ham-D score was 2, a 90% reduction. Both of these are normative scores, and he no longer met criteria for an Axis I (or II) disorder. He had received no additional interval treatment.

Allan's response to IPT treatment evokes observations of what worked and did not work during his course of treatment, as well as a discussion of how his case generalizes to the PTSD population. Like so many patients with PTSD, Allan entered treatment interpersonally mistrustful and affectively deadened. These two characteristic symptoms make IPT well suited for this population but also create unique challenges. Engaging the patient in the therapeutic relationship and identifying, normalizing, and actively encouraging the expression of affect are crucial components of successful IPT treatment. The patient with PTSD may meet this challenge with trepidation, but in our experience, this process is less aversive than the prospect of facing traumatic reminders in prolonged exposure.

Allan's core difficulty with trust preceded his most recent trauma and may have resulted from childhood trauma. The kidnapping and his subsequent encounters with the legal and mental health systems reinforced and exacerbated this pre-existing vulnerability. It is not unusual for patients with PTSD to present a proximate trauma and later reveal a longer pattern of victimization (Cloitre et al., 1997; Davidson et al., 1991). Although Allan desperately wanted to feel better, he began treatment not yet ready to open up and freely enter a collaborative relationship. We expect this reticence in PTSD, and find it important to help patients articulate these feelings and anticipate the process of treatment. The beginning phase of therapy necessarily focused on building a therapeutic alliance to help Allan to trust the therapist enough to take emotional and interpersonal risks.

Allan's case illustrates the well-established connection between the quality of early attachments and the later development of psychiatric problems. Disruptions in early relationships with one's caregiver, and childhood trauma in particular, leave individuals vulnerable to a host of later problems, including the development of anxiety disorders (Fonagy et al., 1996; Slade et al., 2005; Stovall-McClough & Cloitre, 2006). Allan's mother did not protect him from his abusive stepfather. Besides exposing him to violence, she sent Allan the message that the abuse was his fault. From a very young age, Allan could not guarantee his safety. Combined with his mother's dismissive style, these factors suggest that Allan did not develop a secure attachment to his parents. Rather, his adult stance of "not caring" and walking away rather than expressing his feelings may represent the adult outgrowth of an insecure, avoidant attachment style. We hypothesize that premorbid insecure attachment, a difficulty in establishing basic trust, leaves individuals with weaker support networks and limited ability to call on them in crisis. This makes them vulnerable to subsequent interpersonal disruptions after traumatic experiences, and hence to developing PTSD (Markowitz et al., 2009, p. 135).

As part of this research study, in collaboration with Kevin Meehan, Ph.D., we are measuring change in reflective functioning (RF). RF is the capacity to understand one's own and others' emotional mental states. The ability to reflect has been linked to attachment security and protects against developing psychiatric disorders (Fonagy et al., 1991, 1996, 2005). Allan's ability to reflect on his and on others' feelings was understandably quite constricted at the start of treatment. Allan's early history had convinced him that the world is a dangerous place and women are disappointing. The kidnapping, with its interpersonal betrayal by the woman who set him up (and by the DA), brought these ideas into stark relief. Cloitre et al. (1997) note that "abuse which occurs during childhood profoundly interferes with the developmental tasks of that period, mainly self–other relatedness and self-integration" (p. 438). Although a young adult, Allan had not achieved a consolidated sense of self. This vulnerability compounded his difficulty with affect regulation. After the trauma, as any sense of safety he might have had unraveled, he retreated into avoidance. This was the only way he knew to protect himself from becoming overwhelmed by the anxiety, disappointment, and anger the trauma triggered. Working in treatment to verbalize his current experience, to make meaning of what happened to him, and to understand how his behavior affected other people, raised his RF from a very low 2.5 to a meaningfully improved 3.5 (of a possible 9), allowing him another, more effective mode of affect regulation.

Patients with PTSD not uncommonly present with comorbid Cluster B personality disorders, another well-established consequence of early attachment difficulties (Fonagy et al., 1995, 1996). Indeed, individuals with a personality disorder face a higher risk for developing PTSD (Axelrod et al., 2005; Golier et al., 2003), often have a more chronic, debilitating course of illness (Hembree et al., 2004; Southwick et al., 1993), and may have a higher risk for revictimization (Golier et al., 2003; Yen at al., 2002). Patients like Allan who carry a diagnosis of borderline personality disorder have demonstrated poorer response to prolonged exposure, which may even be contraindicated for certain patients who do not have the internal resources to handle it (Feeny et al., 2002; Lanius et al., 2010; Simon et al., 2002,). IPT for PTSD allows the therapist to address affective and interpersonal pathology more directly and may be a particularly good alternative for this group.

These common aspects of the PTSD diagnosis make IPT treatment for PTSD slightly different than for treating major depression. For both diagnoses, therapists need to help patients name affects, to understand them as interpersonal responses (e.g., anger) or symptoms (hopelessness), and to use this emotional understanding to respond to interpersonal encounters. In treating PTSD, the therapist can expect the patient to be emotionally distanced in a way depressed patients rarely are. The therapist needs to work even more than with a depressed patient to detoxify affects as powerful but not dangerous. The feel of IPT sessions with patients with PTSD— even those, like Allan, with comorbid major depressive disorder—differs considerably from those with major depression alone. Depressed patients may dislike their affects, but they usually cannot help but feel them. Patients with PTSD have walled off their feelings and are wary of removing the barrier.

The need to build a therapeutic alliance with an emotionally inchoate patient before tackling the interpersonal focus resembles the adaptation of IPT for borderline personality disorder; in treating comorbid PTSD and borderline personality disorder, familiarization with both manuals is helpful (Markowitz et al., 2007; for IPT for borderline personality disorder, see Chapter 11). Furthermore, while patients with PTSD may present with what appear to be characterological traits, it is important not to prejudge them as they often lift with treatment of the Axis I syndrome. Indeed, Allan met SCID II criteria for borderline personality disorder at study entry and no longer met criteria at study termination, suggesting that his presentation may have reflected his PTSD more than an underlying personality disorder. Regardless, with a patient like Allan, the IPT therapist may also need to work more concretely on rudimentary relationship and affect regulatory skills than would be necessary with a patient presenting with a simple depression or simple trauma.

Allan's central difficulty with trust is typical of PTSD, and the beginning of treatment often felt like a concrete expression of his approach–avoid conflict. Allan created distance in the room with his sunglasses and "the face." On the other hand, he was sensitive to any interventions that felt "manualized" or impersonal, expressing his wish for and fear of attachment. Allan's tendency to distance himself in his interpersonal relationships complicated creating the intimate, vital relationship essential to a successful treatment.

As with many emotionally detached patients with PTSD, it was not until therapy was half over that he had formed enough of an alliance that he could actively participate in usual aspects of IPT. Unsurprisingly, at his week seven assessments midway through treatment, his CAPS and Ham-D scores remained virtually unchanged from his baseline. Patients with PTSD avoid emotional exposure in the same way that they avoid situational exposure. Figuring out how to trust and how to express feelings were integral parts of the therapeutic process, and Allan's ultimate success in establishing a working alliance was a tremendous therapeutic gain. IPT allowed Allan and his therapist to work at an affective level tolerable enough for him to stay in therapy without dropping out. In working with this population, one must be aware of this tension. Ideally, the therapist avoids both a distant, intellectualized treatment and overwhelming the patient with an intolerable level of intimacy and affective expression.

While IPT is an affect-focused treatment, the therapist must bear in mind the task in which he or she is asking the patient to engage. Many patients (particularly those with comorbid Axis II disorders) may develop PTSD because they lack the skills to experience strong emotions in a contained way. Allan demonstrated this difficulty as he began to directly experience his anger. Although his suppression of emotions clearly impaired many aspects of his life, it was familiar, and avoiding feelings caused little or no subjective distress—although he was quite anxious and depressed. As he began to experience anger, he felt flooded and overwhelmed. Role-playing in sessions became important to successfully working on this issue: practicing effective communication in the session modeled appropriate behavior and began to teach Allan rudimentary affect regulatory skills. This intervention is relevant for combat veterans, who often associate angry affect with violent acts. It is important to normalize emotion while simultaneously helping the patient to modulate its expression.

During role-play, Allan often directly challenged the therapist, using his at times acerbic wit and sarcasm to poke holes in her suggestions. At first, Allan's attitude left her feeling frustrated, as Allan seemed more determined to prove her wrong than to solve the problem he had presented. As a beginning IPT therapist, it is easy to become mired in the patient's reluctance to engage in role-playing. The exercise often requires significant redirection and discipline to help the patient focus. Over time, however, the therapist ultimately recognized the contradiction between Allan's descriptions of himself outside of session and his behavior in session. In his outside relationships, Allan depicted himself as meek, unable to get anyone to hear his point of view. In session, Allan proved so sharp and articulate that the therapist often found herself tongue-tied. Pointing this out to Allan gave him concrete proof that he was capable of making himself heard; his self-perception was inaccurate. Role-play allowed Allan to learn from the therapist's modeling and helped the therapist to fine-tune her interventions, as the role-playing revealed both Allan's interpersonal limitations and his strengths. These practice exercises led him to take greater interpersonal risks outside sessions. A man with much to be angry about, he began to be able to express that anger more appropriately to others. Although Allan did not always achieve desired outcomes in his encounters, he successfully re-entered the interpersonal world, increasing his level of social support by re-engaging with his college roommate and attending social functions again. Mobilizing social supports is particularly important as termination approaches and the patient can no longer rely on the therapist.

During the second half of treatment, both patient and therapist began to feel time pressure. While at times they both felt that Allan needed more sessions to adequately complete the therapeutic process, the short-term model has distinct advantages for this population. For a patient like Allan with an avoidant style and (at least an apparent) Cluster B personality disorder, the prospect of an open-ended, long-term treatment might well have been intolerable. The boundary created by the finite number of sessions seemed to free him to open up more than he might have otherwise. Further, the intensity of short-term treatment makes it more difficult for patient and therapist to skirt primary issues: the time pressure increases the affective intensity of therapy. Finally, confronting termination in a structured setting facilitated Allan's work on attachment and loss. Ultimately, termination empowered him, engendering a feeling of mastery: that in fact he could tolerate loss and disappointment and still lead a productive and satisfying life.

Allan's presentation is fairly typical for patients with PTSD, although the diagnosis is a heterogeneous one. Affectively numb, these patients often withdraw from relationships either because they serve as reminders of trauma, or because they have lost interest due to detachment and a sense of foreshortened future. Like Allan, patients with PTSD frequently have trauma histories that predate the index trauma and may emerge over the course of treatment. Through treatment, Allan relocated his vitality—not an easy endeavor for him, as his greater range of emotional experience forced him to grapple with painful affects and ideas. However, this allowed him to reconnect with others, and to develop enough confidence in himself that he could embark on a career path and think about tackling longstanding issues with close family members. While Allan had not remitted at termination (and many patients with PTSD do not), he left feeling like more of a man. Communicating to Allan that he was capable of continuing the therapeutic work on his own, without the therapist's support, was important in helping him to consolidate the gains he had made. Three months after treatment, he was no longer symptomatic and had remitted, having internalized the lessons learned during his therapy.

ACKNOWLEDGMENT

Supported in part by grant R01 MH079078 from the National Institute of Mental Health (Markowitz, Principal Investigator).

SUGGESTED READING

American Psychiatric Association: Practice guideline for the treatment of patients with acute stress disorder and posttraumatic stress disorder. American Journal of Psychiatry 2004;161:3–31

Bleiberg KL, Markowitz JC: Interpersonal psychotherapy for posttraumatic stress disorder. American Journal of Psychiatry 2005;162(1):181–183

Brewin CR, Andrews JD: Meta-analysis of risk factors for posttraumatic stress disorder in trauma-exposed adults. Journal of Consulting and Clinical Psychology 2000;68:748–766

Feeny NC, Zoellner LA, Foa EB: Treatment outcome for chronic PTSD among female assault victims with borderline personality characteristics: a preliminary examination. Journal of Personality Disorders 2002;16:30–40

Lipsitz JD, Fyer AJ, Markowitz JC, Cherry S: An open trial of interpersonal psychotherapy for social phobia. American Journal of Psychiatry 1999;156(11): 1814–1816

Krupnick JL, Green BL, Stockton JM, Krause E, Mete M: Group interpersonal psychotherapy for low-income women with posttraumatic stress disorder. Psychotherapy Research 2008;18(5):497–507

Markowitz M: Adaptations of interpersonal psychotherapy. Psychiatric Annals 2006;36(8):559–563

Markowitz JC, Milrod B, Bleiberg K, Marshall, RD: Interpersonal factors in understanding and treating posttraumatic stress disorder. Journal of Psychiatric Practice 2009;15(2):133–140

Ozer EJ, Best SR, Lipsey TL, Weiss DS: Predictors of posttraumatic stress disorder
    and symptoms in adults: a meta-analysis. Psychological Bulletin 2003;129:52–73
Robertson M, Rushton PJ, Bartrum MD, Ray R: Group-based interpersonal psy-
    chotherapy for posttraumatic stress disorder: theoretical and clinical aspects.
    International Journal of Group Psychotherapy 2004;54(2):145–175
Robertson M, Rushton P, Batrim D, Moore E, Morris P: Open trial of interper-
    sonal psychotherapy for posttraumatic stress disorder. Australasian Psychiatry
    2007;15(5):375–379

Interpersonal Psychotherapy for Social Anxiety Disorder

JOSHUA D. LIPSITZ

Paula's voice trembled as she described the experience that led to her seeking treatment. During a meeting two months before with an important client, Paula, an attorney, experienced the most intense state of panic she had had ever endured. Her hands became cold and clammy. Her heart was beating so loudly it seemed like others could hear it, and she felt beads of sweat forming on her forehead. Most distressing of all was the tightening in her throat, which made her feel she would not be able to finish her sentence. Paula remembered looking around and everyone appearing to be distant and unreal except for a young associate who appearing to be smiling—"as if he were laughing at me." She excused herself and went to the restroom to splash water on her face. Returning to the meeting, she managed to get through, avoiding eye contact and speaking as little as possible. Afterward she felt exhausted and got nothing done for the remainder of the day.

PAULA: I've had this stage fright problem for as long as I can remember, and I am kind of shy around people I don't know well, but I usually managed to work around it. In college I got a C in speech class because I read every speech word for word from the text. In law school I dreaded the mock trials and would have knots in my stomach for weeks. I loved law but I knew all along that being a trial attorney was definitely not an option for me. Most lawyers don't do trials, so this was not a big problem. Since this happened, though, I feel like I've completely lost whatever confidence I did have. Every meeting feels like I'm on trial and everyone around me is the judge and jury. I'm really not sure how long I can go on like this!

ADAPTATION OF IPT FOR SOCIAL ANXIETY DISORDER (SAD)

Excessive social anxiety can be a distressing and disabling problem. Social anxiety disorder (SAD; also called social phobia) is defined as excessive fear of one or more social situations due to concern about scrutiny or potential embarrassment, which leads to significant distress or impairment in functioning (APA, 1994). Epidemiological studies indicate that up to 13% of the population will experience SAD in their lifetimes (Kessler et al., 2005; Wacker et al., 1992). The most commonly feared social situation is public speaking, but fears include a range of routine daily situations. Up to 80% to 90% of people who seek treatment for SAD have generalized SAD, defined as excessive fear in most social situations (Liebowitz et al., 1992). SAD typically begins by adolescence (Magee et al., 1996). Left untreated, its course is generally chronic (Bruce et al., 2005; Reich et al., 1994), with highest prevalence in early adulthood (Wittchen & Fehm, 2003). SAD is associated with significant impairment in work and social functioning (Schneier et al., 1994), impaired quality of life (Simon et al., 2002), and considerable economic cost to society (Lipsitz & Schneier, 2000). SAD often co-occurs with other psychiatric disorders, particularly other anxiety, mood, and substance use disorders (Magee et al., 1996). Because SAD onset typically precedes other disorders (Magee et al., 1996; Angst, 1993), it may be a risk factor for later psychopathology.

Predominant psychological models of SAD emphasize a complex interplay of cognitive and behavioral factors that maintain SAD. The two best-studied formulations (Clark & Wells, 1995; Rapee & Heimberg, 1997) highlight a range of cognitive features, including stable core beliefs, attentional and interpretation biases, overestimation of threat, negative self-perception, and internally focused attention. These cognitive factors interact with actual avoidance or subtle avoidance maneuvers, known as safety behaviors (Wells et al., 1995), which are meant to minimize the risk of adverse outcomes. This cognitive-behavioral constellation precludes direct processing of potentially corrective feedback. This model forms the foundation of efficacious cognitive-behavioral therapy (CBT) treatments for SAD (Clark et al., 2006; Heimberg et al., 1998); some evidence indicates that cognitive changes mediate these benefits (Hofmann, 2004).

Interpersonal theory of SAD (Alden & Taylor, 2004; Lipsitz & Markowitz, 1997) implicates self-perpetuating cycles of social interactions as contributing, reciprocally and over time, to increasing social anxiety and avoidance (Alden & Taylor, 2004). Interpersonal theory focuses on real rather than imagined or misperceived interpersonal consequences of anxious behaviors (Alden & Wallace, 1995). Research suggests that there is often a "kernel of truth" in perceptions of adverse and negative reactions (Spence et al., 1999), which creates a negative interactional pattern always involving at least two players. Blöte and Westenberg (2007), for example, assessed adolescents' perceptions of negative class reactions during a public speaking task. They found that socially anxious adolescents' perceptions of negative class treatment were not exaggerated but rather consistent with ratings of other students. This focus on interactional patterns rather than behavior *per se* or internal processing of experience suggests that there is a place for a more interactional therapeutic strategy (e.g., assertively challenging critical reactions rather than re-interpreting them), such as that IPT espouses.

Second, the interpersonal approach sees important interpersonal relationships and the individual's primary role in society as providing an important context for development and maintenance of psychopathology (Klerman et al., 1984; Sullivan, 1953). In SAD, social anxiety *per se* is, and its immediate consequences are focused mostly on strangers and acquaintances, less so on close friends and family. However, a growing body of research indicates that SAD is associated with a range of difficulties in close relationships (Alden & Taylor, 2004; Davila & Beck, 2002; Neal & Edelmann, 2003). Interpersonal difficulties include fewer close friends in adolescence (Beidel et al., 1999), fewer heterosexual relationships in college (Dodge et al., 1987), greater likelihood of remaining unmarried (Schneier et al., 1992), more problems with intimacy in romantic relationships (Wenzel, 2002), and relationships characterized by dependence and unassertiveness (Davila & Beck, 2002; Stangier et al., 2006). Some of these interpersonal difficulties emerge in childhood and adolescence in the form of peer neglect and rejection as well as harassment, teasing, and bullying (Beidel et al., 1999; Crick et al., 1993; LaGreca & Lopez, 1998; Storch & Masia-Warner, 2004). Beidel et al. (1999) found that children and adolescents with SAD experienced distress due to lack of friendships. The interpersonal model sees these difficulties not merely as sequelae of social anxiety and avoidance but as interacting reciprocally to help develop and maintain this disorder. Interactional patterns that characterize SAD are understood within the context of broader difficulties of human attachment (Ainsworth & Bowlby, 1991; Bowlby, 1973).

The role of close relationships in SAD is supported by additional lines of research. Cuming and Rapee (2010) found that for women, social anxiety was associated with decreased self-exposure even within intimate relationships. When Grewen et al. (2003) randomized couples to "warm contact" or no contact immediately prior to a recorded speech task, individuals receiving warm contact demonstrated lower blood pressure and lower heart rate compared to the low-contact group. This suggests that features of a close relationship may moderate the effects of feared social situations for the socially anxious. Finally, Russel et al. (2011) recently found that emotionally secure situations led to increased pro-social behavior for the socially anxious, suggesting that engaging aspects of the real social situation can help the individual overcome social anxiety and avoidance.

INTERPERSONAL PROBLEM AREAS IN IPT FOR SAD

In IPT for SAD, the most common interpersonal problem is role transition, followed by role dispute. The two are also sometimes a combined focus of IPT. Grief is rarely a compelling context for understanding SAD, although we have, on occasion, used this formulation. Interpersonal deficits, while inevitably appropriate for nearly all patients with generalized SAD, is too global and also overlaps too much with the definition of SAD. As such this formation may reinforce feelings of demoralization rather than introduce a new perspective and instill hope (goals of IPT). We therefore recommend that when using interpersonal deficits as a focal IPT problem area, the therapist reformulate this as "role insecurity," emphasizing that the individual's latent abilities are being held back by SAD.

An individual's interpersonal approach may need fine-tuning, including encouragement in assertiveness, expressing anger and other emotions. In IPT for SAD, it is expected that social skills will emerge and develop naturally as the patient's social anxiety is understood and treated. Finally, therapists may propose a "therapeutic role transition" (adapted from dysthymic disorder by Markowitz, 1998; see Chapter 6) in which receiving the diagnosis of SAD itself—clarifying the impact of the disorder and thereby externalizing the symptoms that patients had previously experienced as their personality and identity—provokes patients to adjust how they see themselves and what they expect in social situations.

STAGES OF IPT FOR SAD

IPT for SAD follows the three standard phases of IPT (Weissman et al., 2007). The initial phase (sessions 1–3) includes (1) a thorough review of symptoms, (2) an assessment of current and past relationships (the interpersonal inventory), and (3) the identification of symptoms as part of a known disorder. For IPT for SAD, this part was modified to focus specifically on symptoms of SAD as part of a treatable anxiety disorder. The therapist identifies physical, emotional, and cognitive symptoms of SAD as part of the same treatable syndrome. Physical symptoms are often a powerful part of the experience of patients with anxiety disorders, and for some individuals with SAD a physical symptom (e.g., blushing, sweating) becomes a prominent focus of social fear. For patients with a comorbid diagnosis of depression, both diagnoses are explained to the patient. The patient is given the "sick role" in order to alleviate some of the emotional burden of having become impaired. The therapist then proposes a link between SAD and one or sometimes two specific interpersonal problem areas, and contracts with the patient to work on this problem for the next several weeks. Studies of IPT for SAD have used durations of fourteen weeks and sixteen weeks.

The rationale given to patients is as follows: "IPT sees your social anxiety as closely connected to your interpersonal relationships and how you interact with other people. The way the social anxiety has affected you may be very obvious to you. But it is equally true that the quality of your relationships and how you interact with others affects your social anxiety. IPT focuses on your relationships and how you feel about yourself in social situations. Looking at your feelings within these relationships, expressing these feelings, and making some improvements, for example, by handling interpersonal encounters differently, will decrease the social anxiety disorder."

In the middle phase (Sessions 4–13), the therapist works with the patient to address the interpersonal problem area(s). The therapist encourages the patient to express feelings about relationships, then helps the patient to clarify and accept the full range of these feelings regarding the problem area, including negative affects such as anger. Next, the therapist helps the patient ameliorate, adjust to, or find ways to cope better with this problem. Activities might range from expressing strong emotions about a lost role or relationship to role-playing a more assertive response to a current dispute. The therapist maintains the focus of each session on the specific problem area(s). Finally, the therapist reinforces the link between progress or lack of progress in the problem area and change in frequency and severity of panic disorder symptoms.

In the final or termination phase (Sessions 14–16), the therapist and patient review progress, consolidate gains, and prepare for challenging situations and experiences in the future. The therapist encourages the patient to discuss progress or lack thereof and to express feelings about termination. The goals during this phase are to give up the therapeutic relationship and establish a sense of competence to deal with social phobia independently. This involves, first, an explicit discussion of termination, highlighting that this is a time of potential grieving and increased vulnerability. For the patient who may have been reluctant to establish new relationships and share feelings, the prospect of ending the therapy may be especially unsettling. The therapist states explicitly that termination is often a difficult phase that involves saying goodbye and losing a source of support and assistance. This may evoke some sadness and anxiety, which are natural and healthy signals of a separation. Some symptoms may worsen or resurface during termination; this is usually temporary. Just as bereavement may lead to increased feelings of vulnerability and waves of emotion that may intensify SAD symptoms, termination may trigger such feelings on a smaller, more transient scale. Second, therapist and patient review progress, identifying areas of success and failure with an eye toward consolidating gains and identifying and preparing for future goals.

ASSESSING SYMPTOM CHANGE IN IPT FOR SAD

An essential feature of IPT is the tracking of symptom change. Although the content of the therapy may focus on interpersonal situations and not on symptoms *per se*, we continuously track the changes in therapy. Although it is possible to informally ask about symptoms and severity, it is important to use some dimensional form of rating (1–10, 1–100) to help reinforce that anxiety is not black and white and that incremental progress is still progress. SAD symptoms are best evaluated using a systematic scale. There are various scales available for measuring severity of SAD symptoms.

The Liebowitz Social Anxiety Scale (LSAS; Liebowitz et al., 1992) is a 24-item, clinician-rated scale that provides separate scores for fear and avoidance in social versus performance situations as well as a total score of overall SAD severity. It is widely used in CBT and pharmacological treatment studies for SAD (Heimberg et al., 1998; Liebowitz et al., 1992). The LSAS has high internal consistency and correlates highly with other SAD measures. It also has an efficient, self-report version that has high convergence with the clinician version (Fresco et al., 2001). Another option to consider is the Social Phobia Inventory (Connor et al., 2000).

In interpreting progress, the clinician should keep in mind that while social anxiety may be experienced in a range of situations, there are typically a few or perhaps only one salient situation that currently affects the patient's life. As such, overall change in symptoms—based on totaling many situations, as in the LSAS—may not always accurately reflect the level of clinically meaningful change in the salient context.

When working with patients with SAD, it is important to be sensitive to the patient's possible efforts to put on an agreeable face and add a positive spin to be polite and please the therapist. Many patients with SAD have trouble expressing dissatisfaction, especially in situations of authority. The therapist should convey explicitly that it is okay not to be improving, okay to express dissatisfactions to the therapist, and important to share this information so that they can plan accordingly. Indeed, the avoidance of such expression is a symptom of SAD.

STATE OF THE EMPIRICAL EVIDENCE FOR IPT FOR SAD

After a promising initial open trial (Lipsitz et al., 1999), an initial fourteen-week controlled trial compared IPT to supportive therapy for SAD. Both treatments yielded statistically significant and clinically meaningful pre-to-post improvement, but IPT was not significantly superior to supportive dynamic therapy on most measures (Lipsitz et al., 2008). However, the use of same therapists for both treatments may have limited differentiation in how the two approaches were administered, and statistical power to find group differences was limited (N = 70). Results of two European trials support the efficacy of IPT for SAD. Borge et al. (2008) showed that IPT was equivalent to CBT for treatment of very severe SAD in a multimodal inpatient treatment. Stangier et al. (in press) showed that IPT was superior to waitlist control, yielding pre-to-post effect sizes comparable to those obtained in many CBT trials. However, in that sample a particularly efficacious form of CBT, with a range of interventions including videotape exposure, outperformed IPT on clinician-rated outcome measures. Based on the limited accumulated research IPT for SAD to date, it should be considered at this point an alternative rather than first-line treatment, as CBT has garnered more extensive and robust empirical support (Rodebaugh et al., 2004). Further research on IPT for social phobia is needed. Based on strong efficacy of IPT for depression and suggestive data from the two-site German trial indicating that IPT seemed to perform well for patients with comorbid SAD and depression (E. Schramm, personal communication, 2007), IPT may be especially worth considering in the fairly common and challenging instance of SAD that co-occurs with major depression.

CASE EXAMPLE

History of Present Illness

Paula, a thirty-six-year-old white woman of Italian-American heritage, described a long history of mild to moderate social phobia in a variety of situations, "at least since middle school." She could not identify a precise date of onset. Paula experienced social anxiety at parties, when meeting strangers, and when talking to authority figures, and when younger became very anxious when dating. However, her biggest fear always involved speaking or making a presentation in front of a group of people. She experienced moderate to severe anxiety in any group of more than two people. In almost every meeting she dreaded being turned to for input. Prior to a formal presentation she would become anxious for days and often had trouble sleeping the night before. During the presentation she experienced palpitations, sweating, and feeling that she was choking and would not be able to continue speaking.

Paula said she had considered seeking treatment several times over the past years but felt embarrassed about her anxiety and also feared that her husband and others would find out and think less of her. Recently the problem had become more acute, especially at work. An associate attorney for seven years, she was expecting to make partner in her firm in the coming year. However, she now felt that her social anxiety might jeopardize her chances, and most people at her stage either made partner or moved on to a different job. Even for the short term she was not sure how long she could keep functioning with this level of anxiety and worried that this could be affecting her health.

At the initial session Paula's total score on the LSAS (Liebowitz et al., 1992) was 78, in the clinical range for generalized SAD.

Interpersonal Inventory

Paula described a stable and generally satisfying relationship with Bill, her thirty-seven-year-old husband of eleven years. Bill, himself gregarious and socially confident, knew that Paula experienced "stage fright" but was not aware to what degree this problem had become a focus of her life. During the second session, Paula informed the therapist that she had not yet told Bill she was seeking therapy. She feared he would think her a weakling. Paula said she was satisfied and fulfilled in her role as mother of two children, ages eight and five years, and felt she was able to be an active mother despite often working long hours in her job. She did not lack confidence in her maternal role, although she felt anxious interacting with teachers and sometimes with other parents at parties and clubs and during other activities. She occasionally experienced the typical pressures juggling the demands of her job and her family, but felt she was managing all of this pretty well and did not see this as a major problem in her life.

Paula said she was casually friendly but not close with a few colleagues at work. She felt close to one partner in the firm, whom she had worked with in the past and whom she viewed as something of a mentor and also her advocate. She had one close friend who had started with her in the firm but had cut back to part time as she began having children; Paula saw her less and less. She felt she had not grown close with other colleagues but insisted this was not unusual in her firm, as people were very driven and there was little time for socializing. However, she did acknowledge that some colleagues seemed to carve out friendships and chat together, whereas she did not feel she had this kind of group. When asked about friendships outside of work, she said she felt that her family and career didn't allow time for other close relationships and that she had lost touch with most of her friends from college and law school. In none of her close relationships did she feel comfortable talking about her anxiety. She worried that if others knew "the truth" they would see her as weak and a failure.

In describing other family connections, Paula portrayed a striking emotional distance from her mother and her two siblings. Her father, a schoolteacher, died when she was twenty-six. She recalled that after this loss she assumed a position of leadership within the family. She arranged the funeral and took primary responsibility for her mother, who went through a difficult period at first. Paula described her older brother and younger sister as underachievers who had little ambition and little in common with her. After her mother recovered, Paula drifted further and further away from her mother and siblings, and although they all lived within an hour's drive she saw them less and less. Paula reflected that in many ways she had "left them behind. It's like I needed to escape so I could make something of my life." She had seen in her father a more kindred spirit who enjoyed reading and debating politics, even though he was not ambitious in his professional life.

Psychiatric, Family, and Medical History

Paula reported a single episode of major depression at age twenty-four that lasted three to four months. She experienced two months or so of depressed mood following her father's death but as she was able to function this was considered uncomplicated bereavement. Paula denied persistent depressed mood or other current symptoms of depression. However, the day after the intense panic during the meeting she recalled a fleeting wish that something would happen, like a car accident, so that she would not have to face this situation again. She denied any history of substance abuse, but acknowledged that during college and law school she drank a little too much at parties and gatherings to try to take the edge off her anxiety. Paula denied experiencing spontaneous panic attacks but felt that her physical symptoms, particularly the feeling of choking, definitely increased her sense of anxiety in social situations and had become a focus. She reported generally good physical health and was not taking any prescription medications regularly. When her anxiety recently increased, she started taking an herbal remedy that was supposed to reduce anxiety. She was still taking this before presentations but did not think it helped much.

Differential Diagnosis and Indication for IPT

Paula's anxiety, although persistent throughout the day and recently triggering full-blown panic attacks, was clearly focused on fear of scrutiny and embarrassment, consistent with the diagnosis of SAD. In addition to the most salient situation, meetings and presentations, Paula had excessive anxiety in several situations that led to her not staying in touch with old friends, making few new friends, not enjoying and often avoiding leisure and social events, and having occasional problems with family members (e.g., she refused to join her husband at his annual holiday party). A diagnosis of panic disorder would be considered if the current anxiety were secondary to occurrence of spontaneous panic attacks. Generalized anxiety disorder would apply if Paula felt pressured and stressed at work and experienced considerable worry and anxiety throughout the day due to concerns that were not about social situations or specific concerns about scrutiny. Likewise, there was no evidence of a trauma that would suggest posttraumatic stress disorder. There was no clear evidence of current depressive symptoms. Paula was distressed, felt demoralized by her symptoms, and occasionally had trouble sleeping due to anxiety, but she did not experience persistent depressed mood or symptoms associated with a diagnosis of major depression. Finally, Paula denied problems with alcohol or drugs either due to efforts to cope with anxiety or as precipitants of increased anxiety or panic feelings.

IPT Formulation

Paula noted that beginning the process of becoming partner was linked in time to exacerbation of her SAD symptoms. In SAD it is unusual for onset to begin immediately before seeking treatment. Instead, most patients seeking treatment have experienced symptoms for years and often report having felt this way for as long as they can remember. For this reason, we attempt to identify acute stressors—events that seem linked to a worsening of symptoms or a greater impact or salience of social phobia symptoms in the patient's life. This was the most obvious and proximal event.

Paula also seemed to be experiencing ongoing tensions and emotional distance from her family of origin (mother, sister, and brother), which might be described as a role dispute. Paula's emotional tone when describing these difficulties varied between distant and removed to sad and angry. The dispute raised the therapist's attention for two additional reasons. First, Paula conveyed warmth toward her own family and her husband's family, but not her family of origin. In Paula's working-class Italian background, close relationships, especially with mother, were the norm. On the other hand, it was not clear how connected this role dispute might be to her SAD and, based on the longstanding impasses, the therapist did not expect her to resonate with this issue as a focus of therapy. The therapist therefore opted to stay with the more proximal and obvious difficulty rather than propose the role dispute.

THERAPIST: The symptoms you are describing fit the criteria for social anxiety disorder, also called social phobia. Social anxiety disorder is one of the most common mental health problems, and it affects all types of people from all walks of life, including successful professionals such as yourself. [Psychoeducation] There are many theories about what causes some people to develop social anxiety disorder while others don't. Most agree that there is a combination of biological and environmental factors. Left untreated, social anxiety disorder tends to be pretty chronic, and some people have it for much of their lives. [Medical model] Social anxiety disorder can cause a lot of distress and really gets in the way of your doing what you want to do. Up until now you've felt that you are to blame when actually social anxiety disorder has held you back, kind of like running with a cast on your leg. [Offering the sick role]. The good news is that social anxiety is treatable, not your fault, and treatments get most people better. [Instilling hope] The main treatments are focused psychotherapies and medications.

In interpersonal therapy we focus on how social anxiety disorder relates to the important relationships in your life and the important roles you assume in society. You described your social anxiety becoming more of a problem as you became eligible for making partner, which is certainly a major transition that comes with many pluses but maybe also some problems. I propose that we work on this important life change you are going through over the next eleven weeks. In doing so we will overcome the social anxiety disorder. How does that sound to you?

PAULA: Are you saying I have fear of success or something like that? Because I have been working on making partner for the last seven years and I feel I'm really trying hard.

THERAPIST: No, I'm not saying that you have a fear of success. Clearly you've already achieved considerable success, which is all the more impressive given that you've been struggling with social anxiety disorder, which can really get in the way of presentations, social interactions, and so on. However, the process of shifting to a new role, what we call a role transition, is sometimes more complicated than people realize, and there may be strong feelings that go along with making this shift.

In the ensuing discussion, the therapist added that the transition to partner might be a special challenge because of her background and feelings about where she was coming from and where she was going. Raised in a working-class neighborhood, Paula was the first in her family to attain a graduate degree. Her economic means were well above that of her parents, siblings, other relatives, and childhood friends. There were few lawyers and no other women of Italian ethnicity in her firm. Furthermore, most of her colleagues seemed to come from privileged backgrounds, families of successful professionals. Paula did not initially connect her social phobia to her humble roots or feeling different from others, and she pointed out to the therapist that there were certainly other people at the firm who came from poor economic backgrounds and did not seem to have this trouble. The therapist pointed out that social phobia was common and most people are not aware of others who have it. By the end of the discussion Paula seemed to accept the general idea of the therapy and the importance of the current role transition in her life. As she was eager to see change, she liked the idea of having a specific time limit. However, she remained a bit skeptical about the possibility of changing something that had been with her for years.

THERAPIST: It sounds like you're comfortable with this plan. So I propose that we work on this transition over the next eleven weeks with the goal of conquering your social anxiety disorder. My hope is that within two months or so your social anxiety will lessen significantly and will stop being a problem for you. If this does not happen, we will then consider other options to help you get better. [contract]

PAULA: OK. I sure wish I could be as optimistic as you.

Session 4

The therapy began focusing on Paula's role transition from a more junior position to a more senior role with more authority and responsibility. She initially discussed feeling that she was somehow different from other people who became partner. She soon confided to the therapist that she often felt like an "imposter" who had convinced people she was more competent than she really was. She shared doubts about her ability to "play with the big boys." Although Paula knew intellectually that she was as capable of doing the work as anyone, she always felt that there was something that did not fit and was not as natural for her. She recalled how comforting it was when, as a new associate, she always had someone looking out for her and checking her decisions. "It's like I want to be on my own, but I also would still like someone to be looking out for me." Paula described her anxiety about having the last word and having to take responsibility for her decisions, no matter what other people said. The therapist clarified that this was something positive about her old role and it was natural to have apprehensions about giving up this sense of security.

Paula also described difficulty confronting someone directly when she disagreed. She often worried that she would "get too angry" or "too upset" and things would get "ugly." She recalled that at one recent meeting she was listening to a partner criticize her and wanted to defend her work. However, she felt frozen and afraid that if she spoke up "things would get out of control." She recalled that when she was newer to the firm it felt like people were always looking out for her or that she was not expected to stick her neck out. The themes of avoiding conflict and of dependency arose again several times in subsequent sessions. The therapist encouraged Paula to talk about why it was hard to get angry and what consequences she feared. On some occasions, the therapist offered to role-play difficult conversations to ease Paula into confronting others.

Middle sessions began using the standard IPT query, "How have things been since we last met?" When asked about the level of her SAD symptoms over the past week, Paula said that she had felt hopeful in the beginning of the week (i.e., following the previous session) that maybe things could change. However, the day before the session she attended an important meeting and noticed once again that she was very anxious. She felt powerless and sat quietly waiting for the meeting to end, which left her feeling discouraged. She focused initially on her physical symptoms.

THERAPIST: In terms of this transition we've been talking about, how did this make you feel?
PAULA: Like some voice inside was telling me: maybe you're not ready for this after all. I felt like I was a first-year associate surrounded by people who all knew more than me and were all more capable than me."
THERAPIST: How did you feel?
PAULA: Helpless . . . Small [silence] . . . Angry.
THERAPIST: Angry about what?
PAULA: Because . . . screw them! I'm as good as any of them. I work as hard as anyone. Why does it seem to be so easy for everyone else?

This discussion continued for much of the session and Paula seemed to become increasingly expressive about her feelings of frustration and anger. The therapist in turn validated these feelings.

Session 5

Continuing on the theme of the role transition, Paula observed that she had felt more comfortable with junior employees and less so with peers and superiors, and she felt this tied in to the role transition. She went on to discuss a colleague, Mark, who had started at the firm the same year as she and with whom she had been friendly in the past. However, Mark had made partner a year earlier because "he knows how to play the game" and "whether he knows or not, he says it like he knows it." She said she now felt he was too good for her and admitted that she had been trying to avoid talking to him. The therapist helped Paula examine her mixed feelings about Mark: how on the one hand she felt a kinship and shared history, but on the other hand he was now somehow different because things seemed to come too easily for him. As Paula talked about this she seemed to soften her critical stance, and finally said Mark "was really an OK guy" and that she missed not chatting with him. The therapist suggested that Paula could try chatting with Mark and that it might help to hear about his experiences and his own transition.

The therapist continued to point out the interactional relationship of SAD—that these feelings about her role added fuel to the SAD, but that SAD in turn made it more difficult for her to feel secure in her role. Regarding Mark, Paula's SAD made her reluctant to enlist support and feedback from someone who shared a similar experience and maybe could support her or help her feel better about the changes. In this way she was not enlisting an effective support system to help her through and needed to explore ways she could change this.

Toward the end of the session, Paula raised her continued frustration with social anxiety in meetings: "I am finding that these discussions are helpful for putting things in perspective and planning for the future, but for now the anxiety is my main concern, and it may have lessened a bit but at times it's still unbearable. When am I going to start feeling like I can put this behind me?"

The therapist provided encouragement about Paula's work so far and reminded her that it sometimes took time for anxiety to decrease. During the middle phase of IPT, some patients begin spontaneously to build their new perspective on their symptoms and report feeling or beginning to behave differently in social situations. Some patients, however, particularly those with prominent physical symptoms, will need more direct encouragement to take concrete positive steps between sessions. In contrast to CBT approaches that develop a systematic hierarchy and a program of repeated exposures to feared situations, the IPT therapist may encourage the patient in a general way to take advantage of the brief time in therapy by taking positive and unfamiliar steps. The patient is free to decide when, how, and in what situation to make these steps.

THERAPIST: During the time we're working together in therapy, I encourage you to assume a more active role in social situations. Social anxiety disorder wants you to stay in the passive role and wait for others to call the shots. You may have to step out of your comfort zone more than you're accustomed to. But you will see that you have more options than you think.

Session 6

Paula had asked her colleague Mark to lunch and was surprised at how receptive he was. The lunch went well, and it helped her to remember that they had been friends and he still seemed to feel friendly toward her. He also shared some of his own recent challenges, including a recent mistake that had almost been very costly for the firm and led one of the senior partners to react very harshly. Paula then shared some of her worries about her own process. She found Mark supportive. After discussing her feelings about this meeting, Paula reflected that she had gotten into "us-and-them" thinking that was making the transition seem more scary than it really was: "I am realizing that he . . . that *they* are not really that different from me. partners are not perfect. Everyone has their challenges and we all screw up sometimes. Even 'perfect' Mark."

Paula went on to discuss her fear that others would be disappointed in her if they knew what was really going on with her social anxiety. She had finally mustered the courage to talk to Bill about being in therapy, but said she played down her distress and portrayed this as something more like coaching to help her communicate more effectively. Paula feared that Bill would see her as weak if he knew the extent of her social anxiety. In our clinical work with patients with social phobia, it is striking how many do not confide to significant others their distress due to SAD and their seeking treatment. This reflects the stance of anxious insecure attachment, which increases risk and contributes to persistence of psychopathology, in contrast to social support, which is protective against risk (Markowitz et al., 2009).

We encourage the patient to find ways of enlisting the support of the partner (or other close relative, friend, or close coworker) in overcoming social anxiety, with the explicit goal of turning him or her into an ally, rather than another source of stress and social pressure. The therapist, trying to help Paula clarify her feelings, asked her how she could be sure that Bill would react this way. She said she was not sure, but guessed she was afraid to find out. The therapist reflected that the current situation left her trapped and also feeling as if Bill were on the other side rather than on her side. He suggested that they role-play a conversation in which she was more upfront with Bill about her distress. They did this, and Paula said she felt closer to being able to do this with Bill.

Session 7

The day before the session, Paula had a frank talk with Bill and shared tearfully how distressed she had been and how overwhelming the SAD had become. She told the therapist that she felt a weight had been lifted from her shoulders. Contrary to her fears, Bill remained supportive and said he was confident that she would get through this challenge as she had many others, and that he would support any decision she made on her career. Although she was still not sure there was a substantial difference in her social anxiety, she expressed more optimism that things could change in the future.

Sessions 8 and 9

Paula continued talking about the role transition, focusing more now on specific problems she anticipated having. At the same time, she reported that over the past two weeks she had made incremental progress in her social anxiety symptoms at work. She had begun speaking up at meetings even when she was not asked. She said that the therapy helped her understand that she did not "need permission" to put her opinions forward. She noticed that when she volunteered spontaneously it felt less threatening the next time she spoke. The therapist gave positive feedback for this spontaneous decision to take charge of the interaction. He reinforced the interactive nature of social anxiety and that she would continue to feel differently as she also behaved differently.

Paula then shared that she was distressed by something else that had happened this past week that she wanted to discuss. She had recently backed out of a family gathering. Her mother, who did not usually challenge her excuse that she was busy with work, snapped at her and accused her of being "too good for everyone else" in the family. Recounting this conversation, Paula clearly felt hurt. Initially expressing anger at her mother for lashing out, the therapist invited her to talk more about what she and her mother expected from each other. Paula discussed her own feelings of disappointment in her family. The therapist then asked if she wanted to let her mother know how she was feeling. Paula fell silent and said, "In a way, she's right. I do feel I'm too good for my family. The truth is, I could have come to the party but I made an excuse because I simply have trouble being around them. I have so little in common with them. I have nothing to say." Paula proceeded to relate the history of her problems with her siblings and how they had grown further and further apart over the years. In recounting the history she spoke with disdain about their lack of professional achievement and drive.

THERAPIST: It sounds like your relationship with your mom and siblings is something that's not so easy to dismiss. In a way, this also may be related to the role transition you are going through.

PAULA: I don't really see what you mean. How does getting annoyed by my family have anything to do with my career?

THERAPIST: I'm just raising the possibility that your family background is making this transition harder for you to swallow. Your mother says you are too good for everyone else in the family. You describe yourself as "escaping from your family" and kind of disapprove of everyone else. Maybe your difficulty in feeling accepted where you came from is making it harder to be comfortable about who you are now becoming.

PAULA: I have so little to do with them. It's like we live on different planets It's hard to imagine that how I feel about them could have any impact on how I feel about myself.

THERAPIST: It may not be, but when you talk about being an "imposter," it's like the real you is broken or not good enough. And where you come from is part of who you are.

PAULA: I look at Bill and his parents and I think, that's my family now. That's why I'm surprised that it bothered me so much when my mother gave me a hard time about not coming.

THERAPIST: It's not so easy to leave a family.

For the remainder of this session and much of the next one, Paula continued talking about her feelings about her mother and siblings. She related the history of her distancing herself from them after she had assumed more responsibility. She recalled feeling resentful that the more responsibility she took on, the less her siblings seemed to do, and further that her mother never seemed to appreciate her. The therapist asked if she had ever expressed this feeling to her mother. Paula said she hadn't. After eliciting and clarifying feelings about why this was difficult, the therapist suggested they role-play a conversation with Paula's mother—which they did.

Sessions 10 and 11

During the next week Paula called her sister, with whom she had not spoken for months. Her sister was surprised but seemed pleased to hear from her. She confided in Paula that her husband had been having trouble at his job and seemed to seek Paula's advice on possible options for him. Paula felt happy at having initiated this conversation and said it made her feel a bit less judgmental of her sister. She said she was not sure whether this would lead to any great closeness between them. However, afterward she had the idea of inviting her mother and her siblings over for brunch one Sunday. She even mentioned this to her husband, but was not sure when she would schedule this. "I really don't see us becoming one of those families on TV that have the big Thanksgiving dinners together, but I think it feels better that we can be on better terms."

The following week Paula said she planned to tell her mother that she had felt hurt when her mother called her a snob, and perhaps also that she did not feel that she ever appreciated her. She did call her mother intending to say this, but could not bring herself to open up. The therapist reassured her that this was a very difficult step and might take some time. He reflected that Paula had taken many important steps in a relatively short amount of time. Paula reported she had been interacting more easily at work and had had much less anxiety in a recent meeting: "I think the fears were still there, but they were much more in the background and didn't get in the way so much."

Termination

At Session 12, Paula reported a continued decrease in social anxiety. She still experienced anxiety in the moment, but she worried less ahead of time and did not feel immobilized by her anxiety. She said she felt more in control, "like I have a choice to feel this way or not." Her LSAS total score had fallen from 78 to 28, indicating only mild social anxiety in a range of situations. The therapist pointed out that there were only two more sessions left after this one, and that this was sometimes a challenging time for maintaining gains and preparing for time after therapy. Paula said that she was feeling she was now on the right track even though she was still more anxious than most people. During the termination, the therapist reminded Paula that the purpose of therapy was not to solve all problems, but to provide tools and new experiences to help her get through a difficult phase and change course for the future. They recapped important steps Paula took during therapy, including her greater assertiveness and willingness to assume a leadership role in social situations, and more willingness to risk vulnerability in close relationships. He directed Paula's attention to external sources of support (her husband, Mark, friends, and even her family of origin) whom she had already begun to use more effectively.

THERAPIST: The bottom line is that although things have begun to change and there will be others to stand up for you, you also have to get used to being your own advocate. When you take risks as you've been doing, you will have to be the one to remind yourself to ease up and not be so harsh, since I won't be there to help you do that.

During the termination phase, the therapist also raised potential areas for future progress and identified and anticipated potential pitfalls. During the next-to-last session, the therapist and Paula role-played an imagined, unsuccessful social experience (a meeting in which she had trouble expressing herself), with the therapist playing Paula and Paula playing the therapist, attempting to help put things in perspective. After this Paula suggested that she check in with an update a month or so after therapy. The therapist said this was an excellent idea and that they could do this by phone or, if Paula preferred, they could hold a follow-up session four to six weeks after the last session. During the last session Paula expressed appreciation for the therapy and optimism about her ability to continue, but some sadness about leaving the therapist.

DISCUSSION

A thorough assessment of the broader issues in Paula's interpersonal life led to an initial IPT formulation and course of therapy that was beneficial in reducing SAD symptoms. Paula, like many patients with SAD, needed concrete encouragement to move out of her comfort zone and begin building on her understanding of SAD and her current interpersonal challenges. The therapy might have concluded successfully without addressing the added component of her estrangement from her family and making steps toward better relations. However, this additional problem area seemed to closely complement that overall thrust.

Paula was an engaged, motivated patient who had only mild difficulty sharing thoughts and feelings in one-to-one conversation. Thus the feel of the sessions was fairly smooth and comfortable. Some patients with more severe SAD, especially those with comorbid avoidant personality disorder, experience intense anxiety in the session itself and may speak only tersely. In such cases, the therapist needs to provide explicit encouragement and guide the conversation with more initial questions and gentle prompts. Over time, the therapist should allow the patient more space and sometimes longer moments of silence to help him or her to talk more freely.

Paula's LSAS score remained at 28 in the final session, which is below the diagnostic range. However, as is often the case in SAD, some excessive anxiety persisted in some situations. In this sense, the change in SAD may feel less dramatic than, for example, remission from an episode of major depression where the patient feels (completely) "better" (i.e., virtually free of depressive symptoms). At the same time, the levels of distress and disability are markedly lower than prior to treatment. Paula no longer doubted her ability to manage at work and was far more effective in communicating and in reaching out professionally and socially. Paula took important steps to greater acceptance and comfort in her role of increasing responsibility and made initial steps toward addressing a lasting and nagging schism between her and her family of origin.

SUGGESTED READING

Alden LE, Taylor CT: Interpersonal processes in social phobia. Clinical Psychology Review 2004;24:857–882

Lipsitz JD, Gur M, Vermes D, et al.: A randomized trial of interpersonal therapy versus supportive therapy for social anxiety disorder. Depression and Anxiety 2008;25:542–553

Lipsitz JD, Markowitz JC, Cherry S, Fyer AJ: Open trial of interpersonal psychotherapy for the treatment of social phobia. American Journal of Psychiatry 1999;156:1814–1816

Lipsitz JD, Marshall RD: Alternative psychotherapy approaches for social anxiety disorder. Psychiatric Clinics of North America 2001;24:817–829

Interpersonal Psychotherapy for Borderline Personality Disorder

KATHRYN L. BLEIBERG AND JOHN C. MARKOWITZ

Previous research on IPT has focused on Axis I disorders, not personality disorders. Borderline personality disorder (BPD) is the first personality disorder for which IPT has been adapted (Angus & Gillies, 1994; Markowitz et al., 2006, 2007). There are several reasons to try to treat BPD with IPT. DSM-IV defines borderline personality disorder as a "pervasive pattern of instability of interpersonal relationships, self-image and affects, and marked impulsivity" (APA, 1994). To meet the diagnosis, a patient must meet five out of nine diagnostic criteria, including several that reflect interpersonal functioning: "frantic efforts to avoid real or imagined abandonment," "a pattern of unstable and intense relationships characterized by alternating between extremes of idealization and devaluation," "inappropriate, affective instability due to marked reactivity of mood," "chronic feelings or emptiness," and "intense anger or difficulty controlling anger." Difficulties in interpersonal functioning and managing affects—hallmarks of BPD—are problems that not only are targeted but are the focal points in IPT.

The diagnosis of BPD carries a stigma and has been considered difficult to treat. Patients with BPD often evoke fear and avoidance in clinicians. Recent research indicates that the prognosis for BPD may be far better than traditionally believed (Grilo et al., 2004; Shea et al., 2002; Zanarini et al., 2010a, 2010b). The use of the medical model in IPT can help reduce the stigma and provide hope for improvement as it does for patients with mood disorders. The IPT therapist encourages patients by explaining that although their symptoms and suffering may feel interminable, the symptoms and related impairment of BPD lessen over time for most patients; treatment can hasten improvement and increase the chances of achieving remission.

given the high comorbidity and overlap of BPD with mood disorders, it ...ied clinically reasonable to modify IPT for this population.

ADAPTATIONS

Gillies et al. were the first to adapt IPT for patients with BPD (Angus & Gillies, 1994; Weissman et al., 2000, Chapter 23). They enrolled thirteen patients with BPD in a pilot study comprising twelve weekly sessions of IPT. They planned to compare IPT to relationship management therapy (RMT; Dawson, 1988; Marziali & Munroe-Blum, 1994) in a randomized pilot trial of twelve weekly sessions and six monthly follow-up visits. Unable to retain patients in the RMT group, the investigators treated all of the remaining patients with IPT. They added a fifth potential problem area, "self-image," to reflect the unstable sense of self and identity disturbance characteristic of many patients with BPD. Twelve of the thirteen patients completed twelve sessions. Although the results were never published, the investigators reported that overall pathology and self-reported symptoms declined.

We conducted an open trial of IPT for BPD at the New York State Psychiatric Institute, altering the usual IPT approach to meet the needs of patients with BPD in several ways. Some of these changes were conceptual and necessitated by the shift of focus from an acute Axis I disorder to a chronic Axis II diagnosis (Markowitz, Skodol, & Bleiberg, 2006).

We extended the length of treatment to address the expected difficulties in forming and maintaining the treatment alliance as well as the chronicity of BPD. The typical IPT format of twelve to sixteen weeks was expanded to include an acute treatment phase of eighteen sessions in sixteen weeks, followed by a continuation phase of sixteen weekly sessions for patients who tolerated the acute phase. The initial phase was largely devoted to developing and cementing the treatment alliance. Since separation and abandonment are central issues for patients with BPD, termination is addressed well in advance and given greater attention than in standard IPT. The IPT therapist is optimistic and encouraging—a cheerleader for the patient in his or her fight against illness—and focuses on relationships outside of the office. The therapist is flexible about rescheduling sessions—even more so than in standard IPT—to allow for cancellations, which are common among this patient population, and to demonstrate a commitment to working with the patient. These factors can minimize the chance of conflict with the therapist and help foster a positive alliance.

Nevertheless, tensions in the therapeutic relationship are almost inevitable when working with patients with BPD. Should a conflict arise in which the patient has negative feelings towards the therapist and communicates these feelings in an explosive, impulsive way, the IPT therapist uses the conflict as an opportunity to help the patient understand her feelings and explore options for expressing her feelings more moderately and effectively. The therapist explores, validates, and normalizes the patient's feelings when appropriate (Markowitz & Milrod, 2011) and may even apologize. Once the conflict resolves, the focus of treatment returns to other relationships.

As in standard IPT, the therapist employs the medical model, defining BPD as a treatable illness that is not the patient's fault, diminishing the patient's guilt about symptoms and shifting blame from self to the illness. We conceptualized BPD as a mood-inflected chronic illness similar to dysthymic disorder (see Chapter 6), but interspersed with ineffective outbursts of anger and impulsivity. The therapist provides psychoeducation about BPD, explaining what it does and does not mean, clarifying misconceptions about the syndrome. Unlike depressed patients, who tend to avoid expressing anger, patients with BPD tend to express anger in impulsive, explosive, and self-destructive ways. The IPT therapist helps patients with BPD, like patients with depression, learn how to assert themselves and express their anger more effectively. The therapist validates and normalizes the patient's angry feelings when appropriate, explaining that anger is a normal emotion, but one that patients with BPD have difficulty tolerating and expressing.

Patients with suicide risk—common among individuals with BPD—were included in the pilot adaptation study, whereas it is often an exclusion criterion for treatment outcome studies. Suicidal ideation and self-destructive behavior are addressed by allowing patients to remain on stable doses of medications initiated prior to study entry and by providing frequent assessments and the opportunity for brief (ten minute) phone contact with the therapist between sessions (Markowitz, Skodol, & Bleiberg, 2006). The phone check-ins were also intended to maintain continuity and the treatment alliance. Surprisingly, few patients used them when they were offered.

We enrolled eleven subjects in our study, all of whom met DSM-IV criteria for BPD and for current or past mood disorders. Several also met criteria for comorbid Axis II disorders. Four subjects dropped out during the acute phase, and all but one of the eight remaining subjects completed the continuation phase. Six of the seven subjects who completed the study no longer met full criteria for BPD. Symptoms of depression and social functioning also improved. These responders seemed to have gained an understanding about their feelings and a greater ability to manage relationships (Markowitz, in press).

Bellino et al. (Bellino, Rinaldi, & Bogetto, 2010) subsequently applied IPT for BPD in a randomized trial comparing fluoxetine 20 to 40 mg daily alone to fluoxetine combined with IPT for BPD. Their sample of fifty-five patients met diagnostic criteria for BPD but no comorbid Axis I or Axis II disorders. The authors reported only completer analyses (N = 44). Over thirty-two weeks, fluoxetine alone yielded a response rate of 46% and fluoxetine plus IPT for BPD a not significantly different 55% response rate based on at least a 50% decrease in BPD Severity Index score (Arntz et al., 2003). Both treatments lowered depressive symptoms equally. The small sample size limits statistical power to find differences between two active treatment conditions. Patients receiving IPT for BPD had greater decreases in anxiety symptoms, greater improvements in psychological and social functioning, and greater improvements in interpersonal relationships, impulsivity, and affective instability (Bellino et al., 2010).

The data from the initial studies are fragmentary but promising. They suggest the need for further study and a published manual. It is premature to judge whether IPT will emerge as an efficacious treatment for BPD. The following is a case illustration from our pilot study of the implementation of IPT adapted for BPD.

CASE EXAMPLE

Susan is a thirty-year-old, married mother of a fourteen-month-old daughter and stepmother to her husband's five-year-old twin daughters from a previous marriage.

She presented with borderline personality and major depressive disorder. She was referred to the treatment study of IPT for BPD by an emergency room psychiatrist. Susan reported that Mark, her husband of two years, brought her to the ER after she "blew up at him" and threw a cell phone on the floor. Mark called the police, who advised him to take her to the ER. Susan's chief complaint was: "I have my moods . . . after I explode I feel bad." She stated, "I don't think my husband appreciates what I do . . . We used to be able to talk, but now he's just frustrated with me." She reported that she was eager to participate in the IPT study in order to save her marriage.

Susan related that since the birth of her daughter, she and her husband had been fighting frequently. Their arguments often concerned taking care of Mark's twin daughters, whose joint custody he shared with his ex-wife. Susan described having frequent angry outbursts in which she became "upset," threw things, and yelled "mean things" at her husband. She reported feeling "alone" and "empty," and that "nobody understands who I am." Susan reported a history of unstable relationships with men, impulsive spending resulting in thousands of dollars worth of credit card debt, periodically superficially cutting her thigh with razor blades, chronic feelings of emptiness, anger outbursts, and difficulty trusting others. She frequently felt that her husband was abandoning her and the twins, and she had difficulty trusting him. At times Susan idealized her husband, at other times hated him; he was "everything" to her one day, and then when annoyed, she could easily imagine living without him.

In addition to meeting Diagnostic Interview for Personality Disorders (DIPD; Zanarini et al., 1987) criteria for BPD, Susan reported a major depressive episode beginning shortly after the birth of her daughter, and she continued to suffer from depressed mood, anhedonia, inappropriate guilt, feelings of worthlessness, and low appetite about half of the time. She reported intermittently feeling that life was not worth living, although she denied ever wanting to kill herself. She acknowledged that when she felt life was not worthwhile she would cut her thigh with a razor blade, and often did this after an argument with a boyfriend. On two occasions she took six sleeping pills—three times the recommended dosage—to "get rid of the pain." She described having the urge to cut herself and take sleeping pills since moving in with her husband, but claimed that she had not done so because of her daughter.

Although not meeting full criteria for anorexia nervosa, she described periods of excessive dieting and/or exercise when she would become underweight, but not amenorrheic. She reported that these periods lasted anywhere from a few days to a couple of months, began in her teens and persisted to the present day. She met criteria for alcohol abuse in full remission since her mid-20s, but denied ever abusing other substances or any history of psychotic symptoms. Susan had never received psychotherapy, but was treated for several months after the birth of her daughter by a psychiatrist who prescribed antidepressant and anxiolytic medication. She reported finding the medication somewhat helpful.

Susan was a thin, buxom, attractive, heavily made-up woman with short brown hair who appeared her stated age. She was fashionably dressed in casual, form-fitted clothing. Her movements were normal and voluntary; her speech was slightly pressured. Her mood was depressed and anxious, with a somewhat shallow, mildly labile affect. She denied suicidal ideation or any thoughts of hurting herself. There was no evidence of a thought disorder or psychotic symptoms, and her sensorium was grossly clear.

Initial Phase

Susan signed informed consent to participate in our pilot study of IPT for BPD. She was evaluated for study entry by a highly trained independent evaluator using the DIPD-IV to diagnose BPD and the SCID to diagnosis Axis I disorders.

In the initial sessions (Sessions 1–4) of acute treatment, I [KLB] obtained Susan's psychiatric history, set the treatment framework, and began to build a therapeutic alliance. In the first session, I explained that IPT is a time-limited, diagnosis-targeted therapy that focuses on how recent life events affect mood, and how mood symptoms make it difficult to handle current life events, and especially interpersonal interactions. I explained that our sessions would focus not on the past but on her current relationships and difficulties, such as the problems in her marriage—a role dispute. I said that we would work together for sixteen weeks; at the end of that time, we would decide together whether it made sense for her to continue for another sixteen weeks. Based on her evaluation for study entry and my review of her symptoms, I determined that Susan met criteria for BPD. I gave her the diagnosis and the "sick role" (Weissman et al., 2007):

THERAPIST: You have an illness called borderline personality disorder, which is treatable and not your fault … From my perspective, borderline personality disorder means that you have trouble in handling relationships with other people and the strong feelings, such as anger and depression, that you feel in interacting with them.

I asked whether this made sense to her, and she agreed that it did. She reported that she had not heard of BPD until she was given the diagnosis in the ER and was glad to hear that it was treatable. As she also met criteria for major depression in partial remission, I provided psychoeducation about both syndromes and reviewed her specific symptoms. We discussed what BPD did and did not mean. I noted that over the years the term had acquired an unfairly "bad reputation," but that we could be hopeful about her improvement. By the end of the first session, Susan said she felt hopeful that she would feel better and be able to improve her situation with her husband. I was somewhat concerned that Susan was so positive; I wondered if she was experiencing but unable to express uncomfortable or negative feelings like many patients with BPD.

In taking a thorough psychiatric history, I conducted an interpersonal inventory, a careful review of Susan's past and current social functioning and social relationships. The goal of the interpersonal inventory is to help both the therapist and patient understand how the patient interacts with other people; to identify her social supports, if any; and to determine how recent relationships might have contributed to or have been affected by BPD symptoms. Patients with BPD report that their anger outbursts alienate people close to them and make it difficult to form relationships. They describe difficulty forming or maintaining relationships because they have difficulty trusting others. They may end relationships prematurely because they irrationally fear abandonment or feel unable to handle even a minor conflict. The interpersonal inventory provides a framework for understanding the social and interpersonal context in which the borderline features present and should lead to a treatment focus.

Susan reported having grown up in Florida and having spent little time either outside her hometown or apart from her family. She attended a local college and lived close to home. She had an older sister to whom she spoke a few times a year. Susan reported that her parents argued frequently when she was growing up and were never affectionate towards one another: "Sometimes it seemed as though they were leading separate lives." In recent years, her parents seemed to be getting along better. Until meeting her husband, she had felt very close to her parents and described her mother as her "best friend." Her parents initially disapproved of the marriage because of her brief engagement, her moving to the Northeast, and her husband's previous divorce. At the time she began the study, she and her parents we getting along, although still not as close as they had been in the past. She denied knowing of psychiatric illness in her family.

When asked about past physical or sexual abuse, she admitted that from about twelve to fourteen years of age, a close family friend who visited with his wife several times a year would look at her in ways that made her uncomfortable, make inappropriate comments about her body, groped her, and tried to kiss her when he was alone with her in her bedroom on a couple of occasions. When asked if she remembered how she felt when this man behaved inappropriately she said, "I guess I was scared and confused." She reported never having told her parents or sister about what this man did, and that she stopped seeing him when her parents' relationship with him ended abruptly after the man and his wife separated.

Susan reported that she had "no friends"; one woman whom she described as an acquaintance was the wife of a friend of her husband's. She partly attributed her lack of relationships to her difficulty trusting people. She explained that she feared opening up to people lest they use what she told them against her in the future. In addition, she often felt that she did not know what to say in social situations. When asked if she had befriended other mothers with young children in her neighborhood, she said she had not because she feared that they would not like her, and that she did not know what to say to them. (I remarked to myself that this deserved exploration in future IPT sessions.) She reported spending her time alone with her daughter or caring for both her daughter and twin step-daughters.

Although she had few relationships with female peers, she reported that since beginning high school, she was "always dating someone" who tended to be "very controlling." Susan reported a history of relationships with men that had extreme ups and downs. The man she dated prior to meeting her husband had been physically abusive towards her and abused alcohol. Despite this, she often feared that he would leave her.

Susan had met her husband two-and-a-half years before at a Florida resort where they were each attending conferences for work. At the time, she was living in Florida, he in New Jersey. Beginning a long-distance relationship, they married after five months. The patient quit her job of ten years as an insurance broker and moved from her small Florida town to an upper-middle-class New Jersey suburb to become a stay-at-home wife and mother.

Susan had "always wanted to have children" and became pregnant shortly after marrying. Her pregnancy and delivery were normal and uneventful. She reported that she became depressed and anxious shortly after her daughter's birth. Susan conceded that she had not expected that marrying her husband and becoming a stepmother would be so difficult. She had to take care of the twins three or four afternoons and nights each week and at least two weekends each month. The twins' mother lived nearby. Since her husband and the twins' mother worked full-time, Susan spent more time caring for the twins than did their father and mother. She felt annoyed at having to spend so much time caring for them while receiving no appreciation or recognition from her husband. She told me she wanted to spend more time alone with her daughter and with her husband, but was unsure if her feelings were appropriate. I told her: "It's *normal* for you to want that. You can trust your feelings about that. We can explore how you can spend more time without the twins."

Susan reported that Mark had grown "emotionally distant" since their daughter's birth. She explained that he was angry at her for her frequent anger outbursts in the past year. She described him as unsympathetic to her complaints about having to care for and spend so much time with his children—because, as he often reminded her, "You knew I had two children when you married me."

At the end of the initial phase of acute treatment (Session 4), I suggested that we choose one or at most two issues to focus on. As in IPT for major depression, IPT treatment for BPD usually focuses on one of four interpersonal problem areas: a role dispute, a role transition, grief, or (if none of the preceding is possible) interpersonal deficits. I connected Susan's symptoms of BPD as well as depression to her interpersonal situation in an IPT formulation (Markowitz & Swartz, 2007).

Inasmuch as Susan's chief complaint focused on problems in her marriage, my formulation underscored that she was in the midst of a role dispute—her conflict with her husband about spending time with his daughters. I presented the formulation to susan:

THERAPIST: It seems that the main difficulty you've been having is your conflict with your husband about spending time with his daughters. In IPT we call a marital conflict like yours a *role dispute*. You and he have very different ideas about how to handle a complicated family situation, and you've understandably been feeling ignored, hurt, and angry. There's a connection between what's happening in your life and what you're feeling. Role disputes can trigger symptoms of borderline personality disorder and, conversely, symptoms of borderline personality disorder can make it difficult to handle role disputes. Your disagreements with your husband about his daughters make you angry, and since borderline personality disorder makes managing angry feelings difficult, you are struggling to manage this already difficult conflict.

At times you may handle things ineffectively, which will create further conflict and make you feel worse. On the other hand, if we can help you to understand and use your feelings effectively, that should make both the situation better and your mood better. Does that make sense to you?

SUSAN: Yes.

THERAPIST: This is *not* your fault, and you can learn how to better manage this role dispute as well as the symptoms of borderline personality disorder. You are also in the midst of multiple *role transitions*—becoming a wife, a mother, and a stepmother, giving up your career, and moving from the South to the Northeast. Borderline personality disorder makes it difficult for you to manage such transitions as well. We should pick one, or at most two, problems to focus on in our work together. Perhaps we should focus on resolving your role dispute with your husband, since that seems to be bothering you the most; and, if we have time, we can address the transitions. Does this make sense to you?

This formulation made sense to Susan, who agreed that resolving the role dispute should be the focus of the treatment. We agreed that the role transitions would be a secondary focus, time permitting. This agreement on a focus led us into the second phase of treatment.

Acute Middle Phase

During the middle phase (Sessions 5–13), we worked on resolving Susan's interpersonal problem areas. I continued to provide contextual psychoeducation about BPD and to explore with her how BPD influenced social functioning, and I repeatedly linked her symptoms to her role dispute and multiple role transitions. I began each session by asking: "How have you been feeling since we last met?" This opening question elicits affect and brings forth an interval history of events between sessions, as in this example.

SUSAN: I'm nervous because the twins are staying over this weekend.
THERAPIST: Tell me more about that. What are you nervous about?
SUSAN: I just think it is too busy with all three kids, and my husband won't pay attention to me and my daughter. I wish it could just be the three of us sometimes.
THERAPIST: What's it like for you when you get nervous?
SUSAN: I get really irritable and I feel nervous—I can't relax.
THERAPIST: Have you told your husband how you feel, and that you would like to spend more time together without the twins?
SUSAN: I've tried, but he always gets mad.

At this point, I conducted a communication analysis, asking Susan to recount exactly what she said to her husband, how she said it, her husband's response, how that made her feel, and how she then responded. The analysis revealed that Susan became irritable, argumentative, and anxious before the twins were to stay over, or when her husband announced that the twins were coming over on a day when she wasn't expecting them. On occasion she would ask angrily, "Why do *we* always have to have them over?" In response, Mark would get angry and accuse her of not loving the twins, which would further enrage her.

I validated her feeling angry about the situation. I then reiterated that she had difficulty managing negative or uncomfortable emotions, explaining that people with BPD tend to feel overwhelmed by such feelings. I noted that her wish to have a break from the twins was appropriate—normalizing her anger and resentment. The goal was to express the anger effectively. It was not her fault that she was prone to angry outbursts, but she could learn to communicate her anger in a more moderate and effective way. I suggested that we explore ways to communicate her feelings so that her husband might better understand her needs. "What other options do you have?"

We role-played her telling her husband that she does care about the twins, but that she also enjoys having time with her husband and daughter. Further, the time without the twins is less hectic, and she would appreciate having a break, as she takes care of all three children several days each week. Role-play allowed Susan to rehearse both the content and the tone of her communication. She was then able to express this to Mark calmly, and he was somewhat more receptive. The sense that she had some control over her environment and her emotions, and had succeeded in a new approach, in turn improved Susan's mood.

We explored her options:

THERAPIST: How could you plan more for more time alone with your daughter and husband?

SUSAN: I guess I could suggest that my husband's parents take care of the twins one afternoon. They could sleep over at his parents' house.

THERAPIST: That's a great idea! What would it be like for you to suggest this?

SUSAN: I think I could do that.

THERAPIST: What could you say to him?

SUSAN: I would say: "Would it be okay if the twins stayed with your parents one night, so we can have a night alone with our daughter?"

THERAPIST: How do you think your husband might respond?

SUSAN: I think he might be okay with it.

THERAPIST: You sound hesitant. Are you concerned that he might not be okay with your asking?

SUSAN: He may accuse me of not wanting to be with his children, like he always does.

THERAPIST: What could you say if your husband does that?

SUSAN: I guess I could tell him that I do want to be with them, but that sometimes I would like a little time alone with him and our daughter. I think it is important for our daughter that she has time just with us.

THERAPIST: How do you think he might respond?

With a little more confidence, Susan said: "That might work." We then discussed contingencies: how she could react to different responses her husband might have at this point.

Susan often perceived her husband to be abandoning her. I noted that this tendency was a symptom of BPD, but wondered if her husband was, in fact, neglecting her at times. She found herself feeling very angry and abandoned when her husband was around the twins. She reported that on the weekends that the twins stayed with them, he "ignored" her and her daughter, and chose activities that only the twins would enjoy. When asked how she managed these angry feelings, she reported that she would become depressed, withdraw, and snap at him. She admitted also to a strong desire to cut herself, but felt unable to do so because her daughter was around. I asked why she wanted to hurt *herself* when she really felt angry at her husband. I connected this to BPD, a reflection of her difficulty managing anger that was valid and normal, but difficult for her to tolerate. I validated her wanting to spend her weekends doing activities that she enjoyed. Susan was able to acknowledge that her husband was not, in fact, abandoning her, but was not considering her needs as much as she would like.

We explored ways of handling this situation better. For example, she could initiate activities that she liked. I encouraged *her* to explore options, rather than providing them to her. We explored options for activities that she wanted to do and role-played suggesting these activities to her husband. Susan feared that if she suggested alternative activities, he would reject her ideas. I acknowledged the risk of rejection. Susan then decided it was unlikely that her husband would reject her suggestions and ultimately took the risk of suggesting family activities. Her husband was agreeable, which made her feel good. After this positive experience, Susan continued to suggest family activities.

Despite her attending sessions, better managing her anger reactions, and communicating more effectively, Susan reported that Mark remained emotionally distant. Susan felt that he did not recognize the efforts she was making to improve her symptoms and their relationship. We role-played asking her husband to be more supportive. She told him that she appreciated that he had endured a lot when she was having frequent temper outbursts, but that it would be helpful if he could acknowledge the progress she was making and support her efforts to better manage her anger. She also explained BPD to him and spontaneously gave him the book *Stop Walking on Eggshells: Taking Your Life Back When Someone You Care About Has Borderline Personality Disorder*, which she had discovered in a bookstore. Her husband conceded that he had been holding a grudge and not making the efforts he should have to improve their relationship.

End of Acute Phase

At the beginning of the acute termination phase (Sessions 14–18), I began discussing with Susan whether we should continue working together for an additional sixteen weeks. I felt that further treatment was warranted. Susan was compliant with treatment and her symptoms were improving; she felt less depressed, better able to control her anger and to enjoy things, and experienced fewer, less intense urges to cut herself. Her score on the Beck Depression Inventory (BDI), which had been as high as 16 at the beginning of the acute phase and consistent with depression of mild/moderate severity, fell to 10, indicating mild depression. Her Hamilton Depression Rating Scale (Ham-D) score, which had been 6 at baseline, rose to 10. The slight increase in Susan's score on the Ham-D seemed more likely due to an increase in awareness of her symptoms than to a meaningful worsening of her depressive symptoms. Regardless, a score of 10 on the Ham-D falls in mild depression range. Her score on the Clinical Global Impressions Scale (CGI) fell from 4 to 2, indicating significant improvement.

Susan had generally attended sessions promptly and seemed engaged, but I remained concerned that she had never shown any signs of anger in the treatment. Unfortunately, conflicts with her husband continued despite her efforts to improve their relationship. I congratulated her on her progress and proposed that we continue for the additional sixteen weeks on improving her marriage, symptoms, and mood. At this point, I was concerned that Mark's behavior was contributing significantly to their conflicts and planned to discuss this with Susan as it became further evident.

Continuation Phase

Sessions continued to focus on resolving the interpersonal problem areas, as disputes between Susan and her husband continued. For example, Susan reported that her husband sometimes would not call when he was going to be late coming home from work, and was unreachable by cell phone.

She arrived one day tearful and anxious and reported having an argument with her husband the night before about his not calling.

THERAPIST: How did it make you feel when he didn't call?
SUSAN: It made me mad. I don't think he is cheating on me or anything, but I feel like he doesn't care about me. I don't know whether to make dinner for him or if I should wait to eat with him.

I asked her what she did when she realized that he was late. She explained that she tried his cell phone but he did not answer. I agreed that it was understandable that she was upset by his not calling, and asked her how she handled the situation.

SUSAN: I ignored him when he got home because the kids were there. After we put the kids to bed, I yelled at him. He told me that he was with clients so he couldn't call and that I was acting crazy.
THERAPIST: How did you feel when he said that?
SUSAN: I don't know . . . frustrated . . . I still feel like he should call.
THERAPIST [validating her frustration]: Your husband equates your anger with "acting crazy," but maybe it's reasonable to be angry when he leaves you not knowing where he is. Particularly when you've made it clear to him that you're sensitive to feeling abandoned.

I asked her if there was something Mark could have said that might have made her feel better.

SUSAN [after thinking for a while]: He could have apologized and said that next time he would call when he knew he was going to be late.
THERAPIST: That sounds reasonable. What would it be like for you to ask him to call you when he knows he is going to be late?

Susan responded that she could try to ask him.

I validated and normalized Susan's feelings and reactions to her husband—it was appropriate for her to feel angry. Her role dispute was influenced by how she handled her feelings, but her husband also played a role. In fact, it became increasingly evident to Susan and to me that the conflicts in her marriage might reflect her husband's behavior as much as or more than her own. I explained to Susan that individuals with BPD tend to get into relationships that have extreme ups and downs and that both partners may contribute to the conflicts. I stated further that this is not her fault, and that she could try to get her husband to behave better. We explored the option of their seeing a marital therapist when she completed the study, as it seemed that her work in individual treatment was not improving her marriage as much as she had hoped—even though she was doing her part. The shift of marital responsibility to include her husband came as an insight and relief for Susan.

In addition to working on her role dispute, we addressed her role transitions. Having moved to the Northeast and become a full-time mother, Susan had become socially isolated. I noted how difficult transitions could be, and that they influenced her mood. I emphasized that social supports help to buffer the impact of such changes. In Florida, Susan was used to seeing her family weekly and her work colleagues daily. I helped Susan mourn the loss of those relationships and to explore options for forming new ones. Susan started calling her mother more and began for the first time to tell her about her problems with her husband. She also made plans to visit her mother in Florida. We explored opportunities for meeting other mothers and role-played initiating conversations with them in the local playground. Susan began having play dates with other mothers and their children.

By the end of the continuation phase, Susan was able to better control her anger, express her thoughts and feelings, and handle conflicts. Her behavior had become less impulsive. She admitted that at times she still felt "sort of abandoned" when her husband spent time with one of the twins, but quickly was able to realize that she was not being abandoned. While she and her husband were relating somewhat better, she reported feeling unhappy in her marriage and recognized that the ongoing conflicts in her marriage were not entirely her fault. Despite Susan's efforts to communicate her feelings and to ask for help with the children in more appropriate ways, she reported that Mark continued to invalidate her feelings and to refuse to compromise.

Susan recognized that her anger towards her husband was valid and that her feelings about the many transitions she had made were justified. Moreover, she felt increasingly suspicious that Mark might be having an affair, as he reported needing to stay late at work more frequently and was often cold towards her. She felt good about her ability to better manage and express her anger and realized that her husband needed to make more of an effort to be supportive and considerate and to make compromises. She was usually able to express her thoughts and feelings clearly, directly, and firmly, without screaming. Susan felt less alone because she was speaking more with her parents more and with other women.

Termination

I began preparing Susan for termination early in the continuation phase by reminding her how many weeks and sessions we had remaining. I initiated more explicit discussions about termination toward the middle of the continuation phase. I asked her how she was feeling about ending treatment. Susan admitted feeling anxious about losing the weekly support of our sessions but was reluctant to consider further treatment with another therapist.

At the beginning of the acute phase I had explained that we would be working together for up to 32 weeks and that the study policy was that therapists did not continue working with patients beyond the end of the study. As we moved closer to termination, I let her know that I was sad that we could not continue, as I very much enjoyed working with her, but that I felt confident she could maintain the gains she had made during our work together. I hoped in sharing my sadness about terminating that I would be modeling an appropriate expression of sadness, and that she might feel less abandoned. I hoped that expressing my confidence in her ability to maintain her progress would serve to reinforce her independence. I noted that *she* had worked very hard in our sessions and that the changes she experienced were due to *her* efforts. In fact, by the end of treatment she expressed curiosity about how she would fare on her own, and knew that if she ran into difficulty she could pursue treatment elsewhere. She denied feeling abandoned by me.

When I inquired about her feelings about the treatment, Susan said that she found it helpful to think of BPD as an illness. She stated that it felt good to better understand what she was experiencing, that it was not her fault, and that she had not had control over her symptoms. She reported that although role-playing felt awkward at first, it was very helpful in preparing her for conversations with her husband.

At termination, Susan no longer met criteria for BPD, and her depressive symptoms had remitted. Her score on the BDI was 7 and her Ham-D score was 1, both scores reflecting euthymia. Her CGI score was 2 (much improved). She felt less self-critical and better able to enjoy things. Given the persisting problems in her marriage, Susan understandably continued feeling sad and frustrated about her situation, but these feelings did not interfere with her functioning.

DISCUSSION

Susan differed from other patients with BPD in this study in several ways. She denied ever feeling any anger towards the therapist or the study personnel. She denied any negative feelings about the constraints of the study or having to complete the periodic assessments. In fact, she repeatedly expressed feeling grateful for the treatment she was receiving. I doubted that, in fact, she had no negative feelings towards me or the staff, and wondered whether she was suppressing or lying about having negative feelings. It was hard to believe that she had no feelings of abandonment or criticisms about the treatment. At the same time, this may illustrate how starved for connection Susan was: it may have been a relief to have someone to talk to. Prior to our sessions she did not speak to anyone about what she was experiencing. Possibly the positive connection with me encouraged her to seek support from others. For the most part, Susan was very cooperative. She showed up for every scheduled appointment, but on several occasions during the acute phase of the study, she did not answer her phone when we had planned a telephone check-in. She had difficulty explaining why she hadn't answered the telephone, but reported that she tended not to answer when she felt down or overwhelmed. I repeatedly emphasized that these depressed moments were ideal times for us to check in by phone, and that perhaps she would feel better if we spoke. I wondered if she did not want to talk to me but felt unable to tell me. Eventually, she did answer her phone when we were scheduled to speak.

Unlike Susan, many patients with BPD will idealize their therapist at one moment and then devalue and even become rageful towards the therapist in the next. The IPT therapist does not focus on the therapeutic relationship to help the patient learn to tolerate and integrate mixed feelings. The therapist validates the patient's anger if appropriate and may even apologize for upsetting him or her, but then refocuses the patient on other significant relationships and explores the positive and negative feelings the patient has about the people in his or her life (Markowitz et al., 2006, 2007). Another patient in our pilot study often became enraged at the therapist, seemingly out of the blue and without provocation. She would arrive at the session, appear sullenly angry, not speak to the therapist and ignore the therapist's questions. After about fifteen minutes, the patient would curse at the therapist and storm out of the office. The therapist would call her and invite her to return, explaining that she would like to talk to the patient about what she was feeling. Once she returned to the office for the next session, the patient revealed that she had been angry about a conflict she had had with someone else just before the session, and was angry that the therapist didn't care and couldn't do anything about to help her.

THERAPIST: I am really glad you told me that. I am sorry if I did something that made you feel I don't care about you. I do care and I would like to help. Difficulty dealing with conflicts with others like the one you described with your friend is exactly what brought you here and just what we should be working on. You can learn to handle relationships better and feel better. Let's talk about what happened with your friend.

After a few more similar outbursts in the office, the patient was able to laugh at herself and joke with the therapist that she was tough for sticking by her. Eventually the patient was able to stay in the office and express what she was feeling more directly and less explosively.

Susan acknowledged having the urge to cut, but did not. Nonetheless, she did admit to engaging in self-destructive tendencies such as excessive dieting and spending sprees. As she learned to pay closer attention to her feelings in the course of therapy, she recognized both that interpersonal encounters triggered dieting and that her mood worsened when she ate too little food; she then reported making an effort to eat better. In fact, she had regained a healthier weight by the end of treatment. More broadly, I tried to help her see that her impulses to cut, spend, and diet came in response to interpersonal disappointments or frustrations, a connection she became increasingly able to make on her own.

Unlike Susan, most patients in the study have been single. Nevertheless, Susan's relationship history, her history of sexual assault, her exposure to her parents' marital discord, her impulsive decision to marry and uproot her life, and her choice of partner were typical of patients with BPD.

More work could have been done to help Susan form new, healthier relationships. Given that patients with BPD often engage in unstable relationships with troubled individuals, it may be difficult for the therapist to identify any "healthy" social supports. Indeed, Susan had no close female friends to lean on when she was having difficulties in her marriage. Fortunately, IPT teaches social skills and helps people form new relationships. However, helping patients with BPD form new relationships can be particularly challenging.

Patients with BPD have difficulty trusting others and intense fears of abandonment. The IPT therapist explores these issues with the patient, elicits related feelings, and labels these uncomfortable and excessive feelings as symptoms of BPD—symptoms that are treatable and that can be managed with increased awareness.

I have worked with several patients with BPD who reported fearing being judged and rejected by others because of their histories of unhealthy relationships and self-destructive behaviors. Not all have been as comfortable with the label as Susan, but it generally provides an explanation for confusing symptoms and a target for treatment. While they may feel proud of the improvement of their BPD symptoms and functioning in relationships, they see themselves as damaged as a result of having BPD and assume that others will perceive them as damaged also. They fear that others will not understand BPD and why they were unable to manage their symptoms sooner. They may choose friends whom they perceive to be similarly damaged or have difficulties trusting others because they imagine that such friends or partners may be "safer."

Sticking with the medical model, I identify shame about their past behaviors and negative self-concept as characteristic of patients with BPD and a challenge for the patient's transition to getting well and forming healthier relationships. I help patients identify their strengths and positive traits and accomplishments, despite suffering from a debilitating illness. I point out that while the painful past experiences related to the illness have been a significant part of their life to date, they are only *part* of their history and identity. The patient is not the illness. I remind patients that the past negative experiences are related to BPD, an illness that is not their fault, but that they are fully responsible for working hard in therapy to overcome their illness. I invite patients to role-play speaking about their past to potential healthy partners in ways that feel safe, and ideally empowering for the patient. I acknowledge that it can feel uncomfortable and risky—for anyone—to share past painful experiences, but that they may be pleasantly surprised by how people respond.

IPT is a practical, relationship-focused treatment. Susan's symptomatic improvement presumably reflected her gains in social functioning and resolution of problem areas (Markowitz, Bleiberg, Christos, & Levitan, 2006). By the end of treatment she had made progress in partially resolving her marital role dispute, and appropriately recognized her husband's role in their persisting difficulties. She could comfort herself that she had been doing her best to improve matters, with some success. She felt good about her role as a mother to her biological daughter and also about her capacity to care for three young children at the same time. She also had made considerable progress in resolving her role transitions. Just as importantly, she had learned to make the connection between painful affects such as sadness and anger and their interpersonal context, and to use such feelings to understand and respond to life, where she had previously felt overwhelmed by them and out of control.

ACKNOWLEDGMENT

Funded in part by an Independent Investigator Award to Dr. Markowitz from the National Alliance for Research on Schizophrenia and Depression (NARSAD) and by grant MH079078 from the National Institute of Mental Health.

Treating Major Depression in Diverse Populations

12

Treatment of Adolescent Depression with Interpersonal Psychotherapy

LAURA MUFSON, LAURIE REIDER LEWIS, MEREDITH
GUNLICKS-STOESSEL, AND JAMI F. YOUNG

We adapted IPT for depressed adolescents (IPT-A) hoping to build upon the research demonstrating its efficacy with depressed adults. The interpersonal model seemed appropriate for adolescents given their focus on interpersonal relationships and the significant developmental changes that occur in these relationships, such as separation and individuation from parents and increased focus on peer and romantic relationships. IPT-A strategies help adolescents to bolster self-confidence and make steps toward increasing independence while helping them to understand how they still depend on others and how they can negotiate their relationships more successfully (Mufson, Dorta, Moreau & Weissman, 2004).

The use of IPT-A is supported by research on the qualities of relationships and types of stressors common in adolescence. Common interpersonal stressors associated with depression in adolescents include problems with peers (Brunstein-Klomek, Marrocco, Kleinman, et al., 2007) and conflictual and unsupportive relationships with parents (Sheeber et al., 2007). Depressed adolescents display more negative affect in interactions with parents than healthy adolescents (Sanders, Dadds, Johnston, & Cash, 1992; Sheeber, Allen, Davis, & Sorensen, 2000). The negative affect in turn interferes with adolescents' ability to communicate or solve problems effectively, increasing their risk for more interpersonal difficulties and subsequent depression (Gotlib & Hammen, 1992). As IPT-A targets these communication and problem-solving impairments in both family and peer relationships, we believed this treatment would benefit depressed adolescents.

IPT-A is designed for adolescents with mild to moderate depressive severity who meet criteria for a DSM-IV depression diagnosis and can be treated as outpatients. Adolescents suffering from comorbidities including anxiety disorders, attention-deficit/hyperactivity disorder, and oppositional defiant disorder have been successfully treated with IPT-A, although IPT-A is most effective when depression is the primary diagnosis and comorbidity is limited. IPT-A is not indicated for adolescents whose IQ lies in the mentally retarded range, are actively suicidal, homicidal, or abusing substances, or suffer from psychotic symptoms or bipolar disorder.

ADAPTATIONS MADE FOR THE ADOLESCENT MODEL

Several specific adaptations make the treatment more relevant for adolescents. IPT-A is typically delivered once weekly for twelve sessions, rather than the sixteen sessions often used with adults, because adolescents find shorter treatment duration appealing. If needed, treatment can be extended to sixteen sessions, but generally not beyond that point to maintain its time-limited structure. When deemed beneficial, the adolescent may taper to biweekly continuation therapy sessions to help prevent relapse and to address a specific issue, such as switching schools. The adolescent model of IPT relies on the same four interpersonal problem areas as the adult model. Within these four problem areas, however, IPT-A has been adapted to address the specific interpersonal issues relevant to adolescence, such as coping with parental separation or divorce; developing greater independence from parents; negotiating peer relationships, peer pressure, or teasing; and developing romantic relationships.

IPT-A also involves parents in treatment. Therapists invite parents to participate in each phase of treatment to educate them about the therapeutic process, to support the adolescent's treatment, and, when appropriate, to work directly on the interpersonal problem area in dyadic sessions with the adolescent.

The adolescent model revises the "sick role" as a "limited sick role." Similar to the adult model, the therapist explains that like someone with a medical illness, adolescents who have depression may not be able to do as many things or do things as well as before the depression developed. However, in contrast to adult IPT, which may recommend that patients reduce their involvement in activities until they begin to feel better (such as reduce work responsibilities or get help in the home), IPT-A discourages adolescents from cutting back activities. The reason for this limited sick role is the developmental importance for adolescents to be in school and resume schoolwork as soon as possible. The IPT-A therapist encourages the adolescent to push himself or herself to do normal activities like school, homework, and house chores as much as possible and not to give in to the feeling that he or she can't do them. This more limited sick role emphasizes doing the activity but revising expectations, recognizing that the outcome or performance may fall below the pre-depression level. The therapist tells the adolescent that it will get easier and the outcomes will improve as the depression lessens. Most importantly, the therapist explains the limited sick role to the parents, because they often blame the adolescent for lowered performance and may view it as laziness or oppositionality. Parents learn that the lack of motivation and fatigue are symptoms of depression, and to blame the illness, not their child. They are told to encourage the adolescent's activities supportively and to refrain from criticizing the quality of the performance.

Treatment techniques are modified to be developmentally appropriate. While adults may be able to describe their feelings in an open-ended way, in IPT-A adolescents rate their mood on a weekly basis using a 1-to-10 scale. This more concrete method makes it easier for adolescents to track changes in their mood. In our

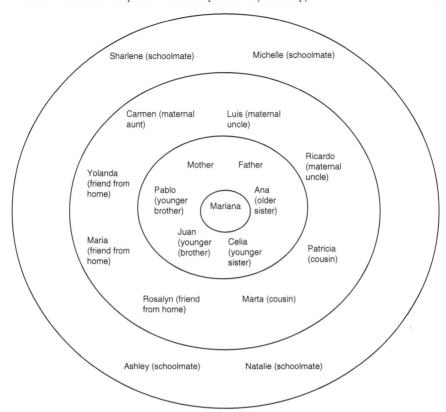

Figure 12.1 Mariana's Closeness Circle (the names have been changed to maintain confidentiality)

experience, adolescents tend to present their emotions in one of two ways. Some adolescents feel their emotions intensely and can easily express them, but have little awareness of how events relate to their feelings. Others can easily describe events in their lives, but do so without any mention of emotion. The therapist works with the adolescent to help find the missing link to either the feelings or the event.

During the interpersonal inventory, the therapist uses a visual aid, a "closeness circle," to help identify the important people in the adolescent's life. The adolescent writes his or her name in the innermost of a series of concentric circles and places names of the people in his or her life in the surrounding circles according to the closeness of each relationship (Fig. 12.1). This may help the adolescent begin to visualize differences in feelings and experiences of the people in his or her life. It also helps the therapist quickly assess the paucity of and/or difficulties in significant relationships.

IPT-A includes increased teaching of basic social and communication skills and greater focus on perspective-taking and problem-solving skills to help adolescents better negotiate disputes with others. Common communication techniques therapists use include:

1. Selecting an optimal time to initiate a conversation
2. Communicating feelings and opinions directly ("I" statements)

3. Attempting to see the problem from the other person's perspective and to begin a conversation with an empathic statement ("give to get") such as, "Mom, I know that you have been working extra hours lately and I know that it's been hard, but I was hoping that I might be able to go out Saturday night instead of babysitting for you. . ."
4. Being specific when discussing a problem and focusing on the problem at hand (avoiding "you always" or "you never")
5. Generating possible solutions prior to the conversation and being willing to compromise

To facilitate the acquisition of these communication skills and to help adolescents remember to use them outside of therapy sessions, a "Teen Tips" handout lists the communication skills and gives examples of how to use them (Appendix 1). The therapist selects and introduces each technique as it becomes relevant for the particular interpersonal interaction the therapist and adolescent are discussing. Lastly, IPT-A offers specific strategies for dealing with other depression-related problems that can affect adolescents' ability to engage in and use the treatment, such as academic difficulties, school refusal, and involvement of child protective services.

OVERVIEW OF EMPIRICAL EVIDENCE

Three clinical trials demonstrate the efficacy and effectiveness of IPT for depressed adolescents (Mufson, Dorta, Wickramratne, et al., 2004; Mufson, Weissman, Moreau, & Garfinkel, 1999; Rossello & Bernal, 1999). The initial efficacy study (Mufson et al., 1999) indicated an average effect size of 0.54; 75% of depressed adolescents receiving IPT-A compared to 46% in the control group (clinical management) recovered, with a score of 6 or less on the 24-item Hamilton Rating Scale for Depression (Ham-D) at week twelve. The effectiveness study conducted in the school-based health clinics (Mufson et al., 2004) indicated an average effect size of 0.50 for IPT-A compared to usual care (TAU). Adolescents in the IPT-A condition reported significantly greater decreases in depressive symptoms than those in TAU at week twelve. Fifty percent of adolescents in IPT-A and 34% in TAU met the Ham-D recovery criteria of 6 or less. Differences on depression indicators between the two groups emerged at week eight of treatment. Patients in IPT-A experienced significantly greater overall improvement in functioning as measured by the Children's Global Assessment Scale and the Social Adjustment Scale-Self-report (SAS-SR) than those in TAU. The IPT-A results show a moderate to large effect size for decreasing depression symptoms and improving global and social functioning compared to control groups that include clinical monitoring, waitlist, and TAU (Mufson et al., 1999, 2004; Rossello & Bernal, 1999).

The APA Task Force distinguished between IPT-A as a theoretical orientation and as a specific manualized approach (Mufson, Dorta, Moreau & Weissman, 2004). Rossello and Bernal (1999) adapted their own manual for Puerto Rican adolescents from the adult IPT manual. Although not the manual used by the Mufson team, it still followed the general IPT strategies and techniques. Consequently, the IPT-A manualized protocol used in the Mufson studies meets criteria for a probably efficacious intervention by the APA Task Force guidelines, as all IPT-A studies were conducted by one research group, the treatment developer. As a theoretical orientation, IPT-A meets criteria for a well-established treatment for adolescent depression according to the APA Task Force guidelines (David-Ferdon & Kaslow, 2009). Most importantly, IPT-A is one of few empirically supported psychotherapies to have been transported to and implemented in community settings with demonstrated effectiveness when delivered by community therapists.

CASE EXAMPLE

Reason for Referral and Chief Complaint

Mariana, a thirteen-year-old monolingual Spanish-speaking girl of Central American descent, presented for an outpatient psychiatric evaluation at a local children's hospital accompanied by her biological mother. Mariana's mother stated she was seeking treatment for Mariana's increasingly disruptive and oppositional behavior at home. She reported that Mariana was frequently argumentative and disrespectful towards her, and often targeted her five-year-old brother Juan through hurtful remarks and aggressive behaviors.

Mariana spoke in a low mumble, her affect constricted and sad as she described her symptoms. She corroborated her mother's report of externalizing symptoms. In addition, Mariana endorsed depressive symptoms: irritable and sad mood, anhedonia, social withdrawal, attention and concentration difficulties, trouble falling asleep, and variable appetite resulting in moderate fluctuations in weight. She reported recent suicidal ideation, a passive wish to die in order to escape current difficulties, although she denied current and active ideation, intent, and plan. She had begun self-injurious behaviors, scratching her arm about twice a week with paper clips. No scars were visible. Mariana explained that the scratches never drew blood, nor did she injure herself with intent to die. She reported scratching herself following conflicts with family members, particularly her mother. Mariana completed the self-report version of the Columbia Diagnostic Interview Scale for Children [DISC] Depression Scale (CDS) (Shaffer & Fisher, 2000). This 22-item questionnaire assesses depressive symptoms per DSM-IV criteria in adolescents ages eleven and over. Scores range from 0 to 22. Scores higher than 12 indicate that a diagnosis of depression is likely. One out of fifty teens scores 16 and above, which indicates a depression diagnosis is highly likely. Mariana scored 18.

Additional symptom review revealed no comorbid psychiatric, substance, or medical disorders, nor evidence of manic or hypomanic episodes. Mariana described feeling "nervous" much of the time; however, further diagnostic interviewing clarified this as a restless irritability more typical of an adolescent unipolar depression than of an anxiety disorder.

History of Presenting Problem and Psychosocial History

Mariana and her mother observed that her behavioral and depressive symptoms had developed over the past seven or eight months, about four months after Mariana arrived in the United States from a small, impoverished town in her home country. Mariana was the second of five children born to her biological parents.

Mariana's mother reported having immigrated to the United States illegally five years ago, along with Mariana's older sister, seeking a better quality of life. Unable to afford bringing all of her children at once, she left Mariana, then eight, and her younger sister in the care of close family friends. After three years with this family, Mariana and her sister moved in with their maternal aunt. Mariana then reportedly began skipping school and grew increasingly irritable, belligerent, oppositional, and non-compliant with adult requests.

Mariana's mother reported that Mariana's father struggled with substance abuse, and when intoxicated he often verbally abused her and, on occasion, the children. The mother's immigration to the United States was partly an attempt to escape Mariana's father and remove the children from his care. Mariana's father remained in the home country for about one year, during which time he had no contact with Mariana or her sister. About a year later, he followed Mariana's mother to the United States. Although they reside separately, Mariana's parents have maintained intermittent contact. Prior to reaching the United States, Mariana did not know the details of her parents' continued relationship, nor that her parents had two more biological children together while Mariana and her parents were separated.

Approximately one year ago, Mariana's mother arranged for Mariana's immigration to the United States but could not afford to send for Mariana's sister as well. Mariana now resides with her biological mother, older biological sister, and two younger biological brothers in a one-room apartment that offers limited space and privacy. Mariana's mother earns some money working as a cleaning woman. Her father, through odd jobs in supermarkets and restaurants, provides financial support when possible, but the family's financial resources are limited.

The therapist obtained input from personnel at the middle school where Mariana was enrolled as an eighth-grade bilingual, regular education student. Teachers described her as well-behaved, motivated, and focused in the classroom, receiving average grades of B's and C's. Mariana described having had a rich social and extra-curricular life in her home country. She particularly enjoyed playing team sports such as basketball. While she currently reported having friends, she had become increasingly isolated and anhedonic over the past seven or eight months, preferring to come home immediately after school to watch television rather than socializing or participating in after-school activities. Based on the intake, the evaluating therapist assigned Mariana a Children's Global Assessment Score (C-GAS) (Shaffer, Gould, Brasic, et al., 1983) of 55. The scale ranges from 1 to 100, with 100 representing the optimal level of mental health and adaptive functioning, and scores below 61 signifying significant impairment resulting from a psychiatric disorder (Bird, Canino, Rubio-Stipec & Ribera, 1987).

Diagnosis and Treatment Planning

The therapist informed Mariana and her mother that Mariana met DSM-IV criteria for a major depressive disorder and presented evidence-based treatment options of IPT-A, cognitive-behavioral therapy, and pharmacotherapy. Mariana's mother expressed reluctance to proceed with psychotropic medication but said she would reconsider if Mariana's symptoms did not improve. The therapist recommended IPT-A due to the interpersonal aspects of Mariana's depression. Because of Mariana's history of passive suicidal ideation and self-injurious behavior, the evaluating thera-pist, Mariana's mother, and Mariana collaborated on a safety plan that included giving the family the hospital's emergency phone number in case symptoms wors-ened, clearing the home of potential threats to Mariana's safety such as pills or razors, and agreeing that Mariana would tell her mother if she began to feel worse.

Initial Phase

The first goal for Session 1 was to reevaluate Mariana's symptoms and confirm the diagnosis of a depressive disorder to establish her appropriateness for IPT-A treat-ment. Mariana continued to endorse the same symptoms of depression as at intake, including passive suicidal ideation. She denied active suicidal ideation, plan, and intent. She added that she now felt sleepy throughout the day. The therapist intro-duced Mariana to the mood rating by asking her to rate her average mood during the past week on a scale of 1 to 10, with 10 representing the most negative and 1 the most positive. Mariana endorsed an average mood rating of 7/10. The therapist also asked her to provide mood ratings for the times during the week when she had felt the worst and when she felt the best, and to describe the events associated with her moods. She reported an 8/10 in response to negative interactions with her mother and brother, and a 4/10 following a positive outing with her sister. The therapist explained that they would review Mariana's depression symptoms and mood rating at the start of each session to understand how positive and negative changes in her mood related to interpersonal events and to track her progress in therapy.

A second goal of the session was to provide psychoeducation to Mariana and her mother about depression and its impact on psychosocial and behavioral functioning. The therapist introduced them to the idea of the limited sick role, which conceptual-ized Mariana's depressive illness as akin to a medical illness: "Just as a medical illness or physical impairment can result in limited functioning and the need to make adjustments, so can depression." The therapist explained that Mariana should be encouraged to do as many of her normal activities as possible, including schoolwork and household chores. However, she might not do them as well as prior to her depres-sion. The family was told that as Mariana's symptoms improved, she would begin to perform better, emphasizing the time-limited nature of the situation.

At first, Mariana's mother was reluctant to consider that Mariana might not be capable of meeting expectations in completing household chores due to her depres-sion. She became more amenable once it was clarified that the goal of treatment, and an essential ingredient in recovery, was reengagement in daily activities, and that this was a treatable aspect of the depression illness. Since parents of depressed children are often depressed themselves, the therapist reviewed the mother's symptoms to determine whether she needed adjunctive treatment to be able to support Mariana's recovery. Mariana's mother did not meet current criteria for a depressive disorder. However, during the discussion, the mother did recall past experiences of depression and its concomitant difficulties. This enabled her to empathize more with Mariana's condition.

The third goal of the session was to describe the IPT-A approach to treating depression, focusing on understanding the link between depressive symptoms and current difficulties in significant relationships. The therapist indicated they would together identify the interpersonal difficulties most closely related to Mariana's depression and then identify and practice skills to improve her relationships and ultimately improve her mood. By the end of the session, Mariana's affect was brighter, and she expressed relief in feeling understood and supported by the therapist: "So, I'm not crazy." Still, she expressed skepticism that things could actually change at home. Mariana's generally positive response to the initial session and treatment plan outline made the therapist hopeful about her capacity to engage in and benefit from treatment. Mariana's mother's level of engagement with the treatment plan was also heartening.

Session 2 began as did most sessions, with the therapist asking: "How have things been since we last met?" This question gives the therapist a snapshot of problems from the past week and gives the adolescent a chance to talk about what is on her mind so that she can then focus on depression-related events. Mariana reported no overall change in depressive symptoms since the previous session, and rated her average mood for the week 7/10. She observed that her mood declines mostly related to disagreements with her mother about household chores and caretaking responsibilities for her younger siblings.

Mariana and the therapist initiated the interpersonal inventory by completing the closeness circle (see Fig. 12.1). The therapist explained that because Mariana's closeness circle included so many people, they would not be able to discuss each relationship but would focus on those Mariana considered most important and most related to her mood in either positive or negative ways. She gave Mariana the choice to select whom she wanted to discuss first. For each relationship, the therapist asked about the frequency and content of Mariana's interactions with the person, the relationship's terms and expectations, positive and negative aspects, how the relationship had changed since Mariana became depressed, and changes Mariana would like to make in the relationship.

Mariana chose to discuss her relationship with her mother first, as it affected her the most. She described her sense of loss when her mother emigrated, and her feelings of longing for their reunification. She recounted frustration, disappointment, and betrayal upon seeing her mother again after their years of separation, only to learn about her mother's other children and ongoing relationship with Mariana's father. Although Mariana had attempted to express her feelings to her mother, she felt that her mother did not listen to her and was routinely distracted by the demands of her other children and by household responsibilities. She reported feeling easily angered and irritated by her mother's requests, which mostly concerned the need to complete household chores.

Discussing her brother, Juan, she described resenting having to help take care of him and her other younger brother when she essentially felt uncared for herself. These feelings were now exacerbated by Mariana's mother's recent medical complications from a gallstone. She hesitantly, albeit honestly, admitted to behaving aggressively on occasion towards Juan but denied an active intent to harm him. Nonetheless, she was reluctant to assume responsibility for these behaviors, instead blaming her brother for being bothersome. When discussing the sister who remained in her home country, Mariana said she attempted to maintain regular contact, but cost and her sister's irregular access to telephones and computers made communication challenging. Mariana reported struggling with guilt over having left her behind.

At the end of the session, the therapist talked with Mariana's mother about her medical status and resultant greater need to rely on Mariana for household and care-taking responsibilities. The therapist validated the mother's situation, but questioned whether Mariana could meet these expectations given her depression and need to focus on her own well-being, and whether other children could also help out. They generated strategies to adjust these expectations and make alternate child care and household chore arrangements for consideration, and devised an alternate plan. Mariana was given an opportunity to select three chores (making her bed every morning, folding and putting away her clothes, and washing and putting away her own dishes after meals) that seemed to be reasonable expectations for an adolescent. Mariana's mother recruited her sister to equitably share a greater portion of the child care responsibility to the extent the sister's own busy work schedule permitted, but Mariana found even this limited assistance was an improvement.

During Sessions 3 and 4, Mariana continued to experience depressive symptoms, including sadness, depressed mood, increased tearfulness, irritability, disturbed appetite and sleep, feelings of guilt, gastrointestinal discomfort, attention and con-centration difficulties, loneliness, "boredom," "laziness," "loneliness," and feeling hopeless regarding her family's poverty and unstable immigrant status. She denied suicidal ideation and self-injurious behaviors. Mariana's moods at the start of Sessions 3 and 4 were 5/10 and 6/10 respectively. When asked to rate her lowest mood since the previous session, Mariana both times reported a 9/10, linking the worsening mood to a dispute with her mother. She reported increasing anxiety and uncertainty about an upcoming change in school at the start of the new school year, in conjunction with difficulty in learning English.

These sessions focused on completing Mariana's interpersonal inventory. Mariana had greater difficulty discussing her father, who had recently reentered her life after a prolonged separation. Unlike her relationship with her mother, Mariana did not long for closeness with him. Rather, she wished to maintain physical and emotional distance, as she doubted his intentions and ability to remain a positive, stable pres-ence in the family's life. Furthermore, she was confused about the nature of her par-ents' relationship, and had trouble accepting that her mother had hidden their history over the years prior to Mariana's arrival in the United States. That her father lived in another city but consistently visited the family every month, often under the influ-ence of substances, reinforced Mariana's feelings of instability, and made it difficult for them to form a close attachment.

The friends Mariana placed on her closeness circle came from her hometown. She spoke about how much she missed them, and how difficult it had been to make close friends since moving to the States.

The initial treatment phase concluded with the therapist presenting the proposed problem area formulation to Mariana. Based on the interpersonal inventory, both a role transition and a role dispute seemed appropriate formulations. Because the con-flict with her mother occurred in the context of several life transitions, the therapist decided to formulate the case as primarily a role transition, with disputes as a sec-ondary problem arising from transition difficulties. The therapist told Mariana that after reviewing her important relationships, Mariana's depression seemed linked with multiple transitions, including Mariana's move to the United States, which involved adjusting to a new country, school, culture, language, and siblings, and more generally, her father's inconsistent involvement and role in the family.

The therapist also highlighted past stressful transitions that likely increased Mariana's vulnerability to depression, such as her mother's departure for the United States and the subsequent changes in her living situation years before. She noted Mariana's great difficulty in communicating her feelings and needs directly and appropriately within relationships, particularly with her mother. As a result, the therapist explained, "You tend act out your feelings through your behavior: for example, the times when you have hit your brother instead of expressing them through your words." This pattern further alienated others and isolated Mariana, which compounded her depression. Her current communication difficulty was hurting her ability to adaptively manage her multiple transitions, increasing her conflict with her mother, and exacerbating Mariana's depressed mood.

To ensure that Mariana understood the formulation, the therapist asked her to explain it using her own words, which Mariana was able to do. Mariana agreed with these observations and expressed relief at the recognition of these challenges she had experienced. She liked that the next phase of treatment would focus on practical ways to manage these transitions and interpersonal disputes by discussing situations that might occur between sessions. At the end of Session 4, Mariana's mother informed the therapist that she would be having gallbladder surgery. She anticipated a long recovery and could not confirm when she would again be able to accompany Mariana to session. She and the therapist agreed to maintain contact by phone.

Middle Phase

Mariana appeared sad and withdrawn when she arrived for Session 5. She stated that she was "bad," with a current mood of 7/10, and an average of "9 or 9.9/10" for the week. She endorsed sadness, irritability, lethargy, decreased appetite, and feelings of worthlessness and guilt. Mariana also reported increased daily thoughts of wanting to die in order to escape current stressors. On three occasions she had thought about throwing herself into oncoming traffic. She denied current active ideation. Mariana explained that her father had arrived in town about five days prior for a ten-day family visit and was staying in Mariana's family's apartment. Two days after his arrival, he and Mariana argued about Mariana's treatment of Juan. Mariana reported he screamed at her, calling her a "bad girl," "ungrateful," and "disrespectful." Her father prohibited further interactions with her brother. She admitted to yelling back at him in anger and walking away in the middle of the argument. Mariana and her father had not spoken since. Mariana felt hurt and angry at him, as well as abandoned by her mother, who had not intervened. Furthermore, she was feeling apprehensive about starting the school year in a new school the next week.

Asked which event of the past week had most upset her, Mariana cited her difficulties with her father. The therapist emphasized the link between the events surrounding her father—his arrival and their fight—and her mood. It was important to help Mariana articulate her feelings about her father and his past and current role in her life so that she could understand how these feelings were currently affecting their relationship. She described her anger at his verbal abuse of her and her mother in the past, and now again towards her. She expressed ambivalence about his presence in her life: she wanted a father, but was disappointed by his inability to be a stable emotional, physical, and financial presence. On some level, she blamed him for her mother's departure to the United States. Mariana was confused about his current role in her family's life, as the status of her parents' relationship remained unclear. The therapist asked Mariana: "What would it be like to communicate your feelings about the current situation directly to your parents—to tell them that you are sad or angry or confused, for example—instead of refusing to speak to your father?" Mariana predicted they would not listen to what she had to say. The therapist asked whether she was willing to experiment with different approaches to communicating her feelings to see if they could understand her, which might help her to feel better. Mariana thought nothing would help, and grew more sullen and withdrawn.

The therapist pointed out how Mariana's mood deteriorated when discussing her relationship with her father. She appeared sad, angry, helpless, and hopeless about her ability to change her family situation. Mariana nodded in agreement but remained quiet. The therapist asked Mariana to rate her mood again, which had worsened to a "9 or 10/10." On reassessment, Mariana endorsed active thoughts of wanting to die. She did not state a specific plan to harm herself, but could not contract for safety. The therapist called Mariana's mother, informed her of Mariana's status, and asked her to come to the hospital to meet them. Mariana's mother arrived and corroborated Mariana's report of the week's events. Mariana continued to endorse active suicidal ideation and remained unable to contract for safety. She was admitted to the Children's Comprehensive Psychiatry Emergency Program (CPEP), where she remained overnight for monitoring and evaluation.

The therapist met with Mariana and her mother and father in a crisis session the next day, immediately upon her discharge from the Children's CPEP, where she had been evaluated and deemed stable. Mariana reported an overall mood of 4/10. The session began by revisiting the precipitants of Mariana's ER admission. Mariana expressed feeling "bad" about the argument with her father, while her parents articulated frustration with Mariana's irritability, defiance, and impatient behavior towards her younger brother. Mariana and her parents recognized how their feelings, and their difficulty communicating these feelings appropriately, led to an escalation in conflict.

The therapist provided the family with additional psychoeducation about depression, explaining, "Mariana is depressed. A central feature of adolescent depression is irritability. It is important to encourage her direct communication of feelings and respectful behavior while also recognizing how her depressed feelings are currently influencing how she behaves. The goal of therapy is to help Mariana feel and behave better. Given the many changes you have experienced as individuals and as a family these past few years, I imagine that you both can relate to the many life changes that Mariana has experienced, and is now experiencing. She feels sadness, confusion, and anger about these changes. She also feels hopeless and helpless about making things better, which is part of what led her to feel she did not want to live." Mariana's parents said they understood, and her father commented on everyone's need to "do their part" in improving relationships within the family.

An additional therapeutic goal was short-term problem solving in potential areas for dispute over the next few days so as to avoid exacerbating the crisis. The first area of conflict was Mariana's behavior towards her brother. She found him "hyperactive" and annoying. Her parents explained that he just wanted to play with her. The therapist asked if it was possible to schedule short periods of supervised playtime for Mariana and Juan to give him the positive attention he wanted while also allowing her longer "break" periods from interacting with him. They agreed to experiment with this plan. The second conflict concerned Mariana's free time. She loved to watch television and did not like sharing the TV with other family members. Mariana and her parents devised a TV schedule to which all members would adhere. They also brainstormed positive activities they could engage in together such as watching movies, shopping, and playing games so that Mariana would remain supervised and her time would be structured. When an adolescent presents with safety concerns, parental involvement is increased temporarily to enlist them to help ensure their child's safety and to make changes to decrease immediate triggers in the child's environment.

At the end of the session, the therapist, Mariana, and her parents reviewed safety-planning procedures. Mariana understood that she should tell her parents if she had suicidal thoughts. Her parents knew to call 911 or proceed to the ER with any significant concerns about Mariana's safety.

Afterwards, the therapist briefly met individually with Mariana to assess her reaction to the session and to reaffirm their alliance. She reminded Mariana of their earlier discussion of the boundaries of confidentiality and how her safety concerns had warranted sharing some of this information with her parents. The therapist reminded her that they would be resuming individual sessions with the hope that Mariana would begin to work with her parents at home between sessions. Mariana expressed comfort with the session's process and outcome, and understood the therapist's involving her parents more actively in treatment to help ensure Mariana's physical safety and emotional stability, as well as to address family interactions contributing to her deteriorating mood. She expressed surprise and relief at how both parents responded to her distress, and especially appreciated her father's acknowledgment of shared responsibility for her difficulties. She agreed to return for another session two days later.

In the second crisis session, Mariana's mood was brighter: she reported feeling "fine," 3 or 4/10. She denied self-harming thoughts or actions. The therapist encouraged Mariana to connect interpersonal interactions to her improved mood. She had been heartened by the previous session's outcome and was enjoying spending time with both parents in structured, "fun" activities. The therapist praised Mariana's willingness to communicate her feelings to her parents in the prior session and her collaboration with them in planning for the weekend. She encouraged Mariana to maintain open communication with her parents by talking to them about her feelings about their relationship and changes she was experiencing as they arose. She and Mariana practiced what Mariana could say to her parents if things did not go according to plan over the weekend, and how Mariana could share any feelings or thoughts of wanting to hurt herself.

The therapist addressed how Mariana was feeling about starting school in a few days. Mariana was still nervous. She expressed anxiety about meeting new people and apprehension about her ability to manage English classes. Mariana and the therapist revisited how Mariana had managed previous school transitions. Mariana recalled how her initial awkwardness faded over time as she began to talk to other kids in classes and to build friendships through involvement in after-school activities. Mariana and the therapist used these past experiences to brainstorm a list of "conversation starters" through which to engage others. Mariana and the therapist discussed ways she could seek help within the school for any academic difficulties if she was struggling with English language problems. They agreed that the first few days might be challenging as she adjusted to new demands, and that she could "forgive" herself accordingly.

The therapist then met briefly with Mariana's father, who had accompanied her to the session. He noted improvements in Mariana's mood and behavior. The therapist highlighted the positive impact of his participation in Mariana's treatment on her mood and functioning. This facilitated discussion about his role in Mariana's and the family's life. He explained that he and Mariana's mother were working towards reconciliation, with plans for him to visit for longer periods of time. He also reported no longer using substances. He and the therapist discussed ways to clearly communicate these plans to Mariana, and to discuss feelings associated with these changes. They reviewed recommendations for safety and activity planning for the coming weekend, and scheduled a session with Mariana for the following week.

In Session 6, Mariana rated her average mood for the week 2/10. She attributed her improvement to positive interactions with family members as well as a successful first day of school. She liked the idea of scheduling family and individual activities, and practiced expressing this to her parents so that they could continue to do this together. At school, she had used a few "conversation starters" to talk to two other Spanish-speaking classmates. They teamed up to help one another navigate their new school building, figure out their schedules, and eat lunch together. Mariana's worst mood for the week was 8/10 following a dispute with her mother over watching television. The therapist and Mariana conducted a communication analysis to dissect this.

THERAPIST: What do you think led up to the argument?

MARIANA: I was watching my favorite soap opera, and my mother interrupted me like she always does to ask if I could wash dishes. There were only fifteen minutes left and she couldn't wait. I hate it when she does that!

THERAPIST: What did you say to her then?

MARIANA: I told her to wait until my show was over to talk to me.

THERAPIST: How exactly did you do that? Like, what words did you use and in what tone of voice did you speak to her?

MARIANA: I said something like: "Leave me alone and don't come until my show is over in fifteen minutes."

THERAPIST: Okay. What happened next?

MARIANA: She walked away, but then came back five minutes later and yelled at me for not doing the dishes.

THERAPIST: What did you do then?

MARIANA: I screamed back at her: "Why can't you just wait until my soap opera is over?!"

THERAPIST: And then?

MARIANA: My mother lectured me about how I need to respect authority, and that I need to do what I am asked to do around the house without questions. She then told me I watched television too much and turned off the TV.

THERAPIST: And what did you do?

MARIANA: I screamed back at her that I was not going to do the dishes.

The therapist encouraged Mariana to name the specific feelings—sadness, anger, helplessness, and frustration—she had in response to the interaction. Mariana explained that watching soap operas was important to her because they reconnected her to her home country, language, and culture. She felt that her mother did not understand this. They then focused on how Mariana communicated her feelings and needs. Based on her observations of Mariana during interactions with her parents, the therapist pointed out the nonverbal means through which Mariana "talked" to her parents when upset. Through crossed arms or waving hands, indirect eye contact, shrugs of her shoulders, and a sucking of her teeth, Mariana expressed a dismissive, "I don't care" attitude. Mariana also admitted to using a whiny or aggressive tone of voice that was likely to aggravate her mother. The therapist encouraged Mariana to consider from her mother's perspective why she might have gotten upset with Mariana. Mariana began to recognize the numerous responsibilities her mother juggled, that her mother's expectations for assistance were realistic, and that her communication style might be affecting the way her mother and other family members responded to her.

For the remainder of the session, Mariana and the therapist role-played using communication strategies to improve her interactions with her mother, such as "I" statements (e.g., "Mom, I feel annoyed when you interrupt me during my special TV time"); communicating an understanding of her mother's perspective, or "give to get" (e.g., "Mom, I understand that you are feeling stressed and need help around the house and the dishes needed to be cleaned; I just would like to do them after my soap opera is finished"), and finding the right time to have a conversation. (See Appendix 1). She also practiced making these statements with a more relaxed, open, and direct nonverbal stance.

After role-playing different scenarios, Mariana felt comfortable approaching her mother later that evening before going to bed and saying: "I felt sad and frustrated about what happened between us this week, and I know that you did too. I understand that you need me to help, and I would like to. Watching my soap operas is important to me because it's one way I feel connected to home. Can we agree upon a set time when I do the dishes every day as long as you agree not to interrupt me when I am watching my soap opera?" She and the therapist practiced how to respond if Mariana's mother reacted poorly, with a focus on considering each other's perspectives. Mariana agreed to report on the outcome of her interpersonal experiment during the coming week.

In Session 7, Mariana continued to report an average mood of 2/10. She remained less irritable and sad, more socially engaged and energetic, with more stable eating and sleeping habits. At her worst during the week, 5/10, Mariana attributed her mood decrease to feeling uncomfortable in hot weather rather than as a result of a negative interpersonal interaction. Mariana and the therapist reviewed the outcome of the week's interpersonal experiment. She and her mother agreed upon a time for her to complete daily chores that did not interfere with Mariana's television watching. Mariana felt empowered and recognized how the new communication strategies she was beginning to use yielded more positive interpersonal interactions with family members, thereby improving her mood. Mariana and the therapist used the session practicing how to communicate her appreciation of recent positive interactions to her mother and father, and identifying other interpersonal situations in which she could use similar communication strategies. At the session's end, the therapist reminded Mariana that there would be two more middle-phase sessions before proceeding to the termination phase of treatment.

In Session 8, Mariana endorsed a mood rating of 4/10 for the week. Her mother had been unable to accompany her to the session as planned due to protracted recovery from the gallbladder surgery. Consequently, Mariana's mother had again increased demands on Mariana to assume more housekeeping and child care activities, and they had to curtail their recreational time together. The therapist asked how Mariana felt about this most recent life change. They discussed Mariana's ambivalent feelings: she was worried about her mother's health, and sad that they could not spend more time together after a period of increased closeness. She was also angry and frustrated at having to increase her responsibilities around the house, and felt guilty about these feelings given her mother's condition. Furthermore, she resented that her older sister, who worked evenings, seemed to get away with doing less than Mariana to help out at home.

The therapist validated Mariana's feelings. They also considered Mariana's mother's perspective given the unexpected complication of her current illness, which helped Mariana to differentiate the current circumstances surrounding her mother's illness from past situations when she had felt abandoned by her mother. The therapist highlighted Mariana's recent interpersonal experiment, which demonstrated that Mariana felt better when she expressed her feelings and needs directly to her mother along with problem-solving. Mariana agreed that she felt worse when she assumed a passive, helpless approach to managing conflict with her parents. They considered a goal for Mariana to speak with her mother and sister to determine a more equitable plan for dealing with the present situation.

Using a decision analysis, the therapist and Mariana took turns brainstorming possible alternatives. Next, the therapist helped Mariana to evaluate the options and to choose the option to try first: Mariana proposing to her mother and sister a list of chores and child care responsibilities, with a schedule of who was responsible for what and when based on each sister's schedule. The family's positive response thus far to structuring activities made this seem viable. They role-played a conversation in which Mariana used "I" statements to articulate her feelings and "give to get" statements to communicate understanding of her mother's situation. Mariana anticipated that her sister might argue that her work schedule was too variable to commit to a set timetable. Mariana employed the "give to get" strategy in deciding to offer to be on "standby" for last-minute changes in her sister's schedule as long as her sister would pay Mariana back with an equal amount of time spent on household responsibilities at another point. She departed the session motivated by her plan.

In Session 9 Mariana reported an average mood of 5/10. She endorsed slight increases in sleepiness, anergia, irritability, decreased appetite, and feelings of boredom. She denied thoughts and behaviors of self-harm. At its worst this past week, Mariana's mood was a 6/10 following a disagreement with her father and maternal uncles about TV use. She described a positive outcome to the conversation with her mother and sister as practiced during the previous session, but complained that her father's return to the household, along with visits by her maternal uncles, complicated their ability to implement their plan as originally designed. Her parents' announcement that her father was moving back to live with them permanently also affected her mood rating. Mariana felt conflicted about this change. Adding another person to the family's small, already crowded apartment made her feel she had no privacy or control over her favored leisure activity of watching television.

She conceded that one positive aspect of her father's return was adding someone else to share household chore and child care responsibilities.

The therapist reviewed successful strategies that Mariana had been using in previous weeks and her improved communication, and helped Mariana work on negotiating a revised television-watching plan. She also encouraged Mariana to expand her use of free time through involvement in a local basketball program. This would allow Mariana to reengage in a sport she had enjoyed in her home country and to spend less time in her house. It would increase her socialization with Spanish-speaking peers in her neighborhood, as most of her school friends lived far from her. Mariana recognized the potentially positive impact on her mood, and role-played calling the director of the basketball program to ask about registering.

Termination Phase

At the beginning of Session 10, the therapist reminded Mariana that only three sessions remained and that their focus would shift to reviewing the course of therapy while continuing to work on communication and problem-solving skills. Mariana reported consistent improvement in her depressive symptoms. She felt happier and less irritable, and was eating and sleeping well. She had not experienced suicidal ideation or self-harm urges since her admission to the psychiatric ER over six weeks earlier. Her average mood rating for the week was 2/10; at its worst, after disagreeing with her father about TV watching, it increased to 3/10. The therapist and Mariana compared her current symptoms to those she had reported when treatment began and linked her work in therapy to her mood improvement. They reviewed her disputes with family members, which had decreased in frequency and intensity, to examine the new repertoire of communication and negotiation skills learned over the course of treatment. Mariana recalled her progress with using "I" statements to communicate her feelings and needs to her family members. She acknowledged greater awareness of the nonverbal messages she relayed through facial expressions and stance, and the impact these messages had on others' moods. They reviewed her use of such strategies as "striking while the iron is cold" and "give to get," which helped Mariana recognize the importance of timing in interpersonal interactions and the role of perspective taking in positive social interactions. She was becoming better versed in problem solving and the need to compromise at times. As a result of this new approach to relationships, Mariana felt closer to her family and was cultivating a growing network of school friends with similar ethnic and linguistic backgrounds. These positive changes helped her feel more "content" about her life in the United States.

Mariana's mother joined the session for the remaining fifteen minutes to allow the therapist to check in on the parents' perception of Mariana's depression and to help plan for the termination phase. Most of Mariana's treatment had been individual therapy, but her mother had joined parts of sessions both to support Mariana's efforts and to address specific parent–child conflicts that were contributing to the depression. Parental involvement in IPT-A varies according to the identified problem area as well as the safety concerns related to the adolescent's depression. Mariana's mother participated both to support Mariana and to learn better ways to communicate and negotiate with her. Her mother listed the improvements in Mariana's behavior, communication style, and mood at home. The quality of family relationships had improved, ameliorating everyone's mood. The therapist encouraged the mother to commend Mariana for her progress during their joint time together, which she later did. The therapist communicated empathy with Mariana's struggles at home, and identified the strategies that Mariana had used to manage the recent transitions in her family, social, and school life more effectively.

When considering future roadblocks to adaptive interpersonal functioning, Mariana reflected upon her avoidant style in overwhelming situations. She recognized her tendency to withdraw and isolate herself when she felt bad or confused about how to negotiate problems. Mariana recently had begun to notice a similar avoidant pattern in her approach to school. She admitted that excessive television watching after school was one way to avoid feeling helpless, frustrated, and sad about her declining academic performance and continuing struggles in a monolingual English-language classroom. Mariana had begun to arrive late to school three or four times per week over the past 2 weeks. She agreed that deterioration in her school functioning could worsen her depression. She and the therapist role-played how to speak with her teachers and guidance counselor about her academic difficulties and the possibility of switching school programs.

In Session 11 Mariana rated her average mood 2/10. She and the therapist reviewed her discussions with school personnel, about which Mariana felt good. She and her mother worked with the guidance counselor to enroll her in an after-school homework program for Spanish-speaking students at her school. She had arrived on time for school every day this past week. This, coupled with renewed efforts to complete as much of her homework as possible on time, resulted in a positive mood. She also had fewer disputes with her father over the television because she was more engaged in completing her schoolwork.

Mariana and the therapist spent the session focusing on possible challenging future situations and interpersonal strategies she could use in these situations. They identified a potential upcoming stressor in her probable change of school setting from a monolingual English program to a bilingual program. Feeling comfortable in her peer group and now adjusted to the rhythms and structure of her current school, Mariana was saddened to make yet another life change, although she could list the benefits of making this change. They discussed the importance of communicating her feelings and needs to her parents and appropriate school personnel as soon as they arose. They reviewed the strategies she had used to ease her transition into her current school setting, such as "conversation starters" and proactive involvement in extracurricular activities, highlighting how these could be useful in any new setting.

Mariana and the therapist addressed another upcoming transition: her movement out of weekly therapy and how that might feel for her. Mariana expressed pride about her progress in therapy and confidence in her developing abilities to communicate and solve problems more effectively. The therapist emphasized that Mariana's progress resulted from her regular attendance at sessions, her efforts to express her feelings more directly, and her willingness to learn new strategies through activities such as role-plays and interpersonal experiments. Mariana acknowledged sadness about leaving the therapist. The therapist modeled the expression of affect by affirming Mariana's feelings and acknowledging that she would miss Mariana.

Mariana's mother accompanied her to the final weekly session, Session 12, to join its latter part. Mariana and the therapist met alone first to highlight her accomplishments in treatment, review her feelings about terminating, and decide what would be discussed with her mother. The therapist helped Mariana to consider the distinction between sadness about saying goodbye to the therapist and a relapse of her depression. Mariana's mother joined the session and attested to Mariana's progress in communicating more directly and respectfully, complying with parental demands at home, and improving relationships with all family members, all of which coincided with the improvement in Mariana's mood. The therapist felt rewarded to see how playfully and lovingly Mariana acted towards her brothers while her mother spoke. She pointed this out to Mariana and her mother as another of her accomplishments in therapy.

Mariana's final CDS score of 4 indicated that presence of depression was "very unlikely." A C-GAS of 75 also reflected Mariana's improvement while accommodating some remaining school difficulties. Together, Mariana, her mother, and the therapist examined a graph of Mariana's mood ratings since the start of her treatment, and celebrated its downward trend. The therapist praised Mariana for her hard work in therapy and also congratulated Mariana's mother for supporting Mariana's treatment. The mother joked about learning useful communication skills such as "I" statements and "striking while the iron is cold" from Mariana.

Her mother's remaining concern was about Mariana's school functioning. She noted Mariana's recent efforts to improve in this area but still worried about the effect of Mariana's inappropriate school placement on her motivation and mood. This provided an opportunity to review the warning signs of depression with both the mother and Mariana, including sustained increases in irritability, sad mood, social withdrawal, appetite changes, and any passive suicidal ideation and urges for self-harm. Mariana and her mother agreed to monitor these depressive symptoms. Given Mariana's unstable school situation and her mother's need for additional support in negotiating the school system, they agreed that Mariana would continue to come for post-treatment follow-up sessions every other week for 8 weeks to see if the therapist could help them change the school placement.

Follow-up

Mariana and her mother attended four more sessions on an every-other-week basis. Mariana continued to report improved mood and maintained gains in family and social functioning. With the therapist's help, Mariana's mother reinforced Mariana's positive gains through praise and modeling effective communication strategies learned in treatment. During this time Mariana faced another new but exciting transition: the family planned to move to a new, larger apartment. Mariana's school placement and academic struggles unfortunately continued. The follow-up sessions focused on assisting Mariana's mother in negotiating with the Board of Education. After the two months, Mariana and her mother agreed that they felt stable and could proceed independently with managing Mariana's school placement. Both felt comfortable returning to treatment or contacting the therapist in the future as needed.

Summary

This case illustrates the interplay between the role transitions and disputes problem areas to provide an interpersonal framework for understanding a complex story of an adolescent's struggle with family relationships and depression. While the transitions contributed to the rise of the depression, they also generated conflict between Mariana and her parents that needed to be addressed in the context of these stressful life changes. The number of stressors and transitions the adolescent experienced could easily have left the therapist feeling overwhelmed, but IPT-A provided the therapist with a structure to prioritize and identify which interpersonal problem was most related to the current depression. The therapist focused on this problem to quickly improve symptoms and functioning, while acknowledging the adolescent's past history within a developmental and interpersonal context. This adolescent was fortunate that her family was receptive to understanding her struggles and willing to change their behavior to support her improvement. When families are less responsive or amenable to change, the therapist needs to help the adolescent develop realistic expectations consistent with his or her circumstances, and to seek other supportive relationships.

Mariana and her family benefited because the therapy was conducted in Spanish by a bilingual, bicultural clinician, allowing the application of IPT-A strategies within appropriate cultural context and norms. Consequently, the therapist was able to address the adolescent's role in performing household duties in light of cultural expectations for Hispanic girls, and adjust communication strategies for consistency with Latino parental expectations for *respeto* or respect from their children. The therapist understood cultural nuances of how feelings are communicated within Latino culture and with whom different strategies would be appropriate. (See Chapter 16.)

A pivotal intervention in the treatment was the suicidal crisis that necessitated a visit to the CPEP. While the therapist conducted additional crisis sessions following the adolescent's discharge, the interventions remained consistent with IPT-A principles and strategies and mobilized the family to make changes sooner than they might have otherwise. IPT-A maintains the flexibility to allow one or two crisis sessions within the twelve-week treatment if needed without disrupting its length, by seeing the adolescent more than once a week during the crisis period. The main objectives of the interpersonal interventions were to decrease family conflict and increase pleasurable family activities. The therapist worked to improve the adolescent's communication strategies, including her communication style with her parents. Although basic, this strategy greatly improved her ability to explain her emotions to her family and to elicit needed support to address difficulties with her siblings and her school.

Finally, the case illustrates that with adolescents, even when the interpersonal problem has dissipated and depression symptoms have remitted, other issues frequently require therapist attention or referral for more services. School difficulties are common, and academic improvements may lag behind remission of the depression due to identification of learning difficulties or the realization that a different school placement is required. This may necessitate continuation sessions to help the family address the problem or may require referral to another agency better equipped to resolve it. It is critical for the IPT-A therapist to assess and address such issues, which could be risk factors for depressive relapse or recurrence. The case illustrates the universality of the problem areas, the way in which transitions and disputes are often intertwined for adolescents, and the ability to address cultural differences within the IPT-A framework.

SUGGESTED READINGS

Mufson L: Interpersonal psychotherapy: perspective on the treatment of a depressed adolescent. In Barnhill JW, ed. The Approach to the Psychiatric Patient. New York: American Psychiatric Publishing, Inc., 2008:289–292

Mufson L: Interpersonal psychotherapy for depressed adolescents (IPT-A): extending the reach from research to community settings. Journal of the Association of Child and Adolescent Mental Health 2010;15(2):66–72

Mufson L, Dorta KP, Moreau D, Weissman MM: Interpersonal Psychotherapy for Depressed Adolescents (2nd ed.). New York: Guilford Press, 2004

Mufson L, Dorta KP, Wickramaratne P, Nomura Y, Olfson M, Weissman MM: A randomized effectiveness trial of interpersonal psychotherapy for depressed adolescents. Archives of General Psychiatry 2004;61, 577–584

Mufson L, Weissman MM, Moreau D, Garfinkel R:. Efficacy of interpersonal psychotherapy for depressed adolescents. Archives of General Psychiatry 1999;56:573–579

APPENDIX 1: TEEN TIPS

1. Aim For Good Timing

Make "appointments" with people when you want to have an important conversation. Pick a time to do it when you feel they would be most able to focus and listen.

Example: *"Mom, I know you are very busy during the week. There's something I want to talk to you about when you will not be rushed or stressed. Can we talk on Saturday after we clean?"*

2. Strike While The Iron Is Cold

Wait until you feel calm to have a discussion about the problem or conflict—don't try to work it out if you are both feeling too angry and are yelling at each other.

Example: *"Dad, I am feeling really angry at the moment and I think you are too, and I don't want to discuss this now because we are too upset. Maybe in an hour after we cool off, we can talk about it."*

3. Give To Get; Start With A Positive Statement That Shows You Understand How They Feel

Example: *"Dad, I know how much you love me and worry about my safety when I am out at night, but ..."*

Example: *"Mom, I know you are concerned about the time I am spending on the phone, but I have an important question to ask Susan about the homework . . . can I use the phone for 20 minutes?"*

4. Use "I" statements to communicate feelings

Start a sentence with a statement about your feelings, not a statement about what someone is doing to you or a blaming statement.

Example: *"I feel frustrated and angry when you insist on my being home by 7 p.m. on Saturday nights because it seems like you don't trust me to be on my own with my friends."*

NOT

"You don't trust me or my friends, and that really makes me mad."

Don't assume they can read your mind. Tell them how you are feeling.

Examples: *"Mom, I feel sad when you . . ."; "Dad, I feel you don't trust me . . ."*

5. Have A Few Solutions In Mind To Solve A Problem

If you want to work something out, do a little prep work! Come up with three or four compromises to whatever you are arguing about.

Example: *"Dad, I know you how much you worry about me when I go out after 7 p.m. on Saturday nights. But I feel really angry and embarrassed when you call me every five minutes on my cell phone. I love you, and I don't want to feel this way. Can we talk about some ideas that may make you feel less worried when I go out and that won't be so difficult for me?"*

Solutions:

1. If I call you every hour (every two hours)?
2. If I let you speak with my friend's parents when I go to her house, and that I call you if I leave there so you know where I am?
3. If I call you when we get to the movies, and then again when we leave so you will know when to expect me at home? I promise I will call you immediately if we change plans.

6. Don't Give Up!

Remember, it takes a LONG time to learn to do something differently. You and your parents/friends are used to handling things a certain way for a long time. You will need to try these new communication strategies more than once. KEEP TRYING!

13

Interpersonal Psychotherapy for Peripartum Depression

KATHRYN L. BLEIBERG

Major depression during the antepartum and postpartum periods is fairly common among women. It is estimated that about 10% to 12% of women experience depression during pregnancy (Spinelli & Endicott, 2003) and 10% to 15% of women experience postpartum depression (Halbreich & Karkun, 2006). Symptoms of depression during the antepartum and postpartum periods can be misattributed—by depressed, pregnant, and postpartum women and those around them—to pregnancy or a "normal" reaction to life with a newborn. Many women who are pregnant or taking care of a newborn report getting little sleep, complain of fatigue or physical discomfort, and report appetite disturbance and decreased libido—all somatic symptoms of depression. Postpartum women may similarly assume that symptoms like insomnia, fatigue, anhedonia, and low motivation are "normal" or are related to having a difficult child (Weissman et al., 2000).

Depression during pregnancy not only causes suffering in the pregnant woman but can compromise fetal development. Depressed pregnant women are at risk for not obtaining adequate prenatal care, for poor nutrition due to depression-related low appetite, and for engaging in other unhealthy behaviors such as cigarette use and alcohol abuse during pregnancy (Spinelli & Endicott, 2003). Depression during pregnancy has also been associated with an increased risk for pregnancy complications (Wisner, 2009).

Postpartum depression (PPD) can interfere with a new mother's ability to bond with her baby and has been associated with insecure attachment and other cognitive, emotional, and behavioral problems in children (Wisner, 2006). Furthermore, PPD can negatively affect a woman's relationship with her partner. Depression during the antepartum and postpartum periods carries a greater burden of illness than at other times during a woman's life as it often affects infants, children, and partners (Birndorf & Sachs, 2008).

Given the prevalence of depression related to childbearing and the potential negative impact of depression on both mothers and their children, it is crucial to identify and treat peripartum depression. Pregnant and breastfeeding women and doctors generally prefer to avoid antidepressant medication when possible because of the potential adverse effects on their babies (Birndorf & Sacks, 2008). Although the limited observational research to date suggests that many psychiatric medications are relatively safe for use during pregnancy, the U.S. Food and Drug Administration (FDA) has yet to identify any of these medications as safe. Current knowledge about the use of antidepressants during pregnancy and lactation is complicated by the lack of systematic and prospective data. Pregnant women have historically been excluded from randomized controlled trials, and studying the effects of medications on a developing fetus or nursing baby has raised ethical concerns (Birndorf & Sacks, 2008; Wisner et al, 2009). Thus, nonpharmacological treatments for these women are preferable when possible.

IPT is a great treatment option for these women for several reasons. First, antepartum and postpartum depression are life-event–based illnesses, and IPT is a life-event–based treatment. They are distinguished from other subtypes of mood disorders not so much by symptoms as by timing: they are defined by major transitions in a woman's life (Halbreich & Karkun, 2006). In fact, the DSM-IV does not distinguish major depression that occurs antepartum or postpartum as a distinct mood disorder. The DSM-IV includes a qualifier of "postpartum onset" for women with major depression that begins within four weeks of giving birth (APA, 1994).

Pregnancy and having children inevitably affect relationships with one's partner, other children, parents, friends, employers, colleagues, and others, often leading to interpersonal conflicts on which IPT can focus. The demands of motherhood force new mothers to reconfigure their priorities and adjust their expectations of themselves in relationships and other areas in their life. Thus, childbearing involves major role transitions often involving interpersonal conflicts—focal problem areas that IPT targets (Weissman et al., 2000).

The time limit of IPT appeals to pregnant women and new mothers. Pregnant women often feel a sense of urgency to feel better as they want to be able to enjoy their pregnancy and feel better before their baby arrives. Some fear the potential impact of their depression on their unborn child. They may anticipate not having time for treatment once the baby comes. New mothers are often overwhelmed by the new responsibilities of caring for a new baby, which may make a focused, time-limited psychotherapy seem manageable. The fact that IPT is the most tested psychotherapy and has the most demonstrated efficacy for the treatment of peripartum depression is encouraging for these women, who feel they do not have time to try different treatments.

Unfortunately, depression and other mental disorders still carry a stigma, which deters some from seeking treatment. Depression during and following pregnancy carries an added stigma. Women who experience negative feelings about their pregnancy or motherhood often feel ashamed and unable to share their feelings with others. The use of the medical model in IPT can help reduce this stigma. The IPT therapist explains that these are major life transitions that are challenging for most women and that it is *normal* to have both negative and positive feelings about them. The therapist tells the patient that major depression at any time in a woman's life is an illness that is not her fault.

In the event that a women reports symptoms that are severe and that interfere with her ability to make use of psychotherapy, a consultation with a psychiatrist specializing in the use of psychotropic medications during pregnancy and lactation should be considered. Fortunately, IPT's medical model makes it is compatible with pharmacotherapy.

As IPT is a natural fit for this population, adaptations require minimal changes to the basic IPT approach.

ADAPTATIONS AND RESEARCH

Antepartum Depression

Spinelli and Endicott (2003) adapted IPT for antepartum depression, conceptualizing pregnancy as a role transition. This captures both the physical changes and the life changes related to pregnancy. In her manual, Spinelli added a fifth problem area called "complicated pregnancy" to reflect a variety of pregnancy-related issues such as unwanted pregnancy, obstetrical problems, and partner abandonment. Therapists were sensitive to the unpredictable nature of pregnancy and offered phone sessions to accommodate patients on bedrest and with delivery complications.

Spinelli and Endicott enrolled fifty bilingual pregnant women in a sixteen-week randomized controlled trial comparing IPT to a parenting education control. Thirty-eight patients were included in intention-to-treat analyses. Depression improved significantly in the IPT group compared to the control group. There was also a significant correlation between improved mood and the mother's ability to interact with her infant. The researchers recognized several limitations of their study. There was a high attrition rate in both groups, and the sample sizes used in the analyses were small. The researchers attributed the high attrition rate to several factors. Several women left after delivery and one after a stillbirth. Single mothers had difficulty meeting the demands of child care and work to attend sessions. Two women left the study after being reunited with their partners, who had been incarcerated. Other women were lost to treatment and follow-up because of disconnected phone numbers. Most of the subjects were impoverished, poorly educated recent immigrants from the Dominican Republic. Many reported unstable and traumatic circumstance that were likely impediments to treatment. While it is important to address this understudied population with multiple risk factors for antepartum depression, the study results were limited by the homogeneity of the sample. Nevertheless, the results suggest that further research is warranted. Spinelli is currently replicating her earlier study among a larger and more diverse sample of pregnant women.

Grote et al. (2009) also attempted to address antenatal depression among a group of pregnant socioeconomically disadvantaged women. They compared enhanced usual prenatal care in a large, urban obstetrics and gynecology (OB-GYN) clinic to brief interpersonal psychotherapy (IPT-B) derived from IPT and enhanced to make it culturally relevant to women who are socioeconomically disadvantaged. The enhanced IPT-B treatment consisted of an engagement session followed by eight sessions of IPT-B before birth, and maintenance IPT for up to 6 months postpartum. Fifty-five non–treatment-seeking depressed pregnant women were included in intention-to-treat analyses. The IPT-B group showed a significantly greater reduction in depressive symptoms during pregnancy as well as six months postpartum compared to the control group. The IPT group also showed significant improvements in social function at six months postpartum.

Postpartum Depression

O'Hara et al. (2000) adapted IPT for PPD. One hundred twenty women were randomized to either 12 weeks of IPT or to a waitlist control group. Ninety-nine patients completed the study and were included in the analyses. Intention-to-treat analyses, which were conducted for the depression measures, showed that patients treated with IPT reported a significantly greater rate of recovery of their depression compared to women in the control group: 32% of women in the IPT group recovered versus only 15% of the women in the control. Completer analyses were conducted for measures of depression and psychosocial adjustment and showed that the IPT group reported significantly greater declines on all measures of depressive symptoms and significant improvement on measures of social adjustment. The women in the IPT group were followed for eighteen months after treatment. Nylen et al. (2010) examined the rate of recurrence among the women who responded to acute IPT and the rate of subsequent recovery among the women who had not recovered by the end of treatment. They found that more than half of the women who recovered from acute treatment sustained recovery over the eighteen-month follow-up period. A large majority (over 80%) of the women who had not recovered with acute treatment recovered at some point during follow-up. The researchers concluded that IPT resulted in long-term benefits among both responders and nonresponders to acute treatment. They suggest that continuation IPT might accelerate the rate of recovery of those who do not recover with acute treatment. O'Hara, Stuart et al. continue to study the efficacy and uses of IPT for this population.

IPT Modified for Group

Several researchers have adapted IPT in group format for the treatment of antepartum and postpartum depression. The group format enables patients to meet other women who are also struggling with pregnancy and the transition to motherhood. This helps normalize a new mother's experience, reduces isolation, and helps reduce the stigma associated with peripartum depression.

Zlotnick et al. (2001, 2006) developed a group intervention based on IPT principles to reduce the risk of PPD among financially disadvantaged pregnant women. After piloting the intervention among a group of thirty-seven women and obtaining promising results, the researchers replicated the study among a group of ninety-nine pregnant women on public assistance who were determined to be at risk for PPD. The intervention—the ROSE Program (Reach Out, Stand Strong, Essentials for new mothers)—consisted of four sixty-minute group sessions over a four-week period and one fifty-minute individual booster session after delivery. The intervention was designed to help these women improve their close relationships and social support systems, and to successfully manage their role transition to motherhood. Women were randomly assigned to receive the intervention plus standard antenatal care or to standard antenatal care alone. Eighty-six of the ninety-nine women completed the study and were assessed three months after delivery. Six of the women dropped out because they moved out of state. Women who received the intervention were significantly less likely (4%) than the women in the standard care condition (20%) to develop PPD. However, no significant differences between the groups were found on measures assessing depression severity and social adjustment. Nevertheless, the data support that this IPT-based intervention may be effective in preventing PPD. The researchers suggest further study is warranted to determine whether additional sessions during the postpartum period would improve the outcomes and whether the intervention can be used in other settings.

Klier et al. (2001) in Vienna, Austria, adapted IPT for group for the treatment of PPD. The adaptation included additional problem areas related to childbirth and motherhood. They piloted the treatment in an open trial of seventeen women who were four to forty-five weeks postpartum and had developed symptoms of depression—fifteen with major depression and two with minor depression within six months postpartum. Each subject received two sixty-minute individual sessions, followed by nine weekly ninety-minute group sessions and one sixty-minute individual termination session. Ten women were enrolled in one group and seven in the other. Eleven women completed the treatment and thirteen were available for a follow-up. The majority of the women who completed treatment reported a significant improvement of their symptoms at the follow-up assessment. This study was limited by its small sample size, high dropout rate, and lack of a control group, blind raters, and treatment adherence monitoring.

Mulcahy et al. (2010) conducted a randomized controlled trial comparing IPT group therapy for PPD to treatment as usual (TAU) in a sample of depressed women who were up to a year postpartum in a community setting in the Australian Capital Territory. A treatment manual for IPT intervention was developed during in an earlier pilot study (Reay et al., 2006) Over an eight-week period, subjects in the IPT group received two individual sessions, eight two-hour group therapy sessions, and a two-hour psychoeducational session for partners. TAU included all other options for support and treatment for PPD, including, but not limited to, antidepressant medication, individual therapy, and group therapy. Fifty-seven women were randomized, but seven withdrew before completing baseline assessments. The fifty patients who completed baseline questionnaires were included in intention-to-treat analyses. Two of these patients dropped out of the study. While depression scores in both groups improved significantly by the end of treatment, the IPT group reported significantly greater improvement and a significantly higher rate of recovery at three-month follow-up than the TAU group. At follow-up the IPT group also showed significant improvement in their relationship with their partners, other social supports, and their infants.

Perinatal Bereavement

IPT also makes intuitive sense for the treatment of depression following pregnancy loss. Women who suffer miscarriage often plan to try to conceive again and, therefore, prefer to avoid antidepressant medications. I have found it straightforward and very helpful to conceptualize depression following perinatal bereavement using the grief problem area. The IPT therapist helps the patient mourn the loss of the child and a family life that she had hoped for, planned for, and fantasized about. Pregnancy loss can lead to discord in a grieving couple: each may feel differently about the loss, express the grief differently, and grieve at a different pace. IPT targets such conflicts and can lead to lasting improvements in how a couple communicates about affectively charged subjects, including future pregnancies and the related transitions.

Treatment of depression following pregnancy loss is an opportunity to provide women with tools to minimize the potential for a recurrence of symptoms during subsequent pregnancies and postpartum. During the termination phase, the IPT therapist educates the patient about her potential for relapse and explores anticipated potentially stressful events that could trigger symptoms. The therapist explores what the patient anticipates she will feel while trying to conceive again, during a subsequent pregnancy and postpartum, and they can discuss coping strategies.

Neugebauer et al. (2006, 2007) conducted a pilot study of phone-administered interpersonal counseling (IPC) adapted to treat subthreshold major depression among women who had sought medical care for miscarriage. IPC is a briefer, more highly scripted version of IPT that was adapted from IPT for use by non-mental health professionals in primary care settings to treat patients with mild depressive symptoms. The researchers developed a treatment manual that focused on facilitating the mourning process, psychoeducation about depression, and seeking social support. Nineteen women were randomized to either the IPC or TAU, which consisted of whatever support or treatment the women sought on their own. Women in IPC were given the option of having up to six weekly sessions. Intention-to-treat analysis showed a significantly greater decline of depressive symptoms in the IPC group versus the TAU group. While depressive symptoms improved, the study had several limitations, including a small sample size and treatment by only one clinician. Nevertheless, the data from the IPC study are promising and suggest the utility of a larger, randomized controlled trial of the adaptation of IPT for depression following pregnancy loss.

Other research on pregnancy-related depression is underway. For example, Koszycki et al. at the University of Ottawa conducted a randomized controlled trial comparing twelve weekly sessions of IPT to twelve weekly sessions of brief supportive psychotherapy for the treatment of major depressive disorder among a small sample of women struggling with infertility. These women often feel a great sense of loss and shame about their inability to conceive without medical intervention. After exhausting fertility treatment options, some face the loss of being able to conceive and parent their own biological child. The data from this study are not yet published, but the results are encouraging: Koszycki reports a trend for the women treated with IPT to show greater reduction of their depressive symptoms. Analysis of six-month follow-up data is underway.

Based on the literature described here, IPT is the best-tested psychotherapy for peripartum mood disorders and has generally worked well. Therapists can offer IPT with confidence. The following case illustrates the implementation of IPT adapted for PPD.

CASE EXAMPLE

Ellen, a thirty-eight-year-old, married mother of a six-month-old daughter, presented with major depressive disorder. Her daughter's pediatrician referred her to me for consultation after she confided to the pediatrician that she was having a difficult time. Ellen's chief complaint was: "I can't stop crying . . .I love my daughter, but I didn't know that it was going to be so hard to be a mother." She added, "I worry about something bad happening to her." She said she was ashamed that she felt this way but knew she needed help. Her husband of four years also thought that she needed help and felt at a loss about how to help her.

Ellen related that her pregnancy with her daughter, Sara, was planned and that she conceived via intrauterine insemination. She remembered feeling "ecstatic" when she learned that she was pregnant and felt "great" for most of her pregnancy. She reported that she started to feel down towards the end of her pregnancy, when she began feeling very uncomfortable and could no longer exercise. Her mood worsened shortly after Sara was born. Ellen had a difficult time breastfeeding initially and despite several meetings with a lactation consultant could not breastfeed exclusively. She reported feeling "like a failure" when her pediatrician told her she had to supplement the breast milk with formula when her baby was one month old.

At this point, Ellen met full criteria for major depressive disorder. She reported a depressed mood, anhedonia, inappropriate guilt, poor appetite, and difficulty sleeping despite feeling exhausted. She felt overwhelmed and unable to enjoy taking care of Sara, but did enjoy playing with her intermittently. Ellen related feeling very down on herself and stated that she felt like "a bad mother" because she felt depressed and lacked confidence about her ability to care for her baby. Lonely and isolated, she felt her husband and others could not understand how she was feeling. She admitted to feeling somewhat hopeless about feeling better, but denied ever feeling that life was not worth living or having thoughts of hurting herself. She denied ever wanting to hurt Sara or having intrusive thoughts about harming her, but reported worrying excessively about something bad happening to Sara.

Ellen first met criteria for major depression during her freshman year of college. She reported having met with a college counselor weekly for much of her freshman year and said she found the counseling "somewhat helpful." She reported having another episode when her relationship with her college boyfriend ended during her first year after graduating from college, but did not seek treatment. She noted that this third, most recent episode was worse than the previous episodes in that the symptoms were lasting longer and that she was much more anxious and isolated. Ellen did not meet criteria for any other Axis I or II disorders. She reported having as many as six drinks a day with friends on a few occasions during college, but did not meet criteria for alcohol abuse. She denied drinking any alcohol during her pregnancy or since Sara was born. She denied ever using recreational drugs and had no history of psychotic symptoms.

Ellen reported that her general health was good. She reported that her menstrual cycle had always been regular and denied ever having been pregnant prior to conceiving Sara. She denied a history of thyroid disease or any other chronic or serious illnesses. She was bothered by seasonal allergies and took Claritin as needed. For the past few years she had been taking a prenatal vitamin daily and denied taking any other medications.

Mental Status Examination

Ellen was a tall, slender woman with blond, shoulder-length hair who appeared her stated age. She wore no makeup and was casually but neatly dressed in leggings, an oversized long-sleeved shirt, and sneakers. Her movements were mildly agitated, her speech was fluent and unpressured, and she avoided steady eye contact. Her mood was depressed and anxious and her affect congruent and nonlabile, tearful and tired. She was cooperative and friendly. There was no evidence of a thought disorder. She denied suicidal and homicidal ideation. She was oriented times three and her sensorium was grossly clear. Her insight was good in that she recognized that she was depressed.

It seemed appropriate to recommend IPT to Ellen for several reasons. First, she wanted to avoid taking medication. Had her symptoms been more severe, I would have referred her for a consultation for medication. In the event that her symptoms worsened, IPT is compatible with pharmacotherapy. Ellen reported feeling guilty that she had not written any thank-you notes for baby gifts and that she was having difficulty responding to email messages. Unlike cognitive-behavioral therapy (CBT), which often involves completing dysfunctional thought records, IPT does not involve "homework" or any written exercises that might feel burdensome to an overwhelmed new mother. IPT also directly addresses the social isolation and difficulty communicating that Ellen described. Finally, given IPT's demonstrated efficacy and time limit, I knew that I could offer IPT with optimism and confidence that she could feel better.

Initial Phase

In the initial sessions (Sessions 1–3) of acute treatment, I obtained Ellen's psychiatric history, set the framework for treatment, and began to build a therapeutic alliance. In the first session, I explained that IPT is a time-limited, diagnosis-targeted therapy that focuses on how recent life events affect mood and how mood symptoms make it difficult to handle current life events, especially interpersonal interactions. I explained that our sessions would focus not on the past but on current relationships and difficulties, such as her difficulty in making the transition to motherhood—a role transition. I explained that IPT has been shown in clinical studies to be effective for the treatment of various types of depression, including postpartum depression. I told Ellen that we would work together for twelve weeks; at the end of that time, we would decide together whether it made sense for us to continue working together. I administered the Hamilton Depression Rating Scale (Ham-D; Hamilton, 1960) and she scored 25, consistent with moderately severe depression. She also completed the Edinburgh Postnatal Depression Scale (EPDS, Cox et al., 1987), a 10-item self-report scale developed to adjust for the neurovegetative symptoms that are a normal part of the postpartum period. Women who score above 12 on the EPDS are likely to be suffering from depression; Ellen scored 24.

Based on my review of her symptoms and these scales, I determined that Ellen met criteria for major depressive disorder with postpartum onset. I gave her the diagnosis and the "sick role" (Weissman et al., 2007):

THERAPIST: You have an illness called major depression. Depression after having a baby is referred to as "postpartum depression." Depression is a very common illness, treatable and not your fault. You can feel better. When people are depressed, they often do not feel like socializing with friends as you described. Give yourself a break: this is how you are feeling for now, but you have started treatment and working on feeling better.

I asked her if this made sense.

ELLEN: Sort of. I just don't understand why this would happen *now*. I thought I would be so happy when the baby was born. I've always wanted to be a mom and we worked so hard to conceive her.
THERAPIST: Becoming a mother is a *major* life transition that shakes up various parts of your life and relationships. Even if you want a change like this, like having a baby, the transition can still be very challenging. Most women find the transition to motherhood challenging.

Ellen agreed that this made sense. I provided psychoeducation about PPD and reviewed her specific symptoms. I explained that her history of depression made her vulnerable to a recurrence of symptoms in the setting of stressful life events, like having a baby. I emphasized that this was not her fault and that her symptoms were treatable. I acknowledged the stigma related to PPD. I explained that women often feel ashamed that they have negative feelings about their baby and motherhood and unfortunately don't share these feelings or seek help if they are depressed. In fact, it is normal to have both positive and negative feelings. We also discussed how she could explain PPD to her husband, Joe, and others. By the end of the first, consultation session, Ellen reported feeling relieved that she was "not going crazy," that other new mothers also have a hard time, and that she could feel better.

In taking a thorough psychiatric history, I conducted an interpersonal inventory, a careful review of Ellen's past and current social functioning and social relationships. The goal of the interpersonal inventory is to help both the therapist and patient understand how the patient interacts with other people; to identify her social supports, if any; and to determine how recent relationships might have contributed to or have been affected by the depression. Depressed individuals tend to withdraw from others. They tend to avoid seeking support when they feel down because they fear burdening others with their problems. They have difficulty asserting their needs in relationships, but feel disappointed when their expectations of others are not met. Depressed individuals tend to avoid expressing anger and other negative feelings towards others. The IPT therapist helps the depressed patient learn to identify and tolerate such affects, then how to assert herself and express her anger more effectively. The interpersonal inventory provides a framework for understanding the social and interpersonal context that contributed to the current depressive episode and should provide a treatment focus.

Ellen reported that she grew up in New York City and attended a good liberal arts college in Pennsylvania. She had an older brother with whom she felt close and spoke weekly. She and Joe visited him, his wife, and their children, ages three and five, about once a month. Ellen described having good relationships with her parents, who lived nearby. Since her daughter was born, she spoke to her mother daily and saw her several times a week. Her mother would come over a few times a week to help her take care of the baby. Ellen explained that she felt "uncomfortable" accepting her mother's help: "I'm used to being very independent. I don't like having to rely on her." She suspected that her mother had suffered from depression in the past and that her brother was depressed when he was in high school. She denied knowing of any other psychiatric illness in her family.

Ellen reported that she had several close female friends: one from elementary school, a few from high school and college, and a couple she met through work. She described herself as "shy at first" when meeting new people, but eventually able to open up and form lasting friendships. She admitted that she tended to avoid conflict when angry at her friends. She explained that instead of telling her friends how she felt, she would keep her feelings to herself, feel down, and avoid phone calls or contact for at least a few days until the feelings dissipated. She had not seen many of her friends since the baby was born. They offered to come over, but she was embarrassed that her apartment was a mess and she felt too overwhelmed to enter-tain guests. In addition, Ellen felt self-conscious about her appearance: it was some-times difficult to take a shower while taking care of the baby and she had not lost all of the weight she had gained during her pregnancy. Ellen explained that about half of her friends also had children, but that they had started their families six or seven years earlier, so none of her close friends had babies. She had not yet met any other new moms.

Ellen reported that she began dating in high school and had a few relationships with men before meeting Joe, each one lasting two or three years. She met Joe while working as the head of the recruiting department at a prestigious Manhattan law firm. Joe, an attorney at another firm, met her at a career fair where they were each presenting their respective firms. They married after dating for two years. She related that she and Joe "had a lot of fun together" before their daughter was born. She described him as a "really nice guy." When asked how they handle conflict, Ellen said that they generally got along well, but that when she was angry at him, she tended to be "passive aggressive" and had difficulty telling him how she felt. She would become withdrawn, irritable, and terse until he asked her why she was upset. Ellen described a longstanding difficulty asserting herself with others—a difficulty that was exacer-bated in the setting of depression and that would be addressed in IPT.

Ellen had worked in legal recruiting since graduating from college, quickly work-ing her way up to heading a recruiting department where she managed a team of ten people. While very successful in her field, she reported feeling unfulfilled intellectu-ally and tired of the very long hours her job required. Ellen and Joe agreed that it made sense for her to leave her job when the baby arrived. They planned to have more than one child and assumed that she would pursue a different career after stay-ing home to take care of their children for a few years. When I asked her how she felt about leaving her job, she replied: "I don't miss the work and the stress, but I miss being with other adults and getting out of the apartment." I asked her how she felt about not earning money and relying on her husband's income. She replied that she felt a little uncomfortable, as she had been financially independent for over fifteen years, but had saved a lot of money.

Ellen was "so excited to have a baby." She and Joe began trying to conceive about a year after marrying. She denied ever having been pregnant prior to conceiving her daughter. At thirty-seven, after a year of unsuccessful attempts, her OB-GYN recommended intrauterine insemination to improve her chances of conceiving. Ellen became pregnant after their third insemination procedure. She and Joe "were ecstatic" when they learned she was pregnant. An avid exerciser, Ellen exercised throughout her pregnancy and "felt great" most of the time. As she approached term and grew more uncomfortable and tired, however, she felt unable to exercise as much and began feeling "like I was losing myself." She reported that Joe was affectionate and doted on her throughout her pregnancy, and that she felt very close to him. He was beside her in the birthing room for the delivery and tried to be helpful, but was very anxious; at times she felt like she had to calm him down.

Ellen reported that while her delivery was normal and uneventful, she had a difficult time nursing her baby in the hospital and received assistance from a lactation consultant. "I didn't think breastfeeding would be so difficult . . . I felt incompetent as soon as my daughter was born." After bringing Sara home, her nursing difficulties continued. Despite following the lactation consultant's instructions, she could not produce enough milk to feed her daughter. Her pediatrician told her to supplement the breast milk with formula. She "felt like a failure" and became more depressed. Ellen also related becoming increasingly anxious about Sara getting sick or hurt:

ELLEN: I feel like I have no idea what I am doing . . . I'm used to working really hard and getting things done . . . Everyone else makes it look so easy.

THERAPIST: You are so hard on yourself! You are right—you've been an expert at your job at the firm and highly effective. Being a mother is a brand-new role for you, and you're not expected to be an expert right away. We can work on your feeling more comfortable as a mother.

Ellen described Joe as somewhat helpful with the baby, but wished that he would do more and give her a break. When I asked her if he knew what she wanted, she answered: "He should know . . . I am obviously exhausted." She resented that he had the freedom to have lunch with his colleagues and get out of the house every day. When I asked if she had shared these feelings with him, she stated that she had not. Although they had not been arguing, Ellen related feeling distant from him. She reported his supportive response when she told him what she had learned about PPD, and he frequently told her that he thought she was a great mother.

On the morning of our third session, Ellen's mother, who was scheduled to watch the baby during our session, became ill. Ellen called me and asked if she could bring her baby to our session. I agreed that she could. Although I generally find it distracting for both the patient and me to have a baby in session, it is helpful to see how a depressed new mother interacts with her baby. I also appreciated and wanted to accommodate Ellen's interest in keeping our appointment. She arrived with the baby prepared with everything the baby could need for the excursion to my office. Ellen seemed natural and relaxed holding her daughter, who appeared well taken care of. She made loving and happy faces at her daughter. She seemed connected to her baby and did not resemble the incompetent mother she had described. I shared my observations with Ellen, and she replied, tearfully, "I want to believe you. I am relieved that you think so."

Indeed, I felt relieved too. Unlike Ellen, depressed new mothers can appear uncomfortable with their babies, seem unable or unsure how to hold or care for them, or emotionally disconnected from their babies. When working with women with PPD, therapists often have to deal with concerns about the health of both mother and child. Therapists may feel uncomfortable raising concerns about the depressed mother's capacity to care for her child or about the potential impact of her untreated illness on her baby. Patients may feel criticized, resulting in a rupture in the treatment. The medical model and the sick role can be helpful: depression does make it difficult to care for a child and to emotionally connect, so it is not the new mother's fault. The IPT therapist can encourage the patient to get help taking care of her baby from another caregiver while she is still depressed. The therapist tells the patient that she is not expected to know how to do everything in her new role and that she can learn how to care for their baby. I have referred patients with very poor insight and judgment about taking care of their babies to mother–infant specialists who work with mothers having difficulty bonding with and taking care of their babies. In New York State, mental health professionals are obligated to report mothers who describe behaving in ways that put their children in imminent danger to the Office of Children and Family Services. Similarly, therapists working with depressed pregnant women who are not practicing good prenatal care or using substances that can potentially harm the fetus may feel compelled to address the health of the developing fetus.

Concluding the initial phase of acute treatment (Session 3), I suggested that we choose one or at most two issues to focus on. IPT for major depression usually focuses one of four interpersonal problem areas: a role dispute, a role transition, grief, or (if none of the preceding fits) interpersonal deficits. Women with PPD by definition are in the midst of a role transition, which often also involves a role dispute, so the interpersonal deficits problem area is never a focus. I connected Ellen's symptoms of depression to her interpersonal situation in an IPT formulation (Markowitz & Swartz, 2007).

As Ellen's chief complaint focused on her adjustment to motherhood, my formulation emphasized her role transition into motherhood:

THERAPIST: You have been having a difficult time adjusting to becoming a mother. In IPT we call any shift to a major new role a *role transition*. There have been many changes in your life since Sara was born. For example, you gave up your career. You're used to being an expert at your job, but you're now in a new role that feels unfamiliar. You are used to being very independent, but now need to rely on others to help you. Before Sara was born, you spent a lot more time with other adults—your husband, colleagues, and friends. You also used to have a lot more freedom to take care of yourself. There's a connection between what is happening in your life and your mood. Role transitions can trigger symptoms of depression in vulnerable individuals, and, conversely, depressive symptoms can make it difficult to handle role transitions. If we can help you navigate this transition to motherhood, your mood should improve. Also, if we can help you to better understand and manage your depressive symptoms, you'll be better able to deal with this major life change.

I asked her if this made sense. She agreed that it did.

THERAPIST: In addition, your relationship with your husband has changed since your baby was born—the two of you have had to negotiate the new responsibilities of parenting and have less time for each other. From what you've told me, you've had difficulty expressing how you feel to Joe and you two have been in conflict. Depression affects how people function in relationships. People with depression tend to withdraw from others and have difficulty asserting themselves. I think that if you can express your needs more effectively to him, you'll be able to feel more connected to him and feel better. Does this make sense to you?

She said it did. Ellen agreed that working on her role transition should be the focus of treatment. With this agreement we entered the middle phase of treatment.

At the end of the acute phase, I repeated the Ham-D and also had Ellen complete another EPDS. Her Ham-D score fell to 19 and her EPDS score to 20. We reviewed together that the improvement in her scores reflected her feeling somewhat less depressed, more hopeful, and less anxious.

Middle Phase

During the middle phase (Sessions 4–9) we worked on resolving Ellen's interpersonal problem areas. I continued to provide psychoeducation about PPD and to explore how it affected her social functioning, and I repeatedly linked her symptoms to her role transitions and role dispute.

During the initial phase, I identified Ellen's old roles and acknowledged her sense of loss. Thus, I had already begun to encourage Ellen to mourn the loss of her old roles—an important task in helping patients with role transitions. We continued this discussion in the middle phase of treatment. I encouraged Ellen to explore how she could regain some of what she missed about her life before Sara's birth. We explored how she could find time to exercise, go on dates with her husband, and spend time with other adults.

In one of the first sessions, Ellen asked me if I had children. I told her that I was happy to answer her question, but that her question was more important than the answer. She explained that she thought that if I did, then I "looked like I had figured out how to manage both a job and children." She had wondered about how other women can "have children and a life." As IPT does not focus on the therapeutic relationship, I gently redirected the patient. I used this as an opportunity for exploring options and to encourage Ellen to reconnect with old friends and to form new relationships.

THERAPIST: I do have children. It's great that you are interested in learning about how other women meet the demands of motherhood. How can you learn more about what other new moms are doing?

ELLEN: I guess I could ask my friends who have children, but their children are older.

THERAPIST: Great idea! Since your friends made it through this difficult time in the past, could it still be helpful to ask them?

ELLEN: I suppose so.

THERAPIST: What could you ask them?

ELLEN: I guess I'd want to know how they managed to do everything when their kids were babies.

THERAPIST: Great! What would it be like for you to ask that?

ELLEN: I guess it would be okay.

THERAPIST: You sound hesitant.

ELLEN: I just don't want to burden them and make them think I'm stupid.

THERAPIST: When people are depressed they feel down on themselves and, therefore, fear they will burden others when they reach out for help. In fact, getting social support from others is so important for improving your mood. You're allowed to have needs too. Does this make sense?

ELLEN: Yes.

THERAPIST: I appreciate that we're talking about your trying something new and different, but I bet you will be pleasantly surprised.

Role-playing asking her friends for help allowed Ellen to practice her communication skills, rehearsing the content and tone of what she might say, and to begin to feel more comfortable reaching out for support. I encouraged Ellen to explore options for meeting new mothers: "You mentioned that your friends have children who are older. What options do you have for meeting other new mothers?" Ellen said that she had heard of groups for new mothers getting together with their babies. She was concerned that the mothers in these groups would be much younger than she. We explored options for finding out about existing groups with women her age and possibly forming a group herself.

Ellen reported in the next session that she had spoken with a couple of her old friends. They were happy to hear from her and to share their experiences. When she admitted her embarrassment about her own and her apartment's appearance, they reminded her that their homes were still messy and that they too had often not been able to shower when their children were infants. They agreed that carrying the remaining baby weight was frustrating, but assured her she would lose it within the year. They also reminded Ellen how helpful and supportive she had been to them when they had newborns and said that they would love to see her and help her out with her daughter. Ellen accepted her friends' offers and scheduled dates for them to visit with her.

Ellen's success in reaching out to her friends improved her mood. It gave her a greater sense of control over her situation and inspired her to reach out to others. She reported that after speaking with her friends, she began initiating conversations with women who appeared to be around her age and were mothers of a young baby. For example, she met a woman in her pediatrician's office who invited her to a playgroup she was forming with a couple of other women.

I began each session by asking: "How have you been feeling since we last met?" This opening question elicits affect and an interval history of events between sessions. In one session Ellen responded, "'I am so frustrated with Joe."

THERAPIST: Tell me more about that. What are you frustrated about?

ELLEN: He still doesn't help out enough with the baby. I wish he had more of a relationship with her.

THERAPIST: Have you told Joe how you feel?
ELLEN: Sort of.

I conducted a communication analysis, asking Ellen to recount exactly what she said to Joe, how she said it, his response, how that made her feel, and how she then responded. Ellen had called her husband at work to complain that she needed more help with the baby, but did not specify that she wanted more help from *him*. In response, Joe asked Ellen if she would like to hire a babysitter. Ellen explained that she wanted more help from him at night and on the weekends when he was not working, but felt guilty asking him because he worked so hard at his job. I pointed out it was great that she appreciated how hard he worked, but that she was working hard too. Her guilt was a symptom of depression. Furthermore, her husband would not be able to understand what she wanted unless she were specific about what she wanted. I empathized that it was difficult for her to assert her needs given her depression, and I suggested that we explore ways to communicate her feelings so that Joe might better understand her needs.

We role-played asking Joe to help her more with the baby when he was home. Ellen acknowledged that he worked hard, but avowed that she did too, and that she wanted him to take care of the baby so that she could have a break. She also wanted to share more of the experience of parenting with him. To Ellen's surprise, Joe revealed that he would like to do more, but felt unsure of himself with Sara and needed more direction from her. He said that she was the "expert" in taking care of their child. Ellen said that her husband's compliment made her feel good.

He also admitted that he missed spending time alone with her. Before Sara was born they would frequently attend work functions together and enjoyed trying new restaurants and going to art museums. Joe went out with colleagues a few times since the baby was born, but missed sharing the experience with Ellen. She realized that becoming a father was a big transition for Joe, too.

Ellen and Joe agreed that a babysitter would be helpful for her when he was work to give her a break. They also agreed that they needed a babysitter to take care of Sara so that they could go out alone. We explored options for babysitters. Ellen's parents had offered to babysit more, but she had been reluctant. When I asked her why she replied:

ELLEN: I don't want to bother my parents. Also, my mom is constantly telling me what to do with Sara.
THERAPIST: What do you mean?
ELLEN: My mom has spent a lot of time with my brother and his kids and she is always telling me how *they* do things.
THERAPIST: Can you give me an example?
ELLEN: The other day I was telling her that I am starting to try solid foods with Sara, and she told me that my brother has this little food processor that is really great for making baby food.
THERAPIST: How did that make you feel?
ELLEN: Annoyed. It makes me feel like she thinks I don't know what I am doing and that my brother and sister-in-law are perfect parents.

I wondered if, in fact, Ellen's mother was being critical or if Ellen was being hyper-sensitive, which patients with depression can be.

THERAPIST: How did you respond to your mother?

ELLEN: I told her I'd think about it.

THERAPIST: Have you let your mom know how you feel when she tells you about things your brother and sister-in-law have done?

ELLEN: No, because she will just get defensive.

THERAPIST: What do you mean?

ELLEN: She'll say she was just trying to help.

I asked her if it was possible that, in fact, her mother *was* just trying to help, and she agreed that it was possible, but still annoying. I told Ellen that people often give unsolicited advice to new parents, but that when you are depressed it can be hard not to perceive the advice as criticism. Patients with depression are down on themselves and assume that others are down on them too. We explored options for responding to her mother's advice and role-played. Ellen decided to tell her mother how she felt. Her mother admitted that she was eager to help her, particularly since she had been struggling with depression. In addition, Ellen's mom had received very little guidance from her own mother or any of her peers when she became a mother and wanted to offer her daughter the support she wished she had been given. She assured Ellen that she thought she was a great mother to Sara. Ellen reported feeling better about clearing the air and gradually started asking for more help from her parents.

In addition to discussing what Ellen had lost, we discussed what she had gained by becoming a mother. She did enjoy her time with Sara and said that playing allowed her to be silly. She felt good that she was usually able to intuit what Sara needed when she cried and comfort her in a way that others could not. She also gained a new appreciation of her own parents and the challenges they faced raising her brother and her. They were younger and had fewer financial resources and supports than she did when they first became parents. Her parents were playful with Sara and able to take good care of Sara when she and her husband were out. Once she felt better able to communicate, she appreciated being able to spend more time with her parents than she could when she was working long hours at her law firm.

Ellen was increasingly excited by her new skills in speaking up with her husband, family, and friends. By Session 9, her score on the Ham-D had fallen to 12, consistent with mild depression, and her EPDS score to 12.

Termination Phase

During the final sessions (Sessions 10–12), we focused on consolidating Ellen's gains. She felt increasingly confident as a mother and enjoyed being with her daughter more. At times she felt a little guilty about wanting time for herself or apart from her daughter, but was able to recognize that it is normal to want to have time separate from one's children and to do things she used to enjoy before becoming a mother. Ellen continued to assert herself more effectively and was less hesitant to reach out for help. She felt more comfortable asking for help and realized that the experience was similar to her having to delegate tasks when she ran the recruiting department at her firm. She resumed exercising, which made her feel better about her body and enhanced her mood. She was able to better connect with her old friends and her brother and sister-in-law who had kids; until she had her baby, she had not fully appreciated what their lives had been like. Ellen acknowledged that she and Joe were communicating better than they had before having a baby.

I complimented her on the hard work she had done in treatment with me. I also provided psychoeducation about her risk of relapse and discussed relapse prevention. Given that this had been Ellen's third episode of depression, she had a great than 90% chance of a recurrence without further treatment. I encouraged her to pay particular attention to her mood in the setting of any potentially stressful life events—transitions, conflicts, deaths—as she now appreciated the connection between her mood and what is going on in her life. I reminded her that she had found a treatment that worked for her and that she could continue treatment to maintain her progress or return for "booster" sessions if she needed to ward off or began experiencing a recurrence of depressive symptoms.

By Session 12, Ellen's score on the Ham-D had fallen to 7, which is considered euthymic, and her EPDS to 4. To her surprise, Ellen wanted to consider going back to work part-time. She admitted to feeling increasingly uncomfortable not earning money and, while she enjoyed being with her daughter, she missed the stimulation and connection with adults that she enjoyed at work. She also reported feeling self-conscious at times about "just being a mother" and worried that she would not have anything interesting to talk about with other adults. In addition, Ellen and Joe had started to talk about having a second child. While she denied feeling depressed, she wanted to continue treatment with me to learn to better manage intermittent uncomfortable feelings and to explore going back to work and getting pregnant again. I agreed that it was a good idea to continue weekly sessions. IPT had helped her, and she was at great risk for relapse in the setting of two potential role transitions (returning to work and a second pregnancy). We agreed to continue meeting weekly for another twelve weeks to maintain her progress and planned to reassess the need for further treatment at that time.

DISCUSSION

Ellen's case includes some of the issues that often arise in treating women with PPD. Other important issues frequently affect the postpartum transition. While Ellen struggled with her new role as "just a mom," women who return to work after having a baby often struggle with incorporating their new role as mother with their old role as employee. They describe feeling unable to do a good job at work or at home, feel guilty about not spending enough time with their children, and feel they are failing at their jobs. The return to work is yet another role transition. I help these women evaluate and readjust their expectations of themselves as mother and as employee. When appropriate, I encourage patients to mourn the loss of being able to give their job "110 percent" and help them learn to set boundaries with their work in a way that they felt unable to before having a child. Ultimately, these patients often find themselves being more efficient at work because their time is more limited, and feel empowered being able to set a boundary between their career and family.

I have worked with a number of mothers whose babies were born prematurely and with medical complications, and were treated for weeks in a neonatal intensive care unit (NICU). I have conceptualized these cases as role transitions but identified the role transition as the transition to being a mother of a sick baby. I help these women mourn the loss of their wish for and fantasy of having a healthy newborn. Some new mothers struggle with babies who are difficult to soothe or have difficulty sleeping or feeding. Some women develop major depression in the setting of having their second or third child, struggling with taking care of more than one child and the changes this causes in their relationships with older children.

Ellen's husband was very supportive of her. Other women report more marital discord or even abandonment by the baby's father. Some report ambivalence towards their new baby because he or she is related to a father who is absent or abusive, especially if the baby resembles the father. New mothers who report that their pregnancies were unwanted or unplanned also struggle with ambivalence about their baby and regret about not terminating their pregnancy.

Having children often activates feelings and thoughts about one's own parents. Women who are adoptees may experience increased anger at their birth parents and a greater appreciation for their adoptive parents. Experiencing the bond with their own biological child makes them wonder how their parent could have given them up. On the other hand, others who now appreciate the challenges of parenthood may better understand the decision to give a child up for adoption.

Single mothers by choice report struggling with isolation and not being able to share the experience and child care responsibilities with a partner. They often fear being criticized for their decision to have a child on their own and have difficulty reaching out for help.

Similar issues arise when working with women who are depressed during pregnancy. However, working with women antepartum is an opportunity to anticipate and address these issues, prepare a woman for the transition to motherhood, and treat depression before giving birth.

Working with women with perinatal bereavement presents additional challenges. These women often describe traumatic pregnancy losses that can be difficult for the therapist to hear about. Telling the story of the loss is generally cathartic for the patient, who may not have shared the story with others for fear of upsetting them. Addressing the social isolation among women with perinatal bereavement can be particularly challenging for the IPT therapist. These women often have peers who have children or are pregnant, and they report feeling very uncomfortable being around them. Nevertheless, the IPT therapist can help them reconnect with peers and form new relationships. In some cases, augmenting IPT with a pregnancy loss support group can be helpful. The IPT therapist instills hope that the patient will recover from her depression, but cannot promise that a woman will get pregnant again; in some cases, pregnancy loss leads to the diagnosis of a fertility problem. While this provides some women with hope that they will be able to carry a pregnancy to term, they may also mourn the loss of conceiving or carrying a child without medical intervention.

Like Ellen, depressed pregnant and postpartum patients often want to know if the therapist has children. They explain that a therapist with children is more likely to relate to the challenges of pregnancy and motherhood. I explain to patients that while there are common experiences among new mothers, each woman's experience is unique and our goal in therapy is to help each woman identify *her* feelings and thoughts about motherhood and the options that will work best for *her* to manage the transition. Conversely, in my experience, the majority of patients who have experienced a pregnancy loss do not want to know if I have children. They report that if I do have children, I can't appreciate their emotional pain. Furthermore, they feel that they cannot feel comfortable expressing jealousy and anger towards other people who have children. A therapist's pregnancy affects patients in different ways. Among patients who have experienced loss, the therapist's announcement of her pregnancy can result in a therapeutic rupture or even termination of the treatment. For those who are pregnant or postpartum, a pregnancy can evoke competitive feelings with a therapist. The IPT therapist does not focus on the transference, but she does encourage the patient and compliment her efforts to express her feelings.

It should be noted that pregnancy, pregnancy loss, and the transition to parenthood affect men too, and they are also vulnerable to depression during these times. In fact, they struggle with many of the same issues that women experience. However, the literature on peripartum mood disorders and the mental health community have historically focused on women, and men are generally less likely to seek treatment. In recent years, PPD in new fathers has started to be acknowledged in the media and by mental health professionals. IPT would be a great option for these men too.

Many factors can influence a woman's experience of having a baby and make her vulnerable to depression during the peripartum period. While there are common themes among women with peripartum depression, each woman's experience with pregnancy, motherhood, and pregnancy loss is unique and can be addressed with IPT.

SUGGESTED READING

Bennett S, Indman P: Beyond the Blues: A Guide to Understanding and Treating Prenatal and Postpartum Depression. California: Moodswings Press, 2003

Jaffe J, Diamond MO, Diamond DJ: Unsung Lullabies. New York: St. Martin's Press, 2005

Kohn I, Moffit PL: A Silent Sorrow. New York: Routledge, 2000

Leon IG: When A Baby Dies. New York: Ballou Press, 1990

Shields B: Down Came the Rain: My Journey Through Postpartum Depression. New York: Hyperion, 2005

Stone SD, Menkin AE: Perinatal and Postpartum Mood Disorders: Perspectives and a Treatment Guide for Mental Health Professionals New York: Springer Publishing, 2008

14

Using Interpersonal Psychotherapy with Older Individuals

MARK D. MILLER AND CHARLES F. REYNOLDS III

IPT is a good fit for older individuals. Although depression secondary to grief can occur at any age, the deaths of spouses, friends, or other relatives are more common in those aged sixty and older. IPT is an intuitively good fit for addressing the meaning of these losses and encouraging or rekindling the mourning process. Role transitions common to later life include retirement (Miller et al., 2003), relocation, increasing medical burden (and associated disability) (Lyness et al., 2006), awareness of cognitive decline, and ceasing to drive, as well as anticipation of the final role transition from living to dying (Miller, Wolfson, Frank, et al., 1998). The potential for role disputes declines for some couples, who seem to grow more comfortable over years of shared experiences and practice resolving their differences. Other couples experience increased interpersonal tension in late life due to their illness burden, greater interpersonal proximity following retirement, or the caregiving burden for an ill, failing, or dementing spouse. Sometimes role disputes in older patients involve ill, addicted, or financially dependent children or grandchildren as well.

Older individuals whose IPT focus is interpersonal deficit report a long history of unsatisfying relationships, isolation, or estrangement that may reflect poor interpersonal skills related to lifelong maladaptive personality traits. Some older individuals with borderline personality profiles, however, can show a mellowing of intense interpersonal interactions as they settle into a pattern where they maintain an optimal distance in key supportive relationships. Other older individuals, however, can face a crisis and resultant major depressive episode when aging or illness takes its toll on perceived desirability, or when they perceive influence upon others to decline with waning ability to compensate because of shrinking opportunities to seek fame, fortune, or stature.

IPT provides practical, user-friendly tools for addressing these common issues. Even the psychotherapy-naïve individual can benefit immediately from IPT's psychoeducational component. Other IPT features easily acceptable for older individuals include its short-term, pragmatic orientation and a format that feels conversational rather than jargon-filled and artificial. In our experience implementing IPT in research protocols, we felt no need to modify IPT for an older population other than accommodating for hearing loss and transportation problems, and sometimes using shorter sessions if chronic pain intruded. Telephone sessions were sometimes used to maintain therapeutic momentum when travel to and from the visits was difficult due to inclement weather or illness (Miller et al., 2008).

A thorough scholarly review of the accumulated evidence supporting the use of IPT for depressed late-life individuals exists in book form (Hinrichsen & Clougherty, 2006). We will briefly review key studies our group carried out in Pittsburgh before turning to our detailed case study.

Following the maintenance studies of Frank et al. (Frank et al., 1990, Frank, Kupfer, et al., 1991; Frank, Prien, et al., 1991) (see Chapter 19), who compared recurrence rates using double randomization to antidepressant medication versus placebo as well as IPT versus clinical management (CM) in midlife patients, our group similarly tested the efficacy of nortriptyline versus placebo and IPT versus CM in subjects over age sixty with recurrent major depression. In the Maintenance Therapies in Late Life Depression (MTLD) (Reynolds et al., 1999), one hundred eighty-six subjects (mean age sixty-eight) received combined IPT and nortriptyline acutely. Those who achieved and maintained a Hamilton-17 Rating Scale for Depression score (Hamilton, 1960) of 10 or less for three consecutive weeks were randomized to three years of monthly treatment. All three active treatment arms—nortriptyline + IPT, placebo + IPT, nortriptyline + CM, and placebo + CM—were statistically superior (in descending order) to placebo and CM. This study was not designed to test the acute-phase efficacy of IPT, as all subjects received combined therapy (nortriptyline and IPT). Systematically applying IPT to recruited subjects with major depression who did not necessarily come seeking psychotherapy provided invaluable experience about the acceptability and practicality of IPT to older individuals. A few subjects balked at the idea of "required talking therapy," but even subjects who would not have sought psychotherapy found the psychoeducation useful and informative, and the vast majority assimilated the IPT process and became willing collaborative partners.

We conducted a *post hoc* sub-analysis of subjects receiving only placebo in order to examine the effect of IPT alone without an active medication effect. This showed no significant difference in recurrence rates between patients receiving monthly IPT versus CM for patients whose acute-phase IPT focus was role transition or grief (Miller et al., 2003). When the original focus was role dispute, however, 100% (14/14) of patients randomized to CM had a recurrence of major depression within three years of monthly follow-up, compared to 46% (5/11) randomized to monthly IPT sessions (without medication). These subgroup data, although small in sample size, argue for monthly maintenance IPT for patients whose IPT focus is role dispute. Those with an acute-phase IPT focus of role transition or unresolved grief appeared to resolve these problem areas within the twelve to sixteen weekly sessions of acute-phase IPT, so that monthly maintenance IPT did not offer differential protection against a new major depressive episode. For role disputes, however, we hypothesize that the healthier coping strategies learned in acute IPT dissipated over time in CM patients but were continually renewed for those receiving monthly IPT sessions, which provided a protective effect in the absence of antidepressant medication against recurrence of major depression.

Another study (MTLD-II) of similar design targeted the "old-old" (mean age seventy-eight, vs. sixty-eight in MTLD-I) (Reynolds et al., 2006). Because cognitive impairment is commonly comorbid in this cohort, we included depressed individuals with a Mini Mental Status Exam (MMSE) (Folstein et al., 1975) score as low as 17 out of a possible 30 points (scores of 17–25 indicate mild cognitive impairment). In preparation for MTLD-II, we worried about cognitive impairment interfering with IPT delivery in patients with memory impairment and anticipated receiving more anxious calls from concerned caregivers than we had for younger geriatric patients in MTLD-I. The two-year follow-up results found paroxetine superior to placebo in preventing major depressive relapse but showed no statistically significant separation between depressed patients who received paroxetine combined with IPT versus CM.

Why did IPT protect against major depressive recurrence in MTLD-I but not in MTLD-II? Training and supervision of therapists were identical in both studies, and some of the same therapists participated in both studies. Attendance and retention rates did not differ between the MTLD-I and MTLD-II cohorts. The MTLLD-II cohort was on average ten years older and had greater medical burden and more cognitive impairment. These factors may been important in themselves—or perhaps, because of them, our therapists took a generally more purely supportive approach to this cohort, which may have inadvertently made it harder to detect a difference in recurrence rates between the maintenance IPT and CM groups, as both took a supportive stance. In retrospect, caregivers received more frequent supportive contact in MTLD-II than MTLD-I due to frequent family and caregiver requests for advice on managing the identified patient, and maintenance-phase CM sessions tended to be longer (thirty minutes in MTLD-II vs. ten to fifteen minutes on average in MTLD-1) (Carreira et al., 2008).

A third study examined subjects aged sixty and older to test whether partial responders to a fixed 10-mg dose of escitalopram for six weeks could reach remission by sequentially adding a sixteen-week course of IPT. All partial responders at six weeks (defined as a Hamilton Rating Scale for Depression [Ham-D] score of 11–14 [Hamilton, 1960]) were randomized to either an increase of escitalopram to 20 mg daily or to the same dosage increase of 20 mg plus weekly IPT sessions for sixteen additional weeks. Results showed a clear benefit for longer-term treatment with higher-dose escitalopram but failed to show added benefit for IPT augmentation. From these results one could conclude that IPT had little therapeutic potency combined with medication, or that the medication effect was so powerful that IPT added no measurable advantage (Reynolds et al., 2010).

CASE EXAMPLE

This case illustrates the use of IPT in a late-life patient in two stages. The first stage outlines the use of IPT for major depression, which our patient Mr. Jones was diagnosed with and treated successfully for using combined antidepressant medication and IPT. At this first encounter, Mr. Jones showed some mild memory loss as well. Eighteen months after completing acute IPT, he showed more prominent cognitive impairment as well as a recurrence of major depression as he struggled with his continued role in the family business. Traditional individual IPT could not resolve this struggle due to his memory impairment and executive dysfunction. Thus, we undertook to engage concerned family members in the therapeutic process to better understand the scenario and to seek opportunities to facilitate the most reasonable course of action.

Mr. Jones, a seventy-five-year-old married white businessman, presented for help accompanied by his wife, Sarah, who had encouraged him to get treatment. Mr. Jones described feeling depressed and kept saying that he did not know why, as he really had nothing to complain about. He was not sleeping well, had trouble rising in the morning, and felt listless and sometimes useless. He denied ever feeling suicidal but said he sometimes asked himself what the point of life was.

Mr. Jones was a self-made man who had built a successful steel fabrication business he started shortly after graduating from a local two-year college. Three of his four children were employed in the business. They had plenty of work despite the economic downturn and actually had trouble finding enough qualified help. He worked six days per week but managed to take time to play golf and spend time with his grandchildren, although these pastimes no longer seemed to give him as much pleasure. All of his contemporaries were retired and spent hours on the golf course followed by drinking, a lifestyle he never really liked or wanted. His business seemed to be running well; he knew he could take more time off if he wanted to, but he enjoyed his business and found that it was an engrained habit to get up daily and go to work, which was located quite close to his home.

Mr. Jones had never been depressed like this before and had never had any mental health treatment or severe physical health problems either. He was normal weight, took Lipitor for high cholesterol and Flomax for an enlarged prostate, but had never had any surgery or serious illness. He drank alcohol socially. Sarah asked to join one meeting during his evaluation and reported he was driving too aggressively after he had had a couple of drinks on the golf course. Mr. Jones had not noticed this but agreed to limit himself to one drink. Advised to abstain completely from alcohol during the acute treatment for his depression, he said he would try. His wife voiced no further complaints about his driving, and his subsequent alcohol intake seemed minimal.

Mr. Jones' father was an Eastern European immigrant who came to work in the steel mills and died at age fifty. His mother died of breast cancer when he was still in high school. Mr. Jones was the youngest of four brothers, two of whom had died already of cancer; he visited the third on holidays. Mr. Jones had four children: two daughters and one son worked with him in the family business, and his other daughter was married and lived in a distant city. None of his biologic relatives suffered from mental illness, to his knowledge, except alcohol abuse in both of his deceased brothers.

In providing an interpersonal inventory, Mr. Jones described having a pleasant and cooperative relationship with his wife. His eldest child, Rita, worked in the office and helped to manage the business, his son Stephen supervised the installation crews for the steel, and his youngest daughter, Gloria, was the bookkeeper. Rita was married with two young children, Stephen had two children and was struggling with a contentious divorce, and Gloria was unmarried. Mr. Jones deemed himself a workaholic because he spent so much time at work building up his business. He enjoyed the work and had made friendships with a number of his regular customers. He played golf with a handful of contemporaries but could not name a close friend or confidant he met on a one-on-one basis. He had known a few of his friends since high school. Mr. and Mrs. Jones socialized with some of these men and their wives by going to restaurants. He and his wife rented a Florida condominium for two winter weeks when business was slow, and their children sometimes visited them there. He belonged to no organized religion and his only hobby, beyond his weekly golf game, was more of a wish: he had purchased a potter's wheel to take up ceramics but had never gotten around to setting it up.

Mr. Jones met DSM-IV criteria for major depressive disorder with an initial Ham-D score of 28. He agreed to participate in a depression treatment study in which he would receive antidepressant medication and IPT.

In the initial sessions, although Mr. Jones said he could not put a finger on a reason for feeling depressed, he began describing considerable anxiety about his future. He could see that all his contemporaries had retired and were leading lives of leisure, mostly playing golf. Mr. Jones feared that lifestyle would not suit him. He liked his work and was proud that his company provided a livelihood for three of his children. At age seventy-five, he knew he would not be able to work forever, however, but he could not seem to define an endpoint. He felt like a boat adrift in the currents. His wife was encouraging him to cut back and to cultivate hobbies like the ceramics he had never started. He feared being bored. He said he was thinking a lot about retirement but could not reach any decision, and that it bothered him that he could not. Even though Mr. Jones had not retired, his IPT therapist was thinking about his presentation as a role transition as Mr. Jones was struggling with whether to retire or not, and asked him whether he thought that this issue was the most salient on his mind. Mr. Jones agreed that it was and agreed to explore it further.

This dialog illustrates the use of IPT in the middle phase to explore in depth Mr. Jones' feelings about his future and his potential choices:

THERAPIST: Last week we began talking about the role you see yourself playing in your business in the future. Have you given it more thought this week?

MR. JONES: Yes I have. I am still not sure what I should do. I just can't imagine being idle all day without a purpose, especially when I know there is work that I could be doing [pauses reflectively], work I have actually enjoyed.

THERAPIST: Yes, I can see that you struggle with these questions of whether, how, and when to consider a pullback from the business of some kind. It seems that this struggle has been consuming a lot of your energy, to the point where it has resulted in your becoming depressed.

MR. JONES: Yes, I think that is correct. I have not been able to come to terms with it, or to put it aside, either.

THERAPIST: Would you like to take a closer look at this question today, then?

MR. JONES: Yes, that would be good.

THERAPIST: Let me play the devil's advocate for a moment and ask, Why don't you just keep on working and forget about retirement?

MR. JONES: I thought about that, just keep working until I drop dead on the job or something. I wouldn't mind it for myself, but my wife is pressuring me to cut back, like working is not good for my health or something. She asks me why I don't retire like everyone else my age. I am seventy-five, you know.

THERAPIST: Yes, I am aware of that, and it is true that most people have retired by the time they reach your age, but what are your feelings about it?

MR. JONES: When I try to imagine being retired, fully retired, I think I would wake up and wonder what is going on in the plant, what orders are being filled and how many are pending, etc. I guess it is in my blood by now or something. I get a big kick out of seeing custom product installed to the customer's satisfaction . . . and I like to see checks headed to the bank too! Of course, business is not all fun, there are always headaches . . . those I won't miss.

THERAPIST: So it seems clear that you get a great deal of satisfaction from watching your business work like it is supposed to . . . you make a quality product . . . the customer is happy, hopefully, they pay you for your service, you make a living as do your employees, including three of your children, and you feel proud of your accomplishment. Do I have that about right?

MR. JONES: Yes, that about sums it up.

THERAPIST: So why do you continue to struggle as you do?

MR. JONES: That's just it! I can't seem to make a decision one way or the other.

THERAPIST: You told me earlier your wife is pressuring you to retire. How does that affect you?

MR. JONES: Yeah, she wants me to take up a hobby and cut back and act my age or something. I never was much for hobbies, but I did buy that potter's wheel, which is still in the box. I'll get around to it someday, but I just don't seem to have the time.

THERAPIST: What is your feeling about your wife's stated preference for you to cut back your time working?

MR. JONES: She is trying to be helpful, that's all. We have always had a good relationship and she has never interfered with my business decisions. She says it is ultimately up to me but that she thinks I should slow down and enjoy my "golden years" before it's too late.

THERAPIST: What do you say to her?

MR. JONES: I tell her that I know she is right on some level, that it is perfectly legitimate for me to cut back and act like every other retired person. I know my good health won't last forever either, so I know she is also right that I should probably capitalize on my good fortune of good health and a sustaining business and do something else. [pauses pensively] The problem for me is, when I look around at what else there is, and none of it excites me.

THERAPIST: Lots of retired couples take time to travel and do more things together. Do you feel your wife is advocating for that in what she is saying to you?

MR. JONES: I don't think so. She is pretty much of a homebody. We go to Florida every winter and all she can talk about is when the kids are coming to visit. I see her for lunch every day when I am working since I can walk home from the plant, so it is not like we don't see a lot of each other. No, I don't think her reasons for me to retire are selfish ones at all. She just does not want to see me work myself into the ground.

THERAPIST: I see. [pause] Do you see this retirement dilemma as all or none? Have you considered a compromise plan, something in between?

MR. JONES: Do you mean like a phase-out plan or partial retirement?

THERAPIST: Yes, something like that. What are your feelings about it?

MR. JONES: I have sort of been trying to do that, it is just that we are short-handed at work and I feel bad about leaving all the work to the staff. I feel guilty, I guess, if I am on the golf course and two miles away, they are scrambling to fill orders.

THERAPIST: Do you need to hire more help to meet your workload so that you would not feel so guilty being around less?

MR. JONES: Yes, we thought about that. It is hard to find skilled people these days and you have to watch the bottom line too. I have a lot of loyal employees because I have not had to lay off anyone when things slow up.

THERAPIST: I see, but you said yourself that you know you will not be able to keep working forever; at some point they will need to look for additional help, right?

MR. JONES: I suppose we could hire someone to be the extra hands that I am helping out, but it is really about me . . . whether I am ready for that or not.

THERAPIST: I can see you really are struggling with this.

MR. JONES: Yes, I seem to think about it all the time. I can't seem to just make a decision and go with it.

THERAPIST: Well, to play the devil's advocate again, not making a decision to change anything is a decision in its own right. Maybe you are voting for the status quo by not making any move in the retirement direction. Maybe you are saying that you wish to continue as is until something else forces a change upon you?

MR. JONES: Maybe I am, but I can't seem to get the issue out of mind.

THERAPIST: Well, that's why you're here, right? We are trying explore what your true feelings are on the matter and to help you to chart a course for your future, including the option of keeping everything just as it is for the time being, right?

MR. JONES: Yes, I like the way you put that.

THERAPIST: Do you feel that we are exploring the correct subject matter that has been weighing on you to the point that it has brought on depression, or might there be another issue that you find stressful as well?

MR. JONES: No, I think we are in the right place for exploration. Everything else in my life seems to be doing OK. Sometimes I forget what it was that I wanted to say to someone, but I guess that is to be expected for my age.

THERAPIST: Your memory testing that we did as part of the study actually did show some mild memory impairment that was a bit more than one would expect for someone at your age and with your education. You scored 25 out of a possible 30 points on that paper-and-pencil test called the Mini Mental Status Exam.

MR. JONES: Yes, I recall that they told me that. I don't really think it is a big deal, though. It is that retirement thing that just bugs me every day.

THERAPIST: I see.

MR. JONES: Something just occurred to me as we are talking. Now that we have talked about this subject from every angle, I never thought that doing nothing was an option. I guess no one is insisting that I do anything different really. They have made suggestions, my wife, my kids, and my golf buddies that is, but there is nothing stopping me from just saying no, I don't want to retire yet, period, end of story. I can just announce that I intend to keep working until further notice and if they don't like it, well tough, it's my decision.

THERAPIST: It seems that you feel some relief in being able to say that you do not intend to cut back significantly on working at this time.

MR. JONES: You're damn right! It's my company, isn't it?

THERAPIST: It certainly is. You seem suddenly passionate about defending your right to keep working as long as you please.

MR. JONES: Yes, I guess I do. If only I felt as confident out there about making such a decision.

THERAPIST: Well, how about talking more about the ways in which you might express your opinion to these various individuals and how you would defend your position if they were to challenge you on it?

MR. jones: That sounds good to me. Let's see, I'll start with my wife. . .

Exchanges like this continued over the ensuing weekly sessions. He received feedback from his wife, kids, and golf buddies that they understood his wish to keep working as long as he could or until he changed his mind at some point in the future. Mr. Jones had been struggling to weigh the relative merits of the arguments for and against retirement that others put to him without adequately exploring his own feelings. His IPT therapist felt her role was to help him to complete this subjective exploration and then help him to examine his own preference against the caveats raised by others. Mr. Jones seemed to be responding to this work in IPT: his Ham-D score dropped from 24 to 14, he reported sleeping soundly for the first time in months, and he actually enjoyed golfing after realizing that he had been avoiding going to avoid those who chided him for not retiring to play more often. After twelve weeks, Mr. Jones' Ham-D had fallen to a score of 8 for two consecutive weeks and his major depression was declared remitted.

The IPT techniques used to relieve Mr. Jones' depressive symptoms (in addition to his antidepressant medication) were (1) clarification of his social role within the company and in his larger social sphere; (2) decision analysis about whether, when, and how to begin implementing a retirement strategy; and (3) communication analysis to explore how he heard and responded to the queries of others in his interpersonal inventory about his plans for retirement. Helping Mr. Jones to first clarify his own preference for continuing to work was the necessary first step for him to explore how to present his decision to others and to defend it, if necessary, in the face of opposition from those he cared about.

As per the study protocol, Mr. Jones entered the follow-up phase, where he was assessed monthly for signs of worsening depression and annually for cognitive status for two years.

Mr. Jones remained well for over a year and one half in monthly follow-up visits as he continued working daily in a hands-on way in the company he had built. Unfortunately, his memory continued to deteriorate during this period, making his work more frustrating for him and a dilemma for those who worked with him: they noted his struggles and increasingly his mistakes, which usually involved forgetting important steps in a given project. Mr. Jones, aware of these errors, was frustrated with his performance and again began questioning whether he should retire as he felt he was no longer doing a good job. This resurgent retirement dilemma now seemed clearly related to his cognitive decline. Once again, he felt paralyzed by inability to decide upon the best course of action. His Ham-D score of depressive severity rose from consistent monthly scores below 10 to 22. Cognitive retesting confirmed a significant drop in his Folstein MMSE score from 25 to 18, and he now met DSM-IV-TR criteria (and on standardized cognitive tests) for dementia, a diagnosis confirmed by independent experts at the Pittsburgh Alzheimer's Disease Research center. Mr. Jones was offered another course of IPT, only this time using IPT adapted for use with cognitive impairment and depression (IPT-ci).

Before returning to Mr. Jones' clinical course, we will provide background and justification for IPT-ci.

ADAPTATION OF IPT FOR COGNITIVE IMPAIRMENT

The clinical experience we gained in applying IPT to the MTLD-II cohort of older individuals, of whom 24% had clinically significant cognitive impairment, caused us to rethink the utility of traditionally delivered IPT for older patients who had features of both depression and cognitive impairment. Accompanying caregivers in this study frequently asked the IPT therapists for offhand management advice in the waiting room, which usually reflected their limited understanding of the identified patients' executive dysfunction more than their memory loss or depression. Executive dysfunction can manifest as impairment in various higher-order cognitive functions such as insight, judgment, and complex problem solving presenting as impairments in one or more areas: social graces, initiative, planning, impulse control, empathy, and multitasking (shifting attention or focus without becoming confused). These abilities require multiple brain regions to communicate efficiently with each other. Thus, any brain disease that damages these neural circuits, such as strokes or Alzheimer's disease, can produce executive dysfunction.

Besides being frustrated with the identified patient's memory loss, caregiving family members frequently misread or misattribute signs of executive dysfunction as willful opposition, laziness, or even meanness. Caregiver reactions based on these misunderstandings can provoke further maladaptive responses and role disputes.

Researchers now define cognitive impairment on a spectrum from normal to so-called minimal cognitive impairment (MCI) (Lingler et al., 2006) to frank dementia, defined as significant memory loss that compromises functioning plus at least one other area of cognitive impairment. When meeting for the first time an older patient who has depression and some degree of cognitive impairment, it can be a puzzle to unravel how the depression and cognitive impairment (as well as any underlying medical illness) contribute to the clinical picture. Even facing memory impairment sufficient to impede a psychotherapy that builds upon work done in prior sessions, we concluded that the IPT approach was useful and viable with some modifications. We preserved the basic tenets of IPT such as the interpersonal inventory, ample psychoeducation, assigning the sick role, and establishing a focus with therapeutic efforts directed toward improving social role functioning. We saw a gap on the spectrum between psychotherapeutic approaches designed to help depressed elders and social casework for patients with cognitive impairment, with IPT-ci an ideal middle of that spectrum, especially in the early stages of cognitive impairment when caregivers frequently do not fully understand what they are observing.

Combining our IPT experience in MTLD-II with our psychiatric experience treating geriatric patients at a multidisciplinary treatment center (Benedum Geriatric Center), we formed a work group to discuss and test modifications of IPT. Since caregivers had many questions and were often beginning to take on more supervisory or helping roles with their cognitively impaired family members, we concluded it was crucial to modify IPT to integrate the caregiver into the IPT treatment process.

We define a caregiver as anyone who worries about, provides surveillance for, or assists an older individual for either cognitive decline or depression. We experimented with various refinements we then collectively named IPT-ci, for "cognitive impairment," and subsequently published an IPT-ci manual (Miller, 2009) as a guide for clinicians.

Table 14.1 outlines key modifications of IPT-ci.

We define "steady state" as the point when (1) both the identified patient and caregiver(s) are educated to their appropriate level of comprehension about depression and cognitive impairment/dementia, (2) a biomedical workup has determined potential medical causes for depression or specific subtypes of cognitive impairment, (3) trials of appropriate psychotropic medications have been attempted, (4) depressive symptoms and dementia-related problem behaviors have been minimized, and (5) quality of life has been maximized for the identified patient, taking cognitive status into account.

Social casework for cognitively impaired patients focuses on completing a diagnostic workup, assessing safety, finding helping services or new housing arrangements, and preparing for long-term contingencies like a nursing home or other long-term care facility. By virtue of its roots in psychotherapy, IPT-ci seeks to understand the patient's presentation in the broadest context, including changes in social roles for not just the identified patient but caregivers as well. Traditional IPT techniques can be used insofar as a given older patient can collaborate with the psychotherapist, while specific IPT-ci techniques can help to bridge the gap of understanding between the identified patient and caregivers and can serve as a forum for joint or individual problem solving and role dispute resolution.

Absent a death that triggers grieving, identified patients who are keenly aware of and upset by their cognitive impairment are considered to be in a role transition from

Table 14.1. COMPARING TRADITIONAL IPT AND IPT-ci

Traditional IPT	IPT for Cognitive Impairment
Format: One-to-one patient–therapist visits, with rare involvement of significant others	**Format:** Full engagement of identified patient plus caregiver(s); flexible use of individual sessions with either the patient or caregiver(s); option of joint problem-solving sessions as indicated
Focus: Reducing depressive symptoms	**Focus:** Assessment and treatment of both depressive symptoms and cognitive impairment/dementia
Duration: Twelve to sixteen weekly sessions with contract for planned termination. Optional monthly maintenance IPT sessions (IPT-M) for patients at high recurrence risk.	**Duration:** Roughly weekly sessions to engage patient and caregiver(s); complete workup for cognitive impairment and depression; goal of a "steady state"; follow-up visits spaced appropriately for the lifetime of the identified patient

normal cognitive ability to less so. Caregivers are recognized as often experiencing their own role transitions as they position themselves to supervise and provide more direct assistance: this position may prove uncomfortable, unwelcome, or even a role reversal. To understand the complete picture, which the identified patient may be unable to provide, the IPT-ci therapist must assess the caregivers' ability to give care, understand other stressors the caregivers may be struggling with, engage them in education about what they are observing, and sometimes elicit their help to implement changes to improve the social role function of identified patients when the patients cannot implement such changes themselves.

Using techniques to indirectly benefit the identified patient by working with or through a caregiver obviously departs from traditional IPT, which focuses on the interface between the patient and the therapist, with infrequent input or visits from others in the patient's interpersonal inventory. IPT-ci targets the interface between the identified patients and caregiver(s) who live with them or at least observe the effect of cognitive impairment on their daily function. Collaborative work with caregivers in addition to the identified patient allows the IPT-ci therapist a fuller understanding of the patient's functioning as well as an opportunity to clarify, educate, and bridge gaps in understanding that can reduce future role disputes. Collaboratively seeking to implement changes that encourage better function and higher quality of life for the identified patient is the ultimate goal of IPT-ci, including but not limited to resolution of depressive symptoms.

Caregivers are not patients *per se*, even though they may benefit from the IPT-ci therapist's efforts. Caregivers may require referral for their own therapy or other services., a subject we will return to after considering the evolution of the case of Mr. Jones, whose cognitive impairment has worsened to meet criteria for dementia.

CASE EXAMPLE: COMBINED PATIENT AND CAREGIVER INTERVENTION IN IPT-ci

Mr. Jones had made progress in his initial course of IPT focusing on his role transition facing retirement from his family business. The combination of antidepressant medication and IPT helped him feel better about deciding to continue his routine as long as he felt he was contributing in a meaningful way. During eighteen months of monthly maintenance medication management sessions, however, Mr. Jones began to complain more loudly that he felt unsure of himself and felt frustrated at work as it was now harder to contribute meaningfully, and that this made him feel more depressed. His Ham-D score rose to 22. Neuropsychological testing, performed as part of the research protocol at predetermined intervals over eighteen months, determined that Mr. Jones had declined from minimal cognitive impairment to dementia in a pattern that suggested probable Alzheimer's disease. His MMSE score dropped from 25 to 18, and other cognitive test batteries declined. He wondered aloud if he should bother to go to the office anymore. He followed these thoughts with counter-arguments that he would not know what to do with himself if he were no longer working.

After re-engaging with Mr. Jones and exploring this issue in depth, the IPT therapist recognized that Mr. Jones' ability to continue working was in jeopardy. As Mr. Jones could not describe clearly how others around him were reacting to his now-obvious cognitive changes, the therapist offered to host a family meeting to explore this issue. Mr. Jones readily agreed.

In his prior IPT course, Mr. Jones had been a full partner in the treatment process despite mild memory loss consistent with minimal cognitive impairment. He had been able to consider the issue of retirement from several points of view (including the suggestions of his wife, children, and peers), and with his therapist's help had explored his own feelings about what he really wanted for himself. Having decided to continue working for the time being, his mood improved and he seemed content.

As his cognitive impairment gradually but significantly worsened, eighteen months later Mr. Jones reported making work errors that were potentially costly to the company. This made him question his worth to the enterprise. A bigger problem than memory loss was his declining executive function. Good judgment and complex problem solving can be challenges in the business world even with fully functional brain capacity. Although from all indications Mr. Jones had once operated as a very effective chief operating officer, his dementia was taking a toll on his insight, judgment, problem-solving ability, and ability to grasp the "big picture." His IPT-ci therapist could see that the problem was not confined to memory impairment: Mr. Jones' ability to lead and to effectively delegate ongoing decisions was gone, as his wife and daughter confirmed.

How can one carry out IPT or any psychotherapy that requires intact memory to build upon prior work with a cognitively impaired patient? How can a therapist help a patient whose depression is relapsing from changes in his work ability and work relationships wrought by a brain disease like Alzheimer's disease? The IPT-ci therapist seeks the best understanding possible of the problem (Mr. Jones' declining ability to work effectively or contribute meaningfully) and to incorporate other sources of information (with permission) to help grasp the "big picture" more completely than the patient himself can, given his cognitive impairment. Although IPT-ci shares one goal of traditional IPT, to resolve depressive symptoms, the role of cognitive impairment in worsening Mr. Jones' depression could not be ignored. IPT-ci confronts cognitive impairment head on to assess its severity and its disruption of the patient's social roles. The IPT-ci therapist seeks to understand how the depression and the cognitive impairment conspire to reduce effective social role functioning while asking the question: "Who else might be willing to assist the identified patient to make meaningful changes to help reduce his or her depressive symptoms?" Traditional IPT might provide limited help to Mr. Jones in one-to-one weekly sessions if cognitive impairment limits his recall, insight, and understanding of the complex agendas of others around him in the workplace. If the IPT-ci therapist, understanding the common presentations of cognitive impairment, can gather enough information from all available sources to formulate a cogent assessment that includes the contribution of cognitive impairment to the depressive symptom picture, perhaps he or she can work realistically with the identified patient and involved caretakers. These techniques depart from traditional IPT by engaging and educating caregivers and potentially having separate or joint meetings with caregivers and the identified patient to orchestrate changes to help relieve the identified patient's depression. IPT-ci deliberately shifts from a position of advocacy by working solely with the patient to a willingness to engage, educate, and enlist the assistance of interested caregivers who may help to reduce the identified patient's depressive symptom burden.

Mr. Jones' IPT-ci therapist invited all interested family members Mr. Jones wished to attend. He came to the meeting with his wife and his youngest daughter Gloria.

THERAPIST: I want to welcome all of you. The purpose of this meeting is to better understand the issues surrounding your father and husband's depression and the struggles he has expressed about how to pull back or retire from the business.

SARAH: I don't work in the business, so I really can't comment, but he has changed, and he doesn't seem sure about what to do with himself anymore.

MR. JONES: I go to work every day, but I can't seem to get a grip on what is happening. We are short-staffed, and so I try to help out, but I make too many mistakes.

THERAPIST: Can you be more specific?

MR. JONES: Yes. I get to working on drawings from a draftsman, and I forget where I put things. Sometimes the things get caught, but if they are missed and the steel goes out to a job site, it can be very expensive to have to cut and burn it to make it fit.

THERAPIST: If I could ask a direct question, Mr. Jones, do you think your memory loss interferes with your ability to handle the jobs you do?

MR. JONES: Definitely. I spend half my day looking for things I misplaced.

THERAPIST: As I understand it, you have three children who work for this business, correct? One daughter manages the front office and oversees the orders and overall operation, your son manages the installation, and Gloria, who is here today, is the bookkeeper. Do I have that right so far?

MR. JONES: Yes.

THERAPIST: You told me you have about twenty total employees and that you have built this business from scratch over thirty-five years and now have quite a loyal following of customers.

MR. JONES: Yes, that's true.

THERAPIST: You must be very proud of this business that you created and that is able to employ three of your children.

MR. JONES: Yes, I guess I am.

THERAPIST: So you don't want mistakes hurting your bottom line, but you also don't want mistakes hurting the good reputation of the good-quality work that you have earned.

MR. JONES: That's correct.

THERAPIST: Let me ask you this, then. Do you feel that your kids and your employees know what they are doing at this point, so that you don't have to continue working in the way that you describe as increasingly harder for you to handle?

MR. JONES: Yes, they can handle it.

THERAPIST: Then why do you still go to work if it is so hard for you?

MR. JONES: Habit, I guess. I wouldn't know what to do with myself. I have friends who play golf every day for hours and are retired full time, and they sit around and bullshit about nothing. It never did much for me. Working has always been second nature to me since I was a young boy, and besides, the fabrication building is just one hundred yards from my house, so it's just my routine to get up every day and go there.

THERAPIST: I see.

THERAPIST: [To Gloria] Do you have an opinion about your father's work and how it affects him emotionally?

GLORIA: It's true, he does have trouble keeping up with projects, but we keep an eye on him, and we have taken more things away from him, but since we are short-handed lately we've needed all the help we can get. I don't think he is ready to just walk out of there and retire. This business is too much a part of him. . . . [hangs her head and pauses] There is something else. [looks at father] I'm sorry, but there are some personalities that are playing a role here. This person does not like to delegate either. She looks over his shoulder 24/7, and that's fine . . . let's just leave it that she doesn't delegate either. This person should be here today.

THERAPIST: Are you speaking about your sister, then?

GLORIA: Yes. She needs to be taken down a peg or two.

SARAH: It's true. She is too bossy, and she needs to be settled down.

THERAPIST: I'm getting a picture of tension between you two sisters regarding how the business should be run. What about your brother?

GLORIA: He has been going through a bad divorce and that is about all he can handle right now.

THERAPIST: I see.

THERAPIST: [To Sarah] You mentioned that your older daughter needs to be settled down a bit. Is this something your husband would have handled in prior years that he is not seemingly able to do now?

SARAH: Yes, definitely.

THERAPIST: [To Mr. Jones] Do you want to comment on that?

MR. JONES: It's true. I've never been what you call a confrontative person. I never wanted to browbeat anyone. [Head hung, folding a tissue in his hands]

THERAPIST: Would you say that in previous years you felt more comfortable than you do now knowing the best decisions to make to run the company?

MR. JONES: Yes, that's true. I just don't seem to know what to do anymore. I spend my day going from one place to another, and I try to be helpful, but at the end of the day, I don't seem to have accomplished much.

THERAPIST: [To Gloria] I'm getting the impression that you wish your father would be more authoritative towards your sister, who seems to be running the operation these days.

GLORIA: That's right. No one voted her in to be CEO, but she acts like it. [Looks towards father] I'm sorry, but that's the truth.

MR. jones: You're right. She can be bossy, but I just don't know where to start some-times, so I guess I haven't been doing anything.

At this point it had become clear to me that in addition to memory loss, the pre-ceding exchange demonstrates Mr. Jones' executive dysfunction in his decreased ability to make authoritative decisions, which requires weighing many options, pros, cons, and projected outcomes. This has resulted in the *de facto* rise to power of his oldest daughter, who is absent, and the resentment expressed by his younger daugh-ter, Gloria. It's clear to me that the rest of the family was hoping Mr. Jones would "just take control and straighten things out and settle some people down," meaning his eldest daughter, but has not done so due to executive impairment. I decided to try to: (1) provide psychoeducation about executive impairment; (2) acknowledge that the retirement issue is complicated by intrafamilial role disputes; and (3) acknowledge that the patient's self-esteem is under great pressure from the perception that he should do something, yet he cannot figure out what that should be, and that his inability to "execute a plan" is due to executive dysfunction that the family has not yet recognized.

I see an opportunity within the remaining time to bridge the gap between the patient and the family, who have a distorted view of his current ability, and to seek opportunities for maintaining his self-esteem and helping him to minimize his depressive symptoms while coming to terms with his difficulties in conducting his business.

THERAPIST: Mr. Jones, there seems to be some tension between your daughters about just how this business should be run, and your wife and Gloria seem to feel that the situation calls for you to do something about it. Do you sometimes feel pushed into the role of good cop, bad cop?

MR. JONES: Yes. It grieves me, but I don't know what to do about it.

THERAPIST: If, for example, you were unable to be a part of this business any longer due to illness or some other reason, do you think there would be a shake-up after you left for good?

MR. JONES: I would hope not, but I know there has been tension.

THERAPIST: [To Gloria] What's your opinion?

GLORIA: Big time!! I want him to retire whenever he wants to, but if he walked out of the business tomorrow, I don't think it would survive.

THERAPIST: Wow! Those are strong words.

MR. jones: That's what I say. I'm aware that it's not a good situation.

Now it's clear that the current hot issue is less about mistakes he makes due to memory loss than that his perceived lack of leadership has left a void. It is clear to me that Mr. Jones cannot manage sorting through these issues on his own, and that he feels guilty in retreating from confronting them. Again, I am cognizant that Mr. Jones is the identified patient and that my role is to try to ameliorate his depressive symptoms by helping him cope with the role transition to partial or complete retirement as well as the role dispute he cannot effectively negotiate concerning business decisions. I decide to try some concrete suggestions and clarifications before ending the session.

THERAPIST: If I might sum up a bit, it seems clear that you, Mr. Jones, are having a hard time at work these days for two reasons. Your memory loss impairs accuracy, and it's a constant source of great frustration for you. When individuals suffer memory loss, other areas of brain function can suffer as well. Making the complex decisions required to run a business with all its demands means that many parts of the brain must work together efficiently to weigh the pros and cons of each decision, to actually come to a conclusion on a particular decision, and then to constantly evaluate how well that decision worked or did not work. Memory is one factor involved, but logical thinking, reasoning, and problem solving are also very important. I think it's fair to say that these other areas have been weakened by the same disease process that causes your memory loss, namely probable early Alzheimer's disease, as we discussed earlier. In other words, it's not your fault that you cannot grasp the big picture and make strategic decisions as well as you did 10 or 20 years ago, it's the result of the disease process your brain is suffering from. It's just no longer possible for you to make hard decisions and to work as effectively and as efficiently as you once did. Are you all with me so far?

ALL: Yes, go on.

THERAPIST: It also seems clear to me with regard to your business, that a succession plan has never been discussed or agreed to by all parties, am I correct?

MR. JONES: That's true. It just seems to have evolved on its own.

THERAPIST: I would like to make some concrete suggestions that I think would be helpful here. Is that okay with you?

MR. JONES: Sure, go ahead.

THERAPIST: I would first like everyone to understand, including those who are not here today, that Mr. Jones cannot be expected to make all the tough decisions anymore—through no fault of his own, as it's due to Alzheimer's disease. The same illness that has brought on memory loss has also robbed him of some decision-making capabilities. Does this make sense?

ALL: Yes.

THERAPIST: I think the time is not right to talk about formal retirement yet. He does not want it but also feels deeply frustrated with how many things aren't going well. It's not a simple matter of yes or no. Perhaps we need to allow him to gradually cut back and phase out at his own pace that feels right to him.

GLORIA AND SARAH: We agree with that.

THERAPIST: I also think that a serious discussion needs to take place among the children about how to best run the family business going forward. Am I right that no such discussion has taken place?

GLORIA: That's true.

THERAPIST: The fact is, your father already struggles with memory loss, and now declining decision-making ability. If this is Alzheimer's disease, as we suspect it to be, his ability to participate may be further compromised over time, not to mention his voiced wish to pull back to some degree or other. The result of all this is that the three of you sooner or later must find a way to cooperate, resolve your differences, and make the business thrive if it is going to continue to provide you with a livelihood for the long term.

GLORIA: Yes, that's true.

THERAPIST: [To Gloria] Can you call a meeting of your siblings and have such a discussion?

GLORIA: Yes.

THERAPIST: Good. It really seems overdue, and waiting for your father to solve these issues has not worked satisfactorily up to now, right?

GLORIA: You are correct.

THERAPIST: [To Mr. Jones] Am I saying anything that does not seem right to you, Mr. Jones?

MR. JONES: No, you've hit the nail on the head.

THERAPIST: As it is soon time to stop for today, are there any questions any of you have? Have you found this family meeting to be helpful?"

GLORIA AND SARAH: Yes.

THERAPIST: Would you like to have a follow-up meeting to see how things are going?

ALL: Yes.

THERAPIST: Okay. I'll see you, Mr. Jones, next week, and we'll talk about a time for another meeting.

Next Week: Follow-up Visit with Mr. Jones Alone

THERAPIST: How do you think the meeting went last week?

MR. JONES: I thought it was good. I guess I never realized how much I've been avoiding this issue of how my kids are going to run the company. They are all good kids, but they don't always get along and see eye to eye. It was good to have everything put on the table and now I realize I wasn't doing my job by avoiding the issue of who is to take responsibility for what.

Mr. Jones feels some guilt for not acting in a timely fashion, which has been damaging to his self-esteem and his mood. I decide to remind him of the important role he has played throughout his lifetime, even though his capability to run the company as a CEO is now lacking.

THERAPIST: Well, let's review for a moment. You created this business thirty-five years ago, correct? You built it from scratch, and it has been providing a livelihood for you and your family, including your adult children who have entered the business and continue to receive a livelihood from it, correct?

MR. JONES: Yes, that's true.

THERAPIST: So even though you acknowledge that it's hard for you to keep track of what's going on in the business today, it really isn't your fault. You would do so if you could, but your brain won't allow you to due to the illness your brain is suffering from. Are you with me so far?

MR. JONES: Yes, I am.

THERAPIST: The other thing I want to point out is: this business would not be here today if you hadn't built it up to what it is. And even though you might not be able to run it as efficiently as you once did, it's still a viable business you have created that you should give yourself credit for.

MR. JONES: I guess so, but I don't think about it from that point of view very often.

THERAPIST: I think you should. You are at a crossroads in your life where you are trying to figure out how to gradually pull back due to your age and your memory problems, which we've discussed, but you are having a hard time figuring out how to do that.

MR. JONES: I don't know how to go about it. I just don't know what to do anymore.

THERAPIST: Well, we've discussed that, let me remind you. Your memory and your problem-solving ability is affected, so that perhaps it is time to turn more of the reins over to the people whose memories are intact, like your children, although they need to figure out how to work together to keep the company running like you intended it to. That's why I suggested that the three of your kids meet and work out their differences to have a strategy for managing the business long term, so that it will be a relief for you to see them cooperating on their own.

MR. JONES: Yes, that's been overdue.

THERAPIST: I'm aware of other family-owned companies where the founder, as he's aged, takes on more of an emeritus status, where he makes an appearance in the plant and walks around and says hello and checks on the quality of the product, but really doesn't have to do any of the day-to-day operational work, which has been turned over to others. Do you think it's time for you to think about such a role for yourself?

MR. JONES: Yes, I just can't contribute in a meaningful way anymore.

THERAPIST: The impression I got from Gloria is that you *do* contribute in a meaning-ful way just by showing up, because you still are the CEO of the company even though your daughter Rita handles most of the day-to-day operations. You are the founder who represents the legacy of this company and the quality of the product you deliver. I would think you'd be very proud of that.

MR. JONES: Yes. I guess I am.

THERAPIST: Well, maybe you should think about your new role as presiding over the transition to having your children run the whole thing. Could you see yourself as partially retired and come and go as you want? Do you think your kids would be agreeable to that?

MR. JONES: I think they would. I think they are capable of running this business without me.

THERAPIST: Well, just to be clear. It's not that they don't want you there, or don't appreciate you being there. I think they have all been careful not to pressure you to retire until such time that you are completely ready. The business decisions that come up every day can't wait, however, and there hasn't been a very clear succession plan up to now if you are no longer making all of the big decisions.

MR. JONES: That's true.

THERAPIST: So perhaps, with your blessing, your children will find a way to work out their differences and essentially take over the running of the company completely and allow you to come and go as the founder. What do you say about that?

MR. JONES: I agree. I think that's the best role for me, if they can do it.

THERAPIST: I don't think they have much choice at this point. If this business is going to survive long term, they must find a way to cooperate.

MR. jones: I guess you're right.

The above dialog departs somewhat from traditional IPT, whose goal is to help patients first decide what they feel, explore what they really want, then devise and implement strategies to pursue those goals. In IPT-ci there is tacit recognition that the patient can no longer do all of these things, and that preservation of self-esteem in light of accomplishments already achieved, as well as seeking new roles commensurate with his or her current capabilities, is the realistic and achievable goal. There is room for creativity and interpersonal negotiation skills by the IPT-ci therapist that can affect outcome in such cases.

IPT-ci might therefore seem more supportive, more directive, and more paternalistic than traditional IPT, but the goal is for the IPT-ci therapist to use his or her own cognitive ability to steer the patient toward what the therapist has come to understand to be the patient's wishes (synthesized from all available information), which he or she can no longer achieve or perhaps even fully articulate. Mr. Jones desperately wanted to remain with the business he had built but could not figure out how to do so. As his children and his wife did not fully appreciate that he could no longer lead the company, the therapist suggested that they needed to work things out for themselves so that their much-respected father could stop worrying about the business and, while they were at it, help him figure out some role he could still play within his capability that would not leave him frustrated. After ample psychoeducation and having once introduced the concept of elder statesman inspecting the plant's work as an achievable role for Mr. Jones, his family quickly embraced the concept and helped to implement it. Mr. Jones was able to maintain a role as "semi-retired founder of the company," allowing him to come and go as he pleased without necessary involvement in day-to-day operations. Mr. Jones expressed relief for these changes that constituted his new life, and his mood improved.

Family Meeting, Two Months Later

THERAPIST: So how are things going, particularly in how you are now handling your role in the business, Mr. Jones?

MR. JONES: I cut back. Sometimes I don't go into the office until ten o'clock in the morning, and then I leave early. My memory seems to be getting worse. I can't seem to keep track of much of anything anymore.

GLORIA: That's not true, Daddy. You've been working on the plans for the Oliver structure.

MR. JONES: Not really. Stephen has been doing most of the project.

GLORIA: But you've been helping. The two of you have been doing it together.

MR. jones: I guess I have been helping, but he has really been doing the work.

His daughter clearly wants Mr. Jones to have a continued presence in the company, even though it's beyond his capabilities. I note this and decide to return to this issue later to make other suggestions about buoying his self-esteem in this transition.

MR. jones: I've tried to spend more time doing some pottery. I always wanted to do that, and I have a pottery wheel at home that I set up, but I can't seem to figure out the directions of how to do it.

THERAPIST: Well, that's very good. Having hobbies can give you pleasure and are a great way to help with the transition from helping working full time to partial or full retirement.

MR. JONES: I just wish I could get that wheel working right so I could throw some pots on the wheel.

THERAPIST: Perhaps you can ask your pottery instructor if he can come help you set it up. It's probably easy for him to do so, and it would be worth paying some money to help you.

MR. JONES: Yes that's a good idea. I never thought of that.

THERAPIST: [To Gloria and Sarah] How do the rest of you feel your father/husband has been doing?

GLORIA: He has cut back. We've taken more and more things off of him so that he doesn't have to feel burdened by the details.

THERAPIST: OK. And what's your feeling about the role your father still plays in the business?

GLORIA: I think it's important for him to come around every day and see that things are going OK. It wouldn't be right for him to just quit coming in altogether.

THERAPIST: I think you are absolutely correct. I think he needs to keep a role in the company of some kind, even if it is more the role of the respected elder statesman whom everyone respects for forming the company in the first place.

GLORIA: Yes, we try to do that and give him tasks that we know that he can handle.

SARAH: He has cut back. I think he should cut back some more though.

THERAPIST: What's your opinion about what would be appropriate for him at this point?

SARAH: I think it should be 50/50—hobbies and work. He is not quite there yet. I would like to see him cut back further.

MR. JONES: [shrugs] I guess. There is not much I can do at the business anyway.

THERAPIST: Mr. Jones has been talking about his transition from working full time to part time to partial retirement. I've reminded him several times that there would be no business were it not for his hard work and tenacity that got the business to where it is today, and that he should remember that every time he walks into the building, as I'm sure the employees are well aware. Wouldn't you agree?

GLORIA: Yes. We have tried to send that message to him. It's been hard for him to pull back, but we are trying to help him to do so as he is ready.

THERAPIST: [To Gloria] The last time we met, we talked about your meeting among your siblings to see what could be worked out about how the three of you can figure out how to work together better, so that your father no longer feels he has to play good cop/bad cop with regard to the differences between you all. Can you say something about how that went?

GLORIA: Yes, we had a meeting. There is better agreement between us. We have to all agree that we just have different personalities, and we are never going to be perfect together, but it is working better, and we do now all realize that we have to pull together to run the company and let our father transition to partial or full retirement as he wishes and not have to worry about it, which I think was weighing on him heavily.

THERAPIST: Good! I'm glad you were able to have that discussion, because clearly you are the ones who are going to need to pull together to keep this company running.

SARAH: I think the increased dose of his antidepressant has helped his mood. He is less quiet now, and he interacts more with people.

THERAPIST: I agree with you. I think he needed a dose adjustment and going forward, it's going to be important to keep his medication adjusted properly as well as to provide a forum for him to discuss these and any other issues that he wishes to help him cope with his everyday life. Mr. Jones, do you feel that you are tolerating the medication?

MR. JONES: Yes, I don't seem to have any side effects with them. I guess they have been helpful to me.

THERAPIST: Okay. I want to say thanks to everyone for coming in for another family meeting, and we can do this again in the future as the situation dictates, but I think you've all pulled together to figure out what's best for your father/husband, and this has been helpful to him.

THERAPIST: [To Mr. Jones] Mr. Jones, I'll shut the tape off now, and we'll discuss making a follow-up appointment.

MR. jones: Okay.

In two additional years of individual visits and occasional reports by phone or accompanying visits from family members, Mr. Jones complained of progressively worsening cognitive impairment, easily observable in his language errors and his frustration with worsening memory. His MMSE fell to 16. His mood, however, remained euthymic with a Ham-D score of 6. He was maintained long term on antidepressant and cognitive enhancer medications. Mr. Jones described his role in the company as consisting of increasingly brief visits as the busy environment confused him. His new "job" was to bring in the mail and to take the checks to the bank, "something," he added, "you never get enough of."

DISCUSSION

The difference between trying to help Mr. Jones with IPT initially compared to the second round necessarily included his worsening cognitive impairment and its effect on his work role. Family meetings made clear that Mr. Jones' wife and daughter were becoming caregivers, providing more surveillance and trying to steer him to gradually pull back from work he was obviously finding too stressful to perform. Mrs. Jones and Gloria initially did not understand that his cognitive impairment directly affected his ability to make complex business decisions and manage employee interpersonal conflicts. Diplomatically educating Mr. Jones' family about his cognitive limitations was important to allow them to readjust their expectations of his performance to realistic levels. This psychoeducation indirectly benefited Mr. Jones, as the family could then better help him to reassess his role in his company and maintain his self-esteem with appropriate increases in social support, rather than harboring unrealistic expectations that he would somehow return to his former authoritative self.

It became clear that Mr. Jones' family neither wanted to see him highly frustrated attempting work he could no longer manage, nor to feel pushed into retirement, as they knew that his whole life's focus and purpose was tied to his business. The role of the IPT-ci therapist was to first grasp the big picture and all contributing elements (identified patient role and ability, caregiver agendas, workplace demands, etc.), and then to explore possible interventions in this role transition scenario that best advocated for Mr. Jones by helping all parties to understand the reality of his cognitive impairment and to prepare them to appropriately help him decide how to move forward. This needed to be done in a way that was not continuously demoralizing and helped to maintain his self-esteem and preserve his role as the company's respected founder, while allowing him to remain confident that his children were now cooperating to keep the business going.

In traditional IPT, the therapist provides a forum for the patient to explore the agreed-upon focus in sufficient depth to understand it. The goal of IPT is to use the realized understanding of the problem focus to implement change, thus relieving depressive symptoms. In contrast, the patient who suffers from cognitive impairment often has limited ability to use insight, process complex information, see problems from multiple angles, and integrate the specific problem area into the larger sphere of the social community within which he or she operates. Although traditional IPT is often no longer possible for such a patient, the therapist can still assess the problem area, solicit other concerned parties to jointly explore greater understanding of the problem area, and incorporate their participation into a treatment plan to benefit the identified patient, reducing depressive symptoms and helping to realign unrealistic expectations about current cognitive abilities. The IPT-ci therapist acts more like a surrogate or advocate for the identified patient's best interests to the extent that the patient can no longer fulfill that role due to cognitive impairment.

One could argue that the IPT-ci therapist's actions might appear paternalistic rather than facilitating the patient's ability to better understand his or her own feelings about the identified problem area. On the contrary, the IPT-ci therapist does his or her best to determine the patient's struggle that precipitated the depression, taking any cognitive impairment into account, and then to help the identified patient to understand the overview pieced together from all available sources. This must be done before trying to help the identified patient to implement the most effective coping strategy commensurate with current (realistic) cognitive ability. This might mean, for example, helping the patient to cope with and plan alternative strategies for ceasing to drive an automobile if such a restriction is mandated or inevitable.

A preliminary task to achieve before implementing changes that involve the participation of others is to assess the caregiver's understanding of the identified patient's cognitive impairment and to correct any unrealistic conclusions. A thorough understanding of basic gerontology is a prerequisite. Once educated and realistic in their expectations, caregivers can be approached to help implement appropriate changes in conjunction with changes the identified patient is attempting to achieve desired goals.

In the case of Mr. Jones, all concerned parties could see his frustration at work, but they needed help to understand the role his executive dysfunction played in limiting his work role. Once educated about Mr. Jones' cognitive disability, they could support efforts to convert his company role to one he could manage, allowing him to preserve his self-esteem while relieving him of the burden of responsibility.

Caregiver agendas that run counter to the IPT-ci therapist's view of the best course of advocacy for the identified patient may also need appropriate negotiation. Insofar as the identified patient cannot always be his or her own best advocate due to cognitive impairment, the IPT-ci therapist tries to orchestrate what might be a series of steps, like a conductor of a symphony, to seek the participation of all willing parties who want to help relieve the depression, maintaining the highest self-esteem, independence, and quality of life possible for the identified patient.

A Word about Caregivers

Mr. Jones' wife and daughter were not IPT patients *per se*. The IPT-ci therapist did not solicit their overall life problems but rather engaged, educated, and worked with them where their misunderstanding of depression and cognitive impairment complicated their interpersonal relationships with Mr. Jones and his role in the family business. IPT-ci engages caregiver(s) not as patients but as significant others who desire help adjusting to new caregiving roles and to maximize their ability to cope with the identified patient's current status. Should the caregiver need help with other issues, the IPT-ci therapist makes referrals, which might include individual psychotherapy for the caregivers themselves. This demarcation allows the IPT-ci therapist to focus on the identified patient's needs and not try to act as therapist for caregivers. Establishing this position is important since, in rare instances where elder abuse might emerge, the IPT-ci therapist must be prepared to advocate for the identified patient even if it means reporting a caregiver to the AREA AGENCY ON AGING or other appropriate protective service. Caregivers may well benefit from IPT-ci as their understanding of the patient improves and they focus on the reality of the identified patient's cognitive ability, but this is incidental to the goal of improving the identified patient's supportive social environment.

The goal of IPT-ci interventions for an older depressed individual with cognitive impairment is to achieve and maintain an optimized, steady state of function commensurate with the patient's current cognitive ability, maintaining readiness to reassess new problems, mood changes, and further cognitive decline over time. If an older individual is cognitively intact, IPT can be applied as it is for younger patients to resolve depressive symptoms. If cognitive impairment is the presenting complaint, whether or not comorbid with depression, the IPT-ci model can be useful to help caregivers and the identified patient maintain optimal function consistent with current cognitive ability and maintain regular follow-up visits at an interval appropriate to evaluate and facilitate coping strategies for the patient's lifetime.

Presentation of IPT-ci at conferences and meetings has yielded feedback from geriatric clinicians that its concepts are useful. Other clinicians report having intuitively evolved a similar working strategy, and that IPT-ci clarified and integrated their experience. Perhaps the best use of IPT-ci is as a teaching format for the next generation of healthcare professionals planning to do psychotherapy with the exploding population of individuals developing cognitive impairment. No systematic research studies have yet evaluated IPT-ci. One recent Quality Improvement Pilot Project using social workers to implement IPT-ci at the Benedum Geriatric Center in Pittsburgh showed a statistically significant drop in mean PHQ-9 scores (therapist rated) in 10 cognitively impaired subjects from 17.6 at baseline to 10.2, 9.1 and 7.5 at 3, 6, and 12 months respectively (unpublished data).

Working in Late-Life Settings

The themes illustrated in Mr. Jones' case are common in geriatric settings. We therefore recommend background familiarity with gerontology and geriatric psychology/psychiatry as prerequisite to IPT-ci. Master's-level social workers working in geriatric settings may be ideally suited to understand care options as well as to learn the IPT-ci skills of tactfully interviewing impaired patients in the company of family members, to understand common presentations of cognitive impairment, and to explain test results and observations to both caregivers and patients with limited insight. Working on a collaborative team that includes primary care physicians, neuropsychologists, and geriatric psychiatrists is ideal. More details for successfully implementing IPT-ci are available elsewhere (Miller, 2009).

SUGGESTED READING

Arean PA, Hegel MT, Reynolds CF: Treating depression in older medical patients with psychotherapy. Journal of Clinical Geropsychology 2001;7:93–104

Arean PA, Reynolds CF: The impact of psychosocial factors on late-life depression. Biological Psychiatry 2005;58:277–282

Bharucha AJ, Dew MA, Miller MD, Borson S, Reynolds CF: Psychotherapy in long-term care settings: A review. Journal of the American Medical Directors Association 2006;7:568–580

Butters MA, Young JB, Lopez O, Aizenstein HJ, Mulsant BH, Reynolds CF, DeKosky ST, Becker JT: Pathways linking late-life depression to mild cognitive impairment and dementia. Dialogues in Clinical Neuroscience 2008;10:345–357

Dombrovski AY, Lenze EJ, Dew MA, Mulsant BH, Pollock BG, Houck PR, Reynolds CF: Maintenance treatment for old-age depression preserves health-related quality of life: A randomized, controlled trial of paroxetine and interpersonal psychotherapy. Journal of American Geriatrics Society 2007; 55:1325–1332

Dombrovski AY, Mulsant BH, Houck PR, Mazumdar S, Lenze EJ, Andreescu C, Cyranowski JM, Reynolds CF: Residual symptoms and recurrence during maintenance treatment of late-life depression. Journal of Affective Disorders 2007;103:77–82

Karp JF, Skidmore E, Lotz M, Lenze E, Dew MA, Reynolds CF: Use of the late life function and disability instrument to assess disability in major depression. Journal of American Geriatrics Society 2009;57:1612–1619

Karp JF, Weiner D, Seligman K, Butters M, Miller M, Frank E, Stack J, Mulsant BM, Pollock B, Dew MA, Kupfer DJ, Reynolds CF: Body pain and treatment response in late-life depression. American Journal of Geriatric Psychiatry 2005;13:188–194

Lenze EJ, Dew MA, Mazumdar S, Begley AE, Cornes C, Miller MD, Imber SD, Frank E, Kupfer DJ, Reynolds CF: Combined pharmacotherapy and psychotherapy as maintenance treatment for late life depression: Effects on social adjustment. American Journal of Psychiatry 2002;159:466–468

Lenze EJ, Mulsant BH, Mohlman J, Shear MK, Dew MA, Schulz R, Miller MD, Tracey B, Reynolds CF: Generalized anxiety disorder in late life: Longitudinal course and comorbidity with Major Depressive Disorder. American Journal of Geriatric Psychiatry 2005;13:77–80

Martire LM, Schulz R, Reynolds CF, Morse JQ, Butters MA, Hinrichsen GA: Impact of close family members on older adults' early response to depression treatment. Psychology and Aging 2008;23:447–452

Miller MD, Reynolds CF: Expanding the usefulness of Interpersonal Psychotherapy (IPT) for depressed elders with co-morbid cognitive impairment. International Journal of Geriatric Psychiatry 2007;22:101–105

Miller MD, Richards V, Zuckoff A, Martire LM, Morse J, Frank E, Reynolds CF: A model for modifying interpersonal psychotherapy (IPT) for depressed elders with cognitive impairment. Clinical Gerontologist 2007;30:79–101

Taylor MP, Reynolds CF, Frank E, Cornes C, Miller MD, Stack JA, Begley AE, Mazumdar S, Dew MA, Kupfer DJ: Which elderly depressed patients remain well on maintenance interpersonal psychotherapy alone? Report from the Pittsburgh study of maintenance therapies in late-life depression. Depression and Anxiety 1999;10:55–60

15

Interpersonal Psychotherapy for Medically Ill Depressed Patients

MARCELA HOFFER, JOHN C. MARKOWITZ,
AND CARLOS BLANCO

IPT relates depressive symptoms to interpersonal difficulties, with the goals of diminishing the depressive symptoms and improving the patient's interpersonal functioning. This chapter describes therapeutic work with a woman presenting with two medical illnesses: breast cancer and major depressive disorder (MDD). Medical illnesses are dramatic life events that affect the individual's life in profound ways. To quote some of our patients struggling with breast cancer on how the illness affected their lives:

> "It was like a bucket of cold water on my head."
> "It will never be the same as before, when I wasn't ill."
> "I feel strange, like I'm not myself. My life has been shaken up dramatically."

IPT fits a depressed medically ill population nicely. These patients face a built-in, dramatic role transition, the kind of life-changing event IPT therapists like to work with. In our experience of treating depressed women with breast cancer with IPT, patients often have difficulties making the role transitions particularly concerning physical symptoms (pain, chemotherapy), loss of parts of their body (hair and breasts), fertility, and consequently dealing with meaningful relationships. Facing the possibility of dying as well as challenges in romantic and sexual relationships were also difficult adjustments. Each transition also requires "reevaluation of responsibilities to others and oneself" (Markowitz, Klerman, & Perry, 1992). IPT therapists encourage medically ill patients to take action such as adhering to treatment regimens, following healthy lifestyles, and resisting social isolation. The therapists work with patients to assist them in adjusting to the new roles and being able to negotiate with doctors, ask for help and support, and find the new and more positive aspects of their new lives in the aftermath of the unwanted change.

Patients sometimes have *two* medical illnesses as part of their role transition: in this example, breast cancer and MDD. This conjunction of psychiatric and other medical disorders can help to reinforce the medical model of IPT. Medical illness or its treatment, however, may complicate the diagnosis of major depression by making the neurovegetative symptoms of depression such as sleep, appetite, or fatigue more difficult to interpret.

RESEARCH SUPPORT

Several empirical studies have examined the efficacy of IPT in individuals with MDD and medical illness. Klerman et al. (1987) investigated the efficacy of a brief psychosocial intervention (Interpersonal Counseling) for sub-syndromal symptoms of stress and distress among 64 patients in primary care. The results of this pilot study indicated more rapid reduction of symptoms and improvement in emotional symptoms and psychosocial functioning compared to an untreated group. Subsequent studies with medically ill and post-miscarriage patients (e.g., Mossey et al., 1996; Neugebauer et al., 2006) have also found benefits for this shorter (six session) version of IPT designed for delivery by clinicians without mental health training.

In 1996, Schulberg et al. treated MDD in two hundred seventy-six patients in a primary care practice and showed that pharmacotherapy with nortriptyline and IPT each treated major depression more effectively than usual care. van Schaik et al. (2006) found IPT more effective than usual general practitioner care in treating elderly patients with a diagnosis of moderate to severe MDD in general practice. Markowitz et al. (1998) found IPT to have equal efficacy to pharmacotherapy plus supportive therapy, and greater efficacy than cognitive-behavioral therapy or supportive therapy alone, for one hundred one depressed HIV-positive patients. Ransom et al. (2008) observed that a six-session, telephone-delivered IPT for HIV-infected rural individuals (N = 79) with depression showed greater reductions in depressive symptoms and in overall levels of psychiatric distress than a usual-care control group. A negative study by Lesperance et al. (2007) documented the efficacy of citalopram administered in conjunction with weekly clinical management for MDD among patients with coronary artery disease but found no evidence of added value of IPT over clinical management.

Thus, although not all studies have been positive, the evidence generally supports the utility of IPT with depressed medically ill individuals.

CASE EXAMPLE

History of Present Illness

Juana was a forty-eight-year-old Mexican separated mother of three who immigrated to the United States with her husband in 1993 at the age of thirty-one. She has three daughters, ages twenty-one, twenty-three, and twenty-six, and had been separated from her husband for nine years at the time of referral for treatment by her oncologist due to increasing depressive symptoms. The clinic in which Juana was treated was part of a study of psychotherapies for depression for patients with breast cancer.

Assessment Process

A psychiatrist at the clinic conducted the initial evaluation and learned that Juana had been diagnosed with breast cancer in July 2005. She had a total mastectomy of her right breast in September 2005. She underwent chemotherapy, which she tolerated well, and continued with a new course of tamoxifen in March 2006. Juana started to feel depressed after being diagnosed with cancer. She tried not to be alone but endorsed feelings of isolation, crying spells, increased and decreased appetite, lack of energy, hopelessness, worthless, difficulty sleeping, and nightmares. She clarified that the anorexia and low energy preceded her chemotherapy. She denied suicidal thoughts.

Juana was a well-groomed, carefully dressed Hispanic woman with short, patchy hair, appearing roughly her stated age. Her movements were mildly agitated and her speech was fluent and slightly pressured. Her mood was depressed and anxious, with a congruent, sometimes tearful, nonlabile affect. Thinking was goal-directed. She denied suicidal ideation. Sensorium was grossly clear and she was fully oriented. Her insight into her depression was poor. She reported having trouble with short-term memory as well as having poor concentration.

At the initial interview, Juana scored 22 on the Hamilton Depression Rating Scale (Ham-D; Hamilton, 1960), indicating moderately severe depression, and met criteria for recurrent MDD according to the SCID-I/P (Spitzer et al., 1994), endorsing symptoms of depressed mood, anhedonia, weight loss, insomnia, psychomotor retardation, fatigue, and social isolation.

Juana recalled a prior depressive episode at the time she moved to the United States: "It wasn't what I expected," she said. Even though she had difficulties in the role transition of adjusting to the new country, she quickly found work and established a steady social network. Her depression lasted less than a year and spontaneously remitted without treatment. She denied other depressive episodes. She subsequently functioned well, living a busy life that included a long-term relationship, a full-time job, and her own apartment.

After being diagnosed with breast cancer, she decided to move to New York from Pennsylvania for her surgery and chemotherapy. She wanted to live closer to the treating hospital. As a consequence, Juana lost her steady waitressing job and moved in with her sister. Shortly thereafter, Juana's sister was evicted from her apartment for failure to pay her rent. Juana then had to move to a shelter, where she continues to live. She has been struggling to move to an apartment but has been waitlisted for eight months. In addition, Juana had lost her nephew in the Caribbean in a car accident in November 2009. Paul, her boyfriend, abandoned her due to jealousy in January 2010.

Interpersonal Inventory

Juana had had a four-year relationship with Paul, a man twenty years younger than she. They had met in the restaurant where she worked, and according to Juana, "it was supportive and beautiful for a long time." She became close not only to Paul but to his family, spending time with his mother and sister at their home, which became like her own. When undergoing chemotherapy, Juana felt relieved calling and sharing her fears with people, particularly old friends and an ex-boyfriend (i.e., employing social supports—something that we encourage in IPT and that protects against psychopathology). According to her, Paul found some text messages she had written and became very upset and distant, accusing Juana of sexual interest in the text recipient. Since then, he had withdrawn. Juana felt that Paul had been supportive when her illness began but couldn't handle what he claimed was a betrayal on her part. She also considered he had found an excuse to leave her after she got ill with cancer. Juana became increasingly alone and withdrawn following Paul's withdrawal.

We discussed how difficult it was for her to reach out when she was depressed. She lacked the energy and motivation to ask for help. Particularly with her daughters, she had trouble showing this "weak" and vulnerable side of hers. I explored with her how it felt to protect them as opposed to having them help her. She looked at me and said that she had never before realized that she had needs. She had a hard time accepting her needs and showing them to her daughters. I encouraged the idea of communicating with Maria, her oldest daughter, at least to ask her what it would be like if she moved in with her temporarily. I acknowledged that even though Juana refused to actually do it, we could explore her feelings: What does it mean to ask for help? How does it feel to reach out to others? How does it feel when you don't reach out to others? How different do you feel when you have problems and you share them with significant others as opposed to not doing so?

Working Towards the Formulation

Juana came to treatment feeling "too many things have happened" to her. She was shocked that all these "tragedies" could have happened to just one person. Until she was diagnosed with breast cancer, her life had felt "pretty normal and full." Juana was satisfied with her job, social network, and romantic relationship. Her diagnosis of breast cancer led to a series of losses that left Juana alone, without one breast, jobless, and in a homeless shelter. Her move to her sister's apartment in New York cost her her restaurant job, and she became financially dependent on her boyfriend and sister. During her surgery and initial recovery, Paul decided to leave her, her sister was evicted, and Juana ended up living in a small room with one of her daughters in a shelter.

In IPT we help patients link their depressive state to an interpersonal problem area (grief, role transition, role disputes, or insufficient social relationships). When I started working with Juana, she was having difficulties formulating and really comprehending the turn her life had taken. It was as if she were still trying to "catch up" with a new, overwhelmingly challenging life. I understood the case as a role transition that started with her cancer diagnosis. When we started discussing it, we found many different effects the diagnosis had produced. She couldn't believe and felt it overwhelming and impossible that so many things were happening to the same human being.

All areas of her life were affected. Juana described feeling as if this were not happening to her, feeling as if her life were not real. She sometimes described her life as "the feeling you get when you wake up from a dream" except that this life, with all these losses, was her actual life. Her depression started to make "sense," particularly because of her sense of general instability in her life and the extreme series of losses and changes she had been through. The diagnosis of breast cancer might have triggered the depression, but Juana emphasized the subsequent series of negative events as superseding the cancer itself. I realized that she had difficulties connecting to her fears, particularly the fears surrounding the loss of her breast, her health, her hair. She always tried to distance herself from painful feelings. Focusing on her material losses might be serving to distract her from feeling the pain and threat of her breast cancer.

While I had no intention of minimizing the severity of the other setbacks in her life, I felt it would be important to ensure that treatment included exploration of her feelings about the effects of breast cancer and its treatment on her life.

When formulating the problem area, I considered the following factors: basic needs to survive, threat of the recurrence of her treated cancer, the loss of her breast, her body image and sense of womanhood, and the loss of her boyfriend. Juana talked extensively about the pain she felt in having limited space of her own and feeling lonely. Yet clearly her breast cancer had triggered her downward trajectory and still represented a major life threat.

Beginning Sessions

We started each session with my asking Juana how she had been during the previous week. We dedicated a few minutes to discussing the progression of symptoms.

In Session 1, we discussed Juana's depression and its symptoms. She was relieved to understand that her illnesses were common ones, not particular to her. I stressed that sometimes depressed people blame themselves for the illness, but that the depressive illness, like breast cancer, was treatable and not her fault. When discussing her symptoms, she started to make associations between her mood changes and the changes that had occurred in her life. Juana began to relate her sense of despair and sadness to the losses she had undergone. She was extremely upset about not being able to support herself financially since having lost her job. And she was missing her boyfriend: she felt a tremendous sense of emptiness after Paul distanced himself from her.

We discussed the length of the treatment (twelve weekly sessions) and some of the basic characteristics of IPT: that we would focus on the present and on the interaction between mood and events in this brief treatment. We also started the interpersonal inventory to explore her relationships and their patterns, particularly relationships that might have contributed to Juana's depression or might provide needed social support. Juana started to talk about her boyfriend. She discussed being confused about where the relationship stood, particularly because Paul was giving her mixed messages: remaining sexually involved with her but also saying he didn't want to be in a relationship.

I began Session 2 by asking: "How have things been since we last met?" Juana continued discussing her relationship with Paul, before and after her cancer diagnosis. Before she was diagnosed, and in the first few years of the relationship, she described him as supportive, loving, and caring. She enjoyed his company, and he was very protective and "present" for her. She also spent much time with his sisters and mother, who had become good friends. The relationship had lasted four years.

I pointed out a contradiction: that wanting a purely sexual relationship with her didn't sound at all supportive on Paul's part. Juana disregarded what I said. After her diagnosis, Paul had used an excuse to distance himself from her, claiming that he had been "insulted" and couldn't forgive her text messages to an old boyfriend. Juana had been struggling with anxiety and had needed to share her cancer news with everyone, including the former boyfriend. She discussed feeling confused and hopeful at the same time. Paul was being very close to her, even sexually, yet still claimed that he didn't want a relationship. She felt that he could take time to decide what he really wanted to do with her. I asked her about her feelings towards him, but she seemed detached. I asked her to describe their relationship in the present and in the past. Juana described having a very committed relationship with Paul. They used to share time and activities together, such as family gatherings and going out with friends. She added that he was very helpful to her with practical things: picking her up from work, running errands for her, etc. She said she realized that those close times together were gone; the only thing they were sharing now was a sexual relationship.

We discussed that her confusion arose from her attributing a meaning to his behavior, particularly when he was physically intimate with her. She understood him to love her, although he still was choosing not to be with her. She equated sex with love and commitment. We started discussing the link between Paul distancing himself at such a crucial moment in her life and her depression. His withdrawal constituted the loss of an important piece in her social support system. Juana didn't believe her depression was connected to Paul's withdrawal because she still believed he loved her.

We also started discussing how much her cancer might have scared him away. I attempted to bring up the issue of the loss of her breast in the context of their intimate relationship. Juana dismissed it as unimportant. I got the feeling she couldn't talk about it yet: it was too painful. We agreed that her cancer had hit her life as a "tsunami," leaving her vulnerable in many areas. We agreed that her depression was associated with the sudden, severe challenges of her new life. The way I formulated the problem area (the role transition) was:

THERAPIST: We have been discussing that you are suffering from an episode of major depression, measured by your Hamilton Rating Scale for Depression score of 22. Depression can feel like it's your fault, but it isn't; and fortunately, it's a treatable illness. From what we've been discussing together, your depression seems to be associated with the overwhelming recent events in your life. In particular, your depression might be related to the sudden changes that have taken place since you were diagnosed with cancer. You have had to adjust and make many changes in so many areas: relationships, work, and your own body. We call this a role transition. What would be like for you if we focus in the next 10 weeks on helping you work on this role transition? If you can figure out how to handle and improve your life situation, your life will no longer feel so out of control, and your depression will very likely improve as well. How does this sound to you?

Juana agreed with this formulation and said she was willing to discuss these issues. Presenting the formulation in Session 2 permitted an early shift into the middle phase of acute IPT.

In Session 3 Juana continued talking about Paul in the context of the difficult turn in her life since her cancer diagnosis. I tried to elicit affect by asking questions such as: "How did you feel about his distancing himself in such a difficult moment for you?" Juana became angry. She started to feel vengeful and angry, and replied: "How did he dare leave me like that?" She became upset not only at Paul but at the turn her life had taken. She talked at length about her quiet, enjoyable former life in Pennsylvania. She again recounted having had a steady waitressing job and how she would spend weekends with Paul and his family. Because of her illness, however, she had had to move to New York, where she felt much more lonely.

We discussed her feelings about these losses. She missed her life as it had been before, quiet and stable. She cried and shared her distress at being alone, and ill. We started to look at ways in which she could communicate to Paul how she felt.

JUANA: I would like to tell him that I was hurt and betrayed; that I had thought that he was a different person and, most importantly, that I was looking for someone who would be a real partner and companion, not someone who would walk away in the most challenging moments of my life.
THERAPIST: How can you do that?
JUANA: I am feeling scared of saying these things. I don't know how to.
THERAPIST: Is it possible that you might feel angry at him, in which case it may be difficult for you to confront him?

She agreed. We decided to role-play to help her practice her communication skills. We first discussed her feelings about Paul and what she would like to accomplish. Juana confided how angry she was, and that she had been able to communicate with him in the past but now felt unable to tell him her real feelings. She wanted to try to assert herself more this time to express her real feelings without getting just vengeful and critical. She wanted to express, calmly, how deeply hurt she was. In role-play, she was able to switch roles, being herself and Paul. She was able to express her anger and disappointment, and that she recognized that he was making excuses to distance himself.

JUANA: I need to talk to you. Calmly . . . I have to tell you a few things I have been feeling. Is that okay?
PAUL: Yes.
JUANA: I am so upset with you. I realized that you left me during one of the most difficult and challenging times in my entire life. What kind of a man are you?
PAUL: Well . . . I felt you were not loyal to me. You were interested in somebody else.
JUANA: Do you understand that I had cancer? Do you understand what that is for a person? By the way, I was with you 100%. And I needed you by my side. You were my man . . . and you left me. I am very upset and very disappointed.
PAUL: I am sorry. I am really sorry.

Juana shared her feelings of empowerment and relief after expressing her feelings to me as Paul. We discussed the importance of her doing this in a calm, organized way, as opposed to just expressing angry aggression to him. We worked on both the content and the tone of her confrontation.

Middle Phase

Juana came to Session 4 feeling really upset, physically and emotionally. She had had a bad reaction to chemotherapy. She had started a new medication regimen and was having all sorts of physical symptoms, including fatigue, stomach ache, and painful mouth sores. We explored the different options she might have with her chemotherapy regimen. Juana decided she would discuss this with her oncologist. We talked about her asking about the possibility of switching back to the previous regimen, on which she had had only minor reactions, or at least telling her oncologist that she wasn't feeling well and asking whether there might be a better and more tolerable treatment.

We discussed how new it was for her to be able to ask for what she needed: to ask for a different option that could make her feel better. Juana felt good about that. She realized that she usually didn't act that way—even when not depressed, but especially now—and reported feeling somewhat empowered by the thought of being able to bring up the issue with her doctor.

Questions we worked on were: How entitled did Juana feel to ask questions? How comfortable did she feel addressing these issues? Did she feel understood by her doctor? Could she really ask for what she wanted? Juana realized that sometimes she had difficulties in asking certain questions. We worked on her feelings of intimidation. She talked about being a Mexican in an English-dominant culture. Juana rehearsed through role-play a dialog with her doctor and nurse. In this, she was able to express her concerns about the side effects she was having and to ask for an alternative treatment. Some anger arose during the role-play, particularly about her side effects.

I used this moment to bring up the issue of her cancer, her experience and emotional reaction to it. It seemed to be easier for Juana to experience and react to somatic challenges than emotional ones. Juana was more comfortable becoming angry and frustrated with side effects than in having an emotional reaction towards her illness. She was feeling very discouraged and disappointed, particularly that she couldn't perform her normal activities. I normalized her feelings, especially her anger at feeling badly physically and about being ill. Juana again had trouble accepting this. She rationalized that "those medications are for my well-being" and that "I shouldn't be angry about it because the medicine is going to protect me." I told Juana that it was okay to feel angry, even when doctors are trying to provide the best medical treatment: side effects can still be annoying, and so can the fact of having breast cancer. I normalized her anger. We discussed that people often get upset and angry when they are undergoing chemotherapy. Juana briefly discussed being angry but switched to a different topic, focusing more on her accomplishments. I asked her if talking about anger was upsetting to her, but she said she really wanted to talk about something else.

By the end of the session, Juana started describing her strengths, which were associated with activity. I was torn between pushing Juana to confront and tolerate her feelings more, and allowing this depressed woman to bolster her sense of her strengths.

Juana came to Session 5 feeling better. She reported having more energy and being in a much better mood. She was able to visit friends and be more social. Juana had had a chance to discuss her treatment options with her doctor, after which they decided to stop her regimen for a week. We agreed that her sense of well-being was probably two-fold. First, she felt better physically, without side effects. Second, she felt empowered by having been able to confront the doctor and make a positive change in her life. We discussed her self-efficacy in making this happen. I also pointed out her greater use of social supports in seeing her friends.

The idea of her being the agent of change led her to review her experience of losing her breast. She discussed how difficult it was for her to go through the surgery. Juana recalled a discussion in which her oncologist offered her the possibility of having only a partial mastectomy. She refused, explaining that she wanted to live, to survive, and wanted to "take everything that is ill out." She felt that a full mastectomy was the only way for her to feel safe. I addressed her powerful will to live. I asked her how it felt to go through this experience of losing her breast. Juana started to cry. We talked about how natural and human it is to feel sad about such a loss. She talked about fighting that feeling and criticizing herself for having such feelings. We also discussed the meaning of mourning and some of its common symptoms. In her case, she had lost a breast, a part of her body, a part of her feminine body. Juana talked about how scared she was to be confronted with such a great loss. She described her experience of losing a breast as "feeling less like a woman, less attractive." She shared fears of "not ever being loved again" by a man due to the loss of a breast. She talked about her anticipation of rejection and her consequent isolation from social situations and avoidance of potential relationships. She spoke about how it was easier to be alone and avoid any painful situation that would remind her of the loss of her breast. She also discussed how "inferior" she felt in comparison to other women. She felt "less of a woman," as if she couldn't be loved, or compete with women who were "intact." We discussed how it was possible that her "man" could love her despite her deformity and not be concerned with her physical loss.

Juana started to talk about her sense of empowerment within the chaos of illness and loss. She described that she was starting to feel the pain of what she had been through, recognizing the tremendous loss and the deep fear she had experienced. Nonetheless, she focused more on her strengths. She talked about her desire to live and have a good life for herself. She described the empowering life events that had happened within the context of her cancer. She started really putting into perspective her past relationship when she realized that Paul had left her during an extremely difficult moment. She freely expressed her anger and disappointment toward him for leaving her in one of the most difficult and painful moments of her life, while she had still believed he loved her. She realized that he was not the type of man she wanted to have in her life. She talked about how the cancer had opened her eyes to exactly the type of relationship she wished to have. She talked about a new ability to consider options, not to stay stuck and "depressed in the bed." That she was living in a shelter led her to be "on the go"; every morning she would wake up and start looking for a place to stay.

I phoned Juana the next week because she had missed her appointment. She sounded very depressed and hopeless. She told me that she had been trying so hard to get disability benefits and "nobody is helping me." She had been contacting agencies and found no help at all. I spent time on the phone feeling completely stuck and hopeless myself. What would be my arguments in a situation that seemed to have no way out? I contemplated my own limits as I was listening to her. She then told me that she was so disappointed that she didn't feel like seeing doctors or psychologists because she had lost trust in them as well. She told me she didn't see the purpose in it "if everything fails at the end."

I empathized and validated the way she was feeling. I told her how angry I would feel in so frustrating, so surreal a situation. She agreed with me and owned her anger against the world, the agencies, and the huge obstacles she was now facing. I also repeated that she—one more time—was still fighting, was still voicing her feelings and her disagreements with a system that was obviously ill equipped. During this conversation, I felt her becoming emotionally alive. She asked what I thought she could do next. I pointed out to her that she was again contemplating options, brainstorming about ideas to achieve her goal. She told me she was considering contacting a Hispanic channel news program to get them to publicize her situation and put some pressure on her issue. She also thought about recontacting a legal aid lawyer, although she had previously done so with discouraging results.

This session raised a dilemma. Juana's despair elicited my urge to help her in a more concrete manner, to try to assist her in obtaining disability benefits. I quickly recognized, however, that my job was not to help her materially but to support her emotional issues, to empathize with her, encourage her, to find options so that she would persevere in sorting out her own role transition. Offering direct instrumental help might have helped to cement our treatment alliance but would have set up a potentially uncomfortable precedent for her expectations of my role.

Juana arrived for Session 6 looking and sounding much better. She said that she was feeling good. When I asked her to tell me more about that positive feeling, she replied that she was feeling "pretty strong," physically and emotionally. I asked her whether she had any thoughts, feelings, or reactions from the previous session. She said she had a hard time thinking about what we discussed. I empathized and reminded her that we had started discussing what it meant for her to connect to the pain of her illness, her loss of her breast. She said that actually it wasn't so bad to talk about those issues. She felt better mentally, calmer, and more hopeful. She discussed at length her many activities with friends and family in the past week: going out to eat at a restaurant, going to see a movie, and going to the park. I reinforced that having social supports was as an antidote to her depression. She realized that having a supportive social network was allowing her to survive financially, as everyone was helping her out with money. Adding to the social network, she had resumed going to church. She said something like: "My strength is mediated by God." I told her it was a great partnership she had with God, because she was also actively working towards getting better, both emotional and physically. When I said that, she made a connection to her decision to leave Paul. She again experienced deep anger towards him. She told me that she didn't understand how he could leave her at a time when she was so weak that she literally needed him to walk and hold her arm so she wouldn't fall.

Juana arrived for Session 7 feeling frustrated. She had been trying to get disability, without success. She had been doing what she could be expected to do and more. As she described it, the agency was being neither helpful nor effective. Once more, I was confronted with my own sense of hopelessness as Juana kept bumping into walls and obstacles. She told me that she was confident in her workers from the agency but at the same time was starting to doubt their efficacy and integrity and felt she was being lied to and that they were not doing their job. Juana repeated that she felt cheated and added that she hadn't chosen to have cancer, be unable to work, and have no money to pay her rent. She was becoming more upset, and I empathized with her. I felt that my words weren't enough, reflecting this sense of social unfairness she had been dealing with. Having allowed her to express her distress at some length, I validated her feelings. Once again I cited her unbeatable strength, her ability not to crack under pressure and to keep going, despite these circumstances. She agreed and said that in a funny way, her difficulties gave her strength to try to find what she really needed for herself. I asked her whether she had ever experienced such a sense of power and will to make something happen. She couldn't remember a similar situation.

I asked her to think for a moment that her life was mine and I was sharing it with her. Then I asked her what her reactions would be. Although not a typical IPT intervention, I felt it was a direct way for her to experience what I had been saying about her strength. She started to laugh. She told me she was laughing because she thought: "I wouldn't be able to survive what this person is going through." My idea was for her to connect with her amazing spirit and her unwillingness to give up, particularly because she was facing so many real obstacles that I was afraid she would, at some point, decide to give up. This session, however, she left with a sense of hope.

Juana came to Session 8 and reported feeling not so well. She described a series of events the prior week that led her to be down, disappointed, and hopeless. We connected her mood change to these setbacks. However, I had been thinking a lot about how all her material losses had distracted her from really connecting to her deepest fears and feelings. I decided to share that idea with her. She reacted with surprise. I emphasized that I wasn't denying the severity of her financial situation. I told her that her feeling down and hopeless could be associated with her having cancer, that she lost her breast and hair, and also that she might have faced the idea of dying.

She paused for a second, looked me in the eye, and told me that she didn't want to talk about that. When I asked why, she became tearful. I encouraged her to tell me what made her tearful. She said that she didn't want to die; that she was terrified of dying; that if she laid down her arms, she could also let herself die. I encouraged her to keep talking about it. She cried and talked about the fear she went through before the surgery. She told me that she had always been used to being strong, sort of a fighter, her entire life; that people would come to her for help and advice; that she wasn't allowed to be weak. I told her how difficult it must have been for her to hold herself together without being able to be vulnerable, what an effort she had to make. I told her that connecting to our feelings doesn't kill us, and allowing ourselves to feel the most vulnerable feelings can help us to understand situations and make us stronger. She agreed, and her facial expression softened. I told her that at the moment that she allowed herself to let her tears come, she was being extremely strong; she was in the process of becoming whole, and possibly by connecting to and tolerating her feelings, she would feel less hopeless and less depressed.

We talked at length about the normalcy of painful feelings when we go through extreme situations like having cancer. I asked her how it felt to let those tears come. She said it was okay. I asked how new this experience was for her. She said that she usually tried to choke her tears. I kept silent at points to let her feel her feelings, but also periodically encouraged her to realize that she had allowed herself to feel strong emotions and hadn't died (her original fear). She agreed. She told me that she never associated tears or pain with strength. I asked how that experience was for her, and she told me that it was new (she was a bit shy about it) but felt more released. She also expressed how when she allowed herself to have her feelings, she started to connect to the fear of getting ill again. She realized that being disconnected prevented her from having fears but—at the same time—made her feel "numb and dead inside." Juana scored 16 on the Ham-D, indicating mild to moderate depression, an improvement in her symptoms since the beginning of treatment.

In Session 9 Juana seemed a bit distressed. I asked how she had been during the previous week. She said that she was feeling slightly better, particularly more hopeful. I asked whether she had any feelings about our last session. She said that she was thinking about our conversation on feelings. She added that she wanted to talk about another loss: herself. Surprised and curious, I asked what she meant. She explained how painful it had been for her to realize that she hadn't taken care of or paid attention to herself during these years. She realized that by being "strong" for everybody else, she had forgotten her own needs. She realized that she had maintained a relationship with a younger man and had been taking care of him, supporting him emotionally; she was the giver, the caretaker. I encouraged her to explore how that made her feel. She said it made her angry, frustrated with herself for allowing that to happen. She also realized now why she had had so much difficulty reaching out and asking for help. She talked at length about the association between her lack of awareness of her needs and reaching out. Why should she if she didn't "need" anything? I noticed that at that point, she looked more alive, full of life and feelings. I asked how she was feeling and remarked on what I had noticed. She agreed. She told me that she felt as if she were waking up from a deep dream.

Termination Phase

In Session 10 Juana said she was doing well. Before asking her to elaborate on her positive feelings, I expressed to her that we would start focusing on termination, since we had three more sessions together. She smiled and told me that "my life seems chaotic but I feel hopeful and okay." She added that the sessions were helpful, and she was already feeling much better. Luckily, she had been approved for disability benefits. I congratulated her, particularly for the extreme effort and accomplishment. It had been all her doing. I had a feeling that now she would be more available emotionally to discuss other "losses" in her life, more related to her illness. I asked her what it would be like to focus on the impact her illness had on her body, her femininity, and her relationship, including her sexual relationship. She said: "Yes, why not?" I asked what her reaction was when I mentioned the impact of the cancer on her life. She said that her first reaction while she was listening to me was shame. I asked her to tell me more. She said that she felt extremely ashamed of her body; that she had tremendous difficulties getting undressed, showing her body to her boyfriend after the surgery. I encouraged her to discuss what made her feel ashamed about her body. She said she was afraid that her boyfriend would be "freaked out"; she felt that she wasn't "woman enough" and, most importantly, she was scared that he would leave her. I asked her to tell me more about the romantic and sexual relationship between them. She said she felt that he had trouble being sexual after her surgery. He became more distant, didn't want to be intimate and to have sex as often as before. I encouraged her to discuss her feelings associated with his distance.

She said that she felt abandoned; she felt that there was something wrong with her, something ugly in her body. We discussed how painful it was for her to reveal and expose her "wounded" body to him. I asked her about her anger, particularly associated with Paul's distancing himself. She agreed: she told me that she hated him. She felt deeply hurt and angry. She said that he wasn't capable of loving her as she was. She told me that she felt deeply hurt by his inability to contain her emotionally in her pain, in her loss. We agreed on the normalcy of such a feeling. We discussed the importance of her connecting to her anger towards him as a way of counteracting her self-criticism. She continued talking about how much she missed who she was before: her "intact" body, healthy and vibrant. She discussed feeling old, different, non-sexual, unattractive. We talked about how negative feelings about herself and decreased libido were part of her depressive experience. She didn't feel like having sex. I also told her about the effects of tamoxifen on her loss of libido. In any case, she needed pure acceptance from her boyfriend and felt that she didn't get that. She cried while discussing his emotional distance and unavailability.

In Session 11 Juana reported she was feeling well. She said that our last discussion was "painful and helpful" at the same time. I asked her to elaborate how it was helpful. She described having "pretty poisonous feelings and thoughts" about her body and her womanhood. She said that by discussing them, she felt a great release. She added that in a way she felt like reconnecting again with her body "in a friendly way." I asked her to discuss this. She said that after the surgery, she completely detached from her body. She pretended her body didn't exist anymore. She had difficulties accepting her new body, with all these "scars and wounds." She talked about even feeling scared of looking at herself. I asked how different her body was compared to before the surgery. She said that actually it wasn't that different: the anticipatory fear was worse than the reality. She discussed how, in a strange way, discussing these feelings put things at ease, especially how she felt with her body. She described feeling like "sort of a new woman." During this session I was aware that we only had this session and another one left to discuss termination issues. Because of her sense of independence, I chose to use most of this session to let her discuss such an important piece of her process. In any case, I did bring up the issue of termination. She said that she felt okay with this process. She was used to dealing with "everything on her own" but still deeply appreciated having these conversations together. I told her how much I admired her courage to explore these painful and scary feelings. I asked her how helpful these conversations were for her. She said that she had never had these kinds of dialogs with anybody. She realized that she felt relieved after our discussions. She also said that she learned "a few things about life and relationships." She added that she had learned new ways of communicating. I asked her how she felt about terminating this short therapy. She said she was "okay," would miss having these conversations, but that she felt pretty strong already. When I asked what she meant, she replied that she felt her emotional vocabulary had expanded. She knew herself better and understood what she really would like to have in a relationship with a man. I told her what an amazing process she had gone through. We discussed how she dealt with several losses in her life, including her breast, her "intact body," and her boyfriend. We talked about how much better she felt now compared to the beginning of treatment. She realized that she was doing okay but might face challenges in the future, and talked about what she would do if she started feeling depressed again. Juana said: "Well, I'm not alone anymore." She said she would look for professional help instead of becoming scared and isolated. She was reassured that she could always contact the clinic if she needed help.

In Session 12 Juana looked good. She was smiling and reported feeling well. I told her that she looked happy. She told me that she felt a big weight "has come off my back." I asked her to talk a bit about that. She expressed how much effort she had been making to keep her emotions away. She realized that she had done so out of fear of the unknown. She had been afraid of letting go. She had felt afraid of "feeling too much" and then not knowing what the consequences would be. I asked her how she felt now, after having the experience of connecting and feeling her emotions. She said, "It wasn't as bad as I thought." We discussed her ability now to "apply this new knowledge in her life." She talked about feeling like "she had completed a training . . . sort of," in which her emotional vocabulary had expanded. Juana thanked me. She had tears in her eyes.

Juana scored 9 on the Ham-D, indicating very mild depressive symptoms and a significant decrease from 22 at the beginning of treatment.

DISCUSSION

IPT nicely frames the situation of medically ill depressed patients. Some interesting issues arise in working with this population.

First, as depression begins to lift, many patients reframe the role transition of their medical illness as having a silver lining, "a blessing in disguise," as one patient described it. The illness gives them a chance to take a serious look inward, to evaluate, reconsider, and embrace their real needs. Some patients describe the illness as a turning point, after which they addressed aspects in their lives that they had previously avoided. Having a serious illness and facing the prospect of death is an opportunity to reevaluate life from a different, more introspective, and deeper perspective. Patients who have felt crushed by a role transition can feel resilient in having confronted and at least partially resolved it. This was obviously the case for Juana.

Another woman with breast cancer realized that she had been the stronger one in her relationship, and the financial and emotional caretaker for the whole family. When she got sick, she continued working, taking only a few days off for surgery. She had believed that she couldn't take the time off because her family would not survive financially. After that experience, she started to reexamine her twenty-five-year relationship with her husband. She was able to recognize and understand her deep resentment and anger towards him. She started to make changes to take care of herself, giving herself permission to ask for things, set limits, and be vulnerable. Patients may see how numb their lives have been up to that point. A patient talked about a sense of "awakening," as if the illness were actually knocking on her door to force her to look at what had long been dormant or "dead," making her life dull and meaningless.

We may hypothesize that facing the possibility of one's own death may alter one's perspective, make one pay attention to what is really important in life, to one's deepest desires and real fulfillment (Markowitz et al., 1995). Illness and the prospect of death may paradoxically provide a second chance to really live, leaving trivialities behind. Patients have frequently described this "now or never" attitude towards life. They felt they had to live fully; they dared to attempt what they never had done before. Having a serious illness pushed them to realize that life is not a dress rehearsal.

Second, this reevaluation allows many patients to focus on the more positive and constructive aspects of enduring such a painful and frightening experience. From the therapist's perspective, this was a surprise. I had anticipated difficulties in finding positive aspects of illness as a role transition. I was happily surprised to observe how patients regained a more positive outlook on life and on themselves as depressed symptoms decreased, and their ability to make changes towards a more fulfilled and richer emotional life.

A third interesting issue that arose involved understanding medical illness and depression from an interpersonal perspective. Addressing difficulties in social support and communication helped patients to assert themselves and advocate and negotiate for themselves in addressing medical decisions and postsurgical planning with medical staff.

During vulnerable times such as surgery or chemotherapy, patients face inevitable fears: of death, disability, disfigurement, the loss of health, fertility, youth, etc. This is an obvious time to ask for help and support from family and friends. Yet patients struggling with depression have difficulty feeling self-confident enough to assert their needs. They have trouble making decisions and plans. IPT, in focusing on interpersonal and communication problems, appears to be a good therapeutic approach to help these patients negotiate and better communicate their needs with their doctors, nurses, family, and friends. One patient vacillated about whether to stay with her abusive mother or go to her supportive daughter, whom she didn't want to bother. She also did not feel comfortable asking her son because she did not want him to miss work.

Another patient struggled both with chemotherapy side effects and with fears of telling her doctor about them. Role-playing proved effective in validating her feelings and communicating her needs to her oncologist. Like Juana, she was finally able to switch to a medication with fewer side effects, and moreover felt more comfortable that her doctor understood her. This is a frequent theme for depressed medically ill patients: they often fear bothering or antagonizing their doctor or treatment team with questions, side effects, etc. One role of the IPT therapist is to help empower depressed patients to speak up. This has benefits both in treating depression (by improving self-assertion, control over one's environment, and ideally the therapeutic relationship with the medical doctor) and improving medical treatment of the comorbid disorder.

Fourth, another important aspect of IPT treatment is that psychoeducation about depression helps depressed medical patients to feel less burdened as they understand that difficulty in making decisions, difficulty in advocating for themselves, and feeling self-doubt or lack of confidence stems from their depressive disorder. In our experience, patients learn to blame the depression instead of blaming themselves. This seems even more important than usual in IPT in working with a population experiencing two medical illnesses (e.g., breast cancer and major depression).

Finally, another aspect I discovered in working with these patients is the sense of their heroism in struggling with breast cancer. I started to feel (and see) Juana as a warrior with intensity, an unbeatable will, determined to survive and determined to make the right choices in her life. I felt connected to her and admired her. I told her how amazingly strong she was. I shared my admiration of having her in front of me, telling me her life story, trying to make sense of it, trying to express and share her pain and feelings in general. She had lost so much, and yet she was still fighting. What amazed me was her refusal to give up, even at the most difficult times. My only caveat would be that it is important not to rush to tell the patient this, to reflect it back after having developed a relationship and understood the full range of the patient's life situation.

ACKNOWLEDGMENTS

Supported in part by National Cancer Institute grant R01 CA133050, "Interpersonal Psychotherapy for Depression in Breast Cancer," and NIMH grant R01 MH076051, "Improving the Effectiveness of Treatment for Depression in Hispanics," to Dr. Blanco; and support from the New York State Psychiatric Institute

SUGGESTED READING

Markowitz JC, Klerman GL, Clougherty KF, Spielman LA, Jacobsberg LB, Fishman B, Frances AJ, Kocsis JH, Perry SW: Individual psychotherapies for depressed HIV-positive patients. American Journal of Psychiatry 1995;152:1504–1509

Markowitz JC, Klerman GL, Perry SW: Interpersonal psychotherapy of depressed HIV-seropositive patients. Hospital and Community Psychiatry 1992;43:885–890

16

Interpersonal Therapy and Cultural Issues

The Case of Hispanic Patients

SAPANA R. PATEL AND ROBERTO LEWIS-FERNÁNDEZ

In 2002, Hispanics represented approximately 13% of the national population, becoming the largest U.S. minority group (Ramirez & de la Cruz, 2003). The majority of Hispanics in the United States were of Mexican origin (67%), followed by Central and South Americans (14%), Puerto Ricans (9%), Cubans (4%), and "other Hispanics" (7%; Ramirez & de la Cruz, 2003). A Surgeon General's report concluded that, like other racial and ethnic minorities, Hispanics experience disparate mental health care compared to non-Hispanic whites (Department of Health and Human Services [DHHS], 2001). Although prevalence rates differ according to immigration status and levels of acculturation, mental disorders such as major depression are generally just as prevalent among Hispanics as among non-Hispanic whites (Kessler et al., 2003; Vega, Sribney, Aguilar-Gaxiola, & Kolody, 2004). The impact of major depression has been estimated to be a leading cause of disability worldwide (Murray & Lopez, 1996).

The minimal involvement of Hispanics in psychotherapy studies (Elkin et al., 1989; Navarro, 1993) has raised concern about whether empirically supported treatments such as IPT, tested mainly in samples of majority white women, apply to cultural minorities (Bernal, Bonilla, & Bellido, 1995; Bernal & Scharron del Rio, 2001; Miranda, Nakamura & Bernal, 2003). Clinicians need to adapt empirically supported treatments in order to meet the cultural needs of Spanish-speaking patients of varied national origins and to retain them in treatment. Several frameworks for adapting psychotherapy to culturally diverse populations exist. They begin by transforming knowledge about a patient's culture into strategies used within the clinical encounter (Bernal, Bonilla, & Bellido, 1995; Bernal & Scharron del Rio, 2001; Comas Diaz & Jacobsen, 1987; Domenech-Rodriguez & Wieling, 2004; Hwang, 2006; Miranda, Nakamura, & Bernal, 2003; Roselló & Bernal, 1996; Sue, Zane, & Young, 1994). In this chapter, a brief literature review and case illustration will describe how IPT is compatible with Hispanic culture and can be adapted for working with Hispanic populations.

IPT AND HISPANICS

Culturally competent mental health care includes the selection of treatments that fit with Hispanic culture (Marin, 1991; Miranda, Nakamura, et al., 2003; Rogler et al., 1987). IPT is congruent with the cultural expectations of Hispanics for several reasons. First, the literature suggests that the key goals of mental health for Hispanics are to regain the ability to function and contribute to society, and to make and maintain relationships, beyond mere remission of symptoms (Bernal et al., 1995; Guarnaccia & Martinez, 2003; Szapocznik et al., 1994). These goals are highly congruent with IPT's focus on mobilizing social supports and improving interpersonal relations and psychosocial functioning, although IPT goes a step further and specifically links improvements in those domains with symptom improvement. Second, the emphasis on interpersonal relatedness that exists within Hispanic cultures makes IPT a particularly well-suited treatment modality. Interpersonal conflicts in marriage and the family have been reported as common issues in psychotherapy for Hispanics (Comas-Diaz, 1985, Delgado & Humm-Delgado; Organista & Muñoz, 1996). For example, generational gaps between parents and children about assimilating to U.S. culture may result in clashing value systems that contribute to role disputes. These elements are important in considering best-fit treatments for diverse populations because patient preferences for treatment and how treatment matches their culture influence treatment entry and retention (Dwight-Johnson et al., 2001; Fairhurst & Dowrick, 1996; Jaycox et al., 2006). Research on IPT's effectiveness for Hispanics is limited (Roselló & Bernal, 1999; Markowitz et al., 2000; Mufson et al., 1999, 2004). Adaptations include one published study of a preliminary adaptation of IPT for depressed, low-income, Spanish-monolingual Hispanics in New York City (Markowitz et al., 2009).

CULTURAL ASSESSMENT

A key dimension of cultural competency involves cultural assessment. The term *Hispanic* covers heterogeneous populations: it refers to many cultures from the Spanish-speaking countries of Central and South America, as well as Mexico, the Caribbean, and Spain. The term refers more to an ethnic class that has some common attributes but encompasses diverse cultures that can vary considerably in practices and values. Hispanic cultures also vary in their sociopolitical histories, which reflect varying migratory patterns and possibly differential risk for psychiatric illness (e.g., Lee, Markides, & Ray, 1997; Moscicki, Rae, Regier, & Locke, 1987).

An additional consideration for differences is acculturation, the process of adjusting to the host culture (Balls Organista, Organista, & Kurasaki, 2003). Acculturation may affect dominant language and adoption of American values. Thus, given the range of cultural contexts, it is critical to understand the specific cultural factors of individual patients.

The most comprehensive and best-operationalized of existing models for cultural assessment in mental health is the Cultural Formulation (CF; Lewis-Fernández &

Diaz, 2002). The CF model supplements a standard intake evaluation by highlighting the effect of culture on the patient's identity, personality development, symptomatology, explanatory models of illness, help-seeking preferences, stressors and supports, therapeutic relationships, and outcome expectations. The CF has five sections: cultural identity, cultural explanations of illness, cultural levels related to psychosocial environment and functioning, cultural elements of the clinician–patient relationship, and overall cultural assessment.

The cultural formulation facilitates the clinical process. It can inform the interpersonal inventory and IPT formulation, allowing the therapist to present the formulation using the patient's language and notions of illness. For example, a therapist might de-emphasize the medical model for a patient who believes that depression is a test from God. A cultural assessment may also flag common areas of clinical concern among Hispanic patients. Organista (2000) reviewed a number of studies and concluded that family and marriage conflicts are common problem areas among Hispanic patients. Other problems that commonly arise among Hispanic migrants include stressful life events associated with the migration process, reduced social support due to family/social displacement, and feelings of separation and loneliness. Finally, Hispanic values, beliefs, and explanatory models of illness are likely to vary from individual to individual. For example, a highly educated, third-generation Mexican-American patient will likely demonstrate cultural differences in comparison with a patient of limited educational background who recently immigrated from rural Mexico. A cultural assessment provides the detailed information about a patient's cultural background that allows hypothesis generation rather than reliance on assumptions based on generalizations. The relevance of the cultural adaptations discussed below will vary according to the information obtained from a cultural assessment.

ADAPTATIONS FOR HISPANICS: INTERPERSONAL STYLES AND VALUES

Establishing a therapeutic alliance is a fundamental component of all psychotherapeutic approaches. It has been demonstrated to predict successful treatment outcome among Hispanic psychotherapy patients (Bernal, Bonilla, Padilla-Cotto, & Perez-Prado, 1998). For several decades, authors have discussed key values among Hispanics (e.g., Marin, 1991; Stevens, 1973; Triandis, Marin, Lisansky, & Betancourt, 1984). Embodying these values in the way we relate with Hispanic patients will help engage Hispanic patients in the treatment process and enhance the therapeutic alliance. We describe these values before reporting a detailed case to illustrate how they were applied within the context of treatment.

Simpatía is a "permanent personal quality where an individual is perceived as likeable, fun to be with, and easy going, and seems to strive for harmony in interpersonal relations" (Triandis et al., 1984). Although such a style may characterize many therapeutic interactions with non-Hispanics, expressing *simpatía* with Hispanic patients requires warmth and kindness of a more overt and expressive quality. It includes avoiding a neutral, passive demeanor that may characterize some clinical stances—albeit not IPT. Not achieving *simpatía* can have significant consequences: focus groups with Hispanic patients suggest perceived coldness among practitioners is a barrier to treatment (Guarnaccia & Martínez, 2003). As psychotherapy occasionally requires confrontation or "limit-setting," such encounters require warmth and an emphasis on positive aspects. For example, if a patient were to arrive late for appointments repeatedly, a *simpatico* response overtly expresses gladness for his or her arrival, concern for his or her having been delayed (e.g., transportation difficulty), and appreciation for his or her effort.

Authors have also discussed *formalismo*, a certain degree of formality characterizing interactions (e.g., Miranda et al., 1996). Notable examples involve addressing patients as *Señor* or *Señora/Señorita* followed by their last name, as well as use of the word *usted*, the formal word for *you*. Hispanic culture prescribes a related value of *respeto* (respect) towards older individuals in positions of authority, parents, and relatives, even towards males and husbands for women with traditional gender roles (Comas-Díaz & Duncan, 1985). *Respeto* and *formalismo* are relevant for engaging the patient because they help to delineate the therapist's role with the patient and vice versa.

Personalismo involves personalized interactions with patients. It is consistent with the value described by Delgado (1983), that Hispanic patients prefer to interact with individuals versus institutions. For example, telephone calls to confirm or reschedule appointments made personally by the clinician are one way to achieve this personal relating. Miranda et al. (1996) also suggest remembering the names of children and family members and asking about them during sessions. Interactions with Hispanic patients should balance *personalismo* and *formalismo*, rather than overemphasizing one or the other.

Fatalismo has been described as the belief among many Hispanics that their problems reflect fate and cannot be changed (Flores, 2000). This idea is a barrier to IPT, a treatment that strives to help patients to express feelings, and to confront and solve problems through understanding of interpersonal relationships. To overcome this barrier, a strong treatment alliance is essential. It is not uncommon for religion to play a role in *fatalismo*: Hispanic patients may view their problems as God's will. Organista (2000) has described effective techniques for working within devout patients' belief in God's will in order to motivate active coping.

Familismo has been described as a strength of Hispanic culture (Sabogal, Marín, Otero-Sabogal, Marín, & Perez-Stable, 1987). It refers to a strong reliance on the family for meeting psychological, social, and security needs. A strong orientation of *familismo* commonly involves the sacrifice of individual needs to meet those of the family (Comas-Díaz & Duncan, 1985). *Familismo* provides information regarding potential barriers to treatment, such as individual behaviors that run counter to family needs. At the same time, *familismo* highlights a source of motivation that clinicians can emphasize when advocating problem solving to improve interpersonal functioning.

CASE EXAMPLE

The following case of Señor A[1] comes from a weekly IPT supervision for monolingual Spanish-speaking patients of mixed regional origins and low socioeconomic

---

1. The concepts of respeto and formalismo are important for engaging Hispanic patients, helping to delineate the therapist's role with the patient and vice versa. Hence we shall refer to the patient as "Señor A."

status living in upper Manhattan. We describe treatment themes, cultural considerations, and IPT's congruence in addressing these below and in the discussion.

History of Present Illness

Sr. A is a fifty-three-year-old Venezuelan man who presented for treatment of "fatigue, depression and a lot of worry about my life." After prolonged unemployment and anxiety about his family's financial situation, Sr. A reported feeling like a "victim of the system in the United States because of a lack of opportunity," which led him to feel "angry with life." His symptoms included anhedonia, psychomotor agitation, agitation, depressed mood, insomnia, and "emotional pain." Sr. A denied any suicidal or homicidal ideation since the current depressive episode began.

He reported a history of depression and anxiety dating back to 2000 when a workplace accident injured his back. During his rehabilitation, Sr. A became depressed and suicidal and was hospitalized in a psychiatric inpatient unit, during which time he received little benefit from group therapy. After his discharge, he experienced a major depressive relapse and could not return to work due to difficulty concentrating, anhedonia, tension, and worry about his health, finances, and family. He sought treatment for depression from a Cuban psychiatrist for seven months and received antidepressant medications for one year, with moderate benefit. Sr. A discontinued his medications out of concern that "medications mess up the brain and interact with other medications." After stopping medication, his mood symptoms worsened and he presented to the Hispanic Treatment Program seeking IPT. He believed IPT would "give me strength and the ability to communicate better and be less angry with people."

Psychiatric, Family, and Medical History

Sr. A's history of unipolar depression and generalized anxiety disorder dated back to age thirty-six. He reported the single hospitalization for suicidal ideation. The only known family member with a psychiatric illness was his brother, who was diagnosed and treated for schizophrenia. Sr. A suffered from hypertension for which he had been prescribed but refused to take medication. Instead, Sr. A treated his hypertension with natural remedies. Sr. A's mother and father both suffered from heart disease, and his father had died from a myocardial infarction.

Interpersonal Inventory and Cultural Formulation

To better understand how Sr. A's relationships had evolved during his migration and acculturation to U.S. society, the therapist conducted a cultural formulation in addition to the interpersonal inventory. To track clinical progress and depressive symptoms, the Hamilton Depression Scale 17-item (Ham-D-17) was administered to Sr. A at the beginning, midpoint, and termination of treatment. Upon beginning treatment, the Ham-D score was 27, indicating severe depression. The interpersonal inventory and cultural formulation were introduced as follows:

THERAPIST: Señor A, I'd like to take some time to do two interviews that will help me understand the nature of what brings you to treatment and your experience in the context of your cultural background.

Sr. A received this enthusiastically as a perceived sign of *respeto* and *formalismo*. The interviews took place over two sessions.

Sr. A was born in a northern South American country and is the second of five children. He reported a pleasant childhood and a secure relationship with his parents and siblings. His father passed away suddenly at age forty-seven of cardiovascular disease, which was the first loss Sr. A experienced in his life. He reported multiple romantic relationships during his adolescence and mid-twenties, stating that he was an "athlete and quite popular when he was younger." His most significant relationship was with a woman he met while studying naturopathic medicine in another Latin American country. He found this relationship exciting and a source of comfort and security while he was away from his family and friends in his country of origin.

Sr. A had three children with this woman (now ages thirty, twenty-seven, and eighteen) and described many disputes before eventually separating from her and his children because he wanted to move back to his country and she refused to accompany him. He supported his three children throughout the years and remained in contact with them at the time he presented for treatment. As a young adult back in his home country, Sr. A described himself as religious, active, and competitive, spending most of his time in his successful naturopathic medicine practice, attending church, and competing as a player on a national sports team. He recounted this time in his life with nostalgia and pride and reported a shift when the political climate changed in his country. In 1988, Sr. A migrated to the United States "for a better life," citing political insecurity and abuse as reasons for leaving his country.

He had little family presence in the United States and his social support system mainly comprised his girlfriend and two young children, his church members, pastor, and a few friends he had made since immigrating twenty years earlier. The most important person in his life was his girlfriend, twenty years younger than he, whom he met through the local evangelical church. He described this relationship as supportive, nurturing, and intense. Sr. A and his girlfriend had two infants, nineteen and four months old, at home to care for. Their relationship had become strained as he was the family's sole provider but was currently unemployed. He did manual labor, managing lift trucks, after immigrating to the United States. In 2000 he was injured on the job when one of the lifts broke and exploded. He sustained injuries to his back, including two herniated lumbar discs. Sr. A viewed the accident as part of his illness, claiming: "My body has many physical problems, and I cannot function in the way I am used to and have relied upon both emotionally and physically." Prior to his accident, he believed himself an extrovert, outgoing, and someone who experienced very little negative emotion. He felt this way of being had left him unprepared for the "internal world of emotional experience" that he had had to face since the accident. Sr. A now views himself as "weak and incompetent," both emotionally and physically, but he found this difficult to discuss with his girlfriend and during IPT sessions.

Sr. A described his girlfriend as understanding of his periodic unemployment until recently, and that their religious faith and devotion saved them from worse marital conflicts. He had strong Christian beliefs about his emotional problems, stating that his depression was a "*Prueba de Dios* [test from God]" and that his devotion and prayer would see him though his depression and anxiety, adding, "*Dios me ayuda* [God will help me]." Sr. A prefers natural remedies, spiritual help, or vocational rehabilitation to psychiatric help and feared the addictive potential of antidepressant medications.

In his attempts to rehabilitate, Sr. A felt unable to adjust after the accident because of the limited opportunities available to him in the United States. This was reminiscent of the environment just before he left his country. He complained of limited knowledge about vocational rehabilitation and assistance and said that his lack of motivation held him back from pursuing these programs. Sr. A received disability for a time but perceived a "lack of respect and coldness from the disability experience and people I interacted with during this process." This led him to feel angry and hostile towards most people around him; he cited an "opening of his senses to the harsh, cold manner in which human beings with vulnerabilities are treated." When his employer expected him to return to work, Sr. A felt he needed to rediscover his path, yet was frustrated and unmotivated in knowing how to do so.

Although the treatment was delivered by a Spanish-speaking therapist, the therapist, an Indian American psychologist, and Sr. A, of Latin American descent, came from different cultural backgrounds. Sr. A and the therapist communicated effectively in Spanish but faced barriers and gaps in understanding when discussing the role of Christian faith in recovery. They turned these barriers into a therapeutic opportunity, as described below.

Overall, the interpersonal inventory and cultural formulation allowed rapport building and set the stage for the therapeutic relationship in a way that acknowledged the cultural aspects considered key in Sr. A's formulation and treatment.

IPT Formulation

It was clear to the therapist that Sr. A was experiencing a role transition, with some evidence for a role dispute with his girlfriend. The therapist began psychoeducation about depression, his symptoms, and the course and effectiveness of treatment. During this exchange Sr. A seemed hesitant and unwilling to accept that his experience was a result of biomedical phenomena rather than something existential and spiritual. As he believed that this role transition was a test from God, the therapist decided to de-emphasize (but not fully abandon) the medical model and assignment of the sick role. The therapist presented this formulation to Sr. A:

THERAPIST: These symptoms that you have been telling me about are a part of depression, which is a treatable illness. The depression is connected to the life transition you experienced after the accident you suffered at the workplace. You have explained to me that your transition was from once being a strong, virile, admired man in your country, to now an injured manual laborer in the U.S. who feels weak, frustrated, and victimized by the "cold, callous, and self-serving" people surrounding you here. Much in the way you have been telling me about some of the recent arguments with your girlfriend and how they make you feel, depression is affected by and affects relationships. Interpersonal therapy has been shown to be highly effective in treating depression. You have told me a little bit about how it has been difficult to get along with others, and in this therapy we will try to understand what current stresses and relationships in your life may be contributing to the depression, and how your depressed feelings affect how you interact in your relationships. This therapy is going to help you transition out of feeling depressed, inadequate, and frustrated into feeling healthier and happier.

Sr. A willingly accepted this formulation, adding that he felt this role transition was "similar to my experience when I first immigrated to this country." At the end of this session the therapist asked Sr. A about his role transition after immigration and how he was able to cope and adjust to his new life in the United States. He attributed his ease of adjustment and assimilation at the time to meeting with extended family members and finding a church, a pastor, and a social group who helped provide a community for him and helped him navigate employment and other opportunities.

Middle Phase

The focus of treatment was his role transition since the accident and the ensuing role dispute with his girlfriend as the sole provider for the family. He subsequently set goals for treatment: to overcome anxiety and depression related to feeling unproductive, to relearn how to make a living and provide for his family, and to feel less anger and hostility in interacting with his girlfriend and others around him.

During subsequent IPT sessions the therapist began each session asking Sr. A about his thoughts and feelings about himself since the accident and how things were going in his relationship with his girlfriend. The therapist found it challenging to elicit Sr. A's feelings about this transition for two cultural reasons. He avoided discussing his feelings because they entailed the unappealing, culturally dystonic role of a weak male unable to provide for his family. Providing and sacrificing for the family is part of the ethos of *familismo* and an important part of Sr. A's identity, one that had made him feel competent and proud but now elicited feelings of inadequacy, low self-esteem, and sadness. Sr. A also revealed that discussing his feelings would contradict his strong belief in God, in whose hands matters lay.

The therapist reframed the importance of emotional expression by using cultural idioms such as *desahogarse* to describe *unburdening oneself* of painful emotions. The therapist also facilitated his expressing emotions within the context of Biblical passages and interpretations. It was important during this phase and throughout treatment that the therapist took a stance characterized by *simpatia* and *formalismo*. "Señor A, you [formal: *usted*] mentioned that during the past week reading from the Bible and reflecting on your experience and emotions has helped your mood. As I had mentioned to you, I am not familiar with the Bible as you are. You mentioned that sharing the word of God is the evangelical way and I wonder if you would be willing to share with me passages that you feel relate to your experience since the accident, or even how you have been interacting with your girlfriend."

Sr. A was enthusiastic about this idea and each week recited Biblical passages that he believed pertained to his experience and emotions. Discussing his immigration experience and perceived social injustice freed Sr. A from feeling trapped and allowed him to explore options such as vocational rehabilitation and practical solutions to his immediate life problems.

As he felt more comfortable expressing his emotions, Sr. A experienced relief in his mood symptoms. Through the use of Bible passages and role-plays in session, he began to express his emotions more freely to his girlfriend and his pastor. Sr. A reported less irritability and conflict with his partner, which gradually led to decreased social isolation overall, as he and his family began to socialize at church outings and extended family gatherings.

Having achieved two of his three goals for treatment, the therapist and Sr. A began to explore steps that he could take to become more productive and to find employment. The therapist introduced this idea of problem solving by using another Hispanic concept, *poner de su parte* (the need to do one's part), to encourage patient agency in confronting or resolving conflicts. Interactions at church presented Sr. A with the opportunity to give conferences at church meetings. Sr. A also partnered with a friend who owned a natural medicine store in his neighborhood to write a natural medicine newsletter for sale in the store. At week twelve, Sr. A also began doing volunteer work caring for the elderly, and delivering sermons over a local Hispanic religious radio station.

Termination Phase

Sr. A believed that prayer and waiting patiently brought him to therapy. By termination of treatment, he reported an improvement in his mood symptoms (Ham-D-17 score = 8) and attributed this to the love of God, the therapy, the opportunity to start vocational rehabilitation, and his conducting religious services over the radio.

DISCUSSION

IPT appeared culturally congruent in the case of Sr. A. Focusing on relationship issues is consistent with Hispanic cultures, and IPT was flexibly adaptable to the cultural tensions that arose. Cultural adaptations that were implemented focused on incorporating cultural experiences—spirituality, acculturation, familism—into IPT in order to help Sr. A understand interpersonal problem areas, and gradual, modeled expression of emotion while preserving equanimity. The therapist had to subtly alter the IPT model in this case. De-emphasizing the medical model for this naturopath, who held distinct beliefs about health, and integrating his religious beliefs in the treatment were important in orienting Sr. A to therapy and facilitating expression and communication of distress. His gender role expectations, which ranged from personal virility to more extreme masculinity, crucially influenced the role transition and dispute contributing to the depression. IPT engaged these expectations by exploring culturally syntonic ways to develop a more desirable gender-based sense of self within cultural bounds. Based on the psychotherapy adaptation literature, some general principles applied in the care of Sr. A might generalize to other minority cultures in other parts of the world, including orientation to therapy, using cultural bridges and metaphors, understanding culturally influenced models of illness, framing treatment concepts within cultural beliefs, and treatment in the patient's native language (e.g., Domenech-Rodríguez & Wieling, 2004; Griner & Smith, 2006; Hwang, 2006; Ying, 2001).

In our general supervision of cases, several salient issues arose when working with depressed Hispanic patients, including time-limited treatment and deference to therapists for guidance and needed resources (Markowitz et al., 2009). Patients at times construed time-limited treatment as potential abandonment. Coming from intensely social cultures, patients saw therapy as a relationship they did not expect to end. Therapists provided an orientation to therapy by educating patients about time-limited psychotherapy at the outset and acknowledging that it differed from the usual handling of problems in their social network. Therapists reassured: "As we work together, I'll check in with you to see how you feel about the process and how our work fits with your world outside the office." Nonetheless, termination was sometimes difficult and IPT was sometimes extended beyond the initial time frame.

Many depressed patients desperately needed concrete resources and related their distress to lack of housing and other needs. They saw their therapists as more successful, better integrated into mainstream culture, and better positioned than them to acquire these goods. (See also Chapter 17 for work with low-income patients.) Patients therefore often appeared passively resigned, expecting therapists to resolve their claims or to direct them, rather than having to act themselves. They often seemed unable to navigate English-language–based procedures for obtaining needed benefits. Depression magnifies such passivity. The precariousness of patients' environments furthered some therapists' wishes to make suggestions or referrals for concrete services.

Obtaining needed services might indeed relieve environmental stress, yet psychotherapy typically arms patients to achieve such goals themselves. Thus therapists, without rejecting patients' requests, focused on the patient's role in IPT. Although occasionally offering concrete advice, therapists predominantly asked what patients had already tried, and what options remained to try, in order to meet their needs. Role-playing viable options then prepared patients for attempting them, as in the case of Sr. A.

In any clinical encounter, therapists need to be aware of their own feelings and prejudices as well as patients' diagnoses, character, and cultural and socioeconomic backgrounds. These factors have differing impacts in different cases, requiring therapists to respond sensitively and flexibly, and complicating generalization about what "works" with a particular cultural group. Every adaptation of IPT has required determining the salient issues of the treatment population, which vary among depressed adolescents, depressed geriatric patients, and depressed HIV-positive patients, for example. Similarly, IPT with Spanish-speaking immigrants in New York City likely differs slightly from IPT with, say, Scandinavian or Ugandan patients (Bolton et al., 2003; Griner & Smitth, 2006). IPT appears sufficiently flexible to maintain its general structure, with some adjustment, with varied patients.

SUGGESTED READING

Balls Organista P, Organista KC, Kurasaki K: (2003). The relationship between acculturation and ethnic minority mental health. In Chun KM, Balls Organista P,

Marin G (Eds.): Acculturation: Advances in Theory, Measurement, and Applied Research. Washington, D.C.: American Psychological Association., 139–161

Bernal G, Bonilla J, Bellido C: Ecological validity and cultural sensitivity for outcome research: Issues for the cultural adaptation and development of psychosocial treatments with Hispanics. Journal of Abnormal Child Psychology 1995;23:67–82

Bernal G, Bonilla J, Padilla-Cotto L, Perez-Prado EM: Factors associated to outcome in psychotherapy: An effectiveness study in Puerto Rico. Journal of Clinical Psychology 1998;54:329–342

Bernal G, Scharro-del-Rio MR: Are empirically supported treatments valid for ethnic minorities? Toward an alternative approach for treatment research. Cultural Diversity & Ethnic Minority Psychology 2001;7:328–342

Bolton P, Bass J, Neugebauer R, Verdeli H, Clougherty KF, Wickramaratne P, Speelman L, Ndogoni L, Weissman M: Group interpersonal psychotherapy for depression in rural Uganda: a randomized controlled trial. Journal of the American Medical Association 2003;289:3117–3124

Comas-Díaz, L, Duncan JW: The cultural context: A factor in assertiveness training with mainland Puerto Rican women. Psychology of Women Quarterly 1985;9:463–476

Comas-Díaz L, Jacobsen FM: Ethnocultural identification in psychotherapy. Psychiatry 1987;50:232–241

Cooper LA, Gonzales J, Gallo JJ, Rost KM, Meredith LS, Rubenstein LV, et al.: The acceptability of treatment for depression among African-American, Hispanic, and White primary care clients. Medical Care 2003;41:479–489

Delgado M: Hispanics and group work: A review of the literature. Ethnicity in Group Work Practice 1984;7:85–96

Delgado M: Hispanics and psychotherapeutic groups. International Journal of Group Psychotherapy 1983;33:507–520

Department of Health and Human Services: Mental Health: Culture, Race, and Ethnicity—A Supplement to Mental Health: A Report of the Surgeon General. (DHHS Publication No. SMA-01-3613) Rockville, MD: U.S. Department of Health and Human Services, Substance Abuse and Mental Health Services Administration, Center for Mental Health Services, 2001

Domenech-Rodríguez M, Wieling E: Developing culturally appropriate evidence based treatments for interventions with ethnic minority populations. In Rastogi M, Wieling E (Eds.): Voices of Color: First Person Accounts of Ethnic Minority Therapists. Thousand Oaks, CA: Sage Publications, 2004:313–333

Dwight-Johnson M, Unutzer J, Sherbourne C, Tang L, Wells KB: Can quality improvement programs for depression in primary care address patient preferences for treatment? Medical Care 2001;39:934–944

Elkin I, Shea MT, Watkins JT, Imber SD, Sotsky SM, Collins JE, Glass DR, Pilkonis PA, Leber WR, Docherty JP, Fiester SJ, Parloff MB: National Institute of Mental Health Treatment of Depression Collaborative Research Program: general effectiveness of treatments. Archives of General Psychiatry 1989;46:971–982

Fairhurst K, Dowrick C: Problems with recruitment in a randomized controlled trial of counseling in general practice: causes and implications. Journal of Health Services Research and Policy 1996;1:77–80

Flores G: Culture and the client-physician relationship: achieving cultural competency in healthcare. Journal of Pediatrics 2000;136:14–23

Griner D, Smith TB: Culturally adapted mental health interventions: a meta-analytic review. Psychotherapy: Theory, Research, Practice, Training 2006;43:531–548

Guarnaccia PJ, Martinez I: "It's like Going Through an Earthquake": Anthropological Perspectives on Depression From Focus Groups with Latino Immigrants. Paper Presented at Mount Sinai Medical Center, New York, 2003

Hu T, Snowden LR, Jerrell JM, Nguyen TD: Ethnic populations in public mental health: services choice and level of use. American Journal of Public Health 1991;81:1429–1434

Hwang W-C: The psychotherapy adaptation and modification framework. American Psychologist 2006;61:702–715

Jaycox LH, Asarnow JR, Sherbourne CD, Rea MM, LaBorde AP, Wells KB: Adolescent primary care patients' preferences for depression treatment. Admin Policy Mental Health Serv Res 2006;33:198–207

Kessler RC, Berglund P, Demler O, Jin R, Koretz D, Merikangas K, et al.: The epidemiology of major depressive disorder: Results from the National Comorbidity Survey Replication (NCS-R). Journal of the American Medical Association 2003;289:3095–3105

Lee DJ, Markides KS, Ray LA: Epidemiology of self-reported past heavy drinking in Hispanic adults. Ethnicity and Health 1997;2:77–88

Lewis-Fernández R, Díaz N: The Cultural Formulation: A method for assessing cultural factors affecting the clinical encounter. Psychiatric Quarterly 2002;73: 271–295

Marin G: Defining culturally appropriate community interventions: Hispanics as a case study. Journal of Community Psychology 1991;21:149–161

Markowitz JC, Patel SA, Balan I, McNamara M, Blanco C, Yellow Horse Brave Heart M, Buttacavoli Sosa S, Lewis-Fernández R. Towards an adaptation of interpersonal psychotherapy for depressed Hispanic patients. Journal of Clinical Psychiatry 2009:70:214–222

Markowitz JC, Spielman LA, Sullivan M, Fishman B: An exploratory study of ethnicity and psychotherapy outcome among HIV-positive patients with depressive symptoms. Journal of Psychotherapy Practice and Research 2000;9:226–231

Miranda J, Azocar F, Organista KC, Muñoz RF, Lieberman A: Recruiting and retaining low-income Latinos in psychotherapy research. Journal of Consulting and Clinical Psychology 1996;64:868–874

Miranda J, Nakamura R, Bernal G: Including ethnic minorities in mental health intervention research: A practical approach to a long-standing problem. Culture, Medicine, and Psychiatry 2003;27:463–481

Moscicki EE, Rae DS, Regier DA, Locke BZ: The Hispanic Health and Nutrition Survey: Depression among Mexican-Americans, Cuban-Americans, and Puerto Ricans. In Garcia M, Arana J (Eds.): Research Agenda for Hispanics. Chicago: University of Illinois Press, 1987:145–159

Mufson L, Dorta KP, Wickramaratne P, Nomura Y, Olfson M, Weissman MM: A randomized effectiveness trial of interpersonal psychotherapy for depressed adolescents. Arch Gen Psychiatry 2004;61:577–584

Mufson L, Weissman MM, Moreau D, Garfinkel R: Efficacy of interpersonal psychotherapy for depressed adolescents. Archives of General Psychiatry 1999;56: 573–579

Murray CJL, Lopez AD: Evidence-based health policy: lessons from the Global Burden of Disease Study. Science 1996;274:740–743

Navarro AM: Efectividad de las psicoterapias con Latinos en los Estados Unidos: Una revision meta-analitica. Interamerican Journal of Psychology 1993;27:131–146

Organista KC: Latinos. In White JR, Freeman AS (Eds.): Cognitive-Behavioral Group Therapy. Washington, D.C.: American Psychological Association, 2000, 281–303

Organista KC, Muñoz RF: Cognitive behavioral therapy with Latinos. Cognitive and Behavioral Practice 1996;3:255–270

Ramirez RR, de la Cruz GP: The Hispanic population in the United States: March 2002. Current Population Reports, P20–545. Washington, DC: U.S. Census Bureau, 2003

Rogler LH, Malgady RG, Constantino G, Blumenthal R: What do culturally sensitive mental health services mean? The case of Hispanics. American Psychologist 1987;42:565–570

Rosello J, Bernal G: The efficacy of cognitive-behavioral and interpersonal treatments for depression in Puerto Rican adolescents. Journal of Consulting and Clinical Psychology 1999;67:734–745

Sabogal F, Marin G, Otero-Sabogal R, Marin BV, Perez-Stable EJ: Hispanic familism and acculturation: What changes and what doesn't? Hispanic Journal of Behavioral Sciences 1987;9:397–412

Scheffler RM, Miller AB: Demand analysis of mental health service use among ethnic subpopulations. Inquiry 1989;26:202–215

Stevens E: *Machismo* and marianismo. Transaction/Society 1973;10:57–63

Sue PW, Sue DP: Counseling the Culturally Different. New York: John Wiley and Sons, 1990

Sue S, Zane N, Young K: Research on psychotherapy with culturally diverse populations. In Bergin AE, Garfield SL (Eds.): Handbook of Psychotherapy and Behavior Change, 4th ed. New York: John Wiley & Sons, 1994:783–817

Szapocznik J, Williams RA: Brief strategic family therapy: Twenty-five years of interplay among theory, research and practice in adolescent behavior problems and drug abuse. Clinical Child & Family Psychology Review 2000;3:117–134

Triandis HC, Marin G, Betancourt H, Lisansky J, Chang B: Dimensions of Familism Among Hispanics and Mainstream Navy Recruits. Technical Report No. 14, Department of Psychology, University of Illinois, Champaign,1982

Triandis HC, Marin G, Lisansky J, Betancourt H: *Simpatìa* as a cultural script of Hispanics. Journal of Personality and Social Psychology 1984;47:1363–1375

Ying Y-W: Psychotherapy with traumatized southeast Asian refugees. Clinical Social Work Journal 2001;29: 65–78

17

Interpersonal Psychotherapy for Women with Depression Living on Low Incomes

NANCY K. GROTE, HOLLY A. SWARTZ,
AND ALLAN ZUCKOFF

Individuals of low socioeconomic status (SES) have higher prevalence rates of major depression than the general population (DHHS, 1999, 2001; Kessler et al., 2003; Lorant et al., 2003; McMillan et al., 2010; Williams & Collins, 1995). A meta-analysis by Lorant et al. (2003), based on fifty-six studies, showed that individuals with low SES had a higher risk of major depression or clinically significant depressive symptoms than individuals with high SES, and this association was not limited to the bottom SES group but persisted across the social spectrum. This meta-analysis measured SES by education, income, or work status.

Although the association between SES and major depression applies across genders, this chapter focuses on women with depression living on low incomes, who face significant barriers to treatment access, engagement, and retention. Women are twice as likely as men to experience a lifetime episode of major depression (Weissman & Klerman, 1977; Wolk et al., 1995). High levels of depressive symptoms are common in young minority women (Kessler et al., 1994) and in pregnant and postpartum mothers and mothers on low incomes: 20% to 25% meet criteria for major or minor depression (Hobfall et al., 1995; Miranda et al., 1998; 2003; Scholle et al., 2003; Siefert et al., 2004) compared to 9% to 13% of their middle-income peers (Gotlib et al., 1991; O'Hara & Swain, 1996).

Despite this increased risk for and prevalence of depression in low-income women (DHHS, 1999; Perez-Stable et al., 1990), many either do not seek mental health services or drop out after an initial visit or after their acute distress abates (Greeno et al., 1999; Miranda et al., 1998; Leaf et al., 1985; Sue et al., 1991). In the National Comorbidity Survey replication, Wang et al. (2005) found that most people with mental disorders, especially those from racial/ethnic minorities and those on low incomes, either remain untreated or receive minimal, inadequate treatment. Thus, failure to engage and retain low-income and minority individuals with depression in efficacious mental health services constitutes a critical public health problem (DHHS, 1999, 2001).

In this chapter, we review the effectiveness of IPT for depressed women on low incomes and highlight the multiple chronic stressors and barriers to care they face. We describe adaptations and additions to IPT we have made in our work with depressed, low-income women who face practical, psychological, and cultural barriers to treatment engagement and retention. A case example demonstrates these modifications in the delivery of IPT.

RESEARCH ON IPT WITH WOMEN WITH DEPRESSION LIVING ON LOW INCOMES

Promising evidence for the effectiveness of IPT in this population has emerged from 11 studies specifically treating depressed, socioeconomically disadvantaged women. Although IPT was sometimes shortened and, in many studies, flexibly delivered—on the telephone, in the home, in prison, or in a destigmatizing setting such as a prenatal clinic or a school health class—most of these studies provide little information (except Beeber et al., 2008, and Talbot & Gamble, 2008) about how the researchers adapted IPT to address psychological or cultural barriers to care, including the culture of poverty and race/ethnicity. Two open trials and three randomized controlled trials focused on women with a depressive disorder or symptoms and other psychiatric comorbidities (e.g., an anxiety disorder or substance abuse), psychosocial vulnerabilities (e.g., imprisonment, immigrant status), or medical illness (HIV-AIDS). Acute IPT sessions lasted fifty to sixty minutes, unless otherwise specified.

Talbot et al. (2005) conducted a pilot open trial of sixteen sessions of IPT in a community mental health center with twenty-five socioeconomically disadvantaged women with major depression who reported childhood sexual abuse. Most had a comorbid anxiety disorder, such as PTSD. Talbot and Gamble (2008) described how IPT was modified to accommodate the stressful lives of the women in the sample who were living on low incomes. Modifications included an expanded treatment duration (from sixteen to thirty-two weeks to increase treatment participation) and an engagement analysis in initial IPT sessions to help patients overcome social and practical barriers to care. Significant improvements in depression and psychological functioning, but not social functioning, were observed at ten, twenty-four, and thirty-six weeks after baseline. In another open trial (Johnson & Zlotnick, 2008), twenty-five female prisoners with depression or dysthymic disorder and at least one substance abuse disorder, who were enrolled in a substance abuse treatment program, received twenty-four sessions of an interpersonally based group intervention over eight weeks. Group IPT was adapted to address the treatment needs of female prisoners, including addressing substance use-specific social support and communication problems, interpersonal consequences of sexual and physical assaults, disrupted family and friendship relationships resulting from women's entry into or attempted exit from drug- or crime-involved lifestyles, and reactions to loss or potential loss of children to the child welfare system. Prison substance use counselors who received IPT training co-led the group treatment. At post-treatment, depressive severity and perceived social support had improved, and 75% of participants no longer met criteria for any depressive disorder.

A small randomized trial (Ransom et al., 2008) treating seventy-nine rural, financially disadvantaged individuals (84% male) with major depression or dysthymia and an HIV-AIDS diagnosis showed that six sessions of telephone-delivered IPT significantly reduced depressive severity and psychiatric symptoms compared to usual care. Clinically meaningful change (Jacobson & Truax, 1991) in depressive symptoms was higher in the IPT group (23%) than in the usual care group (9%).

Beeber et al. (2004, 2010) conducted two randomized trials for Early Head Start mothers with depressive symptoms, providing eight IPT sessions in the 2004 trial (n = 16 African-American and white, non-Hispanic mothers) and eleven IPT sessions in the 2010 trial (n = 80 new immigrant Latina mothers with limited English fluency) of nurse-delivered, in-home, culturally tailored IPT (plus five follow-up booster sessions) or usual care (no therapeutic intervention until data collection completed). IPT mothers showed significantly greater decrease in depressive symptoms (1) at eight and sixteen weeks after baseline in the 2004 trial and (2) at post-treatment and four weeks post-treatment in the 2010 trial. At four weeks post-treatment, more IPT mothers (78%) than usual-care mothers (53%) scored below the depression cutoff of 16 on the CES-D (Center for Epidemiology Studies-Depression; Radloff, 1977). Beeber et al. (2008) described culturally enhancing IPT in their 2010 trial by partnering with bilingual Early Head Start staff who screened Latina women for the study using the CES-D Spanish version, provided Spanish translation during treatment sessions in a destigmatizing home setting, and assisted the women in meeting their survival needs, such as obtaining housing, food, transportation, health care, and resources for their children's schooling.

Six studies (two open trials, four randomized controlled trials) of IPT with low-income, pregnant women at risk for or having a depressive disorder yielded positive results. An open trial (Miller et al., 2008) treated eleven predominantly financially disadvantaged, pregnant adolescents with major depression in an urban public school with twelve sessions of group IPT. Depressive symptoms significantly decreased: at post-treatment 73% no longer met criteria for major depression. These gains were maintained at the two-week postpartum follow-up. In two trials of thirty-seven and ninety-nine financially disadvantaged women receiving care in a prenatal clinic who were at risk for postpartum depression, Zlotnick et al. (2001, 2006) randomly assigned subjects to receive four ninety-minute sessions of IPT-oriented group intervention, entitled ROSE (Reach Out, Stand strong, Essentials for new mothers), in addition to standard antenatal care. ROSE subjects were significantly less likely than those receiving standard antenatal care alone to develop postpartum depression within three months after delivery (2001 study: 0% vs. 33%; 2006 study: 4% vs. 20%). The 2006 study found no group differences in depressive severity three months postpartum. Similarly, in a small randomized controlled trial, Crockett, Zlotnick, et al. (2008) reported that thirty-six low-income, rural African-American pregnant women at risk for postpartum depression who received the ROSE intervention showed better adjustment three months postpartum than the usual care group, but there were no group differences in depressive severity.

Finally, an open trial (n = 13) and a small randomized controlled trial (n = 53) by Grote et al. (2004, 2009) supported the effectiveness of brief IPT (eight sessions, plus a pre-therapy "engagement" session) and monthly maintenance IPT (until six months postpartum) in reducing antenatal depression diagnoses and depressive symptoms and improving social functioning for socioeconomically disadvantaged, pregnant, depressed women. Because most women in both trials reported childhood trauma and recurrent depression, which are risk factors for depressive relapse (Frank et al., 1993), IPT maintenance sessions to prevent depressive relapse were an integral part of the 2009 trial design. In the latter study, 68% of the brief IPT group received an average of six IPT maintenance sessions. In the 2004 open trial, brief IPT significantly reduced depressive severity and major depression diagnoses at post-treatment (from 83% to 0%) and six months postpartum (from 83% to 8%). In the 2009 study, more women in brief IPT than in usual care showed a 50% improvement in depressive severity post-treatment (80% vs. 21%) and six months postpartum (88% vs. 25%), and fewer women in brief IPT than usual care met criteria for major depression post-treatment (5% vs. 42%) and six months postpartum (0% vs. 30%). Grote et al. (2004, 2009) enhanced IPT to make treatment relevant for the cultures of poverty and race/ethnicity and to address treatment ambivalence and barriers to care.

CHALLENGES AND BARRIERS TO CARE

Women on low incomes experience more frequent, more threatening, and more uncontrollable life events and chronic stressors than the general population, including food insufficiency; crowded, inadequate housing; community crime, violence, and discrimination; unemployment or under-employment; substance abuse or addiction in their families and neighborhoods; limited access to transportation, and, at times, imprisonment of their partners (Belle, 1990; Grote et al., 2007; Siefert et al., 2004). Their social networks can be conduits of stress as well as sources of support (Riley & Eckenrode, 1986). Epidemiologic and qualitative research (Armstrong et al., 1984; Diamond & Factor, 1994; Hunt & Andrews, 1992; Maynard et al, 1997) has identified practical barriers to service use by low-income populations, including cost, lack of insurance, inconvenient or inaccessible clinic locations, transportation difficulties, limited clinic hours, and child care problems. Many low-income individuals experience so many economic and practical difficulties that they may see treatment as just one more burden (Hall et al., 1985).

Psychological barriers that depressed, low-income women face include mental health stigma and discrimination (Brown et al., 2010; Cooper et al., 2003); their own, family members', or friends' negative experiences with treatment; the heavy burden of depression; and distrust of helping professionals because of prior childhood and adult trauma. Evidence from OB/GYN clinics suggests that women on low incomes experience high levels of sexual/physical abuse in both childhood and adulthood (Miranda et al., 1998). Some epidemiologic data indicate that traumatic childhood events, including physical, sexual, and emotional abuse, correlate with low SES (i.e., welfare status) of the affected individual's family of origin (Menard et al., 2004). Recurrent childhood abuse and neglect have been linked to greater risk for PTSD and major depression in adulthood and greater risk of PTSD from subsequent trauma (Breslau et al., 1999, 2008; Widom, 2007). Childhood interpersonal trauma is associated with insecure adult attachment styles, including dismissing or fearful attachment (Mickelson et al, 1997). A dismissing attachment style is characterized by low trust of others and strong self-reliance, while a fearful attachment style comprises low trust of others, approach–avoidance behavior, and cautious independence (Ciechanowski et al., 2002). Although partially adaptive strategies for dealing with adversity, these attachment styles (strong self-reliance and cautious independence) complicate engagement, collaboration, and adherence in psychotherapy (Dozier, 1990; Tyrell et al., 2001) and in health care regimens (Ciechanowski et al., 2001).

Cultural barriers to care for depressed, low-income women of color include provider ignorance of or insensitivity to cultural perspectives on mental health, including somatic symptoms as indicators of depression, coping mechanisms such as spirituality or prayer (Mays et al., 1996), and the importance of family (Markowitz et al., 2009; Rossello & Bernal, 1999). Compared to white peers of similarly disadvantaged SES, economically disadvantaged individuals of color may question the quality of available prevention and treatment services, given societal racism (Broman, 1996; Snowden, 2001; Thomas et al., 1994).

In brief, to effectively engage and retain depressed low-income individuals, IPT must address practical, psychological, and cultural barriers to care. In our view, the IPT therapist needs to show that treatment is relevant to the complex, acutely and chronically stressful culture of living in poverty by (1) helping depressed women address basic material needs and (2) reducing treatment burden by providing shorter, more accessible, flexibly delivered treatment. The IPT therapist needs to resolve psychological barriers to care by explicitly addressing treatment ambivalence and depression stigma before treatment begins and reaching out continually to engage and retain women mistrustful of treatment (Tyrell et al., 2001). Lastly, the IPT therapist must demonstrate the relevance of treatment to racial/ethnic culture by respecting culturally based indicators and views of depression, finding out before treatment begins whether and how the therapist's race/ethnicity matters, and affirming and incorporating cultural coping strategies and strengths in the treatment process (Cooper et al., 2003).

ADAPTATION AND ADDITIONS TO IPT

Brief IPT

The rationale for developing a briefer form of IPT was two-fold. First, Swartz et al. (2002) developed a briefer version of IPT to reduce treatment burden for mothers who face practical barriers to care, including financial and time constraints. A second reason to shorten IPT was the paucity of empirical evidence linking increased therapy "dosage" to enhanced therapeutic effects (Gunderson, Fonagy, & Gabbard, 2002). Conversely, a small literature suggested that eight psychotherapy sessions may suffice to treat depression for some individuals (Howard, Kopta, Krause, & Orlinsky, 1986; Shapiro et al., 1994). Patients and therapists work harder and faster when the number of psychotherapy sessions is limited from the outset (Reynolds et al., 1996), thereby hastening the onset of antidepressant effects.

Based on these clinical and empirical observations, Swartz et al. (2004) developed "brief IPT." Its eight weekly individual sessions retain the theory, targets, tactics, and techniques of IPT, employing strategies to distill its key ingredients and hasten its course. Five studies have empirically supported brief IPT, which demonstrated an onset of action comparable to pharmacotherapy (Grote et al., 2004, 2009; Swartz et al., 2004, 2006, 2008). A treatment manual is available on request (Swartz et al., unpublished).

Standard IPT is already a brief, time-limited treatment. "Brief IPT" intensifies the time limit, heightening the patient's motivation to achieve symptom relief still faster. The initial IPT phase is limited to two sessions and constricts the interpersonal inventory to current relationships. The goals of the initial phase, however, remain the same. At the end of the first session, the therapist gives a provisional, rapid case formulation that may be modified in the second session. The therapist and patient collaboratively select only one focal problem area, ideally a problem that can be managed in eight sessions. Brief IPT avoids the problem area of interpersonal deficits.

The middle phase of brief IPT (Sessions 3–7) comprises five sessions. In addition to standard IPT techniques of communication analysis, decision analysis, role-playing, etc., therapists borrow from behavioral therapy, using behavioral activation strategies to increase the patient's experience of pleasure and accomplishment to reduce depressive symptoms (Jacobson et al., 2001; Lewinsohn, 1974). They *explicitly* assign weekly behavioral homework, preferably with an interpersonal emphasis, in a graded approach to encourage the patient to engage in previously gratifying or productive activities, based on the patient's anergia (Beck, 1995). No other cognitive or behavioral techniques are employed. Further, during the middle phase, therapists typically ask patients to carry out weekly interpersonal homework assignments to engage patients in the change process and to address and resolve the focal interpersonal problem area, whereas standard IPT does not assign homework. Brief IPT homework assignments are developed collaboratively between therapist and patient and might include discussing a conflict-laden issue with a partner, exploring part-time job opportunities, or enrolling in a parenting class.

Although the conclusion of brief IPT begins in Session 7 and ends in Session 8, the end of treatment never lies far from the minds of patient and therapist. Ending brief IPT is handled like a graduation, as in standard IPT, focusing on the patient's accomplishments, emotional reactions to the end of acute treatment, relapse prevention, and future needs. For patients who have not or have only partially responded to brief IPT, options include additional sessions, the addition of antidepressant medication, or an alternative treatment. For patients with histories of trauma and recurrent or chronic depression, clinical logic suggests following successful brief IPT with continuation or maintenance IPT sessions to solidify treatment response and prevent relapse (APA, 2010).

Pretreatment Engagement Session

Brief IPT is typically administered following a single, forty-five- to sixty-minute engagement session to increase the likelihood that patients will participate in psychotherapy (Zuckoff et al., 2008). While IPT includes well-specified strategies for developing a therapeutic alliance, it does not explicitly explore treatment ambivalence or reasons why the depressed woman may not want treatment, nor does it address impediments to care. The initial engagement session is not a treatment session, but occurs *before* the patient has committed to treatment. Nor is it a psychosocial assessment. It focuses on the patient's perceptions of her depression, motivation for change, treatment ambivalence, and specific obstacles she faces to participating in psychotherapy. This pretreatment engagement strategy has a theoretical foundation (described below) distinct from IPT, comprises five components designed to enhance motivation for treatment engagement, is described in a manual (Zuckoff et al., unpublished), and has received preliminary empirical support (Grote et al., 2007; Swartz et al., 2007). In a small randomized controlled trial with depressed, low-income, pregnant women in a public care prenatal clinic who were assigned to receive the engagement session and eight sessions of brief IPT, Grote et al. (2007) found that 96% of the women attended an initial brief IPT treatment session and 68% completed a course of treatment. Of women assigned to receive usual care (referral to behavioral health services located in the same prenatal clinic), only 36% attended an initial treatment session and only 7% completed standard depression treatment. Similarly, in an open trial, Swartz et al. (2007) found that of thirteen depressed mothers offered the engagement interview and brief IPT, eleven agreed to participate in the engagement interview; eleven (100%) attended an initial treatment session, and ten (91%) completed a course of brief IPT.

We drew on the theoretical foundations of ethnographic interviewing (Schensul et al., 1999) and motivational interviewing (Miller & Rollnick, 2002) in designing our engagement strategy to address practical, psychological, and cultural treatment impediments collaboratively with depressed mothers and expectant depressed mothers. During ethnographic interviewing, an interviewer seeks unbiased understanding of the perspectives, experiences, and values of an individual from a different culture and assumes the role of a friendly, interested learner, relinquishing control and inviting the interviewee to be the expert or teacher (Schensul et al., 1999). Because many depressed impoverished individuals may differ from their treating clinicians in cultural background and chronically stressful life circumstances, we addressed potential cultural biases in our engagement intervention. Motivational interviewing is a client-centered, goal-oriented, therapeutic method for enhancing motivation for change by helping clients resolve ambivalence (Miller & Rollnick, 2002). As we expected, based on clinical experience, that depressed, socioeconomically disadvantaged women would have ambivalence about attending treatment for various reasons, we saw motivational interviewing as a potentially valuable element of engagement. Further, we felt that the directive components of motivational interviewing could help move individuals toward the desired outcome of the engagement session (viz., participation in depression treatment), as we were decidedly not neutral about resolving the patient's ambivalence over treatment seeking.

The engagement session integrates ethnographic and motivational interviewing techniques to address and resolve barriers to mental health care treatment ambivalence. The clinician uses open-ended questions; expresses empathy through reflective listening; recognizes and affirms a woman's strengths and resilience in dealing with past and current adversity (Stack, 1975); responds to resistance by "rolling with" it through the motivational interviewing techniques of double-sided reflection, amplified reflection, reframing, and emphasizing personal choice and control; evokes and strengthens "change talk" (Miller & Rollnick, 2002) and adherence talk (Zweben & Zuckoff, 2002); and uses the "elicit–provide–elicit" technique (Miller & Rollnick, 2002) when providing the patient with psychoeducation about depression and its treatment. The engagement session also addresses race, gender, and cultural barriers: the clinician encourages a woman to voice concerns about aspects of depression treatment she considers culturally unacceptable, such as working with a therapist from a different racial, ethnic, or economic background (Grote et al., 2007). Using open-ended questions, expressing empathy through reflective listening, and affirming strengths are basic therapeutic techniques familiar to IPT practitioners.

The engagement session includes five manualized components (Zuckoff et al., unpublished) delivered flexibly over forty-five to sixty minutes to meet a patient's specific needs: (1) eliciting the story, crystallizing the patient's perceived dilemma(s), and highlighting motivation for change (how the patient has been feeling and how it interferes with her life); (2a) identifying treatment ambivalence, exploring why the woman would *not* want treatment through eliciting negative views about treatment or previous negative treatment experiences of the woman, her family members, or friends; (2b) identifying her coping mechanisms for previous and current adversity or depression, such as strong self-reliance (Ciechanowski et al., 2002) or spirituality and prayer (Boyd-Franklin & Lockwood, 1999; Cooper et al., 2001); (2c) developing discrepancy between where the patient is and where she wants to be, and finding out what the patient wants and does not want in a therapist; (3) feedback and psychoeducation about depression and various treatment options using the "elicit–provide–elicit" technique; (4) probing for and problem-solving specific practical, psychological, and cultural barriers to treatment seeking; and (5) eliciting an explicit commitment to treatment, affirming the patient's strengths, and offering hope.

Miller and Rollnick (2002) found that after successfully addressing treatment ambivalence, eliciting the patient's verbal commitment to treatment strongly predicts subsequent treatment adherence. If the patient addresses topics in a different order than specified here, the therapist follows the patient and not the outline. Although the initial IPT assessment sessions may cover material in some of the engagement components (items 1, 2, 3, and 5), during the engagement session the therapist assumes that the patient has not committed to treatment and employs specific motivational interviewing techniques (not typical of IPT) that target treatment ambivalence and enhance motivation for change, such as double-sided reflections, amplified reflections, eliciting change talk, and developing discrepancy.

Making Brief IPT Relevant to the Culture of Poverty

To reduce stigma and enhance access to treatment for women suffering acute and chronic stressors of poverty, we delivered the engagement session and brief IPT sessions in a large primary care OB/GYN clinic serving socioeconomically disadvantaged women. When participants could not attend treatment, we conducted telephone sessions to maintain continuity, an effective practice in delivering antidepressant psychotherapy and pharmacotherapy (Simon et al., 2004). If a woman missed an in-person or phone session, we employed extensive outreach to re-engage her in treatment (e.g., phone calls, notes, spontaneous contact in the OB/GYN clinic).

Finally, we integrated a *case management component* into brief IPT to make treatment relevant to economically disadvantaged women, for whom multiple stressful social problems and depression are closely linked (Belle, 1990). We use "case management" as shorthand for facilitating access to and helping to negotiate specific social services (i.e., job training, housing, food, legal services, household and baby supplies)

304 TREATING MAJOR DEPRESSION IN DIVERSE POPULATIONS

upon which individuals on low incomes rely to meet their own and their family's basic needs (Germain, 1983; Kemp et al., 1997). Clearly, social and economic problems associated with depression are not always easily resolved. Adding a case management component to brief IPT treatment aimed to help women manage these problems through partnering with relevant social services to obtain needed resources. Following Maslow's influential theory (1943), we thought that by beginning to address basic needs, treatment could move to the psychological level focusing on managing interpersonal difficulties. If basic needs are not met, the depressed woman is likely to reprioritize those needs until they begin to be reasonably satisfied.

Miranda et al. (2003) demonstrated the benefits of enhancing an evidence-based psychotherapy with case management. They found significantly greater improvement in depression symptoms in the intervention group (especially for Spanish-speaking patients) than the usual-care control group, which did not receive case management services. In the study by Grote et al. (2009), the usual-care group received case management from prenatal clinic social workers, whereas the brief IPT group received supplemental case management integrated into the IPT treatment. As the women in brief IPT became significantly less depressed over time compared to those in the usual-care group, integrating case management into brief IPT may have improved depression, which in turn may have facilitated their pursuit of needed social services.

How is case management integrated into brief IPT? During the initial part of the engagement session (the story), the therapist probes not only for acute interpersonal stressors most linked with the woman's depression, but also for chronic stressors such as living in an unsafe neighborhood, lacking adequate shelter or food, and being unemployed. During the psychoeducational component of the engagement session, while describing antidepressant treatment options (e.g., brief IPT and/or medication), the therapist informs the woman that enhanced brief IPT would not only help her address her interpersonal difficulties but would help her obtain her basic material needs as best she can. For our studies with depressed, economically disadvantaged expectant mothers (Grote et al., 2004, 2009), we compiled a comprehensive list of social services (food, housing, job training, household and baby supplies, legal services, etc.) indexed by both neighborhood and type of service, to which we could refer women after brief IPT began.

During the assessment phase, while conducting the interpersonal inventory, the brief IPT therapist continues to explore whether the woman's basic needs are being met. Supplementing the interpersonal formulation of the woman's depression, the therapist emphasizes facilitating her access to needed social services or negotiating existing services more effectively. During each session of the middle phase of treatment, the therapist focuses on the interpersonal problem area most linked with the woman's depression and, if indicated, discusses how she can meet her basic needs. To this end, IPT may include encouraging the woman to become more active in seeking the needed social services that she and the therapist have identified. In other words, IPT is used to empower the woman to access services to meet her own and her family's basic needs. Clinical observations from a randomized controlled trial with fifty-three low-income, depressed, pregnant African-American and white women (Grote et al. 2009) revealed that while adding case management took little time away from an IPT focus, this enhancement made the therapy more relevant to economically disadvantaged expectant mothers because it matched not only their interpersonal but also their survival concerns.

Making Brief IPT Relevant to the Culture of Race/Ethnicity

To address relevance for economically disadvantaged individuals of different races and ethnicities, we enhanced brief IPT treatment to reflect seven of the eight components delineated in the culturally centered framework of Bernal et al.: persons, metaphors, concepts, content, goals, methods, contexts, and language (Conner & Grote, 2008; Bernal et al., 1995) (see Chapter 16). We addressed *persons* by employing therapists trained in cultural competence and experienced in working with impoverished racial/ethnic minorities. We used *metaphors* by displaying culturally relevant pictures of racially and ethnically diverse infants in therapists' offices and using stories from the participants' cultural background to reinforce treatment goals. For *concepts,* therapists provided education about depression in a manner congruent with the patient's cultural perspectives—for example, by using the word "stressed" instead of "depressed" if a participant desired, to minimize her perceived stigma of depression. Using the patient's preferred term, such as "stress," to describe her depressive symptoms did not contradict viewing her symptoms through the medical model, with its biopsychosocial components. Rather, giving their experiences culturally acceptable labels ("stress") enabled women to accept their adversity as a legitimate illness both consonant with the IPT model and personally relevant. As in standard IPT, we addressed *content* by exploring coping mechanisms and cultural resources, such as spirituality or the importance of family, which had helped participants through past adversity, and by building on these resources during treatment. Therapists helped patients develop personally and culturally relevant treatment *goals. Methods* involved intensive outreach and shortening therapy to reduce participant burden. *Contexts* incorporated the pragmatic additions described above making brief IPT relevant to the culture of poverty. As we treated only English-speaking women, we did not address the eighth component of *language* by providing bilingual therapists or interpreters.

Preliminary data from our randomized controlled trial suggest that brief IPT, augmented as just described, may be more effective than usual care in promoting treatment engagement and retention and in ameliorating antenatal depression, preventing postpartum depression, and improving social and maternal role functioning (Grote et al., 2009).

CASE EXAMPLE

Helen was a thirty-one-year-old, unmarried, primiparous African-American woman of Baptist faith who lived in an apartment with her two dogs in a poor, urban neighborhood. She worked the night shift, part-time, in the inventory department of a large supermarket. Helen was twenty-eight weeks pregnant and receiving maternal support services for women on Medicaid from her local public health center. Maternal support services had connected her to prenatal care, provided nutritional advice, identified her depression, and referred her for mental health treatment. At initial screening, she met criteria for major depression and scored 19, a moderately severe level of depressive symptoms, on the PHQ-9, a scale ranging from 0 to 27 (higher scores indicate more depression symptoms) (Kroenke et al., 2001).

Engagement Session

Before Helen committed to brief IPT, the therapist conducted an engagement session, explaining that the purpose was to get to know her better, explore her concerns about and preferences for treatment, examine barriers to treatment, and decide whether or not she wanted treatment. During the first section of the engagement session, "eliciting the story," the therapist asked Helen how she was feeling lately and what she thought was contributing to it. Helen acknowledged that she was depressed and that her "boyfriend" Hank, the baby's father, was unreliable and unsupportive of her unplanned pregnancy. She had maintained an off-and-on relationship with Hank for 3 years. Her pregnancy had come as a complete surprise, as her family doctor had told Helen that she could not get pregnant. She had decided to keep the baby for religious reasons, but feared her depression might prevent her from being the kind of mother she wanted to be; becoming a good mother was Helen's primary motivation for seeking treatment. The therapist offered an empathic, affirming reflection of her dilemma:

THERAPIST: You decided to keep this baby because you felt so strongly that it was the right decision, even though you knew it would be hard. The most important thing to you now is to be the best mother you can be, but being pregnant without Hank's support is leaving you feeling overwhelmed, and making you wonder how you can do it. Coming to us for therapy is really a way for you to take care of yourself and your baby at the same time.

When probed about other stressors, Helen described worries about not getting enough work hours, obtaining safe housing, repairing her car, and affording baby furniture and supplies. The therapist validated Helen's need for help with these situations in order to be the mother she wanted to be for her baby.

During the second section of the engagement session, "treatment history, coping mechanisms, and views of treatment," Helen reported having attended a two-year alcohol treatment program in her early twenties and having been sober ever since. She said the program had helped her by reconnecting her with God as a source of support and guidance, and by giving her tools to deal with challenges to her recovery. In dealing with adversity, she typically prayed to God, relied mostly upon herself, and did not like to ask anyone for financial help except Hank, upon whom she depended for getting to work when her car broke down. Helen did not want to take antidepressant medication, which she feared was addictive, and did not want to tell a therapist her business lest child protective services take away her baby. She was concerned that a therapist from a different cultural background might not understand her life and might judge her:

THERAPIST: And even if you're assured that our therapy sessions would be confidential, except in certain instances, I'm wondering whether you might be concerned that I can't understand what you're up against? I don't live your life, there's an obvious difference between us: I'm white, and you're African-American. Does that come into play? Do you wonder about that? Some of my patients have had this concern.

HELEN: Yeah—like, in the sense that you have an understanding, but you—you've never lived it. You have no idea.

THERAPIST: I haven't walked in your shoes.

HELEN: Right. You have no idea. And that also does come into play. 'Cause you go in there and they tell you what the textbook says, "Hey, this is what you should do." But, like I said, in theory that sounds good, but you know—at home, like I am a black woman. You know, I just can't do that. Or, not that I can't do that, but reality—

THERAPIST: I wouldn't choose to.

HELEN: Exactly. Reality is totally different. We come from two different cultures. And two different environments, you know? I have to make sure—I have to watch my back when I walk in my neighborhood. And I'm pretty sure my therapist doesn't have to watch her back when she walks in her neighborhood. *If I had a therapist.* You know, it's a totally different aspect, and a totally different perspective and point of view. And yeah, that does—definitely comes into play. Because, if you can't totally understand where I'm coming from, then how can you help me?

THERAPIST: Right. So let me put this back to you. I'm interested in your feelings about this. What would you want your therapist to understand and to do about this difference of your life from her life?

HELEN: Well. . . See, that's the thing. It would be kind of hard, because they've never experienced it. But they have to understand that, you know, this is my life, and this is not like some case in a book. This is really what I live every day. You know? Come up to my house and see this is where I live. This is reality. But how a therapist would actually try to reach that understanding? I'm not too sure about that. You know, I always hear about these workplaces on the commercials about diversity training and stuff like that, and you really can't unless you've lived it, you know?

THERAPIST: It's not the same to learn about it in the classroom or something like that.

HELEN: Right. Right.

THERAPIST: So, let me see, see if this makes any sense. At least part of what you're saying is, certainly any therapist who's gonna have any chance at being helpful to you has got to come in with a kind of humility.

HELEN: Right.

THERAPIST: She really needs to understand, and to show you she understands, that she has not walked in your shoes. She cannot start from the standpoint of thinking that she knows exactly what you should do.

HELEN: Exactly. Exactly.

THERAPIST: And any therapist who does that is going to just lose you.

HELEN: Because everybody is different. Everyone has their own story. And everybody has a why to their own story. It's not, "Okay, she's depressed, she has to do this."

THERAPIST: You're not a standard case . . .

HELEN: Right.

THERAPIST: Yeah. So, that is definitely one of the things that would have to happen, is that the therapist would have to come in willing and interested in learning about who you are—

HELEN: And being open.

THERAPIST: —and letting you teach her about that. Open to learning about what she can't possibly know.

HELEN: Exactly.

After discussing what Helen would want in a therapist, the therapist moved to the third section of the session, providing psychoeducation about depression and treatment options using the "elicit–provide–elicit" technique. She asked Helen what she already knew about depression and its treatment (elicit), asked permission to tell Helen more (provide), and then elicited Helen's reactions to this information (elicit). During the fourth section, the therapist explored other practical, psychological, and cultural barriers to care and collaboratively strove to address each barrier that Helen mentioned through problem solving. In the final section, the therapist summarized Helen's story and her motivation to feel better before her baby's birth, affirmed her strengths (e.g., her commitment to her faith, determination to feel better, ability to stand up for herself, and insistence on being treated with respect), and offered hope that brief IPT might help as it had helped others like her. By the end of the engagement session, Helen committed to giving treatment a try.

Initial Brief IPT Sessions (Sessions 1 and 2)

Psychiatric, Family, and Medical History

Helen's baseline PHQ-9 score, in this first brief IPT session, had dropped from 19 at the initial screening to 16. In describing her psychiatric, family, and medical history, Helen reported having been molested from the ages of eleven to fifteen by her maternal grandfather, who had also molested her mother as a child and adolescent. When she told her mother about the molestation at age fifteen, it stopped. Helen met current criteria for PTSD, experiencing nightmares a couple of times a month. Although Helen did not meet criteria for dysthymia, she reported having been intermittently depressed since age fourteen, but could not enumerate how many depressive episodes she had experienced. She started drinking when she was fourteen and met criteria for alcohol dependence at age twenty, when she entered the substance abuse treatment program. Her father had had alcoholism as long as she could remember and was currently drinking. Her mother had untreated lifetime depression, while her younger brother was receiving antidepressant medication.

Helen reported currently smoking half a pack of cigarettes a day and being treated for chlamydia she had contracted from Hank. Otherwise, her health was good. Despite the comorbid diagnosis of PTSD, for which IPT appears to be a promising treatment alternative to cognitive-behavioral therapy (Krupnick et al., 2008; Markowitz et al., 2009), the therapist judged it appropriate to focus upon Helen's depression using brief IPT because her depressive symptoms seemed most onerous. Because of her childhood trauma and recurrent depressive history, the therapeutic plan from the outset was to provide monthly IPT maintenance sessions once Helen achieved remission and after acute treatment ended (Frank et al., 1993).

TIMELINE

To determine Helen's history of present illness, the therapist developed a timeline connecting the onset and persistence of Helen's depressive symptoms to stressful interpersonal events. Helen reported having begun to feel mildly depressed off and on when Hank began to see other women about 3 years before. Helen broke off the relationship despite fears of loneliness, but always reunited with him. Since then, they had chronic fights about his unreliability, insensitivity to her feelings, and cheating. They had an off-and-on relationship. About seven months before, around Halloween, Helen was surprised to learn that she was pregnant. Her depressive symptoms worsened significantly, she slept little, and she worried about how she would care for the baby and find safe housing with little money. When she told Hank about the unexpected pregnancy, he told her to get an abortion so the pregnancy wouldn't ruin her figure. Helen replied that they weren't married, "so you can't tell me what I can and cannot do," and decided to keep the baby for religious reasons.

Although generally able to work, she became even more depressed, especially during the Christmas holidays, when she would "lose days." Hank, since learning of the pregnancy, never offered to support her and never asked her how she and the baby were doing. Although contact became more sporadic, their interactions remained antagonistic, which lowered Helen's mood even more. Helen stated, "I think I'm depressed because this is my first time being a mom. So I'm thinking of things that I'm going to have to do on my own, how I'm gonna do them, knowing that I'm not going to have a father there. My own daddy was never there for me, and I know how this baby is gonna feel without a daddy."

INTERPERSONAL INVENTORY

The therapist and Helen initially explored her relationship with Hank, as well as the acute and chronic financial stressors she was confronting. Hank was important not only for emotional reasons but for pragmatic concerns: he helped her pay the rent or repair her car and loaned her money to pay the bills. When they first started dating, Helen remembered Hank as thoughtful, giving her a ring for her birthday and helping her with finances. She initially liked him because he was tall with dark hair, funny, and like a big teddy bear: "I gave him a piece of my heart because I loved him." About nine months after they started dating, he joined a motorcycle club and began drinking more heavily and seeing other women. Helen and Hank started their ongoing pattern of chronically arguing, breaking up, and reuniting. Helen reflected, "I always throw myself back out there with him after the arguments or after he's been with someone else, so I ask myself, `Why do I keep doing this?'" Communication analysis revealed that their arguments typically lacked resolution:

THERAPIST: So then what did you say to him after he came back two months later?

HELEN: I was like, "Why are you even calling me? You started seeing somebody." And he was like, "I ain't seein' anybody." And I was like, "You know what, I don't have 'stupid' written across my forehead. So when you decide to stop cheating on me, then maybe you can call me and talk to me." I said, "Until then, don't treat me like a doormat. I'm not your doormat."

THERAPIST: So you were able to express to him how angry and betrayed you felt. How did he respond or how did you guys resolve that?

HELEN: He says . . . "So whatever. I gotta go." That's always, a lot of his reaction, "I gotta go."

THERAPIST: So how did you feel when he said that?

HELEN: I felt disgusted with him and worn out.

THERAPIST: And then at some point, you guys got back together. And did you talk about what happened?

HELEN: Yeah. I mean, he came back and he said that he was sorry and I'm like, "Well, what are you doing on my doorstep?" He said he was no longer with whatever her name was. So we started seeing each other again, but it lasted only a couple of months until he started messing around again.

Despite strongly doubting that Hank would ultimately step up and father their baby, Helen never abandoned hope that he might do so. Further into the interpersonal inventory, the therapist explored Helen's relationships with other important people in her life, focusing on those who were supportive or potentially so. Since having achieved sobriety in her early twenties, Helen had become very close to her mother, who had been depressed for as long as Helen could remember. Helen attributed much of her mother's depression to living with her very critical and negative stepfather. Helen and her mother talked nearly every day on the phone, confiding in and often comforting each other. Helen remarked, "I would take a bullet for my mother." In the past, Helen had partially supported her mother and stepfather financially, despite having little money herself. When asked how she handled conflict with her mother, Helen described telling her mother that she was pregnant, a conversation that had a successful resolution:

THERAPIST: How did that conversation go? What did you say to her?

HELEN: "Mom, there's something I really want to talk to you about and I'm afraid to talk to you. I'm afraid to tell you." "Well," she said, "You can tell me anything. Are you okay, are you hurt?" "No, I'm not hurt, Mom, I'm okay"; and then it just came out of my mouth, "I'm pregnant." And then she just said: "WHAT?" And then that's when she kind of reamed me a little bit and I said, "Well, that's why I didn't want to tell ya."

THERAPIST: And what did she say to you?

HELEN: She asked, "How long have you been with him? I thought you guys broke up!" So, I said, "Yeah, we broke up, we broke up a few times, Mom." "Yeah, I know, but I thought you weren't back with him." And, I said, "Well, you know, can't say I don't have feelings for him. If I didn't have feelings for him, Mom, I wouldn't have been with him for what, the past almost three years."

THERAPIST: I guess I'm wondering how you felt when she said that to you.

HELEN: It hurt my feelings. It hurt my feelings because I wanted her to just understand and help me through it because at that time, that's when I was like, what do I do?

THERAPIST: I see. Did you tell her how you felt?

HELEN: Yeah, when I called her back. And she said she was sorry for saying the things that she said and reacting that way, but she goes, "I was just, I was shocked," and I said, "Well you're not the only one. I was just as shocked and in denial." And then she said, "What are you going to do?" and I said, "I don't know."

Helen also reported having a good friend, Rhonda, and an amicable neighbor, Judy, whom she occasionally visited and could confide in, but since becoming more depressed she had reduced contact with them. She was also fond of several female friends in her workplace and at church. Helen maintained good relations with her father but spent little time with him because of his drinking. Her brother was somewhat supportive but had married a controlling and demanding woman, so Helen kept her distance. Regarding caring about the baby after "she" was born, Helen most worried about her ability to financially support her child and afford the things she would need, including safe housing. Shifting into the case management component of brief IPT, the therapist learned that Helen lived in a dilapidated apartment building in a crime-ridden neighborhood. She did not want to move in with her alcoholic father or her mother and negativistic stepfather, but she earned just enough money to disqualify her for federal housing assistance. Helen also worried whether she could afford to take the three months of leave her workplace allowed, and wondered who would care for the baby on nights when she returned to work. Helen was relieved to discover that the therapist could help her investigate sources of rent assistance, and she expressed appreciation for the therapist's offer of information about a day care program for babies of low-income, working mothers.

CASE FORMULATION

Based on the timeline and interpersonal inventory, the therapist provided Helen with the tentative formulation that the onset of her depression appeared linked both to her chronic role dispute with Hank and to her "complicated pregnancy," a role transition involving psychosocial complications such as an unplanned pregnancy, lack of social or financial resources, or medical complications (Spinelli, 2001). The therapist explained to Helen that her pregnancy seemed to have several complications: that it was a big, unexpected change in her life; that she was concerned about getting emotional and financial support from Hank; and that she was worried that her financial and medical illness, such as chlamydia, would hurt her baby. Helen readily agreed with this formulation. Then the therapist asked Helen which of the two problem areas seemed more immediately concerning and manageable to work on, given her level of depressive symptoms and the time constraints of the therapy. They discussed the chronicity of Helen's conflict with Hank and how it wore her out, worsening her mood. They agreed that the remaining six weekly acute treatment sessions would be best spent achieving depressive remission before the birth by focusing on the complicated pregnancy and helping Helen prepare for the challenges of motherhood, including activating her social supports, deciding how to manage her financial and workplace concerns, and discussing her medical illness with her obstetrician. The therapist conveyed to Helen the expectation of a time limit for the acute phase of therapy—that she would likely achieve full or partial improvement from her depression after six more weekly brief IPT sessions. The therapist suggested that after Helen's depression remitted and the baby was born, she might have more energy to address her longstanding dispute with Hank (which was at an impasse) during the monthly maintenance IPT phase. The therapist explained that the main purpose of monthly IPT maintenance was to help Helen sustain her recovery from depression after the acute-phase weekly brief IPT sessions ended.

BRIEF IPT HOMEWORK

At the end of the first and second IPT sessions, the therapist encouraged Helen to do something during the week to give herself a break, such as engaging in a previously pleasurable activity with someone she liked. Helen decided to see a movie with Rhonda for pleasure and to clean her apartment for a sense of accomplishment. The therapist worked with Helen on specifying when she would do these activities, what might interfere, and how likely it was that she could do them. The therapist asked Helen how she planned to buffer the downturn in her mood were she to have contact with Hank. Helen planned to rely on coping strategies that had helped her mood in the past, like talking to her mother and praying in church for guidance. At this point, Helen decided not to ask Hank for what she needed because she was sure conflict would ensue that would make her feel worse.

Brief IPT Middle Sessions

The primary therapeutic goal of the middle phase was to help Helen manage her complicated pregnancy, which was linked to the onset of her major depressive episode. Subgoals included: (1) encouraging Helen to express her feelings in session, as feelings convey important information about what she needed; (2) encouraging Helen to activate social supports and ask family and friends for what she needed to prepare for the baby's birth, thereby moderating her interpersonal style of self-reliance; (3) building on the reliable strategies Helen had used to buffer the downturn in mood that resulted from interacting with Hank; (4) figuring out what instrumental role, if any, Hank might play if he chose to become involved as a father; (5) connecting Helen with the requisite social services to meet her basic needs in preparation for the baby, such as safe housing and child care while she worked; (6) supporting Helen's decisions about whether to have a cesarean section because of her chlamydia, and communicating her needs and wishes to her obstetrician; and (7) prescribing weekly between-session activities with an interpersonal focus, if possible, to increase Helen's pleasure and accomplishment as she prepared for the transition to motherhood. This homework was designed to complement the IPT goal of managing her complicated pregnancy. We will illustrate how the therapist worked with Helen on subgoals 1, 2, 3, 5 and 7 in the middle sessions.

Here the therapist checks on fluctuations in Helen's mood related to events during the past week, inquires about Helen's homework assignment, and finds opportunities to give her credit for reducing or trying to manage her depressive symptoms. Note that Helen's mood improved after she engaged in activities designed to increase pleasure or accomplishment, a strategy that the therapist highlighted.

THERAPIST: So, Helen, this is the third of our eight weekly sessions. As I was saying, on the PHQ your score went down to 9 from 14 last week and from 16 the week before. How have you been since we last met? And what's been happening?

HELEN: It's been pretty good. I think a lot of it had to do with the whole family thing—Easter. That was special to me and that made me feel good that I could spend time with my family. I did go to my dad's. Everybody waited for me to get there and I didn't think that everybody was going to be there. I was late getting there.

THERAPIST: So everybody was anticipating your arrival, and waiting for you and you didn't really know that everyone was going to be there, just waiting for you.

HELEN: And I know the reason why everybody wanted to see me, because I'm pregnant.

THERAPIST: So folks in the family are pretty excited about you being pregnant and wanted to see you.

HELEN: Yeah, it was nice, except my dad started drinking and had to go to bed early.

THERAPIST: So it seems that, although your dad's going to bed early was disappointing, you really enjoyed yourself overall.

HELEN: Yeah.

THERAPIST: And I'm also wondering what else you did this week to improve your mood.

HELEN: Well, like we talked about last week, I cleaned my apartment and that made me feel good, and I went to see Rhonda, but we didn't go to a movie because she couldn't get a babysitter for her kids.

THERAPIST: That's great! So your mood improved when you took the initiative to clean your apartment. And you managed to spend time with Rhonda even though you couldn't go to a movie. How was that for you?

HELEN: We just sat around her place and talked about life—I asked her for a little bit of advice about Hank and she asked me for a little bit of advice about her husband. Her husband doesn't treat her like a wife, more like a floor mat, and it really hurts her. I try to comfort her on that. She's a good person, so we kind of support each other.

THERAPIST: Well, that's cool—your friendship; you support each other. So talking to Rhonda also helped your mood. Were there other times last week when your mood went down?

HELEN: My mood went down where I was down in the dumps a bit.

THERAPIST: What was going on?

HELEN: Hank. He was going through my mind. I was wondering how Hank was doing.

THERAPIST: Okay, so you were feeling pretty depressed when you started to think about . . .

HELEN: Him.

THERAPIST: When was that in terms of the week?

HELEN: It was on Easter and the day after. I think I was kind of hoping that he would call me and try to talk to me. No, that didn't happen. So I cried a lot and lay in my bed for a while.

THERAPIST: So you were holding out hope maybe he'd check in just to see how you're doing. And he didn't. That's when your mood went down, pretty significantly, to almost feeling very depressed. What did you do to bring it back up?

HELEN: Well, to bring it back up, I called my mom and talked to her a little bit and it helped. I just kind of told myself to do a little praying to God to help me get through this, to get over my feelings for him, and went from there.

THERAPIST: So when you're able to pray to God and also reach out to somebody, like your mom, or Rhonda, your mood goes up. That's great! Do you see the connection between what you did and your mood improving?

HELEN: Yeah, I do.

THERAPIST: Like if you talk to them about what's happened . . . Were you talking to your mom about Hank or just talking to her about other things?

HELEN: A little about Hank, just to get it off my chest, and then life in general. 'Cause Mom will ask me, "Well, what else is wrong?" And I'll tell her that I'm worried about being able to afford better housing and child care when I go back to work after my baby girl is born.

The following excerpt illustrates the integration of case management into brief IPT. The therapist and Helen chip away at the financial stressors associated with her pregnancy, such as housing. They employ IPT techniques of decision analysis (problem solving) and role-playing or coaching. For homework, the therapist encouraged Helen to begin to investigate specific housing services and to increase her interpersonal pleasure.

THERAPIST: So, in our time together, because we have a limited amount of time, it's, how do we build up the supports so that you can stay independent, and get in your own, safer place when the baby comes?

HELEN: The only thing I can say, honestly, is that I'll be hosed if I don't get help from Hank. I don't know where to go or what to do after, to find a place. I don't know about any of the state stuff, how much they can help you. I'm even worried about losing the apartment I have right now, if I take maternity leave for three months with no real paycheck.

THERAPIST: And I know you've depended on Hank in the past . . .

HELEN: But he's not coming through for me anymore.

THERAPIST: You're really angry at Hank for letting you down.

HELEN: I sure am.

THERAPIST: So what do you think of this idea—instead of counting on Hank, it may be more helpful to break this down a little bit and think about what else you can do each week without Hank to make it a little more manageable.

HELEN: Yeah, that's what I have to do.

THERAPIST: I know you've tried to reach your caseworker at the DOH [Department of Health] to find out about rent assistance. How was that?

HELEN: She never called me back after I called a dozen times. I have a mind to go down there and rip her a new one. All I want is information about what's out there and if there is anything I can qualify for.

THERAPIST: Sounds pretty frustrating trying to get your caseworker to respond, reasonably so. You feel you'll get better results if you actually go to the DOH office to talk with her or someone else. That's great! I know there is a federal program from HUD [Housing and Urban Development] to help working folks get low-income housing. If you were to go to DOH and talk to your caseworker, what would you say?

HELEN: I'm not sure—maybe I could ask about that HUD thing and if I could apply . . .

THERAPIST: Would it help if we practice how that talk might go?

HELEN: Sure, that would help.

THERAPIST: OK, so I'll be your caseworker and let's have that conversation. What would you say to me?

Helen and the therapist role-played for five minutes, then debriefed. The therapist praised Helen's ability to ask for what she needed from the caseworker and made a couple of suggestions. They agreed that for homework, Helen would go to the DOH office during the next week or so to ask about applying for the HUD program, which she eventually did.

In the following excerpt, Helen describes going to court to support Hank, who rebuffs her and ultimately is court-ordered to jail for two months for failing to follow up on DUI charges. Helen has less contact with him thereafter and more time to focus on preparing for motherhood without him. The therapist makes it safe for Helen to express her grief and anger over not being able to count on Hank during her pregnancy and commends Helen for using IPT strategies to buffer her mood to comfort herself. Then they continue to work on the financial stressors associated with her pregnancy, such as finding affordable child care for her nighttime work hours. Treatment again integrates case management with the IPT techniques facilitating the expression of affect, problem solving, and role coaching. For weekly homework, Helen planned to investigate child care sources, talk to her manager about changing her work schedule, and shop for baby clothes with Rhonda.

THERAPIST: So, Helen, this is the fifth of our eight weekly sessions and it looks like your depression score on the PHQ-9 went up to 11 this week and that you've felt bad about yourself or like a failure. Last week it was at a 6: I'm wondering what's been going on since we last met and what's contributed to your feeling so down?

HELEN: I was really down in the dumps. I was crying.

THERAPIST: So you really felt bad and let it out. Were you down and crying for the entire week?

HELEN: No, I guess just on Friday and the weekend. Then I lost it on Monday at work.

THERAPIST: Tell me a little bit about what happened when you say "lost it."

HELEN: I was crying because, how am I going to do this by myself? It's hard for me to accept that.

THERAPIST: You really feel alone in all of this and had so hoped that Hank would be by your side, supporting you.

HELEN: Yeah, that's it.

THERAPIST: And I know he was going to court last Friday. Is that when all these feelings came up? I know you were on the fence as to whether you were going to go or not.

HELEN: So, it was like a last-minute decision and then on the way there I started thinking I shouldn't do this because he's probably going to bring his girlfriend. So I see him and he looks at me and says with a scowl on this face, "What are you doing here?"

THERAPIST: So you made the decision to go, and then he makes the comment with a hurtful look on his face and doesn't really acknowledge your support and you feel terribly hurt and unappreciated and mad at him.

HELEN: Right, and I was mad at myself for even going!

THERAPIST: So you beat yourself up a bit, which is part of the depression talking. Then what did you do after that? How did you make yourself feel better?

HELEN: To make myself feel better, I cried. I cried all the way home. And I prayed and that's when I kind of asked the Lord to ... I don't even want to have even any kind of connection with him whatsoever in my heart, mind, or my soul. Lord, just take my feelings away of my caring for him because I know that he doesn't care for me.

THERAPIST: So you spent a lot of this weekend, crying—kind of giving it up to God. I think your religious faith has given you strength through all this. Did you feel a sense of relief, or were you still hurt and angry?

HELEN: I felt somewhat of a relief and then I also talked to my mom. Then I talked to Rhonda, and she asked me how I was doing, and I kind of lost it on the phone with her that time. She's like, "Everything's going to be okay. I'm really sorry he's done that to you." She tried to comfort me, which was nice and I ended up feeling better.

THERAPIST: I know that you are experiencing a lot of grief around the amount of time you and Hank were together and the kinds of dreams you had for your relationship and for your baby girl. And I think you're adjusting to the idea that it's not gonna happen the way you wanted.

HELEN: That's right.

THERAPIST: So despite how sad and hurt you feel about Hank, you've still been able to reach out to folks—God, your mom, and Rhonda—which makes you feel better. That shows how strong you are, Helen—being able to ask for comfort. Step by step, you've been reaching out to people for comfort and doing some pleasurable things and that's bringing you back into balance.

HELEN: Yeah, and I also asked the girls at work about child care when they saw me crying and asked me what was wrong. I told them I am really worried about being able to find a babysitter at two in the morning. I'm pretty sure that's the shift I'm gonna end up starting at, after the baby.

THERAPIST: So despite how lousy you felt about Hank over the weekend and at work on Monday, you were still able to bring up your worries about child care to your coworkers and ask for their help. That's great! What did they say?

HELEN: They said they know a woman, Tracy, who can take babies into her home when their mothers or fathers are working the night shift and they are going to give me her number to call. I'm also worried about how much Tracy would charge and I wonder whether the state can help me pay for child care.

THERAPIST: It seems really helpful for you to be getting information right now about child care, so you can feel less anxious. You felt encouraged to hear about a potential child care arrangement at night, especially because your mom can't take care of the baby on a regular basis.

HELEN: Yeah.

THERAPIST: At the same time, you're concerned about being able to afford it. I know about a state program called Child Care Connections that helps working mothers partially pay for child care while they work. Would you like me to find the number for you?

HELEN: Yeah, thanks. Maybe I could give them a call this week and that woman Tracy as well.

THERAPIST: So you would like to follow up and get more information about all of this next week—good idea! Do you think anything might get in the way of your doing this?

HELEN: Only if I'm too tired.

THERAPIST: So at the end of the session, let's talk about breaking all this down into parts and figuring out when you might take some of these steps.

HELEN: OK.

THERAPIST: I was also wondering, as you think about work, if you could ideally change your schedule, what would that look like for you?

HELEN: Well, I'd really like to be working the four-to-midnight shift, but I would have to be retrained and I don't know how good I'd been at anything else but stacking and organizing the inventory. And I don't want to rock the boat—I can't afford to lose my job. I've been there for two years and I like it. After all, beggars can't be choosers.

THERAPIST: So you're concerned that if you bring up changing your work hours to your supervisor, he or she might let you go.

HELEN: She. I don't want her to think I have a bad attitude.

THERAPIST: So you don't want her to get the wrong idea if you were to raise the issue with her. What's her name?

HELEN: Lois.

THERAPIST: Do you know how the company handles the situation with other pregnant employees?

HELEN: I've heard it's a pretty family-friendly company, but I'm not sure what that means, to tell you the truth. I could talk to my coworkers and try to find out whether they give new moms better work hours. If I got the evening shift, I could spend the day with my baby girl instead of having to sleep it off.

THERAPIST: Talking to your coworkers is a really good start, Helen. Let's see what you find out this week and then we can discuss where you go from there in terms of talking to Lois. How does that sound?

HELEN: Good.

THERAPIST: And since you're planning to take on more challenges this week and gather more information, what I want to know is, how are you going to give yourself some pleasure, something rewarding that perhaps you can do with someone else?

HELEN: Not a problem. My good childhood friend, Brenda, is coming to town next week and we are planning to go out to eat somewhere and talk and talk and talk. We're very close and been through some hard things together.

THERAPIST: Well, Helen, I'm impressed with all that you've done and plan to do to improve your mood and to chip away at this complicated pregnancy. I know that one of the biggest complications is your sadness and anger about Hank, but you have also figured out ways to buffer your mood and bring it back up when he lets you down, hard as that is. You know, recovery from depression can be kind of jagged, meaning that you may start to feel a little better and then something may happen where you start feeling worse, but ideally, you can manage it so you are starting to feel better more days of the week. That's what you're doing!

Termination/Graduation from Acute Brief IPT

During part of the seventh and all of the eighth brief IPT sessions, the therapist handled Helen's shift from acute brief IPT treatment to maintenance IPT as a graduation. By Session 7, Helen's PHQ-9 depression score had dropped to 6; by Session 8, it was 5. The therapist reviewed with Helen all she had accomplished: (1) applying for low-income housing from HUD, getting onto a waiting list, and preparing her apartment for her baby; (2) speaking to Lois, her work supervisor, about changing her work hours, being switched to the evening shift, and retraining to handle the supermarket produce section; (3) investigating Tracy's home day care for her baby and applying for state child care assistance; (4) discussing childbirth options with her obstetrician to prevent chlamydia from infecting the baby, and opting for a cesarean section; (5) reaching out to family, friends, and church to maintain a steady mood; and (6) putting her chronic dispute with Hank on the back burner. Helen acknowledged it was easier to get things done the less she interacted with Hank, who called her occasionally from jail and was due to get out the week before the baby was to be born. For relapse prevention, whenever experiencing a downturn in mood, Helen planned to use the coping strategies that had previously served her well: praying, reaching out to others, speaking up for what she needed, and problem-solving with her mom or Rhonda. She liked the idea of having six to eight monthly maintenance IPT sessions between the end of acute treatment and six months postpartum to maintain her progress and to prepare to deal with Hank re-entering the picture as a father after their daughter's birth.

During the weeks before Helen gave birth, she was given two baby showers by her church friends and her friends at work. Helen felt supported and cared for when she delivered a healthy baby girl, whom she named Sienna. Hank never assumed a paternal role and kept his usual distance off and on. Helen stayed well and continued maintenance IPT until Sienna's 6-month birthday.

DISCUSSION

The case of Helen, a pregnant, depressed, thirty-one-year-old African-American woman living on a low income, illustrates how the therapist worked with Helen to make IPT relevant to the culture of poverty with its multiple stressors, as well as to important cultural values and practices such as prayer. IPT was delivered in an eight-session format following an initial engagement session to better understand Helen's perspective on her symptoms and treatment. During brief IPT, the therapist tried to weave case management into standard IPT practice and techniques, which included (1) increasing pleasurable or accomplishment activities, preferably with an interpersonal emphasis, (2) facilitating the expression of affect, including hurt and anger, (3) communication analysis, (4) decision analysis, and (5) role-playing or coaching of assertiveness skills.

The therapist's biggest challenge was to honor Helen's grief and anger over Hank's unreliability and unsupportiveness (qualities that Helen found intolerable only after she became pregnant), while helping her to focus on the challenges she faced in preparing for motherhood. The therapist felt the pull of wanting to help Helen resolve her dispute with Hank, perhaps through Helen's dissolving the relationship, but their three-year history of unresolved conflict over differing expectations of the relationship suggested that this approach might lead the therapist and Helen into a quagmire, take up the whole session, and worsen Helen's depression. The therapist had to remind herself in every session to allow Helen time to talk about Hank, but also to move on so that Helen could feel empowered to face motherhood with other supports in place and financial problems addressed.

Another challenge for the therapist was how to respond when Helen did not complete homework assignments to inquire about housing assistance and child care services. Helen usually followed through with some pleasurable, interpersonal weekly activity. The therapist took a non-blaming approach when asking Helen about what interfered with homework completion, commenting that the depression may have interfered or that Helen may have had a good reason to delay or not do the planned activity. For example, by the time Helen gave birth, she had not enrolled Sienna in Tracy's day care as she had planned. The therapist explored the reasons with Helen and learned that not only had Helen been waiting to hear about receiving state assistance, but that she was ambivalent about sending Sienna to Tracy's. Helen said she preferred having family or friends come to her house to care for Sienna rather than packing her up on workdays. Indeed, when Helen's three-month maternity leave ended and her part-time evening shift began, Helen had cultivated a patchwork arrangement with family and friends to care for Sienna either in her or their homes.

During maintenance IPT, the therapist was concerned about Helen experiencing a depressive relapse because of her vulnerability to Hank's entreaties to reunite and to the increased financial stress posed by the national economic downturn. Helen did not relapse, however. During the acute brief IPT, Helen learned to solve challenges without Hank's support, to ask help from others who could meet her needs, to proactively enlist the aid of social services, and to resume involvement with her church community. During maintenance IPT, Helen had become more determined to set limits with and require more of Hank. The therapist continued to support Helen in this regard. As for the financial stressors, safer housing was not available, but Helen did not lose her job as many friends and family members did. When family members pressured Helen to lend them money, the therapist supported Helen in diplomatically setting reasonable limits with them as well.

Women who confront the chronic stressors associated with poverty face increased risk for depression and forgoing the treatment interventions that can bring relief. Patients like Helen may lack the time or opportunity to identify or differentiate among their feelings as they focus their energy on meeting basic survival needs. In brief IPT, as in standard IPT, depressed patients on low incomes learn that their feelings give them important information about what they need emotionally and materially for survival, and that they can ask the help of appropriate, receptive people and sources to meet their needs. Like Helen, they feel understood and validated by the therapist's use of "feeling words" to reflect their emotions, and they engage more readily in therapy when they can express their wishes and fears about treatment and learn that the therapist can help them find ways to meet their material as well as their emotional needs. Thus, we have found that brief IPT, enhanced with an engagement session and integrated with case management, is well suited to meeting the depression treatment needs of this difficult-to-reach population.

ACKNOWLEDGMENTS

This work was supported by grants from the National Institute of Mental Health: 67595, 64518, and 30915 and from funds received from the NIH/NCRR/GCRC Grant MO1-RR000056.

SUGGESTED READING

Beeber LS, Perreira KM, Schwartz T: Supporting the mental health of mothers raising children in poverty: how do we target them for intervention studies? Annals of the New York Academy of Sciences 2008;1136:86–10

Bernal G, Bonilla J, Bellido C: Ecological validity and cultural sensitivity for outcome research: Issues for cultural adaptation and development of psychosocial treatments with Hispanics. Journal of Abnormal Child Psychology 1995;23:67–82

Boyd-Franklin N, Lockwood T: Spirituality and religion: Implications for psychotherapy with African American clients and families. In Walsh F (Ed.): Spiritual Resources in Family Therapy. New York: Guilford, 1999:90–103

Conner KO, Grote NK: A model for enhancing the cultural relevance of empirically-supported mental health interventions. Families in Society 2008;89:1–9

Grote NK, Zuckoff A, Swartz HA, Bledsoe SE, Geibel SL: Engaging women who are depressed and economically disadvantaged in mental health treatment. Social Work 2007;52:295–308

Markowitz JC, Patel SR, Balan I, McNamara M, Blanco C, Brave Heart MYH, Sosa S, Lewis-Fernández R: Towards an adaptation of interpersonal psychotherapy for depressed Hispanic patients. Journal of Clinical Psychiatry 2009;70:214–222

Miranda J, Azocar F, Organista K, Dwyer E, Areane P: Treatment of depression among impoverished primary care patients from ethnic minority groups. Psychiatric Services 2003;54:219–225

Rossello J, Bernal G: The efficacy of cognitive-behavioral and interpersonal treatments for depression in Puerto Rican adolescents. Journal of Consulting and Clinical Psychology 1999;67:734–745

Snowden LR: Barriers to effective mental health services for African Americans. Mental Health Services Research 2001;3:181–187

Stack C: All Our Kin. New York: Harper & Row, 1975

Sue S, Fujino DC, Hu LT, Takeuchi DT, Zane NW: Community mental health services for ethnic minority groups: A test of the cultural responsiveness hypothesis. Journal of Consulting & Clinical Psychology 1991;59:533–540

Zuckoff A, Swartz HA, Grote NK: Motivational interviewing as a prelude to psychotherapy of depression. In Arkowitz H, Westra H, Miller WR, Rollnick S (Eds.): Motivational Interviewing in the Treatment of Psychological Problems. New York: Guilford Press, 2008:109–144

18

Interpersonal Psychotherapy in Developing Countries

HELENA VERDELI, CHARLES D.R. BAILY,
CHRISTINE NANYONDO, JESSICA A. KEITH,
AND ORI ELIS

Cross-national, epidemiologic studies have documented that depression in the developing world is both highly prevalent and associated with a range of devastating consequences: loss of economic productivity, disability, and increased morbidity and mortality from other illnesses, including infectious diseases (Prince et al., 2007; Weissman et al., 1996). Uganda, which during the past twenty years has been overwhelmed by the AIDS epidemic, offers a case in point. World Vision, a nongovernmental organization (NGO) working in the Masaka and Rakai districts in the southwest part of the country, had invested large sums in micro-finance projects designed to restore and empower the local communities, but the results did not reflect the extent of the effort and investment. World Vision officials hypothesized that there might be barriers to local development that remained unaddressed (Verdeli, Bolton, & Speelman, 2009). In 2000, they partnered with investigators at Johns Hopkins (P.I.: Paul Bolton) to survey the mental health needs of these communities.

The mental health survey revealed a staggering 21% point prevalence rate of major depression (as assessed by the Hopkins Symptom Checklist), accompanied by significant functional impairment (Bolton, Wilk, & Ndogoni, 2004). Two depression syndromes, *Okwekyawa* and *Okwekubagiza*, were identified, which roughly translated from the local language Luganda as "self-loathing" and "self-pity," respectively. These frequently comorbid conditions collectively encompassed all DSM-IV depression symptoms, as well as some local ones, such as "hatred towards the world" and "ingratitude for assistance." The local community recognized these two syndromes as consequences of the AIDS epidemic as well as of other illnesses, bereavement, war, natural disasters, disagreements with family members and neighbors, unemployment, life changes such as getting married, dealing with a husband's decision to marry a new wife (polygamy is practiced in Uganda), change in social status, and poverty (Verdeli et al., 2003; Wilk & Bolton, 2002).

Although depressed people in the community typically turned to traditional healers for treatment of *Okwekyawa* and *Okwekubagiza,* the local healers reported feeling unable to treat these disorders. The lack of availability and high cost of physicians and mental health professionals left few treatment options available to people in the region with these syndromes. After participating in the mental health survey, community members expressed the desire for treatment to combat *Okwekyawa* and *Okwekubagiza.* Antidepressants were rejected due to their high cost and the lack of available medical personnel. After having considered potential psychotherapy options, Bolton et al. proposed that IPT would be a good match for the local community, given its relational orientation, emphasis on use of affect, and the precedent for its use in a group format (Verdeli et al., 2003). The connection made explicitly in IPT between life events and the onset of depression also made the treatment a good fit for this population, within which there was widespread recognition that *Okwekyawa* and *Okwekubagiza* were precipitated by the multiple problems besetting the community.

In collaboration with World Vision, Bolton et al. tested the effectiveness of group IPT modified for the cultural context of southwestern Uganda (IPT-GU), compared to a treatment-as-usual (TAU) control condition, in a clustered randomized controlled trial conducted in 2002. Participants in the study were chosen from thirty villages in the Masaka and Rakai districts. Eligible participants were men and women, age eighteen or over, who met study criteria for a current major depressive episode or sub-syndromal depressive episode (defined as one criterion short of a full DSM-IV major depressive episode diagnosis) and who were not actively suicidal. Potential participants were initially identified by local facilitators and healers in each village, who were asked to list adults believed to have *Okwekyawa* or *Okwekubagiza.* Local interviewers contacted these individuals, obtained their consent, and screened them for inclusion. Two hundred forty-eight people meeting these criteria were randomized to the IPT-GU and TAU control conditions. Participants included men and women, ages eighteen to seventy-eight years. To create single-sex treatment groups, half of the thirty villages were designated for female participants and half for males (Bolton et al., 2003).

Participants' depressive symptomatology was measured with the depression section of the Hopkins Symptom Checklist (D-HSCL) (Derogatis, Lipman, Rickels, Uhlenhut, & Covi, 1974), validated for local use with ethnographic and quantitative methods by Bolton et al. (2001). Because cutoff points for major depression on the D-HSCL had not been established for the study population, a previously validated algorithm (Bolton, Neugebauer, & Ndogoni, 2002) using DSM-IV symptom criteria and functioning criteria was used to assess presence or absence of depression. Functioning, an outcome of particular interest for the study, was assessed with an instrument developed locally that included gender-specific tasks that community members had reported were most important to the welfare of themselves, their families, and their communities. All assessments were administered at baseline, termination, and six-month follow-up.

Outcome analyses (Bass et al., 2006; Bolton et al., 2003) found IPT-GU superior to TAU in reducing depression symptoms and functional impairment. At the end of the

16-week treatment, 94% of participants who received IPT-GU versus 45% of participants in the TAU condition no longer met the modified DSM-IV criteria for depression. The mean reduction in depression score from baseline to termination was 17.5 for the IPT-GU arm and 3.6 for the TAU arm ($p < 0.001$) (Bolton et al., 2003). At the 6-month follow-up, only 12% of those in the IPT-GU condition and 55% of those in the TAU arm met the modified DSM-IV depression criteria. The mean reduction in depression score from baseline to six-month follow-up was 17.5 for the IPT-GU arm and 4.0 for the TAU arm ($p < 0.001$) (Bass et al., 2006). The IPT-GU arm also experienced a significantly greater reduction in functional impairment than TAU by treatment termination and at six-month follow-up. At termination, functional impairment decreased 8.0 points in the IPT-GU group versus 3.8 points for the control group ($p < 0.001$) (Bolton et al., 2003). These results were maintained at the six-month follow-up (Bass et al., 2006).

Given the effectiveness of IPT-GU in the study, World Vision has continued to disseminate the treatment in southwestern Uganda, providing IPT groups in the villages assigned to the TAU condition in the original randomized controlled trial, as well as in other communities in the region. In addition, groups have continued to meet in the villages that received IPT-GU in the study. A recent study involving follow-up interviews in communities that received IPT-GU showed that, even after the active treatment ended, communities perceived the groups as continuing to have a positive impact on a variety of outcomes, ranging from greater social cohesion to increased economic productivity (Lewandowski, Verdeli, & Bolton, in preparation). World Vision is scaling up IPT-GU treatment throughout regions of sub-Saharan Africa heavily affected by the HIV/AIDS crisis. An open trial of IPT for the treatment of depression in adults in rural Kenya has yielded promising results, and initiatives to provide the treatment in regions of Swaziland, Lesotho, Malawi, Democratic Republic of Congo, South Africa, and Zambia are underway (Ndogoni, 2009). Finally, Bolton et al. (2007) conducted a randomized controlled trial that included group IPT for depressed adolescents in northern Uganda who had been affected by war and displacement. IPT-GU was adapted to meet the clinical, developmental, and other regional particularities of the population (Verdeli et al., 2008). The study found that compared to a waitlist control condition and Creative Play, an active group treatment routinely conducted by NGOs in the area, IPT was effective in reducing depression symptoms among girls. There was a nonsignificant trend for boys (the study was not powered to detect sex differences).

ADAPTING IPT-GU

To adapt group IPT for the population of southwestern Uganda, a dialog among the researchers, the group facilitator trainees who were to become the therapists in the trial, and members of the local community was set in motion. Much of this occurred during a two-week IPT "boot camp" in which facilitators-in-training were immersed in IPT didactics and participated in extensive role-plays focused on IPT strategies. The facilitators were all young Ugandans from the local region who had been hired by World Vision to work in the trial. They were bilingual in English and Luganda and had obtained at least a high school education. None had prior mental health or counseling training or experience.

A training manual had been drafted with the understanding that it would be adapted on site, based on the training experience and feedback from the trainee facilitators about what would make sense in the local culture (Clougherty, Verdeli, & Weissman, 2003). The language of IPT was simplified: for example, the interpersonal problem area of grief became "death of loved one(s)," interpersonal disputes became "disagreements," role transitions became "life changes," and interpersonal deficits became "loneliness and social isolation." Similarly, the level of structure of the therapy was increased to respond to the training needs of lay facilitators. Trainee feedback was instrumental in further adapting the manual during the training period. For example, because the trainees suggested that men might overshadow women in a mixed-sex group, it was decided to have single-sex groups. Groups with male members had male facilitators and groups with female members had female facilitators. In addition, an attempt was made to match group members approximately by age, so that members could better relate to each other. Unlike a traditional IPT format in which the individual or group meets the therapist at a set time and place, the schedule remained flexible to allow for village events and rituals that the entire community attended, although meetings had to be rescheduled within the same week (Verdeli et al., 2003).

In addition to these adaptations to the treatment structure, the IPT problem areas themselves were examined for cultural appropriateness—that is, whether these constructs fit the local context. During the therapist training, it was noted that individuals in this community are socialized to participate in communal activities daily, and are expected to do so. Further discussions with members of the community and local facilitators indicated that the social withdrawal characteristic of interpersonal deficits tended not to precede depression among this population, but rather followed it. Therefore, the interpersonal deficits problem area was not deemed particularly relevant and was not used in the group members' case formulations and treatment (Verdeli et al., 2003). However, the same investigators found that in other parts of Africa, interpersonal deficits were considered a trigger of depression. For instance, when adapting group IPT for war-affected adolescents in internally displaced persons camps in Gulu, in northern Uganda, it became clear that some participants, abducted and raised by the rebels to become child soldiers, presented with profound social isolation. The interpersonal deficits problem area was therefore included in group IPT for that population (Verdeli et al., 2008).

The treatment adapted and used in Uganda was group IPT rather than group Interpersonal Counseling (IPC), a simplified, brief version of the treatment developed for use in primary care with patients with low levels of depression symptoms (often secondary to a medical illness) rather than a full major depression diagnosis (Weissman, Markowitz, & Klerman, 2007). Some colleagues have been confused with regard to this point, perhaps because IPT-GU was more structured than standard IPT and administered by non-mental health professionals. However, unlike IPC, the IPT-GU adaptation was a full, sixteen-week intervention for people presenting with major depression.

IPT-GU: INTERVENTION

Single-sex groups comprising one facilitator and six to eight participants met in private settings in the local village for approximately ninety minutes on a weekly basis for sixteen weeks. Group facilitators were supervised on a weekly basis by two on-site psychologists on the staff of World Vision. They sent regular written progress reports to the IPT trainers, Helen Verdeli and Kathleen Clougherty, from whom they received weekly supervision via phone or email. In the clinical trial, active suicidal ideation was an exclusion criterion. The few potential participants who were excluded on this basis were referred to the on-site psychologists. Thoughts of death and passive suicidal ideation were nevertheless common among group members who participated in the study, and these were monitored closely by group facilitators and the supervising psychologists.

Four Phases of Intervention

Pre-group Phase (Two Individual Sessions)

Before beginning IPT-GU group meetings, members attended two individual pre-group meetings in which group facilitators introduced themselves and discussed the purpose of the study and the various participating organizations and individuals. The facilitators also established expectations of what the treatment would involve, and in particular clarified that, unlike many NGO-sponsored programs, no material goods or services would be provided. Initially, many prospective members protested: "Give me money, then I will no longer be depressed," declared one man. Others expressed doubt about the potential of group psychotherapy to help them: "I cannot find solutions to my problems, how can I help others?" and "How can others with Okwekyawa help me?" The facilitators encouraged them to try the groups, suggesting that the meetings might assist members in learning to live a life without *Okwekyawa* and *Okwekubagiza*, which compounded the burden they experienced from other life struggles. The adage "Give a man a fish and he will eat for a day. Teach a man to fish and he will eat for a lifetime" was frequently employed.

Facilitators then gauged group members' current depression symptoms and functioning and provided psychoeducation, emphasizing that depression is a legitimate illness, that it is not the person's fault, and that it is treatable. Facilitators also clarified that members were not experiencing madness, as many of them feared. Members were then assigned the "sick role" (using comments such as, "You may not be able to do all you need or want to do for a while, until you start feeling better. Who can step in and help you during this time?") to temporarily relieve them of certain overwhelming social obligations. Next, facilitators conducted the interpersonal inventory to learn about the circumstances surrounding the onset and maintenance of members' depression and to identify the appropriate interpersonal problem area(s) and goals for treatment.

Initial Phase (Four Sessions)

During this phase, group members (who typically already knew each other from the community) learned about each other's symptoms and stories, and group facilitators attempted to ensure that all members felt safe and comfortable talking openly in the group setting. Facilitators reiterated that depression is a treatable illness and explained the group rules and frequency of meetings. They also began to discuss the interpersonal problems linked to the depression, and explored previous strategies group members had employed to deal with their situations.

At each of the sixteen sessions, group members were asked to report on any improvement or worsening of their symptoms over the previous week. Group facilitators reviewed which depression symptoms participants had endorsed, and asked them to describe the past week's events that contributed to the state of their mood. Participants were then encouraged to make connections between their experiences and their current mood.

MIDDLE PHASE (10 SESSIONS)

The goals of the middle phase of treatment were for group members to talk about their interpersonal problems and to attempt to make appropriate changes to manage those problems. These sessions revolved around the identified problem areas, and how to decrease difficulties therein.

In the original group adaptation of IPT for eating disorders, all patients were assigned the interpersonal deficits problem area, thus avoiding the potential difficulty in managing multiple different problem areas among group members (Wilfley et al., 2000; see Chapter 8). However, in the IPT-GU group members presented with different problem areas (and often more than one), and this served an important therapeutic function within the groups. Members were made aware of each other's problem areas in the initial phase of treatment, and were subsequently updated on these on a weekly basis as each member took it in turn at the beginning of every session to describe his or her progress over the previous seven days. The goal was for members to ruminate less about their own difficulties, develop a sense of mastery, and generate new perspectives by strategizing, solving problems, and offering advice and support in relation to other people's problem areas. In addition, many of the IPT techniques used were relevant across the different problem areas.

Death of Loved One(s). With HIV prevalence rates in Ugandan adults as high as 15% during the 1990s (Kirungi, Musinguzi, Opio, & Madraa, 2002), almost everyone in the groups had lost someone to HIV/AIDS, and some members were suffering from the illness themselves. When multiple deaths had occurred in one person's life, group facilitators tried to focus on the most recent death, or the death that was most likely the trigger of the current depressive episode. Traditional IPT reconstructs the relationship with the lost loved one, giving the patient a chance to construct a narrative that reflects the complexities of the relationship with the deceased. However, one issue in developing such narratives in this community was an intolerance of mentioning the dead negatively—as a local saying goes, "the dead are living among us." The challenge was therefore to assist awareness of both positive and negative aspects of relationships with the deceased without criticizing them directly. In one instance, a widow had to make peace with her husband for taking a second wife prior to his death and to decide whether to construct a relationship with her. With the help of her group she was able to express how hurt she had felt when her husband had taken this second wife, without criticizing him overtly. Whenever possible, the groups aimed to honor the memory of the deceased. Many members had not been able to conduct the proper honoring rituals at the time of their loved one's passing away, due to multiple deaths, a lack of resources, and, in many cases, the anergia associated with their depression.

Disagreements. Interpersonal disputes often require understanding differences of expectation and communication patterns among the parties involved. In southwestern Uganda, it proved necessary to explore ways to communicate expectations that were appropriate and acceptable within the local culture (see also Chapter 16). In the United States, direct confrontation is often rewarded in such situations, and frequently that is the IPT therapist's goal. However, in Uganda direct communications are seen as inappropriate, especially for women, and so alternate strategies had to be conceived. For example, a group member could find someone who had more social power to relay the information and conduct the negotiations. In one instance, a group member knew she could not talk to her husband directly, so she implored an older man from her husband's family to persuade the husband to use condoms so that she would not contract HIV and their children would not become orphans. In another instance, a member's husband was coming home drunk demanding to have sex with her in front of the children. The group suggested that she send the children outside and go into the bedroom so that they would not witness the intercourse. The group also suggested that she work at night making mats to sell for extra money to buy a TV, so that the husband would watch TV instead of becoming abusive. (This strategy worked.)

Life Changes. In traditional IPT, the work in role transitions involves identifying both the positive and negative aspects of the previous and current roles. However, frequently there was no positive aspect to the transitions group members experienced: devastation due to poverty, HIV/AIDS, and war. Instead, facilitators had to place emphasis on aspects of their lives that they could control: learning new skills; setting concrete, achievable goals; and finding advocates to help them achieve their goals. The objective was to empower group members and give them agency to explore options, act, and ask for help in achieving goals, instead of succumbing to the powerlessness that so often accompanies depression.

Despite these adaptations, the basic IPT strategies used in the middle phase of treatment remained operative in this setting: clarifying the depressogenic interpersonal situation and its impact on the person; assisting in generating options to manage the situation, thus reducing the person's sense of hopelessness; encouraging the person to identify advocates and supporters, thus reducing the sense of helplessness; and increasing a sense of interpersonal mastery.

TERMINATION (TWO SESSIONS)

The termination phase reviewed changes in symptoms and problems. Group members strategized with facilitators about how to deal with future problems that might trigger depression. During this time, members were encouraged to express how they felt about the group ending, and to explore ways that they could continue to be sources of support for each other, even after the group officially came to a close.

CASE EXAMPLE

Interviewers from the team who conducted the mental health survey for the randomized controlled trial in southwestern Uganda in 2001 assessed Amadi, a fifty-nine-year-old Catholic woman from a village outside Masaka, for depression. Her score on the locally adapted version of the Hopkins Symptom Checklist was 26, indicating a high level of depression. Her function score was 15, indicating moderate impairment. She met criteria for both *Okwekubagiza*, endorsing symptoms such as feeling sad and worthless and crying easily, and *Okwekyawa*, endorsing additional symptoms such as irritability, hating the world, and social withdrawal.

Pre-group Meetings

C.N., the IPT group facilitator for Amadi's village, walked around the village enrolling people whom the survey team had identified as eligible for the IPT-GU study. When she approached Amadi's home, it at first appeared deserted. Upon reaching the door, however, she saw Amadi sitting inside in the semi-gloom. She looked disheveled, exhausted, and weak, and did not come to the door to greet C.N., as is the local custom. When C.N. told Amadi that she was there to describe a therapy group she would be running and to see if Amadi wanted to participate, she mumbled in a quiet voice that she could come in.

That day, C.N. spoke with Amadi for about ninety minutes. Amadi described herself as numb and hopeless. She reported symptoms consistent with major depression, including persistent sadness and irritability, apathy, low energy, difficulty concentrating, trouble sleeping, loss of appetite leading to significant weight loss, feelings of guilt and worthlessness, and psychomotor retardation. Although many of these symptoms dated back ten years to the death of her eldest son, she had lost four more children since then and her symptoms appeared to have intensified over time, to the point that she was now experiencing them daily. She stated that she kept her rosary with her at all times "to protect" her against suicidal thoughts, but that she resented God for granting her a long life.

C.N. suggested in her notes that "Amadi was alive, but not really living." Amadi reported having profound difficulty in carrying out her familial roles as a wife, mother, and grandmother, and in her occupation as a mat-weaver. She told C.N. that she felt unable to grow food for herself and her family, could not concentrate enough to mix the colors for her mats, lacked the energy to look after her house and *shamba* (garden), and could not even take care of her own hygiene.

When Amadi had finished describing her situation, C.N. provided some psycho-education on depression and assigned her the sick role. She explained to Amadi that she was suffering from a combination of *Okwekubagiza* and *Okwekyawa* that was compromising her ability to take care of herself, her family, and her community. She explained that this was an illness rather than madness, told her that the illness was not her fault, and attempted to provide her with hope that the treatment would help her to get better. Amadi shook her head, stating that all the talk in the world would not bring back her children. C.N. also explained that it would probably take a while before she was able to mix colors for her mats again correctly, but that she should expect to see significant improvement in the next four months, and asked her whether there was anyone who could help with her mat-making in the meantime. Amadi responded that she had only one close friend, Bacia, but that she had recently become gravely ill. When, following the protocol, C.N. clarified that she would not receive any material goods in the group, Amadi declared that she had no use for other people's charity.

Amadi's husband then entered the house, and as Amadi sat hunched over with her eyes to the ground, he reminisced about how she had been before the onset of her depression: energetic and loving, a strong, "fierce lady" who voiced her opinion, took excellent care of her house, was a good wife, and most of all was an excellent mother to their nine children. She had frequently offered help and advice to other mothers, and worked diligently as a mat-weaver.

The following week, C.N. returned to Amadi's home to complete the interpersonal inventory and share the interpersonal formulation and contract. Slowly, over these two initial sessions, she learned that in the past ten years Amadi and her husband had lost five of their nine children (three of them to the AIDS epidemic), some of whom had spouses and children. In addition to their loss, Amadi and her husband now found themselves burdened with caring for their deceased children's families, instead of their sons and daughters supporting them in their old age as they had planned.

Over the years, Amadi had become so withdrawn and uncommunicative with her remaining children and grandchildren that they had ceased to visit. Exasperated by Amadi staying at home and crying constantly, her husband spent as much time out of the house as possible. In addition, Amadi isolated herself from other people in the village, to the point where she no longer responded when her neighbors or her fellow churchgoers greeted her. Although several women from the village had come to see her, she had turned each of them away, telling them that until they had experienced the death of their own children they could not understand what she was going through. Sometimes Amadi was visited by other women who had lost children, but she spoke to them little.

After gathering all this information, C.N. concluded that the trigger of Amadi's depression was grief, which had been compounded with each additional loss. Amadi spoke most about the deaths of her two youngest sons, both of whom had died shortly after graduating from university. One had died three years earlier in a car accident and the second the following year from "the illness" (HIV/AIDS). C.N. decided to focus Amadi's treatment, at least initially, around mourning the loss of these two sons.

Together, C.N. and Amadi set two goals for treatment. The first was for Amadi to think of the children she had lost without experiencing such intense sadness and hopelessness. The second, proposed by Amadi, was to be able to return to her work on her *shamba* and making mats. Amadi rejected a third goal of improving her relationships with her remaining children.

Initial Phase (Weeks 1–4 of Group Treatment)

The IPT group in which Amadi participated consisted of the facilitator (C.N.) and eight women, ranging in age from forty-five to seventy, with three women in their late forties; two, including Amadi, in their fifties; two in their sixties; and one in her seventies. Like Amadi, four other members of the group were bereaved following the deaths of one or more loved ones, either recently or dating back many years. A number of group members were struggling with disagreements with those close to them. For example, one group member fought frequently with her husband; another had a conflict with her son, who accused her of being a witch. Women in the group also struggled with lack of resources and financial losses, such as a husband's recent unemployment, as well as illness. All group members started treatment experiencing high levels of sadness and hopelessness, and most noted they had been crying very frequently. They all seemed to be intensely worried about their problems and had difficulty functioning in their lives.

The first four group sessions were structured around the *initial phase* of IPT, during which group members become acquainted with each other. At the beginning of the first session, the women appeared anxious, sad, and withdrawn. When C.N. asked them to share their experiences, silence enveloped the group. Finally, Amadi volunteered to speak, but broke down before she could complete her first sentence. Through her tears, she recounted that the death of her beloved youngest son, following so many other losses, had robbed her of any remaining hope and happiness. "Nothing good will happen now," she declared, almost defiantly. Prompted by C.N., she described how she learned of his death and suffered through the funeral rituals. She said that he had been living in a city several hours away, and that although she had received word from her sister-in-law that he was ill, she had not realized the extent and rapidity of his decline. "One day my husband's sister came to me with the news of his death, I never even got to say goodbye," she reflected sadly. She continued that, during the burial period, she had refused food for days, developed diarrhea, and at one point collapsed. In addition, she revealed to C.N. and the group that her daughter had recently disappeared and, in her words, "not even a mutilated body was recovered for burial." Responding to Amadi's outpouring of grief, the group commiserated with her, shedding tears for the next half-hour. One group member placed her hand on Amadi's back to comfort her, while another gently cradled Amadi's head in her lap. An air of hopelessness and despondency filled the room. When asked to come up with a plan for the week, Amadi told the group that she had no plan except to "put everything to God."

At the beginning of the second session, when each member described changes in their depression since the previous week, Amadi reported worsening of her symptoms, especially her sadness and loneliness, which she attributed to the death of her close friend, Bacia. She also reported feeling increasingly weak herself. When C.N. asked her about her past and recent relationship with Bacia, Amadi reported that they had worked together making mats for many years, and that she had been the godmother to Bacia's first son. Amadi also revealed that they had shared in their grief when Bacia lost a daughter to "the illness" several years earlier. "She was the only one who could understand me," Amadi added.

By the third session, the group members' support for each other had increased: they were better able to comfort those in the group who were bereaved and started offering each other suggestions more directly. C.N. facilitated this process by prompting the members to express their feelings and support, as well as to give advice to one another: "I can see the pain in your faces as Amadi is talking about her son. What would you like to tell Amadi right now?" However, Amadi seemed to have further deteriorated since the second session: she was thinking obsessively about her dead children, could not stop crying or force herself to eat or sleep, and was losing strength with each passing day. As the session closed, the group's weekly plan for Amadi was that she try to dig in her *shamba* to take her mind off her lost loved ones, and go to bed earlier in an effort to rest.

At the beginning of the fourth session, C.N. noticed some members smiling shyly when they met for the group, while two more arrived together in a pair. During the session she observed that the women were beginning to establish eye contact when addressing one another, and when one member broke down discussing a recent argument with her son, the others comforted her without the hesitancy and self-consciousness they had shown during previous sessions. Slowly, a change was coming over the group. Above and beyond offering practical advice, support, and encouragement to their fellow members, it seemed to C.N. that they were beginning to establish a collective bond, trust each other more, and empathize more deeply with one another. C.N. noticed, for the first time, some improvements in Amadi, too. She announced during the symptom review that she had been going to bed earlier and that her sleep and appetite had somewhat improved. She attributed these improvements to encouragement from the group, an increasing awareness that others in the group were going through similar situations, and praying regularly. She was somewhat more proactive than in previous sessions, offering advice to another member for the first time, encouraging her to take time to rest and to find comfort and strength through prayer.

Middle Phase (Weeks 5–14 of Group Treatment)

By the fifth session, the beginning of the *middle phase* of treatment, Amadi was sleeping better, her appetite was increasing, and her anhedonia was beginning to dissipate. This progress mirrored that of most of the other women in the group, who, with a few exceptions, by the fifth session had begun to show a more positive attitude and initiative toward action. The group members, as a whole, seemed to have become closer, and were more comfortable supporting and making suggestions to one another. In her group notes, C.N. wrote that group members were now interacting with each other more directly rather than looking to her to take the lead.

Amadi was unable to attend the sixth and seventh sessions because she had contracted malaria. During her absence, C.N. went to visit her and found that, after two weeks of being sick, Amadi was unable to walk and was both emotionally and physically drained. C.N. discovered that two group members had visited Amadi as well, for which Amadi had been grateful. Amadi recounted that they had asked about her mood, and that when she replied that she was fine they had suggested that her "eyes said otherwise," at which point Amadi had revealed that her current frailty reminded her of her successive children's deterioration with the illness. Through this anecdote, C.N. was pleased to see some of the aspects of the IPT-GU meetings being translated into "real life" beyond the group.

When Amadi returned to the group for the eighth session, she had maintained her improvements in sleep and appetite, and was no longer ruminating as much over the deaths of her children. She told the other members that she had been missing the meetings and her fellow group members, and that she felt determined to take care of her physical health in order to maintain the small gains she had made in her emotional health. During the session, the group asked her about her relationships with her lost children. Amadi spoke of her youngest sons' accomplishments and how proud she had been when they had graduated from university. She also reflected on her sorrow that her relationship with her daughter had not been good over the two years prior to her disappearance. She reported having felt hurt that, since moving to a town several hours away, her daughter had rarely returned home. A group member asked her whether her depressed state interfered with making her daughter feel welcome. Amadi thought for a moment before acknowledging that her *Okwekubagiza* and *Okwekyawa* symptoms had probably played a part in their strained relationship.

By Session 9, for the first time, the majority of Amadi's symptoms had improved and none had worsened. She reported not only better sleep and appetite, but also improved concentration. She felt more energized and, perhaps most remarkably, her sadness had begun to lift. In addition, with medical care her health was steadily improving and she was doing all she could to help herself heal. In this session, she volunteered to take part in a role-play for the first time, playing the part of a sister-in-law whom a younger group member was planning to ask for help in persuading her husband not to come home drunk and yell at her in front of their children.

By the tenth session, group members were noticing changes in Amadi as well. She played herself in a role-play asking her husband and children for assistance in the home without the conversation escalating into an argument. Later in the session, in contrast to anything the group had seen thus far, Amadi revealed herself to have a sense of humor, making the entire group burst into laughter when she quipped that it was a "miracle" that a group of women was able to keep what they were discussing during their meetings to themselves.

Like Amadi, the other group members showed noticeable improvement in their symptoms between Sessions 6 and 10, despite physical illnesses and the loss of loved ones during this period. Most reported that they were less sad and tearful, that they were sleeping and eating better, and that they were finally able to focus on important tasks such as weeding their land and making and selling mats and baskets. Previous shyness and hesitancy in sharing with the group seemed to have disappeared almost entirely over this period, as the women appeared to have developed a trust in each other and the confidentiality of the group. During these sessions group members also revealed many things to each other that they had not mentioned previously; for example, one woman bravely shared her pain about her son's imprisonment for stealing. In another memorable moment, from the ninth session, one member pronounced to the rest of the group that they had all "lost treasures," but that to give in to their depression would mean giving up on the treasures that remained and letting their lives slip away to nothingness. The women agreed collectively to use this new opportunity the group had given them to embrace life by becoming more active in the community.

Between the tenth and eleventh sessions, as discussed and planned by the members during the previous meeting, several women who had lost relatives, including Amadi, decided to visit the graves of their loved ones in order to grieve their losses formally. Once there, they cleared the entire graveyard, which had been overtaken by weeds, and planted flowers that they had brought for the occasion. The women then conducted a memorial ceremony in honor of the deceased, verbally praising them, and telling them how much they were loved and missed. The experience served not only to commemorate those who had died, but also to create a sense of purpose and greater solidarity among them.

By the eleventh week, and thereafter, Amadi reported improvement in all of her symptoms. For the first time, and with the group's encouragement, she was not talking about those who had died, but about her remaining children and grandchildren. For reasons she had struggled to put into words up to that point, she stated that before it had been too painful to see the children who were left, as it had brought back memories of those who had died, and because of her belief that it was only a matter of time before they were taken from her as well. Her fellow group members urged Amadi to recontact loved ones and rebuild long-neglected relationships. Most of her family and friends accepted her back into their lives with understanding and warmth, and as a result she was able to replace much of the resentment she had harbored towards them with love and hope for their future. She began to discuss the possibility of one of her son's getting a new job in a larger, nearby town in order to support the family, and she now felt closer to her remaining daughter, who had come to visit recently. Amadi invited her grandson to weed her *shamba* with her, cooked for the family again, and visited neighbors she had long shunned.

As the weeks progressed, Amadi dug and plowed her *shamba*, restoring it effectively. She told the group that hearing other members' stories had given her the courage to stop crying, "get out of my blanket," and start making mats again. She surprised herself by making two mats without any problems, and continued throughout the remaining weeks to make mats for sale. She announced proudly that she was mixing her colors flawlessly. She came to the thirteenth session in a colorful *gomesi* (dress); the group smiled and clapped when they saw her, and reminded her of the drab shawls she had worn in the first few sessions. In her weekly notes, C.N. wrote that whereas Amadi had entered the group without hope, she was now looking toward the future, taking care of herself, and participating more in the lives of her family and community.

Amadi attributed her improvement to the suggestions and support that she received from the group members and from C.N., whom she saw as someone who truly cared about her and empathized with what she had been through. Along with other members, Amadi repeatedly thanked World Vision for bringing IPT to her, noting that it was not until she joined the group that she was able to function normally—for the first time in ten years. During the fourteenth session, Amadi declared, "I am now at the top of the mountain, but it was not easy to climb. I feel better. At the start, I wanted to go back in the valley, but the group pushed [me] up. Thank you, C.N. and members."

The other group members paralleled Amadi in their improvement. Some of the women expressed the resolution of their grieving state over lost loved ones. They said that they had been able to resume work again, and some had even started new businesses. All the group members found ways to share the benefits of the group with the community. One woman took it upon herself to make sure that village children were attending the local school; another helped a neighbor resolve a dispute about the proceeds from a shared plot of land by asking her brother-in-law, an important man in the village, to intercede. Since so many, like Amadi, had lost loved ones to HIV-related illnesses, all of the women agreed to sit down with their sons and daughters to discuss both the dangers of HIV infection and the necessary prevention measures. In addition to her familial responsibilities, Amadi herself even took on a new role as a *ssenga*, a wise, older woman who advises young girls on how to become good women and wives.

Termination (Weeks 15–16 of Treatment)

By the last two sessions of IPT-GU, the group members spent most of their time sharing their improvements with each other. They also made plans to continue to meet after the group officially ended. At the final meeting, Amadi gave C.N. a recently finished mat. C.N.'s entry for that session read, "The week was so wonderful. Life has changed for her! She is sleeping, eating, [and sheds] no more tears. The husband also noticed this . . . the home is at peace. The grandchildren are happy to see their grand-mother well again. For ten years, life had become useless, and for four years she had no energy. But now she is strong."

Follow-up

At her interview two weeks after treatment ended, Amadi endorsed almost no prob-lems in any of the functioning areas assessed and no major depression symptoms. As they had planned in the final sessions, in the six months following treatment Amadi and her IPT group members carried on meeting informally on a monthly basis, con-tinuing to provide support and encouragement to each other and also to help each other with suggestions for new economic ventures.

At her six-month follow-up evaluation, Amadi reported that she never missed the group's monthly meetings. She said that they helped to give her the ongoing strength to work long hours making mats to provide additional income for her family. In addition, she noted that following the recent loss of her eldest grandson, counseling from the group comforted her greatly. Other members related that she assumed something of a leadership role in the meetings—ensuring that the group stayed focused on feelings, encouraging members to explore their commonalities, and insisting that each of the women maintain confidentiality at all times. The evaluation indicated that Amadi continued to have few difficulties in functioning and no major depression symptoms.

DISCUSSION

Raging communicable diseases, poverty, and violence dominate the global humani-tarian aid agenda. In the face of these enormous adversities, one understands the skepticism towards addressing the high rates of depression that frequently accom-pany them. In southwestern Uganda, one fifth of the people surveyed had depression symptoms and impaired functioning (Bolton, Wilk, & Ndogoni, 2004). While adapt-ing IPT for the local communities, the team found that people's demoralization was at times so paralyzing that they resigned themselves to their suffering and did not take advantage of the resources, albeit meager, that were available to them to improve their life conditions.

IPT was developed as a treatment for acute depression focusing on the interpersonal trigger(s) of the most recent depressive episode (Klerman, Weissman, Rounsaville, & Chevron, 1984), and the majority of evidence for its efficacy is based on studies conducted in Western countries with patients with episodic major depression. Studies conducted in the United States suggest that IPT is as effective as medication in treating severe depression over sixteen weeks (Elkin et al., 1989; Markowitz et al., 1998). Amadi's case, and the randomized controlled trial of which it was a part, indicate a similar impact of IPT in Uganda. The dramatic improvement in Amadi's depression is striking given the severity of her symptoms, her poor occupational and social functioning at baseline, and the ten-year chronicity of her depressive episode.

As the case study illustrates, IPT-GU provided an antidepressant intervention that capitalized on the strong interpersonal orientation which permeates the way people in this region experience and react to the world. It has become a cliché to contrast so-called collectivist cultures in non-Western, especially resource-poor areas, with individualistic Western society. However, the southern Ugandan affinity for an interpersonal perspective, which views human relationships not only as a potential cause of sickness and suffering but also as a mechanism for recovery and growth, goes far beyond this generalization. In the words of an African proverb, "I am a person through other people." The recognition and detailed exploration of emotions are part and parcel of the interpersonal focus of IPT (as compared to the emphasis on cognitions and the monitoring of behavior in cognitive-behavioral therapy). Recognition of affect in other people's tone, facial expressions, and gestures appeared to come naturally both to the local therapists and group members who participated in IPT-GU. The ease with which group members related to each other appears to have been an important component of the treatment's success.

In addition to its specific effects on depression symptoms, IPT-GU also yielded significant improvements in functioning. This functional change extended beyond the improved social and occupational functioning seen in many Western IPT patients to encompass increased involvement in community projects. As observed in Amadi's group, when IPT-GU group members started reporting noticeable improvements in their symptoms, they typically decided to translate these personal gains into active contributions in their communities, entirely of their own accord (Lewandowski et al., in preparation).

The following aspects of Amadi's case highlight some characteristics of IPT-GU.

IPT-GU and Grief

Although it was not formally assessed as part of the study, in addition to depression, Amadi appears to have met several criteria for complicated grief. This syndrome, although not included in the DSM-IV, is receiving increased clinical and research attention. Its features include bitterness and anger over the death of the loved one, preoccupation with thoughts about him or her, and pangs of severe emotion and yearning for the deceased. It is frequently comorbid with both depression and PTSD (Shear, Frank, Houck, & Reynolds, 2005). Several studies have shown that treatments for bereavement-related depression have little impact on complicated grief symptoms. In their study of ninety-five men and women with complicated grief, Shear et al. (2005) found that a targeted complicated grief treatment (CGT) developed for the study was significantly more efficacious than individual IPT. However, in that study some defining aspects of IPT grief work were omitted to differentiate it from CGT, such as talking about the death scene. A second study by Shear et al. is currently investigating the impact of "full force" individual IPT on complicated grief.

In Amadi's case, IPT-GU seemed very effective in alleviating complicated grief symptoms, including her anger over her children's deaths, her obsessive rumination and longing for them, and her intense bouts of emotional pain. Based on the case notes, it appears that several factors contributed to the alleviation of Amadi's grief symptoms. The treatment allowed her to express her grief openly; the group contained her emotions and made her feel supported; listening to other group members' stories of lost loved ones helped her break the sense of isolation stemming from her grief; and talking about her deceased children gave her the opportunity to honor their memory. The treatment appears to have helped Amadi to accept the hard reality of her multiple losses.

The treatment also provided a link to the present by enabling Amadi to see how her grief for children lost was affecting her current interpersonal relationships. By role-playing interpersonal skills that had atrophied over her years of grieving, she began to refocus her thoughts and energy on her remaining family members and loved ones and her role in the community.

Use of Affect

Encouraging Amadi to explore and express her affect was central to her treatment. People who have undergone painful loss of loved ones often fear that if they allow themselves to experience and express their emotions openly, they will not be able to stop and their feelings will engulf them. However, the group appears to have given Amadi a safe haven to express her grief. Over time the group discovered collectively that they could contain their feelings, taking ownership of their emotions without being overwhelmed by them. For Amadi, allowing herself to experience her grief at an affective level appears gradually to have replaced her obsessive ruminations about her children's deaths.

While C.N. and the group members appear to have recognized the importance of processing their emotions during sessions, they advocated, especially early in treatment, that between sessions Amadi "not think all the time," and instead focus her energy on digging in her *shamba*. Encouraging the expression of painful emotions in the safety of the therapeutic environment while helping patients to contain those feelings between sessions is a challenging task in IPT. However, Amadi appears to have maintained this balance. Working her land appears not only to have suspended her ruminations and distracted her from her grief, but also to have helped lift her anergia and given her a sense of purpose and accomplishment.

Breaking Social Isolation

As treatment progressed, the group increasingly encouraged Amadi to break her social isolation by restoring her relationships with family and friends. This went hand in hand with her grief therapy: with the group's support, Amadi was able to acknowledge that her deceased children were gone forever, and to move on by renewing ties to loved ones around her. Breaking her social isolation also worked in parallel with increasing her engagement in more interpersonal activities.

At the beginning of treatment, Amadi displayed the anger and interpersonal hostility that people who have experienced multiple losses often feel. However, the group's encouragement appears to have helped Amadi gain renewed faith in others and enjoyment of their company. This was poignantly demonstrated by her light-hearted reflection towards the end of treatment about the "miracle" of a group of eight women mutually respecting the confidentiality of their discussions. As Amadi's hostility towards others lifted, she could re-access sources of interpersonal support within her community on which she had turned her back. For example, she started to greet her neighbors again, and once more become an active participant in the church she attended.

Role Development

Although Amadi's specified problem area was grief, in IPT-GU (as in many treatments for grief) exploring the role transition precipitated by the death of loved ones was also an important aspect of the work. At the beginning of treatment, Amadi seemed to regard her grieving mother role as an important part of her identity. Several group members suggested that their depression was all that they had left of their relationship with the people they had lost. They described feeling that the intensity of their grief showed how much they had valued the relationship. In her notes, C.N. suggested that they appeared afraid that if they no longer felt that pain it would mean they no longer cared about those they had lost.

The IPT "sick role" was used to reframe Amadi's depression as a current illness, rather than a permanent identity. It also gave her the mental space to reduce expectations and focus on combating her depression, to "not think," as the group put it, and, in doing so, reduce her sense of sadness, guilt, and burden.

As her symptoms began to lift, the group challenged Amadi to move beyond the sick role by taking on more responsibility and resuming old roles as a mother, grandmother, and mat-weaver. The new role as *ssenga* Amadi assumed towards the end of treatment gave her an additional sense of purpose, mastery, and fulfillment.

Functional Improvement

Mental health professionals, humanitarian aid groups, and economists bring differing perspectives to the question of the functional impairment that accompanies mental health problems. Colleagues from other parts of the world have criticized the American approach to psychopathology for excessively emphasizing improved functioning and a prosaic preoccupation with the patient's ability to live, work, and contribute to society, to the relative detriment of more philosophical or spiritual concerns. Similarly, from a development perspective, the justification for treating mental health needs in resource-poor areas, despite the apparently more immediate challenges imposed by poverty, is often made in economic terms. Indeed, the overall disease burden is frequently measured by developmental economists in disability-adjusted life years (DALYs), the amount of time lost due to living in less than full health and having one's ability to work compromised. Within this framework, depression is estimated to be the fourth highest contributor to DALYs worldwide (Murray & Lopez, 1997).

If such arguments appear reductionist and utilitarian, they seem to have had real and direct relevance to Amadi. She and her husband, both approaching their 60s, had envisaged that their children, particularly the recent university graduates, would help support them in old age. Their deaths therefore represented an economic blow as well as an emotional one. Furthermore, Amadi's lack of energy and concentration meant that she had allowed her land to become overgrown and could not mix the colors correctly for her mat-making. Moreover, Amadi's suffering, which confined her to days spent at home grieving, distracted her husband to the point that he was finding it hard to work also. Recultivating the land and restoring her mat business were therefore important goals of therapy for Amadi, not only serving a therapeutic function by helping lift her anergia and giving her a sense of purpose and mastery, but also helping herself and her family survive.

Role of the Group

In their group adaptation of IPT, Wilfley et al. (2000) encouraged the use of the group as a laboratory through which to identify maladaptive communication patterns, both outside and within the group. In the IPT-GU adaptation the team sought to facilitate a similar form of group process, but with a specific focus on building an environment of cohesion and support (Verdeli et al., 2003). In Amadi's case, the group format apparently played a key role in her improvement by making her aware that she was not alone in her suffering. She stated during the 6-month follow-up evaluation, "I found out that I was not alone." The group provided her with a supportive community and offered her advice based on the members' multiple perspectives. Prior to treatment, Amadi had dismissed suggestions from other community members to rest or spend more time with her family, on occasion interpreting their comments as thinly veiled criticism. However, as the group dynamic developed, she took great strength from group members offering similar advice, their words encouraging her to take active steps between sessions to combat her depression. In addition, through the use of role-plays, the therapy enabled Amadi to "relearn" important aspects of social communication, such as greeting neighbors and paying attention to her appearance.

Role of the Therapist

The implementation of IPT-GU followed the World Health Organization's task-shifting model, in which the challenge presented by a dearth of trained professionals and lack of financial resources is overcome by delegating tasks to less specialized staff (WHO, 2007). C.N. and her fellow therapists had no mental health experience prior to their IPT-GU training. However, the treatment they learned during a two-week intensive training provided them with a clear structure. As they were all from the region, they were able to provide invaluable local knowledge that helped fine-tune the adaptation of the treatment during the training. During the trial they received weekly supervision from experienced mental health workers who had attended the training, and who themselves were in regular contact with the U.S. trainers.

Provided with this task-shifting framework, they were able to deliver the treatment effectively, as the results of the trial showed.

C.N. vividly remembers this first group she facilitated, and how it felt as a shy twenty-three-year-old presenting herself nervously at the first session to this group of older women, many of whom bore the pessimism and bitterness of having struggled with depression for years. However, despite the initial hesitance of the group, she resisted the temptation to over-insert herself during meetings, something that can challenge even seasoned therapists. As a result, she enabled a positive group process to develop among the members, and this became an important vector for change. She understood that learning to overcome problems for oneself is a vital component in combating the helplessness and hopelessness of depression, and used the group to model this practice. This aspect of treatment has special relevance in a resource-poor area such as southwestern Uganda, where assistance often takes the form of handouts from aid agencies.

C.N. went on to conduct many more IPT groups in the region through the sponsoring organization, World Vision. She also returned to university to complete a master's degree in psychological counseling, and has received specialized training in treating complicated grief, trauma, and working with people with HIV. In 2007, as part of a scaling up of the treatment, she attended the IPT "Training of Trainers" in Nairobi, Kenya; since then, she has trained and supervised other IPT therapists in Uganda, thus broadening the reach of the treatment. She plans to complete a doctorate and conduct treatment research combining antiretroviral treatment (ART) with group IPT in HIV-positive patients with comorbid depression.

CONCLUSION

Based on C.N.'s notes, all the members in Amadi's group of older, mostly chronically depressed women responded well to the treatment. C.N. attributed this to their respect for one another, their diligence in working towards goals, their active participation, and their willingness to embrace psychotherapy despite their initial skepticism. In her notes, C.N. observed that during the pre-group sessions, Amadi stated that she did not believe that talking alone could help her overcome the depression that had plagued her for so long. Four months later, she reported in her final session that her husband and granddaughter had both asked what sort of treatment she was receiving that allowed her to sleep, eat, and no longer cry or lose things. Many of Amadi's fellow group members' suggestions and her own weekly goals revolved around reworking her long-neglected, overgrown land. In therapeutic terms, this served the function of combating her neurovegetative symptoms, distracting her from depressive ruminations about her deceased children, and providing her with a sense of purpose and mastery. In functional terms, digging her land enabled her to interact with other members of her family and community. In economic terms, it was taking one step closer to self-reliance. There is also a symbolic meaning to Amadi's rediscovery of her connection with the land. Within the rich symbolism of southwestern Ugandan culture, the land is a metaphor for people themselves. We view Amadi's cultivation and attention to her land after years of neglect as a sign of her renewed investment in life.

SUGGESTED READING

Bolton P, Tang AM: An alternative approach to cross-cultural function assessment. Social Psychiatry and Psychiatric Epidemiology 2002;37:537–543

Clougherty KF, Verdeli H, Mufson LH, Young JF: Interpersonal psychotherapy: effectiveness trials in rural Uganda and New York City. Psychiatric Annals 2006; 36:566–572

Using Interpersonal Psychotherapy in Differing Formats

19

Maintenance Interpersonal Psychotherapy (IPT-M)

MARK D. MILLER, ELLEN FRANK,
AND JESSICA C. LEVENSON

Since the discovery of effective psychotherapeutic and pharmacotherapeutic acute treatments for depression, the problem of how to prevent relapse and recurrence has been a vexing one. If a biologic disturbance of homeostasis in brain chemistry underlies some cases of recurrent depression, then withdrawing an effective dose of pharmacotherapy could increase the risk of recurrence. Similarly, the stress-diathesis model of depression suggests that some individuals lack adequate coping strategies to effectively manage the stress they face, which can trigger a depressive episode. If psychotherapy can help these individuals to learn better coping strategies, their depression can be diminished or eliminated. However, if these more effective coping strategies fade over time without reinforcement, the former maladaptive coping patterns could return, resulting in new episodes of major depression. There is also no reason to think that these two paths to recurrence are completely distinct from each other; both factors may interact in the same individual to provoke a recurrence.

Researchers have tried to tease apart the benefits of pharmacotherapy and psychotherapy in preventing recurrences of major depression. Because some individuals have strong preferences for one modality over another and patient preference influences treatment outcome (Kocsis et al., 2009), multiple strategies are needed. Some individuals' depressive symptoms respond poorly to monotherapy and thus require combination approaches or alternative treatments.

We will describe some of the studies designed to test the protective effects of maintenance pharmacotherapy and psychotherapy against relapse and recurrence. With pharmacotherapy, judging long-term efficacy simply requires monitoring patients on a given dose of medication over time. Psychotherapeutic interventions raise other issues. For example, so long as participants are feeling the burden of depressive symptoms and can identify specific struggles they would like to work on in therapy, they are often highly motivated to work hard and collaboratively, but what motivation do they have to continue psychotherapy once they feel well? Certainly, some patients are willing to continue psychotherapy for benefits other than depression prophylaxis, such as self-discovery or pursuit of the "examined life"; however, if the goal is prophylaxis of subsequent depressive episodes, there are a very limited number of psychotherapies for which there is evidence of preventive efficacy. One of these is IPT.

With evidence accumulating that IPT was an effective short-term treatment for acute major depression (DiMascio et al., 1979; Elkin et al., 1989), a logical extension of this work was to ask how well a maintenance form of IPT could prevent relapses and recurrences of major depression. Although IPT was created as an acute treatment for major depression using techniques designed to improve social functioning, unipolar recurrent major depression is a chronic, recurring condition that often requires a long-term strategy to prevent recurrences, each one of which can further damage remaining interpersonal relationships in a vicious cycle. Would IPT work at a reduced frequency compared to the weekly session used in treating the acute episode? Should sessions of a maintenance version of IPT (IPT-M) differ from those of acute IPT? What specific goals should IPT-M pursue to achieve protection against recurrence, and what specific techniques would serve that end?

To address these questions, Frank (1991) described IPT-M and noted several ways in which it differs from IPT: (1) The goal of IPT is to achieve acute remission of a depressive episode, whereas the goal of IPT-M is to prevent recurrences; (2) The interval for IPT-M is typically monthly, versus weekly in acute-phase IPT; and (3) While one or at most two interpersonal foci are addressed in acute IPT, IPT-M potentially addresses multiple foci. Additionally, of course, IPT-M lacks the time pressure associated with most acute forms of IPT.

Originally, the rationale for using IPT in a maintenance format grew out of research to prevent major depressive recurrences using antidepressant medications. Findings from this research informed the description of IPT-M seen above. Large collaborative studies in the United States (Prien et al., 1984) and Great Britain (Glen, Johnson, & Shepherd, 1984) show unequivocally that individuals with recurrent major depression who were stabilized on antidepressant medication were far more likely to suffer a recurrence if they were tapered to placebo than those who continued to take medication long term. Unfortunately, however, patients with recurrent unipolar depression who were treated to remission of an index episode of major depression with antidepressant medication still carried a 50% or lower chance of surviving for three years without another major depressive episode (recurrence) even if they stayed on antidepressant medication throughout. Thus, there was a relatively high likelihood of recurrence even with continued antidepressant pharmacotherapy.

In concert with this work on the development of a maintenance form of IPT, we sought to clarify the terminology used to describe the course of depression, terminology that has proven critical to subsequent understanding of the phases of depressive illness and the interventions appropriate to each phase. These efforts are illustrated in Table 19.1 and Figure 19.1.

Noting the poor long-term stability of remission in patients with recurrent depression, researchers at the University of Pittsburgh (Frank et al., 1990) studied

Table 19.1. DEFINITIONS

Term	Definition
Response	Persisting depressive symptoms after treatment, but no longer meeting severity criteria for major depressive disorder
Remission	An extended period (three to four weeks) during which there are no longer any signs of significant depression
Relapse	Return of depressive symptoms, during remission but before recovery, that suffice to diagnose major depression
Recovery	Remission that extends for a specified period of time: sixteen weeks is the standard in research settings
Recurrence	A new episode of major depression occurring after recovery has been achieved

(Adapted from Frank, Prien, et al., 1991)

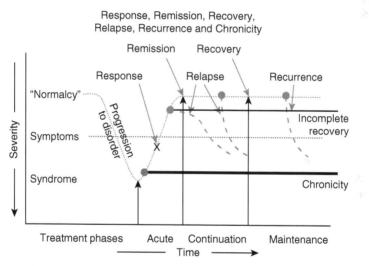

Figure 19.1 The Kupfer diagram shows these terms in graphic form. (Adapted with permission from Kupfer DJ. Journal of Clinical Psychiatry 1991;52(suppl 5):28–34.)

two questions: (1) Could different pharmacotherapy techniques lengthen the inter-episode euthymic interval (perhaps by maintaining the same dose of pharmacotherapy that had achieved remission—something that had not been done in previous pharmacotherapy maintenance trials), and (2) Could the addition of a psychotherapy improve the outcome further? While the original study of IPT (Klerman, Dimascio, Weissman, Prusoff, & Paykel, 1974) was a continuation treatment trial, this was the first time that any psychotherapy had been conceptualized as possibly having the capacity to prevent recurrence in patients who had achieved sustained remission. Although it was common for patients to continue particularly psychoanalytic psychotherapy for many, many years, the goal of such treatment was the exploration of intrapsychic conflict, not the prevention of depressive recurrence per se, as in IPT-M.

Having observed persistent deficits in social functioning even in those patients who had remained well in the maintenance phase of the Prien et al. (1984) pharmacotherapy study, the investigators (Frank et al., 1990) decided to study IPT as opposed to other forms of psychotherapy in an effort to address what they thought might represent a vulnerability factor for recurrence. Indeed, a study of psychotherapy as a long-term maintenance treatment in patients who had achieved remission had not been designed and carried out before this time. They hypothesized that IPT could work by improving social functioning, thus creating a stress-buffering effect that could augment any protection the pharmacotherapy provided. The study design combined the antidepressant imipramine (150–300 mg per day) and weekly IPT as acute treatment, followed by a seventeen-week continuation period of stability after achieving depressive symptom remission, which was defined as a Hamilton Rating Scale for Depression (Ham-D; Hamilton, 1960) score of 7 or less for three consecutive weeks. Participants who remained in remission for a total of twenty weeks were then randomly assigned to one of five treatment conditions for three years of prophylactic treatment: (1) IPT-M alone, (2) IPT-M plus imipramine at the dose that achieved remission, (3) IPT-M plus placebo, (4) Clinical management (CM) plus imipramine, and (5) CM plus placebo. All participants had monthly visits for three years or until they suffered a recurrence of major depression, defined as a Ham-D score of more than 15 at two evaluations a week apart and the confirmation of the presence of an episode of major depression by a research psychiatrist not otherwise involved in the study and blinded to the participant's treatment assignment.

All participants were between ages twenty-one and sixty-five; individuals who screened positive for bipolar disorder, psychotic spectrum disorders, or borderline or antisocial personality disorder were excluded (Frank et al., 1990). Only those participants whose acute episode remitted while receiving combined treatment with imipramine and IPT were randomized into the three-year maintenance phase. Patients assigned to IPT received monthly IPT-M sessions, whereas those assigned to monthly CM received general therapist support, surveillance for side effects, and encouragement to remain adherent to their treatment, an approach consistent with a "medication check," but without specific psychotherapeutic elements. The monthly "dose" was selected as one that was sufficiently infrequent to be reasonable from a cost standpoint and sufficiently frequent to permit continuity of focus. Still, a scheduled "dose" of psychotherapy this low had not been studied in any previous psychotherapy trials. Figure 19.2 illustrates the results of this study, showing a highly statistically significant protective effect for patients receiving maintenance imipramine (continued at the dose that achieved remission), with or without IPT-M, compared to the subgroup assigned to placebo and CM.

On average, imipramine and imipramine plus IPT-M prevented a recurrence four times longer than the placebo plus CM. The IPT-M alone and IPT-M plus placebo groups were both statistically superior to the group receiving CM plus placebo, with the IPT-M alone group surviving an average fifty-four weeks without a recurrence and IPT-M plus placebo group surviving seventy-four weeks, versus an average of twenty-one weeks for the CM plus placebo group.

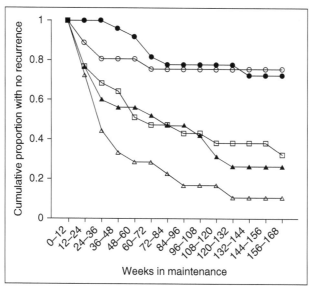

Outcome of the maintenance therapies in recurrent depression protocol. Open circles represent group that underwent medication clinic and active imipramine; solid circles, interpersonal psychotherapy and active imipramine; squares, interpersonal psychotherapy alone; solid triangles, interpersonal psychotherapy and placebo; and open triangles, medication clinic and placebo.

Figure 19.2 (Frank et al., 1990) Copyright © 1990 American Medical Association. All rights reserved.

The lack of an additive effect in lengthening the time to recurrence for patients receiving combination imipramine plus IPT-M likely reflects a ceiling effect: those receiving full-dose active imipramine, with or without IPT-M, had such a low risk of recurrence that there was essentially no room to improve upon those outcomes. The late Daniel Freedman, then editor of the *Archives of General Psychiatry*, on discussing the upcoming publication of this report in his journal, noted to the PI that it hadn't been a "fair fight" since they had used the highest doses of medication and the lowest doses of psychotherapy ever studied.

In the maintenance phase, all participants received either IPT-M or CM provided by the same therapist who had provided IPT in the acute phase in order to avoid a withdrawal-of-therapist effect. To be certain that therapists adhered to the randomly allocated treatment, a rating instrument was developed for independent raters to evaluate audiotaped maintenance sessions (Frank, Kupfer, Wagner, McEachran, & Cornes, 1991). The rating scale needed to distinguish IPT-M sessions from CM sessions (discriminant function) and to distinguish whether sessions contained predominantly IPT elements versus those of cognitive-behavioral therapy (CBT) or psychodynamic psychotherapy (contaminant function). Trained undergraduate students unaware of treatment assignment and the number of weeks in maintenance treatment rated a seven-minute segment that commenced five minutes into the session using the 27-item Therapy Rating Scale (TRS; Wagner, Frank, & Steiner, 1992). This scale rated interpersonal elements, somatic elements (indicative of CM), and cognitive elements (indicating CBT contamination). Meticulous analysis of a large number of variables (age, gender, severity of index episode, etc.) revealed a surprising finding: therapist–patient dyads that showed high interpersonal specificity (above the median) versus low interpersonal specificity (below the median) had longer euthymic intervals before suffering a recurrence. High specificity can be thought of as the extent to which the session was characterized by interpersonal interventions and was free of "contaminant" (somatic, cognitive, psychoanalytic) interventions. Although there were no detectable differences among individual *therapists* in overall treatment specificity across all cells, patients in patient–therapist *dyads* with high interpersonal specificity survived significantly longer before suffering a recurrence than the low-specificity group (see Fig. 19.2). The difference observed between high- and low-specificity dyads appeared to stem from the high-specificity group maintaining a sustained focus on the IPT foci of grief, role transition, role dispute, or interpersonal deficits. There was no difference in depressive severity between the two groups initially or over time (Frank et al., 1991).

IPT-M FOR LATE-LIFE DEPRESSION

A similar design was employed to study a sample of older depressed participants (Reynolds et al., 1999), the details of which are outlined in Chapter 14. That study's notable finding was improved social adjustment among patients randomized to combined treatment with nortriptyline and IPT relative to either monotherapy. This finding resembles that found among adult (non-geriatric) patients whose social adjustment improved with combined therapy with antidepressants and IPT (Weissman, Klerman, Paykel, Prusoff, & Hanson, 1974). Interestingly, the Social Adjustment Scale (Weissman, Kasl, & Klerman, 1976) scores obtained at three-month intervals over three years showed that patients who maintained their social adjustment during maintenance showed a 5.3% rate of recurrence versus 26.3% for patients whose Social Adjustment Scale scores declined (Lenze et al., 2002), although it is impossible to know whether this is a cause or effect of recurrence, or some combination of the two.

In this older population, recurrence rates differed among participants randomly assigned to IPT plus placebo versus CM plus placebo only when the IPT focus in the acute treatment phase was role dispute, not when it was role transition or grief (Miller, Frank, Cornes, Houck, & Reynolds, 2003). We hypothesized that the latter two foci were adequately resolved in the acute phase, whereas the tendency to revert to maladaptive coping strategies in the role dispute subgroup placed those participants at greater risk for recurrence unless they continued to receive IPT-M, which reinforced and helped them to maintain the better coping strategies they had learned in the acute phase. Some caution is warranted in making these inferences, however, as the numbers of participants in these subsets are few.

A second study of late-life depression examined the effect of paroxetine plus monthly CM, placebo plus monthly CM, paroxetine plus monthly IPT-M, or placebo plus monthly IPT-M on an older group of late-life adults (aged seventy and older) who recently remitted from an episode of major depression (Reynolds et al., 2006). Paroxetine plus IPT-M was not more efficacious than paroxetine plus CM, but it was more efficacious than IPT-M plus placebo at preventing recurrence. However, the authors note that IPT-M plus placebo may have been less successful in this study because the patients in this study endorsed more cognitive impairment and comorbid medical disorders (Reynolds III et al., 2006).

IPT MODERATES THE ROLE OF STRESS TO HELP PREVENT RECURRENCES

The correlation between psychosocial stressors and the onset of a major depressive episode is well documented. It therefore stands to reason that if IPT can help depressed patients to learn new skills, it should improve the quality of their interpersonal relationships, increase social support, and thereby relieve depressive symptoms. A maintenance paradigm of continued practice over time and a willingness to examine alternate coping strategies for newly encountered psychosocial problems could thus prove efficacious in reducing the risk of a new depressive episode even in the absence of antidepressant medication. Specific benefits of IPT-M over pharmacotherapy alone include the fact that although pharmacotherapy might serve to provide a kind of safety net in terms of patients' reaction to any severe life stress, no one would expect antidepressant medication to assist a patient in processing the emotional meaning and implications of the death of a loved one or some other major loss that occurred during the maintenance phase.

In addition to any practice effect from more sessions that reinforce IPT principles, new problems, of course, arise in the lives of remitted patients, so having regular booster sessions is helpful to review effective coping strategies and pitfalls in interpersonal strategies that led to depressions in the past. Regular access to IPT-M can also continue to assist patients in problem solving and finding solutions to new problems that they encounter as maintenance treatment continues.

MAINTENANCE IPT AND PERSONALITY PATHOLOGY

The extent to which personality disorders or traits predict risk for depressive episodes is a complex subject. IPT recognizes the literature acknowledging this association but makes no attempt to alter personality in short-term treatment (Klerman, Weissman, Rounsaville, & Chevron, 1984; Weissman et al., 2000). IPT focuses on reducing depressive symptoms by exploring ways to improve social role functioning. Cyranowski et al. (2004) assessed personality traits that reached the severity level of a personality disorder using the SCID-II rating instrument (First, Gibbon, Spitzer, & Williams, 1997) in one hundred twenty-five women with major depression after participants remitted from their index episode of major depression. Of the sample, 21.6% met criteria for a personality disorder, and this subgroup as a whole, compared to the entire sample, showed an earlier age of onset, more prior major depressive episodes, and a greater requirement for adjunctive medication required to achieve remission. The presence of a comorbid personality disorder also predicted higher recurrence rates and a shorter time to recurrence during a two-year maintenance phase, with nearly all of the recurrences occurring within the first year. The women who remained euthymic during the two-year treatment period showed measurable declines in personality pathology ratings over time. Although IPT makes no attempt to change personality traits *per se*, it is intriguing that cluster C personality severity declined with treatment, possibly suggesting that IPT-M may reduce the social role impairment that often accompanies criteria for personality disorder. Unresolved role disputes, for example, are common for individuals with personality disorders and can lead to divorce, terminated employment, and eventual estrangement or isolation (poor social function) from otherwise supportive social relationships. Another interpretation of these findings, however, is that although the SCID-II was assessed after participants had remitted from their index major depressive episode, some of the criteria used to determine a personality disorder diagnosis may have reflected a depressive diathesis that resolved more completely over time with continued treatment. In other words, chronic depression itself often induces poor social functioning and disrupted relationships, which can, in turn, further erode social support in a downward spiral that can make an individual appear to meet criteria for a personality disorder (Markowitz, 1998) (see Chapter 6). Continued treatment that yields long-term euthymia may reverse this downward spiral. In other words, sustained improvement in social functioning may encourage more satisfying relationships that then increase further social support. In this scenario, such an individual might meet apparent criteria for a personality disorder early on but not later in his or her continued recovery.

WHAT IS THE OPTIMAL FREQUENCY OF IPT-M?

Early trials of IPT-M used monthly follow-up visits comparable to follow-up visits for pharmacotherapy. Subsequently, various doses of IPT-M (weekly, bimonthly, or monthly) were compared in a randomized controlled trial of two hundred thirty-three women (age twenty to sixty) with recurrent depression scoring at least 15 or greater on the Ham-D (Hamilton, 1960) at baseline who sought nonpharmacologic treatment for an acute episode of major depression, (Frank et al., 2007). All participants were treated acutely with weekly IPT for at least four weeks; if they had not achieved a 33% reduction in Ham-D scores by then, the dose of IPT was increased to twice weekly. Remission was defined as three consecutive weekly Ham-D scores of 7 or less. Those who did not respond to weekly or twice-weekly IPT were offered the addition of an SSRI antidepressant for the acute episode. After a minimum of twelve weeks (and a maximum of twenty-four weeks) of study participation, those who were able to remain in remission for five additional weeks after achieving remission were then randomly assigned to maintenance therapy with IPT-M weekly, every two weeks or monthly for two years or until a recurrence of major depression. Those women who required the addition of SSRI to achieve remission were stabilized in continuation treatment for seventeen additional weeks before randomization to IPT-M alone, with careful monitoring of drug withdrawal and with clear discussion of the potential risk of recurrence off of antidepressant medication. Results showed that among seventy-four participants who achieved remission with IPT alone in the acute phase and finished two years of maintenance follow-up, fifty-five remained euthymic and nineteen (26%) suffered a recurrence. The mean time to recurrence was thirty-six weeks. There was no difference in time to recurrence between any of the IPT-M doses (weekly, every two weeks, or monthly). Of those participants who needed combined IPT and antidepressant medication to achieve a remission in the acute phase, twenty-six completed two years of maintenance, with thirteen (50%) suffering a recurrence. The authors concluded that IPT-M appears to be an effective maintenance treatment for recurrent depression in those who achieved remission with IPT alone, regardless of whether participants received weekly, every-two-weeks, or monthly follow-up sessions. However, they acknowledged that other factors in addition to the frequency of visits, such as treatment fidelity and treatment intensity, may also play a role. The authors further concluded that IPT-M alone could not be recommended for those participants who required combined treatment with antidepressant medication to achieve remission of their index episode. There was no difference in baseline Ham-D scores or the number of prior lifetime episodes between the IPT-alone responders acutely compared to the group that required sequential therapy, although there were more participants with comorbid panic symptoms in the latter group.

SUMMARY OF RESEARCH USING IPT-M

These research results suggest that IPT-M can play an important role in preventing recurrences of major depressive episodes, particularly among those who achieve remission with IPT alone. Combining IPT-M with antidepressant medication may have synergistic, bidirectional effects: antidepressant medication can reduce depressed mood, irritability, impulsivity, and anxiety, thus making interpersonal interaction more pleasant and more prone to positive, reciprocal affective experiences. Antidepressant medication may also provide a kind of neurobiological safety net in the face of life stress. IPT can develop and maintain better interpersonal skills to help resolve role disputes that could otherwise become impasses, leading to demoralization and potentially new major depressive episodes.

The science behind preventing recurrences still has far to go. Stable remission rates remain stubbornly low despite the use of rigorous stepped pharmacotherapy algorithms, as in the STAR*D trial (Warden, Rush, Trivedi, Fava, & Wisniewski, 2007). How to decide which recovered patients require IPT-M (either alone or combined with pharmacotherapy) to maintain euthymia awaits further research into a variety of other factors, such as interactions among personality traits, coping style, stress level, IPT focus, genetic vulnerability, and past traumas. In the one study of variable dosing of IPT-M frequency, we can conclude that women with histories of recurrent depression who achieve remission with IPT alone can be protected from a recurrence over two years with IPT-M alone delivered on a monthly basis (Frank et al., 2007).

CASE EXAMPLE

The following case describes the acute and maintenance phases of IPT for a depressed woman we will call Lauren who is going through a role transition (retirement). She appears to lack assertiveness and accepts many social roles passively; this often leads to resentment, which she has a hard time expressing. In the course of IPT, she gains greater awareness of her own pattern of behavior and works on strategies for change that she finds to be difficult to implement. IPT-M provides an additional opportunity to recognize her own pattern of drifting back into old maladaptive patterns of behavior that contributed to prior depressions, and to practice new, more adaptive coping strategies as new challenges arise in her life.

Lauren, a sixty-five-year-old married white Protestant woman, was referred for evaluation of depressive symptoms that began eight months after retiring from her career as a medical-surgical nurse in a general hospital. She was tearful throughout much of the initial interview, with her body slumped forward as she folded and refolded the tissue in her hands that she used to dry her frequent tears. At one point she asked the therapist if she was wasting his time, which could be better spent with other patients. She was clearly quite depressed but resisted the idea when it was reflected back to her, arguing that she had never thought of herself as someone who "took time to feel sorry for myself."

Lauren met DSM-IV (APA, 2000) criteria for a major depressive episode; her Ham-D (Hamilton, 1960) score of 30 indicated severe depression. She had what sounded like one prior major depressive episode while caring for her husband following a work injury. She described having had a terrible time getting out of bed, feeling low and blue, and losing eighteen pounds, but never sought or received any kind of treatment from mental health professionals. Her personal physician had offered her a trial of an antidepressant, but she had refused. She described an apparent spontaneous recovery from this episode that coincided with her return to work after taking time off without pay under the Family Medical Leave Act to care for her injured husband. Lauren drank alcohol only in small amounts on holidays and did not abuse other substances.

Lauren's interpersonal style could best be described as passive and highly responsive to the needs of others. She had a good work history as a nurse and was well liked and respected at work, within her family, and in her church. Lauren said she tried her best in her role as nurse and considered her occupation to be as much a religious mission to assist others as a livelihood. She tried her best to adapt to new work environments she was assigned without pressing for assignments she preferred. She noted with some "annoyance" that she always seemed to be the nurse transferred to the area of greatest need, although she never complained. She worked well independently, not seeming to depend upon others to complete tasks or to feel a sense of satisfaction from her efforts; therefore, she did not appear to meet criteria for dependent personality disorder or any other Axis II disorder.

Lauren reportedly tried her best to be a good mother, wife, nurse, and member of her community. She attended church regularly and participated in fundraisers there. Lauren definitely sounded like more of a follower than a leader: vacation plans always deferred to her husband's preference for the warmth of the beach, and she always submitted to her work transfers. She described her own needs as simply "to see that everything got done and then to curl up with a good book." She was pleased with how her two daughters had turned out and she expressed hope that her daughter Karen would get married and settle down to raise a family.

There was a family history of what could have been depression: she recollected that her mother "took to her bed" for weeks at a time but never received any treatment. Her father drank heavily during his forties and fifties but managed to cease thereafter. Her only sister, two years older, showed no history of mental illness.

Lauren eventually agreed to treatment and contracted for twelve to sixteen weekly sessions of IPT. Lauren said she was eager to retire "to be free to do some other things," and had taken the first opportunity to retire that her job setting allowed. The interpersonal inventory revealed a thirty-eight-year marriage to her only husband, Frank, who had been disabled in an industrial accident ten years prior and stayed at home. He was functional in the sense that he could drive a car, shop, and do small jobs around the house, but he walked with a severe limp and had balance problems that he worked on in a daily home physical therapy regimen he had learned during his rehabilitation. Lauren had two daughters: Alice, who lived in town with her husband and a two-year-old granddaughter Melissa, and Karen, who lived alone, a ten-hour drive away. Her father had died twenty years earlier. Her mother was in a nursing home in the city where her one sister lived; the sister "kept an eye on her." Lauren attended Sunday church services on weekends when she did not work and was friendly with members of a church group who baked holiday cookies for fundraising, but she could not identify a confidant or close friend whom she went out of her way to see.

She said she had liked being a nurse but was tired of the early hours and felt that she had devoted "enough of myself" to the service of others. Two of her former work colleagues had called to inquire about her since her retirement, wondering when they might get together, but she had not responded, stating that she knew they were busy and had families and that she did not want to bother them.

Lauren said in several different ways that retirement was not turning out the way she had envisioned it. She described her retirement dream as arising every morning and making her own plan for how she wanted to spend her day. She loved to read and hoped to read more, and perhaps to volunteer in the local library reading to younger children.

Lauren agreed with the therapist's suggestion that they focus their work on her role transition from working to retired status, as her depression seemed clearly to begin since she stopped working. They began by discussing her expectations for the roles she anticipated playing during retirement, which were (1) to be freed from the regimentation of work and the necessity to rise early in the morning; (2) to choose day by day what she wanted to do; and (3) to spend more time with books and in the local library, where she thought she might look into volunteering.

The reality of her retirement had taken a different course, one that made her feel she was on a treadmill. Her daughter Alice had obtained a part-time job shortly after Lauren retired, creating a mad scramble to find day care for Melissa. "As if by default," in Lauren's words, she began to babysit for Melissa as Alice's employment date loomed. Everyone was relieved and contented with the plan, except one. Lauren said that she felt that it was the duty expected of her since she had retired and was "free" to fill the need for babysitting, even though Alice had not actually asked whether she would mind. Once Alice's new job got rolling, the search for new babysitters had ceased, as Lauren felt everyone but she was satisfied with the arrangement. She wanted to make it clear to the therapist that she loved spending time with Melissa, that there was no problem there. She could not help feeling some resentment, however, that everyone just assumed that she would be happy to jump into another caregiving role when she so looked forward to getting a break from all the caregiving she had done over the years: raising her own family, nursing her husband back to health after his accident, and devoting herself to her patients as a nurse for thirty-five years. She quickly followed these statements with guilty ruminations about how she should not be complaining and that she should be happy and proud to be of service to a grandchild so loving and cute.

Her tendency to criticize herself was becoming clear as a longstanding pattern in which she would take on caretaking tasks without questioning whether she really wanted to or not. For example, Lauren felt an obligation throughout life, as a nurse, to attend to the health needs of those around her when they became sick, feeling it her duty to answer questions, check wound healing, and drive extended family members and some members of her church to and from their doctor appointments. She felt some satisfaction at the appreciation they always showed her, but she was beginning to feel weary and burdened by all the responsibility, and yet could not imagine herself saying "no" to any requests made of her.

This background set the stage for the middle phase of IPT, with repeated rounds of communication analysis, clarification, and decision analysis to try to better understand how Lauren came to find herself in her current situation. Role-play was used to practice strategies in which she could risk bringing up the subject of babysitting with her daughter for renegotiation, but these imagined forays were often followed by a retreat to the safety of her usual role as the dutiful caregiver, not questioning whether this was the role she wanted at this time in her life. When asked what she wanted for herself, Lauren frequently referred to the needs of Alice's family, their limited income, and how she "had no right" to ask Alice to pay for day care when she could provide it herself at no cost to them. Saying aloud that she would prefer not to babysit four days per week was very hard for her to practice even in the safety of the therapist's office. It was particularly hard for her to admit to feeling angry emotions, preferring to use words like "annoyed" as the strongest descriptors. The IPT therapist validated her feelings at every opportunity and tried to help her to explore ways to express her angry feelings. Lauren struggled with admitting angry feelings to herself, let alone expressing it to others.

Continued clarification that she had the right to decide her own future and had the capability to exercise that right if she chose to coincided with a brightening of her affect, an elevation in her posture, and a glimmer of a sense of humor. Her Ham-D score also fell from 30 to 14 over the same time period, and she was no longer having tearful episodes. The therapist pointed out the association repeatedly, with Lauren slowly gaining confidence that she "probably" could speak up more for herself.

With continued encouragement and role-play practice, Lauren finally asked for a few minutes of her daughter's time and summoned her courage to state clearly that she loved her granddaughter and was happy to help out with babysitting, but that she had been looking forward to having more time to also do other things during her retirement. She proposed that she continue to babysit two days per week but was able to bring herself to ask whether Alice could continue to search for other babysitting options for the other two weekdays she worked. To Lauren's surprise and relief, Alice readily agreed and asked her why she had not said anything sooner. Alice clarified that she and her husband could well afford to pay for that level of day care and thanked her mother for having done it all up to then. She went on to say that she wanted her mother to be able to enjoy her retirement in any way she saw fit, and that she knew it was her own responsibility to arrange for child care.

In her next session, the therapist helped Lauren to modestly celebrate the courage she showed in voicing her needs, perhaps for the first time in her life, even though she could construe it as causing someone else distress. The relief she felt from proving she could do something she found very difficult also required more work to continually link her action to the positive reaction she received and her reduction in depressive symptoms.

The therapist tried to consolidate Lauren's willingness to allow herself to be "at least a little selfish" by first exploring within herself what she really wanted, to then forge a plan of action for carrying it out, to practice stating her case clearly, and finally to be prepared to stand her ground if challenged. For example, they discussed how Lauren might have felt like reversing herself had her daughter been upset with her request or had she accused Lauren of selfishness, for example. They discussed these hypothetical outcomes that could not be predicted *a priori* and shored up her newfound courage to speak up for herself, as the following dialog will illustrate. The discussion particularly focused on the difference between selfishness (implying an excess of self-centered-ness) and self-protectiveness (something everyone should have at least some of).

THERAPIST: I think you did a fine job confronting your fear of speaking out for your-self and making your preference heard loud and clear.

LAUREN: Thank you! I could not have done it without your help.

THERAPIST: I am happy to do so, but I was merely the facilitator; you are the one who summoned her courage to do something that has been very hard for you to even consider.

LAUREN: I suppose you are right.

THERAPIST: In this instance, your daughter responded very positively to your request and actually asked why you had not spoken up earlier. You were heard and action was being taken to remedy your displeasure, right?

LAUREN: Right. It felt good that it all turned out as it did.

THERAPIST: Yes, I can see that in your expression and in the uprightness of your body language. I recall when we first met, you were bent over with your head hung, feeling very badly at the time.

LAUREN: Yes, I remember that. I don't feel that way now.

THERAPIST: That is precisely the point I am trying to make. Can you see that your taking action to present your true preference (after you have taken the time to figure out what it really is) can make you feel more free and fulfilled and excited about life—the opposite of feeling depressed, really?

LAUREN: Yes, I see the connection.

THERAPIST: I want to make sure that you see that your actions do matter when they are a reflection of your true preferences, particularly when negative emotions of anger or resentment are acknowledged, first to yourself, and then expressed in appropriate ways to others. Do you see that not doing so can make you feel demoralized or depressed?

LAUREN: I never thought about it quite that way, but I do understand what you mean. You are saying that if I remain true to myself and speak my mind, especially when I am stewing inside about something, I won't end up depressed.

THERAPIST: Yes, that is it in a nutshell. [pause] I think it would be helpful for us to consider how you might have handled the situation if you did not get such a positive response from your daughter. Do you think you would have been ready to stand your ground even if she was critical of your request?

LAUREN: I am not sure; that is a tough one.

THERAPIST: Would you like to try doing some role-play to practice what you might say and how you would handle your own feelings as they come up during such a conversation between you, with me playing the role of your daughter who reacts as if you are being selfish?

LAUREN: OK, I guess it would be good for me to try, but I've got to tell you, it is already making me nervous inside.

THERAPIST: All the more reason to practice here in the soundproof confines of this office, right?

LAUREN: Right . . . I guess.

In the remaining four weeks of a sixteen-week course of IPT, the therapist encouraged Lauren to continue to look for ways to advocate for herself by learning to pause in the face of any new explicit or implied requests for help and to give herself time to carefully examine her own preferences before agreeing or refusing to help. From these discussions, Lauren realized that she had probably been afraid to stand up for herself from an early age. She recalled growing up in a strict, religious family where "back-talking" was not tolerated and often punished.

The possibility of exercising the planned termination of their weekly IPT sessions caused Lauren to voice concern that she felt that she was just beginning to learn what it was like to be able to say "no," and that she did not yet feel very good at self-advocacy. She had never imagined that she would ever engage in talking therapy, but she could now see that it could be very helpful. She admitted that she could probably use twenty more sessions and that she really appreciated the therapist's help. At this point the option of maintenance IPT was discussed as an alternative to the planned termination in the original contract as a means to continue to practice self-advocacy in other situations, but also to have ample opportunity to practice decision making on her own between monthly sessions. The last acute sessions were spent solidifying the connection between the demoralization she suffered when she felt "that trapped feeling again," meaning those times when she had let herself fall into another obligation without first considering all of its implications that committed her time and energy, often with no end point in sight. The therapist put it another way: that Lauren had the power to minimize or prevent future depression from overtaking her by continuing to be true to herself, by revealing her true feelings, first inwardly, and then strategizing about how best to present them to others. Her therapist gave her votes of confidence at every opportunity, saying he believed that her new skills would serve her well in the future and that she could continue to apply them on her own but that they would meet for monthly hour-long sessions to review her progress.

Discussion of the Acute Phase

It was quickly apparent that Lauren routinely and almost automatically made herself available for the needs of others without questioning the impact this would have on her own preferences. Her therapist explored this pattern using IPT techniques of clarification, communication analysis, decision analysis, and role-play to help her to see the connection between her action/inaction and the consequences on her mood. The affects of anger and resentment for being committed to tasks she did not really want to do and her guilt feelings for admitting the same and concluding that such feelings were selfish and thus counter to her religious beliefs were explored, clarified, and validated. Allowing herself to be "just a little selfish" was normalized as something everyone needed to do to find a balance between self-advocacy and service to others. As she began to better understand these connections and her latent power to change them, her mood began to lift. Repeated role-play readied her to summon her courage to more effectively advocate for herself. Termination sought to consolidate her progress by applying the same techniques to other situations and to implement them accordingly.

As IPT does not explore early life relationships in depth, despite the likely connection between her strict upbringing and her current interpersonal relations with others, the therapist acknowledged her spontaneous insights but did not explore them further in order to keep IPT focused on her current relationships and life situations that had triggered the depressive episode. The chosen focus of role transition seemed obvious given the timing of the onset of her depression and her voiced disappointment about her retirement not working out as planned. One could also consider a role dispute focus, as Lauren's inability to confront or negotiate with her daughter seemed to complicate the role transition of her retirement with emotions of feeling trapped, angry, and depressed by this new, unanticipated commitment. Role dispute was not chosen as the focus since her daughter was not aware of Lauren's distress; the struggle was all within Lauren and kept secret from her daughter.

Maintenance Phase

In their first monthly IPT-M session, Lauren confirmed that her decision to halve her babysitting had been the right decision for her. She reported various pleasures in experimenting with craft hobbies like needlepoint art, exploring local antique stores, and actually making arrangements for part-time volunteering in the library as she had originally intended. Her mood remained in a range of Ham-D scores between 5 and 9.

In their sixth month of maintenance treatment, Lauren said she wanted to bring up something she had not previously discussed. It had to do with her husband, Frank. Perhaps the rapport that she had built with her therapist in the acute treatment and subsequent months of IPT-M emboldened her to reveal that she was afraid of Frank. He sometimes had a bad temper and yelled loudly, she said. She noted that his temper had seemed sharper since his accident and that she went to great lengths not to cross or upset him. She denied fearing physical contact, as he had never even threatened that in all of their married life, but she described cringing in anticipation of his verbal tirades. When asked to elaborate, she painted a picture of Frank as having been a hard-working heavy equipment operator, a "can-do" kind of guy who could get things done. His accident had knocked him unconscious and crushed his leg and pelvis. He required several surgeries and months of physical rehabilitation, and he was eventually awarded disability from workman's compensation. No brain damage was diagnosed, but the therapist wondered about possible closed head injury and subsequent behavioral changes.

When asked what specifically bothered her about her husband's tendency to show verbal outbursts and how she felt about it, Lauren had to think for a minute. She then responded by giving the example that every morning, her husband rose, had a light breakfast, and put himself through lengthy exercises to strengthen his vestibular system and then walk with his cane for a mile or more in their neighborhood or, in inclement weather, at their local indoor shopping mall. When asked to clarify how this related to her feelings of fear and anxiety anticipating a possible verbal outburst, Lauren revealed that she had been accompanying him on his morning walks on days she did not babysit, before beginning her own daily activities. She said that her husband seemed to enjoy her company, and she deliberately paced her stride to match his slow cadence to be supportive of his rehabilitation efforts. If they went to the mall, she accompanied him when he stopped for coffee or a chat with other mall-walkers he had met over the years. She mostly observed his interactions with these other retired men without entering into their conversations, and when pressed for how she felt about being there, she admitted that she was often bored. When asked directly if she disliked accompanying him on these daily walks, Lauren paused, and said she felt guilty for saying so but admitted that she usually could not wait for them to end so that she could get on with her own plans for the day.

When the therapist then asked why she continued doing what she disliked (confrontation), she said she was afraid to stop, fearing it might trigger a negative reaction in her husband, who might be disapproving or see her as uninterested in his welfare. Follow-up inquiry into why she could not just share her true feelings with her husband, even if he did express disappointment, revealed her fear and anxious anticipation that he could unleash another verbal tirade directed at her. A discussion followed of other times in her life when arguments with her husband had led to verbal outbursts on his part and how afraid she was to provoke him again. On these occasions he would raise his voice, which she described as "booming," and belittle her with statements such as "there is no way I am ever going to agree to that" or "I can't believe you could be so stupid to think that." She recalls feeling embarrassed and humiliated with these outbursts, as she felt her children and even the neighbors could hear his loud voice, and she secretly vowed to herself that she would do anything to avoid future occurrences of the same. From his accumulated knowledge of their communication analysis, her therapist pointed out that these outbursts were now rare, usually arising only between her husband and son-in-law when they discussed their political differences. She agreed and said that her son-in-law rarely discussed politics with him any longer for that very reason.

At this point, the IPT therapist pointed out that this scenario sounded similar to the babysitting situation with her daughter, as the following dialog will illustrate.

THERAPIST: Do you notice that when you perceive that people need something from you, your first impulse is to begin to think about how you might accommodate them—perhaps out of compassion, perhaps to gain their favor, or perhaps to avoid having them be annoyed or angry with you if you declined to help out?

LAUREN: Do you mean when I jumped in to babysit for my granddaughter?

THERAPIST: Yes, and also when you "volunteered" to walk with your husband every morning.

LAUREN: Oh, I see what you are getting at now.

THERAPIST: What connection is coming into focus for you right now?

LAUREN: You are connecting the two incidents to point out that I jump into situations that become like duties for me before I think through, in my heart of hearts, whether I really want to do it or not, what the cost will be to me.

THERAPIST: Can you share with me what you are feeling inside when you make these volunteering decisions?

LAUREN: [Pauses, thinking] I guess I feel that I do not want to disappoint them. If I am able to help out, I was raised to believe that you should contribute your own efforts at every opportunity.

THERAPIST: I accept that a helping attitude was inculcated into you when you were a child, but now that you are a fully responsive adult, how would you feel about making the choice to commit yourself by including your own preferences in the decision making?

LAUREN: Do you mean to ask myself what I would rather do instead of volunteering to be helpful?

THERAPIST: Yes, in these two examples you admitted to me that you did not want to babysit four days a week in your new retirement regimen, and you also told me that you would prefer to get up every morning and have the luxury of planning your own day after all the years you trudged off to the hospital before dawn, yet you volunteer to do otherwise, specifically go with your husband even though you are bored and eager to get on with your own day's agenda.

LAUREN: I see what you mean. I am not very good at saying what I really want, I guess.

THERAPIST: Perhaps this depression that has weighed you down for these past years has made you too timid for your own good. I recall that when you confronted your daughter about cutting back on babysitting and she agreed to do so, you told me that you felt better about yourself—more confident and less depressed.

LAUREN: You are right, I did. I struggled with a mix of feelings. I felt some guilt that I could be doing it and that I would be forcing them to spend money on a babysitter instead of me. I also felt nervous that my daughter might be disappointed in me or lower her opinion of me. In the end, I did realize that I was also feeling angry and resentful that, once again, I was the fallback for everyone who needed something. I have to say I did feel relief when I said something to her and she seemed to get my intention correctly and said I had the right to choose my own schedule in retirement. I felt a huge relief, and you are right, I felt lighter and happier to realize that my wishes could also be taken seriously, not just everyone else's.

THERAPIST: In light of what you just described, what are your feelings now about the situation you find yourself in with your husband?

LAUREN: I guess you expect me to have a talk with him about this, too.

THERAPIST: I am not the one in your shoes. I suspect you have already been coming to that conclusion on your own, but your feelings of anxiety about him potentially having a verbal outburst are making you hesitate.

LAUREN: You are right on both counts. I have been thinking about saying something, and I knew you would ask me about it coming in here today.

THERAPIST: Can you talk about your feelings about it right now?

LAUREN: I guess I feel a bit bolder than I used to, I mean about speaking up for myself. It is just that we have been getting along so well in general, I just hate to rock the boat.

THERAPIST: But you are still walking on eggshells around him, as if his temper might erupt at any moment. From the conversations you have described having with your husband, he sounds to me to be a pretty reasonable person to deal with lately . . . Could it be that you are being overly cautious by going out of your way not to provoke him?

LAUREN: Maybe I am. I guess I am. I just don't want to take a chance.

THERAPIST: So let's stick with this for a moment. If you stated your case honestly and clearly about not wanting to go with him on these daily walks, what if he reacts with disappointment? How would you feel about that, and how would you handle it?

LAUREN: I would be afraid he might yell at me; that's why I am not sure I want to try.

THERAPIST: Okay, but you told me in our earlier work together that you hoped your life would change for the better by not always continuing the pattern of doing things for others at your own expense.

LAUREN: Yes, that is about it.

THERAPIST: Have you been considering how you might approach this problem differently?

LAUREN: I guess I could just take a chance and say I don't want to go, and hope that he is OK with it.

THERAPIST: OK, what specifically might you say to Frank?

LAUREN: I guess I could just say that I don't want to walk today because I have something else I need to do.

THERAPIST: OK, how about this: if you pretend I am Frank for a moment, would you like to practice saying to me what you would like to say to him?

LAUREN: I guess I could try.

THERAPIST: Good, start whenever you are ready.

LAUREN: Frank, can I talk to you for a minute?

THERAPIST: Yes, what is it?

LAUREN: It's about your morning walks. I was thinking of doing some different things in the morning instead of going with you every time.

THERAPIST: Oh? What brings this on?

LAUREN: I just feel there are so many things I want to do and try now that I am retired, and there does not seem to be enough time in the day.

THERAPIST: Uh-huh.

LAUREN: I would still go with you sometimes but just not every time. Would that be OK with you?

THERAPIST: Just do what you want.

LAUREN: You're not mad at me for asking this, are you?

THERAPIST: Why would you think I might be mad?

LAUREN: I just thought you expected my company.

THERAPIST: Look, I have been doing this for years by myself while you were at work. Why would you think I can't do it on my own? Just do what you want.

THERAPIST: OK, I am going to change roles back to being your therapist. How did that feel to you?

LAUREN: A little scary, except I knew you would not yell at me.

THERAPIST: Are you convinced that your husband will yell at you?

LAUREN: No, not really; it's just that I'm not used to speaking up for myself. I guess it's like an ingrained fear in me or something.

THERAPIST: Yes, we have talked about how feeling depressed can make you more timid and even give up on expecting to get anything to go your way for a change, right?

LAUREN: Right.

THERAPIST: When you don't advocate for yourself, you start to feel angry and resentful inside, negative feelings that over time can leave you feeling demoralized about how your life is going at times, feelings that, when repeated over and over in various situations you encounter, have led to serious depression in your past. Right?

LAUREN: Yes, you are right. I guess I could just give it a try.

THERAPIST: And if he balks at your plan or appears disappointed with you, or even loses his cool again, how are you feeling right now about your preparedness to respond if that should happen?

LAUREN: I guess I should be prepared to stand my ground, right?

THERAPIST: I want you to do what is best for you.

LAUREN: I guess I could say that it isn't fair to me, to need to feel committed to always walking with you now that I've retired, since I paid my dues with all those years I worked and cared for all of the family needs, including taking care of you after your accident. All I am asking for is some flexibility to make my own schedule for a change . . . [pauses] and I would go on to say that I was not planning to do any less housework, cooking, shopping, or laundry, just the freedom to plan my own day and that you should not hold it against me. Something like that.

THERAPIST: How did that sound to you saying it out loud?

LAUREN: OK, I guess.

THERAPIST: Very good. That sounds like you are preparing to defend your position, which reflects how you are really feeling. I really like what you came up with. How did it feel to you saying it?

LAUREN: [sighs] Like a big relief, I guess.

THERAPIST: Are you ready to have such a conversation for real now with your husband?

LAUREN: Yes, if you think I am . . . I mean, yes.

THERAPIST: Good. Very good. I have no doubt you can do this and that you'll be glad you did so in retrospect, whatever your husband's reaction might be. You have the right to say these things as an individual who has self-respect and insists on respect for your point of view from the other important people in your life, even if they disagree with your conclusion.

LAUREN: Yes, you are absolutely right.

THERAPIST: Would you tell me straight out if you disagreed with me?

LAUREN: What do you mean?

THERAPIST: I mean that as a person who stands her ground and expresses her true opinions would be expected to do so with her therapist as well.

LAUREN: OK, I get it now. You are asking if I could manage to disagree with you, even though you are the teacher and I am the pupil, so to speak.

THERAPIST: Yes.

LAUREN: I don't know. It hasn't come up yet [pauses] but I will give it some thought. As a matter of fact, I disagree with you on one thing: that it is not always the best idea to share all of your feelings; sometimes it is best to leave some things unsaid.

THERAPIST: Can you say more about what you mean?

LAUREN: Like, you have to weigh what you think the impact of your words will be on others and then decide if you want to go through with it.

THERAPIST: And what if you conclude that your feelings are better left unsaid but you are left carrying around feeling angry or resentful inside?

LAUREN: Well, I guess that is the crux of the matter, isn't it. At that point I would have to make the choice about taking a risk.

THERAPIST: Do you feel you have the right to express your feelings even if it makes someone hearing them feel bad or angry or some other negative emotion?

LAUREN: Hmm [pauses]. Yes, theoretically, some things just need to be said regardless. Mind you, that is not what I usually do, but I suppose I ought to do it more often.

THERAPIST: That brings us right back to your dilemma of what to say or not say to Frank, doesn't it. Are you ready to find an opportunity to have this conversation with your husband and come back next month and talk about how it went?

LAUREN: Yes, I think I am ready. No, I am definitely ready.

Drawing the comparison with the babysitting issue and the need to figure out the best way to speak about her dilemma with her husband in hopes of renegotiating her participation in the morning walks was not nearly as difficult for Lauren to grasp as the babysitting issue had been during the acute phase of IPT. Having made this clarification, the therapist was gratified to see Lauren already beginning to formulate her own strategy for approaching this similar but new situation. As they would not meet again for another month, Lauren had ample opportunity to work on this new problem by herself. Lauren was willing to practice what she was planning to say in a role-play as they had done previously. The result of confronting her husband was again a positive experience for her, as her husband basically said he enjoyed her company when she wanted to come along, but that he had been following this routine for years when she was still working and was used to doing it alone. He clearly said she could come when she wanted to and decline when she had better things to do. No outburst resulted, which had been Lauren's greatest fear.

In subsequent monthly sessions, Lauren continued to recount instances where she chose to assert herself in various situations, such as saying "excuse me" when someone stepped in front of her in a checkout line in order to "correct their mistake." The therapist, pleased with her progress, pointed out nuances in the interactions she described as evidence that she was operating in a new, more assertive way, particularly when her internal "unfairness antennae" sent out a signal, as she put it. She remained euthymic for three years of monthly IPT-M without antidepressant medication until they mutually agreed it was time to terminate.

Discussion of Maintenance Phase

The fear Lauren described of being more assertive with her husband may have had roots in reality at some point in the past: a critical father she feared to speak out to, and Frank's irritability toward her and the children after his accident. Lauren seemed to continue to learn from new situations that the payoff for practicing being more assertive and speaking her mind was feeling freer and not suffering from the demoralization or depression that had previously accompanied remaining silently resentful and angry about committing herself to another "treadmill" of obligated service. Could the issue of asserting herself to her husband have been resolved had IPT ended with the acute phase? One would hope it would have following the work of consolidation with which the acute phase ended; however, the added value of IPT-M in this case was to give Lauren the opportunity to continue to practice her new skills with the therapist, whom she had learned to trust. The hesitation Lauren showed when the therapist pointed out the similar pattern between the babysitting and the morning walks issue with her husband indicated that she could benefit from reminders of the work they had done previously. This reminder seemed to trigger her other skills of strategizing how to approach the issue, for which she seemed to need less and less guidance over time.

The extra opportunities of ongoing therapy are a clear benefit of IPT-M for individuals like Lauren who struggle to be assertive for their own good as the added practice of being more assertive that is repeatedly linked with the lifting of her depressed mood builds confidence that she can avoid future depression by remaining true to her new, more assertive stance. The therapist encouraged her to search and struggle to find her own answers until he felt she was getting stuck, after which he provided a modicum of direct guidance. He also acknowledged that she connected the fear of her husband's rage with memories of a critical father but did not explore that subject further. Rather, the focus remained on the here and now, where attempts at change can be experimented with in real time.

Termination in acute IPT after twelve to sixteen sessions is made easier by maintaining the patient's efforts for change in interpersonal relationships or social roles outside of the therapy office, thus reducing the intensity of transferential attachment. In Lauren's case, her role transition to retirement, her reluctance to negotiate her babysitting duties with her daughter, and her perceived requirement to exercise daily with her husband were all influenced by her apparent life-long pattern of not being very assertive. The therapist assumed that the demoralization and depression she felt discouraged her from risking further self-assertion. With the help of IPT in the acute phase and with added reinforcement of IPT gains in the IPT-M phase, Lauren was able to develop a steadier pattern of interpersonal interactions in which she asserted her preferences more regularly and more carefully considered the pros and cons of commitments before agreeing to them. These efforts appeared to help prevent further episodes of depression over the three years of follow-up.

SUMMARY OF IPT-M

IPT-M has a proven track record of preventing depressive recurrences in two double-blind, placebo-controlled studies of recurrent unipolar major depression in adults and in one of two studies in late-life patients. Lauren's case illustrates the value of IPT-M. She maintained euthymia over a three-year period. Lauren's passive interpersonal style, which may have been a consequence of recurrent depression, made it hard for her to speak up for herself, putting others' needs ahead of her own and then suffering unexpressed resentment that culminated in depressed mood and feelings of hopelessness. She recognized this in IPT and subsequently worked on more effective interpersonal strategies for expressing her wishes. This did not come easily to Lauren, but with steady support and encouragement she was able to realize the benefits of confronting her fears of reprisal and rejection for speaking her mind. IPT-M alone (without the added benefit of maintenance pharmacotherapy) allowed Lauren to refresh her own commitment to self-assertion before jumping into commitments she might later have resented. Life events continued to challenge Lauren to practice her new coping strategies, the results of which helped her to remain free of a major depressive recurrence for three years.

Perhaps future research will allow more accurate predictions of who is at highest risk for recurrence, so that IPT-M can most effectively maintain euthymia and prevent recurrences, especially for patients who refuse, cannot tolerate, or fail to respond to antidepressant pharmacotherapy.

20

Interpersonal Psychotherapy for Group (IPT-G)

R. ROBINSON WELCH, MONICA S. MILLS, AND DENISE E. WILFLEY

Interest in adapting IPT to the group format (IPT-G) emerged in 1989 when Wilfley et al. developed a research protocol to compare cognitive-behavioral therapy (CBT) and IPT to treat non-purging bulimia nervosa (now known as binge eating disorder), using group as the intervention modality. Since then, IPT-G has been applied more broadly and is currently used to treat a range of patient populations and disorders. IPT-G has been investigated in the elderly (Scocco et al., 2002), adolescents (Rossello et al., 2008), pregnant adolescents (Miller et al., 2008), and veterans (Ray & Webster, 2010), with results indicating improved outcomes following IPT-G treatment. IPT-G also shows promise in the treatment of various disorders, including posttraumatic stress disorder (PTSD) (Campanini et al., 2010; Krupnick et al., 2008; Ray & Webster, 2010), depression (Bass et al., 2006; Rossello et al., 2008; Levkovitz et al., 2000; MacKenzie & Grabovac, 2001), postnatal depression (Klier et al., 2001; Mulcahy et al., 2010; Reay et al., 2006), depressive symptoms (Rossello et al., 2008), trauma spectrum disorders (Schaal et al., 2009), and binge eating disorder (Wilfley, 2000; Wilfley et al., 1993). The potential utility of IPT-G appears vast, and continued investigation across populations and disorders is certainly warranted.

OVERVIEW OF IPT-G

In altering an established individually focused intervention to a group format, it is necessary to consider the potential for diminishing the potency or delivery of the intervention. Conducting behavioral analysis, problem solving, or other traditionally individually focused interventions in a group setting requires involvement of not just the individual patient, but of the other group members. Thus, an intervention must be altered to include an interactive component when administering it in a group. Individually based IPT incorporates a wide range of specific interventions, and the goals and strategies prescribed to address the four problem areas—grief, interpersonal role disputes, role transitions, and interpersonal deficits—lend themselves well to the group modality. In fact, given the *interpersonal* focus of IPT, the group setting is arguably an ideal format in which to administer IPT.

ADVANTAGES OF IPT ADMINISTERED VIA GROUP MODALITY

IPT-G capitalizes on the fact that groups, by definition, are interpersonal and therefore provide a natural delivery platform on which to apply the strategies of IPT (Wilfley et al., 2000). Due to the range of social interactions that can occur in the group context, interpersonal skills developed in group therapy may be more readily transferable to participants' social lives than those developed in one-on-one individual therapy. Furthermore, groups where membership is based on diagnostic similarity (e.g., depression, binge eating, PTSD) offer a radically altered social environment for patients who have become isolated from others. Group participation alone, therefore, may help patients break patterns of social isolation and self-stigmatization that contribute to the maintenance of the disorder (Wilfley et al., 1998). Additionally, the group context may help to normalize patients' symptoms and alleviate concerns that they are alone in their psychiatric disorder (Kaplan & Sadock, 2007).

IPT-G IN COMPARISON TO OTHER GROUP
THERAPY MODELS

IPT-G differs from other group therapy models in the same ways in which IPT differs from other individual psychotherapies (see Weissman et al., 2000, for an overview comparing IPT to other therapies). In addition, several aspects make IPT-G different compared to other group modalities, including the following:

- *IPT-G is semistructured.* While IPT-G is structured in having distinct phases of treatment, strategies for addressing interpersonal goals, and focus on identified interpersonal problem areas, therapists' facilitation of the group sessions is less structured than in cognitive or behavioral group formats. IPT-G lacks an established agenda and pre-established thematic discussions, and the interactive process among group members is completely open.
- *IPT-G is focused on outside personal relationships.* IPT-G therapists place less emphasis on intragroup processes and relationships, and focus work on changing current interpersonal relationships outside of the group context.
- *IPT-G is action-oriented.* IPT-G members are expected to transfer the skills and insights developed during the group sessions to their interpersonal relationships outside the group. Towards this end, group members must

work on their individual goals each day and must be willing to discuss their relevant progress and/or challenges during the group treatment sessions.

For a more complete overview of distinctions across time-limited group therapies, see Table 20.1.

IPT-G TECHNIQUES

Maintaining the Focus on Current Interpersonal Relationships

Throughout the course of IPT-G, it is important to maintain a focus on current interpersonal relationships. The therapist must consistently keep each member's problem area and associated goals in mind while acting as necessary to refocus discussions that veer off track. Vague or symptom-laden discussions should be diverted to refocus members on specific and personal accounts of targeted interpersonal problems. Tangential discussions should be interrupted or related back to the central themes and goals of treatment. This approach emphasizes topics of personal emotional importance to members. By continuously reinforcing the connections among members and highlighting their relevance to the group as a whole, the therapist can maintain focus when members shy away from addressing problems directly while in group.

Linking Problem Areas

Each of the four problem areas addressed in IPT-G falls within the context of interpersonal relationships. Accordingly, certain problem areas share strategies with others. This similarity allows therapists to link one member's work with another's. For example, the tasks of developing or reestablishing social relationships and exploring feelings associated with the problem context apply to all four interpersonal problem areas. While integrating the four problem areas might seem problematic and create challenges in directly addressing members' identified problems, group members can actually benefit from reflecting on how another member's issue may relate to their own lives, even if it does not fall within their identified problem area. Moreover, many members will have a secondary problem area to address. Linking the various problem areas helps to encourage common work among group members and often enhances the sense of cohesion among group members.

Harnessing Member-to-Member Relationships

The group setting provides members with the opportunity to notice and comment on their reactions to each other. These interactions, which may include confrontation and clarification as well as support, can give group members awareness of their own contribution to the development of unsatisfying encounters with others. The group provides an ideal setting for patients with depression and eating disorders, many of whom share an interpersonal style of avoiding expression of negative

Table 20.1. Comparison of Time-Limited Group Models

Model	CBT	IPT-G Interpersonal	Yalom Interpersonal/ Interactional	Psychodynamic
Time frame	Time-limited	Time-limited	Time-limited, longer term	Time-limited, longer term
Group schedule	Closed	Closed	Open/closed	Open/closed
Composition criteria	Common diagnosis or situation (e.g., binge eating, depression)	Common diagnosis or situation (e.g., binge eating, depression)	Common interactional capacity	Common interactional capacity
Formal pre-group preparation	Moderate: Incorporated into early sessions	High: Incorporated into early sessions	Low	Low
Therapist style	High activity	Moderate activity	Low/moderate Activity	Low/moderate activity
Group structure	High: Programmed sessions	Moderate: Problem areas/goals established and actively kept in focus	Low/moderate	Low/moderate
Process focus	Low group process focus (managed to preserve teaching environment)	Moderate group process focus (managed to preserve group integrity, not interpreted)	High "here-and-now" group process focus (interpreted re: interpersonal conflict)	High "here-and-now" group process focus (interpreted re: intrapsychic conflict)

Homework	Written homework and behavior change expected	Changing interpersonal/social patterns expected	Not formally prescribed	Not formally prescribed
Mediating strategies	Identify and block negative cognitions	Identify and alter current interpersonal/social coping	Promote here-and-now interpersonal learning and existential awareness	Identify and understand interpersonal and intrapsychic conflicts
Focus on affect	Low/moderate	Moderate (identification of excessive or blocked affect re: current interpersonal tensions)	Moderate/high	Moderate/high
Extragroup socializing	Permitted, perhaps encouraged re: assigned tasks	No	No	No

feelings due to fears of rejection. In the group environment, these patients can experiment with discussing these feelings and receive feedback on how well they have expressed themselves—a process that enhances skill in successful conflict resolution.

INDIVIDUAL IPT TECHNIQUES TAILORED TO GROUP FORMAT

Clarification

In the short term, the goal of clarification is to increase members' awareness of what they have actually communicated. This technique is useful when a group member has said something in an unusual way or when the therapist wants to highlight a connection that the member seems to be making. To facilitate clarification, the therapist can ask a group member to repeat or rephrase a statement. Clarification is also helpful when a conflict arises among group members. By slowing members down, it allows them to explore the meaning of their feelings. In addition, the therapist should call attention to contradictions in group members' statements. For example, the member's affective expression may be discrepant with his or her verbal discussion.

Communication Analysis

This technique is used to identify communication difficulties and to help members learn to communicate more effectively. By asking an individual group member to recall in detail a recent interaction or argument with a significant other, the therapist can identify difficulties in communication and underlying assumptions that the group member makes about others' thoughts or feelings. Other members can then share their reactions with the speaker. After exploring associated issues, the group can suggest alternatives to poor communication.

Encouragement of Affect

Learning awareness of internal feelings leads to learning to express, accept, and understand what such feelings mean. Two specific techniques available to this end include prompting the member (1) to acknowledge and accept painful affects, and (2) to use his or her affective experiences to bring about desired interpersonal changes. The group facilitates the first technique, providing an environment where group members can express their feelings. Group members may be unassertive and not feel anger when their rights are violated, or they may be unassertive and feel anger but lack the courage to express it directly. In such cases, it is important for the therapist to facilitate such affective expression.

The second technique involves teaching group members how to use affect in interpersonal relationships. The therapist can assist group members in identifying their feelings and in understanding the catalyst for such feelings. For instance, when a group member expresses frustration towards a coworker regarding a contentious interaction that day, working with the member to identify the specific feelings associated with that interaction and to understand what it was about the interaction that led to such feelings can be particularly useful. By learning to identify, understand, and acknowledge their feelings, members can learn to distinguish between real-life situations that are best managed by expressing affect and those best managed by suppressing affect.

Supporting Active Progress towards Goals

It is generally best to encourage members to examine feelings and expectations first, before moving on to try out new behaviors. With regard to the example above, the therapist and group can work with the member to identify potential strategies for effectively managing the feelings towards the coworker and encourage him or her to engage in such strategies. Then, once group members attempt new behaviors, the group can help individual members to evaluate their outcomes and decide whether they need a different course of action. Ongoing assessment of progress and highlighting of changes are necessary to help members translate in-group discussions to outside application in their daily lives and to recognize the effect of changing interpersonal functioning on their symptoms.

Summarizing

A review of important group themes that emerge during sessions can have a supportive, clarifying, and unifying effect on group members. Sometimes a member will spontaneously provide a summary, while other times the therapist can comment on significant themes. At the end of each session, it is useful for the therapist to review the themes covered throughout the group and highlight significant aspects of the group discussion related to members' identified goals. If deemed useful, the therapist can send written group summaries to members following each session.

TIMELINE AND STRUCTURE

Groups often take time to become cohesive, a necessary development if members are to engage in psychological work together. Cohesion follows the development of a basic sense of trust in the other group members, a sense that the group is a safe and supportive environment. Groups of less than 16 sessions often encounter constraints on the therapeutic possibilities, as they spend most of the first half of treatment becoming a true working environment, and most of the second half in the shadow of termination. To allow adequate time to foster cohesion and engage in the formal work of IPT, we recommend that IPT-G groups comprise twenty ninety-minute sessions.

In addition to these twenty sessions of group psychotherapy, three individual meetings over a five-month time period should take place. Individual meetings should occur at pretreatment (two hours), mid-treatment (one hour), and posttreatment (one hour). We recommend that group size range from seven to nine members with one or two group leaders, depending on resources and training needs. The initial phase (Sessions 1–5) of IPT-G is devoted to managing negative feelings and developing positive group norms as group members test out and refine their individual target problem area(s). In the intermediate phase (Sessions 6–15), group members work toward common goals and practice newly acquired social skills inside and outside the group. The final, termination phase of treatment (Sessions 16–20) consolidates gains the group members have made during treatment and prepares them for the termination of the group. Specifically, the therapist works to help group members to feel confident in their ability to apply the skills and understanding acquired during treatment once they no longer have support of the group. Some members may express reluctance to discuss the pending termination of the group, and such feelings are addressed and processed directly to help manage this sense of "loss" and prepare members for future work on their own.

While most effective in the format outlined above, IPT-G has proven useful under more constrained timelines as well. For instance, IPT-G can be employed intensively in day treatment programs or inpatient settings that schedule several group sessions per day (Schramm et al., 2008; see Chapter 21). In such settings, patients can establish short-term interpersonal treatment goals and address them both within the group and the treatment ward milieu. Therapists may take on a more instructional role in working with more severely impaired patients in these settings. An outpatient or day treatment program can use brief, open group IPT-G to address acute situational problems. Such groups might extend eight sessions over the course of several months with a constantly changing membership. Group sessions must be highly structured in this model, and the group functions as a supportive audience, providing encouragement and ideas.

Group Composition

The double constraints of a time limit and the group format render diagnostic homogeneous composition essential. IPT-G groups should be composed on the basis of specific criteria, such as depression or binge eating. Homogeneous composition brings common target problems that enhance motivation and facilitate the rapid emergence of a working focus for the group. This promotes early cohesion and expedites movement through the crucial early stages of group development. It creates an environment where the members feel almost immediately understood, often in contrast to their experiences in the outside world. For example, members of a binge eating group experience relief at being able to talk about details of their eating behavior that have likely been kept a carefully guarded secret. This instant sense of membership allows the group to move forward rapidly, allowing more time for advanced interactional work.

We recommend that groups begin with seven to nine members. Losing a member or two is not uncommon, but if membership drops below six it becomes increasingly difficult to maintain a strong interactive group atmosphere. Group membership should ideally be closed, with all members beginning and ending together; in reality, adding members over the first two or three sessions (only) may prove necessary. This should be minimized, as any change in membership reconfigures the group's relationship balance and sets back the level of group work.

Group composition requires system-level thinking. As a general rule, it is useful to identify patients who may not fit into the group or may impede group progress.

Specific considerations in selecting IPT-G group members include whether an individual fully meets the purpose of the group (e.g., binge eating, major depression); a single member who is significantly older or younger than the rest; a single member of a particular gender; active suicidal ideation or an acute, severe current stress situation, which might monopolize group discussion during the early sessions and be more appropriately treated in individual IPT; inability to identify focal problem areas during assessment; a highly defended personality style, making the individual likely to intellectualize the nature of his or her own interpersonal problems, and those of others; low motivation; availability for all group session dates; and more than three members with moderate personality pathology. These considerations are not intended as absolute criteria but rather as a screening guide to alert the therapist to possible difficulties. Seasoned therapists adept at IPT may certainly be able to manage individuals who fall into some of the aforementioned categories, such as those experiencing acute distress or who are highly intellectualized, and such therapists may choose to include these individuals in group treatment. Overall, only *major* discrepancies across potential group members matter; minor fine-tuning of membership is generally unnecessary.

PHASES OF IPT-G

Each of the three IPT phases has specific strategies and tasks for therapists and patients (Weissman et al., 2000). These phases are defined to guide therapists in helping individuals to identify problem areas, work on their goals, and consolidate their work in treatment. Although these same phases reflect an individual's progression in IPT-G, they do not reflect the stages of group development, nor do they necessarily provide intervention strategies for fostering healthy group development. As such, a stage-oriented group approach (MacKenzie, 1994) complements the structure of the therapeutic tasks and the three phases of IPT. This model of group development parallels the developmental sequence of the three IPT phases (Table 20.2).

Therapist Activity Level in IPT-G

How "active" a therapist is during group psychotherapy sessions can vary widely, ranging from using a detailed agenda to maintain control of process, to moderate control through group exercises and active focusing techniques, to relatively unstructured groups that have only a general common direction or thematic focus. Therapist activity level for IPT-G falls in the middle of this range, with the therapist maintaining an active stance to keep members focused and engaged regarding predetermined areas of clinical relevance, while allowing the group to pursue pertinent issues that arise, as well as noting interactions within the group. Maintaining this stance is crucial, as a constantly shifting structure will fragment the group and impede effective group development.

The IPT-G therapist's role involves greater emphasis on maintaining constructive group properties and less on specific therapist interventions. Strategic group management establishes structure, with the expectation that much of the therapeutic potential will arise through the vehicle of group interaction rather than from the

Table 20.2. LINKING THE PHASES OF IPT TO THE STAGES OF GROUP
DEVELOPMENT

IPT Phases/ Tasks	Group Stages	Members' Work	Therapist Interventions
Initial Sessions 1–5: Identify problem areas	*Engagement* Session 1 & 2	Members seek structure as they grapple with the anxiety of being in a group and sharing their problems.	Therapist establishes a structure that encourages appropriate self-disclosure and facilitates norms for effective communication.
	Differentiation Sessions 3–5	Members work to manage negative feelings over interpersonal differences as these emerge in the group.	Therapist helps members understand their reactions in the context of interpersonal differences in their outside social lives.
Intermediate Sessions 6–15: Work on goals	*Work* Sessions 6–15	Members work out differences and strive toward common goals.	Therapist facilitates connections among members as they share their work with each other and encourages practice of newly acquired social skills inside and outside the group.
Termination Sessions 16–20: Consolidate treatment	*Termination* Sessions 16–20	Members struggle with how to manage the impending loss of connection with other group members.	Therapist helps members to consolidate their work and to plan continued work and assists members in grieving over loss of the group.

therapist directly. Particularly in the early phase of the group, the therapist must pay attention to developing a cohesive working group environment. Once positive group process norms are established, the specific issues of individual members can receive greater attention. The therapist encourages active application to outside relationships and encourages the group to review and discuss how they are implementing and experiencing these changes. The therapist does not emphasize specific intragroup interactions, managing rather than exploring these. Although active, the therapist's role largely consists of promoting therapeutic group activity: hence members may experience the therapist as a facilitator who sits, to some extent, in the background.

Maintaining a Focus on Each Individual's Work

The challenge of adapting individual psychotherapy to the group modality lies in maintaining an intensive focus on individual patients' problem areas while avoiding the trap of merely providing individual therapy in a group setting. To establish a therapeutic stance compatible with IPT, yet appropriate for the group format, we recommend that therapists (1) schedule individual meetings with patients, (2) conduct a thorough assessment using a diagnostic interview, serially applied symptom severity rating scales, and the interpersonal inventory to establish interpersonal treatment goals prior to the first group meeting, (3) provide a thorough orientation to IPT-G, (4) mail weekly group summaries to group members, and (5) use interventions informed by group stage development theory.

INDIVIDUAL MEETINGS

Individual meetings compensate for the loss of the sustained, exclusive attention that patients receive in individual psychotherapy. First, in a pre-group individual meeting, therapists focus on identifying interpersonal problem areas, establishing an explicit treatment contract to work on problem areas, and preparing patients for group treatment. At the midpoint of the intermediate phase (between Sessions 10 and 11), a mid-treatment individual meeting provides an opportunity for the therapist to conduct a detailed review of each patient's progress and to refine interpersonal goals. The final individual meeting should occur within a week of the final group session. This posttreatment individual meeting develops an individualized plan for each patient's continued work on his or her interpersonal goals.

DIAGNOSTIC INTERVIEW AND INTERPERSONAL INVENTORY

The first portion of the pre-group meeting is used to assess the patient's interpersonal history through standard diagnostic interview and administration of the interpersonal inventory (Weissman et al., 2000). The interview establishes a DSM-IV diagnosis, along with a general formulation that pulls together past development, current stress, and relevant psychological issues. The therapist may then decide whether the patient is suitable for the group being planned.

Patients should be informed if a disorder has been diagnosed, with the intention of assigning to the patient a "sick role." The therapist should review symptoms, explain them as part of the disorder, and describe the relevant course of treatment. As with individual IPT, the "sick role" temporarily relieves each group member of responsibility for his or her current state, placing the blame, instead, on the diagnosed disorder. Furthermore, assignment of the "sick role" allows each member to receive compensatory (if time-limited) care that has not been adequately received, or felt as received, from others, and informs the patient of the obligation to cooperate with treatment.

The interpersonal inventory allows the therapist to identify targeted interpersonal problem(s) (i.e., interpersonal deficits, role disputes, role transitions, or grief) and to formulate prescriptions for change. In individual IPT, the first few sessions involve a detailed examination of the patient's interpersonal history via the interpersonal inventory, and the formulation of problem areas and goals that will guide the therapeutic work. Because this luxury of time is not available in the group IPT format, the therapist must rapidly discern and evaluate patients' interpersonal problem areas during the pre-group meeting and develop target goals that will become the focus of each patient's group work. Target goals should refer to specific persons, specific events, and specific interpersonal themes. This ensures particularizing the target goals in language that maximizes personal meaning for the patient. Having identified a goal, the therapist will want to match concrete ideas for change, collaboratively identifying the specific steps the patient will take to improve relationships and socialization. The therapist should provide these goals to the patient in writing and address them with the patient throughout the course of group treatment.

Here are case examples for each of the four problem areas:

Grief. The death of your wife four years ago was a very difficult time. Her lengthy illness with cancer occupied a great deal of your time and energy, and her demanding nature complicated your caring for her. From your description, it appears that you never really addressed the actual event of her death: you looked after all the funeral arrangements, and then returned directly to work. You have acted responsibly in caring for your three young children since then, though perhaps this focus also diverted you from dealing with both the grief and the anger you describe experiencing.

Goal: Unresolved grief is a common trigger for depression. You will need to let yourself go back in time to re-experience all that was happening around the time of your wife's death. This will be a complicated but important task. On the one hand, you adored your wife; on the other hand, her rather forceful personality became increasingly demanding during her illness. You may help this process of working through the grief by going through pictures or letters you have from your wife and also talking to good friends who were involved at the time. You might also think of reconnecting with her by visiting her grave, something you've been avoiding. The group will provide an opportunity to talk about your wife from both the positive and not-so-positive perspectives and give you an opportunity to let yourself grieve.

Interpersonal Disputes. You describe your current depression as being directly connected to a lengthy intimate relationship about which you feel quite ambivalent. On the one hand, you question whether James will allow it to progress from its present state into a full and committed relationship; on the other, you find yourself quite dependent on the relationship to fulfill your legitimate emotional needs for a close bond with someone. You feel that this impasse affects your feelings about yourself and your future.

Goal: No one can make this decision for you, but it is important that you resolve it, by either negotiating a commitment for a future with him or resolving that the relationship must end. It is important to break out of the stuck position in which you have felt yourself trapped for several years. The group will provide an opportunity to explore this relationship and especially the emotions it evokes for you. Talking about the implications of the alternatives and getting ideas from others in the group may help you in your decision.

Role Transition. You see yourself as somewhat sheltered and naïve and feel very much under parental supervision, even though your parents live abroad. You are acutely aware of your parents' admonitions, which are always in your mind, and you describe these negative messages as continually reinforcing your depression. Although you do wish to maintain connections with your parents, you feel that the current ways of interacting are damaging to you. You want to move on to make your own decisions in your life.

Goal: Your goal is to begin setting clear boundaries with your parents. This will entail standing up for yourself and setting limits on your parents' influence so that you are not as enmeshed in their expectations (or at least your ideas of their expectations). Part of this task is to come to terms with just how emotional you feel about this situation, while maintaining control of your feelings. The group will provide an opportunity to talk about these issues, including your emotions as you experience them in the group, and to develop strategies that allow you to react less to your parents and increase your social network to include more peer relationships.

Interpersonal Deficits. You describe yourself as quite socially isolated, even though you have a variety of potential creative interests that you could share in social groups. From your descriptions, you can be quite open and friendly in the workplace, but this changes immediately when you leave work. Depression generally responds to an increase in interpersonal contact and support.

Goal: It would be helpful to become more actively involved in social organizations associated with your interests. Your membership would be an opportunity to talk to others and perhaps develop some ongoing friendships. You would also have an opportunity to lower your anxiety about how people might see you and whether that corresponds to your view that you are ugly. It will be important to discuss this goal with the group and use the group sessions to monitor efforts to become more involved and self-disclosing.

Finally, before the patient begins the group sessions, the therapist must prepare each patient for group treatment by linking each patient's individual goals to those of the group as a whole. We encourage patients to think of the group as an "interpersonal laboratory" where they can develop ties to others, examine naturally occurring "impasses" in the formation of intimate relationships in detail, and experiment with new approaches to handling interpersonal problems. We stress to patients that they should not use the group as a substitute for a social network, but use it instead to work on modifying their current interpersonal situations or intensifying important existing relationships.

Orientation to IPT-G

Almost everyone joining a group will have some apprehension, so the chance to discuss the proposed group in detail is reassuring. The process of doing so establishes basic rapport between the therapist and patient, which helps to sustain members through the early sessions. An open discussion about the group's duration, including the date of the final session, allows the therapist to respond to concerns or questions about the rationale for a time-limited approach. In time-limited groups

Table 20.3. SUMMARY CHECKLIST FOR PRE-GROUP MEETING

1. Discuss chief complaint and symptoms/syndrome.
2. Obtain history of symptoms.
3. Assign patient the "sick role."
4. Establish whether or not there is a history of prior treatments for the disorders or other
5. psychiatric problems.
6. Assess patient's expectations about psychotherapy.
7. Reassure patient about positive prognosis.
8. Explain IPT and its basic assumptions.
9. Complete an interpersonal inventory (i.e., a detailed review of important relationships):
   - Review past interpersonal functioning (e.g., family, school, social life).
   - Examine current interpersonal functioning (e.g., family, work, social life)
   - Identify the interpersonal precipitants of episodes of symptoms.
10. Translate symptoms into an interpersonal context.
11. Explain IPT techniques.
12. Contract for administrative details (i.e., length of sessions, frequency, duration of treatment, appointment times).
13. Provide feedback to patient regarding general understanding of IPT problem area(s), interpersonal target goals, and interpersonal triggers.
14. Collaborate on a contract regarding the treatment goals.
15. Explain tasks in working toward treatment goals.

such as IPT-G, therapists stress the importance of attendance and punctuality to patients before group treatment begins. We explain that attendance and punctuality have broader implications than in individual therapy because of the deleterious effect on the entire group. We specify the number of sessions that can be missed, recommending no more than four absences for a 20-session group.

Socializing between group members outside of group sessions deserves discussion. As IPT-G highlights the interactional process, we strongly discourage such contact. In the age of Facebook it is difficult to prevent group members from having outside contact. Nonetheless, we clarify as members begin that IPT-G is intensive psychotherapy, and that becoming social friends with other group members may complicate using the group effectively. Confidentiality always deserves discussion, as it will concern almost everyone. (See Table 20.3 for a summary checklist for the individual pre-group meeting.)

Weekly Group Summaries

Therapists can provide group members with weekly group summaries (a method adapted from Yalom, 1995) that they prepare following each session and mail to group members at least twenty-four hours before the next session. (All group members receive the same mailed set. To protect confidentiality and patient identity, it is imperative to use only group members' initials throughout these summaries and to ensure that mailings accord with HIPPA guidelines.) These four- or five-page summaries include a discussion of the transactions that occurred during each session and their implications for each patient's recovery, notes about the group process, the common interpersonal problems of those in the group, and how to use the group most effectively. Because writing group summaries can be time-intensive, an alternative may be the use of *self-help manuals*. In this approach, which has not received formal study, all group members receive the same self-help manuals with the instruction to read them during the course of treatment.

Interventions Informed by Group Stage Development Theory

Maintaining the important individual focus in IPT-G requires attention to developmental processes that characterize time-limited groups. The group's developmental sequence emerges naturally, and it is essential for therapists to understand the stages of group development in order to manage the group effectively while maintaining the interpersonal focus IPT requires (see Table 20.2). Attending to normative transitions in the group intensifies cohesion, prevents premature dropout, and assists patients in making otherwise difficult interpersonal transitions. Informed therapists who can predict critical transition points across group sessions and use "stage-appropriate" interventions are more likely to effectively facilitate the work of group members.

THE IPT GROUP

Initial Phase

The tasks of the initial phase of treatment are to refine and consolidate, at a group level, the tasks introduced in the individual pre-group meetings. By helping group members to make preliminary connections between their symptoms and relationship difficulties, the therapist sets in motion a productive momentum. The therapist then amplifies this momentum as members begin to learn to work together as a group. Sessions 1 to 5 represent IPT-G's initial phase, during which the therapist has the following objectives:

- To cultivate positive group norms and group cohesion
- To emphasize the commonality of symptoms and how they will be addressed
- To educate members about IPT-G theory and their role in treatment
- To review the interpersonal inventory of each group member and link his or her symptoms to the interpersonal context
- To consolidate the principal problem area and establish a treatment contract.

Session 1: Getting Started

The main objective in this first group meeting is to help members join the group without overdisclosing information. Given the extensive pre-group preparation and

Table 20.4. SUMMARY CHECKLIST FOR SESSION 1

Therapist Tasks

1. Start and end group on time.
2. Welcome and introduce members.
3. Cultivate positive group norms and cohesion:
4. Reiterate the common diagnosis, and generate the expectation of recovery.
   - Educate about IPT treatment, group structure, and process issues.
   - Encourage all members to join in the discussion of interpersonal problem areas and associated target goals, using information gleaned in pre-group interviews.
   - Begin to facilitate member self-disclosure.

Individual Patient Tasks

1. Introduce self (including details regarding reason for joining group, work stress, activities, significant others).
2. Begin to understand IPT treatment structure and group process.
3. Develop feelings of connection to other members.
4. Reveal and begin to clarify initial target goals.
5. Perceive an expectation of recovery.

goal formulation in IPT-G, members not uncommonly come "charging out of the gate" during the first session. When this occurs, the therapist should educate the group and encourage members to proceed slowly, assuring them that there will be plenty of time for them to get to know one another. (See Table 20.4 for a summary checklist covering Session 1.)

The following excerpt comes from a first session of IPT-G for depression. The therapist begins by orienting members to the process of sharing a little about themselves and their goals:

THERAPIST: Today you will begin to communicate with people you don't know and find out what it's like to be in a group. Talk a little bit about who you are and what brings you here. And then, if you feel like you can, maybe share a little bit about some of the goals that you have set for yourself or some of the things that you think you're going to be interested in working on over the next twenty weeks. Next session, we will start talking more about the important people in your life and the people that you're really needing to make changes with. So, that's how we'll have things unfold over at least the next couple of sessions. Again, as things come up, and as issues come up with the goals, we'll want to talk about that with you. Who would like to start?

SAMANTHA: I will. My name's Samantha. I've been a secretary for many years. I have a great husband, a terrific little toddler. So, externally, everything just seems great, but I've been really depressed. I just got the group goals as I was leaving for tonight's session. I didn't really get to look at them, except at the traffic lights.

THERAPIST: One of the things we had talked about being important [in the pre-group interviews] was what other group members have been talking about today, about not feeling validated. And I think that was one of the things you talked about, too. So not being validated by your parents and then not feeling like you've been able to let other people give you positive feedback or say good things about you, especially even your husband . . .

SAMANTHA: Yeah.

THERAPIST: That seemed like a real important connection.

SAMANTHA: It was. Just after I had met with you, it was just—I sat out in my car and I cried. I've thought about it a lot since I met with you both. It touched on things. And I mean I've had therapy for years, and nothing ever struck a chord for me like it did in my session with you both.

THERAPIST: Also, I think you mentioned difficulties in your work situation as well. You find yourself feeling frustrated, not feeling like you have the right to speak up.

SAMANTHA: Right.

THERAPIST: Right. And I think—Caroline, you had mentioned that, too, not feeling like you had the right to express yourself.

CAROLINE: For me, it is more with my family, not so much work situations. I don't want to hurt anyone's feelings so I tend to keep it to myself. I don't want to feel like a burden.

THERAPIST: . . . so, feeling it is not okay to share your feelings.

SAMANTHA: . . . uh, that's creating a problem more and more within myself and in my relationships.

CAROLINE: For me too. It is so hard, though, to do that.

THERAPIST: Is anyone else connecting with this issue?

Notice how the therapist assists Samantha by bringing in information from the pre-group meetings and guides her to clarify her goals, while encouraging others to join the discussion.

Session 2: The Role of Members

The group climate intensifies in Session 2 as members reveal more about themselves, their relationships, and their emotional reactions. The group is on track if members can discuss key people in their lives, begin to show signs of connection to each other, and demonstrate some understanding of the association between symptoms and interpersonal functioning. The therapist focuses in this session on members learning to identify and manage the emotions they experience in the group. Some members might hint at feeling overwhelmed by emotions. Members may also worry about "fitting in" with the group or whether the group will be help them. It is useful, therefore, to urge members to stick with the process, and let them know they will likely feel more comfortable as they come to trust each other more. (See Table 20.5 for a summary checklist covering Session 2.)

By the second session, the initial review of target goals in Session 1 will likely lead members to discuss ways in which they have begun to apply new approaches to their problem areas. In this excerpt from an IPT-G binge eating group, notice how the

Table 20.5. SUMMARY CHECKLIST FOR SESSION 2

Therapist Tasks

1. Start and end group on time.
2. Review introductions and important structural aspects of IPT, as needed.
3. Teach members their role in IPT treatment.
4. Cultivate positive group norms:
   - Encourage all members to join discussion of interpersonal relationships related to target goals.
   - Continue to assist members in making connections among target goals, difficulties managing relationships, and associated symptoms.
   - Facilitate member self-disclosure and awareness of feelings.
   - Help members begin to modify goals and to understand how to apply them.

Individual Patient Tasks

1. Deepen feelings of connection to other members.
2. Continue to learn how to use group structure and process to work on target goals.
3. Review significant interpersonal relationships.
4. Continue to make connections among target goals, difficulties managing relationships, and associated symptoms.
5. Begin to share more about self and feelings.
6. Begin to modify target goals, and understand how to apply them in daily life.

therapist redirects Robert's focus on his symptoms to an awareness of his struggles in his current relationships with his wife and father:

THERAPIST: Many of the goals you have created center on the important people in your lives. Much of the binge eating centers on either difficulties in relationships or lack of relationships. As you share more about how your goals are fitting, also talk more about these important people. Not only does it give us more information, so we understand you more fully, but it also gives us the opportunity to help you achieve some of these relationship goals.

ROBERT: Well, for me, last week was a pretty mellow week as far as my eating. I spent a lot of hours at work, so I didn't have a whole lot of hours to eat, which was good. I had an episode Sunday, though. When I finished my work, I went in and started cooking, and I didn't stop until I got a phone call. Thank goodness he called me last night because I would've eaten all the way through till this morning.

CO-THERAPIST: One of the things you shared with me, and I think a lot of you have talked about this, is that eating is a way to unwind, you know, and to kind of de-stress. Instead of talking to or doing something with someone, a friend or spouse, you turn to food.

ROBERT: Boy, did I unwind, right on the refrigerator . . .

CO-THERAPIST: How are some of the other things going with working on your goals, with your relationship with your wife?

ROBERT: Good. My wife and I are actually talking quite a bit more. She's not used to that, so she's kind of wondering. But then she knows why I'm asking her questions and then talking to her more, because of the group and my goals. She's pretty private herself and doesn't talk a lot either. So it's weird for us to do that. You know, it's like I try to sneak the information out of her.

CO-THERAPIST: So, that was one of the things you're working on, to share more? It's great that you're already trying to do that. I think a few others have that as a goal also.

ROBERT: Yeah, sharing with her more in general and also about how I feel about my father. He's out of the hospital. I haven't known him for very long, since we were only recently reunited, so I want to keep him around as much as I can.

NANCY: It's good to hear that he's doing better.

JEANNE: I think I told you that my daughter found me after many years—she was adopted out. . .

In this example, the therapist was able to keep the group discussion focused on relevant tasks, while encouraging Robert for beginning to work towards his goals.

Sessions 3–5: The End of the Initial Phase

Sessions 3 to 5 are geared toward preparing members for the next step—the stage in which much of the "work" is done. During this stage, members continue to refine their target goals while beginning to work on them on a daily basis. The expectation is that by Session 5, the majority of group members will have begun addressing one or two target goals.

Since members will know each other better by this time, they will be in a better position to provide meaningful and helpful feedback to each other. At this stage, the therapist encourages members to ask for comments or reactions from other members as a way to help others feel less isolated and to promote reality testing. Some members may interpret the term *feedback* as an opportunity to "give advice." Members should be specifically guided to provide positive feedback, as this is a powerful tool that addresses core self-esteem issues.

During Sessions 3 to 5, it may become evident to the group therapist(s) that certain members are struggling in the tasks of goal setting or daily application. Some members may feel unsure where to begin their endeavors, and feel overwhelmed about how and where to begin. The therapist can help them refine their goals and decide where to begin by encouraging them to choose a specific initial goal, so that they will feel less overwhelmed.

The following excerpt comes from the third session of a group for patients with major depression. In earlier sessions, Mary was active, almost dominating the group as members discussed depression and its effects. In the third session, the therapist effectively brings in other members to address the issue Mary raises and to assist her in thinking about taking steps toward working on it.

MARY: Well, this has been a week from hell. My mother called and insisted I go over and help clean her house. Then, my son got the flu, so I had to look after him.

To top it all off, my sister called and wanted me to come over and meet her new boyfriend. By Saturday, I had all I could take. So, I told my husband he would have to look after everything, and I went to bed.

THERAPIST: It does sound like it's been difficult. You had described yourself at the beginning as not being able to set limits due to your depression, and it sounds like that theme was going on this week. Carol, you had said that this was the sort of problem you often encounter. What do you make of what Mary is reporting?

CAROL: Well, I know just what she's going through. Mary, you just need to get up your courage and learn to say "no." After our meeting last week, I went home and actually told my husband he has to help out more with the kids. And, you know, he said, "Okay." I almost fell over!

JOHN: I agree, because you don't have trouble speaking up in here, Mary.

As illustrated here, members often need assistance in learning how to begin to take concrete steps to work on goals. This task will become the primary focus of the intermediate sessions.

While the end of the initial phase in individual IPT is marked by the formulation identifying the patient's problem area and the focus and goals of treatment, in group IPT-G such tasks are completed *prior* to beginning group sessions. As such, therapists conducting IPT-G will find that group members are already experiencing a deeper level of affect by the end of the first phase in group IPT, which should be readily apparent during the last session of this phase. This change reveals an awareness of the depth of distress members have been experiencing and provides strong motivation for further work. If all group members have been participating effectively to this point, the therapist may simply acknowledge that the group seems ready to move forward with their work. To gauge this readiness more systematically, group therapists can check with members in Session 5 to ensure that all have made the necessary connections between their symptoms, interpersonal problem areas, and associated target goals. (See Table 20.6 for a summary checklist covering Sessions 3 to 5.)

Intermediate Phase

The bulk of work on problem areas occurs during the intermediate phase. To help members reach their goals, the therapist introduces the IPT strategies specific to each problem area (Table 20.7). The therapist promotes the work of the intermediate phase by keeping the group on task, guiding members to:

- Maintain a focus on discussing issues related to their problem areas
- Increase self-disclosure
- Connect to and learn from other group members
- Express their emotional reactions primarily in relation to addressing their target goals and interacting with the therapist and with other members
- Implement changes based on problem areas in outside circumstances and in the group
- Remain motivated to continue in current group treatment, despite concerns about upcoming treatment termination and associated feelings of loss and fear

Table 20.6. SUMMARY CHECKLIST FOR SESSIONS 3 TO 5

Therapist Tasks

1. Start and end group on time.
2. Ensure that members have a clear understanding of IPT rationale and roles of the therapist and members.
3. Cultivate positive groups norms:
   - Maximize member self-disclosure, and heighten awareness of feeling states.
   - Keep group member discussions centered on current problem areas.
   - Continue to assist members in making connections between target goals and difficulties managing relationships.
   - Encourage members to discuss problems, changes, and successes in applying target goals.
4. Work with members who are struggling to make connections, and encourage them to note the efforts of others as a way to assist them in pushing their work forward.
5. Prepare members to enter the work stage.

Individual Patient Tasks

1. Deepen feelings of connection to other members.
2. Continue to learn how to use group structure and process to work on target goals.
3. Continue to make connections among target goals, difficulties in interpersonal relationships, and symptoms.
4. Modify target goals.
5. Begin applying target goals to daily life outside of group.
6. Share problems, changes, and successes in applying target goals.
7. Solidify goals.
8. Discuss feelings regarding the end of the initial phase.

GRIEF

A cohesive group can powerfully support a member working through grief issues. The group can validate the member's feelings and question unrealistic, guilty ideas or distortions that may accompany the disclosure of details of the event. The diversity of grief experiences among members of a typical group provides a rich source of consolation, reassurance, and corrective reorientation. One group member might tell another, "I know just what you were experiencing. I thought I'd never get over it, but I finally did and found some peace about the whole situation. Just keep at it." Group members can provide such genuinely constructive comments with great expertise. Since death is a universal experience, the group can usually address the related issues with an immediate understanding that is less easily achieved in the other problem areas.

Table 20.7. INTERPERSONAL PROBLEM AREA GOALS AND STRATEGIES

	Goals	Strategies
Grief	1. Facilitate the mourning process. 2. Help the patient re-establish interest and relationships to substitute for what was lost.	1. Reconstruct the patient's relationships with the deceased. 2. Describe the sequence and consequences of events just prior to, during, and after the death. 3. Explore associated feelings (negative and positive). 4. Help the patient consider ways of becoming re-involved with others.
Interpersonal role disputes	1. Identify the dispute. 2. Help the patient choose a plan of action. 3. Modify the patient's expectations or faulty communications to bring about a satisfactory resolution.	1. Determine the stage of the dispute. 2. Understand how nonreciprocal role expectations relate to the dispute.
Role transitions	1. Help the patient to mourn and accept the loss of the old role. 2. Help the patient to regard the new role as more positive. 3. Help the patient to restore self-esteem by developing a sense of mastery regarding demands of new roles.	1. Review positive and negative aspects of old and new roles. 2. Explore feelings about what is lost. 3. Explore feelings about the change itself. 4. Explore opportunities that the new role brings. 5. Realistically evaluate what is lost. 6. Encourage appropriate release of affect. 7. Encourage development of a social support system and of any new skills called for in the new role.
Interpersonal deficits	1. Reduce the patient's social isolation. 2. Encourage formation of new relationships.	1. Review the patient's past significant relationships, including negative and positive aspects. 2. Explore the repetitive patterns in these relationships. 3. Discuss the patient's positive and negative reactions toward both the therapists and the group members, and seek parallels in other relationships.

Interpersonal Role Disputes

Strategies used in the group format resemble those in individual IPT, such as helping members to determine whether there is potential for renegotiation or resolution, if the dispute is at an impasse, or if it is necessary to dissolve the relationship. Within the group context, members can provide feedback to other members struggling with identified role disputes. For instance, in working to help patients understand how nonreciprocal role expectations influence the dispute, the therapist may address questions such as, *What are the issues in the dispute? What are the differences in expectations and values? What are the options? What is the likelihood of finding alternatives? What resources are available to bring about change in the relationship? Are there parallels in other relationships? What is the patient gaining? What unspoken assumptions lie behind the patient's behavior? How is the dispute perpetuated?* Through this discussion, group members can draw upon their own experiences to provide relevant ideas and support (see Wilfley et al., 2000, for elaboration).

Consider this IPT-G member for whom emotional tension experienced within the group directly connected to her outside dispute, allowing a more objective view of her interpersonal challenges:

> Jane spoke at length in early sessions about how controlling her husband was and about the absence of love in their marriage. Several women in the group echoed this theme and pressed Jane to initiate discussing separation. The therapists cautioned against premature advice and encouraged a deeper look at the relationship. This led to the revelation, as the group progressed, that Jane's husband handled most of the child-rearing responsibilities and that Jane continually berated him for his failings, which she viewed as the major trigger for her bingeing/purging episodes. Gradually, the group's attitude changed. The members addressed the high level of control that Jane herself appeared to exert in the home and, indeed, how her initial presentation had dominated the group interaction, evoking some resentment from other members at not getting their fair share of time. This discussion triggered a helpful process for Jane in self-understanding and in beginning to address the role imbalance at home. Most of this work was done by group members, with subtle prompting by the therapist.

Here, the facilitation of an interactive and cohesive group provided a model and a platform on which to practice more effective dispute resolution. The therapist was able to model direct, open, and nonconfrontational communication regarding this core issue with group members.

Role Transitions

The strategies used to address this interpersonal problem area in individual IPT apply within the group format as well, though the group provides the social support system that members with role transitions often lack or underuse. By joining this new group system, members take a first step toward an important aspect of role transitions treatment—finding and connecting to new supports. Having a place to discuss recent role changes helps members to express the associated affect they may experience as overwhelming when alone. As change is a universal experience, many group members can identify with role transition issues and offer empathy and support.

The therapist specifically needs to encourage expression of affect around changes when a patient leaves an old role and assumes a new one. For instance, feelings of disappointment may arise if the old role was one that the patient attempted but did not succeed in. Or, feelings of emptiness may arise if the old role was part of a life phase that has now ended, such as children leaving home. Group members are likely to have experienced such changes and will have feedback to offer by way of common experience.

INTERPERSONAL DEFICITS

While some studies have indicated that patients having interpersonal deficits are particularly difficult to treat with IPT (e.g., Klerman et al., 1984), such individuals generally have more severe interpersonal deficits and profiles consistent with schizoid personality. These individuals are unlikely to tolerate group treatment and may more readily benefit from individual treatment, perhaps engaging in group treatment at a later time. For the purposes of group IPT, the interpersonal deficits problem area is conceptualized as individuals who are unskilled in developing meaningful relationships with others, who therefore are socially isolated or chronically develop unfulfilling relationships despite desiring more meaningful relationships (Wilfley et al., 1998). This more inclusive approach to interpersonal deficits encompasses individuals with relational shortcomings who can benefit from psychotherapeutic treatment.

IPT-G can be particularly effective for those patients with interpersonal deficits. The goals for such patients include reducing social isolation and encouraging the formation of new relationships that they can review and practice during IPT-G sessions. Individuals are diagnosed with the problem area of interpersonal deficits when they have a history of profound and persistent disturbances in social relationships. Many of these difficulties are longstanding, leading to a failure to develop intimate relationships. Such individuals may lack social skills or have pervasive, maladaptive ways of reacting to relationships that prohibit social and emotional development. Often they are socially isolated or so superficially involved that their relationships are chronically unfulfilling. Their relationships are often typified by absence of emotional expression, avoidance of conflict, fear of rejection, and lack of perceived support.

Participation with the group itself is a first step toward reducing isolation and increasing motivation to form new relationships, which addresses the primary goal for this problem area. As the key issue for patients with interpersonal deficits is longstanding and repeated relationship difficulties more severe than in the typical role dispute, members with interpersonal deficits will inevitably experience mixed emotions as they attempt to find their place among the other group members. Others in the group can usually identify with these difficulties, especially the loneliness and fear of rejection that are common among members with interpersonal deficits. This connection with other members is important in allowing those with interpersonal deficits to reveal their relationship difficulties more readily. The IPT group is an ideal setting for identifying interpersonal difficulties *in vivo*, as the interpersonal challenges experienced in outside relationships are likely to surface in interactions with the therapist and other group members. Direct attention to such maladaptive styles of engaging with others can be addressed directly in the group context, and the development of improved interactional behaviors within the group can serve as a model for outside relationships.

Marking the End of the Intermediate Phase

As this phase ends, members are acutely aware that the group will soon end, which may arouse considerable anxiety. The therapist can formally end this phase by saying something like:

> Today's session marks the end of the intermediate phase of treatment. Part of what we need to do today is reflect on what you have achieved in your goals and to express any feelings about ending this stage. We still have time to work on your goals, so you can spend some time today talking about what you have left to do. It's also important to comment on the changes that you see in each other and to discuss the feelings that accompany that aspect of your work together.

It is imperative that all group members participate in this discussion, relaying their concerns about termination and associated feelings, and outlining what they still need to accomplish. The therapist should work to keep the discussion productive and positive, carrying this sentiment through to the termination phase of treatment.

Termination Phase

The termination phase, encompassing the last five sessions, is an essential component of IPT-G. On a basic level, this specified stage gives members the chance to consolidate progress, formally say goodbye, and discuss concerns about relapse and the possible need for future treatment. More poignantly, it is a time when members learn to manage the emotions evoked by ending relationships that they have found useful and meaningful. Hence, many complicated and conflicted feelings come up. How members grapple with their feelings likely determines how each approaches the basic tasks of the phase. When managed successfully, this aspect of treatment can promote motivation and application that continues long after the group ends.

During this significant stage of treatment, therapists encourage the group to confront several themes central to the termination process (Table 20.8). Therapists should discuss termination explicitly and raise the issue of reactions to impending termination in each of the last several sessions. Therapists should conceptualize termination as a formal, powerfully therapeutic part of the treatment. Before the group ends, members should be afforded many opportunities to reveal their feelings about stopping and their methods for managing these feelings.

Inevitably, some members will suggest that the group get together outside the clinical setting and exchange a flurry of telephone numbers and email addresses. The therapist may suggest that the group explore what they want to get out of such a reunion. The therapist needs to maintain a calm firmness about the ending of the group and the importance of talking about it.

Table 20.8. THEMES CENTRAL TO THE TERMINATION PROCESS

1. Recognizing that termination is a time of possible loss, an analogue of grieving
2. Acknowledging negative reactions regarding not getting enough treatment or being abandoned
3. Emphasizing the progress that each member has made, especially in terms of improved relationships and socialization outside of group
4. Maintaining the stance of adopting personal responsibility for continued work on problem areas
5. Discussing concerns about future need for treatment
6. Specifically saying goodbye to each other and to the therapist(s)

A brief vignette from the final session of a group for members with binge eating disorder:

THERAPIST: Today we'd like to take time to give feedback to each other about changes you've made during the course of group. Why don't we start with Marilyn? You've done quite a bit of work and had a breakthrough with your husband.

MARILYN: I did make some good changes in my relationship with my husband, but I don't feel I've made as much progress as I should have if I'd taken better advantage of the group.

THERAPIST: Marilyn, let me stop there. You have a tendency to be overly self-critical at the expense of recognizing the gains you've made. For today, I'd like you to focus on your accomplishments throughout the group process. For instance, you took the time to make connections between your relationships and food. You stuck with it, even though initially you weren't sure how it even applied to you.

MARILYN: I did. I let go of caretaking more, too. I realized I have to take care of myself and that no one will do that for me.

THERAPIST: What have others noticed about Marilyn?

TED: I've seen a shift in you. Even in group you changed, not apologizing as much but being more direct.

THERAPIST: How about you, Ted? What do you think about your own progress?

TED: I've gotten some tools . . . I don't doubt myself as much, so I am more clear with other people now. My relationships at work are better, I think, because I work hard to be more aware of what I think and not to so easily take on the opinions of others. I feel more confident and others respond to that.

THERAPIST: Other feedback for Ted . . .?

Group members should be encouraged to continue until all have commented on their own and each other's progress.

NEGATIVE FEELINGS ABOUT TERMINATION

Therapists should move confidently toward the termination task, which must include both positive and negative dimensions of the group's ending. A hesitant or apologetic therapist stance will impede constructive termination. Encouraging members to verbalize negative feelings limits the potential for members to "bury" these feelings as a resentful residue of the therapeutic experience. The therapist should normalize the sense of loss group members experience, emphasizing that such feelings are typical in preparing for separation from the group and not indicative of depression. Helping members to learn to work through these feelings will allow each member to develop a sense of mastery over his or her fears.

A POTENTIAL TIME FOR GRIEF

As the group nears conclusion, and sometimes well before that, members may develop anxiety about saying goodbye to each other and "going it alone." Since termination ends the connection to other group members and the therapist, it has a theme of loss, an analogue of grief. It is important to state explicitly the possibility of experiencing normal grief-related symptoms, as unacknowledged "grieving" may lead to fears of relapse and an increase in symptoms.

PROGRESS REVIEW

An important aspect of ending the group is encouraging members to discuss the progress they have made and the changes they have witnessed in one another. Crediting each member for changes each has made is important, because members may tend to attribute these changes to therapists, outside circumstances, or the efforts of others. Such misplaced credit could erode members' confidence in their continued success and improvement without further treatment. A review of progress should increase members' self-confidence and awareness of new interpersonal skills. Therapists should encourage group members to recognize the importance of assuming responsibility for monitoring their own lives, their relationships, and their involvement in social activities.

MAINTAINING THERAPEUTIC GAINS

The therapist should direct each member to identify areas that require further attention, as not all goals may have been achieved within the group's time frame. To anticipate future difficulties, the therapist cultivates discussion of preparing for and addressing these challenges should they arise. By discussing these issues openly, group members will grow to understand that continued change and progress require effort comparable to the work they have already been doing. Predicting that setbacks will occur helps members to be realistic about change, and underlines that continued benefits necessitate personal responsibility for applying strategies developed during IPT-G. This important theme counters passivity and undue reliance on others.

Guiding members in a discussion of contingencies for handling future problems will bolster feelings of competence. It is vital to assist members in thinking about warning signs and symptoms that suggest need for future treatment. The therapist may recommend that members discuss potential warning symptoms with significant others, as such indicators can help members and others in their social environment to notice changes much as in the group. Therapists can encourage members to write down and to rehearse strategies to handle such warning signs.

For group members who have not responded to group treatment and continue to experience distress, the therapist should recommend continued psychotherapeutic treatment, perhaps in individual format, and provide relevant referral information. The therapist may determine that pharmacotherapy is warranted for some members upon termination, and should provide referrals for such follow-up accordingly.

FOLLOW-UP VISIT

Four to six months after termination, an individual follow-up visit with each former member allows an assessment of level of functioning and gains or setbacks following group termination. It serves as an incentive for the patient to continue working towards individual goals established during IPT-G. Members who have relapsed may need arrangements for additional treatment at this time.

In summary, termination is a transition marking the end of one format for change and movement toward the beginning of another. Members must become their own "therapists" following their experience in group treatment.

DISCUSSION

IPT-G is an effective and often optimal method for addressing a range of symptoms and disorders. The group format is an ideal milieu to work on interpersonal problems and to develop interpersonal skills with other patients struggling with similar challenges. The group setting offers therapists an opportunity to observe each patient in an interactive setting and identify maladaptive interpersonal patterns. The feedback offered among patients can have powerful effects in fostering change. To adequately implement IPT-G, clinicians must have a working knowledge of IPT theory and practice and of group psychotherapy and practice, as well as specific training in the concepts, strategies, and techniques of IPT-G. Proficiency in administering IPT-G is likely to prove rewarding for therapists due to the established utility of this cost-effective and powerful form of therapy.

SUGGESTED READING

Hilbert A, Saelens BE, Stein RI, Mockus DS, Welch RR, Matt GE, Wilfley DE: Pretreatment and process predictors of outcome in interpersonal and cognitive behavioral psychotherapy for binge eating disorder. Journal of Consulting and Clinical Psychology 2007;75(4):645–651

Wilfley DE, Frank MA, Welch R, Spurrell EB, Rounsaville BJ: Adapting interpersonal psychotherapy to a group format (IPT-G) for binge eating disorder: Toward a model for adapting empirically supported treatments. Psychotherapy Research 1998;8(4):379–391

Wilfley DE, Grilo CM, Rodin J: Group psychotherapy for the treatment of bulimia nervosa and binge eating disorder: Research and clinical methods. In Spira JL (Ed.): Group Therapy for Medically Ill Patients. New York: Guilford Press, 1997:225–295

Wilfley DE, Mackenzie KR, Welch RR, Ayres VE, Weissman MM: Interpersonal Psychotherapy for Group. New York: Basic Books, 2000

Wifley DE, Welch RR, Stein RI, Spurrell EB, Cohen LR, Saelens BE, Dounchis JZ, Frank MA, Wiseman CV, Matt GE: A randomized comparison of group cognitive-behavioral therapy and group interpersonal psychotherapy for the treatment of overweight individuals with binge-eating disorder. Archives of General Psychiatry 2002;59(8):713–721

21

Interpersonal Psychotherapy for Inpatients with Depression

ELISABETH SCHRAMM

RATIONALE

Why did we develop an inpatient treatment program based on the IPT model? In Germany and in many other countries, a high percentage of patients with affective disorders are fully or partially hospitalized for intensive treatment of their illness (Schulz et al., 2006). More than ninety psychiatric and psychotherapeutic clinics in Germany have established specialized depression wards with an average inpatient treatment duration of forty-six days (Wolfersdorf & Müller, 2007). This is far longer—and perhaps more reasonable—than the current U.S. mean inpatient stay of a week or less (e.g., Case et al., 2007).

Recent studies (Wolfersdorf, 1997; Wolfersdorf & Müller, 2007) reveal the need to optimize the cost-effectiveness of traditional treatment strategies for this patient population. This includes reducing the length of stay while at the same time improving short- and long-term outcomes. Because of the high cost of inpatient care, the development and evaluation of effective therapy programs have particular relevance. Psychodynamic and cognitive-behavioral approaches dominated inpatient treatment models for depression in Germany before the introduction of IPT in the mid-1990s. The numerous obvious benefits of the IPT model in a hospital setting (e.g., the simple, plausible rationale and ease of adoption by all members of a treatment team) have led to the widespread dissemination of this method in German (Wolfersdorf & Müller, 2007) and other European inpatient settings.

Originally designed for outpatients, the IPT model has several characteristics that suit it for inpatient use. In addition, IPT has some advantages for hospitalized patients relative to cognitive-behavioral therapy (CBT) or psychodynamic approaches:

1. IPT has proven effective even for **more severely depressed** patients (de Mello et al., 2005; Elkin, 1994). Two thirds of hospitalized depressed patients suffer from severe to extremely severe forms of depression (Wolfersdorf & Müller, 2007).
2. IPT is designed for a **brief duration,** which is mandatory for inpatient treatment.
3. Based on a **medical model,** IPT complements the usual procedures of experienced psychiatrists and works well in combination with antidepressant medication. The rationale is simple and plausible and can be easily explained by the therapist to the patient and the patient's family with the following words:

Interpersonal psychotherapy assumes that depression is an illness that is based on several factors such as genetic vulnerability, biochemical changes, developmental factors, etc. Independent of the causes, depression always occurs in an interpersonal context, which means the individual's relationships and social roles are affected by the disorder. Conversely, those relationships and role fulfillments have an impact on the onset and course of depression. There are several approaches to treating depression, such as antidepressant medication and different forms of psychotherapy.

We will use a combination of IPT and medication to treat your depression because this approach has proven to be effective in more severe forms of depression. Inpatient treatment also involves other interventions, which I will explain to you when we go through your individual treatment plan.

4. IPT is structured and **described in a manual** (Schramm, 2000, 2010; Weissman et al., 2007), which helps to train residents, younger clinicians in training, and nurses relatively quickly.
5. The manual can be used **flexibly** and adapted to the needs of an individual patient, for example a patient who can only be briefly hospitalized. This also enables the therapist to use his or her personal therapeutic style.
6. The IPT principles can be used in the daily clinical hospital routine by **all members of a treatment team:** nurses, social workers, etc. For example, all can collaborate in giving the patient the sick role.
7. Relative to comparable psychological treatments such as CBT, IPT is **less challenging** in requiring information processing by severely disturbed patients, older patients, or less educated patients. The connection of mood to life events is straightforward.
8. Several **modified forms** of IPT exist for subtypes of mood disorders commonly seen in the inpatient setting: for instance, IPT-Late Life for geriatric patients (Hinrichsen & Clougherty, 2006; Miller, 2009), IPT for bipolar patients (Frank, 2005), and IPT for dysthymic patients (Markowitz, 1998).

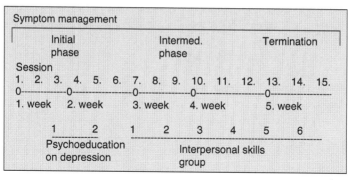

Figure 21.1 IPT treatment program

DEVELOPMENT OF THE CONCEPT

Besides numerous and severe symptoms, hospitalized patients often report suicide risk, comorbid disorders, and a history of treatment resistance. Thus, an intensive treatment program including multidimensional psycho- and pharmacological as well as traditional inpatient treatment strategies (occupational therapy, physiotherapy, etc.) is indicated (Schramm et al., 2007; see Fig. 21.1).

The program we have pioneered has been in operation since 1995 and has developed in several phases.

PHASE I: MODIFICATIONS

To address the special needs of hospitalized and mostly severely depressed patients, we slightly modified the original IPT concept. We transferred some IPT strategies (e.g., psychoeducation about depression) to a group format, added behavioral elements (e.g., structured homework), and systematically integrated different members of the treatment team into the treatment process. The most relevant modifications appear in Table 21.1.

These modifications are described in an additional manual (Schramm, 2000). The modified strategies were tested in single case studies and revised if necessary. The additional group sessions are also manualized (Schramm & Klecha, 2010).

The program was evaluated in two different phases and studies. It augments algorithm-driven pharmacotherapy with twelve to fifteen individual sessions conducted two or three times a week by a medical or psychological psychotherapist, plus eight to twelve group sessions.

Initial Treatment Phase (Three to Six Individual and Two or Three Group Sessions)

IPT treatment starts as soon as the patient has adapted to the inpatient setting (usually after three to five days) and disabling symptoms (including suicidality) are

Table 21.1 IPT in the Inpatient Setting: Modifications and Features

Setting

- The severity of symptoms (e.g., lack of concentration) may require **shorter sessions** (twenty to thirty minutes) at the beginning of therapy.
- An **extended initial phase** (four to eight sessions), focusing on symptom management, acceptance of the diagnosis, and instilling hope is warranted.
- A **higher frequency of sessions** (two or three times per week for approximately five weeks) is usually applied.
- The therapy program is conducted by the entire **ward team**, all of whom should be familiar with the IPT concept. All other interventions should be compatible with it.
- The **active involvement of significant others** is mandatory (with the patient's consent): to educate about the diagnosis, illness, and treatment strategies (including written material), to explain the treatment concept, to encourage the family to accept the patient's sick role, to agree on general treatment goals, and to request familial support in solving interpersonal conflicts and problems.
- Opportunities to **transfer learned strategies** into everyday life are limited in the acute treatment phase and should be compensated by sending inpatients home for a night or weekends (so-called "stress tests") as often as possible.
- **Termination** may be associated with stronger and more complex emotions than in outpatients, as inpatients separate not only from the therapist but also from other patients, the treatment team, and a protective, caretaking environment. In extreme cases (e.g., after an extended hospital stay) the discharge can be dealt with as a role transition in itself.

Content

- **Most hospitalized patients** report suicidal thoughts. A thorough evaluation of acute suicidality and previous suicidal attempts needs to be conducted in each session and suitable interventions (e.g., locking the ward) need to be taken.
- The therapist is even **more active and supportive** (e.g., offering direct help, setting short-term goals) than in outpatient IPT.
- The therapist is even **more flexible** (e.g., regarding the duration of sessions, the length of the initial phase, the frequency of contact with the patient's significant others, networking with the treatment team and other treating healthcare professionals).
- The patient's **acute events and concerns** (e.g., results of physical examinations, conflicts with other patients or treatment team members) may interrupt the work on the determined focus. These events can be addressed as crisis management and ideally integrated in the relevant problem area.
- Direct feedback about the patient's **interpersonal style** from members of the treatment team can be crucial. The setting can be used as a **field to practice**.

sufficiently reduced that the patient can be interviewed and will not be overwhelmed by the requirements of the program. Like in standard IPT, the individual sessions of the initial phase focus on the interpersonal inventory, identification of the relevant problem area, and the treatment contract, whereas delivery of information about depression mainly occurs in a group format. A significant other should attend to

Table 21.2 EXAMPLE OF A SYMPTOM MANAGEMENT FORM FILLED OUT
BY A PATIENT

Present symptom (please name)	Which strategies did you try out? (please describe)	Did it help? 0 = not at all 1 = a bit 2 = it was good 3 = it was very good
Insomnia	Work out in the evening Go to bed late No sleep during the day Sleep ritual (reading) Relaxation exercise	0 1 2 will try out will try out

discuss the content and duration of the treatment program. The individual sessions also provide an opportunity to evaluate whether a patient is able to participate in a group program.

The initial phase may take longer in hospitalized patients because they are usually more symptomatically stressed than outpatients, presenting with suicidal symptoms, severe rumination, and compromised decision-making capacity and motivation. Nurses help the patient to systematically develop and practice strategies for symptom management (Table 21.2).

All other psychoeducational and symptom-coping elements of the initial phase are conducted in two or three group sessions—for instance, providing information about depression and treatment options and giving the sick role. Due to some limitations of acutely ill hospitalized patients such as agitation and poor concentration, group sessions should not exceed one hour in duration, and important messages and facts should be highlighted on a flipchart. An example of the topic "acceptance of the sick role" is:

> We collected some examples of depressive symptoms and realized that depression affects not only your mood but your whole system. I want to discuss with you what it means to suffer from depression and be sick. Which daily duties and tasks are you still able to perform (even with depressive symptoms)? What are your limits? How can you find relief? What are the responsibilities associated with being a patient?

The initial phase concludes when the patient's symptom level allows work on the focal interpersonal problem area.

Intermediate Treatment Phase (Six to Eight Individual and Four to Eight Group Sessions)

In the individual sessions, the therapeutic work focuses on emotional aspects of the relevant problem area, while the group setting is used to enhance problem-solving

Table 21.3 INTERPERSONAL GROUP SESSIONS IN THE INPATIENT SETTING

Module I	Basic interpersonal skills
Two to four sessions	• **Skills:** How to build a social network, basic communication and social skills, interpersonal impact of depressive vs. non-depressive communication, encouragement of new relationships • **Goal:** Overcome isolation and loneliness, find social support, recognize the linkage of interpersonal problems and depression
Module II	Interpersonal conflicts and disputes
Three or four sessions	• **Skills:** How to identify conflicts, create a plan of action, learn communication skills, deal with emotions in conflicts, find solutions • **Goal:** Clarify and solve interpersonal conflicts
Module III	Role transitions and mourning losses
Three or four sessions	• **Skills:** Mourn the loss of old roles, evaluate positive aspects of the new role, build self-esteem, deal with grief, substitute for loss • **Goal:** Successful adaptation to life changes and coping with grief

strategies and interpersonal skills. The training of interpersonal skills takes place once or twice a week for approximately ninety minutes and includes four to ten participants. The group is usually conducted by a clinical psychologist or a psychiatric resident and—depending on the size of the group—co-therapeutically by a psychiatric nurse. The therapists of the individual sessions are psychiatric residents or clinical psychologists, preferably those who conduct the group treatment. The typical IPT problem areas are addressed in three modules: basic interpersonal skills/overcoming social isolation, dealing with interpersonal disputes, and coping with role transition and grieving losses (Table 21.3).

Grief about the death of a significant other turned out to be too stressful and emotionally intense for patients to address in an open group setting. Therefore, the IPT focus "complicated grief" is worked on in individual sessions only. Grief and loss as a part of role transitions are included in module III (role transition).

The program is half open, meaning that newly admitted patients can join at the beginning of each module. Each patient knows his or her personal problem area, which was negotiated in the individual sessions. Each patient is expected to contribute his or her own examples in the relevant group sessions. The examples are worked through using typical IPT strategies: for instance, in role transition, by naming positive and negative aspects of the old and the new roles. The group interventions have a structured and practicing character and include homework. Written material (e.g., about helpful communication strategies) is offered and between-session homework is assigned to facilitate the transfer of learning to everyday situations. Here is an example from the module "interpersonal conflicts":

Now you told us that you wanted to go hiking with your partner last Sunday, but he took off to watch a basketball game without you. You felt frustrated, helpless, and angry. Let's go through this scenario and practice how you can communicate your wish to him in a powerful way. How can you be clear and insistent in negotiating a solution for your different needs? Let's use the guidelines for effective communication which I passed around in the last session.

In addition, the IPT problem areas can be addressed creatively, using traditional inpatient treatment strategies like art or physical therapy. The following example from the art therapy group manual addresses role transitions:

TOPIC: Perception of the old role and expectations for the new role
TASK: Paint a hill. Imagine yourself on the top of this hill. What lies behind you, where are you standing right now, and what is in front of you? Put your imagination into creating the picture.

In the inpatient setting, all interventions on the ward should be compatible with the interpersonal, educative, supportive, and focused character of IPT.

Termination Phase (Two or Three Individual Sessions)

Termination of inpatient treatment takes usually about one inpatient week and means separating not only from the therapist but also from other patients, the treatment team, and a protective, caretaking environment. Emotions surrounding the termination of therapy may be stronger and more complex in inpatients than in outpatients. In extreme cases (e.g., after an extended hospital stay) discharge itself can be dealt with as a role transition. An important goal of termination is to create a smooth transition from full hospital care to outpatient treatment. Most German clinics offer post-hospital treatment programs for two additional weeks where patients can finish inpatient groups or other interventions as outpatients. Outpatient psychotherapy paradoxically usually consists of either CBT or psychodynamic therapy, as only these modalities are reimbursed by the German public health insurance system. Privately insured patients or patients in a special health insurance program usually continue with outpatient IPT.

PHASE II: EVALUATION IN AN OPEN PILOT STUDY

We evaluated the feasibility and effectiveness of the treatment program in a clinical sample of 28 inpatients with non-psychotic major depressive episodes. To ensure high external validity, all comorbid mental disorders except bipolar I and psychotic disorders, organic mental disorders, and primary substance abuse or dependency were allowed. Of Axis II disorders, only borderline and antisocial personality disorders were excluded.

All patients received standard medication (amitriptyline or amitriptyline-N-oxide). The ward team (consisting of a senior physician, a psychiatric resident, clinical psychologists, nurses, a social worker, an occupational therapist, and a physiotherapist) was trained in IPT for twenty hours and had regular group supervision.

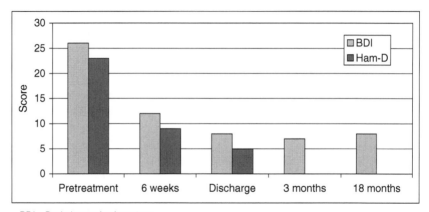

BDI = Beck depression inventory
Ham-D = Hamilton rating scale for depression

Figure 21.2 Mean BDI and Ham-D scores at different time points of evaluation (six weeks posttreatment, discharge, three and twelve months after discharge)

Outcome measures included the 17-item Hamilton Rating Scale for Depression (Ham-D), Beck Depression Inventory (BDI), and measures of social functioning and interpersonal problems (Schramm et al., 2004). The treatment program, comprising twelve individual and eight group sessions (Schramm et al., 2004), yielded significant improvements after six weeks. Gains remained stable three and eighteen months after discharge (Fig. 21.2). The remission rate (Ham-D 7 or less) of 68% (according to the reliable-change index) surpassed that of most other studies investigating outpatient treatment of major depression. The IPT concept appeared promising and was well accepted by both the patients and the treatment team.

PHASE III: COMPARISON WITH STANDARD PSYCHIATRIC TREATMENT IN A RANDOMIZED TRIAL

A subsequent (Schramm et al., 2007) controlled, randomized study compared IPT with usual care. The program was shortened to five weeks and intensified with three weekly individual and eight group sessions, some of which included significant others. One hundred twenty-four patients with major depressive disorder referred for psychiatric hospitalization were randomly assigned either to the combination of IPT and pharmacotherapy (sertraline) or to standard psychiatric care (sertraline plus clinical management [CM]). CM was described in a guideline and defined as psychoeducational, supportive, and empathic, involving three weekly twenty- to twenty-five-minute sessions delivered by psychiatric residents. Exclusion criteria were minimized to increase the generalizability of results: bipolar I disorder, other primary axis I disorders, substance dependence, organic mental disorder, psychotic symptoms, severe cognitive impairment, active suicidal ideation, and borderline and antisocial personality disorders.

The primary outcome measure was the 17-item Ham-D (Hamilton, 1960). Self-evaluated depressive symptoms (BDI) and social functioning were also assessed.

Results are presented in Figure 21.3.

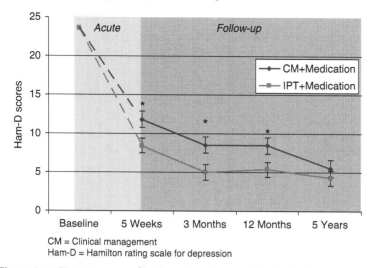

Figure 21.3 Ham-D scores of both treatment groups for the single measure points

Both groups showed significant improvement in depressive symptoms after five weeks, but improvement was significantly greater in the IPT group than the CM group. The response rate (reduction in symptom severity of at least 50% on the Ham-D) was higher among patients who completed IPT (77%) than CM (58%), whereas remission rates (Ham-D 7 or less; 58% vs. 40%) did not statistically differ. Patients who initially responded to IPT exhibited greater treatment gains at the three-month follow-up: only 3% of IPT patients, compared to 25% of CM patients, relapsed ($p = 0.008$). Nine months later, however, this difference was no longer statistically significant. Global and social functioning was higher in the IPT group at both follow-up assessments.

Five years after discharge, patients in both treatment modalities had depressive symptoms significantly reduced from baseline levels, with the time rate of change and acceleration on the Ham-D being higher for patients in the combination therapy condition. Although the contrast between conditions at year five was nonsignificant, 28% of IPT patients showed a sustained remission compared with 11% of CM patients ($p = 0.032$). Patients with traumatic experiences responded significantly better to IPT than to CM.

In summary, the combination of IPT and medication showed short- and long-term benefits even five years after discharge. Future research is needed to compare inpatient IPT to briefer hospital stays followed by outpatient care using the same program.

CASE EXAMPLE

History of present illness

Mike, a forty-seven-year-old business owner, the married father of three daughters, experienced his first episode of depression. His psychiatrist referred him for hospitalization after a suicide attempt. Mike was managing one of the family's wine stores when—two years before—his older brother Jack died of a heart attack. Up to then, Jack had headed the family business, coordinating the roles and ownerships of four brothers: besides Jack and Mike, their younger twin brothers owned parts of the company. The relationship between the siblings, always somewhat tense, escalated after Jack's death to a severe dispute about the role distribution in the business. While Mike was able to grieve Jack's death, he could not stand up to his brothers when they transferred him to one of the family branches in East Germany. He was very upset and felt manipulated, but accepted their decision and moved to East Germany during the week while spending the weekends with his family. However, he was unsuccessful in the East and the branch had to be closed down. As a consequence, there was further conflict with his brothers, and he ended one of their arguments by saying: "In case you still need me in our business, let me know."

Unexpectedly, Mike heard nothing more from his brothers, which so upset him that he took a leave of absence. In the following period of inactivity he became more and more depressed, hopeless, and suicidal. He had extreme fears about the future and suffered from insomnia. His general practitioner prescribed sertraline (50 mg/day) and benzodiazepines (lorazepam up to 3 mg/day). When Mike's depressive symptoms did not improve after six weeks of treatment, he referred him to a psychiatrist. While the psychiatrist was trying to wean him off the benzodiazepines, Mike made a suicide attempt by taking an overdose of lorazepam and was hospitalized for psychiatric treatment. Mike was convinced that the "world would be better off" without him.

Interpersonal Inventory

Mike named his wife Helga as his closest significant other. They met twenty-two years earlier when she worked as a secretary in the family business. They have three teenage daughters together. He described Helga as the most supportive person in his life. Since the birth of their first daughter seventeen years ago, Helga had taken care of the household and the children. The couple had some common interests, such as gardening and training their dogs. They also shared the burden in caring for their disabled daughter. However, Mike's job did not leave much time to spend with his family. Due to Mike's time restrictions the couple had no close friends. His lack of friends, however, reflected not just lack of time but also his lack of social skills. Mike described the relationship with Helga as peaceful: "We understand each other without words. We have known each other for so long and all we want is to live in peace and harmony." His suicide attempt had shocked his wife, particularly when she learned from the note he left for her that he meant his death to be a relief for the family.

Mike listed his deceased brother Jack as his second closest relationship. Jack had been four years older than he. They had grown up together until their parents separated when Mike was ten years old. Jack stayed with his mother, Mike with his father. Jack had always been his role model, and Mike described the early separation from him as a "drama." From then on Mike developed an increasingly avoidant attachment style. Particularly when it came to confronting people, he was always afraid it would end in a final breakup. Therefore, when Mike entered the company, Jack supported and protected him from their younger twin brothers, who often tried to take advantage of Mike.

The patient mentioned his father (but not his deceased mother) as another significant relationship. The father had died nine years earlier from a heart attack. After Mike's parents separated, his father remarried and had twin boys. Mike always felt that he was only "second best" and that his younger brothers had more privileges than he did, but he never dared to express negative feelings in front of his dad for fear of losing him. He admired his father for leading the family business but realized that he was very different from his father's assertive, dominant, and extroverted character.

The patient described his two younger half-brothers as a "power unit" who always got a lot more attention from their parents than he. As long as he could remember, they had taken advantage of and manipulated him. Again, Mike got used to swallowing his anger and despair. As an adult, he had not spent much time with his half-brothers except at the workplace. Currently, Mike was very disappointed with them because they had not contacted him even after they learned about his suicide attempt.

Mike did not want to talk about his mother because he had never forgiven her for leaving him behind with his father when he was a child.

Psychiatric, Family, and Medical History

The patient had had no prior severe depressive episodes and no history of mania or substance use. He did meet criteria for early-onset dysthymic disorder, which remained untreated in the past. Currently, he also fulfilled criteria for benzodiazepine dependency.

Mike's mother had a history of recurrent depressive episodes. There was no other family history of psychiatric illness or treatment. Mike had been physically healthy, with no history of thyroid disease.

Case Formulation

Several life events clearly contributed to the onset of the patient's depressive episode, which was superimposed on dysthymic disorder. Most important was the death of his older brother and the consequent restructuring of the family hierarchy within the business (even though all brothers kept the same number of company shares). Mike anticipated Jack's death for a long time and, supported by his wife, grieved normally, but he could not adapt to the new structure of the company. Due to his anxious-avoidant personality style and probably as a reflection of dysthymic symptoms, Mike was too insecure to follow in Jack's footsteps and abruptly left the business following an argument with his brothers. He had to endure an unintended role transition from business manager to inactivity to being ill. The conflict with his half-brothers remained unresolved, "on hold," and Mike waited passively for a solution. He felt stuck between returning to the family business to deal with his brothers and leaving the business to start a new career. He found neither alternative attractive.

INDIVIDUAL THERAPIST: Mike, we looked at what was going on in your life when you had your first depressive symptoms. Let me summarize what I heard you saying so far. Your oldest brother's death and its consequences for your position in the family business began a series of disputes with others and led to more life changes. You went through the normal grieving process following your brother's loss, but it was hard to stand up for your needs in the company. Your unintended move to the East, the separation from your family, the closing of the company branch in the East, and the arguments with your brothers presented challenges that seemed to overwhelm you. You told me that you are still hoping your brothers will turn to you and make up, but you are losing this hope with each day that you are hospitalized. The marked severity of your depression is reflected by a score of 29 on the Ham-D and 37 in the self-rated BDI questionnaire.

What do you think about us starting to work on the problem area of a "role transition"—that is, your coming to terms with letting go of your old position of being protected by Jack and finding out what your actual choices are and how your new role should look?

MIKE: Yes, that makes sense. I still can't believe what has happened. It seems as if my whole life got out of control and I feel overwhelmed with mixed emotions. I'll be relieved if you help me to sort out the chaos and come to a decision on how to proceed.

INDIVIDUAL THERAPIST: You said it feels as if you lost everything you've worked hard for all your life, you lost Jack and your illusion of a family clan that sticks together in good times and bad. It's very understandable that you got depressed. Once you are able to deal with your complex emotions, it will be easier to figure out what you want for your future and how to deal with your brothers. I also heard you saying that you feel too confused to approach the conflicts with your brothers. However, at a later stage of therapy when things have cleared up, we may want to add the focus of "interpersonal disputes" to our treatment contract.

MIKE: Okay, maybe later; I am not ready for that yet.

Differential Diagnosis and Indication for IPT

Indication: First episode of major depression (superimposed on dysthymia), which occurred in the interpersonal context of the death of a close family member followed by a family conflict and life changes. Acute suicidality and substance dependence (benzodiazepines) made hospitalization necessary. In addition, the patient showed anxious-avoidant and dependent personality traits (without meeting full criteria on the SCID-II; First et al., 1997), which made the adaptation to life changes and dealing with interpersonal conflicts more difficult for the patient.

Middle Phase of Treatment

Besides the individual sessions (which focused on dealing with emotions), Mike participated twice weekly with seven other patients in interpersonal skills training (for content see Table 21.3). The group was conducted by his individual therapist and a psychiatric nurse. In covering the module "coping with role transition and grieving

Table 21.4 POSITIVE AND NEGATIVE ASPECTS OF MIKE'S OLD AND NEW ROLES

	Positive Aspects	Negative Aspects
Old role	• Recognition by employers • Financial security • Feeling safe and familiar	• Dependent on others • Work stress • No leisure time • Conflicts with brothers • Fear of failure
New role	• Chance for a new beginning • More time for family and leisure • Greater independence	• Insecurity for the future • Feeling stuck • Having to start all over again • Unresolved conflicts with brothers

losses," the group explored positive and negative aspects of Mike's old and new roles and listed them on a flip chart (Table 21.4).

GROUP THERAPIST: Mike, can you describe what it was like when you were working in your former role in the family business? What did it mean to you? What did you experience as positive?

It became evident that Mike felt safe in his old role as the head of a small department, which he led from age twenty under the direct guidance and supervision of his older brother Jack. As a manager he felt recognized and respected by his employees and in his community. The business was successful and he was able to take good care of his wife and daughters. He was proud of the company's growth and trusted that the family would support each other in difficult times.

GROUP MEMBER: Mike, when you think back, were there also some negative aspects of your old role?

Mike realized that he had always felt very dependent on his older brother's opinion and advice, even after twenty years in the business. Even though Jack protected him, their younger brothers often delegated to Mike unpleasant tasks such as telling employers their contracts would not be extended or traveling to unattractive sites. Another negative aspect was that he worked so much that he had almost no leisure time.

GROUP THERAPIST: Can you describe your current, new position?

Mike could find no positive aspects in his new role. When Jack died, the twins restructured parts of the company without even asking Mike's opinion or approval. They told him that the business had been mismanaged for the past years and could survive only if Mike followed their lead (e.g., being transferred to the East). Mike was not able to stand up to his brothers. He had felt inferior to them since childhood and thought he had no chance of resisting them. He was afraid that expressing his anger and dislike would lead to a final split-up of the family (as he experienced it when he was ten years old). Besides those fears, he realized that he lacked assertiveness skills. This pattern of conflict avoidance also existed in other relationships.

GROUP MEMBER: Are there any benefits in your new role?

Mike could not think about what might make the new role more attractive. Other group members pointed out that he could see it as a chance for a new beginning and to become more independent. In addition, he finally had more time with his wife and his kids.

Mike talked about his old role as if he still wanted to live it without any changes. As usual, he visibly suppressed anger or disappointment and tried to avoid painful feelings because he was afraid of getting overwhelmed by them. It also became clear that mourning the loss of the old role included mourning the loss of the illusion that his brothers appreciated him. The group therapist assumed that Mike avoided dealing with the current loss because he was afraid of dealing with even more feelings associated with past losses (i.e., the deaths of his father and brother and the early separation from his mother and brother when he was ten years old). In an individual session, the therapist addressed Mike's feelings associated with the role change.

INDIVIDUAL THERAPIST: When you talk about your old position, how does that make you feel?
MIKE: I still cannot believe my old life fell apart like this. I never expected this. I have been a part of this family and our business for as long as I can remember. I refuse to accept that all that I worked for in the past thirty years might be no longer real. I don't feel anything but disbelief.
INDIVIDUAL THERAPIST: Have you thought of saying this to your brothers?

Mike had experienced multiple losses: not only had he lost his old role of leading a small but successful department of the family business, but he was also still mourning the loss of his older brother. To see Jack's work being devalued by his younger brothers and being unable to defend it created intense pain for him.

In the treatment contract Mike and the therapist agreed on the goals of coming to terms and accepting the losses, including the experience of the painful emotions associated with them and working on confronting his brothers with his feelings rather than just avoiding them.

INDIVIDUAL therapist: What do you feel as you become more aware of what you have lost and what is left?
MIKE: I start to get angry and very disappointed with my younger brothers. I thought that we would stick together as a family, but they are only interested in their own profit. And I think that was always the case, even when we were kids; I just did not want to see it. They disrespect the values that Jack implemented in our business: fairness, trust, one for all and all for one. There is not a whole lot left. It is very sad . . . [starts crying] . . . I have never cried in front of another person, sorry, it's a shame! I am ashamed that I am not able to stand up for Jack's and my life's work.

The therapist validated Mike's feelings and reassured him that the mixed and overwhelming emotions would soon be followed by some relief.

INDIVIDUAL THERAPIST: It is very understandable that you feel upset and helpless after all that has happened. It is normal to experience strong feelings when you are betrayed. By accepting this painful mix of emotions and making sense out of it, you will finally feel better again."

MIKE: I never let myself get angry about my brothers. It was against what Jack taught us about loyalty. I always wanted to believe that we are a "family clan," loyal and successful. To realize that the twins deceived me feels as if my whole world view is breaking apart. They do not even care that I almost lost my life! Neither of them nor their wives or kids asked how I am doing. You are right: I do feel upset about them. What they did was not right.

INDIVIDUAL THERAPIST: It is normal that you feel angry about your brothers' breaking the family tradition of loyalty. Most people would feel this way. You are now beginning to deal with it. How does that feel?

MIKE: Feels stronger, not so helpless anymore. I think I have to approach them. I need to get out of my corner.

Once the patient worked through his feelings, he realized that he needed to approach his brothers and negotiate a solution for the impasse they were stuck in. At this point, the treatment contract was extended to include role disputes as an additional problem area. At the beginning of therapy the patient had not felt ready to deal with this focus. After a few more sessions of working on role disputes, Mike made a decision.

MIKE: I feel very relieved to have for the first time expressed my disappointment and anger to you, and I guess I need to do the same with my brothers. I always thought feelings would kill me, but they did not. Now that I can admit that my primary family is and never was what I wanted them to be, I think I do not want to be part of the family business any more. Mainly because I do not want my children to have to go through the same process.

He carefully prepared to approach his brothers by means of role-plays. In individual and group sessions, Mike learned to express his needs and feelings of anger and disappointment. Because he still suffered from symptoms such as insomnia, lack of energy, and concentration, Mike asked the therapist to support him in negotiating a solution and therefore invited the brothers to join a session. When Mike adequately expressed his disappointment and frustration, both brothers apologized, saying that they did not mean to make him depressed and that they too felt overwhelmed and helpless. However, it became clear that the twins' values, expectations, and future plans were very different from Mike's. Therefore, Mike decided to leave the company and buy out a small branch that had been under his leadership for the longest time. For more detailed negotiations the brothers agreed to involve a lawyer.

Mike felt relieved and empowered about finally confronting his brothers. As a result his depressive symptoms decreased: his Ham-D score dropped from 29 to 16, the BDI from 37 to 17.

Termination, Including Maintenance Treatment and Follow-up

After Mike's condition improved, the therapist introduced the termination of treatment. Mike spent the last two weekends and some weekdays at home to test his stressability. He also returned to his former office to collect his belongings. He became tearful describing his feelings associated with leaving the clinic. He described it as his first experience of being "seen and respected as the person I am" with vulnerabilities, emotions, and weaknesses. It deeply touched him to be supported by other patients in group therapy without having to perform. He had some anxiety about being self-employed, but was able to engage Jack's former senior partner in leading the new branch. Mike summarized take-home messages: "Particularly in the group sessions, I learned to express myself and be open with other people even when I do not feel strong or perfect. And I discovered that the company does not equal my life. There is so much more to it that I've neglected so far. In the individual sessions I recognized that my feelings, including my anger, are valid and important. I always thought they would get in my way, but the opposite is the case—they are my motor."

After six weeks of inpatient treatment, maintenance therapy was crucial to a smooth transition. For two weeks after discharge, the patient participated in the clinic's day program to finish his group work and follow-up with his therapist. In addition, he started outpatient therapy with a clinical psychologist. In this less-than-ideal circumstance, the psychologist was not trained in IPT but read the manual after talking to Mike's hospital therapist. Mike continued to take sertraline in the same dosage initially prescribed, and the focus of his outpatient psychotherapy remained role disputes and his new role.

Approximately one year after discharge Mike reported that he had remained euthymic with some ups and downs, despite some legal difficulties with starting his own business: "But I kept negotiating with my brothers because avoiding conflicts does not help. And with the help of a lawyer we found solutions."

Use of Rating Scales Demonstrating Improvement in Symptoms, Functioning, and Other Domains

The patient had an initial score of 29 on the 17-item Ham-D, which indicates intense severity. His BDI score was 37. He met SCID (Spitzer et al., 1994) criteria for a single major depressive episode, dysthymic disorder, and substance (benzodiazepine) dependency. On the SCID-II interview he screened positive for anxious-avoidant and dependent personality traits. His GAF (APA, 1994) score of 42 indicated significantly impaired global functioning.

By the time of hospital discharge, the Ham-D score dropped to 10, the BDI to 12. The GAF score reached 70, indicating an acceptable level of functioning. Benzodiazepines were completely weaned. The anxious-avoidant and dependent traits decreased visibly when the depressive symptoms decreased and when the patient took greater action. He consciously decided not to avoid feelings and conflicts any longer after he recognized this behavior as maladaptive.

DISCUSSION

Mike presented a typical inpatient case insofar as his suicide attempt, benzodiaz-epine dependence, and severe depressive symptoms made hospitalization necessary. During the first two inpatient weeks he was stabilized by the IPT strategies of instill-ing hope, support, and the reassurance that solutions could be found. In addition, he learned symptom management strategies. The benzodiazepines were stepwise sub-stituted by less addictive substances and finally completely withdrawn. At the same time, the dosage of antidepressants was increased and the patient responded. In an early session addressing his suicide attempt, he could truthfully promise that he would not act on any suicidal thoughts. Better stabilized, he was able to overcome his fear to join the group sessions, which he later rated as the most effective part of the treatment program.

The interpersonal context of Mike's depressive symptoms represented several potential foci: grief over Jack's death, role disputes with his twin brothers, and the role transitions related to changes in the structure of the family business and finally the hospitalization. The patient seemed to have a normal grieving process, including being involved in the funeral and other rituals, feeling supported by his wife and family, showing affects usually associated with grief such as sadness, despair, grate-fulness, guilt, anxiety, and anger (even though anger was difficult for Mike to express), being able to reminisce about memories of Jack, and resuming his life after an appro-priate period of time. He did not show signs of complicated grief such as consistent denial, avoidance behavior, preoccupation, longing, nightmares, etc. However, the therapist considered in the case formulation that the loss of Jack added to other losses Mike experienced (e.g., loss of his mother, death of the father, loss of his status in the company). The patient's preference was to begin the therapeutic work on the area of role transitions as he was not ready yet to deal with the role disputes with his brothers.

Mike had a longstanding attachment history of feeling "unwanted" (and as a result showed interpersonally avoidant behavior) by others: by his mother who left him, his father who treated him second best, Jack who left him by death, and his twin brothers who wanted to cut him out of the business. Losing one's mother before the age of ten is a risk factor for depression and could explain Mike's dysthy-mia and anxious attachment. His suicide attempt was triggered by the thought: "The world is better off without me." He also avoided group situations because he did not want to risk the experience of rejection again. To be fully accepted by the therapist and by the group members was an essential experience for him, which gave him enough confidence to finally express his feelings of disappointment, anger, and frus-tration in his individual and the group sessions and later on to his brothers. He real-ized that he had denied the negative aspects of the old role of being a part of the company and that starting a new career also included positive aspects such as inde-pendence. Once he came to terms with his mixed emotions and was able to confront his brothers, he reached the decision to let go of the old role in the company. In therapy, Mike learned interpersonal skills to deal with the new role of independent businessman: for example, he was able to convince Jack's former senior partner to help him build up his own business (using his support and guidance as a substitute for his brother's support).

SUMMARY

In German-speaking and many other countries, inpatient treatment of severe affective disorders constitutes a significant part of health care. IPT was adapted for this patient population on the basis of several obvious advantages of the approach for the inpatient setting. The program usually consists of fifteen individual and eight group sessions combined with medication. It proved to be superior to psychiatric standard treatment in the short term and longer term.

The benefits of inpatient treatment in Mike's case included the possibility of intensely intervening at different levels:

1. Medication treatment—increasing the dosage of sertraline while withdrawing benzodiazepines
2. Suicide prevention, working through the traumatic experiences of committing a suicide attempt, overcoming hopelessness and helplessness, and developing the awareness that he is not isolated if he keeps sharing his feelings
3. The intertwining of individual (work on emotions) and group psychotherapy (work on interpersonal skills)
4. Symptom management: learning strategies from nurses to cope with suicidal thoughts, sleep problems, rumination, etc.
5. Inpatient milieu therapy, in which Mike realized that he was not the only one suffering from a severe mental disorder, felt recognized and supported by others, and grew by supporting others
6. Other therapies: physical and art therapy helped him to change his inactive, avoidant lifestyle and discover his own resources and talents

The limitation of inpatient treatment is the difficulty in transferring insights or learned behavior immediately into everyday life. On the other hand, most severely ill patients need the protected environment and significant support of an inpatient unit to take the first steps to cope with their symptoms and the stressful context of their disorder. Later on, it is useful to transfer the progress stepwise into everyday life to avoid regression, for example by limited discharges over the weekend or transfer to a day clinic program. However, almost all patients find the transition from full inpatient care to returning home to their usual environment a challenge.

Another limitation is that outpatient treatment generally involves a change of psychotherapeutic modality, since in Germany only CBT and psychodynamic therapy are reimbursed by public health insurance. Patients can receive outpatient IPT when they have private insurance or when the therapist presents IPT to the health insurance company as an either a psychodynamic or behavioral approach. Changes to this traditional but inappropriate system are on the way. Future research might compare inpatient IPT to the briefer hospitalizations used in the United States (Markowitz, 2008) followed by outpatient care using the same program. Inpatient treatment might be more costly in the short term but it may have long-term financial benefits.

22

Interpersonal Psychotherapy by Telephone

CARLOS BLANCO, JOSHUA D. LIPSITZ, AND EVE CALIGOR

Although psychotherapy is usually, and probably best, delivered face to face, situations arise in which the patient may not be able to see the therapist in person. This can happen, for example, because the patient may be physically disabled, may live too far from the clinic to make it practical to attend regularly in person (or be away on travel), or may have competing obligations to attend to at home, such as child care. A potential solution is, rather than having the patient visit the therapist, bringing the therapist to the patient. Although home therapy visits have been provided with success in some contexts (Burns et al., 2001), they are typically impractical in terms of required resources.

One easy, relatively inexpensive approach to transporting the therapist is to deliver psychotherapy by telephone. Telephone sessions provide service to individuals who otherwise would not receive care (Nickelson, 1998) and can transcend numerous barriers to treatment, including economic status, weather, comorbid general medical illness, and distance from or availability of transportation to the clinic (Stamm, 1998). Telephone interventions can also overcome the stigma some patients may experience in seeking mental health treatment by allowing them to access care in a private and confidential manner. Furthermore, telephone-administered psychotherapy increases temporal accessibility by permitting more flexible scheduling of treatment. Several studies have demonstrated the acceptability and efficacy of treatment delivered by telephone for a range of behavioral and emotional problems (Day & Schneider, 2002; Green et al., 2002; McNamee et al., 1989; Reese et al., 2002; Zhu et al., 1996).

Telephone-delivered psychotherapy has been used successfully to treat depression. Mohr et al. (2000) randomized thirty-two patients with depressive symptoms and multiple sclerosis to either telephone cognitive-behavioral therapy (CBT) or usual care. Depressive symptoms decreased significantly in the CBT treatment group compared with the usual care group. In a larger study, Simon et al. (2004) randomized six hundred patients who had recently started antidepressants to usual primary care, telephone management, or telephone-delivered CBT. Treatment participation rates were 97% for telephone care management and 93% for telephone-delivered CBT. Compared with usual care, the telephone psychotherapy intervention led to lower mean depression scores, a higher proportion of patients reporting their depression "much improved," and a higher proportion of patients "very satisfied" with depression treatment. There were fewer differences between telephone care management and usual care, suggesting specificity for the telephone CBT intervention.

IPT has also been successfully delivered by telephone. Six studies have examined the efficacy of IPT delivered by telephone. All have focused on populations that had difficulties attending regular clinic visits. The first study explored the feasibility and acceptability of telephone IPT (IPT-T) to reduce psychological distress and to enhance coping during high-dose chemotherapy in breast cancer patients (Donnelly et al., 2000). Patients, who were often housebound, received one weekly session for sixteen weeks. Psychosocial functioning was assessed using standardized measures at study entry, after chemotherapy, and following IPT-T. Accrual and participation supported feasibility: fourteen patients and ten partners were recruited, constituting 82.5% of those eligible. Participants rated their satisfaction with the program between "good" and "excellent." Although providing some initial indication of the usefulness of IPT for breast cancer patients, this study had two important limitations. First, patients' psychiatric diagnoses were not assessed. As a result, the number of patients who had major depressive disorder (MDD) is unknown. Second, no depression-specific scale was used, further limiting the ability to examine the efficacy of IPT in treating depression.

Miller and Weissman (2002) conducted a twelve-week controlled pilot trial of IPT-T in thirty women with MDD, dysthymia, or both who had difficulty attending clinic visits due to time constraints, demands of child care, or finances. Patients were randomly assigned to IPT delivered by telephone (n = 15) or a waitlist control (n = 15). Patients were interviewed at baseline and at twelve weeks by a blinded independent clinical evaluator to assess their symptom level and social functioning. At the end of the study, women in the IPT-T group were rated as having achieved significantly greater improvement in depressive symptoms ($p < 0.02$), increased global functioning (GAS) ($p < 0.02$), and improved work and social functioning ($p < 0.03$–0.05, respectively). Eighty-three percent of the patients had favorable attitudes toward the use of the telephone and saw the telephone as facilitating treatment, and 75% expressed the desire to continue treatment by telephone in the future should the need arise. In contrast, only 25% were willing to accept a referral for face-to-face treatment.

In a third study, Neugebauer et al. (2007) randomized women with a recent history of miscarriage, suffering from minor depression, to usual care or telephone-administered interpersonal counseling (IPC), an abbreviated and simplified form of IPT. Depressive symptom levels were measured and change in symptom levels evaluated by comparing baseline to post-intervention Center for Epidemiologic Studies-Depression (CES-D) scores in an intention-to-treat sample (n = 17) and a completer sub-sample (n = 9). In the intention-to-treat sample, the CES-D mean score declined from 25.4 to 18.8 (mean within-subject change = 6.6, 95% confidence interval [CI] = 1.4–11.6); in the completer sub-sample, it declined from 23.6 to 11.2 (mean within-subject change = 12.3, 95% CI = 4.0–20.7). These findings, although based on a small open trial, further support the efficacy of telephone-administered psychotherapy for depressive disorders.

A study conducted in China examined the effects of an IPT-oriented childbirth psychoeducation intervention on postnatal depression, psychological well-being, and satisfaction with interpersonal relationships in Chinese first-time childbearing women (Gao et al., 2010). The intervention consisted of two ninety-minute antenatal classes and a telephone follow-up within two weeks after delivery. One hundred ninety-four first-time pregnant women were randomly assigned to the intervention group (n = 96) or usual care consisting of routine childbirth education (n = 98). Outcomes of the study included symptoms of postnatal depression, psychological well-being, and satisfaction with interpersonal relationships, which were measured by the Edinburgh Postnatal Depression Scale (EPDS), General Health Questionnaire (GHQ), and Satisfaction with Interpersonal Relationships Scale (SWIRS), respectively. Women receiving the IPT-based intervention had significantly better psychological well-being, fewer depressive symptoms, and better interpersonal relationships six weeks postpartum than those in the usual care group.

A pilot study examined whether brief IPT-T could reduce psychiatric distress among persons living with HIV-AIDS in rural areas in the United States (Ransom et al., 2008). Seventy-nine participants were assigned randomly to usual care or to six sessions of IPT-T. Patients in the IPT-T group continued to receive standard services available to them in the community. Patients receiving IPT-T evidenced greater reductions in depressive symptoms and in overall levels of psychiatric distress compared with those in the control group. Nearly one third of patients receiving IPT-T reported clinically meaningful reductions in psychiatric distress from pre- to post-intervention.

In another recently completed small pilot study, we randomized Hispanic patients to venlafaxine with weekly visits for clinical management (VLX-W), venlafaxine with monthly visits for clinical management (VLX-M), or VLX-M enriched with weekly IPT (VLX-IPT). Patients in the IPT arm had to come to the clinic for Sessions 1, 4, 8, and 12 but were allowed to have all other IPT sessions by telephone. Eight of nine (89%) patients completed the study in the VLX-IPT group, compared to seven of ten in the VLX-W group and five of ten in the VLX-M group. Consistent with the findings of Miller and Weissman regarding the acceptability of IPT-T, six of the patients in VLX-IPT continued treatment at the clinic after the trial ended, whereas no patients in the VLX-W or VLX-M groups returned to treatment despite being offered treatment with other medications. VLX-IPT was superior to the other treatments in retention and outcome. The mean length of treatment of the VLX-IPT, VLX-W, and VLX-M groups was 77.8, 65.1, and 59.5 days (joint SD = 28.3), resulting in a difference in retention length between VLX-IPT and the medication-alone groups of Cohen's $d = 0.72$. Patients in the IPT group had a mean decrease in Hamilton Rating Scale for Depression (Ham-D) scores from 21.1 to 12.6, while the scores of the patients in the VLX-W group decreased from 16.9 to 11.6, and the scores of the patients in the VLX-M group decreased from 16.3 to 12.3. The effect size of combined treatment versus venlafaxine alone was $d = 0.54$, in the moderate range.

The results of these studies, as well as clinical experience, suggest that IPT-T may be a useful alternative for individuals with MDD who have difficulty attending clinic appointments. The findings are based on relatively small samples, however, and thus need replication in larger samples with more rigorous experimental methods.

We also note that, when possible, patients generally prefer face-to-face sessions. Therefore, from the clinical and research points of view, for each session, the patient should have the option of choosing whether IPT will be delivered in person or by telephone. Furthermore, for safety reasons, it may be prudent to agree with the patient that even if most sessions are delivered by telephone, some sessions will be in person. In our experience, having the first and last visit and about one visit a month in person is generally not too onerous for the patient and helps facilitate the estab-lishment and maintenance of a good working alliance and processing of the emo-tions surrounding termination. However, this is only a guideline, and it may need modification depending on the circumstances of the treatment. Our conceptual framework is that IPT-T does not exclude the possibility of face-to-face sessions, but rather that the two modes of delivery can be combined in the same treatment.

Providing therapy by telephone poses several additional challenges to the thera-pist and the patient. Because communication is limited to verbalizations and audible expressions of emotions, important nonverbal communication such as facial expres-sions or shifting of posture is missing. Thus, it is more difficult for both the patient and the therapist to assess each other's emotional state and to create an atmosphere of trust. It is also easy for the therapist and the patient to get distracted while on the telephone (e.g., checking e-mail, doing household chores), which may further decrease the intensity of the treatment. The use of web cameras may help overcome some of these limitations in the future. An additional difficulty is how to ensure the safety of the patient. In an office, it may be easier to assess or intervene when a patient voices suicidal ideation than when the therapy is delivered by telephone. Here again, the use of cell phones may allow calling an ambulance while talking with the patient on the other line. There is certainly a risk that the patient may engage in self-harming behavior without the therapist being able to prevent it. However, this would also be true in many cases in face-to-face therapy, where the therapist often may be unable to physically contain the patient.

To illustrate some of the advantages and challenges posed by the delivery of IPT by telephone, we present a case of a middle-aged woman with a chronic mood disor-der and multiple psychosocial and economic problems. Although the initial plan was to deliver the therapy face to face, the constraints the patient faced made it necessary to provide IPT by telephone. This case also illustrates the need to take into account cultural differences between patient and therapist (see Chapter 16) and how to reach agreement when patient and therapist initially disagree on the goals of the therapy.

CASE EXAMPLE

Ana was a thirty-eight-year-old married Caucasian woman who had three daughters aged two, seven, and fifteen. At the time of treatment, she was living with her hus-band and children in New York City, was receiving public assistance, and had no prominent medical illness.

Ana was referred to the clinic by her fifteen-year-old daughter's therapist, who thought Ana might be depressed. Ana reported having felt depressed for the past four years, having little interest or pleasure in doing things, and experiencing feelings of worthlessness. She reported fatigability and low energy; she had to push herself to manage household chores. She felt guilty about not doing enough for her children and making poor life choices and often felt hopeless and helpless. Ana denied recurrent thoughts of death and had no history of suicide attempts. She reported chronic oversleeping and overeating and was morbidly obese. She felt unattractive particularly because of her weight and felt easily criticized or rejected by others. Her baseline score on the 17-item Hamilton Rating Scale for Depression (Hamilton, 1960) was 25, indicating depression of moderate severity. According to Ana, her symptoms had not substantially changed throughout this episode before coming to treatment. She was assessed with the Structured Clinical Interview for DSM-IV Axis I Disorders (First et al., 1997), on which she did not meet criteria for another lifetime or current psychiatric disorder.

The onset of the recent depressive episode coincided with the worsening of her difficulties with her husband. Ana was increasingly dissatisfied with the limited role that she and her children seemed to play in her husband's life, even though at the same time he expected them to be always available and ready to care for him and try to please him.

Ana's first episode of major depression was at age twenty-eight. This happened immediately after she had discovered that her husband had a second wife and two children in another country. Although Ana had three daughters, she knew that her husband would always favor the other wife because one of these other children was a son. Initially, Ana considered divorcing her husband and confronted him about the situation. However, when she saw that he was not willing to stop seeing his other family, she reasoned that the pain of losing him for a few months every year while he was away (with the other family) was less than the pain of losing him totally. She therefore backed down and tried to accept her predicament. She felt that she slowly grew used to the situation. However, as a result, her relationship became more distant, and she started to feel more isolated and unsupported. She saw a psychiatrist for the first three months after the onset of her depressive symptoms and received medication, but stopped the treatment for financial reasons. This episode slowly remitted over two years. With the onset of her current episode at age thirty-four, Ana consulted a psychologist at a university clinic and initiated therapy. However, she discontinued therapy after two sessions due to "lack of progress."

Consistent with reports of a higher risk for depression in the offspring of mothers with a history of major depression (Weissman et al., 2005), Ana's fifteen-year-old daughter was also depressed. The daughter had been in treatment for depression when Ana was referred to the clinic, although her session attendance had been sporadic. There was no other documented family history of psychiatric disorders.

In developing a plan with this patient, the therapist had to consider a daunting array of symptoms and interpersonal problems: a demeaning and troubled marital relationship, a child's depression, unemployment, low household income, few friends, morbid obesity, and chronic low self-esteem, among other issues. One might question whether it was even feasible to treat this woman with a twelve-week, short-term therapy program. IPT proposes that it is possible to treat an episode of major depression by narrowing the focus to one or two problems. The explicit expectation is that resolving a crisis will improve mood, and that the patient will be able to manage the other problems better once mood improves.

Following the initial evaluation, which was done in person, Ana agreed to begin twelve sessions of weekly interpersonal therapy. After much difficulty negotiating a mutually convenient time, the first forty-five-minute session was scheduled. Two hours before the appointment, Ana canceled because she could not find a babysitter for her two-year-old daughter. The appointment was rescheduled, and Ana's fifteen-year-old daughter agreed to babysit for her two sisters at the clinic. Ten minutes into the session, the two-year-old insisted on entering the room, and the session had to be interrupted for ten minutes until she agreed to return to her sisters. After the second appointment was rescheduled (and missed) three consecutive times, the therapist suggested that the therapy take place over the phone; the duration and periodicity of the sessions were preserved. After this, no session was rescheduled or missed. Ana was never late for her phone sessions, although on occasion the sessions were briefly interrupted by the children coming into her room to ask her a question. The possibility of returning to in-person visits or coordinating them with the child's visit was discussed twice more during the treatment, but Ana stated that she could not afford to pay for a babysitter to look after her children during the visits.

This patient's difficulties in getting to the clinic were seen as a reflection of her life situation and her limited social and economic support. It is consistent with IPT's pragmatic approach to focus on how to get the therapy done rather than to interpret its snags and pitfalls. Likewise, if a patient were to come late to sessions, the IPT therapist would "blame" the depression, reinforce the importance of coming on time, and perhaps even reschedule the session for another day rather than interpret possible resistance.

The first three sessions were devoted to reviewing symptoms, obtaining an interpersonal inventory, understanding current relationships, explaining the medical model of depression and the role of interpersonal relationships in the onset and course of depression, and formulating the focus of the therapy. Ana was born and raised in New York City, the only daughter of an Irish-American family. She lived with her parents until she married. She described her father as a caring person who always had difficulty expressing his love. Her mother frequently devalued Ana's social and intellectual capabilities, criticizing her friends and telling her that she would never be able to go to college.

Before her marriage, Ana's longest relationship had been with a man of her age whom she had dated for four years. The relationship ended when they both realized that the passion had gradually disappeared. Ana met her husband at a party and fell in love with him immediately. She stated that their passion had grown more intense over the years and that sex played a very important role in their relationship. Ana held several administrative jobs until her first pregnancy, when she quit. After that, Ana progressively focused on her new family at the expense of other social contacts. She had intermittently considered returning to work or opening a business but was systematically discouraged by her husband, who insisted it would detract from the care of the children.

In IPT the sessions are used to assess the presenting disorder and broader clinical status and to evaluate the patient's current and past interpersonal relationships, looking for patterns relevant to current relationships. Examining the interactions of these relationships may elucidate the patient's current behavior, expectations, and obstacles to changing her relationship with her husband. In this case, the patient's relationship with her parents was noteworthy for the superficial support and lack of warmth from the father and an undercurrent of criticism from the mother. Fear of rejection was seen as a potential obstacle that could prevent the patient from resolving the dispute with her husband.

In the final phase of the evaluation, the therapist identified for the patient the name of her illness and provided her with the sick role—alleviating the responsibility and sense of guilt for being depressed.

Because the onset of the first episode of depression and the subsequent course were clearly related to marital difficulties, the therapist framed this case as a role dispute. He incorporated Ana's attempts at independence into the therapy by formulating a secondary focus on role transition. This formulation, refined through the course of treatment, helped Ana and the therapist translate the difficulties in the relationship into specific, achievable goals of the therapy. When Ana started treatment, her stated goal was to be able to tolerate her marital situation without suffering. This seemed an unrealistic objective to the therapist, who worked with Ana to develop alternative goals. The therapist repeatedly raised the possibility of reconsidering the marital arrangement, but Ana made it very clear that leaving her husband was not an option she was willing to entertain. After much discussion, Ana and her therapist agreed to work on identifying positive aspects of the relationship with the husband that she would like to promote and aspects that she saw as sources of pain and wanted to change. Throughout the sessions, it became evident that the way she felt in his company, their sexual relationship, and their history together were aspects of the relationship that she cherished and wanted to preserve. Her emotional and economic dependency on her husband, and feeling humiliated at times by him, were aspects she wanted to change. A great deal of time in the sessions was spent obtaining the details of how specific situations developed, how she felt in those situations, normalizing those feelings, and examining what could be alternative, more adaptive behaviors in response to such situations. References to similar situations in the recent past were discussed, but attempts at reconstructing the childhood roots or intrapsychic conflicts underlying those behaviors were avoided.

It is not uncommon for depressed patients to accept too much responsibility for a problem that really involves two people. This patient hoped therapy would help her learn to better adapt to a bad situation. Because our society rejects bigamy, the therapist initially suggested a discussion on how to change that situation:

THERAPIST: Although there are many things you like about your relationship with your husband, it also seems that some aspects of the relationship are quite upsetting to you.

ANA: Yes, most of the time I am with my husband he makes me feel great. But when we get into arguments, he becomes almost a different person and I feel as if he did not care for me. He shouts at me, says all kind of things. I feel humiliated and don't know what to say.

THERAPIST: Have you tried to tell him how you feel in those situations?

ANA: When we are in the middle of those situations I feel too small to say anything. And then, when the situation has passed, I think it is not worth bringing it up because it happens so rarely, that I think it is better to let it go than take the risk of losing the relationship.

THERAPIST: Would you say, then, that you are overall happy with your relationship with your husband and how he makes you feel?

ANA: No, I am not totally happy, I wish things could be different. It obviously does not make me very happy to know he has another family.

THERAPIST: It would difficult for most people to tolerate that situation.

ANA: It is really hard. I would feel much better if he did not have the other family.

THERAPIST: As we speak, I have the impression that you see that situation as something that cannot be changed. Something that is imposed on you and there is nothing you can do to change.

ANA: I really cannot change it. Not unless I left my husband.

THERAPIST: Is that something that you have ever considered?

ANA: Of course I have thought about it, who wouldn't? But I don't think it would be good for my kids if I left him. So, I try not to think too much about it, and try to focus on the good things about our relationship.

THERAPIST: I understand. At the same time, though, it seems that the difficulties in your relationship have contributed to your depression.

ANA: Yes, but I think I would be more depressed if I did not have my husband. I do not want to leave my husband. I just want to learn how to feel less hurt when he does what he does.

The therapist took the patient at her word that she did not wish to leave her husband. The therapist tried to avoid making judgments about explicit reasons or subconscious motivations for her lifestyle choice and instead helped the patient explore ways of initiating change in the relationship to make it less distressing and more satisfying. Limited to a telephone connection, the therapist had to try to be especially attuned to the patient to appreciate the totality of her life and to overcome emotional distance that might lead to a judgmental stance.

Pragmatically, IPT usually does not provide sufficient time to confront problems that the patient does not yet recognize as such. Rather, the therapist works with the patient to select a problem area that makes sense to the patient. Even when IPT cannot alter the nature of the problem, it may help by changing the patient's feeling about the problem and thus its impact on symptoms. Often the mere process of working on the problem, airing the patient's feelings, analyzing the options, and actively selecting a course of action, provides the patient with a sense of control, which neutralizes his or her depressive feelings of powerlessness.

On several occasions during the treatment, the therapist felt uncomfortable with Ana's helplessness and was tempted to shortcut the therapeutic process by immediately offering a solution to the patient's problems. However, the therapist was aware that he did not have "the right answer" to those problems and that he had limited knowledge of the culture of Ana and her husband. He was also careful to avoid substituting Ana's dependency on her husband with a dependency on the therapist himself. Thus, he encouraged Ana to discuss her situation and possible solutions with her close friends, who would be better judges of her cultural norms and provide ongoing support should she decide to deviate from those norms. She would also see them as peers, making it easier for her to disagree with them than it would be to disregard the therapist's advice. Increased contact with her friends would also improve her interpersonal relationships, increase her independence and self-esteem, and strengthen a social network on which to rely upon termination of therapy.

Because IPT emphasizes the "here and now" and problem solving, there is a risk that therapists may be overactive and try to impose their own point of view instead of creating a space in which the patient can express feelings and discuss and rehearse alternative courses of action. In this case, helplessness, a classic depressive symptom, led the therapist to underestimate the patient's ability to solve her problems and to feel that he alone was responsible for the outcome of the case. The therapist's temptation to be too active may be stronger in a telephone relationship, during which there is a lack of eye contact during brief silences. Through awareness of the feelings elicited by the patient, the therapist avoided the temptation of presenting himself as holding the key to the patient's problems or presenting the therapy session as the only place where she could discuss her problems. Thus, the therapist explored other possible sources of interpersonal support and satisfaction that could influence the patient's mood and avoid excessive dependence on the therapist.

As the treatment developed, Ana focused on three specific goals to help resolve the role dispute:

1. *Renegotiation with her husband about their differences of opinion* without giving in to his point of view, but also without allowing the situation to become an argument. Ana identified a pattern in which minimal disagreements would very quickly impair their ability to listen to each other and degenerate into arguments in which her husband would become verbally abusive. She would then feel unappreciated and disrespected, which lowered her self-esteem. Areas of dispute included how much time they should spend together as a family and how to allocate their scarce economic resources.
2. *Weight loss.* Ana stated that her husband enjoyed overweight women. However, she also believed that his encouraging her to stay overweight served the additional purpose of limiting her attractiveness to other men, thus allowing her husband to take her for granted emotionally and sexually.
3. *Work on obtaining a government-guaranteed loan to start a small clothing business.* Ana had some experience in that specific type of business and was able to enlist the help of her former boss to advise her on how to set up the new store. She also found agencies that could help her develop a business plan and other people who would provide accounting and other services for nominal fees to small start-up companies.

Formulating these goals helped Ana focus her energies, test her assumptions about her ability to change her environment and her life, and measure her progress in therapy. As Ana realized how much control she really had over her life, her self-esteem improved, her mood lifted, and she felt much more energetic.

The goals of treatment in a case of role dispute are to help identify and characterize the nature of the dispute and to choose how to address it. The direct approach to the role dispute relies on careful tracking of the sequence of interactions. In this way the patient can make changes in his or her own behavior and expectations that may renegotiate the relationship and lead to decreased conflict. The first goal in Ana's case focused on her communication. She was accustomed to tolerating her husband's lack of attention and worried that bringing up her feelings would lead to fights between them, resulting in her eventually receiving even less attention from him. The therapist examined this expectation and helped her explore ways of expressing how she felt:

THERAPIST: One of the things that you've mentioned several times in the sessions is that you feel you can't tell your husband how you feel.

ANA: Not really. I can communicate very well with him. I feel very connected to him. The only problem is when I get frustrated, he does not want to hear it.

THERAPIST: What do you mean? What happens if you express frustration?

ANA: I don't do it anymore because I think he would leave the room or become verbally abusive.

THERAPIST: Is that what he does, or what you think he would do?

ANA: Well, I'm not sure. I try not to complain so we don't get into arguments, but then I feel more lonely and like I have no one around who understands.

THERAPIST: So when you withhold feelings like frustration, do you feel more connected to your husband?

ANA: I feel a little resentful when I can't tell him how I feel or that I wish he paid more attention to me.

THERAPIST: How does this resentment impact your feelings of connection to him and your feelings of sadness?

ANA: If I'm resentful, I feel less connected to him. When I feel less connected, I feel sad.

THERAPIST: So would it be fair to say that your fear of expressing your feelings makes you feel sad?

ANA: Yes, I think that's true.

THERAPIST: So, in order to avoid irritating your husband and then feeling lonely, you prefer to hold your feelings to yourself, feel resentful and disconnected, and then feel lonely and sad anyway.

ANA: Yes, I feel sad no matter what I do.

THERAPIST: Do you think you would be willing to try this and see what happens?

ANA: What do you mean?

THERAPIST: I was thinking that maybe you could test how your husband would react if you tell him how you feel. Of course, before you do that, we would rehearse the conversation here. That way, when talk to your husband, you would have some practice and would know what to respond depending on what he says or how he reacts.

ANA: I think that may be too risky. I may end up losing more than I win.

THERAPIST: Would you be willing to try something simple, maybe start with some feelings that were a little bit negative, but not too negative, so that it is easier for you and you gain some practice?

ANA: I am willing to try it here in the session, but I don't want to commit to having to confront my husband if I don't feel like it.

THERAPIST: I think that's reasonable. Let's start simple and see what we can do.

The implicit hope in this process is that the partner will meet the patient halfway and that the patient's change will be a catalyst for change in the couple. If both people are motivated, this work is often best accomplished in conjoint sessions. In this case,

Ana's husband was able to hear her concerns more willingly than Ana expected; however, he did not alter his behavior in any significant way. Despite this frustration, Ana still felt relief in expressing how she felt and empowered by the knowledge that she had choices.

The therapy also sought to address the role dispute indirectly, by helping the patient draw on other relationships and activities to neutralize the negative valence of the problematic relationship. To this end, two additional goals were identified: taking steps to start a business and losing weight. The reasoning behind choosing these goals was that by empowering her, it would be easier for Ana to be more assertive regarding her expectations of the relationship with her husband. The patient said that her husband was pleased with her being overweight and commented about how he found heavy women attractive. The patient recognized that obesity was not in her own interest and resolved to try to lose weight. Similarly, she became aware that her distress about her husband was worsened by her financial dependency and limited social contacts. The therapist helped her recognize how this situation satisfied his expectations but frustrated her own. She sought to modify her role in the family by establishing her own source of income. She and her therapist anticipated that her increased independence would facilitate a renegotiation toward a more satisfying relationship with her husband.

An implicit goal in IPT, regardless of the problem area selected, is to demonstrate the link between the interpersonal problem and change in symptoms. Since the patient had already connected the dispute with her husband to her depression, it was left to demonstrate that the converse was also true. When she took a positive step, such as expressing her feelings to her husband more openly, the therapist asked about changes in her mood. Improvements in mood were explicitly linked to changes in the problem area. Further, the therapist congratulated Ana on her progress, encouraging her to seek new opportunities to apply her newly learned skills, and coached her on how to further improve her performance in future situations.

Therapy progressed smoothly from the third through the eighth session. Increasingly, Ana was able to select the appropriate incidents for discussion during the session, consider alternative ways of handling difficult situations, and work toward achieving her stated goals. It became evident that she spent substantial amounts of time thinking about her difficulties outside the sessions and was progressively able to learn how to solve most of them without the therapist's help. During the seventh session, the therapist announced he would be taking a two-week vacation after the tenth session. During the ninth session, two weeks after that announcement, Ana reported that her husband would be returning to his native country for five months. He would be leaving the day after the therapist returned from vacation. Ana felt abandoned by her man, who was going back to his country to visit his other wife and children.

The therapist asked how she found out about his trip and whether they had discussed the situation. Ana said that he had told her casually, as if it was unimportant news. She had felt enraged but was unable to express those feelings because she was afraid that he would be verbally abusive, would hurt her self-esteem, and would make her feel lonely. Instead, she cried, which prompted her husband to tell her that he understood it was a difficult situation but he was proud of her for taking care of the family.

During the therapy session, the therapist asked Ana what had made it difficult to express her feelings more openly, as she had been able to do in the previous weeks.

Ana said that the surprise of the news and the intensity of her emotions made it difficult to express her true feelings to her husband. She also felt trapped by his praise as a good caretaker. Ana and the therapist agreed to spend part of the session role-playing what she might have said so she would feel better prepared on future occasions, and the other part finding ways to cope with her husband's absence, including relying on her friends for companionship and emotional support.

Upon the therapist's return from vacation, Ana stated that she was a little down, but she was clearly not depressed. She scored a 6 on the Ham-D administered at the last session. Ana requested a referral to continue working "on issues." However, she had difficulty articulating those issues. Given the acute stressor of her husband's departure and her history of recurrent major depression, they agreed to extend the treatment for two additional sessions. Ana remained euthymic and continued to work on her goals after the two extra sessions.

In IPT, it is accepted that problems are not always resolved at the end of therapy. Rather, IPT begins a process of change that ideally will continue after the therapy ends. The termination phase in IPT seeks to review and consolidate gains and deal with feelings related to termination. Although feelings of sadness and loss related to therapy ending are discussed, the therapist does not belabor this point. As during the rest of the treatment, the therapist avoids centering the discussion on transferential material and focuses on the here and now of relationships outside the session. Since the goal of IPT termination is to help the patient cope well without therapy, termination provides an opportunity to internalize strategies. In this case, the fact that Ana's husband left during the therapy was presented as a positive opportunity to tackle this experience with the therapist's help. The patient was then able to acquire a new perspective and feel less helpless in coping with this event. Had the departure not yet occurred, the therapist might have attempted to rehearse this scenario and explore ways of coping were this to happen.

Three months after the end of the treatment, the therapist contacted Ana by phone as part of the clinic procedure. Although many of her chronic problems remained, Ana reported feeling considerably better than before treatment. She had lost twenty pounds since her last treatment session, had remained euthymic, and had substantially improved communication with her husband. The start of her business was lagging, however. The therapist informed her that should she become depressed again, she could contact the clinic for a new evaluation and another course of treatment or a referral.

DISCUSSION

This case exemplifies how short-term therapy can be provided by telephone, even for complex cases, and can benefit patients with longstanding problems, even in the setting of limited psychosocial support. Use of medication was considered throughout the treatment. However, the patient's psychological mindedness, her expressed preference for treatment with psychotherapy, her early and good response to treatment, the moderate severity of her depression, and the absence of suicidal ideation made her a good candidate for psychotherapeutic treatment alone.

The patient did not solve all of her problems during the course of this treatment. However, she achieved her main goals of improving her mood and her relationship with her husband, and she felt prepared to face new challenges. Furthermore, during her course of treatment, her fifteen-year-old daughter became more compliant with her own treatment, and her depression also improved. Whether these improvements were related is unknown, although recent evidence suggests that improvement of mood in depressed mothers is associated with improvement in their children's depression (Weissman et al., 2006). It is possible, although far from certain, that Ana may need further antidepressant treatment in the future. Short-term therapy favors new time-limited treatment courses in these situations. If the patient's preferences or situation change, other therapeutic alternatives may need to be considered.

We expect that in the coming years, psychotherapy delivered by telephone or Internet will become progressively more common, as it provides greater flexibility and easier access. Some cognitive-behavioral therapies are sufficiently structured and task-oriented that entire therapies or large parts of therapy can be guided through non-computer interface of using limited text message contact with therapists (Tillfors et al., 2008). Whether IPT lends itself to this type of administration remains to be seen. However, telephone, especially with video augmentation, is certainly possible and with time and practice can closely replicate the warmth and spontaneity of an in-person session. This shift in the mode of delivery will bring important challenges to patients and therapists regarding issues of safety, availability, patient–therapist relationships, and treatment efficacy. There is a need for clinicians and researchers to address those challenges to improve the accessibility and efficacy of psychotherapy.

ACKNOWLEDGMENTS

This work was supported in part by NIH grants MH-15144, MH076051, CA133050, and DA023200 (Dr. Blanco) and MH-01575 (Dr. Lipsitz); a Young Investigator Award from the National Alliance for Research on Schizophrenia and Depression (Dr. Blanco); and the Samuel Priest Rose Research Award and a grant from the Klingenstein Third Generation Foundation to Myrna M. Weissman, Ph.D., and the New York State Psychiatric Institute. Adapted from Blanco C, Lipsitz J, Caligor E: Treatment of chronic depression with a 12-week program of interpersonal psychotherapy. American Journal of Psychiatry 158;3:371–375. Reprinted with permission from the American Journal of Psychiatry, Copyright 2001 American Psychiatric Association.

23

Afterword

MYRNA M. WEISSMAN AND JOHN C. MARKOWITZ

This chapter closes the casebook for now, but the development of IPT does not end here. We hope and expect that IPT will continue to evolve, and that as it does, clinical researchers will develop new applications and new adaptations. Treatments are fluid, living things. There are applications of IPT already under development that do not appear in these pages: for example, IPT as part of treatment triage; IPT for patients with bipolar II disorder; IPT for somatizing patients; IPT for prepubescent depression; conjoint (couples) IPT. There is certainly a place for a computerized version. There will surely be others.

In an era when psychotherapy is under pressure from managed care and other economic forces, when pressures on residency training threaten the integrity of psychotherapy training, and when psychiatry is focusing its science more on genes and neuroimaging than on psychotherapy, anything that sustains the development of psychotherapy skills is a resource. This book will have value only if it teaches and evokes reactions from clinicians. In the interests of healthy growth and debate, we encourage readers to respond to the cases published here. What reactions did you have to the cases? Did the process come through to you? Would you have handled things differently in conducting IPT? What are your opinions? Was reading this useful? What's missing? We further invite you to send us your own (appropriately disguised) IPT treatment cases (mmw3@columbia.edu, jcm42@columbia.edu) with your comments. Perhaps we can include them in a subsequent casebook, and we will try to respond.

REFERENCES

Abbass A: Small group videotape training for psychotherapy skills development. Academic Psychiatry 2004;28:151–155

Agras WS, Walsh T, Fairburn CG, Wilson GT, Kraemer HC: A multicenter comparison of cognitive-behavioral therapy and interpersonal psychotherapy for bulimia nervosa. Archives of General Psychiatry 2000;57:459–466

Ainsworth MD, Bowlby J: An ethological approach to personality development. American Psychologist 1991;46:333–341

Alden LE, Taylor CT: Interpersonal processes in social phobia. Clinical Psychology Review 2004;24:857–882

Alden LE, Wallace ST: Social phobia and social appraisal in successful and unsuccessful social interactions. Behaviour Research and Therapy 1995;33:497–505

Amaya-Jackson L, Davidson JR, Hughes DC, Swartz M, Reynolds V, George LK, Blazer DG: Functional impairment and utilization of services associated with posttraumatic stress in the community. Journal of Traumatic Stress, 1999;12:709–724

American Psychiatric Association: Diagnostic and Statistical Manual of Mental Disorders, 4th ed. Washington, DC: APA, 1994

American Psychiatric Association: Diagnostic and Statistical Manual of Mental Disorders, 4th ed., text revision. Washington, DC: APA, 2000

American Psychiatric Association: Practice guideline for the treatment of patients with acute stress disorder and posttraumatic stress disorder. American Journal of Psychiatry 2004;161:S3–S31

American Psychiatric Association: Practice guideline for the treatment of patients with major depressive disorder (revision). American Journal of Psychiatry 2000;157:1–45

American Psychiatric Association Workgroup on Major Depressive Disorder: Practice guideline for the treatment of patients with major depressive disorder, 3rd edition. American Journal of Psychiatry 2010;167:S1–S152

Angst J: Comorbidity of anxiety, phobia, compulsion and depression. International Clinical Psychopharmacology 1993;8:S21–S25.

Angst F, Stassen HH, Clayton PJ, Angst J: Mortality of patients with mood disorders: follow-up over 34–38 years. Journal of Affective Disorders 2002;68:167–181

Angus L, & Gillies LA: Counseling the borderline client: An interpersonal approach. Canadian Journal of Counseling 1994;28:69–82.

Arcelus J, Whight D, Langham C, Baggott J, McGrain L, Meadows L, Meyer C: A case series evaluation of a modified version of interpersonal psychotherapy (IPT) for the treatment of bulimic eating disorders: a pilot study. European Eating Disorders Revivew 2009;17:260–268

Armstrong H, Ishike D, Heiman J, Mundt J, Womack W: Service utilization by black and white clientele in an urban community mental health center: Revised assessment of an old problem. Community Mental Health Journal 1984; 20:269–281

Arntz A, van den Hoorn M, Cornelis J, Verheul R, van den Bosch WM, de Bie AJ: Reliability and validity of the borderline personality disorder severity index. Journal of Personality disorders 2003;17:45–59

Axelrod SR, Morgan CA, Southwick SM: Symptoms of posttraumatic stress disorder and borderline personality disorder in veterans of Operation Desert Storm. American Journal of Psychiatry 2005;162:270–275

Balls Organista P, Organista KC, Kurasaki K: The relationship between acculturation and ethnic minority mental health. In Chun KM, Balls Organista P, Marin G (Eds.): Acculturation: Advances in Theory, Measurement, and Applied Research. Washington: American Psychological Association, 2003:139–161

Basco MR, Rush JA: Cognitive-Behavioral Therapy for Bipolar Disorder. New York: Guilford Press, 1996

Bass J, Neugebauer R, Clougherty KF, Verdeli H, Wickramaratne P, Ndogoni L, Speelman L, Weissman M, Bolton P: Group interpersonal psychotherapy for depression in rural Uganda: 6-month outcomes: randomised controlled trial. British Journal of Psychiatry 2006;188:567–573

Beck A, Rush A, Shaw B, Emery G: Cognitive Therapy of Depression. New York: Guilford, 1979

Beck AT, Steer RA, Brown GK: Manual for Beck Depression Inventory II (BDI-II). San Antonio, TX: Psychology Corporation, 1996

Beck J: Cognitive Therapy: Basics and Beyond. New York: Guilford Press, 1995

Beeber L, Holditch-Davis D, Belyea M, Funk SG, Canuso R: In-home intervention for depressive symptoms with low-income mothers of infants and toddlers in the United States. Health Care for Women International 2004;25:561–580

Beeber LS, Holditch-Davis D, Perreira K, Schwartz TA, Lewis V, Blanchard H, Canuso R, Goldman BD: Short-term in-home intervention reduces depressive symptoms in early head start Latina mothers of infants and toddlers. Research in Nursing & Health 2010;33:60–76

Beeber LS, Perreira KM, Schwartz T: Supporting the mental health of mothers raising children in poverty: how do we target them for intervention studies? Annals of the New York Academy of Sciences 2008;1136:86–10

Beidel DC, Turner SM, Morris TL: Psychopathology of childhood social phobia. Journal of the American Academy of Child and Adolescent Psychiatry 1999;38:643–650

Belle D: Poverty and women's mental health. American Psychologist 1990;45: 385–389

Bellino S, Rinaldi C, Bogetto F: Adaptation of interpersonal psychotherapy to borderline personality disorder: a comparison of combined therapy and single pharmacotherapy. Canadian Journal of Psychiatry 2010;55:74–81

Bernal G, Bonilla J, Bellido C: Ecological validity and cultural sensitivity for outcome research: Issues for the cultural adaptation and development of psychosocial treatments with Hispanics. Journal of Abnormal Child Psychology 1995;23: 67–82

Bernal G, Bonilla J, Padilla-Cotto L, Perez-Prado EM: Factors associated to outcome in psychotherapy: An effectiveness study in Puerto Rico. Journal of Clinical Psychology 1998;54:329–342

Bernal G, Scharro-del-Rio MR: Are empirically supported treatments valid for ethnic minorities? Toward an alternative approach for treatment research. Cultural Diversity & Ethnic Minority Psychology 2001;7:328–342

Bifulco A, Kwon J, Jacobs C, Moran P, Bunn A, Beer N: Adult attachment style as mediator between childhood neglect/abuse and adult depression and anxiety. Social Psychiatry and Psychiatric Epidemiology 2006;41:796–805

Bifulco A, Moran P, Ball C, Bernazzani O: Adult attachment style. I: Its relationship to clinical depression. Social Psychiatry and Psychiatric Epidemiology 2002; 37:50–59

Bifulco A, Moran P, Ball C, Lillie A: Adult attachment style. II: Its relationship to psychosocial depressive-vulnerability. Social Psychiatry and Psychiatric Epidemiology, 2002;37:60–67

Bird HR, Canino G, Rubio-Stipec M, Ribera JC: Further measure of the psychometric properties of the Children's Global Assessment Scale. Arch of Gen Psychiatry, 1987; 44(9):821–824

Birndorf CA, Sacks AC: To medicate or not: the dilemma of pregnancy and psychiatric illness. In Stone SD, Menkin AE (Eds.): Perinatal and Postpartum Mood Disorders: Perspectives and a Treatment Guide for Mental Health Professionals. New York: Springer Publishing, 2008:237–265

Bishop M, Stein R, Hilbert A, Swenson A, Wilfley DE: A five-year follow-up study of cognitive-behavioral therapy and interpersonal psychotherapy for the treatment of binge eating disorder. Paper presented at the Eating Disorders Research Society, 2007

Blake DD, Weathers FW, Nagy LM, Kaloupek DG, Gusman FD, Charney DS, Keane TM: The development of a Clinician-Administered PTSD Scale. Journal of Traumatic Stress 1995;8:75–90

Blanco C, Okuda M, Markowitz JC, Liu S-M, Grant BF, Hasin DS: The epidemiology of chronic major depressive disorder and dysthymic disorder: results from the National Epidemiologic Survey on Alcohol and Related Conditions. Journal of Clinical Psychiatry 2010;71:1645–1656

Bleiberg KL, Markowitz JC: Interpersonal psychotherapy for posttraumatic stress disorder. American Journal of Psychiatry 2005;162:181–183

Blom MB, Jonker K, Dusseldorp E, Spinhoven P, Hoencamp E, Haffmans J, van Dyck R: Combination treatment for acute depression is superior only when psychotherapy is added to medication. Psychotherapy and Psychosomatics 2007;76:289–297

Blöte AW, Westenberg PM: Socially anxious adolescents' perception of treatment by classmates. Behaviour Research and Therapy 2007;45:189–198

Boelen PA, van den Bout J, de Keijser J: Traumatic grief as a disorder distinct from bereavement related depression or anxiety: A replication study with bereaved mental health care clients. American Journal of Psychiatry 2003;160:1338–1341

Bolton P: Cross-cultural validity and reliability testing of a standard psychiatric assessment instrument without a gold standard. Journal of Nervous and Mental Disease 2001;189:238–242

Bolton P, Bass J, Betancourt T, Speelman L, Onyango G, Clougherty KF, Neugebauer R, Murray L, Verdeli H: Interventions for depression symptoms among adolescent survivors of war and displacement in northern Uganda: a randomized controlled trial. Journal of the American Medical Association 2007;298:519–527

Bolton P, Bass J, Neugebauer R, Verdeli H, Clougherty KF, Wickramaratne P, Speelman L, Ndogoni L, Weissman M: Group interpersonal psychotherapy for depression in rural Uganda: a randomized controlled trial. Journal of the American Medical Association 2003;289:3117–3124

Bolton P, Neugebauer R, Ndogoni L: Prevalence of depression in rural Rwanda based on symptom and functional criteria. Journal of Nervous and Mental Disease 2002;190:631–637

Bolton P, Wilk M, Ndogoni L: Assessment of depression prevalence in rural Uganda using symptom and function criteria. Social Psychiatry and Psychiatric Epidemiology 2004;39:442–447

Bordin E: Theory and research on the therapeutic working alliance: New directions. In Horvath A, Greenberg L (Eds.): The Working Alliance: Theory, Research, and Practice. New York: Wiley, 1994:13–37

Borge FM, Hoffart A, Sexton H, Clark DM, Markowitz JC, McManus F: Residential cognitive therapy versus residential interpersonal therapy for social phobia: A randomized clinical trial. Journal of Anxiety Disorders 2008;22:991–1010

Bowlby J: Attachment and Loss: Vol. I: Attachment. New York: Basic Books, 1969

Bowlby J: Attachment and Loss. New York: Basic Books, 1973

Boyd-Franklin N, Lockwood T: Spirituality and religion: Implications for psychotherapy with African American clients and families. In Walsh F (Ed.): Spiritual Resources in Family Therapy. New York: Guilford, 1999:90–103

Bradley R, Green J, Russ E, Dutra L, Westen D: A multidimensional meta-analysis of psychotherapy for PTSD. American Journal of Psychiatry 2005;162:214–227

Breslau N, Chilcoat H, Kessler R, Davis G: Previous exposure to trauma and PTSD effects of subsequent trauma: Results from the Detroit Area Survey of Trauma. American Journal of Psychiatry 1999;156:902–907

Breslau N, Peterson E, Schultz LR: A second look ot prior trauma and the posttraumatic stress disorder effects of subsequent trauma. Archives of General Psychiatry 2008;65:431–437

Brewin CR, Andrews B, Valentine JD: Meta-analysis of risk factors for posttraumatic stress disorder in trauma-exposed adults. Journal of Consulting and Clinical Psychology 2000;68:748–766

Broman CL: Coping with personal problems. In Neighbors HW, Jackson JS (Eds.): Mental Health in Black America. Thousands Oaks, CA: Sage, 1996:117–129

Brown C, Conner KO, Copeland VC, Grote N, Beach S, Battista D, Reynolds CF: Depression stigma, race, and treatment seeking attitudes and behaviors. Journal of Community Psychology 2010;28:350–368

Browne G, Steiner M, Roberts J, Gafni A, Byrne C, Dunn E, Bell B, Mills M, Chalklin L, Wallik D, Kraemer J: Sertraline and/or interpersonal psychotherapy for patients with dysthymic disorder in primary care: 6 month comparison with longitudinal 2 year follow-up of effectiveness and costs. Journal of Affective Disorders 2002;68:317–330

Bruce SE, Yonkers KA, Otto MW, Eisen JL, Weisberg RB, Pagano M, Shea MT, Keller MB: Influence of psychiatric comorbidity on recovery and recurrence in generalized anxiety disorder, social phobia, and panic disorder: a 12-year prospective study. American Journal of Psychiatry 2005;162:1179–1187

Brunstein Klomek A, Marrocco F, Kleinman M, Schonfeld IS, Gould MS: Bullying, depression, and suicidality in adolescents. Journal of the American Academy of Child and Adolescent Psychiatry 2007;46:40–49.

Burns T, Knapp M, Catty J, Healey A, Henderson J, Watt H, Wright C: Home treatment for mental health problems: a systematic review. Health Technology Assessment 2001;5:1–139

Buysee DJ, Cheng Y, Germain A, Moul DE, Franzen PL, Fletcher M, Monk TH: Night-to-night sleep variability in older adults with and without chronic insomnia. Sleep Medicine 2010;11:56–64

Campanini RF, Schoedl AF, Pupo MC, Costa AC, Krupnick JL, Mello MF: Efficacy of interpersonal therapy-group format adapted to post-traumatic stress disorder: an open-label add-on trial. Depression and Anxiety 2010;27:72–77

Carlson GA, Kotin J, Davenport YB, Adland M: Follow-up of 53 bipolar manic-depressive patients. British Journal of Psychiatry 1974;124:134–139

Carreira K, Miller MD, Frank E, Houck PR, Morse JQ, Dew MA, Butters MA, Reynolds CF: A controlled evaluation of monthly maintenance Interpersonal Psychotherapy in late-life depression with varying levels of cognitive performance. International Journal of Geriatric Psychiatry 2008;23:1110–1113

Case BG, Olfson M, Marcus SC, Siegel C: Trends in the inpatient mental health treatment of children and adolescents in US community hospitals between 1990 and 2000. Archives of General Psychiatry 2007;64:89–96

Chui W, Safer DL, Bryson SW, Agras WS, Wilson GT: A comparison of ethnic groups in the treatment of bulimia nervosa. Eating Behaviors 2007;8:485–491

Ciechanowski P, Hirsch I, Katon W: Interpersonal predictors of HbA1c in patients with Type 1 diabetes. Diabetes Care 2002;25:731–736

Ciechanowski P, Katon W, Russo J, Walker EA: The patient-provider relationship: Attachment theory and adherence to treatment in diabetes. American Journal of Psychiatry 2001;158:29–35

Clark DM, Ehlers A, Hackmann A, McManus F, Fennell M, Grey N, Waddington L, Wild J: Cognitive therapy versus exposure and applied relaxation in social phobia: A randomized controlled trial. Journal of Consulting and Clinical Psychology 2006;74:568–578

Clark DM, Wells A: A cognitive model of social phobia. In: Heimberg R, Liebowitz M, Hope DA, Schneier FR (Eds.): Social Phobia: Diagnosis, Assessment, and Treatment. New York: Guilford, 1995:69–93

Cloitre M, Scarvalone P, Difede JA: Posttraumatic stress disorder, self and interpersonal dysfunction among sexually retraumatized women. Journal of Traumatic Stress 1997;10:437–452

Clougherty KF, Verdeli H, Weissman MM: Interpersonal psychotherapy for a group in Uganda (IPT-GU). Copyrighted unpublished manual, 2003

Comas-Díaz L, Duncan JW: The cultural context: A factor in assertiveness training with mainland Puerto Rican women. Psychology of Women Quarterly 1985;9:463–476

Comas-Díaz L, Jacobsen FM: Ethnocultural identification in psychotherapy. Psychiatry 1987;50:232–241

Conner KO, Grote NK: A model for enhancing the cultural relevance of empirically-supported mental health interventions. Families in Society 2008; 89:1–9

Connor KM, Davidson JR, Churchill LE, Sherwood A, Foa E, Weisler RH: Psychometric properties of the Social Phobia Inventory (SPIN). New self-rating scale. British Journal of Psychiatry 2000;176:379–386

Constantino MJ, Arnow BA, Blasey C, Agras WS: The association between patient characteristics and the therapeutic alliance in cognitive-behavioral and interpersonal therapy for bulimia nervosa. Journal of Consulting and Clinical Psychology 2005;73:203–211

Constantino MJ, Manber R, DeGeorge J, McBride C, Ravitz P, Zuroff D, et al.: Interpersonal styles of chronically depressed outpatients: Profiles and therapeutic change. Psychotherapy: Theory, Research, Practice, Training 2008;45:491–506

Cooper A, Corrigan PW, Watson AC: Mental illness stigma and care seeking. Journal of Nervous and Mental Disease 2003;191:339–341

Cooper LA, Brown C, Ford DE, Vu HT, Powe NR: How important is intrinsic spirituality in depression care? A comparison of the views of White and African American primary care patients. Journal of General Internal Medicine 2001;16:634–638

Cooper LA, Gonzales J, Gallo JJ, Rost KM, Meredith LS, Rubenstein LV, Wang NY, Ford DE: The acceptability of treatment for depression among African-American, Hispanic, and White primary care clients. Medical Care 2003;41:479–489

Cox JL, Holden JM, Sagovsky R: Detection of postnatal depression: development of the 10-item Edinburgh Postnatal Depression Scale. British Journal of Psychiatry 1987;150:782–786

Crick NR, Ladd GW: Children's perceptions of their peer experiences: attributions, loneliness, social anxiety, and social avoidance. Developmental Psychology 1993;29:244–254

Crockett K, Zlotnick C, Davis M, Payne N, Washington R: A depression preventive intervention for rural low-income African-American pregnant women at risk for postpartum depression. Archives of Women's Mental Health 2008;11:319–325

Cuming S, Rapee RM: Social anxiety and self-protective communication style in close relationships. Behaviour Research and Therapy 2010;48:87–96

Cutler NR, Post RM: Life course of illness in untreated manic-depressive patients. Comprehensive Psychiatry 1982;23:101–115

Cyranowski JM, Frank E, Winter E, Rucci P, Novick D, Pilkonis P, Fagiolini A, Swartz HA, Houck P, Kupfer DJ: Personality pathology and outcome in recurrently depressed women over 2 years of maintenance interpersonal psychotherapy. Psychological Medicine 2004;34:659–669

Daly K, Mallinckrodt B: Experienced therapist's approach to psychotherapy for adults with attachment avoidance or attachment anxiety. Journal of Counseling Psychology 2009;56:549–563

David SP, Munafo MR, Johansen-Berg H, Smith SM, Rogers RD, Matthews PM, Walton RT: Ventral striatum/nucleus accumbens activation to smoking-related pictorial cues in smokers and nonsmokers: a functional magnetic resonance imaging study. Biological Psychiatry 2005;58:488–494

David-Ferdon C, Kaslow NJ: Evidence-based psychosocial treatments for child and adolescent depression. Journal of Clinical Child and Adolescent Psychology 2008;37:62–104

Davidson JRT, Hughes D, Blazer D, George LK: Posttraumatic stress disorder in the community: An epidemiological study. Psychological Medicine 1991;21:1–19

Davila J, Beck JG: Is social anxiety associated with impairment in close relationships? A preliminary investigation. Behavior Therapy 2002;33:427–446

Dawson DF: Treatment of the borderline patient, relationship management. Canadian Journal of Psychiatry 1988;33:370–374

Day S, Schneider P: Psychotherapy using distance technology: a comparison of face-to-face, video, and audio treatment. Journal of Counseling Psychology 2002;49:499–503

Delgado M: Hispanics and group work: A review of the literature. Ethnicity in Group Work Practice 1984;7:85–96

Delgado M: Hispanics and psychotherapeutic groups. International Journal of Group Psychotherapy 1983;33:507–520

De Mello MF, De Jesus MJ, Bacaltchuk J, Verdeli H, Neugebauer R: A systematic review of research findings on the efficacy of interpersonal therapy for depressive disorders. European Archives of Psychiatry and Clinical Neuroscience 2005;255:75–82

Department of Health and Human Services: Mental Health: A Report of the Surgeon General. Rockville, MD: U.S. Department of Health and Human Services, Substance Abuse and Mental Health Services Administration, Center for Mental Health Services, National Institutes of Health, National Institute of Mental Health, 1999

Department of Health and Human Services: Mental Health: Culture, Race, and Ethnicity—A supplement to Mental health: A Report of the Surgeon General. (DHHS Publication No. SMA-01–3613) Rockville, MD: U.S. Department of Health and Human Services, Substance Abuse and Mental Health Services Administration, Center for Mental Health Services, 2001

Derogatis LR, Lipman RS, Rickels K, Uhlenhut EH, Covi L: The Hopkins Symptom Checklist (HSCL): A self-report symptom inventory. Behavioral Science 1974;19:1–15

Diamond R, Factor R: Treatment-resistant patients of treatment-resistant systems? Hospital and Community Psychiatry 1994;45:197

DiMascio A, Weissman MM, Prusoff BA, Neu C, Zwilling M, Klerman GL: Differential symptom reduction by drugs and psychotherapy in acute depression. Archives of General Psychiatry 1979;36:1450–1456

Dodge CS, Heimberg RG, Nyman D, O'Brien GT: Daily heterosocial interactions of high and low socially anxious college students: A diary study. Behavior Therapy 1987;18:90–96

Domenech-Rodríguez M, Wieling E: Developing culturally appropriate evidence based treatments for interventions with ethnic minority populations. In Rastogi M, Wieling E (Eds.): Voices of Color: First Person Accounts of Ethnic Minority Therapists. Thousand Oaks: Sage Publications, 2004:313–333

Donnelly JM, Kornblith AB, Fleishman S, Zuckerman E, Raptis G, Hudis CA, Hamilton N, Payne D, Massie MJ, Norton L, Holland JC: A pilot study of interpersonal psychotherapy by telephone with cancer patients and their partners. Psycho-Oncology 2000;9:44–56

Dozier M: Attachment organization and treatment use for adults with serious psychopathological disorders. Development and Psychopathology 1990;2:47–60

Due DL, Huettel SA, Hall WG, Rubin DC: Activation in mesolimbic and visuospatial neural circuits elicited by smoking cues: evidence from functional magnetic resonance imaging. American Journal of Psychiatry 2002;159:954–960

Dwight-Johnson M, Unutzer J, Sherbourne C, Tang L, Wells KB: Can quality improvement programs for depression in primary care address patient preferences for treatment? Medical Care 2001;39:934–944

Ehlers CL, Frank E, Kupfer DJ: Social zeitgebers and biological rhythms: A unified approach to understanding the etiology of depression. Archives of General Psychiatry 1988;45:948–952

Ehlers CL, Kupfer DJ, Frank E, Monk TH: Biological rhythms and depression: The role of zeitgebers and zeitstorers. Depression 1993;1:285–293

Elkin I: The NIMH treatment of Depression Collaborative Research Program: Where we began and where we are. In: Bergin AE, Garfield SL (Eds.): Handbook of Psychotherapy and Behavior Change, 4th ed. New York: Wiley, 1994

Elkin I, Shea MT, Watkins JT, Imber SD, Sotsky SM, Collins JE, Glass DR, Pilkonis PA, Leber WR, Docherty JP, Fiester SJ, Parloff MB: National Institute of Mental Health Treatment of Depression Collaborative Research Program: general effectiveness of treatments. Archives of General Psychiatry 1989;46:971–982

Ellicott A, Hammen C, Gitlin M, Brown G, Jamison K: Life Events and the course of bipolar disorder. American Journal of Psychiatry 1990;147:1194–1198

Eliot TS: Little Gidding. In: The Four Quartets. London: Faber, 1943

Engelberg MJ, Steiger H, Gauvin L, Wonderlich SA: Binge antecedents in bulimic syndromes: an examination of dissociation and negative affect. International Journal of Eating Disorders 2007;40:531–536

Fairburn CG, Jones R, Peveler RC, Hope RA, O'Connor M: Psychotherapy and bulimia nervosa: Longer-term effects of interpersonal psychotherapy, behavior therapy, and cognitive behavior therapy. Archives of General Psychiatry 1993;270:419–428

Fairburn CG, Norman PA, Welch SL, O'Connor ME, Doll HA, Peveler RC: A prospective study of outcome in bulimia nervosa and the long-term effects of three psychological treatments. Archives of General Psychiatry 1995;52:304–312

Fairhurst K, Dowrick C: Problems with recruitment in a randomized controlled trial of counseling in general practice: causes and implications. Journal of Health Services Research and Policy 1996;1:77–80

Feeny NC, Zoellner LA, Foa EB: Treatment outcome for chronic PTSD among female assault victims with borderline personality characteristics: a preliminary examination. Journal of Personality Disorders 2002;16:30–40

Feijó de Mello M, Myczcowisk LM, Menezes PR: A randomized controlled trial comparing moclobemide and moclobemide plus interpersonal psychotherapy in the treatment of dysthymic disorder. Journal of Psychotherapy Practice and Research 2001;10:117–123

First MB, Gibbon M, Spitzer RL, Williams JBW: Structured Clinical Interview for DSM-IV Axis II Personality Disorders. Washington, DC: American Psychiatric Publishing, 1997

First MB, Spitzer RL, Gibbon M, Williams JBW: User's Guide for the Structured Clinical Interview for DSM-IV Axis II Personality Disorders. Washington, DC: American Psychiatric Press, 1997

Flores G: Culture and the client-physician relationship: achieving cultural competency in healthcare. Journal of Pediatrics 2000;136:14–23

Foa EB, Keane TM, Friedman MJ (Eds.): Effective Treatments for PSTD. New York: Guilford, 2000

Foa EB, Kozak MJ: Emotional processing of fear: exposure to corrective information. Psychological Bulletin 1986;99:20–35.

Foa EB, Riggs DS, Massie ED, Yarczower M: The impact of fear activation and anger on the efficacy of exposure treatment for post-traumatic stress disorder. Behavior Therapy 1995;26:487–499

Folstein MF, Folstein SE, McHugh PR: "Mini-mental state": a practical method for grading the cognitive state of patients for the clinician. Journal of Psychiatric Research 1975;12:189–198

Fonagy P, Leigh T, Steele M, Steele H, Kennedy R, Matton K, Target M, Gerber A: The relation of attachment status, psychiatric classification, and response to psychotherapy. Journal of Consulting and Clinical Psychology 1996;64:22–31

Fonagy P, Steele M, Moran G, Steele H, Higgit A: The capacity for understanding mental states: The reflective self in parent and child and its significance for security of attachment. Infant Mental Health Journal 1991;13:200–216

Fonagy P, Steele M, Steele H, Leigh T, Kennedy R, Mattoon G, Target M: Attachment, the reflective self, and borderline states. In Goldberg S, Kerr J (Eds.), Attachment Research: The State of the Art. New York: Analytic Press, 1995:233–278

Fonagy P, Target M: Bridging the transmission gap: An end to an important mystery of attachment research? Attachment & Human Development 2005;7: 333–343

Frank E: Interpersonal and social rhythm therapy prevents prevents depressive symptomatology in bipolar I patients [abstract]. Bipolar Disorders 1999;(suppl 1).

Frank E: Interpersonal psychotherapy as a maintenance treatment for patients with recurrent depression. Psychotherapy and Psychosomatics 1991;28:259–266

Frank E: Treating Bipolar Disorder: A Clinician's Guide to Interpersonal and Social Rhythm Therapy. New York: Guilford Press, 2005

Frank E, Hlastala S, Ritenour A, Houck P, Tu XM, Monk TH, Mallinger AG, Kupfer DJ: Inducing lifestyle regularity in recovering bipolar disorder patients: Results from the maintenance therapies of bipolar disorder protocol. Biological Psychiatry 1997;41:1165–1173

Frank E, Kupfer D, Cornes C, Morris S: Maintenance interpersonal psychotherapy for recurrent depression. In Klerman G, Weissman M (Eds.): New Applications of Interpersonal Psychotherapy. Washington, DC: American Psychiatric Press, 1993:75–102

Frank E, Kupfer DJ, Buysse DJ, Swartz HA, Pilkonis PA, Houck PR, Rucci P, Novick DM, Grochocinski VJ, Stapf DM: Randomized trial of weekly, twice-monthly, and monthly interpersonal psychotherapy as maintenance treatment for women with recurrent depression. American Journal of Psychiatry 2007;164:761–767

Frank E, Kupfer DJ, Cornes C, et al.: Maintenance interpersonal psychotherapy for recurrent depression. In Klerman G, Weissman MM (Eds.): New Applications of Interpersonal Psychotherapy. Washington, DC: American Psychiatric Press, 1993

Frank E, Kupfer DJ, Perel JM, Cornes C, Jarrett DB, Mallinger AG, Thase ME, McEachran AB, Grochocinski VJ: Three-year outcomes for maintenance therapies in recurrent depression. Archives of General Psychiatry 1990;47:1093–1099

Frank E, Kupfer DJ, Thase ME, Mallinger AG, Swartz HA, Fagiolini AM, Grochocinski V, Houck P, Scott J, Thompson W, Monk T: Two-year outcomes for interpersonal and social rhythm therapy in individuals with bipolar I disorder. Archives of General Psychiatry 2005;62:996–1004

Frank E, Kupfer DJ, Wagner EF, McEachran AB, Cornes C: Efficacy of interpersonal psychotherapy as a maintenance treatment of recurrent depression. Contributing factors. Archives of General Psychiatry 1991;48:1053–1059

Frank E, Levenson J: Interpersonal Psychotherapy. New York: American Psychological Association, 2010

Frank E, Prien RF, Jarrett RB, Keller MB, Kupfer DJ, Lavori P, Rush AJ, Weissman MM: Conceptualization and rationale for consensus definitions of terms in major depressive disorder: response, remission, recovery, relapse and recurrence. Archives of General Psychiatry 1991;48:851–885

Frank E, Swartz HA, Kupfer DJ: Interpersonal and social rhythm therapy: Managing the chaos of bipolar disorder. Biological Psychiatry 2000;48:593–604

Frank E, Swartz HA, Mallinger AG, Thase ME, Weaver EV, Kupfer DJ: Adjunctive psychotherapy for bipolar disorder: Effects of changing treatment modality. Journal of Abnormal Psychology 1999;108:579–587

Frank J: Therapeutic factors in psychotherapy. American Journal of Psychotherapy 1971;25:350–361

Fresco DM, Coles ME, Heimberg RG, Liebowitz MR, Hami S, Stein MB, Goetz D: The Liebowitz Social Anxiety Scale: a comparison of the psychometric properties of self-report and clinician-administered formats. Psychological Medicine 2001;31:1025–1035

Gao LL, Chan SW, Li X, Chen S, Hao Y: Evaluation of an interpersonal-psychotherapy-oriented childbirth education programme for Chinese first-time childbearing women: a randomized controlled trial. International Journal of Nursing Studies 2010;47:1208–1216

Germain CB: Using social and physical environments. In Rosenblatt A, Waldfogel D (Eds.): Handbook of Clinical Social Work. San Francisco: Jossey-Bass, 1983: 110–133

Gitlin MJ, Swendsen J, Heller TL, Hammen C: Relapse and impairment in bipolar disorder. American Journal of Psychiatry 1995;152:1635–1640

Glen AIM, Johnson AL, Shepherd M: Continuation therapy with lithium and amitriptyline in unipolar depressive illness: a randomized, double-blind, controlled trial. Psychological Medicine 1984;4:37–50

Golier JA, Yehuda R, Bierer LM, Mitropoulou V, New AS, Schmeidler J, Silverman JM, Siever, LJ: The relationship of borderline personality disorder to posttraumatic stress disorder and traumatic Events. American Journal of Psychiatry 2003;160:2018–2024

Goodwin FK, Jamison KR: Manic Depressive Illness. New York: Oxford University Press, 1990

Goodwin FK, Jamison KR: Manic Depressive Illness (2nd ed.). New York: Oxford University Press, 2007

Gotlib IH, Hammen CL: Psychological Aspects of Depression: Toward a Cognitive-Interpersonal Integration. Chichester, UK: Wiley, 1992

Gotlib IH, Whiffen VE, Wallace PM, Mount JH: Prospective investigation of postpartum depression: factors involved in onset and recovery Journal of Abnormal Psychology 1991;100:122–132

Green B, McAfee T, Hindmarsh M, Madsen L, Caplow M, Buist D: Effectiveness of telephone support in increasing physical activity levels in primary care patients. American Journal of Preventive Medicine 2002;22:177–183

Greeno CG, Anderson CM, Shear MK, Mike G: Initial treatment engagement in a rural community mental health center. Psychiatric Services 1999;50: 1634–1636

Grewen KM, Anderson BJ, Girdler SS, Light KC: Warm partner contact is related to lower cardiovascular reactivity. Behavioral Medicine 2003;29:123–130

Grilo CM, Shea MT, Sanislow CA, Skodol AE, Gunderson JG, Stout RL, Pagano ME, Yen S, Morey LC, Zanarini MC, McGlashan TH: Two-year stability and change in schizotypal, borderline, avoidant and obsessive-compulsive personality disorders. Journal of Consulting and Clinical Psychology 2004;72:767–775

Griner D, Smith TB: Culturally adapted mental health interventions: a meta-analytic review. Psychotherapy: Theory, Research, Practice, Training 2006;43: 531–548

Grote NK, Bledsoe SE, Larkin J, Brown C: Depression in African American and White women with low incomes: the role of chronic stress. Social Work in Public Health 2007;23:59–88

Grote NK, Bledsoe SE, Swartz HA, Frank E: Feasibility of providing culturally relevant, brief interpersonal psychotherapy for antenatal depression in an obstetrics clinic: A pilot study. Research on Social Work Practice 2004;14:397–407

Grote NK, Swartz HA, Geibel SL, Zuckoff A, Houck P, Frank E: Culturally relevant brief interpersonal psychotherapy for perinatal depression. Psychiatric Services 2009;60:313–321

Grote NK, Zuckoff A, Swartz HA, Bledsoe SE, Geibel SL: Engaging women who are depressed and economically disadvantaged in mental health treatment. Social Work 2007;52:295–308

Gruber J, Harvey AG, Wang PW, Brooks JO, Thase ME, Sachs GS, Ketter TA: Sleep functioning in relation to mood, function, and quality of life at entry to the Systematic Treatment Enhancement Program for Bipolar Disorder (STEP-BD). Journal of Affective Disorders 2009;114:41–49

Guarnaccia PJ, Martinez I: "It's like Going Through an Earthquake": Anthropological Perspectives on Depression From Focus Groups with Latino Immigrants. Paper presented at Mount Sinai Medical Center, New York, 2003

Gunderson JG, Fonagy P, Gabbard GO: The place of psychoanalytic treatments within psychiatry. Archives of General Psychiatry 2002;59:505–510

Halbreich U, Karkum S: Cross-cultural and social diversity of prevalence of postpartum depression and depressive symptoms. Journal of Affective Disorders 2006;91:97–111

Hall GC: Psychotherapy research with ethnic minorities: Empirical, ethical, and conceptual issues. Journal of Consulting and Clinical Psychology 2001;69: 502–510

Hamann DM, Wonderlich-Tierney AL, Vander Wal JS: Interpersonal sensitivity predicts bulimic symptomatology cross-sectionally and longitudinally. Eating Behaviors 2009;10:125–127

Hall L, Williams C, Greenberg R: Supports, stressors, and depressive symptoms in low-income mothers of young children. American Journal of Public Health 1985;75:518–522

Hamilton M: A rating scale for depression. Journal of Neurology, Neurosurgery, and Psychiatry 1960;25:56–62

Hamilton M: Rating depressive patients. Journal of Clinical Psychiatry 1980;41: 21–24

Hastings MH, Herzog ED: Clock genes, oscillators, and cellular networks in the suprachiasmatic nuclei. Journal of Biological Rhythms 2004;19:400–413

Haynes PL, Ancoli-Israel S, McQuaid J: Illuminating the impact of habitual behaviors in depression. Chronobiology International 2005;22:279–297

Heimberg RG, Liebowitz MR, Hope DA, Schneier FR, Holt CS, Welkowitz LA, Juster HR, Campeas R, Bruch MA, Cloitre M, Fallon B, Klein DF: Cognitive behavioral group therapy vs phenelzine therapy for social phobia: 12-week outcome. Archives of General Psychiatry. 1998;55:1133–1141

Hellerstein DJ, Little SAS, Samstag LW, Batchelder S, Muran JC, Fedak M, Kreditor D, Rosenthal RN, Winston A: Adding group psychotherapy to medication treatment in dysthymia. Journal of Psychotherapy Practice and Research 2001;10:93–103

Hembree EA, Cahill SP, Foa EB: Impact of personality disorders on treatment outcome for female assault survivors with chronic posttraumatic stress disorder. Journal of Personality Disorders 2004;18:117–127

Henderson S: A development in social psychiatry, the systematic study of social bonds. Journal of Nervous and Mental Disease 1980;168: 63–69

Henderson S, Duncan-Jones P, McAuley H, Ritchie K: The patient's primary group. British Journal of Psychiatry 1978;132:74–86

Hinrichsen GA, Clougherty KF: Interpersonal Psychotherapy for Depressed Older Adults. Washington, DC: American Psychological Association Press, 2006

Hobfoll S, Ritter C, Lavin J, Hulszier M, Cameron R: Depression prevalence and incidence among inner-city pregnant and postpartum women. Journal of Consulting and Clinical Psychology 1995;63:445–453

Hofmann SG: Cognitive mediation of treatment change in social phobia. Journal of Consulting and Clinical Psychology 2004;72:392–398

Hollon SD, Jarrett DB, Nierenberg AA, Thase ME, Madhukar T, Rush J: Psychotherapy and medication in the treatment of adult and geratric depression: which monotherapy or combined treatment? Journal of Clinical Psychiatry 2005;66:455–468

Hollon SD, Thase ME, Markowitz JC: Treatment and prevention of depression. Psychological Science in the Public Interest 2002;3:39–77

Horberg MA, Silverberg MJ, Hurley LB, Towner WJ, Klein DB, Bersoff-Matcha S, Weinberg WG, Antoniskis D, Mogyoros M, Dodge WT, Dobrinich R, Quesenberry CP, Kovach DA: Effects of depression and selective serotonin reuptake inhibitor use on adherence to highly active antiretroviral therapy and on clinical outcomes in HIV-infected patients. Journal of Acquired Immune Deficiency Syndromes 2008;47:384–390

Horowitz MJ, Seigel B, Holen A, Bonanno GA, Milbrath C, Stinson CH: Diagnostic criteria for complicated grief disorder. American Journal of Psychiatry 1997;154:904–910

Horvath A, Symonds B: Relation between working alliance and outcome in psychotherapy: A meta-analysis. Journal of Counseling Psychology 1999;38:139–149

Howard KI, Kopta SM, Krause MS, Orlinsky DE: The dose-effect relationship in psychotherapy. American Psychologist 1986;41:159–164

Hu T, Snowden LR, Jerrell JM, Nguyen TD: Ethnic populations in public mental health: services choice and level of use. American Journal of Public Health 1991;81:1429–1434

Hudson JI, Hiripi E, Pope Jr HG, Kessler RC: The prevalence and correlates of eating disorders in the National Comorbidity Survey Replication. Biological Psychiatry 2007;61:348–358

Hunt C, Andrews G: Drop-out rate as a performance indicator in psychotherapy. Acta Psychiatrica Scandinavica 1992;85:275–278

Hwang W-C: The psychotherapy adaptation and modification framework. American Psychologist 2006;61:702–715

Hyman SE: Goals for research on bipolar disorder: The view from NIMH. Biological Psychiatry 2000;48:436–441

Jacobs MJ, Welch R, Wilfley DE: Interpersonal psychotherapy for anorexia nervosa, bulimia nervosa, and binge eating disorder. In T. Brewerton (Ed.): Clinical Handbook of Eating Disorders: An Integrated Approach. New York: Marcel Dekker, 2004:449–472

Jacobson NS, Martell CR, Dimidjian S: Behavioral activation treatment for depression: returning to contextual roots. Clinical Psychology-Science & Practice 2001;8:255–270

Jacobson NS, Truax P: Clinical significance: A statistical approach to defining meaningful change in psychotherapy research. Journal of Consulting and Clinical Psychology 1991;59:12–19

Jamison KR: Touched With Fire: Manic-Depressive Illness and the Artistic Temperament. New York: The Free Press, 1993

Jaycox LH, Asarnow JR, Sherbourne CD, Rea MM, LaBorde AP, Wells KB: Adolescent primary care patients' preferences for depression treatment. Admin Policy Mental Health Serv Res 2006;33:198–207

Jaycox LH, Foa EB: Obstacles in implementing exposure therapy for PTSD: Case discussions and practical solutions. Clinical Psychology and Psychotherapy 1996; 3:176–184

Johnson SL: Mania and dysregulation in goal pursuit: A review. Clinical Psychology Review 2005;25:241–262

Johnson JE, Zlotnick C: A pilot study of group interpersonal psychotherapy for depression in substance-abusing female prisoners. Journal of Substance Abuse Treatment 2008;34:371–377

Keck PE, McElroy SL, Strakowski SM, West SA, Sax KW, Hawkins JM, Bourne ML, Haggard P: 12-month outcome of patients with bipolar disorder following hospitalization for a manic or mixed episode. American Journal of Psychiatry 1998;155:646–652

Keitner GI, Solomon DA, Ryan CE, Miller IW, Mallinger A, Kupfer DJ, Frank E: Prodromal and residual symptoms in bipolar I disorder. Comprehensive Psychiatry 1996;37:363–367

Kemp S, Whittaker J, Tracy E: Person-Environment Practice: The Social Ecology of Interpersonal Helping. Hawthorne, NY: Aldine de Gruyter, 1997

Kessler RC, Berglund P, Demler O, Jin R, Koretz D, Merikangas K, Rush AJ, Walters EE, Wang PS; National Comorbidity Survey Replication: The epidemiology of major depressive disorder: Results from the National Comorbidity Survey Replication (NCS-R). Journal of the American Medical Association 2003;289:3095–3105

Kessler RC, Chiu WT, Demler O, Walters EE: Prevalence, severity, and comorbidity of 12-month DSM-IV disorders in the National Comorbidity Survey Replication. Archives of General Psychiatry 2005;62:617–627

Kessler RC, McGonagle KA, Zhao S, Nelson CB, Hughes M, Eshleman S, Wittchen HU, Kendler KS: Lifetime and 12-month prevalence of DSM-III-R psychiatric disorders in the United States. Archives of General Psychiatry 1994;51:8–19

Kirungi WL, Musinguzi JB, Opio A, Madraa E: Trends in HIV Prevalence and Sexual Behaviour (1990–2000) in Uganda. Paper presented at the Fourteenth International AIDS Conference. Barcelona, Spain, 2002

Klerman GL, Budman S, Berwick D, Weissman MM, Damico-White J, Demby A, Feldstein M: Efficacy of a brief psychosocial intervention for symptoms of stress and distress among patients in primary care. Medical Care 1987;25: 1078–1088

Klerman GL, DiMascio A, Weissman MM, Prusoff BA, Paykel ES: Treatment of depression by drugs and psychotherapy. American Journal of Psychiatry 1974;131:186–191

Klerman GL, Weissman MM, Rounsaville BJ, Chevron ES: Interpersonal Psychotherapy of Depression. New York: Basic Books, 1984

Klier CM, Muzik M, Rosenblum KL, Lenz G: Interpersonal psychotherapy adapted for the group setting in the treatment of postpartum depression. Journal of Psychotherapy Practice 2001;10:124–131

Klomek AB, Marrocco F, Kleinman M, Schonfeld IS, Gould MS: Bullying, depression, and suicidality in adolescents. Journal of the American Academy of Child and Adolescent Psychiatry 2007;46:40–49

Kocsis JH, Gelenberg AJ, Rothbaum BO, Klein DN, Trivedi MH, Manber R, Keller MB, Leon AC, Wisniewski SR, Arnow BA, Markowitz JC, Thase ME, REVAMP Investigators: Cognitive behavioral analysis system of psychotherapy (CBASP) and brief supportive psychotherapy for augmentation of antidepressant nonresponse in chronic depression: the REVAMP trial. Archives of General Psychiatry 2009;66:1178–1118

Kocsis JH, Leon AC, Markowitz JC, Manber R, Arnow B, Klein DN, Thase ME: Patient preference as a moderator of outcome for chronic depression treated with nefazodone, cognitive behavioral analysis system of psychotherapy, or their combination. Journal of Clinical Psychiatry 2009;70:354–361

Kramer PD: Listening to Prozac. New York: Viking, 1993

Kreger R, Mason P: Stop Walking on Eggshells: Taking Your Life Back When Someone You Care About Has Borderline Personality Disorder. Oakland: New Harbinger, 1998

Kroenke K, Spitzer RL, Williams JB: The PHQ-9: validity of a brief depression severity measure. Journal of General Internal Medicine 2001;16:606–613

Krupnick JL, Green BL, Stockton JM, Krause E, Mete M: Group interpersonal psychotherapy for low-income women with posttraumatic stress disorder. Psychotherapy Research 2008;18:497–507

Kupfer DJ: Long-term treatment of depression. Journal of Clinical Psychiatry 1991;51:S28–S34

La Greca AM, Lopez N: Social anxiety among adolescents: linkages with peer relations and friendships. Journal of Abnormal Child Psychology 1998;26:83–94

Lam D, Wong G: Prodromes, coping strategies, insight, and social functioning in bipolar affective disorders. Psychological Medicine 1997;27:1091–1100

Lam DH, Watkins ER, Hayward P, Bright J, Wright K, Kerr N, Parr-Davis G, Sham P: A randomized controlled study of cognitive therapy for relapse prevention for bipolar affective disorder: Outcome of the first year. Archives of General Psychiatry 2003;60:145–152

Lam D, Wong G, & Sham P: Prodromes, coping strategies and course of illness in bipolar affective disorder – a naturalistic study. Psychological Medicine 2001;31:1387–1402

Lanius RA, Vermetten E, Loewenstein RJ, Brand B, Schmahl C, Bremner JD, Spiegel D: Emotion modulation in PTSD: clinical and neurobiological evidence for a dissociative subtype. American Journal of Psychiatry 2010;167:640–647

Leader JB, Klein DN: Social adjustment in dysthymia, double depression and episodic major depression. Journal of Affective Disorders 1996;37:91–101

Leaf P, Livingston M, Tischler G, Weissman MM, Holzer CE 3rd, Myers JK: Contact with health professionals for the treatment of psychiatric and emotional problems. Medical Care 1985;23:1322–1337

Lee DJ, Markides KS, Ray LA: Epidemiology of self-reported past heavy drinking in Hispanic adults. Ethnicity and Health 1997;2:77–88

Leibenluft E, Moul DE, Schwartz PJ, Madden PA, Wehr TA: A clinical trial of sleep deprivation in combination with antidepressant medication. Psychiatry Research 1993;46:213–227

Leibenluft E, Wehr TA: Is sleep deprivation useful in the treatment of depression? American Journal of Psychiatry 1992;149:159–168

Lenze EJ, Dew MA, Mazumdar S, Begley AE, Cornes C, Miller MD, Imber SD, Frank E, Kupfer DJ, Reynolds CF 3rd: Combined pharmacotherapy and psychotherapy as maintenance treatment for late-life depression: effects on social adjustment. American Journal of Psychiatry 2002;159:466–468

Lesperance F, Frasure-SmithN, Koszycki D, Laliberte MA, van Zyl LT, Baker B, Swenson JR, Ghatavi K, Abramson BL, Dorian P, Guertin MC, CREATE Investigators: Effects of citalopram and interpersonal psychotherapy on depression in patients with coronary artery disease: the Canadian Cardiac Randomized Evaluation of Antidepressant and Psychotherapy Efficacy (CREATE) trial. Journal of the American Medical Association 2007;297:367–379

Levenson JC, Frank E, Cheng Y, Rucci P, Janney CA, Houck P, Forgione RN, Swartz HA, Cyranowski JM, Fagiolini A: (2010) Comparative outcomes among the problem areas of interpersonal psychotherapy for depression. Depression and Anxiety 2010;7:434–440

Levkovitz Y, Shahar G, Native G, Hirsfeld E, Treves I, Krieger I, Fennig S: Group interpersonal psychotherapy for patients with major depression disorder- pilot study. Journal of Affective Disorders 2000;60:191–195

Lewandowski E, Verdeli H, Bolton P: Community impact of group interpersonal psychotherapy in rural Uganda. (in preparation)

Lewinsohn PM: A behavioral approach to depression. In Friedman RJ, Katz M (Eds.): The Psychology of Depression: Contemporary Theory and Research. Oxford: Wiley, 1974:157–178

Lewis-Fernández R, Díaz N: The Cultural Formulation: A method for assessing cultural factors affecting the clinical encounter. Psychiatric Quarterly 2002;73: 271–295

Lichtmacher JE, Eisendrath SJ, Haller E: Implementing interpersonal psycho-therapy in a psychiatry residency training program. Academic Psychiatry 2006; 30385–30391

Liebowitz MR, Schneier F, Campeas R, Hollander E, Hatterer J, Fyer A, Gorman J, Papp L, Davies S, Gully R, et al.: Phenelzine vs atenolol in social phobia: a placebo-controlled comparison. Archives of General Psychiatry 1992;49:290–300

Lingler JH, Nightingale MC, Erlen JA, Kane AL, Reynolds CF, Schulz R, DeKosky ST: Making sense of mild cognitive impairment: A qualitative exploration of the patient's experience. The Gerontologist 2006;46:791–800

Linkowski P: Neuroendocrine profiles in mood disorders. International Journal of Neuropsychopharmacology 2003;6:191–197

Lipsitz JD, Fyer AJ, Markowitz, JC, Cherry, S: An open trial of interpersonal psycho-therapy for social phobia. American Journal of Psychiatry 1999;156:1814–1816

Lipsitz JD, Gur M, Miller NL, Forand N, Vermes D, Fyer AJ: An open pilot study of interpersonal psychotherapy for panic disorder (IPT-PD). Journal of Nervous and Mental Disease 2006;194:440–445

Lipsitz JD, Gur M, Vermes D, Petkova E, Cheng J, Miller N, Laino J, Liebowitz MR, Fyer AJ: A randomized trial of interpersonal therapy versus supportive therapy for social anxiety disorder. Depression and Anxiety 2008;25:542–553

Lipsitz JD, Markowitz JC: Manual of Interpersonal Therapy (IPT) for Social Phobia. Unpublished manuscript. New York: Columbia University, 1997

Lipsitz JD, Schneier FR: Social phobia: epidemiology and cost of illness. Pharmacoeconomics 2000;18:23–32

Lorant V, Deliège D, Eaton W, Robert A, Philippot P, Ansseau M: Socioeconomic inequalities in depression: A meta-analysis. American Journal of Epidemiology 2003;157:98–112

Lyness JM, Niculescu A, Tu X, Reynolds CF, Caine ED: The relationship of medical comorbidity to depression in older, primary care patients. Psychosomatics 2006;47:435–439

MacKenzie KR: Where is here and when is now? The adaptational challenge of mental health reform for group psychotherapy. International Journal of Group Psychotherapy 1994;44:407–428

MacKenzie KR, Grabovac AD: Interpersonal psychotherapy (IPT-G) for depression. Journal of Psychotherapy Practice and Research 2001;10:46–51

Magee WJ, Eaton WW, Wittchen HU, McGonagle KA, Kessler RC: Agoraphobia, simple phobia, and social phobia in the National Comorbidity Survey. Archives of General Psychiatry 1996;53:159–168

Malkoff-Schwartz S, Frank E, Anderson BP, Hlastala SA, Luther JF, Sherrill JT, Houck PR, Kupfer DJ: Social rhythm disruption and stressful life events in the onset of bipolar and unipolar episodes. Psychological Medicine 2000;30:1005–1010

Malkoff-Schwartz S, Frank E, Anderson B, Sherrill JT, Siegel L, Patterson D, Kupfer DJ: Stressful life events and social rhythm disruption in the onset of manic and depressive bipolar episodes. Archives of General Psychiatry 1998;55:702–707

Manning DW, Markowitz JC, Frances AJ: A review of combined psychotherapy and pharmacotherapy in the treatment of depression. Journal of Psychotherapy Practice and Research 1992;1:103–116

Marin G: Defining culturally appropriate community interventions: Hispanics as a case study. Journal of Community Psychology 1991;21:149–161

Marziali E, Munroe-Blum H: Interpersonal Group Psychotherapy for Borderline Personality Disorder. New York: Basic Books, 1994

Markowitz JC: Adaptations of interpersonal psychotherapy. Psychiatric Annals 2006;36:559–563

Markowitz JC: A letter from America: rescuing inpatient psychiatry. Evidence-Based Mental Health 2008;11:68–69

Markowitz JC: Interpersonal handbook for personality disorders. In Widiger T (Ed.): Oxford Handbook of Personality Disorders. New York: Oxford University (in press)

Markowitz JC: Interpersonal psychotherapy for chronic depression. In Session: Journal of Clinical Psychology 2003;59:847–858

Markowitz JC: Interpersonal Psychotherapy for Dysthymic Disorder. Washington, DC: American Psychiatric Press, 1998

Markowitz JC: Psychotherapy of dysthymia. American Journal of Psychiatry 1994;151:1114–1121

Markowitz JC: Psychotherapy of the post-dysthymic patient. Journal of Psychotherapy Practice and Research 1993;2:157–163

Markowitz JC: Teaching interpersonal psychotherapy to psychiatric residents. Academic Psychiatry 1995;19:167–173

Markowitz JC, Bleiberg KL, Christos P, Levitan E: Solving interpersonal problems correlates with symptom improvement in interpersonal psychotherapy: preliminary findings. Journal of Nervous and Mental Disease 2006;194:15–20

Markowitz JC, Bleiberg KL, Pessin H, Skodol AE: Adapting interpersonal psychotherapy for borderline personality disorder. Journal of Mental Health 2007;16: 103–116

Markowitz JC, Klerman GL, Clougherty KF, Spielman LA, Jacobsberg LB, Fishman B, Frances AJ, Kocsis JH, Perry SW: Individual psychotherapies for depressed HIV-positive patients. American Journal of Psychiatry 1995;152:1504–1509

Markowitz JC, Klerman GL, Perry SW: Interpersonal psychotherapy of depressed HIV-seropositive patients. Hospital and Community Psychiatry 1992;43: 885–890

Markowitz JC, Kocsis JH, Bleiberg KL, Christos PJ, Sacks MH: A comparative trial of psychotherapy and pharmacotherapy for "pure" dysthymic patients. Journal of Affective Disorders 2005;89:167–175

Markowitz JC, Kocsis JH, Christos P, Bleiberg K, Carlin A: Pilot study of interpersonal psychotherapy versus supportive psychotherapy for dysthymic patients with secondary alcohol abuse or dependence. Journal of Nervous and Mental Disease 2008;196:468–474

Markowitz JC, Kocsis JH, Fishman B, Spielman LA, Jacobsberg LB, Frances AJ, Klerman GL, Perry SW: Treatment of HIV-positive patients with depressive symptoms. Archives of General Psychiatry 1998;55:452–457

Markowitz JC, Milrod B: The importance of responding to negative affect in psychotherapies. American Journal of Psychiatry 2011;168:124–128

Markowitz JC, Milrod B, Bleiberg KL, Marshall R: Interpersonal factors in understanding and treating posttraumatic stress disorder. Journal of Psychiatric Practice 2009;15:133–140

Markowitz JC, Patel SA, Balan I, McNamara M, Blanco C, Brave Heart MYH, Buttacavoli Sosa S, Lewis-Fernández R. Towards an adaptation of interpersonal psychotherapy for depressed Hispanic patients. Journal of Clinical Psychiatry 2009;70:214–222

Markowitz JC, Skodol AE, Bleiberg K: Interpersonal psychotherapy for borderline personality disorder: possible mechanisms of change. Journal of Clinical Psychology 2006;62:431–444

Markowitz JC, Spielman LA, Sullivan M, Fishman B: An exploratory study of ethnicity and psychotherapy outcome among HIV-positive patients with depressive symptoms. Journal of Psychotherapy Practice and Research 2000;9:226–231

Markowitz JC, Swartz HA: Case formulation in interpersonal psychotherapy of depression. In Eells TD (Ed.): Handbook of Psychotherapy Case Formulation, 2nd ed. New York: Guilford Press, 2007:221–250

Maslow A: A theory of human motivation. Psychological Review 1943;50:370–396

Mays V, Caldwell C, Jackson J (1996): Mental health symptoms and service utilization patterns of help-seeking among African American women. In Neighbors H,

Jackson J, (Eds.): Mental health in Black America, Thousand Oaks, CA: Sage, 1996:161–176

Maynard C, Ehreth J, Cox G, Peterson P, McGann M: Racial differences in the utilization of public mental health services in Washington State. Administration and Policy in Mental Health 1997;24:411–424

McBride C, Zuroff D, Ravitz P, Koestner R, Moskowitz DS, Quilty L, Bagby RM: Autonomous and controlled motivation and interpersonal therapy for depression: Moderating role of recurrent depression. British Journal of Clinical Psychology 2010;49:529–545

McClung CA, Sidiropoulou K, Vitaterna M, Takahashi JS, White FJ, Cooper DR, Nestler EJ: Regulation of dopaminergic transmission and cocaine reward by the clock gene. Proceedings of the National Academy of Sciences 2005;102: 9377–9381

McFarlane AC, Atchison M, Rafalowicz E, Papay P: Physical symptoms in posttraumatic stress disorder. Journal of Psychosomatic Research 1994;38:715–726

McMillan KA, Enns MW, Asmundson GJ, Sareen J: The association between income and distress, mental disorders, and suicidal ideation and attempts: findings from the collaborative psychiatric epidemiology surveys. Journal of Clinical Psychiatry 2010;71:1168–1175

McNamee G, O'Sullivan G, Lelliott P, Marks I: Telephone-guided treatment for housebound agoraphobics with panic disorder: exposure vs. relaxation. Behavior Therapy 1989;20:491–497

Meyer T, Maier S: Is there evidence for social rhythm instability in people at risk for affective disorders? Psychiatry Research 2006;141:103–114

Menard CB, Bandeen-Roche KJ, Chilcoat HD: Epidemiology of multiple childhood traumatic events: Child abuse, parental psychopathology, and other family-level stressors. Social psychiatry and psychiatric epidemiology 2004;39:857–865

Mickelson KD, Kessler RC, Shaver PR: Adult attachment in a nationally representative sample. Journal of Personality and Social Psychology 1997;73:1092–1106

Middleton W, Burnett P, Raphael B, Martinek N: The bereavement response: a cluster analysis. British Journal of Psychiatry 1996;169:167–171

Miklowitz DJ, George EL, Richards JA, Simoneau TL, Suddath RL: A randomized study of family-focused psychoeducation and pharmacotherapy in the outpatient management of bipolar disorder. Archives of General Psychiatry 2003;60:904–911

Miklowitz DJ, Goldstein MJ: Bipolar Disorder: A Family-Focused Treatment Approach. New York: Guilford, 1997

Miklowitz DJ, Otto MW, Frank E, Reilly-Harrington NA, Kogan JN, Sachs GS, Thase ME, Calabrese JR, Marangell LB, Ostacher MJ, Patel MDJ, Thomas MR, Araga M, Gonzalez JM, Wisniewski SR: Intensive psychosocial intervention enhances functioning in patients with bipolar depression: results from a 9-month randomized controlled trial. American Journal of Psychiatry 2007;164:1340–1347

Miklowitz DJ, Otto MW, Frank E, Reilly-Harrington NA, Wisniewski SR, Kogan JN, Nierenberg AA, Calabrese JR, Marangell LB, Gyulai L, Araga M, Gonzalez JM, Shirley ER, Thase ME, Sachs GS: Psychosocial treatments for bipolar depression: A 1-year randomized trial from the systematic treatment enhancement program. Archives of General Psychiatry 2007;64:419–427

Miklowitz DJ, Simoneau TL, George EL, Richards JA, Kalbag A, Sachs-Ericsson N, Suddath R: Family-focused treatment of bipolar disorder: 1-year effects of a psychoeducational program in conjunction with pharmacotherapy. Biological Psychiatry 2000;48:582–592

Miller L, Gur M, Shano A, Weissman M: Interpersonal psychotherapy with pregnant adolescents: two pilot studies. Journal of Child Psychology and Psychiatry 2008;49:733–742

Miller L, Weissman M: Interpersonal psychotherapy delivered over the telephone to recurrent depressives. A pilot study. Depression and Anxiety 2002;16:114–117

Miller MD: Using interpersonal therapy (IPT) with older adults today and tomorrow: A review of the literature and new developments. Current Psychiatry Reports 2008;10:17–22

Miller MD: Clinician's Guide to Interpersonal Psychotherapy in Late Life: Helping Cognitively Impaired or Depressed Elders and their Caregivers. New York: Oxford University Press, 2009

Miller MD, Frank E, Cornes C, Houck PR, Reynolds CF: Value of maintenance interpersonal psychotherapy (IPT) in elder adults with different IPT foci. American Journal of Geriatric Psychiatry 2003;11:97–102

Miller MD, Wolfson L, Frank E, Cornes C, Silberman R, Ehrenpreis L, Zaltman J, Malloy J, Reynolds CF: Using interpersonal psychotherapy (IPT) in a combined psychotherapy/medication research protocol with depressed elders: a descriptive report with case vignettes. Journal of Psychotherapy Practice and Research 1998;7:47–55

Miller NL, Markowitz JC: Interpersonal psychotherapy of depressed patients. Journal of Practical Psychiatry and Behavioral Health 1999;5:63–74

Miller WR, Rollnick S: Motivational Interviewing: Preparing People for Change, 2nd ed. New York: Guilford Press, 2002

Miranda J, Azocar F, Komaromy M, Golding JM: Unmet mental health needs of women in public-sector gynecologic clinics. American Journal of Obstetrics and Gynecology 1998;17:212–217

Miranda J, Azocar F, Organista K, Dwyer E, Areane P: Treatment of depression among impoverished primary care patients from ethnic minority groups. Psychiatric Services 2003;54:219–225

Miranda J, Azocar F, Organista KC, Muñoz RF, Lieberman A: Recruiting and retaining low-income Latinos in psychotherapy research. Journal of Consulting and Clinical Psychology 1996;64:868–874

Miranda J, Nakamura R, Bernal G: Including ethnic minorities in mental health intervention research: A practical approach to a long-standing problem. Culture, Medicine, and Psychiatry 2003;27:463–481

Mohr DC, Likosky W, Bertagnolli A, Goodkin DE, Van Der Wende J, Dwyer P, Dick LP: Telephone-administered cognitive-behavioral therapy for the treatment of depressive symptoms in multiple sclerosis. Journal of Consulting and Clinical Psychology 2000;68:356–361

Molnar GJ, Feeney MG, Fava GA: Duration and symptoms of bipolar prodromes. American Journal of Psychiatry 1988;145:1576–1578

Monk TH, Kupfer DJ, Frank E, Ritenour AM: The Social Rhythm Metric (SRM): Measuring daily social rhythms over 12 weeks. Psychiatry Research 1991;36: 195–207

Moscicki EE, Rae DS, Regier DA, Locke BZ: The Hispanic Health and Nutrition Survey: Depression among Mexican-Americans, Cuban-Americans, and Puerto Ricans. In Garcia M, Arana J (Eds.): Research Agenda for Hispanics. Chicago: University of Illinois Press, 1987:145–159

Mossey JM, Knott KA, Higgins M, Talerico K: Effectiveness of a psychosocial intervention, interpersonal counseling, for subdysthymic depression in medically ill elderly. Journals of Gerontology, Series A: Biological Sciences and Medical Sciences 1996;51A:M172–M178

Mufson L, Dorta K, Moreau D, Weissman M: Initiating the Interpersonal Interview. In Interpersonal Psychotherapy for Depressed Adolescents, 2nd ed. New York: Guilford, 2004

Mufson L, Dorta KP, Wickramaratne P, Nomura Y, Olfson M, Weissman MM: A randomized effectiveness trial of interpersonal psychotherapy for depressed adolescents. Archives of General Psychiatry 2004;61:577–584

Mufson L, Weissman MM, Moreau D, Garfinkel R: Efficacy of interpersonal psychotherapy for depressed adolescents. Archives of General Psychiatry 1999;56: 573–579

Mulcahy R, Reay RE, Wilkinson RB, Owen C: A randomized control trial for the effectiveness of group interpersonal psychotherapy for postnatal depression. Archives of Women's Mental Health 2010;13:125–139

Murray CJL, Lopez AD: Evidence-based health policy: lessons from the Global Burden of Disease Study. Science 1996;274:740–743

Murray CJL, Lopez AD: The Global Burden of Disease: A Comprehensive Assessment of Mortality and Disability from Diseases, Injuries, and Risk Factors in 1990 and Projected to 2020. Boston: Harvard University Press, 1996

Murray CJL, Lopez AD: Global mortality, disability, and the contribution of risk factors. Lancet 1997;349:1436–1442

National Institute for Clinical Excellence: Depression: Management of Depression in Primary and Secondary Care. Clinical Guideline 23 [On-line], 2004. Available: http://www.nice.org.uk/CG23

Navarro AM: Efectividad de las psicoterapias con Latinos en los Estados Unidos: Una revision meta-analitica. Interamerican Journal of Psychology 1993;27:131–146

Neal JA, Edelmann RJ: The etiology of social phobia: toward a developmental profile. Clinical Psychology Review 2003;23:761–786

Neugebauer R, Kline J, Bleiberg K, Baxi L, Markowitz JC, Rosing M, Levin B, Keith J: Preliminary open trial of interpersonal counseling for subsyndromal depression following miscarriage. Depression and Anxiety 2007;24:219–222

Neugebauer R, Kline J, Markowitz JC, Bleiberg K, Baxi L, Rosing M, Levin B, Keith J: Pilot randomized controlled trial of interpersonal counseling for subsyndromal depression following miscarriage. Journal of Clinical Psychiatry 2006;67:1299–1304

Ndogoni L: Dissemination of IPT research findings in Africa: methods and challenges. Paper presented at Third International Conference of the International Society for Interpersonal Psychotherapy: Global Update. New York, 2009

Nickelson D: Telehealth and the evolving health care system: strategic opportunities for professional psychology. Professional Psychology: Research and Practice 1998;29:527

Nusslock R, Abramson LY, Harmon-Jones E, Alloy LB, Hogan ME: A goal-striving life event and the onset of bipolar episodes: Perspective from the Behavioral Approach System (BAS) dysregulation theory. Journal of Abnormal Psychology 2007;116:105–115

Nylen KJ, O'Hara MW, Brock R, Moel J, Gorman L, Stuart S: Predictors of the longitudinal course of postpartum depression following interpersonal psychotherapy. Journal of Consulting and Clinical Psychology 2010;78:757–763

O'Hara MW, Swain AM: Rates and risk of postpartum depression—a meta-analysis. International Review of Psychiatry 1996;8:37–54

O'Hara MW, Stuart S, Gorman LL, Wenzel A: Efficacy of interpersonal psychotherapy for postpartum depression. Archives of General Psychiatry 2000;57:1039–1045

Organista KC: Latinos. In White JR, Freeman AS (Eds.): Cognitive-Behavioral Group Therapy. Washington, DC: American Psychological Association, 2000:281–303

Organista KC, Muñoz RF: Cognitive behavioral therapy with Latinos. Cognitive and Behavioral Practice 1996;3:255–270

Ozer EJ, Best SR, Lipsey TL, Weiss DS: Predictors of posttraumatic stress disorder and symptoms in adults: a meta-analysis. Psychological Bulletin 2003;129: 52–73

Pace-Schott EF, Hobson JA: The neurobiology of sleep: Genetics, cellular physiology and subcortical networks. Nature Review Neuroscience 2002;3:591–605

Parikh S, Segal Z, Grigoriadis S, Ravindran A, Kennedy S, Lam RW, Patten SB: Canadian Network for Mood and Anxiety Treatments (CANMAT): Clinical guidelines for the management of major depressive disorder in adults. II. Psychotherapy alone or in combination with antidepressant medication. Journal of Affective Disorders 2009;117:S15–S25

Patel NC, Delbello MP, Bryan HS, Adler CM, Kowatch RA, Stanford K, Strakowski SM: Open-label lithium for the treatment of adolescents with bipolar depression. Journal of the American Academy of Child & Adolescent Psychiatry 2006;45: 289–297

Paykel ES, Myers JK, Dienelt MN, Klerman GL, Lindenthal JJ, Pepper MP: Life events and depression: a controlled study. Archives of General Psychiatry 1969;21: 753–760

Perez-Stable E, Miranda J, Munoz R, Ying Y: Depression in medical outpatients: underrecognition and misdiagnosis. Archives of Internal Medicine 1990;150: 1083–1088

Pike KM, Hilbert A, Wilfley DE, Fairburn CG, Dohm FA, Walsh BT, Striegel-Moore R: Toward an understanding of risk factors for anorexia nervosa: a case-control study. Psychological Medicine 2008;38:1443–1453

Pike KM, Wilfley D, Hilbert A, Fairburn CG, Dohm FA, Striegel-Moore RH: Antecedent life events of binge-eating disorder. Psychiatry Research 2006;142: 19–29

Polivy J, Herman CP: Causes of eating disorders. Annual Review of Psychology 2002;53:187–213

Power MJ, Champion LA, Aris SJ: The development of a measure of social support: the Significant Others (SOS) Scale. British Journal of Clinical Psychology 1988;27:349–358

Prien RF, Kupfer DJ, Mansky PA, Small JG, Tuason VB, Voss CB, Johnson WE: Drug therapy in the prevention of recurrences in unipolar and bipolar affective disorders. Report of the NIMH Collaborative Study Group comparing lithium carbonate, imipramine, and lithium carbonate-imipramine combination. Archives of General Psychiatry 1984;41:1096–1104

Prien RF, Rush AJ: National Institute of Mental Health workshop report on the treatment of bipolar disorder. Biological Psychiatry 1996;40:215–220

Prigerson HG, Bierhals AJ, Kasl SV, Reynolds CF 3rd, Shear MK, Day N, Beery LC, Newsom JT, Jacobs S: Traumatic grief as a risk factor for mental and physical morbidity. American Journal of Psychiatry 1997;154:616–623

Prigerson HG, Bierhals AJ, Kasl SV, Reynolds CF 3rd, Shear MK, Newsom JT, Jacobs S: Complicated grief as a disorder distinct from bereavement-related depression and anxiety: a replication study. American Journal of Psychiatry 1996;153: 1484–1486

Prigerson HG, Frank E, Kasl SV, Reynolds CF 3rd, Anderson B, Zubenko GS, Houck PR, George CJ, Kupfer DJ: Complicated grief and bereavement related depression as distinct disorders: preliminary empirical validation in elderly bereaved spouses. American Journal of Psychiatry 1995;152:22–30

Prigerson HG, Shear MK, Jacobs SC, Reynolds CF 3rd, Maciejewski PK, Davidson JR, Rosenheck R, Pilkonis PA, Wortman CB, Williams JB, Widiger TA, Frank E, Kupfer DJ, Zisook S: Consensus criteria for traumatic grief: a rationale and pre-liminary empirical test. British Journal of Psychiatry 1999;174:67–73

Prince M, Patel V, Saxena S, Maj M, Maselko J, Phillips MR, Rahman A: No health without mental health. Lancet 2007;370:859–877

Radloff LS: The CES-D Scale: A Self-Report Depression Scale for Research in the General Population. Applied Psychological Measurement 1977;1:385–401

Ramirez RR, de la Cruz GP: The Hispanic population in the United States: March 2002. Current Population Reports, P20–545. Washington, DC: U.S. Census Bureau, 2003

Ransom D, Heckman TG, Anderson T, Garske J, Holroyd K, Basta T: Telephone-delivered, interpersonal psychotherapy for HIV-infected rural persons with depression: a pilot trial. Psychiatric Services 2008;59:871–877

Rapee RM, Heimberg RG: A cognitive-behavioral model of anxiety in social phobia. Behaviour Research and Therapy 1997;35:741–756

Ravindran AV, Anisman H, Merali Z, Charbonneau Y, Telner J, Bialik RJ, Wiens A, Ellis J, Griffiths J: Treatment of primary dysthymia with group cognitive therapy and pharmacotherapy: clinical symptoms and functional impairments. American Journal of Psychiatry 1999;156:1608–1617

Ravitz P, Maunder R, McBride C: Attachment, contemporary interpersonal theory and IPT: An integration of theoretical, clinical, and empirical perspectives. Journal of Contemporary Psychotherapy 2008;38:11–21

Ray RD, Webster R: Group interpersonal psychotherapy for veterans with posttrau-matic stress disorder: a pilot study. International Journal of Group Psychotherapy 2010;60:131–140

Reay R, Fisher Y, Robertson M, Adams E, Owen C, Kumar R: Group interpersonal therapy for postnatal depression: a pilot study. Archives of Women's Mental Health 2006;9:31–39

Reese RJ, Conoley CW, Brossart DF: Effectiveness of telephone counseling: a field-based investigation. Journal of Counseling Psychology 2002;49:233–242

Reich J, Goldenberg I, Goisman R, Vasile R, Keller M: A prospective, follow-along study of the course of social phobia: II. Testing for basic predictors of course. Journal of Nervous and Mental Disease 1994;182:297–301

Reynolds CF, Dew MA, Martire LM, Miller MD, Cyranowski JM, Lenze E, Whyte EM, Mulsant BH, Pollock BG, Karp JF, Gildengers A, Szanto K, Dombrovski AY, Andreescu C, Butters MA, Morse JQ, Houck PR, Bensasi S, Mazumdar S, Stack JA, Frank E: Treating depression to remission in older adults: a controlled evalu-ation of combined interpersonal psychotherapy versus escitalopram with depres-sion care management. International Journal of Geriatric Psychiatry 2010;25: 1134–412010

Reynolds CF III, Dew MA, Pollock BG, Mulsant BH, Frank E, Miller MD, Houck PR, Mazumdar S, Butters MA, Stack JA, Schlernitzauer MA, Whyte EM, Gildengers A,

Karp J, Lenze E, Szanto K, Bensasi S, Kupfer DJ: Maintenance treatment of major depression in old age. New England Journal of Medicine 2006;354: 1130–1138

Reynolds CF, Frank E, Perel JM, Imber SD, Cornes C, Miller MD, Mazumdar S, Houck PR, Dew MA, Stack JA, Pollock BG, Kupfer DJ: Nortriptyline and interpersonal psychotherapy as maintenance therapies for recurrent depression: A randomized controlled trial in patients older than 59 years. Journal of the American Medical Association 1999;281:39–45

Reynolds CF, Miller MD, Pasternak RE, Frank E, Perel JM, Cornes C, Houck PR, Mazumdar S, Dew MA, Kupfer DJ: Treatment of bereavement related major depressive episodes in later life: A controlled study of acute and continuation treatment with nortriptyline and Interpersonal Psychotherapy. American Journal of Psychiatry 1999;156:202–208

Reynolds S, Stiles WB, Barkham M, Shapiro DA: Acceleration of changes in session impact during contrasting time-limited psychotherapies. Journal of Consulting and Clinical Psychology 1996;64:577–586

Rieger E, Van Buren DJ, Bishop M, Tanofsky-Kraff M, Welch R, Wilfley DE: An eating disorder-specific model of interpersonal psychotherapy (IPT-ED): causal pathways and treatment implications. Clin Psychol Rev 2010;30:400–410

Rieger E, Wilfley DE, Stein RI, Marino V, Crow SJ: A comparison of quality of life in obese individuals with and without binge eating disorder. International Journal of Eating Disorders 2005;37:234–240

Riggs DS, Byrn CA, Weathers FW, Litz BT: The quality of the intimate relationships of male Vietnam veterans: problems associated with posttraumatic stress disorder. Journal of Traumatic Stress 1998;11:87–102.

Riley D, Eckenrode J: Social ties: Subgroup differences in costs and benefits. Journal of Personality and Social Psychology 1986;51:770–778

Robertson M, Rushton PJ, Bartrum MD, Ray R: Group-based interpersonal psychotherapy for posttraumatic stress disorder: theoretical and clinical aspects. International Journal of Group Psychotherapy 2004;54:145–175

Robertson M, Rushton P, Batrim D, Moore E, Morris P: Open trial of interpersonal psychotherapy for posttraumatic stress disorder. Australasian Psychiatry 2007;15:375–379

Rodebaugh TL, Holaway RM, Heimberg RG: The treatment of social anxiety disorder. Clinical Psychology Review 2004;24:883–908

Rogler LH, Malgady RG, Constantino G, Blumenthal R: What do culturally sensitive mental health services mean? The case of Hispanics. American Psychologist 1987;42:565–570

Rosselló J, Bernal G: The efficacy of cognitive-behavioral and interpersonal treatments for depression in Puerto Rican adolescents. Journal of Consulting and Clinical Psychology 1999;67:734–745

Rosselló J, Bernal G, Rivera-Medina C: Individual and group CBT and IPT for Puerto Rican adolescents with depressive symptoms. Cultural Diversity and Ethnic Minority Psycholpgy 2008;14:234–245

Rucci P, Frank E, Kostelnik B, Fagiolini A, Mallinger A, Swartz HA, Thase ME, Siegal L, Wilson D, Kupfer DJ: Suicide attempts in patients with bipolar I disorder during acute and maintenance phases of intensive treatment with pharmacotherapy and adjunctive psychotherapy. American Journal of Psychiatry 2002;159:1160–1164

Rush AJ, Thase ME: Psychotherapies for depressive disorders: A review. In: Maj M, Sartorius N (Eds.), Depressive Disorders. New York: Wiley, 1999:161–206

Russell JJ, Moskowitz DS, Zuroff DC, Bleau P, Pinard G, Young SN: Anxiety, emotional security and the interpersonal behavior of individuals with social anxiety disorder. Psychological Medicine 2011;41:545–554

Sabogal F, Marin G, Otero-Sabogal R, Marin BV, Perez-Stable EJ: Hispanic familism and acculturation: What changes and what doesn't? Hispanic Journal of Behavioral Sciences 1987;9:397–412

Sadock BJ, Sadock VA: Group psychotherapy, combined individual and group psychotherapy, and psychodrama. In Kaplan and Sadock's Synopsis of Psychiatry, Behavioral Sciences/Clinical Psychiatry, 10th ed., pp. 934–939. Philadelphia: Lippincott Williams and Wilkins, 2007

Sanders MR, Dadds MR, Johnston BM, Cash R: Childhood depression and conduct disorder: I. Behavioral, affective and cognitive aspects of family problem-solving interactions. Journal of Abnormal Psychology 1992;101:495–504

Schaal S, Elbert T, Neuner F: Narrative exposure therapy versus interpersonal psychotherapy: A pilot randomized controlled trial with Rwandan genocide orphans. Psychotherapy and Psychosomatics 2009;78:298–306

Scheffler RM, Miller AB: Demand analysis of mental health service use among ethnic subpopulations. Inquiry 1989;26:202–215

Schensul SL, Schensul JJ, LeCompte MD: Essential ethnographic methods: Observations, interviews, and questionnaires. Ethnographer's Toolkit 2. Walnut Creek, CA: Alta Mira Press, 1999

Schneier FR, Heckelman LR, Garfinkel R, Campeas R, Fallon BA, Gitow A, Street L, Del Bene D, Liebowitz MR: Functional impairment in social phobia. Journal of Clinical Psychiatry 1994;55:322–331

Schneier FR, Johnson J, Hornig CD, Liebowitz MR, Weissman MM: Social phobia: Comorbidity and morbidity in an epidemiological sample. Archives of General Psychiatry 1992;49:282–288

Scholle SH, Hasket RF, Hanusa BH, Pincus HA, Kupfer DJ: Addressing depression in obstetrics/gynecology practice. General Hospital Psychiatry 2003;25:83–90

Schramm E: Interpersonelle Psychotherapie für das stationäre Setting. Unveröffentlichtes Manual, Universitätsklinikum Freiburg, Abteilung für Psychiatrie und Psychotherapie, 2000

Schramm E (Ed.): Interpersonelle Psychotherapie, 3rd ed., Stuttgart: Schattauer, 2010

Schramm E, Klecha D: Interpersonelle Gruppentherapie. Stuttgart: Schattauer, 2010

Schramm E, van Calker D, Berger M: Wirksamkeit und Wirkfaktoren der Interpersonellen Psychotherapie in der stationären Depressionsbehandlung–Ergebnisse einer Pilotstudie. PPmP 2004;54:65–72.

Schramm E, van Calker D, Dykierek P, Lieb K, Kech S, Zobel I, Leonhart R, Berger Ml: An intensive treatment progran of interpersonal psychotherapy plus pharmacotherapy for depressed in patients: acute and long term results. American Journal of Psychiatry 2007;164:768–777

Schulberg HC, Block MR, Madonia MJ, Scott CP, Rodriguez E, Imber S, Perel J, Lave J, Houck PR, Coulehan JL: Treating major depression in primary care practice: Eight-month clinical outcomes. Archives of General Psychiatry 1996;53:913–919

Schulz H: Health services research in psychosocial medicine. Bundesgesundheitsblatt Gesundheitsforschung Gesundheitsschutz 2006;49:175–187

Scocco P, De Leo D, Frank E: Is interpersonal psychotherapy in a group format a therapeutic option in late-life depression? Clinical Pyschology and Psychotherapy 2002;9:68–75

Scott J, Colom F, Vieta E: A meta-analysis of relapse rates with adjunctive psychological therapies compared to usual psychiatric treatment for bipolar disorders. International Journal of Neuropsychopharmacology 2007;10:123–129

Scott J, Garland A, Moorhead S: A pilot study of cognitive therapy in bipolar disorders. Psychological Medicine 2001;31:459–467

Scott MJ, Stradling SG: Client compliance with exposure treatments for posttraumatic stress disorder. Journal of Traumatic Stress 1997;10:523–526

Shaffer D, Fisher P: Columbia Depression Scale. Unpublished manuscript. New York: Columbia University, 2000

Shaffer D, Gould MS, Brasic J, Ambrosini P, Bird HR, Aluwahlia S: A Children's Global Assessment Scale (CGAS). Archives of General Psychiatry 1983;40: 1228–1231

Shapiro DA, Barkham M, Rees A, Hardy GE, Reynolds S, Startup M: Effects of treatment duration and severity of depression on the effectiveness of cognitive-behavioral and psychodynamic-interpersonal psychotherapy. Journal of Consulting and Clinical Psychology 1994;62:522–534

Shea MT, Stout RL, Gunderson JG, Morey LC, Grilo CM, McGlashan TH, Skodol AE, Dolan-Sewell RT, Dyck IR, Zanarini MC, Keller MB: Short-term diagnostic stability of schizotypal, borderline, avoidant, and obsessive-compulsive personality disorders. American Journal of Psychiatry 2002;159:2036–2041

Shear K, Frank E, Houck P, Reynolds C: Treatment of complicated grief: a randomized controlled trial. Journal of the American Medical Association 2005;293: 2601–2608

Sheeber L, Allen N, Davis B, Sorensen E: Regulation of negative affect during mother-child problem-solving interactions: Adolescent depressive status and family processes. Journal of Abnormal Child Psychology 2000;28:467–479

Sheeber LB, Davis B, Leve C, Hops H, Tildesley E: Adolescents' relationships with their mothers and fathers: Associations with depressive disorder and subdiagnostic symptomatology. Journal of Abnormal Psychology 2007;116:144–154

Shen GHC, Alloy LB, Abramson LY, Sylvia LG: Social rhythm regularity and the onset of affective episodes in bipolar spectrum individuals. Bipolar Disorders 2008;10:520–529

Siefert K, Heflin C, Corcoran M, Williams D: Food insufficiency and physical and mental health in a longitudinal survey of welfare recipients. Journal of Health and Social Behavior 2004;45:171–186

Simon GE, Ludman EJ, Tutty S, Operskalski B, Von Korff M: Telephone psychotherapy and telephone care management for primary care patients starting antidepressant treatment: a randomized controlled trial. Journal of the American Medical Association 2004;292:935–942

Simon NM, Connor KM, Lang AJ, Rauch S, Krulewicz S, LeBeau RT, Davidson JR, Stein MB, Otto MW, Foa EB, Pollack MH: Paroxetine CR augmentation for post-traumatic stress disorder refractory to prolonged exposure therapy. Journal of Clinical Psychiatry 2008;69:400–405

Simon NM, Otto MW, Korbly NB, Peters PM, Nicolaou DC, Pollack MH: Quality of life in social anxiety disorder compared with panic disorder and the general population. Psychiatric Services 2002; 53:714–718

Simon NM, Shear MK, Fagiolini A, Frank E, Zalta A, Thompson EH, Reynolds CF 3rd, Silowash R: Impact of concurrent naturalistic pharmacotherapy on psychotherapy of complicated grief. Psychiatry Research 2008;159:31–36

Simon R: Distinguishing trauma-associated narcissistic symptoms from Posttraumatic Stress Disorder: a diagnostic challenge. Harvard Review of Psychiatry 2002;10: 28–36

Slade A, Grienenberger J, Bernbach E, Levy D, Locker A: Maternal reflective functioning, attachment, and the transmission gap: A preliminary study. Attachment and Human Development 2005;7:283–298

Smith JA, Tarrier N: Prodromal symptoms in manic depressive psychosis. Social Psychiatry and Psychiatric Epidemiology 1992;27:245–248

Snowden LR: Barriers to effective mental health services for African Americans. Mental Health Services Research 2001;3:181–187

Soreca I, Frank E, Kupfer DJ: The phenomenology of bipolar disorder: What drives the high rate of medical burden and determines long-term prognosis? Depression and Anxiety 2009;26:73–82

Southwick SM, Yehuda R, Giller EL: Personality disorders in treatment-seeking combat veterans with posttraumatic stress disorder. American Journal of Psychiatry 1993;150:1020–1023

Spence SH, Donovan C, Brechman-Toussaint M: Social skills, social outcomes, and cognitive features of childhood social phobia. Journal of Abnormal Psychology 1999;108:211–221

Spinelli MG: Interpersonal psychotherapy for depressed antepartum women: A pilot study. American Journal of Psychiatry 1997;154:1028–1030

Spinelli MG: Manual of Interpersonal Psychotherapy for Antepartum Depressed Women (IPT-P). Unpublished manuscript. New York: NY, 2001

Spinelli MG, Endicott J: Controlled trial of interpersonal psychotherapy versus parenting education program for depressed pregnant women. American Journal of Psychiatry 2003;160:555–562

Spitzer RL, Kroenke K, Williams JB: Validation and utility of a self-report version of PRIME-MD: the PHQ primary care study. Journal of the American Medical Association 1999;282:1737–1744

Spitzer RL, Kroenke K, Williams JB, Loewe B: A brief measure for assessing generalized anxiety disorder: the GAD-7. Archives of Internal Medicine 2006;166: 1092–1097

Spitzer RL, Williams JB, Gibbon M, First M: Structured clinical interview for DSM-IV-Patient edition. New York: New York State Psychiatric Institute, Biometrics Research Department, 1994

Stack C: All Our Kin. New York: Harper & Row, 1975

Stamm B: Clinical applications of telehealth in mental health care. Professional Psychology: Research and Practice 1998;29:536–542

Stangier U, Esser F, Leber S, Risch AK, Heidenreich T: Interpersonal problems in social phobia versus unipolar depression. Anxiety 2006;23:418–421

Stangier U, Schramm E, Heidenreich T, Berger M, Clark DM: Cognitive therapy versus interpersonal psychotherapy in social phobia. Archives of General Psychiatry (in press)

Steiger H, Gauvin L, Jabalpurwala S, Seguin JR, Stotland S: Hypersensitivity to social interactions in bulimic syndromes: relationship to binge eating. Journal of Consulting and Clinical Psychology 1999;67:765–775

Steinhausen H.-C: The outcome of anorexia nervosa in the 20th century. American Journal of Psychiatry 2002;159:1284–1293

Stevens E: *Machismo* and *marianismo*. Transaction/Society 1973;10:57–63

Stice E: Risk and maintenance factors for eating pathology: a meta-analytic review. Psychological Bulletin 2002;128:825–848

Storch EA, Masia-Warner C: The relationship of peer victimization to social anxiety and loneliness in adolescent females. Journal of Adolescence 2004;27:351–362

Stovall-McClough K, Cloitre M: Unresolved attachment, PTSD, and dissociation in women with childhood abuse histories. Journal of Consulting and Clinical Psychology 2006;74:219–228

Stroud LR, Tanofsky-Kraff M, Wilfley DE, Salovey P: The Yale Interpersonal Stressor (YIPS): affective, physiological, and behavioral responses to a novel interpersonal rejection paradigm. Annals of Behavioral Medicine 2000;22:204–213

Stuart S: Interpersonal psychotherapy: a guide to the basics. Psychiatric Annals 2006;36:542–549

Stuart S, Robertson M: Interpersonal Psychotherapy: A Clinician's Guide. London: Arnold Publishing, 2003

Sue PW, Sue DP: Counseling the Culturally Different. New York: John Wiley and Sons, 1990

Sue S, Fujino DC, Hu LT, Takeuchi DT, Zane NW: Community mental health services for ethnic minority groups: A test of the cultural responsiveness hypothesis. Journal of Consulting & Clinical Psychology 1991;59:533–540

Sue S, Zane N, Young K: Research on psychotherapy with culturally diverse populations. In Bergin AE, Garfield SL (Eds.): Handbook of Psychotherapy and Behavior Change, Fourth Edition. New York: John Wiley & Sons, 1994:783–817

Sullivan HS: The Interpersonal Theory of Psychiatry. New York: Norton, 1953

Swartz HA, Frank E, Shear MK, Thase ME, Fleming MAD, Scott J: A pilot study of brief interpersonal psychotherapy for depression in women. Psychiatric Services 2004;55:448–450

Swartz HA, Frank E, Zuckoff A, Cyranowski J, Houck P, Cheng Y, Fleming MA, Grote NK, Brent D, Shear MK: Brief interpersonal psychotherapy for depressed mothers whose children are seeking psychiatric treatment. American Journal of Psychiatry 2008;165:1155–1162

Swartz H, Grote NK, Frank E, Bledsoe SE, Fleming MAD, Shear K: Brief interpersonal psychotherapy (IPT-B): A treatment manual. (unpublished)

Swartz HA, Shear MK, Frank E, Cherry CR, Scholle SH, Kupfer DJ: A pilot study of community mental health care for depression in a supermarket setting. Psychiatric Services 2002;53:1132–1137

Swartz HA, Zuckoff AM, Frank E, Spielvogle HN, Shear MK, Fleming MA, Scott J: An open-label trial of enhanced brief interpersonal psychotherapy in depressed mothers whose children are receiving psychiatric treatment. Depression and Anxiety 2006;23:398–404

Swartz H, Zuckoff A, Grote NK, Frank E, Spielvogle H, Bledsoe SE, Shear K: Engaging depressed patients in psychotherapy: Integrating techniques from motivational interviewing and ethnographic interviewing to improve treatment participation. Professional Psychology: Research and Practice 2007;38:430–439

Sylvia LG, Alloy LB, Hafner JA, Gauger MC, Verdon K, Abramson LY: Life events and social rhythms in bipolar spectrum disorders: A prospective study. Behavior Therapy 2009;40:131–141

Szapocznik J, Williams RA: Brief strategic family therapy: Twenty-five years of interplay among theory, research and practice in adolescent behavior problems and drug abuse. Clinical Child & Family Psychology Review 2000;3:117–134

Szapocznik J, Kurtines WM, & Santisteban DA: The interplay of advances among theory, research and application in family interventions for Hispanic behavior problem youth. In R. G. Malgady & O. Rodriguez (Eds.), Theoretical and conceptual issues in Hispanic mental health 1994;156–180

Takahashi JS: Finding new clock components: Past and future. Journal of Biological Rhythms 2004;19:339–347

Talbot N, Gamble S: IPT for women with trauma histories in community mental health care. Journal of Contemporary Psychotherapy 2008;38:35–44

Talbot NL, Conwell Y, O'Hara MW, Stuart S, Ward EA, Gamble SA, Watts A, Tu X: Interpersonal psychotherapy for depressed women with sexual abuse histories: A pilot study in a community mental health center. Journal of Nervous and Mental Disease 2005;193:847–850

Tanofsky-Kraff M, Wilfley DE: Interpersonal psychotherapy for bulimia nervosa and binge-eating disorder. In Grilo CM, Mitchell JE (Eds.): The Treatment of Eating Disorders: A Clinical Handbook. New York: Guilford Press, 2010:271–293

Tanofsky-Kraff M, Wilfley DE, Young JF, Mufson L, Yanovski SZ, Glasofer DR, Salaita CG: Preventing excessive weight gain in adolescents: interpersonal psychotherapy for binge eating. Obesity (Silver Spring) 2007;15:1345–1355

Tanofsky-Kraff M, Wilfley DE, Young JF, Mufson L, Yanovski SZ, Glasofer DR, Salaita CG, Schvey NA: A pilot study of interpersonal psychotherapy for preventing excess weight gain in adolescent girls at-risk for obesity. International Journal of Eating Disorders 2010;43:701–706

Tanofsky-Kraff M, Yanovski SZ, Schvey NA, Olsen CH, Gustafson J, Yanovski JA: A prospective study of loss of control eating for body weight gain in children at high risk for adult obesity. International Journal of Eating Disorders 2009;42:26–30

Thomas SB, Quinn S, Billingsley A, Caldwell C: The characteristics of northern Black churches with community health outreach programs. American Journal of Public Health 1994;84:575–579

Tillfors M, Carlbring P, Furmark T, Lewenhaupt S, Spak M, Eriksson A, Westling BE, Andersson G: Treating university students with social phobia and public speaking fears: internet delivered self help with or without live group exposure sessions. Depression and Anxiety 2008;25:708–717

Triandis HC, Marin G, Betancourt H, Lisansky J, Chang B: Dimensions of Familism Among Hispanics and Mainstream Navy Recruits. Technical Report No. 14, Department of Psychology, University of Illinois, Champaign,1982

Triandis HC, Marin G, Lisansky J, Betancourt H: Simpatìa as a cultural script of Hispanics. Journal of Personality and Social Psychology 1984;47:1363–1375

Tyrell C, Dozier M, Teague G, Fallot R: Effective treatment relationships for persons with serious mental disorders: The importance of attachment states of mind. Journal of Consulting and Clinical Psychology 2001;67:725–733

van Minnen A, Arntz A, Keijsers GP: Prolonged exposure in patients with chronic PTSD: predictors of treatment outcome and dropout. Behaviour Research and Therapy 2002;40:439–457 van Schaik DJ, van Marwijk HW, Ader H, van Dyck R, de Haan M, Penninx B, van der Kooij K, van Hout H, Beekman A: Interpersonal psychotherapy for elderly patients in primary care. American Journal of Geriatric Psychiatry 2006;14:777–786

Vega WA, Sribney WM, Aguilar-Gaxiola S, Kolody B: 12-month prevalence of DSM-III-R psychiatric disorders among Mexican Americans: nativity, social assimilation, and age determinants. Journal of Nervous and Mental Disease. 2004;192:532–41

Verdeli L, Bolton P, Speelman L: IPT in Developing Countries. Workshop at Third International Conference of the International Society for Interpersonal Psychotherapy: Global Update. New York, 2009

Verdeli H, Clougherty K, Bolton P, Seelman L, Ndogoni L, Bass J, Weissman MM: Adapting group interpersonal psychotherapy for a developing country: Experience in rural Uganda. World Psychiatry 2003;2:114–120

Verdeli H, Clougherty K, Onyango G, Lewandowski E, Speelman L, Betancourt T, Neugebauer R, Stein T, Bolton P: Group interpersonal psychotherapy for depressed youth in IDP camps in northern Uganda: Adaptation and training. Child and Adolescent Psychiatry Clinics of North America 2008;17:605–624

Wacker HR, Mullejans R, Klein KH, Battegay R. Identification of cases of anxiety disorders and affective disorders in the community according to ICD-10 and DSM-III-R by using the Composite International Diagnostic Interview (CIDI). International Journal of Methods in Psychiatric Research 1992;2:91–100

Wagner EF, Frank E, Steiner S: Discriminating maintenance treatments for recurrent depression: development and implementation of a rating scale. Journal of Psychotherapy Research and Practice 1992;1:280–290

Wang PS, Lane M, Olfson M, Pincus HA, Wells KB, Kessler RC: Twelve-month use of mental health services in the United States: results from the National Comorbidity Survey Replication. Archives of General Psychiatry 2005;62:629–640

Warden D, Rush AJ, Trivedi MH, Fava M, Wisniewski SR: The STAR*D Project results: a comprehensive review of findings. Current Psychiatry Reports 2007;9:449–459

Weathers FW, Keane TM, Davidson JRT: Clinician-Administered PTSD Scale: A review of the first ten years of research. Depression and Anxiety 2001;13:132–156

Wegner KE, Smyth JM, Crosby RD, Wittrock D, Wonderlich SA, Mitchell JE: An evaluation of the relationship between mood and binge eating in the natural environment using ecological momentary assessment. International Journal of Eating Disorders 2002;32: 352–361

Wehr TA, Goodwin FK: Biological rhythms and psychiatry. In Arieti S, Brody HKH (Eds): American Handbook of Psychiatry, Volume 7. New York: Basic Books, 1981;46–74

Wehr TA, Sack DA, Rosenthal NE: Sleep reduction as a final common pathway in the genesis of mania. American Journal of Psychiatry 1987;144:201–204

Weissman MM: A brief history of interpersonal psychotherapy. Psychiatric Annals 2006;36:553–557

Weissman MM: Cognitive therapy and interpersonal therapy: 30 years later. American Journal of Psychiatry 2007;164:693–696

Weissman MM, Bland RC, Canino GJ, Faravelli C, Greenwald S, Hwu HG, Joyce PR, Karam EG, Lee CK, Lellouch J, Lépine JP, Newman SC, Rubio-Stipec M, Wells JE, Wickramaratne PJ, Wittchen H, Yeh EK: Cross-national epidemiology of major depression and bipolar disorder. Journal of the American Medical Association 1996;276:293–299

Weissman MM, Kasl SV, Klerman GL: Follow-up of depressed women after maintenance treatment. American Journal of Psychiatry 1976;133:757–760

Weissman MM, Klerman GL, Paykel ES, Prusoff B, Hanson B: Treatment effects on the social adjustment of depressed patients. Archives of General Psychiatry 1974;30:771–778

Weissman MM, Klerman GL: Sex differences and the epidemiology of depression. Archives of General Psychiatry 1977;34:98–111

Weissman MM, Markowitz JC, Klerman GL: Comprehensive Guide to Interpersonal Psychotherapy. New York: Basic Books, 2000

Weissman MM, Markowitz JC, Klerman GL: Clinician's Quick Guide to Interpersonal Psychotherapy. New York: Oxford University Press, 2007

Weissman MM, Pilowsy DJ, Wickramaratne PJ, Talati A, Wisniewski SR, Fava M, Hughes CW, Garber J, Malloy E, King CA, Cerda G, Sood AB, Alpert JE, Trivedi MH, Rush AJ, Star*D-Child Team: Remissions in maternal depression and child psychopathology: a STAR*D-child report. Journal of the American Medical Association, 2006;295:1389–1398

Weissman MM, Verdeli H, Gameroff MJ, Bledsoe SE, Betts K, Mufson L, Fitterling H, Wickramaratne P: National survey of psychotherapy training in psychiatry, psychology, and social work. Archives of General Psychiatry 2006;63: 925–934

Weissman MM, Wickramaratne P, Nomura Y, Warner V, Verdeli H, Pilowsky DJ, Grillon C, Bruder G. Families at high and low risk for depression: a 3-generation study. Archives of General Psychiatry 2005;62:29–36.

Wells A, Clark DM, Salkovskis P, et al.: Social phobia: The role of in-situation safety behaviors in maintaining anxiety and negative beliefs. Behavior Therapy 1995;26:153–161

Wells KB, Burnam MA, Rogers WH, Hays R, Camp P: Course of depression for adult outpatients: results from the Medical Outcomes Study. Archives of General Psychiatry 1992;49:788–794

Welsh DK, Nino-Murcia G, Gander PH, Keenan S, Dement WC: Regular 48-hour cycling of sleep duration and mood in a 35-year-old woman: Use of lithium in time isolation. Biological Psychiatry 1986;21:527–537

Wenzel A: Characteristics of close relationships in individuals with social phobia: A preliminary comparison with nonanxious individuals. In: A Clinician's Guide to Maintaining and Enhancing Close Relationships. Mahwah, NJ: Lawrence Erlbaum Associates; 2002:199–213

Widom CS, DuMont K, Czaja SJ: A prospective investigation of major depressive disorder and comorbidity in abused and neglected children grown up. Archives of General Psychiatry 2007;64:49–56

Wilfley DE: Interpersonal Psychotherapy for Binge Eating Disorder (BED) Therapist's Manual, 2008

Wilfley DE: Interpersonal psychotherapy. In Sadock BJ, Sadock VA (Eds.): Kaplan & Sadock's Comprehensive Textbook of Psychiatry, 8th ed., Vol. 2. Baltimore: Lippincott Williams & Wilkins, 2005:2610–2619

Wilfley DE, Agras WS, Telch CF, Rossiter EM, Schneider JA, Cole AG, Sifford LA, Raeburn SD: Group cognitive-behavioral therapy and group interpersonal psychotherapy for the nonpurging bulimic individual: a controlled comparison. Journal of Consulting and Clinical Psychology 1993;61:296–305

Wilfley DE, Frank MA, Welch R, Spurrell EB, Rounsaville BJ: Adapting interpersonal psychotherapy to a group format (IPT-G) for binge eating disorder: Toward a model for adapting empirically supported treatments. Psychotherapy Research 1998;8:379–391

Wilfley DE, MacKenzie KR, Welch RR, Ayres VE, Weissman MM: Interpersonal Psychotherapy for Group. New York: Basic Books, 2000

Wilfley DE, Stein R, Welch R: Interpersonal Psychotherapy. In Treasure J, Schmidt U, van Furth E (Eds.): Handbook of Eating Disorders, 2nd ed. Chichester, England: John Wiley & Sons, 2003:253–267

Wilfley DE, Welch RR, Stein RI, Spurrell EB, Cohen LR, Saelens BE, Dounchis JZ, Frank MA, Wiseman CV, Matt GE: A randomized comparison of group cognitive-behavioral therapy and group interpersonal psychotherapy for the treatment of overweight individuals with binge-eating disorder. Archives of General Psychiatry 2002;59:713–721

Wilk CM, Bolton P: Local perceptions of the mental health effects of the Uganda acquired immunodeficiency syndrome epidemic. Journal of Nervous & Mental Disease 2002;190:394–397

Williams D, Collins C: U.S. socioeconomic and racial differences in health: Patterns and explanations. Annual Review of Sociology 1995;21:349–386

Wilson GT, Shafran R: Eating disorders guidelines from NICE. Lancet 2005;365(9453):79–81

Wilson GT, Wilfley DE, Agras WS, Bryson SW: Psychological treatments of binge eating disorder. Archives of General Psychiatry 2010;67:94–101

Wirz-Justice A: ISAD Committee Chronotherapeutics in Affective Disorders. Sleep and Biological Rhythms 2006;4:84

Wisner KL, Chambers C, Sit DK: Postpartum depression: a major public health problem. Journal of the American Medical Association 2006;296:2616–2618

Wisner KL, Sit DKY, Hanusa BH, Moses-Kolko EL, Bogen DL, Hunker DF, Perel JM, Jones-Ivy S, Bodnar LM, Singer LT: Major depression and antidepressant treatment: impact on pregnancy and neonatal outcomes. American Journal of Psychiatry 2009;166:557–566

Wittchen HU, Fehm L: Epidemiology and natural course of social fears and social phobia. Acta Psychiatrica Scandinavica 2003;108:4–18

Wolfersdorf M: Depressionsstationen/Stationäre Depressionsbehandlung. Konzepte, Erfahrungen, Möglichkeiten heutiger Depressionsbehandlung. Berlin: Springer, 1997

Wolfersdorf M, Müller B: Zur Situation der stationären Depressionsbehandlung in Deutschland. Psychiatr Prax 2007;34:277–280

Wolk SI, Weissman MM: Women and depression: An update. American Psychiatric Press Review of Psychiatry 1995;14:227–259

World Health Organization: Task Shifting to Tackle Health Worker Shortages. Geneva: WHO, 2007

Yalom ID: The Theory and Practice of Group Psychotherapy, 4th ed., New York: Basic Books, 1995

Yen S, Shea MT, Battle CL, Johnson DM, Zlotnick C, Dolan-Sewell R, Skodol AE, Grilo CM, Gunderson JG, Sanislow CA, Zanarini MC, Bender DS, Rettew JB, McGlashan TH: Traumatic exposure and posttraumatic stress disorder in borderline, schizotypal, avoidant, and obsessive-compulsive personality disorders:

findings from the Collaborative Longitudinal Personality Disorders Study. Journal of Nervous and Mental Disease 2002;190;510–518

Ying Y-W: Psychotherapy with traumatized southeast Asian refugees. Clinical Social Work Journal 2001;29:65–78

Zaitsoff SL, Fehon DC, Grilo CM: Social competence and social-emotional isolation and eating disorder psychopathology in female and male adolescent psychiatric inpatients. International Journal of Clinical and Health Psychology 2009;9: 219–228

Zanarini MC, Frankenburg FR, Chauncey DL, Gunderson JG: The Diagnostic Interview for Personality Disorders: interrater and test-retest reliability. Comprehensive Psychiatry 1987;28:467–480

Zanarini MC, Frankenburg FR, Reich DB, Fitzmaurice G: Time to attainment of recovery from borderline personality disorder and stability of recovery: a 10-year prospective follow-up study. American Journal of Psychiatry 2010a;167:663–667

Zanarini MC, Frankenburg FR, Reich DB, Fitzmaurice G: The 10-year course of psychosocial functioning among patients with borderline personality disorder and axis II comparison subjects. Acta Psychiatrica Scandinavica 2010b;122: 103–109

Zhu S, Stretch V, Balabanis M, Rosbrook B, Sadler G, Pierce JP: Telephone counseling for smoking cessation: effects of single-session and multiple-session interventions. Journal of Consulting and Clinical Psychology 1996;64:202–211

Zisook S, Shuchter SR: Early psychological reaction to the stress of widowhood. Psychiatry 1991a;54:320–333

Zisook S, Shuchter SR: Depression throughout the first year after the death of a spouse. American Journal of Psychiatry 1991b;148:1346–1352

Zisook S, Shuchter SR: Major depression associated with widowhood. American Journal of Geriatric Psychiatry 1993;1:316–326

Zlotnick C, Johnson SL, Miller IW, Pearlstein T, Howard M: Postpartum depression in women receiving public assistance: pilot study of an interpersonal-therapy oriented group intervention. American Journal of Psychiatry 2001;158:638–640

Zlotnick C, Miller IW, Pearlstein T, Howard M, Sweeney P: A preventive intervention for pregnant women on public assistance at risk for postpartum depression. American Journal of Psychiatry 2006;163:1443–1445

Zuckoff A, Swartz H, Grote NK, Frank E, Bledsoe SE, Spielvogle H: Engagement session: A treatment manual. (unpublished).

Zuckoff AM, Swartz HA, Grote NK: Motivational Interviewing as a prelude to psychotherapy of depression. In Arkowitz H, Westra H, Miller WR, Rollnick S (Eds.): Motivational Interviewing in the Treatment of Psychological Problems. New York: Guilford Press, 2008:109–144

Zweben A, Zuckoff A: Motivational interviewing and treatment adherence. In Miller WR, Rollnick S: Motivational Interviewing: Preparing People for Change, 2nd ed. New York: Guilford Press, 2002

Made in the USA
Las Vegas, NV
08 February 2021